PL-PM

Languages of Eastern Asia,
Africa, Oceania; Hyperborean,
Indian, and Artificial Languages

Library of Congress Classification
2010

Prepared by the Policy and Standards Division

LIBRARY OF CONGRESS
Cataloging Distribution Service
Washington, D.C.

LIBRARY OF CONGRESS

This edition cumulates all additions and changes to subclasses PL and PM through Weekly List 2010/06, dated February 10, 2010. Additions and changes made subsequent to that date are published in weekly lists posted on the World Wide Web at

<http://www.loc.gov/aba/cataloging/classification/weeklylists/>

and are also available in *Classification Web*, the online Web-based edition of the Library of Congress Classification.

Library of Congress Cataloging-in-Publication Data

Library of Congress.
   Library of Congress classification. PL-PM. Languages of Eastern Asia, Africa, Oceania. Hyperborean, Indian, and artificial languages / prepared by the Policy and Standards Division, Library Services. — 2010 ed.
      p. cm.
   "This edition cumulates all additions and changes to subclasses PL and PM through Weekly list 2010/06, dated February 10, 2010. Additions and changes made subsequent to that date are published in weekly lists posted on the World Wide Web ... and are also available in Classification Web, the online Web-based edition of the Library of Congress classification"—T.p. verso.
   Includes index.
   ISBN 978-0-8444-9508-8
   1. Classification, Library of Congress. 2. Classification—Books—Oriental philology. 3. Classification—Books—African philology. 4. Classification—Books—Indians—Languages. 5. Classification—Books—Philology. I. Library of Congress. Policy and Standards Division. II. Title. III. Title: Languages of Eastern Asia, Africa, Oceania. IV. Title: Hyperborean, Indian, and artificial languages.

   Z696.U5P73 2010
   025.4'64—dc22

                                                                    2010008585

For sale by the Library of Congress Cataloging Distribution Service, 101 Independence Avenue, S.E., Washington, DC 20540-4910. Product catalog available on the Web at **www.loc.gov/cds**.

PREFACE

Class P: Subclasses PL-PM was originally published in 1933 as a component part of the first edition of Class P: Subclasses PJ-PM, *Languages and Literatures of Asia, Africa, Oceania, America; Mixed Languages; Artificial Languages.* That edition was reprinted in 1965 with supplementary pages of additions and changes. A second edition of subclasses PL-PM was issued as a separate publication in 1988 under the title *Languages of Eastern Asia, Africa, Oceania; Hyperborean, Indian, and Artificial Languages.* The 2001 and 2006 editions cumulated additions and changes that had been made between 1988 and 2006. This 2010 edition includes additions and changes made since 2006.

In the Library of Congress classification schedules, classification numbers or spans of numbers that appear in parentheses are formerly valid numbers that are now obsolete. Numbers or spans that appear in angle brackets are optional numbers that have never been used at the Library of Congress but are provided for other libraries that wish to use them. In most cases, a parenthesized or angle-bracketed number is accompanied by a "see" reference directing the user to the actual number that the Library of Congress currently uses, or a note explaining Library of Congress practice.

Access to the online version of the full Library of Congress Classification is available on the World Wide Web by subscription to *Classification Web.* Details about ordering and pricing may be obtained from the Cataloging Distribution Service at

<http://www.loc.gov/cds/>

New or revised numbers and captions are added to the L.C. Classification schedules as a result of development proposals made by the cataloging staff of the Library of Congress and cooperating institutions. Upon approval of these proposals by the weekly editorial meeting of the Policy and Standards Division, new classification records are created or existing records are revised in the master classification database. Weekly lists of newly approved or revised classification numbers and captions are posted on the World Wide Web at

<http://www.loc.gov/aba/cataloging/classification/weeklylists/>

Janis Young, senior cataloging policy specialist in the Policy and Standards Division, is responsible for coordinating the overall intellectual and editorial content of class P and its various subclasses. Kent Griffiths, assistant editor of classification schedules, is responsible for creating new classification records, maintaining the master database, and creating index terms for the captions.

Barbara B. Tillett, Chief
Policy and Standards Division

February 2010

OUTLINE

	Languages of Eastern Asia, Africa, Oceania
	Ural-Altaic languages
	Including Altaic languages
	For Uralic languages see PH1+
1-9.5	General (Table P-PZ8a)
	Samoyedic languages see PH3801+
	Turkic languages
21-29.5	General (Table P-PZ8a)
31	Old Turkic (Kök-Türk)
	Including the Yenesei and Orkhon inscriptions
	Northeastern (Siberian) group
41	General works
43-43.95	Altai (Table P-PZ15a)
44-44.95	Kyrgyz (Table P-PZ15a)
45.A-Z	Other languages, A-Z
45.C48-.C4895	Chulym (Table P-PZ16)
	Karagass see PL45.T63+
45.K45-.K4595	Khakass (Table P-PZ16)
45.N67-.N6795	Northern Altai (Table P-PZ16)
	Oirot see PL43+
45.S55-.S5595	Shor (Table P-PZ16)
	Soyot see PL45.T88+
45.T63-.T6395	Tofa (Irkutskaīa oblast', Russia) (Table P-PZ16)
45.T88-.T8895	Tuvinian (Table P-PZ16)
	Yakut see PL361+
45.Y44-.Y4495	Yellow Uigur (Table P-PZ16)
	Southeastern (Chagatai) group
51	General works
53-53.95	Chagatai (Table P-PZ15a modified)
	Literature
53.9.A-Z	Individual authors or works, A-Z
	Subarrange individual authors by Table P-PZ40 unless otherwise specified
	Subarrange individual works by Table P-PZ43 unless otherwise specified
	e.g.
53.9.A24	Abdülazîz bin Maḥmûd el-İsfahanî, 16th cent. (Table P-PZ40)
53.9.A36	Ahmed Mirza, 15th cent. (Table P-PZ40)
53.9.A44	Alisher Navoiĭ, 1441-1501 (Table P-PZ40)
53.9.B33	Babur, Emperor of Hindustan, 1483-1530 (Table P-PZ40)
53.9.E24	Ebülgâzî Bahadir Han, Khan of Khorezm, 1603-1663 (Table P-PZ40)
53.9.M84	Muḥammed Ṣaliḥ, 1455-1535 (Table P-PZ40)
53.9.R33	Rabghuziĭ, Nosiruddin Burhonuddin, 13th/14th cent. (Table P-PZ40)

	Ural-Altaic languages
	Turkic languages
	Southeastern (Chagatai) group
	Chagatai
	Literature
	Individual authors or works, A-Z -- Continued
53.9.S45	Sekkâkî, 14th/15th cent. (Table P-PZ40)
54.2-.295	Khorezmian Turkic (Table P-PZ15b modified)
	Cf. PK6199.7 Khorezmi (Iranian)
	Literature
54.29.A-Z	Individual authors or works, A-Z
	Subarrange individual authors by Table P-PZ40 unless otherwise specified
	Subarrange individual works by Table P-PZ43 unless otherwise specified
	e.g.
54.29.K87	Kutb, 14th cent. (Table P-PZ40)
54.4-.495	Salar (Table P-PZ15b)
54.6-.695	Uighur (Table P-PZ15b modified)
	Literature
54.69.A-Z	Individual authors or works, A-Z
	Subarrange individual authors by Table P-PZ40 unless otherwise specified
	Subarrange individual works by Table P-PZ43 unless otherwise specified
	e.g.
54.69.Y87	Yūsuf, khāṣṣ-hājib, 11th cent. (Table P-PZ40)
56-56.95	Uzbek (Table P-PZ15a modified)
	Literature
56.9.A-Z	Individual authors or works, A-Z
	Subarrange individual authors by Table P-PZ40 unless otherwise specified
	Subarrange individual works by Table P-PZ43 unless otherwise specified
	e.g.
56.9.F87	Furqat, 1858-1909 (Table P-PZ40)
56.9.H35	Hamza Hakimzoda Niëziĭ, 1889-1929 (Table P-PZ40)
56.9.H39	Haydar Mīrzā, 1499 or 1500-1551 (Table P-PZ40)
(56.9.I19)	ĪAsavi, Akhmed, d. 1166
	see PL95.9.I18
56.9.M57	Miriĭ, Ochildimurod, 1841-1899 (Table P-PZ40)
56.9.M84	Muqimiĭ, 1850 or 1-1903 (Table P-PZ40)
56.9.N63	Nodir, 1743 or 44-1821 (Table P-PZ40)
56.9.O35	Ogahiĭ, Muhammad Rizo Mirob Ėrniëzbek ŭghli, 1809-1874 (Table P-PZ40)
58-58.95	Western Yugur (Table Table P-PZ15a)

	Ural-Altaic languages
	Turkic languages -- Continued
	Northwestern (Kipchak) group
61	General works
63-63.95	Kipchak (Table P-PZ15a)
64-64.95	Armeno-Kipchak (Table P-PZ15a)
(65)	Other languages, A-Z
	see PL66 PL67 PL68 etc.
66-66.95	Crimean Tatar (Table P-PZ15a)
67-67.95	Karachay-Balkar (Table P-PZ15a)
	Balkar
(68-68.4)	Balkar language
	see PL67+
	Balkar literature
68.5	History and criticism
	Collections
	Including translations
68.6	General
68.7	Poetry
68.74	Drama
68.76	Prose
(68.8)	Folk literature
	see subclass GR
68.9.A-Z	Individual authors or works, A-Z
	Subarrange individual authors by Table P-PZ40
	Subarrange individual works by Table P-PZ43
69-69.95	Karaim (Table P-PZ15a)
70-70.95	Kumyk (Table P-PZ15a)
72-72.95	Bashkir (Table P-PZ15a modified)
	Literature
72.9.A-Z	Individual authors or works, A-Z
	Subarrange individual authors by Table P-PZ40
	Subarrange individual works by Table P-PZ43
	e.g.
72.9.I24	ĪAlsygulov, Tadzhetdin, ca. 1767-1838 (Table P-PZ40)
73-73.95	Tatar (Table P-PZ15a)
75-75.95	Karakalpak (Table P-PZ15a)
76-76.95	Kazakh (Table P-PZ15a)
	Kyrgyz see PL44+
77-77.95	Nogai (Table P-PZ15a)
	Southwestern (Oghuz) group
91	General works
95-95.95	Oghuz (Table P-PZ15a modified)
	Literature

	Ural-Altaic languages
	Turkic languages
	Southwestern (Oghuz) group
	Oghuz
	Literature -- Continued
95.9.A-Z	Individual authors or works, A-Z
	Subarrange individual authors by Table P-PZ40 unless otherwise specified
	Subarrange individual works by Table P-PZ43 unless otherwise specified
	e. g.
95.9.I18	Ĭ Asavi, Akhmed, d. 1166 (Table P-PZ40)
95.9.K57-.K573	Kitabi Dădă Gorgud (Table P-PZ43)
101-271	Turkish (Osmanic or Ottoman) (Table P-PZ4 modified)
201-271	Literature (Table P-PZ22 modified)
248.A-Z	Individual authors or works, A-Z
	Subarrange individual authors by Table P-PZ40 unless otherwise specified
	Subarrange individual works by Table P-PZ43 unless otherwise specified
	e.g.
248.A234	Abdal Musa, 14th cent. (Table P-PZ40)
248.A236	Abdi, b. 1857 (Table P-PZ40)
248.A2365	Abdülahad Nûri, 1594 or 5-1651 (Table P-PZ40)
248.A238	Abdülhak Hâmit, 1852-1937 (Table P-PZ40)
248.A24	Abdürrahim Nizameddin Merzifonlu, 15th cent. (Table P-PZ40)
248.A3135	Ahmed Bican, 15th cent. (Table P-PZ40)
248.A31355	Ahmed Celâyir, ca. 1359-1410 (Table P-PZ40)
248.A3136	Ahmed Dâi, fl. 1387-1421 (Table P-PZ40)
248.A314	Ahmedî, 1334?-1413 (Table P-PZ40)
248.A3172	Ahmet Haşim, 1883 or 4-1933 (Table P-PZ40)
248.A31723	Ahmet Hilmi Şehbenderzade, 1865-1913 (Table P-PZ40)
248.A3173	Ahmet Mithat, Efendi, 1844-1912 (Table P-PZ40)
248.A318	Ahmet Rasim, 1864?-1932 (Table P-PZ40)
248.A377	Akyürek, Ahmet Remzi, 1872-1944 (Table P-PZ40)
248.A3777	Âlî, Mustafa bin Ahmet, 1541-1599 (Table P-PZ40)
248.A378	Ali, Turkish poet, 13th cent. (Table P-PZ40)
248.A383	Ali bin Ahmed bin Emîr Ali, fl. 1468-1496 (Table P-PZ40)
248.A623	Ârif Hikmet, 1786-1859 (Table P-PZ40)
248.A678	Âşık Ferkî, ca. 1867-1908 (Table P-PZ40)
248.A69	Âşık Paşa-yı Velî, 1271-1332 (Table P-PZ40)
248.A6925	Âşık Tahirî, 1812-1883 (Table P-PZ40)
248.A693	Âşık Veli, d. 1853 (Table P-PZ40)
	Âşık Veysel, 1894-1973 see PL248.S34

Ural-Altaic languages
Turkic languages
Southwestern (Oghuz) group
Turkish (Osmanic or Ottoman)
Literature
Individual authors or works, A-Z

248.A745	'Aṭā'ī, 'Aṭā Allāh ibn Yaḥyā, 17th cent. (Table P-PZ40)
248.A914	Aynî, Hasan, 1766-1837 (Table P-PZ40)
248.B26	Baki, 1526-1600 (Table P-PZ40)
248.B337	Basîrî, 1466-1534 or 5 (Table P-PZ40)
248.B349	Battal (Table P-PZ43)
248.B412	Behiştî, Ramazan bin Abdu'l-Muhsin, d. 1571 or 2 (Table P-PZ40)
248.B57	Birrî, Mehmet Dede, 1669-1715 or 16 (Table P-PZ40)
248.B62	Bosnalı Muhlis, fl. 1748 (Table P-PZ40)
248.B69	Boztepe, Halil Nihad, 1880-1949 (Table P-PZ40)
248.B8	Burhaneddin, Kadi, 1344-1398 (Table P-PZ40)
248.C2	Ca'fer Çelebi, Tâcî-zâde, 1452-1515 (Table P-PZ40)
248.C43	Cem, Prince, son of Mehmed II, Sultan of the Turks, 1459-1495 (Table P-PZ40)
248.C44	Cenap Şehabettin, 1870-1934 (Table P-PZ40)
248.D25	Dadaloğlu, 1785?-1868? (Table P-PZ40)
248.D365	Dervîş Hayâlî, d. 1470 or 71 (Table P-PZ40)
248.D37	Dervîş Muhammed Yemînî, 16th cent. (Table P-PZ40)
248.D39	Derviş Şemseddin, 15th/16th cent. (Table P-PZ40)
248.D575	Divane Mehmet Çelebi, 16th cent. (Table P-PZ40)
248.E23	Ebü'l-Hayr-ı Rumî, fl. 1480-1489 (Table P-PZ40)
248.E36	Elvan Çelebi, 14th cent. (Table P-PZ40)
248.E77	Es'ad Efendi, Meḥmed, 1685-1753 (Table P-PZ40)
248.E84	Eşref, 1846 or 7-1912 (Table P-PZ40)
248.E85	Eşrefoğlu Rûmî, d. 1496 (Table P-PZ40)
248.F338	Fasîh Ahmet Dede, d. 1699 (Table P-PZ40)
248.F339	Fatin, 1813 or 14-1866 (Table P-PZ40)
248.F42	Fehîm, Undjuzāde Mustafa, 1627?-1647 (Table P-PZ40)
248.F46	Fenayî, d. 1664 or 5 (Table P-PZ40)
248.F47-.F473	Ferec ba'd eş-şidde (Table P-PZ43)
248.F95	Fuzulî, 1495?-1556 (Table P-PZ40)
248.G6	Gökalp, Ziya, 1876-1924 (Table P-PZ40)
248.G67	Güftî, d. 1677 (Table P-PZ40)
248.G84	Gürpınar, Hüseyin Rahmi, 1864-1944 (Table P-PZ40)
248.H22	Ḥalikarnas Balıkçısı, 1886- (Table P-PZ40)

Ural-Altaic languages
Turkic languages
Southwestern (Oghuz) group
Turkish (Osmanic or Ottoman)
Literature
Individual authors or works, A-Z -- Continued

248.H252	Handî (Table P-PZ40)
248.H26	Hasan Ünsî, 1645-1723 (Table P-PZ40)
248.H345	Hayretî, d. 1534 (Table P-PZ40)
248.H47	Hilmî, fl. 1618 (Table P-PZ40)
248.H64	Hoca Mesut, 14th cent. (Table P-PZ40)
248.I335	İbrahim Tennuri, d. 1482 (Table P-PZ40)
248.I815	İslâmî, 14th cent. (Table P-PZ40)
248.I8157	İsmail Beliğ, 1668-1729 or 30 (Table P-PZ40)
248.I818	İsmail Hakkı, Bursalı, 1653-1724 or 5 (Table P-PZ40)
248.I819	İsmetî, Mehmet, 1611-1665 (Table P-PZ40)
	Kabaağaçlı, Cevat Şakir, 1886- see PL248.H22
	Kadi Burhaneddin, 1344-1398 see PL248.B8
248.K2236	Kâ'imî Baba, Hasan, 17th cent. (Table P-PZ40)
248.K24	Karacaoğlan, 17th cent. (Table P-PZ40)
248.K3773	Kaygusuz Abdal, 15th cent. (Table P-PZ40)
248.K3776	Kayserili Mehmet Remzî Efendi, d. 1718 or 19 (Table P-PZ40)
248.K3779	Keçecizade İzzet Molla, 1785-1829 (Table P-PZ40)
248.K42	Kemal, Orhan, 1914-1970 (Table P-PZ40)
	Kemal, Raşit, 1914-1970 see PL248.K42
248.K473	Ketencizade Mehmet Rüştü Efendi, 1834-1916 (Table P-PZ40)
248.K65	Kolaylı, Neyzen Tevfik, 1879-1953 (Table P-PZ40)
248.K774	Kul Himmet, 16th cent. (Table P-PZ40)
248.K775	Kul Nesîmî, 17th cent. (Table P-PZ40)
248.L35	Lâmiî Çelebi, 1472-1532 (Table P-PZ40)
248.L37	Latifî, 1491-1582 (Table P-PZ40)
248.L49	Leylâ Hanım, d. 1847 or 8 (Table P-PZ40)
248.L65	Lokmanî Dede, d. 1519 (Table P-PZ40)
248.M38	Mehmed Ali Çelebi, 1592 or 3-1629 or 30 (Table P-PZ40)
248.M42	Mehmet Âkif, 1873-1936 (Table P-PZ40)
248.M435	Mehmet Vecihi, 1869-1904 (Table P-PZ40)
	Merzifonlu Abdürrahim Rumî, 15th cent. see PL248.A24
248.M476	Mesîḥî, fl. 1518 (Table P-PZ40)
248.M478	Mezâkî, 17th cent. (Table P-PZ40)
248.M52	Misaēlidēs, Euangelinos, 1820-1890 (Table P-PZ40)

Ural-Altaic languages
Turkic languages
Southwestern (Oghuz) group
Turkish (Osmanic or Ottoman)
Literature
Individual authors or works, A-Z -- Continued

248.M76	Müftüoğlu, Ahmed Hikmet, 1870-1927 (Table P-PZ40)
248.M764	Muhammed Bahâeddin Erzincânî, d. 1474 (Table P-PZ40)
248.M85	Murādī, 16th cent. (Table P-PZ40)
248.M872	Mürîdî, 14th/15th cent. (Table P-PZ40)
248.M875	Müseyyeb-nâme (Table P-PZ43)
248.M9	Müştak Baba, 1758?-1831? (Table P-PZ40)
248.N18	Nabi, 1641 or 2-1712 (Table P-PZ40)
	Nâbizâde Nâzım, 1862-1893 see PL248.N34
248.N227	Namık Kemal, 1840-1888 (Table P-PZ40)
248.N34	Nâzım, Nâbizâde, 1862-1893 (Table P-PZ40)
248.N36	Necâtî Bey, d. 1509 (Table P-PZ40)
248.N42	Nedim, Ahmet, 1681-1730 (Table P-PZ40)
248.N425	Nef'î, 1572-1635 (Table P-PZ40)
248.N4295	Nesimi, ca. 1369-ca. 1418 (Table P-PZ40)
248.N4297	Nesîmî-zâde Şeyh İbretî Mustafa Efendi, d. 1757 (Table P-PZ40)
248.N465	Neylî, Mîrzâ-Zâde Ahmed, 1673-1748 (Table P-PZ40)
	Neyzen Tevfik, 1879-1953 see PL248.K65
248.N53	Niyâzî, d. 1693 or 4 (Table P-PZ40)
	Öğütçü, Mehmet Raşit, 1914-1970 see PL248.K42
248.O283	Ömer Seyfeddin, 1884-1920 (Table P-PZ40)
	Orhan Kemal, 1914-1970 see PL248.K42
248.O313	Osman Şems Efendi, 1814-1893 (Table P-PZ40)
248.P485	Pir Mehmet bin Evrenos bin Nureddin Zaifî, d. 1559 (Table P-PZ40)
248.P49	Pir Sultan Abdal, 16th cent. (Table P-PZ40)
	Raşit, Mehmet, 1914-1970 see PL248.K42
248.R36	Recâîzâde Ahmed Cevdet, d. 1831 (Table P-PZ40)
248.R38	Recaizade Mahmut Ekrem, 1847-1914 (Table P-PZ40)
	Rizâyî, 1592 or 3-1629 or 30 see PL248.M38
248.S276	Sabit Alaeddin Ali, 1650-1712 (Table P-PZ40)
248.S282	Sâfî, 15th/16th cent. (Table P-PZ40)
248.S283	Şahidî İbrahim Dede, 1470-1550 (Table P-PZ40)
248.S289	Sâkıb Mustafa Dede, 1652?-1735 (Table P-PZ40)
248.S298	Samipaşazade Sezai, 1860-1936 (Table P-PZ40)
248.S34	Şatiroğlu, Âşik Veysel, 1894-1973 (Table P-PZ40)

Ural-Altaic languages
Turkic languages
Southwestern (Oghuz) group
Turkish (Osmanic or Ottoman)
Literature
Individual authors or works, A-Z -- Continued

248.S359	Şemseddin Sâmî, 1850-1904 (Table P-PZ40)
	For general life and works see PG9621.S34
248.S3593	Şemsî Paşa, d. ca. 1580 (Table P-PZ40)
248.S387	Şeyh Galip, 1757 or 8-1799 (Table P-PZ40)
248.S42	Şeyhoğlu Mustafa, b. ca. 1341 (Table P-PZ40)
248.S455	Sezaî, 1669-1738 (Table P-PZ40)
248.S49	Sinan Paşa, 1440-1486 (Table P-PZ40)
248.S52	Şinasi, İbrahim, 1826-1871 (Table P-PZ40)
248.S73	Süheyli Efendi, 17th cent. (Table P-PZ40)
248.S74	Sükkerî Zekeriyya, d. ca. 1682 (Table P-PZ40)
248.S77	Süleyman, Çelebi, d. 1422? (Table P-PZ40)
248.S773	Süleyman Nazif, 1869-1927 (Table P-PZ40)
248.S7745	Sulṭān Valad, 1226-1312 (Table P-PZ40)
	For his Persian works see PK6549.S84
248.S87	Sûzî Çelebi, d. 1524 or 5 (Table P-PZ40)
(248.T28)	Tarhan, Abdülhak Hâmit, 1852-1937
	see PL248.A238
248.T396	Tevfik Fikret, 1867-1915 (Table P-PZ40)
248.T546	Tokatlı İshak bin Hasan Rızâî, d. ca. 1689 (Table P-PZ40)
248.T885	Tursun Fakih, 13th/14th cent. (Table P-PZ40)
248.V37	Vehbi, ca. 1719-1809 (Table P-PZ40)
248.V48	Veysî, 1561-1628 (Table P-PZ40)
248.V57	Visâlî, 15th cent. (Table P-PZ40)
248.V87	Vuslatî Ali Bey, d. 1688 (Table P-PZ40)
248.Y297	Yazıcıoğlu Mehmet, d. 1451 (Table P-PZ40)
248.Y8	Yunus Emre, d. 1320? (Table P-PZ40)
248.Y86	Yūsuf-i Meddāḥ, 14th cent. (Table P-PZ40)
248.Z37	Zati, 1471 or 2-1546. (Table P-PZ40)
248.Z55	Ziya Paşa, 1825-1880 (Table P-PZ40)
	Translations
(261-265)	From foreign languages into Turkish
	see the original language
271-272	From Turkish into other languages (Table P-PZ30)
311-314	Azerbaijani (Table P-PZ11 modified)
	Literature

Ural-Altaic languages
Turkic languages
Southwestern (Oghuz) group
Azerbaijani
Literature -- Continued

314.A3-.Z5	Individual authors or works, A-Z
	Subarrange individual authors by Table P-PZ40 unless otherwise specified
	Subarrange individual works by Table P-PZ43 unless otherwise specified
	e.g.
314.A45	Ākhund'zādah, Fatḥ 'Alī, 1812-1878 (Table P-PZ40)
314.A539	Ămani, Măhămmăd (Table P-PZ40)
314.A84	Ashyg Ălăsġăr, 1821-1926 (Table P-PZ40)
314.F89	Fuzulî, 1495?-1556 (Table P-PZ40)
314.G32	Gasymbăï Zakir, 1784-1857 (Table P-PZ40)
314.G86	Gurbani, 16th cent. (Table P-PZ40)
314.H25	Ḥagverdīïev, Ăbdŭrrăhimbăï, 1870-1933 (Table P-PZ40)
314.I68	Isa, 11th cent. (Table P-PZ40)
314.I74	Ismā'īl I, Shah of Iran, 1487-1524 (Table P-PZ40)
314.K564	Kishvări, 16th cent. (Table P-PZ40)
314.M27	Mămmădguluzadă, Jălil, 1866-1931 (Table P-PZ40)
314.M6	Mȯ'jȗz, Mirză Ăli, ‡d 1873-1934 (Table P-PZ40)
314.N3	Nărimanov, Năriman, 1870-1925 (Table P-PZ40)
314.N37	Năvvab, Mir Mȯhsȗn, 1833-1913 (Table P-PZ40)
314.N398	Ne'manzadă, Omăr Faig, 1872-1938 (Table P-PZ40)
314.N4	Nesimi, ca. 1369-ca. 1418 (Table P-PZ40)
314.O7	Ordubadi, Mămmăd Săid 1872-1950 (Table P-PZ40)
314.P3	Panakh, Mollă, 1717-1797 (Table P-PZ40)
314.S24	Sabir, 1862-1911 (Table P-PZ40)
314.S27	Sadigi, Sadig băï, 16th/17th cent. (Table P-PZ40)
314.S42	Seïdi, 1775-1836 (Table P-PZ40)
314.S437	Seïid Ăzim Shirvani, 1835-1888 (Table P-PZ40)
314.S519	Shams Maghribī, Muḥammad Shīrīn, 1349?-1406 or 7 (Table P-PZ40)
	Cf. PK6549.S515 New Persian
314.S558	Shȗkȗri, Abdyshȗkȗr (Table P-PZ40)
(314.T3)	Tair-zade, Mirza Alekper, 1862-1911
	see PL314.S24
314.T338	Talybov, Mirză Ăbdȗrrăhim, 1834-1911 (Table P-PZ40)
314.T52	Tibrīzī, Yaḥyá ibn 'Alī, d. 1109 (Table P-PZ40)
	Vagif, 1717-1797 see PL314.P3
314.V3	Vazeh, Mirză Shăfi, 1796?-1852 (Table P-PZ40)

	Ural-Altaic languages
	Turkic languages
	Southwestern (Oghuz) group -- Continued
316-316.95	Gagauz (Table P-PZ15a)
	Kipchak see PL63+
331-334	Turkmen (Table P-PZ11 modified)
	Literature
334.A3-.Z5	Individual authors or works, A-Z

          Subarrange individual authors by Table P-PZ40 unless otherwise specified

          Subarrange individual works by Table P-PZ43 unless otherwise specified

          e.g.

334.A56	Andalyp, Nurmukhammet, 18th cent. (Table P-PZ40)
334.A97	Azady, Dȯvletmămmet, 1700-1760 (Table P-PZ40)
334.K3	Kătibi, Oveztagan, 1803-1881 (Table P-PZ40)
334.K36	Kemine, 1770-1840 (Table P-PZ40)
334.M3	Magtymguly, ca. 1733-ca. 1782 (Table P-PZ40)
334.M36	Mătăji, Annagylych, 1822-1884? (Table P-PZ40)
334.V47	Vepaïy, 15th cent. (Table P-PZ40)
334.Z44	Zelili, Gurbandurdy, 1795-1850 (Table P-PZ40)
361-364	Yakut (Table P-PZ11)
	Bulgaro-Turkic
379	General (Table P-PZ15)
381-384	Chuvash (Table P-PZ11)
	Khakass see PL45.K45+
396-396.95	Khalaj (Table P-PZ15a)
	Mongolian languages
400-400.95	Mongolian language group (Table P-PZ15a)

          Class here works on the Mongolian languages collectively (Oirat, Kalmyk, Buriat, Mongolian, etc.)

401-409.5	Mongolian language (Table P-PZ8a modified)
	Including the Khalkha dialect
402	Tod alphabet
(408-408.9)	Literature
	see PL410+
410-419	Mongolian literature (Table P-PZ24 modified)
419.A-Z	Individual authors or works, A-Z

          Subarrange individual authors by Table P-PZ40 unless otherwise specified

          Subarrange individual works by Table P-PZ43 unless otherwise specified

          e.g.

419.B55	Bluva-bsang-bstan-'jin, fl. 1650-1737 (Table P-PZ40)
419.E733	Ėrdėnė-Khaĭvzun, G., 1855-1915 (Table P-PZ40)
419.G4-.G43	Gesar (Table P-PZ43)

	Ural-Altaic languages
	Mongolian languages
	Mongolian language
	Mongolian literature
	Individual authors or works, A-Z -- Continued
419.I5	Injannasi, 1837-1892 (Table P-PZ40)
419.L83	Lubsangdamba (Table P-PZ40)
419.Q24-.Q243	Qan Qaranġġui (Table P-PZ43)
	Buriat language
427	General works
427.1	Grammar
427.2	Exercises. Readers. Phrase books, etc.
427.25	Style. Composition. Rhetoric
427.3	Etymology
427.4	Dictionaries
	Dialects
427.94	General works
427.95	Special. By name or place, A-Z
428-428.9	Buriat literature (Table P-PZ25)
	Kalmyk language
429	General works
429.1	Grammar
429.2	Exercises. Readers. Phrase books, etc.
429.25	Style. Composition. Rhetoric
429.3	Etymology
429.4	Dictionaries
	Dialects
429.94	General works
429.95	Special. By name or place, A-Z
430-430.9	Kalmyk literature (Table P-PZ25)
431.A-Z	Other languages, A-Z
431.B64-.B6495	Bonan (Table P-PZ16)
431.D3-.D395	Dagur (Table P-PZ16)
431.D47-.D4795	Darkhat (Table P-PZ16)
431.D64-.D6495	Dongxiang (Table P-PZ16)
431.E28-.E2895	Eastern Yugur (Table P-PZ16)
	Khalkha see PL401+
431.K65-.K6595	Khamnigan (Table P-PZ16)
431.M57-.M5795	Moghol (Table P-PZ16)
431.M6-.M695	Monguor (Table P-PZ16)
431.O38-.O3895	Oirat (Table P-PZ16)
431.O8-.O895	Ordos (Table P-PZ16)
(431.P3)	Pao-an
	see PL431.B64
(431.T8)	Tung-hsiang
	see PL431.D64

	Japanese language and literature
	Japanese language
	Lexicography
	Dictionaries -- Continued
	Dictionaries with definitions in same language
674.5	Early works to 1867
675	1868-
677.5	Chinese character dictionaries
677.6	Chinese character glossaries, etc.
	Inscriptions see PL750+
	Bibliography see Z7072
	Japanese literature
	History and criticism
700	Periodicals. Serials
(701)	Yearbooks
	see PL700
702	Societies
703	Congresses
703.5	Museums. Exhibitions
	Arrange by author
	Bibliography
	see Z3308.L5
	Collections
704	Series. Monographs by different authors
705.A-Z	In honor of an individual or institution, A-Z
706	By an individual author
707	Encyclopedias. Dictionaries. Indexes
708	Theory. Philosophy. Aesthetics. Psychology
	Study and teaching
709	General works
710.A-Z	By region or country, A-Z
711.A-Z	By school, A-Z
711.5	Literary research
712	History of literary criticism
	Biography of historians, critics, teachers, and editors
713.A2	Collective
713.A3-Z	Individual, A-Z
	Subarrange each by Table P-PZ50
	Criticism
	Treatises
714.A2	Early works through 1867
714.A3-Z	1868-
715	Addresses, essays, lectures
	History
	General works
	Japanese
716.A2	Early works through 1867

Japanese language and literature
Japanese literature
History and criticism
History
General works
Japanese -- Continued

716.A3-Z	1868-
717	English
718.A-Z	Other languages, A-Z
719	Addresses, essays, lectures
719.5	Outlines, syllabi, tables, etc.
719.6	Examinations, questions, etc.

Kanbungaku (Japanese literature)

719.79	General works
719.8-.888	By period (Table PL1a)

Special aspects and topics

720	Relation to history, civilization, culture, etc.

For relations of individual authors, see the author

Relation to other literatures

720.5	General works
720.55.A-Z	By country or language, A-Z

Class by country when possible

720.6	Translations of foreign literature into Japanese

Translations of Japanese literature

For collections see PL782+

720.7	General works
720.75.A-Z	By language, A-Z
721.A-Z	Special topics, A-Z

Class here general works only
For history of a special form or period, see the form or
period

721.A27	Aesthetics
721.A3	Agricultural colonies
721.A35	Aichi-ken (Japan)
721.A42	Alcoholic beverages
721.A47	Anarchism
721.A48	Animals
721.A49	Animism
721.A5	Aomori-ken (Japan)
721.A63	Archaeology
721.A65	Art
721.A68	Astronomy
721.A75	Atomic bomb. Nuclear weapons and disarmament
721.A85	Autobiography
721.A856	Awaji Island (Japan)
721.A86	Aware (The Japanese word)
721.B57	Birds

Japanese language and literature
Japanese literature
History and criticism
History
Special aspects and topics
Special topics, A-Z -- Continued

721.B59	Birthplaces
721.B63	Body, Human
721.B8	Buddhism
721.B83	Buddhist temple bells
721.B84	Bushido
721.B85	Business enterprises
721.C3	Castles
721.C37	Censorship
721.C4	Characters and characteristics
721.C425	Chiba-ken (Japan)
721.C44	China
721.C45	Christianity
721.C46	Chūjō-hime, 8th cent.
721.C5	Cities
721.C6	Color
721.C64	The Comic
721.C645	Confession
721.C65	Cosmetics
721.C66	Cosmology
721.C68	Country life
721.C7	Courts and courtiers
721.C74	Crime
721.D23	Dadaism
	Daughters and fathers see PL721.F37
721.D3	Dayflower
721.D32	Dazaifu-machi (Japan)
721.D38	Death
721.D39	Democracy
721.D4	Demons
721.D45	Detective and mystery stories
721.D58	Divination
721.D62	Dogs
721.D64	Dōjōji (Kawabe-chō, Wakayama-ken, Japan)
721.D7	Dreams
721.D85	Dwellings
721.E32	Ecology. Environment
721.E35	Ehime-ken (Japan)
	Elderly people, Killing of see PL721.K44
	Environment see PL721.E32
721.E7	Eremitic life. Hermits
721.E74	Erotic literature

	Japanese language and literature
	Japanese literature
	History and criticism
	History
	Special aspects and topics
	Special topics, A-Z -- Continued
721.E8	Ethics
721.E9	Evil
	Fabrics, Textile see PL721.T39
721.F25	Family
721.F26	Fantastic literature
721.F27	Fantasy
721.F3	Farm life
721.F32	Fascism
721.F34	Fate and fatalism
721.F37	Fathers and daughters
721.F4	Festivals
721.F46	Filial piety
721.F48	Flatulence
721.F49	Flowering plums
721.F5	Flowers
721.F64	Folklore
721.F65	Food
721.F66	Fortune-telling
721.F67	Forty-seven Ronin
721.F69	Foxes
721.F75	Fruit
721.F85	Fuji, Mount (Japan)
721.G37	Gardens
721.G44	Gender identity
721.G46	Geography
	Ghosts see PL721.S8
721.G55	Ginza (Tokyo, Japan)
721.G6	Gods
721.G7	Grief
721.G85	Gunma-ken (Japan)
721.H4	Hell
	Hermits see PL721.E7
721.H45	Himeji-shi (Japan)
721.H5	Hiroshima
721.H52	Hiroshima Bombardment, 1945
721.H54	History
721.H57	Hokkaido (Japan)
721.H575	Hollies
721.H58	Homeland
721.H59	Homosexuality
721.H595	Hot springs

Japanese language and literature
Japanese literature
History and criticism
History
Special aspects and topics
Special topics, A-Z -- Continued

721.H6	Hotels, taverns, etc.
	Human body see PL721.B63
721.H85	Humanism
721.H96	Hyōgo-ken (Japan)
721.I22	Ibaraki-ken (Japan)
721.I24	Ichikawa-shi (Japan)
721.I3	Ide-chō (Japan)
721.I34	Identity (Psychology)
721.I42	Imitation
721.I45	Impermanence (Buddhism)
721.I54	Inland Sea region
721.I8	Ise-shi (Japan)
721.I82	Ishikawa-ken (Japan)
721.I94	Izu Peninsula (Japan)
721.J3	Japan
721.J33	Japanese flowering cherry
721.J335	Japanese incense ceremony
721.J34	Japanese tea ceremony
721.K27	Kagawa-ken (Japan)
721.K28	Kagoshima-ken (Japan)
721.K3	Kamakura-shi (Japan)
721.K35	Kanazawa-shi (Japan)
721.K36	Kantō Region (Japan)
721.K44	Killing of the elderly
721.K45	Kinki Region (Japan)
721.K54	Kōbe-shi (Japan)
721.K55	Kōchi-ken (Japan)
721.K6	Korea
721.K65	Koto
721.K88	Kyoto (Japan)
721.K9	Kyūshū Region (Japan)
721.L34	Lakes
721.L39	Laughter
721.L42	Law
721.L52	Life
721.L57	Loneliness
721.L6	Love
721.M33	Man-woman relationships
721.M35	Manchuria (China)
721.M37	Marriage
721.M38	Matsukawa Railroad Accident, 1949

Japanese language and literature
Japanese literature
History and criticism
History
Special aspects and topics
Special topics, A-Z -- Continued

721.M42	Medicine
721.M45	Melancholy
721.M46	Melodrama
721.M47	Metamorphosis
	Mice see PL721.R37
721.M53	Mikawa Region (Japan)
721.M54	Military occupation
721.M55	Minamoto, Yoshitaka, 12th cent.
721.M56	Minamoto, Yoshitsune, 1159-1189
721.M57	Mirrors
721.M577	Modernism
721.M58	Money
721.M59	Moon
721.M6	Mothers
721.M63	Mountains
721.M78	Multiple personality
721.M83	Music
721.M85	Mythology
721.N24	Nagano-ken (Japan)
721.N248	Nagasaki Bombardment, 1945
721.N25	Nagasaki-ken (Japan)
721.N27	Nara-ken (Japan). Nara-shi (Japan)
721.N28	Naruto Strait (Japan)
721.N287	National characteristics
721.N29	Naturalism
721.N3	Nature
721.N47	Nichiren, 1222-1282
721.N5	Nihilism
721.N54	Niigata-ken (Japan)
721.O35	Occupations
721.O37	Odors
721.O4	Okayama-ken (Japan)
721.O45	Old age
	Older people, Killing of see PL721.K44
721.P36	Paper
721.P37	Patriotism
721.P38	Patronage and patrons
721.P4	Peace
721.P47	Pencils
721.P474	Performing arts
721.P5	Plants

Japanese language and literature
Japanese literature
History and criticism
History
Special aspects and topics
Special topics, A-Z -- Continued

721.P6	Politics
721.P72	Prophecies
721.P75	Psychology
721.P77	Psychoses
721.P84	Puns and punning
721.R3	Railroads
721.R37	Rats. Mice
721.R4	Realism
721.R45	Religion
721.R48	Revenge
721.R53	Rice wines
721.R56	Ritual
721.R57	Rivers
721.R62	Roads
721.R64	Romanticism
721.R87	Russo-Japanese War, 1904-1905
721.S23	Saddharmapuṇḍarīka
721.S25	Sado Island (Japan)
721.S26	Saiō
721.S27	San'yō Region (Japan)
721.S3	Science. Science fiction
721.S38	Sea
721.S4	Seasons
721.S45	Self, self-knowledge, self-perception, egoism, etc.
721.S46	Semimaru, 10th cent.?
721.S5	Sex
721.S52	Shades and shadows
721.S524	Shanghai (China)
721.S53	Shiga-ken (Japan)
721.S535	Shimanto River (Japan)
721.S54	Shinto
721.S5415	Shunkan, 1142-1179
721.S542	Sick
721.S547	Sin
721.S55	Sino-Japanese War, 1937-1945
721.S57	Snails
721.S58	Snow
721.S6	Socialism
721.S62	Society and literature
721.S63	Sōka-shi (Japan)
721.S64	Sound

PL

Japanese language and literature
Japanese literature
History and criticism
History
Special aspects and topics
Special topics, A-Z -- Continued

721.S66	Sports
721.S72	Stars
721.S73	State, The
721.S75	Style
721.S76	Suicide
721.S78	Sumida River (Japan)
721.S8	Supernatural. Ghosts
721.S86	Swordsmen
721.S94	Symbolism
721.T3	Taira, Atsumori, 1169-1184
721.T32	Taira, Sadabumi, d. 923
721.T34	Taoism. Taoist influences
721.T345	Tea
	Tea ceremony, Japanese see PL721.J34
(721.T347)	Teachers
	see PL722.T4
721.T348	Tears
721.T35	Technology
721.T39	Textile fabrics
721.T52	Time
721.T55	Tōhoku Region (Japan)
721.T57	Tōkaidō (Japan)
721.T6	Tokyo
721.T64	Toyama-ken (Japan)
721.T68	Tragedy
721.T7	Transportation
721.T75	Travel
721.T78	Tsushima Island (Japan)
721.T95	Twilight
721.U73	Utamakura
721.V39	Vegetables
721.V42	Versification
721.V5	Violence. Violent deaths
721.V69	Voyages to the otherworld
721.W27	Wakayama-ken (Japan)
721.W3	War
721.W4	Weather
721.W55	Winds
721.W65	World War II
721.Y3	Yamanashi-ken (Japan)
721.Y35	Yang, gui-fei, 719-756

	Japanese language and literature
	Japanese literature
	History and criticism
	History
	Special aspects and topics
	Special topics, A-Z -- Continued
721.Y56	Yokohama-shi (Japan)
721.Y58	Yoshino Mountain (Japan)
722.A-Z	Treatment of special classes, races, etc., A-Z
	Class here general works only
	For history of a special form or period, see the form or period
722.A-Z	Treatment of special classes, races, etc., A-Z
722.A45	Ainu
722.A78	Artisans
722.B54	Blind
722.B85	Buraku people
722.C48	Children
722.D34	Daimyo
722.H87	Husbands
722.L32	Labor. Working class
722.L46	Lepers
722.L47	Lesbians
722.L52	Libertines
722.M5	Middle class
722.M66	Mothers
	Older people see PL721.O45
722.O96	Outsiders
	Peasantry see PL722.P4
722.P4	Peasants. Peasantry
722.P58	Physical education teachers
722.P74	Prostitutes
722.S64	Soldiers
722.T4	Teachers
722.W58	Wives
722.W64	Women
	Working class see PL722.L32
722.Y67	Youth
	Awards, prizes
722.5	General works
722.6.A-Z	Special, A-Z
	Biography of authors
	Including memoirs and letters
723	Collective
	Individual
	see PL784+
	Literary landmarks. Homes and haunts of authors

Japanese language and literature
Japanese literature
History and criticism
History
Literary landmarks. Homes and haunts of authors --
Continued

724	General works
724.2.A-Z	By place, A-Z
725	Women authors. Literary relations of women
725.2.A-Z	Other classes of authors, A-Z
725.2.C45	Children
725.2.C47	Christians
725.2.E46	Emperors and empresses
725.2.K67	Koreans
	Laboring class see PL725.2.W65
725.2.M45	Men
725.2.P58	People with disabilities
725.2.W65	Working class
726.1-.88	By period (Table PL1)
	Add number in table to PL726
	Special forms
	Poetry
	General works
727.A2	Early works through 1867
727.A3-Z	1868-
727.5	Addresses, essays, lectures
727.55	Study and teaching
727.65.A-Z	Special topics, A-Z
	Prefer classification by form
	For list of topics see PL721.A+
	By form
	Waka
	Including tanka, chōka, katauta, sedōka
728.A2	Early works through 1867
728.A3-Z	1868-
728.116	Dictionaries, indexes, etc.
728.12	Special topics, A-Z
	For list of topics see PL721.A+
728.13	Treatment of special classes, races, etc., A-Z
	For list of special classes, races, etc. see PL722.A+
728.15	Man'yōshū
728.15.A1	Periodicals, societies, etc.
728.15.A2-.Z7	General works
728.15.Z8	History of Man'yōshū studies
728.16	Dictionaries, indexes, etc.
728.17	Commentaries. Explication

Japanese language and literature
Japanese literature
History and criticism
History
Special forms
Poetry
By form
Waka
Man'yōshū -- Continued

728.172	On selections or parts
728.173	Address, essays, lectures, etc.
728.174	Special aspects
	Including language, etc.
728.175	Special topics, A-Z
	For list of topics see PL721.A+
728.176	Treatment of special classes, races, etc., A-Z
	For list of special classes see PL722.A+
	Imperial anthologies
728.2	Hachidaishū. Sandaishū
728.21	Works on selections or on two or more collections
	Individual anthologies
728.22	Kokin wakashū
728.23	Gosen wakashū
728.24	Shui wakashū
728.25	Go shūi wakashū
728.253	Gyokuyō wakashū
728.26	Kin'yō wakashū
728.27	Shika wakashū
728.28	Senzai wakashū
728.283	Shoku senzai wakashū
728.29	Shin kokin wakashū
728.293	Shin shoku kokin wakashū
728.3	Shin chokusen wakashū
728.32	Shoku Gosen wakashū
728.35	Shin gosen wakashū
728.38	Zoku Go shūi wakashū
728.39	Fūga wakashū
728.42	Shin shūi wakashū
728.43	Shin go shūi wakashū
728.5.A-Z	Other anthologies, A-Z
728.5.C5	Chikurinshō
728.5.D34	Dairi meisho hyakushu
728.5.E54	Eikyū yonen hyakushu
728.5.F8	Fuboko waka shō
728.5.F85	Fūyō wakashū
728.5.H6	Horikawain hyakushu

Japanese language and literature
Japanese literature
History and criticism
History
Special forms
Poetry
By form
Waka
Other anthologies, A-Z -- Continued

728.5.J56	Jisanka
728.5.K3	Kampyō no ontoki kisai no miya utaawase
728.5.K6	Kokin waka rokujō
728.5.K825	Kudaishō
728.5.K94	Kyuān hyakushu
728.5.M68	Motoyoshi Shinnō goshū
728.5.N95	Nyōbō sanjūrokunin utaawase
728.5.O4	Ogura hyakunin isshu
728.5.R6	Rokka waka shū
728.5.R84	Ruijū koshū
728.5.S25	Sanjūrokuninshū
728.5.S34	Shin Man'yōshū
728.5.S35	Shinsen man'yōshū
728.5.S4	Shinsen tsukubashū
728.5.S5	Shin'yō wakashū
728.5.S516	Shōji ninen shodohyakushu
728.5.S52	Shoku senginshū
728.5.S53	Shoku shika wakashū
728.5.T77	Tsukimōde wakashū
728.8-.888	By period (Table PL1a)
	Haiku
729.A1	Periodicals, societies, etc.
729.A2-Z	General works
729.5-.588	By period (Table PL1a)
730	Senryū
	Ballads. Songs
	For songs with music, see class M
731	General works
731.1-.88	By period (Table PL1)
	Add number in table to PL731
	Kanshi (Japanese poetry)
731.89	General works
731.9-.988	By period (Table PL1a)
732.A-Z	Other, A-Z
732.C45	Children's poetry. Children's songs (Texts)
732.D53	Didactic poetry
732.H3	Haikai
732.K6	Kouta

Japanese language and literature
Japanese literature
History and criticism
History
Special forms
Poetry
By form
Other, A-Z -- Continued

732.K94	Kyōka
732.R4	Renga
732.R43	Renku
733.1-.88	By period (Table PL1)

Add number in table to PL733

Drama

Cf. PN2920+ The Japanese theater

General works

734.A2	Early works through 1867
734.A3-Z	1868-
734.4	Dictionaries
734.5	Addresses, essays, lectures, etc.
734.55	Study and teaching
734.6	Digests, synopses, etc.
734.65.A-Z	Special topics, A-Z

Class here general works only; for history of a
special form or period, see the form or period
For list of topics see PL721.A+

By form

735	Nō. Yōkyoku. Utai
736	Kyōgen
737	Kabuki

Puppet plays see PN1978.A+
Shadow plays see PN1979.S5
Motion picture plays see PN1993.5.A3+

737.8	Television plays
738.A-Z	Other, A-Z
738.A44	Amateur drama. Juvenile drama
738.C64	Comedy
738.J6	Jōruri. Sekkyōbushi

Juvenile drama see PL738.A44

738.K68	Kōwaka
738.N35	Naniwabushi

Sekkyōbushi see PL738.J6

739.1-.88	By period (Table PL1)

Add number in table to PL739

Prose. Fiction
General works

740.A2	Early works

Japanese language and literature
Japanese literature
History and criticism
History
Special forms
Prose. Fiction
General works -- Continued

740.A3-Z	1868-
740.5	Addresses, essays, lectures, etc.
740.55	Study and teaching
740.6	Digests, synopses, etc.
740.65.A-Z	Special topics, A-Z

Class here general works only; for history of a
special form or period, see the form or period
For list of topics see PL721.A+

740.66.A-Z	Treatment of special classes, races, etc., A-Z

For list of special classes, races, etc. see
PL722.A+

By form

740.8	Children's stories

Diaries. Travel

741	General works
741.1-.88	By period (Table PL1)

Add number in table to PL741

Essay
Including zuihitsu

742	General works
742.1-.88	By period (Table PL1)

Add number in table to PL742

Fiction see PL740+
Kanbun (Japanese prose)

742.89	General works
742.9-.988	By period (Table PL1a)

Letters

743	General works
743.1-.88	By period (Table PL1)

Add number in table to PL743

744	Romance
745	Short story

Including Sōshi
Wit and humor. Satire

746	General works
746.5	Rakugo

Cf. PN2924.5.R34 Performance
Aphorisms, apothegms, etc. see PN6269+
Maxims see PN6299+
Fables, parables, etc. see PN989.A+

Japanese language and literature
Japanese literature
History and criticism
History
Special forms
Prose. Fiction
By form -- Continued
Proverbs see PN6519.J3
Journalism see PN5401+
747.1-.88   By period (Table PL1)
     Add number in table to PL747
Folk literature
For works on folk songs with music or discussed
from a musical view see ML3750+
(748)   History and criticism
     see GR339+
(749)   Collections
     see GR339+
Tales see GR339+
Folk songs see ML3750+; PL731+
Inscriptions
750   History and criticism
751   Collections
751.5   Juvenile literature
     For special genres, see the genre
Collections
General (Comprehensive, not confined to any one period
or form)
752   Published before 1868
753   Published 1868-
754   Selections
754.5   Haibun
Kanbungaku (Japanese literature)
754.69   General works
754.7-.788   By period (Table PL1a)
755.1-.88   By period (Table PL1)
     Add number in table to PL755
756.A-Z   Special classes of authors, A-Z
756.C5   Children
756.J36   Japanese Americans
756.L33   Laboring class. Working class
756.L46   Lepers
756.P7   Prisoners
756.S65   Soldiers
756.S85   Students
756.T83   Tuberculosis patients
756.W54   Widows

PL

	Japanese language and literature
	Japanese literature
	Collections
	Special classes of authors, A-Z -- Continued
	Working class see PL756.L33
756.W6	Women
756.6.A-Z	Special topics (Prose and verse), A-Z
	For list of topics see PL721.A+
756.65.A-Z	Treatment of special classes, races, etc.
	For list of special classes, races, etc. see PL722.A+
	Special forms
	Poetry
757.A1	Periodicals. Societies. Serials
	General works
757.A2	Early works through 1867
757.A3-Z	1868-
757.3	Concordances, dictionaries, indexes, etc.
757.4.A-Z	Special classes of authors, A-Z
757.4.C45	Children
	Including children with disabilities
	Laboring class see PL757.4.W67
757.4.P45	People with disabilities
757.4.P74	Prisoners
757.4.R35	Railroad workers
757.4.S24	Sailors
757.4.V48	Veterans
757.4.W67	Working class
757.5.A-Z	By topics, A-Z
	Prefer classification by form
	For list of topics see PL721.A+
	By form
	Waka
	Including tanka, chōka, katauta, sedōka
758.A1	Periodicals. Societies. Serials
758.A2-Z	General works
	Man'yōshū
758.15.A11-.A2	Text. By editor
	Translations. By date
758.15.A3	English
758.15.A35	French
758.15.A36	German
758.15.A4-.A59	Other languages (alphabetically)
758.15.A6	Selections. By date
758.155.A-Z	Special topics, A-Z
	For list of special topics see PL721.A+
	Imperial anthologies
758.2	Hachidaishū. Sandaishū

Japanese language and literature
Japanese literature
Collections
Special forms
Poetry
By form
Waka
Imperial anthologies -- Continued

758.21	Works of selections or of two or more collections
	Individual anthologies
758.22	Kokin wakashū (Table PL9)
758.23	Gosen wakashū (Table PL9)
758.24	Shui wakashū (Table PL9)
758.25	Go shūi wakashū (Table PL9)
758.26	Kin'yō wakashū (Table PL9)
758.27	Shika wakashū (Table PL9)
758.28	Senzai wakashū (Table PL9)
758.29	Shin kokin wakashū (Table PL9)
758.3	Shin chokusen wakashū (Table PL9)
758.32	Shoku Gosen wakashū (Table PL9)
758.33	Shoku kokin wakashū (Table PL9)
758.34	Zoku Shūi wakashū (Table PL9)
758.35	Shin gosen wakashū (Table PL9)
758.36	Gyokuyō wakashū (Table PL9)
758.37	Shoku senzai wakashū (Table PL9)
758.38	Zoku Go shūi wakashū (Table PL9)
758.39	Fūga wakashū (Table PL9)
758.4	Shin senzai wakashū (Table PL9)
758.42	Shin shūi wakashū (Table PL9)
758.43	Shin go shūi wakashū (Table PL9)
758.44	Shin shoku kokin wakashū (Table PL9)
758.5.A-Z	Other anthologies, A-Z
758.5.C5	Chikurinshō (Table PL10)
758.5.C56	Chūko sanjūrokunin utawaase (Table PL10)
758.5.D35	Dairi meisho hyakushu (Table PL10)
758.5.E34	Eikyū yonen hyakushu (Table PL10)
758.5.F75	Fuboku waka shō (Table PL10)
758.5.F8	Fūyō wakashū (Table PL10)
758.5.G69	Goyō waka shū (Table PL10)
758.5.H6	Hōji hyakushu (Table PL10)
758.5.H67	Horikawa-in ontoki hyakushu waka (Table PL10)
	Hyakunin isshu see PL758.5.O4
758.5.K25	Kakanshū (Table PL10)
758.5.K3	Kampyō no ontokī kisai no miya utaawase (Table PL10)

Japanese language and literature
Japanese literature
Collections
Special forms
Poetry
By form
Waka
Other anthologies, A-Z -- Continued

758.5.K35	Kangetsu waka shū (Table PL10)
758.5.K56	Kōen tsugiuta (Table PL10)
758.5.K6	Kokin waka rokujō (Table PL10)
758.5.K88	Kyūan hyakushu (Table PL10)
758.5.M35	Mandai wakashū (Table PL10)
758.5.M44	Meirin kashū (Table PL10)
758.5.N53	Nihachi meidai waka shū (Table PL10)
758.5.O4	Ogura hyakunin isshu (Table PL10)
758.5.R5	Rikka waka shū (Table PL10)
758.5.R64	Rokkashō (Table PL10)
758.5.R66	Roppyakuban utaawase (Table PL10)
758.5.R84	Ruijū koshū (Table PL10)
758.5.S18	Sanjūrokuninshū (Table PL10)
	Sankashū see PL788.5
758.5.S4	Sen-gohyakuban utaawase (Table PL10)
758.5.S43	Shakkyō sanjūrokunin kasen (Table PL10)
758.5.S46	Shiehijūichiban shokunin utaawase (Table PL10)
758.5.S47	Shin Man'yōshū (Table PL10)
758.5.S476	Shoku go meidai wakashū (Table PL10)
758.5.S48	Shōyō meisho waka shū (Table PL10)
758.5.S5	Shūfū waka shū (Table PL10)
758.5.S537	Shūi gensō wakashū (Table PL10)
758.5.S54	Shūi shō (Table PL10)
758.5.T35	Tamesue shū (Table PL10)
758.5.T6	Tōnoin sesshōke hyakushu (Table PL10)
758.5.T78	Tsukimōde wakashū (Table PL10)
758.5.U5	Ungyoku waka shū (Table PL10)
758.8-.888	By period (Table PL1a)
	Haiku
759.A1	Periodicals, societies, etc.
759.A2-Z	General works
759.5-.588	By period (Table PL1a)
760	Senryū
	Ballads. Songs
	For songs with music, see class M
761	General works
761.1-.88	By period (Table PL1)
	Add number in table to PL761

Japanese language and literature
 Japanese literature
  Collections
   Special forms
    Poetry
     By form -- Continued
      Kanshi (Japanese poetry)
761.89   General works
761.9-.988   By period (Table PL1a)
762.A-Z   Other, A-Z
762.C55   Children's poetry. Children's songs (Texts)
                For collections of poetry by children see
                  PL757.4.C45
762.H3   Haikai
762.K6   Kouta
762.K9   Kyōka. Comic poetry
762.N34   Nagauta (Texts)
762.P3   Parodies
762.R4   Renga
762.R43   Renku
763.1-.88   By period (Table PL1)
                Add number in table to PL763
            Drama
764.A1   Periodicals, societies, etc.
            General works
764.A2   Early works through 1867
764.A3-Z   1868-
764.5   Selections
            By form
764.7   Comedy
765   Nō. Yōkyoku. Utai
766   Kyōgen
767   Kabuki
            Kamishibai plays see PN1979.K3
            Puppet plays see PN1981
            Shadow plays see PN6120.S5
            Motion picture plays see PN1997.A1
768.A-Z   Other, A-Z
768.A35   Amateur drama. Juvenile drama
768.J6   Jōruri. Sekkyōbushi
             Juvenile drama see PL768.A35
768.K67   Kōwaka
768.O53   One-act plays
768.R34   Radio plays
             Sekkyōbushi see PL768.J6
769.1-.88   By period (Table PL1)
              Add number in table to PL769

Japanese language and literature
Japanese literature
Collections
Special forms -- Continued
Prose. Fiction

770.A1	Periodicals. Societies. Serials
	General works
770.A2	Early works through 1867
770.A3-Z	1868-
770.5	Selections
770.55.A-Z	Special classes of authors, A-Z
770.55.T4	Teachers
770.55.W64	Women
770.6.A-Z	Special topics, A-Z
	For list of topics see PL721.A+
770.7.A-Z	Treatment of special classes, races, etc., A-Z
	For list of special classes, races, etc., see PL722.A+
	By form
	Diaries. Travel
771	General works
771.1-.88	By period (Table PL1)
	Add number in table to PL771
	Essays
	Including zuihitsu
772	General works
772.1-.88	By period (Table PL1)
	Add number in table to PL772
	Fiction see PL770+
	Kanbun (Japanese prose)
772.89	General works
772.9-.988	By period (Table PL1a)
	Letters
773	General works
773.1-.88	By period (Table PL1)
	Add number in table to PL773
774	Romance
775	Short story
	Including Sōshi
	Wit and humor. Satire
776	General works
	By form
776.5	Rakugo
	Cf. PN2924.5.R34 Performance
776.8-.888	By period (Table PL1a)
	Aphorisms and apothegms see PN6277.A+
	Maxims see PN6307.A+

Japanese language and literature
Japanese literature
Collections
Special forms
Prose. Fiction
By form -- Continued
Fables, parables, etc. see PN989.A+
Proverbs see PN6519.J3

777.1-.88	By period (Table PL1)

Add number in table to PL777
Folk literature see GR339+
Folk-songs see M1812
Popular songs see M1813.18
Inscriptions see PL751
Juvenile literature see PZ49.2+
Translations
From foreign languages into Japanese
For collection of translations, see the literature of the
original language
For collections from several languages, see subclass PN
For criticism see PL720.6

782-783	From Japanese into foreign languages (Table P-PZ30 modified)

For criticism see PL720.7+
Chinese

782.C1	General
782.C3	Poetry
782.C5	Drama
782.C8	Prose. Prose fiction

Korean

782.K1	General
782.K3	Poetry
782.K5	Drama
782.K8	Prose. Prose fiction

Individual authors and works
Origins. Early to 794 A.D.

784.A-Z	Anonymous works. By title, A-Z
784.K34-.K343	Kaifūsō (Table P-PZ43)
784.K6	Kojiki

Class here only literary and linguistic studies of this
work
For studies from the viewpoint of religion and
mythology see BL2217.3
For original texts, translations, and general and
historical studies see DS855+

Japanese language and literature
Japanese literature
Individual authors and works
Origins. Early to 794 A.D.
Anonymous works. By title, A-Z -- Continued

784.N5   Nihon shoki
          Class here only literary and linguistic studies of this
              work
          For studies from the viewpoint of religion and
              mythology see BL2217.4
          For original texts, translations, and general and
              historical studies see DS855+

785   Kakinomoto, Hitomaro, fl. 689-700 (Table P-PZ39)
785.2   Ō, Yasumaro, d. 723 (Table P-PZ39)
785.4   Otomo, Yakamochi, 718?-785 (Table P-PZ39)
785.6   Yamabe, Akahito (Table P-PZ39)
785.8   Yamanoue, Okura, 660?-733? (Table P-PZ39)
786.A-Z   Other, A-Z
786.K36   Kasa, Kanamura, fl. 715-733 (Table P-PZ40)
786.K87   Kurumamochi, Chitose, 7th/8th cent. (Table P-PZ40)
786.N8   Nukada no Ōkimi (Table P-PZ40)
786.O68   Ōtomo, Sakanoue no Iratsume, 7th/8th cent. (Table
              P-PZ40)
786.O7   Ōtomo, Tabito, 665-731 (Table P-PZ40)
786.T28   Takahashi, Mushimaro (Table P-PZ40)
786.T3   Takechi, Kurohito, 7th/8th cent. (Table P-PZ40)
(786.Y3) Yamabe, Akahito
              see PL785.6
          Heian period, 794-1185
787.A-Z   Anonymous works. By title, A-Z
787.A7-.A73   Ariake no wakare (Table P-PZ43)
787.B85-.B853 Bunka shūreishū (Table P-PZ43)
787.E5-.E53   Eiga monogatari (Table P-PZ43)
787.H4-.H43   Heichū monogatari (Table P-PZ43)
787.H65-.H653 Honchō monzui (Table P-PZ43)
787.H67-.H673 Honchō reisō (Table P-PZ43)
787.I43   Imakagami
          Class here only literary and linguistic studies of this
              work
          For original texts, translations, and general and
              historical studies see DS856
787.I76-.I763 Irohauta (Table P-PZ43)
787.I8-.I83   Ise monogatari (Table P-PZ43)
787.K36-.K363 Kara monogatari (Table P-PZ43)
787.K6-.K63   Konjaku monogatari (Table P-PZ43)
787.O25-.O253 Ochikubo monogatari (Table P-PZ43)
787.R94-.R943 Ryōjin hishō (Table P-PZ43)

Japanese language and literature
Japanese literature
Individual authors and works
Heian period, 794-1185
Anonymous works. By title, A-Z -- Continued

787.R96-.R963	Ryōunshū (Table P-PZ43)
(787.S2-.S23)	Sagoromo monogatari
	see PL789.R63
787.S94-.S943	Sumiyoshi monogatari (Table P-PZ43)
787.T28-.T283	Takamura monogatari (Table P-PZ43)
787.T3-.T33	Taketori monogatari (Table P-PZ43)
787.T35-.T353	Tamatsukuri Komachishi sōsuisho (Table P-PZ43)
787.T64-.T643	Torikaebaya monogatari (Table P-PZ43)
787.T74-.T743	Tsutsumi Chūnagon monogatari (Table P-PZ43)
787.U7-.U73	Utsubo monogatari (Table P-PZ43)
787.Y27-.Y273	Yamaji no tsuyu (Table P-PZ43)
787.Y3-.Y33	Yamato monogatari (Table P-PZ43)
788	Ariwara, Narihira, 825-880 (Table P-PZ39)
788.2	Izumi Shikibu, b. 974 (Table P-PZ39)
788.3	Ki, Tsurayuki, d. 945 or 6 (Table P-PZ39)
	For his compilation, Kokin wakashū, see PL758.22
788.4	Murasaki Shikibu, b. 978? (Table P-PZ39)
788.5	Saigyō, 1118-1190 (Table P-PZ39)
788.6	Sei Shonagon, b. ca. 967 (Table P-PZ39)
788.7	Sugawara, Michizane, 845-903 (Table P-PZ39)
789.A-Z	Other, A-Z
789.A36	Akazome Emon, ca. 957-ca. 1045 (Table P-PZ40)
789.D3	Daini no Sammi, d. 1077 or 8 (Table P-PZ40)
789.D64	Dōmyō, 974-1020 (Table P-PZ40)
789.E33	Egyō, 10th cent. (Table P-PZ40)
789.F776	Fujiwara, Kanesuke, 877-933 (Table P-PZ40)
789.F778	Fujiwara, Kintō, 966-1041 (Table P-PZ40)
789.F779	Fujiwara, Kiyosuke, 1104-1177 (Table P-PZ40)
789.F782	Fujiwara, Michinaga, 966-1027 (Table P-PZ40)
789.F783	Fujiwara, Morosuke, 908-960 (Table P-PZ40)
789.F784	Fujiwara, Nagatō, 949?-1009? (Table P-PZ40)
789.F786	Fujiwara, Nakabumi, 908-973 (Table P-PZ40)
789.F787	Fujiwara, Norinaga, b. 1109 (Table P-PZ40)
789.F79	Fujiwara, Toshinari, 1114-1204 (Table P-PZ40)
789.F793	Fujiwara, Yorinari, 12th cent. (Table P-PZ40)
789.F8	Fujiwara Michitsuna no haha, d. 995 (Table P-PZ40)
789.G67	Goshirakawa, Emperor of Japan, 1127-1192 (Table P-PZ40)
789.H45	Henjō, 816-890 (Table P-PZ40)
789.H53	Higaki no Ōna, 9th/10th cent. (Table P-PZ40)
789.H6	Hon'in no Jijū, ca. 921-ca. 972 (Table P-PZ40)
789.I82	Inpu Mon'in no Taifu, 1131?-1200? (Table P-PZ40)

Japanese language and literature
Japanese literature
Individual authors and works
Heian period, 794-1185
Other, A-Z -- Continued

789.I83	Ise, d. 939 (Table P-PZ40)
789.I85	Ise no Taifu, 987?-1063? (Table P-PZ40)
(789.J3)	Jakunen, 12th cent.
	see PL789.F793
789.J6	Jōjin Ajari no haha (Table P-PZ40)
789.K4	Kenrei Mon'in Ukyō no Daibu, b. 1157? (Table P-PZ40)
789.K56	Kiyohara, Fukayabu, fl. 908-923 (Table P-PZ40)
789.K58	Kiyohara, Motosuke, 908-990 (Table P-PZ40)
789.K64	Kodai no Mimi, 10th cent. (Table P-PZ40)
	Michitshuna no Haha, ca. 95-995 see PL789.F8
789.M46	Minamoto, Kanezumi, b. 955? (Table P-PZ40)
789.M48	Minamoto, Michichika, ca. 1145-1202 (Table P-PZ40)
789.M49	Minamoto, Michinari, d. 1019 (Table P-PZ40)
789.M496	Minamoto, Shigeyuki, d. 1000 (Table P-PZ40)
789.M5	Minamoto, Toshiyori, ca. 1055-ca. 1129 (Table P-PZ40)
789.M53	Minamoto, Tsunenobu, 1016-1097 (Table P-PZ40)
789.M54	Minamoto, Yorimasa, 1104-1180 (Table P-PZ40)
789.M55	Minamoto no Shigeyuki no Musume, 10th/11th cent. (Table P-PZ40)
789.N54	Nijōin no Sanuki, ca. 1141-ca. 1217 (Table P-PZ40)
789.N64	Nōin, 988-1050? (Table P-PZ40)
789.O42	Ōe, Masafusa, 1041-1111 (Table P-PZ40)
789.O43	Oē, Masahira, 952-1012 (Table P-PZ40)
789.O46	Ōnakatomi, Yoshinobu, 921-991 (Table P-PZ40)
789.O5	Ono, Komachi, 9th cent. (Table P-PZ40)
789.R63	Rokujō Saiin no Senji, d. 1092 (Table P-PZ40)
789.S15	Sagami, b. ca. 998 (Table P-PZ40)
789.S18	Saigū Nyōgo, 929-985 (Table P-PZ40)
789.S2	Sanukino Suke, b. ca. 1079 (Table P-PZ40)
789.S43	Senshi, Princess, daughter of Murakami, Emperor of Japan, 926-967 (Table P-PZ40)
789.S47	Shijō no Miya Shimotsuke, fl. 1045-1068 (Table P-PZ40)
789.S48	Shun'e, b. 1113 (Table P-PZ40)
789.S6	Sone, Yoshitada, 10th cent. (Table P-PZ40)
789.S8	Sugawara Takasue no musume, b. 1008 (Table P-PZ40)
789.S88	Sutoku, Emperor of Japan, 1119-1164 (Table P-PZ40)
789.T33	Tachibana, d. 1085 (Table P-PZ40)

Japanese language and literature
Japanese literature
Individual authors and works
Heian period, 794-1185
Other, A-Z -- Continued

789.T35	Taiken Mon'in Horikawa (Table P-PZ40)
789.U5	Uma no Naishi, b. ca. 954 (Table P-PZ40)
789.Y37	Yasusuke-ō no Haha, fl. 1050-1106 (Table P-PZ40)

Kamakura through Momoyama periods, 1185-1660

790	Anonymous works. By title, A-Z
790.A43-.A433	Akigiri (Table P-PZ43)
790.A48-.A483	Ama no karumo (Table P-PZ43)
790.A94	Azumakagami

                    Class here only literary and linguistic studies of the work
                    For original texts, translations, and general and historical studies see DS859

790.B44-.B443	Benkei monogatari (Table P-PZ43)
790.B86-.B863	Bunshō no sōshi (Table P-PZ43)
790.F84-.F843	Fuji no koromo monogatari emaki (Table P-PZ43)
790.G4-.G43	Genpei seisuiki (Table P-PZ43)
790.G432-.G4323	Genpei tōjōroku (Table P-PZ43)
790.G513-.G5133	Gikeiki (Table P-PZ43)
790.H3-.H33	Heiji monogatari (Table P-PZ43)
790.H4-.H43	Heike monogatari (Table P-PZ43)
790.H6-.H63	Hōgen monogatari (Table P-PZ43)
790.I92-.I923	Iwade shinobu (Table P-PZ43)
790.J5-.J53	Jikkinshō (Table P-PZ43)
790.J55-.J553	Jinkei shō (Table P-PZ43)
790.J86-.J863	Jūnidan sōshi (Table P-PZ43)
790.K28-.K283	Kadō hidensho (Table P-PZ43)
790.K33-.K333	Kaidōki (Table P-PZ43)
790.K34-.K343	Kanginshū (Table P-PZ43)
790.K35-.K353	Kasuga Gongen genki (Table P-PZ43)
790.K37-.K373	Katsuragawa jizōki (Table P-PZ43)
790.K42-.K423	Kaze ni momiji (Table P-PZ43)
790.K43-.K433	Kaze ni tsurenaki monogatari (Table P-PZ43)
790.K63-.K633	Kohon setsuwashū (Table P-PZ43)
790.K64-.K643	Koiji yukashiki daishō (Table P-PZ43)
(790.K65)	Kojidan
	see PL792.M47
790.K67-.K673	Koke no koromo (Table P-PZ43)
790.K69-.K693	Kowata no shigure (Table P-PZ43)
790.K85-.K853	Kumano no honji (Table P-PZ43)
790.M3-.M33	Matsukage Chūnagon monogatari (Table P-PZ43)
790.M34-.M343	Matsura no Miya Monogatari (Table P-PZ43)
790.M66-.M663	Monokusa Tarō (Table P-PZ43)

Japanese language and literature
Japanese literature
Individual authors and works
Kamakura through Momoyama periods, 1185-1660
Anonymous works. By title, A-Z -- Continued

790.S3-.S33	Saigyō monogatari (Table P-PZ43)
790.S35-.S353	Sayogoromo (Table P-PZ43)
790.S4-.S43	Senjūshō (Table P-PZ43)
790.S45-.S453	Shigure (Table P-PZ43)
790.S47-.S473	Shinobine monogatari (Table P-PZ43)
790.S5-.S53	Shiratsuyu (Table P-PZ43)
790.S54-.S543	Shizuka (Table P-PZ43)
790.S55-.S553	Shōjin gyorui monogatari (Table P-PZ43)
790.S56-.S563	Shungyū ekotoba (Table P-PZ43)
790.S6-.S63	Soga monogatari (Table P-PZ43)
790.T3-.T33	Taiheiki (Table P-PZ43)
790.T64-.T643	Tōkan kikō (Table P-PZ43)
790.T65-.T653	Tsurezuregusa shūi (Table P-PZ43)
790.U38-.U383	Uji shūi monogatari (Table P-PZ43)
790.W32-.W323	Waga mi ni tadoru himegimi (Table P-PZ43)
790.Y63-.Y633	Yokobue-zōshi (Table P-PZ43)
790.Y65-.Y653	Yoru no nezame monogatari (Table P-PZ43)
790.Y66-.Y663	Yoshino shūi (Table P-PZ43)
790.Z64-.Z643	Zoku kojidan (Table P-PZ43)
791	Fujiwara, Sadaie, 1162-1241 (Table P-PZ39)
791.2	Kamo, Chōmei, 1153?-1216? (Table P-PZ39)
791.4	Minamoto, Sanetomo, 1192-1219 (Table P-PZ39)
791.6	Yoshida, Kenkō, 1282-1350 (Table P-PZ39)
792.A-Z	Other, A-Z
792.A2	Abutsu Ni, ca. 1209-1283 (Table P-PZ40)
792.A73	Arakida, Moritake, 1473-1549 (Table P-PZ40)
792.A83	Ashikaga, Yoshimasa, 1436-1490 (Table P-PZ40)
792.A86	Asukai, Masatsune, 1170-1221 (Table P-PZ40)
792.A88	Asukai, Masaari, 1241-1301 (Table P-PZ40)
792.B45	Ben no Naishi, 13th cent. (Table P-PZ40)
792.D65	Dogen, 1200-1253 (Table P-PZ40)
792.E35	Eifuku Mon'in, 1271-1342 (Table P-PZ40)
792.F72	Fujiwara, Akiuji, 1207-1274 (Table P-PZ40)
792.F75	Fujiwara, Nobuzane, 1177?-1266? (Table P-PZ40)
792.F8	Fujiwara, Tameie, 1198-1275 (Table P-PZ40)
792.F815	Fujiwara, Tokitomo, 1204?-1265 (Table P-PZ40)
792.F82	Fujiwara, Yoshitsune, 1169-1206 (Table P-PZ40)
792.F825	Fujiwara Toshinari no Musume, 1171?-1254? (Table P-PZ40)
792.F83	Fushimi, Emperor of Japan, 1265-1317 (Table P-PZ40)
792.G44	Genryō, 1458-1491 (Table P-PZ40)

Japanese language and literature
Japanese literature
Individual authors and works
Kamakura through Momoyama periods, 1185-1660
Other, A-Z -- Continued

792.G47	Genshō, b. 1224 (Table P-PZ40)
792.G54	Gidō Shūshin, 1325?-1388 (Table P-PZ40)
792.G56	Gokashiwabara, Emperor of Japan, 1464-1526 (Table P-PZ40)
792.G58	Gosukō-in, 1372-1456 (Table P-PZ40)
792.G6	Gotoba, Emperor of Japan, 1180-1239 (Table P-PZ40)
792.H5	Hino Takemuki, fl. 1329-1349 (Table P-PZ40)
792.H6	Hosokawa, Fujitaka, 1534-1610 (Table P-PZ40)
	Hosokawa, Yūsai, 1534-1610 see PL792.H6
792.I25	Ichijō, Kanera, 1402-1481 (Table P-PZ40)
792.I35	Ikkyū, 1394-1481 (Table P-PZ40)
792.I42	Imagawa, Ryōshun, 1325-1420? (Table P-PZ40)
792.I5	Inawashiro, Kensai, d. 1510 (Table P-PZ40)
792.J33	Jakuren, ca. 1139-1202 (Table P-PZ40)
792.J35	Jakushitsu Genkō, 1290-1367 (Table P-PZ40)
792.J5	Jien, 1155-1225 (Table P-PZ40)
792.K42	Keijo Shūrin, 1440-1518 (Table P-PZ40)
792.K43	Keisei, d. 1268 (Table P-PZ40)
792.K45	Kenshunmon'in Chūnagon, 12th cent. (Table P-PZ40)
792.K52	Kino, Yaichiemon, 16th cent. (Table P-PZ40)
792.K54	Kitabatake, Chikafusa, 1293-1354 (Table P-PZ40)
792.K6	Kojijū, 12th cent. (Table P-PZ40)
792.K62	Konparu, Zenchiku, b. 1405 (Table P-PZ40)
792.K9	Kyōgoku, Tamekane, 1254-1332 (Table P-PZ40)
792.M47	Minamoto, Akikane, 1160-1215 (Table P-PZ40)
792.M5	Minamoto, Ienaga, 1170-1234 (Table P-PZ40)
792.M517	Minamoto, Michitomo, 1171-1227 (Table P-PZ40)
792.M52	Minamoto, Mitsuyuki, 1163-1244 (Table P-PZ40)
792.M54	Minamoto, Tadatomo, d. 1597 (Table P-PZ40)
792.M85	Munenaga, Prince, son of Godaigo, Emperor of Japan, 1312?-1385? (Table P-PZ40)
792.M87	Musō Soseki, 1275-1351 (Table P-PZ40)
792.M9	Myōe, 1173-1232 (Table P-PZ40)
792.N3	Nakanoin Mastada no musume, b. 1258 (Table P-PZ40)
792.N34	Nakatsukasa no Naishi, 13th cent. (Table P-PZ40)
792.N5	Nijō, Yoshimoto, 1320-1388 (Table P-PZ40)
792.N94	Nyogetsu, fl. 1517-1524 (Table P-PZ40)
792.R43	Reizei, Masatame, 1445-1523 (Table P-PZ40)
792.R45	Reizei, Tamehiro, 1450-1526 (Table P-PZ40)

Japanese language and literature
Japanese literature
Individual authors and works
Kamakura through Momoyama periods, 1185-1660
Other, A-Z -- Continued

792.R95	Ryūtatsu, 1527-1611 (Table P-PZ40)
792.S28	Saka, Jūbutsu, fl. 1342 (Table P-PZ40)
792.S3	Satomura, Jōha, 1524?-1602? (Table P-PZ40)
792.S4	Seami, 1363-1443 (Table P-PZ40)
792.S43	Shikishi, Princess of Japan, d. 1201 (Table P-PZ40)
792.S44	Shimada, Sōchō, 1448-1532 (Table P-PZ40)
792.S45	Shinkei, 1406-1475 (Table P-PZ40)
792.S53	Shinshō, 1174-1248 (Table P-PZ40)
792.S55	Shotetsu, 1380-1458 (Table P-PZ40)
792.S56	Shukaku, Prince of Japan, 1150-1202 (Table P-PZ40)
(792.S57)	Shunzei Kyō no musume, d. 1254 see PL792.F825
792.S58	Sōchō, 1448-1532 (Table P-PZ40)
792.S6	Sōgi, 1421-1502 (Table P-PZ40)
792.S92	Satomura, Jōha, 1524?-1602? (Table P-PZ40)
792.T33	Tachibana, Narisue, fl. 1254 (Table P-PZ40)
792.T64	Ton'a, 1289-1372? (Table P-PZ40)
792.T76	Tsuchimikado, Emperor of Japan, 1196-1231 (Table P-PZ40)
792.T78	Tsukubashū (Table P-PZ40)
792.U76	Utsunomiya, Kagetsuna, 1235-1298 (Table P-PZ40)
792.Y36	Yamazaki, Sōkan, 1465-1553 (Table P-PZ40)
792.Y83	Yūa, 1291-1375 (Table P-PZ40)
	Zeami, 1363-1443 see PL792.S4
792.Z44	Zekkai Chūshin, 1336-1405 (Table P-PZ40)
	Early Edo period, 1600-1788
793.A-Z	Anonymous works. By title, A-Z
793.A34-.A343	Abe no Seimei Yamato kotoba (Table P-PZ43)
793.A54-.A543	Amida shijūhachiganki (Table P-PZ43)
793.C48-.C483	Chigusa nikki (Table P-PZ43)
793.G55-.G553	Gion sairei shinkōki (Table P-PZ43)
793.H53-.H533	Hiragana seisuiki (Table P-PZ43)
793.H56-.H563	Hitomotogiku (Table P-PZ43)
793.H58-.H583	Hōmyō dōji (Table P-PZ43)
793.I2-.I23	Ichinotani futaba gunki (Table P-PZ43)
	Ikenie monogatari see PL793.H58+
793.I4-.I43	Imoseyama onna teikin (Table P-PZ43)
793.J53-.J533	Jigabachi monogatari (Table P-PZ43)
793.K33-.K333	Kakinomoto no Ki Sōjō asahiguruma (Table P-PZ43)
793.K35-.K353	Kana de Soga nezashi no fujigane (Table P-PZ43)
793.K38-.K383	Keian Taiheiki (Table P-PZ43)

Japanese language and literature
Japanese literature
Individual authors and works
Early Edo period, 1600-1788
Anonymous works. By title, A-Z -- Continued

793.K394-.K3943	Keisei Awa no Naruto (Table P-PZ43)
793.K45-.K453	Kenuki (Table P-PZ43)
793.K47-.K473	Kichō shiwai (Table P-PZ43)
793.K53-.K533	Kinō wa kyō no monogatari (Table P-PZ43)
793.K87-.K873	Kusunoki Teii hikan (Table P-PZ43)
793.K92-.K923	Kyōbun takaraawase no ki (Table P-PZ43)
793.K94-.K943	Kyōganoko musume dōjōji (Table P-PZ43)
793.K96-.K963	Kyōgenki soto gojūban (Table P-PZ43)
793.M52-.M523	Mikka taiheiki (Table P-PZ43)
793.M56-.M563	Minamoto no Yoritomo, Minamoto no Yoshitsune kosenjo kanekake no matsu (Table P-PZ43)
793.M58-.M583	Miyatogawa monogatari (Table P-PZ43)
793.N47-.N473	Nise monogatari (Table P-PZ43)
793.O36-.O363	Oguri hangan ichidaiki (Table P-PZ43)
793.O38-.O383	Okuni kabuki soshi (Table P-PZ43)
793.O39-.O393	Ōmi Genji senjin yakata (Table P-PZ43)
793.O45-.O453	Ono no Tōfū aoyagi suzuri (Table P-PZ43)
793.O48-.O483	Ōoka seidan (Table P-PZ43)
793.O73-.O733	Ōshū Adachigahara (Table P-PZ43)
793.O87-.O873	Otogi bikuni (Table P-PZ43)
793.S22-.S223	Saimyōji-dono kyōkun hyakushu (Table P-PZ43)
793.S26-.S263	Sanada sandaiki (Table P-PZ43)
793.S42-.S423	Shigure (Table P-PZ43)
	Shiragiku-zōshi see PL793.H56+
793.S48-.S483	Shinzoku, Inutsukubashū (Table P-PZ43)
	Shōshō Kurama monogatari, see PL793.H56+
793.S53-.S533	Shutoku-in, Sanuki denki (Table P-PZ43)
793.S64-.S643	Sōgi shokoku monogatari (Table P-PZ43)
793.T26-.T263	Taishokan (Table P-PZ43)
793.T3-.T33	Takayanagi (Table P-PZ43)
793.T75-.T753	Tsuyu Dono monogatari (Table P-PZ43)
793.U66-.U663	Uo monogatari (or Kakai monogatari) (Table P-PZ43)
793.Y67-.Y673	Yoshitsune azumakudari monogatari (Table P-PZ43)
793.Z47-.Z473	Zeraku monogatari (Table P-PZ43)
793.Z63-.Z633	Zoku Kyōgenki (Table P-PZ43)
793.Z64-.Z643	Zoku Ochikubo monogatari (Table P-PZ43)
793.2	Asai, Ryōi, 1612?1691? (Table P-PZ39)
793.4	Chikamatsu, Monzaemon, 1653-1725 (Table P-PZ39)
793.6	Ejima, Kiseki, 1667-1736 (Table P-PZ39)
793.8	Enomoto, Kikaku, 1661-1707 (Table P-PZ39)
793.85	Fabian, fl. 1583-1607 (Table P-PZ39)
794	Ihara, Saikaku, 1642-1693 (Table P-PZ39)

	Japanese language and literature
	Japanese literature
	Individual authors and works
	Early Edo period, 1600-1788 -- Continued
794.18	Matsunaga, Sekigo, 1592-1657 (Table P-PZ39)
794.2	Matsunaga, Teitoku, 1571-1653 (Table P-PZ39)
794.4	Matsuo, Basho, 1644-1694 (Table P-PZ39)
794.6	Takeda, Izumo, 1691-1756 (Table P-PZ39)
794.7	Taniguchi, Buson, 1716-1784 (Table P-PZ39)
794.8	Ueda, Akinari, 1734-1809 (Table P-PZ39)
	Yosa, Buson, 1716-1784 see PL794.7
795.A-Z	Other, A-Z
795.A57	Amenomori, Hōshū, 1668-1755 (Table P-PZ40)
	Anrakuan Sakuden, 1554-1642 see PL795.S25
795.A72	Arai, Hakuseki, 1657-1725 (Table P-PZ40)
795.A727	Arakida, Hisaoyu, 1746-1804 (Table P-PZ40)
795.A73	Arakida, Rei, 1732-1806 (Table P-PZ40)
795.B33	Baba, Nobutake, fl. 1712-1718 (Table P-PZ40)
795.B35	Baijōken (Table P-PZ40)
795.B37	Baisa-ō, 1675-1763 (Table P-PZ40)
795.B65	Bonchō, d. 1714 (Table P-PZ40)
795.B86	Bunkōdō, fl. 1713-1741 (Table P-PZ40)
795.C53	Chikamatsu, Hanji, d. 1786 or 7 (Table P-PZ40)
795.C54	Chikamatsu, Tōnan, fl. 1769-1780 (Table P-PZ40)
	Chiyo-ni, 1703-1775 see PL795.K25
795.C55	Chōgetsu, 1714-1798 (Table P-PZ40)
795.F83	Fujimoto, Tobun, fl. 1737-1756 (Table P-PZ40)
795.F84	Fujitani, Nariakira, 1738-1779 (Table P-PZ40)
795.G65	Gomizunoo, Emperor of Japan, 1596-1680 (Table P-PZ40)
795.G96	Gyokushiken Yūtōshi, fl. 1687 (Table P-PZ40)
795.H35	Hattori, Nankaku, 1683-1759 (Table P-PZ40)
795.H39	Hayashi, Shunsai, 1618-1680 (Table P-PZ40)
795.H45	Heshikiya, Chōbin, 1700-1734 (Table P-PZ40)
795.H48	Hezutsu, Tōsaku, 1726-1789 (Table P-PZ40)
795.H57	Hiraga, Gennai, 1728?-1780 (Table P-PZ40)
795.H58	Hōjō, Dansui, 1663-1711 (Table P-PZ40)
795.H63-.H633	Honchō nijūshikō (Table P-PZ43)
795.I35	Ichinaka Sanjin Yūsa, 18th cent. (Table P-PZ40)
795.I43	Ikeda, Masanori, 17th cent. (Table P-PZ40)
795.I45	Ikenishi, Gonsui, 1650-1722? (Table P-PZ40)
795.I54	Inoue, Tsū, 1660-1738 (Table P-PZ40)
795.I68	Irie, Jakusu, 1671-1792 (Table P-PZ40)
795.I74	Ishikawa, Jōzan, 1583-1672 (Table P-PZ40)
795.I76	Isogai, Shūya, 17th cent. (Table P-PZ40)
795.I77	Issō, 1731?-1820? (Table P-PZ40)
795.I78	Itō, Jinsai, 1627-1705 (Table P-PZ40)

Japanese language and literature
Japanese literature
Individual authors and works
Early Edo period, 1600-1788
Other, A-Z -- Continued

795.I79	Itō, Kanpō, 1717-1787 (Table P-PZ40)
795.J6	Joraishi (Table P-PZ43)
795.J63	Jōsō, 1662-1704 (Table P-PZ40)
795.K25	Kaga no Chiyo, 1703-1775 (Table P-PZ40)
795.K27	Kagami, Shikō, 1665-1731 (Table P-PZ40)
795.K28	Kagawa, Sen'a, 1646-1735 (Table P-PZ40)
795.K3	Kamijima, Onitsura, 1661-1738 (Table P-PZ40)
795.K32	Kamo, Mabuchi, 1679-1769 (Table P-PZ40)
795.K324	Kanai, Sanshō, 1731-1797 (Table P-PZ40)
795.K327	Karaku Inshi Otohisa (Table P-PZ40)
795.K33	Karasumaru, Mitsuhiro, 1579-1638 (Table P-PZ40)
795.K34	Katō, Kyōtai, 1732-1792 (Table P-PZ40)
795.K35	Katori, Nahiko, 1723-1782 (Table P-PZ40)
795.K36	Kaya, Shirao, 1738-1791 (Table P-PZ40)
795.K4	Keichū, 1640-1701 (Table P-PZ40)
795.K44	Kenshiin, Shimben, 17th cent. (Table P-PZ40)
795.K54	Ki, Kaion, 1663-1742 (Table P-PZ40)
795.K545	Kimura, Kenkadō, 1736-1802 (Table P-PZ40)
795.K547	Kinoshita, Chōshōshi, 1569-1648 (Table P-PZ40)
795.K55	Kinoshita, Jun'an, 1621-1699 (Table P-PZ40)
795.K59	Kitamura, Kigin, 1620-1705 (Table P-PZ40)
795.K62	Kobayashi, Fūgo, 1741 or 2-1791 (Table P-PZ40)
795.K64	Kojima, Hikojūrō, fl. 1681-1704 (Table P-PZ40)
795.K65	Komatsuya, Hyakuki, 1720-1793 (Table P-PZ40)
795.K67	Kōnoike, Zen'emon, 1608-1693? (Table P-PZ40)
795.K87	Kuriyama, Senpo, 1671-1706 (Table P-PZ40)
795.K94	Kyōben, d. 1755 (Table P-PZ40)
795.M34	Matsu, Kanshi, d. 1798 (Table P-PZ40)
795.M36	Matsui, Yukitaka, fl. 1696-1712 (Table P-PZ40)
795.M38	Matsuki, Tantan, 1674-1761 (Table P-PZ40)
795.M47	Mimasuya, Hyōgo, 1660-1704 (Table P-PZ40)
795.M49	Miura, Chora (Table P-PZ40)
795.M53	Miyabe, Manjo, 18th cent. (Table P-PZ40)
795.M55	Miyako no Nishiki, b. 1675 (Table P-PZ40)
795.M64	Mokujiki Gogyō, 1718-1810 (Table P-PZ40)
795.M67	Mori, Hidetoshi, 17th cent. (Table P-PZ40)
795.M69	Motoori, Norinaga, 1730-1801 (Table P-PZ40)
795.M78	Mubaiken, Shōhō, 17th/18th cent. (Table P-PZ40)
795.M8	Mukai, Kyorai, 1651-1704 (Table P-PZ40)
795.M85	Muro, Kyūsō, 1658-1734 (Table P-PZ40)
795.N22	Nabeshima, Naosato, 1718-1770 (Table P-PZ40)
795.N24	Nagawa, Kamesuke, fl. 1772-1789 (Table P-PZ40)

Japanese language and literature
Japanese literature
Individual authors and works
Early Edo period, 1600-1788
Other, A-Z -- Continued

795.N27	Nakamura, Kōzen, fl. 1716 (Table P-PZ40)
795.N3	Nakamura, Seizaburō, d. 1743 (Table P-PZ40)
795.N36	Namiki, Senryū, 1695-1751 (Table P-PZ40)
795.N363	Namiki, Shōzō, 1730-1773 (Table P-PZ40)
795.N38-.N383	Narukami fudō kitayamazakura (Table P-PZ43)
795.N42	Narushima, Nobuyuki, 1689-1760 (Table P-PZ40)
795.N53	Nichisei, 1623-1668 (Table P-PZ40)
795.N57	Nishiki, Bunryū, fl. 1705-1717 (Table P-PZ40)
795.N59	Nishizawa, Ippū, 1665-1731 (Table P-PZ40)
795.N66	Nonaka, En, 1660-1726 (Table P-PZ40)
795.N68	Nonoguchi, Ryūho, 1595-1669 (Table P-PZ40)
795.O35	Ōgimachi, Machiko, 1688-1724 (Table P-PZ40)
795.O36	Ogyū, Sorai, 1666-1728 (Table P-PZ40)
795.O39	Okada, Shinsen, 1737-1799 (Table P-PZ40)
795.O394	Okanishi, Ichū, 1639-1711 (Table P-PZ40)
795.O93	Ōyodo, Michikaze, 1639-1707 (Table P-PZ40)
795.O937	Ozawa, Roan, 1723-1801 (Table P-PZ40)
795.O94	Oze, Hoan, 1554-1630 (Table P-PZ40)
795.R46	Ren'a, 1671?-1729? (Table P-PZ40)
795.R55	Rika Sanjin (Table P-PZ40)
795.R6	Rōka, 1671-1703 (Table P-PZ40)
795.R65	Rokujidō, Sokei, fl. 1660-1674 (Table P-PZ40)
795.R69	Rosen, 1655-1733 (Table P-PZ40)
795.R92	Ryōgen, b. 1612 (Table P-PZ40)
795.R94	Ryōta, 1718-1787 (Table P-PZ40)
795.R96	Ryūkyo, 1695?-1748 (Table P-PZ40)
795.S19	Sairoken Kyōsen, 17th cent. (Table P-PZ40)
795.S23	Saitō, Tokugen, 1559-1647 (Table P-PZ40)
795.S25	Sakuden, 1554-1642 (Table P-PZ40)
795.S29	Satoki, Yoichi, 17th cent. (Table P-PZ40)
795.S34	Sawada, Tōkō, 1732-1796 (Table P-PZ40)
795.S44	Senbai, 1686-1769 (Table P-PZ40)
795.S53	Shaiken, 17th cent. (Table P-PZ40)
795.S56	Shimizu, Shunryū, b. 1626 (Table P-PZ40)
795.S563	Shimokōbe, Shūsui, d. ca. 1797 (Table P-PZ40)
795.S58	Shūen, 1736-1775 (Table P-PZ40)
795.S59	Shurakuken, 17th cent. (Table P-PZ40)
795.S64	Soga, Kyūji, 17th cent. (Table P-PZ40)
795.S66	Sōin, 1605-1681 (Table P-PZ40)
795.S69	Sora, 1649-1710 (Table P-PZ40)
795.S78	Suga, Sensuke, 1728-1779 (Table P-PZ40)
795.S82-.S823	Sugata kurabe deiri no minato (Table P-PZ43)

Japanese language and literature
Japanese literature
Individual authors and works
Early Edo period, 1600-1788
Other, A-Z -- Continued

795.S84-.S843	Sugawara denju tenarai kagami (Table P-PZ43)
795.S95	Suzuki, Seifū, 1646-1722 (Table P-PZ40)
795.S96	Suzuki, Shōsan, 1579-1655 (Table P-PZ40)
795.T34	Takai, Kitō, 1741-1789 (Table P-PZ40)
795.T38	Takayama, Biji, 1649-1718 (Table P-PZ40)
795.T39	Takebe, Ayatari, 1719-1774 (Table P-PZ40)
795.T395	Takeda, Izumo, d. 1747 (Table P-PZ40)
795.T4	Takemoto, Saburobē, fl. 1759-1780 (Table P-PZ40)
795.T415	Tamagusuku, Chōkun, 1684-1734 (Table P-PZ40)
795.T417	Tamekawa, Sōsuke, 1760-1788 (Table P-PZ40)
795.T42	Tani, Bokuin, 1646-1725 (Table P-PZ40)
795.T43	Tasato, Chōchoku, 1703-1773 (Table P-PZ40)
795.T44	Tatara, Ichiryu (Table P-PZ40)
795.T57	Toda, Mosui, 1629-1706 (Table P-PZ40)
795.T64	Tōrindō Chōmaro, 17th/18th cent. (Table P-PZ40)
795.T65	Toshihito, Prince, grandson of Ōgimachi, Emperor of Japan, 1579-1629 (Table P-PZ40)
795.T66	Tsuga, Teishō, 1718-1794? (Table P-PZ40)
795.T68	Tsukudabō Gengen, d. 1770 (Table P-PZ40)
795.T69	Tsumaya, Kasetsusau, 1682-1765 (Table P-PZ40)
795.U33	Ueshima, Onitsura, 1661-1738 (Table P-PZ40)
795.U53	Umeno, Kafū, 18th cent. (Table P-PZ40)
795.U54	Unsui, fl. 1691-1694 (Table P-PZ40)
795.W35	Wakatake, Fuemi (Table P-PZ40)
795.Y35	Yamaoka, Genrin, 1631-1672 (Table P-PZ40)
795.Y357	Yanada, Zeigan, 1672-1757 (Table P-PZ40)
795.Y36	Yanagimoto, Masaoki, d. 1732 (Table P-PZ40)
795.Y37	Yanagisawa, Yoshisato, 1687-1745 (Table P-PZ40)
795.Y38	Yasuda, Abun, fl. 1716-1743 (Table P-PZ40)
795.Y66	Yō, Yōtai, 18th century (Table P-PZ40)
795.Y67	Yokoi, Yayū, 1702-1783 (Table P-PZ40)
795.Y675	Yokoo, Shiyō, 1734-1784 (Table P-PZ40)
795.Y683	Yoshida, Kanshi, d. 1760 (Table P-PZ40)
795.Y685	Yoshida, Takayo, 1665-1713 (Table P-PZ40)
795.Y69	Yoshikawa, Gomei, 1730 or 31-1803 (Table P-PZ40)
	Late Edo period, 1789-1867
796.A-Z	Anonymous works. By title, A-Z
796.E27-.E273	Ehon kyōkun kotowazagusa (Table P-PZ43)
796.E33-.E333	Ehon Saiyū zenden (Table P-PZ43)
796.E35-.E353	Ehon Taikōki (Table P-PZ43)
796.E39-.E393	Ehon tengu no tawamure (Table P-PZ43)
796.E43-.E433	Ehon tsūzoko sangokushi (Table P-PZ43)

Japanese language and literature
Japanese literature
Individual authors and works
Late Edo period, 1789-1867
Anonymous works. By title, A-Z -- Continued

796.F88-.F883	Fūzoku taiheiki (Table P-PZ43)
796.K28-.K283	Kagekiyo (Table P-PZ43)
796.K56-.K563	Kimmon gosan no kiri (Table P-PZ43)
796.K87-.K873	Kurogiuri sugata no deikiaki (Table P-PZ43)
796.M38-.M383	Matsura Gorō Kagechika (Table P-PZ43)
796.M45-.M453	Meiboku sendaihagi (Table P-PZ43)
796.S45-.S453	Sekitori kuruwa no datezome (Table P-PZ43)
796.S54-.S543	Shinsho Taikōki (Table P-PZ43)
796.S57-.S573	Shokōkan wa senjo no mutsugoto, shinkotsu ni wa eiyū no ubugoe, Hiyoshimaru wakagi no sakura (Table P-PZ43)
796.S65-.S653	Sono Ōgiya ukina no koikaze (Table P-PZ43)
796.S67-.S673	Sono yukari hina no omokage (Table P-PZ43)
796.T45-.T453	Teikō Fujin (Table P-PZ43)
796.U54-.U543	Ume no haru gojūsantsugi (Table P-PZ43)
796.U56-.U563	Unpyō zasshi (Table P-PZ43)
796.Y67-.Y673	Yoshitsune chishoki (Table P-PZ43)
	Iwase, Denzō, 1761-1816 see PL798
797	Jippensha, Ikku, 1765-1831 (Table P-PZ39)
797.15	Kikusha-ni, 1753-1826 (Table P-PZ39)
797.2	Kobayashi, Issa, 1763-1827 (Table P-PZ39)
797.4	Ōta, Nampo, 1749-1823 (Table P-PZ39)
797.6	Ryōkan, 1758-1831 (Table P-PZ39)
797.8	Ryūtei, Tanehiko, 1783-1842 (Table P-PZ39)
798	Santō, Kyōden, 1761-1816 (Table P-PZ39)
798.2	Shikitei, Sanba, 1776-1822 (Table P-PZ39)
798.4	Takizawa, Bakin, 1767-1848 (Table P-PZ39)
798.6	Tamenaga, Shunsui, 1790-1844? (Table P-PZ39)
799.A-Z	Other, A-Z
799.A32	Aizawa, Nanjō, 1792-1860 (Table P-PZ40)
799.A34	Akatsuki, Kanenari, 1793 or 4-1861 (Table P-PZ40)
799.A35	Akisato, Ritō, fl. 1780-1814 (Table P-PZ40)
799.A73	Asahiko Shinnō, 1824-1891 (Table P-PZ40)
799.A74	Asaka, Gonsai, 1791-1860 (Table P-PZ40)
799.A75	Asakawa, Zen'an, 1781-1849 (Table P-PZ40)
799.A78	Ashibe no Tazumaru, 1759-1835 (Table P-PZ40)
799.B35	Baitei, Kinga, 1821-1893 (Table P-PZ40)
799.B37	Ban, Kōkei, 1733-1806 (Table P-PZ40)
799.B57	Bisanjin, 1790?-1858 (Table P-PZ40)
799.C44	Chikamatsu, Baishiken, d. 1838 or 9 (Table P-PZ40)
799.C45	Chikamatsu, Tokuzō, 1751 or 2-1810 (Table P-PZ40)
799.C46	Chikamatsu, Yanagi (Table P-PZ40)

Japanese language and literature
Japanese literature
Individual authors and works
Late Edo period, 1789-1867
Other, A-Z -- Continued

799.C49	Chisokukan, Shōkyoku, 19th century (Table P-PZ40)
799.D29	Date, Chihiro, 1803-1877 (Table P-PZ40)
799.E46	Eirakusha, Issui, fl. 1853 (Table P-PZ40)
799.E52	Ema, Saikō, 1787-1861 (Table P-PZ40)
799.E58	Enshō, 1788-1837 (Table P-PZ40)
799.F84	Fujita, Tōko, 1806-1855 (Table P-PZ40)
799.G35	Ganshōsha Hōsai, d. 1807 (Table P-PZ40)
799.G44	Gensō, Kochū, 1776-1831 (Table P-PZ40)
799.G67-.G673	Gotenjiku (Table P-PZ43)
799.H38	Hatanaka, Kansai, d. 1801 (Table P-PZ40)
799.H39	Hayami, Shungyōsai, d. 1823? (Table P-PZ40)
799.H46	Hiraga, Motoyoshi, 1800-1866 (Table P-PZ40)
799.H48	Hirose, Kyokusō, 1807-1863 (Table P-PZ40)
799.H49	Hirose, Tansō, 1782-1856 (Table P-PZ40)
799.H5	Hitomi, Tonei, 1761-1804 (Table P-PZ40)
799.H62	Hoida, Tadatomo, 1792-1847 (Table P-PZ40)
799.H65	Hōseidō, Kisanji, 1735-1813 (Table P-PZ40)
	Hosogi, Anjo see PL799.H67
799.H67	Hosogi, Mizue, 1780-1848 (Table P-PZ40)
799.I25	Ichikawa, Hakuen, 1741-1806 (Table P-PZ40)
799.I27	Ichikawa, Kansai, 1749-1820 (Table P-PZ40)
799.I42	Ikeda, Eisen, 1790-1848 (Table P-PZ40)
799.I43	Ikeda, Tori (Table P-PZ40)
799.I44	Ikenaga, Hadara, d. 1795? (Table P-PZ40)
799.I444	Ikkadō Sansui (Table P-PZ40)
799.I56	Inoue, Shirō, 1742-1812 (Table P-PZ40)
799.I57	Insui Sōjin Nameyasu, 19th cent. (Table P-PZ40)
799.I62	Ippyō, 1771-1840 (Table P-PZ40)
799.I64	Irako, Taishū, 1763-1829 (Table P-PZ40)
799.I65	Iseki, Takako, 1785-1844 (Table P-PZ40)
799.I7	Ishikawa, Masamochi, 1753-1830 (Table P-PZ40)
799.I73	Isoma, Shinji, fl. 1832 (Table P-PZ40)
799.I74	Isshō Koji, fl. 1803 (Table P-PZ40)
799.I8	Iwagaki, Gesshū, 1809-1873 (Table P-PZ40)
799.I83	Iwakumo, Hanaka, 1792-1869 (Table P-PZ40)
799.J35	Jakusō, fl. 1825-1843 (Table P-PZ40)
799.K24	Kagawa, Kageki, 1768-1843 (Table P-PZ40)
799.K245	Kaiho, Gyoson, 1798-1866 (Table P-PZ40)
799.K247	Kakutei, Shūga, fl. 1850-1867 (Table P-PZ40)
799.K25	Kamo, Suetaka, 1754?-1841 or 2 (Table P-PZ40)
799.K253	Kamo, Tsuneharu, 1819-1880 (Table P-PZ40)
799.K26	Kamochi, Masazumi, 1791-1858 (Table P-PZ40)

Japanese language and literature
Japanese literature
Individual authors and works
Late Edo period, 1789-1867
Other, A-Z -- Continued

799.K27	Kan, Sazan, 1748-1827 (Table P-PZ40)
799.K28	Kanazawa, Ryūgyoku, 1778 or 9-1838 (Table P-PZ40)
799.K32	Kasuya, Isomaru, 1764-1848 (Table P-PZ40)
799.K33	Katei, Gasui, fl. 1811 (Table P-PZ40)
	Katō, Chikage, 1735-1808 see PL799.T314
799.K35	Katsushika, Hokusai, 1760-1868 (Table P-PZ40)
799.K357	Kawamura, Sekifu, 1750-1843 (Table P-PZ40)
799.K36	Kawatake, Mokuami, 1816-1893 (Table P-PZ40)
799.K37	Kawatake, Nōshin, d. 1886 (Table P-PZ40)
799.K53	Kikuchi, Gozan, 1769?-1853? (Table P-PZ40)
799.K54	Kinoshita, Takafumi, 1779-1821 (Table P-PZ40)
799.K85	Kumagai, Naoyoshi, 1782-1862 (Table P-PZ40)
799.K87	Kurosawa, Okinamaro, 1795-1859 (Table P-PZ40)
799.K94	Kyokusanjin, d. 1836? (Table P-PZ40)
799.M28	Mantei, Oga, 1818-1890 (Table P-PZ40)
799.M3	Matsudaira, Sadanobu, 1759-1829 (Table P-PZ40)
799.M35	Matsumura, Kabumaru, fl. 1846-1853 (Table P-PZ40)
799.M4	Meimei, 1741-1824 (Table P-PZ40)
799.M47	Minagawa, Kien, 1734-1807 (Table P-PZ40)
799.M49	Miyake, Shōzan, 1718-1801 (Table P-PZ40)
799.M5	Mizuhara, Gyokuso, fl. 1844-1857 (Table P-PZ40)
799.M56	Momosawa, Mutaku, 1738-1810 (Table P-PZ40)
799.M65	Motoori, Haruniwa, 1763-1828 (Table P-PZ40)
799.M85	Murata, Harumi, 1746-1811 (Table P-PZ40)
799.N23	Nakajima, Shūkyo, 1773-1826 (Table P-PZ40)
799.N233	Nakajima, Sōin, 1799?-1855 (Table P-PZ40)
799.N24	Nakamura, Gyogan, 18th-19th cent. (Table P-PZ40)
799.N26	Nakawa, Shimesuke, 1754-1814 (Table P-PZ40)
799.N3	Namiki, Gohei, 1747-1808 (Table P-PZ40)
799.N44	Negishi, Yasumori, 1737-1815 (Table P-PZ40)
799.N56	Ninomiya, Sontoku, 1787-1856 (Table P-PZ40)
799.N57	Nishizawa, Ippō, 1801 or 2-1852 (Table P-PZ40)
799.N6	Nomura, Bōtō, 1806-1867 (Table P-PZ40)
799.O32	Okamoto, Kōseki, 1811-1898 (Table P-PZ40)
799.O35	Okkotsu, Taiken, 1806-1859 (Table P-PZ40)
799.O37	Ōkuma, Kotomichi, 1798-1868 (Table P-PZ40)
799.O87	Ōtsuki, Bankei, 1801-1878 (Table P-PZ40)
799.R34	Rai, San'yō, 1780-1832 (Table P-PZ40)
799.R36	Rakutei, Saiba, 1799-1858 (Table P-PZ40)
799.R4	Rengetsu, 1791-1875 (Table P-PZ40)
799.R55	Rikunyo, 1734?-1801 (Table P-PZ40)

Japanese language and literature
Japanese literature
Individual authors and works
Late Edo period, 1789-1867
Other, A-Z -- Continued

799.R94	Ryōkoku, 1763-1835 (Table P-PZ40)
799.R95	Ryūentei, Tanehisa, fl. 1851-1866 (Table P-PZ40)
799.R96	Ryūkatei Taneka-zu, 1807-1858 (Table P-PZ40)
799.R967	Ryūsuitei Tanekiyo, 1822-1908 (Table P-PZ40)
799.R975	Ryūtei, Senka, 1806-1868 (Table P-PZ40)
	Ryūtei, Tanehiko, 1806-1868 see PL799.R975
799.S13	Saeda, Shigeru, 1741-1832 (Table P-PZ40)
799.S15	Sai, Taitei, b. 1823? (Table P-PZ40)
799.S16	Saigō, Takamori, 1828-1877 (Table P-PZ40)
799.S2	Sakurada, Jisuke, 1734-1806 (Table P-PZ40)
799.S22	Sakurai, Baishitsu, 1769-1852 (Table P-PZ40)
799.S25	Santō, Kyōzan, 1769 or 70-1858 (Table P-PZ40)
799.S28	Satō, Issai, 1772-1859 (Table P-PZ40)
799.S38	Segawa, Jokō, 1757-1833 (Table P-PZ40)
799.S4	Segawa, Jokō, 1806-1881 (Table P-PZ40)
799.S46	Shakkyōan Masui, d. 1847 (Table P-PZ40)
799.S463	Shakuyakutei Nagane, 1767-1845 (Table P-PZ40)
799.S465	Shiba, Shiso, b. 1760? (Table P-PZ40)
799.S47	Shinnyūtei, Fujie, fl. 1860 (Table P-PZ40)
799.S474	Shinrotei, d. 1815 (Table P-PZ40)
799.S77	Sugae, Masumi, 1754-1829 (Table P-PZ40)
799.S8	Suzuki, Bokushi, 1770-1842 (Table P-PZ40)
799.T29	Tachi, Ryūwan, 1762-1844 (Table P-PZ40)
799.T3	Tachibana, Akemi, 1812-1868 (Table P-PZ40)
799.T314	Tachibana, Chikage, 1735-1808 (Table P-PZ40)
799.T32	Tachibana, Moribe, 1781-1849 (Table P-PZ40)
799.T333	Tachibana, Shigeyo (Table P-PZ40)
799.T335	Tadano, Makuzu, 1763?-1825 (Table P-PZ40)
799.T338	Takai, Ranzan, 1762-1838 (Table P-PZ40)
799.T339	Takamiyagusuku, Chōjō, 1744-1802 (Table P-PZ40)
799.T34	Takenouchi, Kakusai, fl. 1770-1826 (Table P-PZ40)
799.T348	Tamboan, Yasō, fl. 1826-1852 (Table P-PZ40)
799.T35	Tamenaga, Shunsui, 1818-1886 (Table P-PZ40)
	Tanbaya, Seizaemon see PL799.T34
799.T52	Tokaen, Michimaro, fl. 1804-1829 (Table P-PZ40)
799.T54	Tominaga, Mubutsu (Table P-PZ40)
799.T6	Tomobayashi, Mitsuhira, 1813-1864 (Table P-PZ40)
799.T64	Tosaka, Kakei, d. 1863 (Table P-PZ40)
799.T73	Tsuruta, Takuchi, 1768-1846 (Table P-PZ40)
799.T75	Tsuruya, Namboku, 1755-1829 (Table P-PZ40)
799.U35	Uematsu, Arinobu, 1758-1813 (Table P-PZ40)
799.U45	Umebori, Kokuga, 1826-1886 (Table P-PZ40)

Japanese language and literature
Japanese literature
Individual authors and works
Late Edo period, 1789-1867
Other, A-Z -- Continued

799.U85	Utagawa, Yoshitaki, 1841-1899 (Table P-PZ40)
799.W38	Watanabe, Shoen, 19th cent. (Table P-PZ40)
799.Y28	Yajima, Gogaku, 19th cent. (Table P-PZ40)
799.Y29-.Y293	Yama mata yama hana no yamagatsu (Table P-PZ43)
799.Y295	Yamada no Kakashi, 1788-1846 (Table P-PZ40)
799.Y34	Yanagawa, Seigan, 1789-1858 (Table P-PZ40)
799.Y67	Yoshida, Gako, fl. 1835-1850 (Table P-PZ40)

Meiji-Taishō period, 1868-1926

800.A-Z	Anonymous works. By title, A-Z
	Subarrange each by Table P-PZ43
801	A
	The author number is determined by the second letter of the name
	Subarrange each author by Table P-PZ40
801.K8	Akutagawa, Ryūnosuke, 1892-1927 (Table P-PZ40)
801.M3	Amada, Guan, 1854-1904 (Table P-PZ40)
801.N45	Andō, Seigaku, 1866-1953 (Table P-PZ40)
801.R5	Arishima, Takeo, 1878-1923 (Table P-PZ40)
802	B
	The author number is determined by the second letter of the name
	Subarrange each author by Table P-PZ40
802.U75	Burnett, Frances Hawks Cameron (Table P-PZ40)
803	Ch
	The author number is determined by the third letter of the name
	Subarrange each author by Table P-PZ40
804	D
	The author number is determined by the second letter of the name
	Subarrange each author by Table P-PZ40
804.A55	Danshūrō Enshi (Table P-PZ40)
804.O35	Doi, Bansui, 1871-1952 (Table P-PZ40)
805	E
	The author number is determined by the second letter of the name
	Subarrange each author by Table P-PZ40
806	Fu
	The author number is determined by the third letter of the name
	Subarrange each author by Table P-PZ40

Japanese language and literature
Japanese literature
Individual authors and works
Meiji-Taisho period, 1868-1926
F -- Continued

806.J56	Fujino, Kohaku, 1871-1895 (Table P-PZ40)
806.J57	Fujisaki, Hōkō, 1874-1930 (Table P-PZ40)
806.K8	Fukumoto, Nichinann, 1857-1921 (Table P-PZ40)
806.T3	Futabatei, Shimei, 1864-1909 (Table P-PZ40)
807	G

The author number is determined by the second letter of
the name
Subarrange each author by Table P-PZ40

808	H

The author number is determined by the second letter of
the name
Subarrange each author by Table P-PZ40
Hasegawa, Tatsunosuke, 1864-1909 see PL806.T3
Hekirurien see PL818.5.T27

808.I4	Higuchi, Ichiyō, 1872-1896 (Table P-PZ40)
809	I

The author number is determined by the second letter of
the name
Subarrange each author by Table P-PZ40

809.N6	Inoue, Kenkabo, 1870-1934 (Table P-PZ40)
809.S49	Ishikawa, Hanzan, 1872- (Table P-PZ40)
809.S5	Ishikawa, Takuboku, 1885-1912 (Table P-PZ40)
809.T53	Itō, Chiyū, 1867-1938 (Table P-PZ40)
809.T6	Itō, Sachio, 1864-1913 (Table P-PZ40)
809.W3	Iwano, Hōmei, 1873-1920 (Table P-PZ40)
809.W37	Iwaya, Sueo, 1870-1933 (Table P-PZ40)
809.Z9	Izumi, Kyōka, 1873-1939 (Table P-PZ40)
809.5	J

The author number is determined by the second letter of
the name
Subarrange each author by Table P-PZ40

809.5.O36	Jōken, Yūshi (Table P-PZ40)
810	K

The author number is determined by the second letter of
the name
Subarrange each author by Table P-PZ40

810.A75	Kanagaki, Robun, 1829-1894 (Table P-PZ40)
810.A82	Katsu, Genzō, 1844-1902 (Table P-PZ40)
810.A86	Kawahigashi, Hekigodō, 1873-1937 (Table P-PZ40)
810.A865	Kawai, Suimei, 1874-1965 (Table P-PZ40)
810.A867	Kawakami, Bizan, 1869-1908 (Table P-PZ40)
810.A9	Kawatake, Mokuami, 1816-1893 (Table P-PZ40)

Japanese language and literature
Japanese literature
Individual authors and works
Meiji-Taisho period, 1868-1926
K -- Continued

810.I8	Kitahara, Hakushū, 1885-1942 (Table P-PZ40)
810.I83	Kitamura, Tōkoku, 1868-1894 (Table P-PZ40)
810.O3	Kōda, Rohan, 1867-1947 (Table P-PZ40)
810.O32	Kodaira, Setsujin, 1872-1958 (Table P-PZ40)
810.O85	Kōtoku, Shūsui, 1871-1911 (Table P-PZ40)
810.O87	Kozai, Shikin, 1868-1933 (Table P-PZ40)
810.U2	Kubo, Inokichi, 1874- (Table P-PZ40)
810.U35	Kuga, Katsunan, 1857-1907 (Table P-PZ40)
810.U5	Kunikida, Doppo, 1871-1908 (Table P-PZ40)
810.U7	Kurata, Hyakuzō, 1891-1943 (Table P-PZ40)
810.U74	Kuroiwa, Ruikō, 1862-1920 (Table P-PZ40)
811	M

The author number is determined by the second letter of
the name
Subarrange each author by Table P-PZ40

811.A8	Masamune, Hakuchō, 1879-1962 (Table P-PZ40)
811.A83	Masaoka, Shiki, 1867-1902 (Table P-PZ40)
811.A88	Matsuse, Seisei, 1869-1937 (Table P-PZ40)
811.E4	Meiji, Emperor of Japan, 1852-1912 (Table P-PZ40)
811.I85	Miura, Chiharu, 1828-1903 (Table P-PZ40)
811.O7	Mori, Ōgai, 1862-1922 (Table P-PZ40)
811.O72	Morita, Raishikyū, 1872-1914 (Table P-PZ40)
811.O75	Morita, Sōhei, 1881-1949 (Table P-PZ40)
	Also called: Morita, Shohei
811.U66	Murai, Gensai (Table P-PZ40)
811.U666	Murai, Unoko, 1870-1916 (Table P-PZ40)
811.U69	Murakami, Kijō, 1865-1938 (Table P-PZ40)
811.U8	Mushaskōji, Saneatsu, 1885- (Table P-PZ40)
812	N

The author number is determined by the second letter of
the name
Subarrange each author by Table P-PZ40

812.A4	Nagai, Kafū, 1879-1959 (Table P-PZ40)
812.A5	Naka, Kansuke, 1885-1965 (Table P-PZ40)
812.A75	Narushima, Ryūhoku, 1837-1884 (Table P-PZ40)
812.A8	Natsume, Sōseki, 1867-1916 (Table P-PZ40)
812.I78	Nishida, Kitarō, 1870-1945 (Table P-PZ40)
812.I79	Nishijima, Reigan, 1883-1958 (Table P-PZ40)
812.O3	Noguchi, Yoné, 1875-1947 (Table P-PZ40)
	Noma, Monzaburō see PL812.O38
812.O38	Noma, Sōryū, 1864-1932 (Table P-PZ40)
812.U36	Nukada, Roppuku, 1890-1948 (Table P-PZ40)

Japanese language and literature
Japanese literature
Individual authors and works
Meiji-Taisho period, 1868-1926 -- Continued
813   O
The author number is determined by the second letter of the name
Subarrange each author by Table P-PZ40
813.C5   Ochiai, Naobumi, 1861-1903 (Table P-PZ40)
813.G33   Ogawa, Usen, 1868-1938 (Table P-PZ40)
813.G85   Oguri, Fūyō, 1875-1926 (Table P-PZ40)
813.K3   Okamoto, Kidō, 1872-1939 (Table P-PZ40)
813.N6   Onoe, Hachirō, 1876-1957 (Table P-PZ40)
                       Onoe, Saishū, 1876-1957 see PL813.N6
813.S33   Osanai, Ihei, b. 1852 (Table P-PZ40)
813.Z3   Ozaki, Kōyō, 1868-1903 (Table P-PZ40)
814   P
The author number is determined by the second letter of the name
Subarrange each author by Table P-PZ40
815   R
The author number is determined by the second letter of the name
Subarrange each author by Table P-PZ40
816   S
The author number is determined by the second letter of the name
Subarrange each author by Table P-PZ40
816.A5   Saitō, Mokichi, 1882-1953 (Table P-PZ40)
816.A53   Sakabe, Teru, 1864-1922 (Table P-PZ40)
816.A543   Sakazaki, Shiran, 1853-1913 (Table P-PZ40)
816.A55   San'yūtei, Enchō, 1839-1900 (Table P-PZ40)
816.H4   Shiba, Shirō, 1853-1922 (Table P-PZ40)
816.H5   Shiga, Naoya, 1883-1971 (Table P-PZ40)
816.H54   Shimamura, Hōgetsu, 1871-1918 (Table P-PZ40)
816.H55   Shimazaki, Tōson, 1872-1943 (Table P-PZ40)
816.H552   Shimazu, Yosoki, b. 1871 (Table P-PZ40)
816.H555   Shimodaira, Katsumi, 1822-1910 (Table P-PZ40)
816.H65   Shōken, Empress, Consort of Meiji, Emperor of
                          Japan, 1850-1914 (Table P-PZ40)
816.U4   Suehiro, Shigeyasu, 1849-1896 (Table P-PZ40)
817   T
The author number is determined by the second letter of the name
Subarrange each author by Table P-PZ40
817.A4   Takahama, Kyoshi, 1874-1959 (Table P-PZ40)
817.A43   Takamura, Kōtarō, 1883-1956 (Table P-PZ40)

Japanese language and literature
Japanese literature
Individual authors and works
Meiji-Taisho period, 1868-1926
T -- Continued

817.A46	Takarai, Bakin, 1852-1928 (Table P-PZ40)
817.A48	Takayama, Chogyū, 1871-1902 (Table P-PZ40)
	Takayama, Rinjiro, 1871-1902 see PL817.A48
817.A53	Takeshiba, Kisui, 1847-1923 (Table P-PZ40)
817.A8	Tayama, Katai, 1871-1930 (Table P-PZ40)
817.A85	Tazawa, Inabune, 1874?-1896 (Table P-PZ40)
817.E55	Terada, Torahiko, 1878-1935 (Table P-PZ40)
817.O33	Toda, Kindō, 1850-1890 (Table P-PZ40)
817.O36	Tokuda, Shūsei, 1871-1943 (Table P-PZ40)
817.O38	Tokutomi, Iichirō, 1863-1957 (Table P-PZ40)
817.O4	Tokutomi, Kenjirō, 1868-1927 (Table P-PZ40)
	Tokutomi, Sohō see PL817.O38
817.S8	Tsubouchi, Shōyō, 1859-1935 (Table P-PZ40)
818	U

> The author number is determined by the second letter of the name
> Subarrange each author by Table P-PZ40

818.T665	Utsumi, Ryōtai, 1834-1892 (Table P-PZ40)
818.5	Wa

> The author number is determined by the third letter of the name
> Subarrange each author by Table P-PZ40

818.5.K28	Wakamatsu, Shizuko, 1864-1896 (Table P-PZ40)
818.5.T27	Watanabe, Katei, 1864-1926 (Table P-PZ40)
819	Y

> The author number is determined by the second letter of the name
> Subarrange each author by Table P-PZ40

819.A515	Yamada, Bimyō, 1868-1910 (Table P-PZ40)
819.O8	Yosano, Akiko, 1878-1942 (Table P-PZ40)
	Yosano, Akiko Hō, 1878-1942 see PL819.O8
819.O82	Yosano, Tekkan, 1873-1935 (Table P-PZ40)
	Yoshimura, Fuyuhiko see PL817.E55
820	Z

> The author number is determined by the second letter of the name
> Subarrange each author by Table P-PZ40

Showa period, 1926-1945

821.A-Z	Anonymous works. By title, A-Z
	Subarrange each by Table P-PZ43

Japanese language and literature
Japanese literature
Individual authors and works
Showa period, 1926-1945 -- Continued

822	A

The author number is determined by the second letter of
the name
Subarrange each author by Table P-PZ40

822.B4	Abe, Tomoji, 1903-1973 (Table P-PZ40)

Asakura, Kikuo, 1903-1945 see PL838.H55
Ashihei, Hino, 1907-1960 see PL829.I5
Asikhei, Khino, 1907-1960 see PL829.I5

823	B

The author number is determined by the second letter of
the name
Subarrange each author by Table P-PZ40

824	Ch

The author number is determined by the third letter of the
name
Subarrange each author by Table P-PZ40

825	D

The author number is determined by the second letter of
the name
Subarrange each author by Table P-PZ40

825.A8	Dazai, Osamu, 1909-1948 (Table P-PZ40)
826	E

The author number is determined by the second letter of
the name
Subarrange each author by Table P-PZ40

826.D6	Edogawa, Ranpo, 1894-1965 (Table P-PZ40)
826.N3	Enchi, Fumiko, 1905- (Table P-PZ40)
827	Fu

The author number is determined by the third letter of the
name
Subarrange each author by Table P-PZ40

827.J5	Fujiwara, Shinji, 1921- (Table P-PZ40)
827.K8	Fukuda, Tsuneari, 1912- (Table P-PZ40)
827.N3	Funabashi, Sechi, 1904- (Table P-PZ40)
828	G

The author number is determined by the second letter of
the name
Subarrange each author by Table P-PZ40

828.E5	Genji, Keita, 1912- (Table P-PZ40)
828.O4	Gomigawa, Jumpei, 1916- (Table P-PZ40)

Gotō, Hisao, 1903- see PL829.A85
Gotō, Toshio, 1903- see PL829.A85

Japanese language and literature
Japanese literature
Individual authors and works
Showa period, 1926-1945 -- Continued

829	H

The author number is determined by the second letter of the name
Subarrange each author by Table P-PZ40

829.A8	Hayashi, Fumiko, 1904-1951 (Table P-PZ40)
829.A85	Hayashi, Fusao, 1903- (Table P-PZ40)
829.I5	Hino, Ashihei, 1907-1960 (Table P-PZ40)
829.I7	Hirabayashi, Taiko, 1905-1972 (Table P-PZ40)
	Hirai, Tarō, 1894-1965 see PL826.D6
	Hiraoka, Kimitaka, 1925-1970 see PL833.I7
829.I76	Hirotsu, Kazuo, 1891-1968 (Table P-PZ40)
829.O7	Hori, Tatsuo, 1904-1953 (Table P-PZ40)
829.O8	Hotta, Yoshie, 1918- (Table P-PZ40)
830	I

The author number is determined by the second letter of the name
Subarrange each author by Table P-PZ40

830.B8	Ibuse, Masuji, 1898- (Table P-PZ40)
830.N6	Inoue, Tomoichirō, 1909- (Table P-PZ40)
830.N63	Inoue, Yasushi, 1907- (Table P-PZ40)
	Ishigami, Gen'ichirō, 1910- see PL830.S64
830.S5	Ishikawa, Jun, 1899- (Table P-PZ40)
830.S55	Ishikawa, Tatsuzō, 1905- (Table P-PZ40)
830.S58	Ishizaka, Yōjirō, 1900- (Table P-PZ40)
830.S64	Isonokami, Gen'ichirō, 1910- (Table P-PZ40)
830.T6	Itō, Sei, 1905-1969 (Table P-PZ40)
	Iwaki, Masura, 1903- see PL830.W225
830.W225	Iwakura, Masaji, 1903- (Table P-PZ40)
830.W33	Iwata, Toyoo, 1893-1969 (Table P-PZ40)
831	J

The author number is determined by the second letter of the name
Subarrange each author by Table P-PZ40

832	K

The author number is determined by the second letter of the name
Subarrange each author by Table P-PZ40

832.A4	Kagawa, Toyohiko, 1888-1960 (Table P-PZ40)
	Cf. BV3457.K3 Kagawa as a missionary
832.A5	Kaionji, Chōgorō, 1901-1977 (Table P-PZ40)
832.A7635	Kataoka, Teppei, 1894-1944 (Table P-PZ40)
832.A9	Kawabata, Yasunari, 1899-1972 (Table P-PZ40)
	Khino, Asikhèĭ, 1907-1960 see PL829.I5

Japanese language and literature
Japanese literature
Individual authors and works
Showa period, 1926-1945
K -- Continued
Khotta, Esie, 1918- see PL829.O8
Kida, Minoru, 1894-1975 see PL842.A43
832.I4	Kikuchi, Hiroshi, 1888-1948 (Table P-PZ40)
	Also called Kikuchi, Kan; Kikuchi, Kwan
832.I5	Kinoshita, Junji, 1914- (Table P-PZ40)
	Kinoshita, Mokutarō, 1885-1945 see PL835.T2
832.I8	Kishida, Kunio, 1890-1954 (Table P-PZ40)
832.I828	Kitabayashi, Tōma, 1904-1968 (Table P-PZ40)
832.O3	Kobayashi, Takiji, 1903-1933 (Table P-PZ40)
832.O36	Koga, Hidemasa, 1908- (Table P-PZ40)
832.O446	Kondō, Ryūtarō, 1926- (Table P-PZ40)
	Kubokawa, Ineko, 1904- see PL838.A8
832.U27	Kubota, Hikoho, 1905- (Table P-PZ40)
832.U3	Kubota, Utsubo, 1877-1967 (Table P-PZ40)
832.U4	Kume, Masao, 1891-1952 (Table P-PZ40)
	Kurita, Shigeru, 1916- see PL828.O4
832.5	L
	Subarrange each author by Table P-PZ40
832.5.L8	Lu, Hsün, 1881-1936 (Table P-PZ40)
	Lu, Xun, 1881-1936 see PL832.5.L8
833	M
	The author number is determined by the second letter of the name
	Subarrange each author by Table P-PZ40
833.I7	Mishima, Yukio, 1925-1970 (Table P-PZ40)
833.I9	Miyamoto, Yuriko, 1899-1951 (Table P-PZ40)
	Moiwa, Sanroku, 1907- see PL834.I7524
	Morimatsu, Keiji, 1904- see PL833.O764
833.O764	Moriyama, Kei, 1904- (Table P-PZ40)
	Muku, Hatojū, 1905- see PL832.U27
833.U7	Murakami, Genzo, 1910- (Table P-PZ40)
833.U75	Muroo, Saisei, 1889-1962 (Table P-PZ40)
834	N
	The author number is determined by the second letter of the name
	Subarrange each author by Table P-PZ40
834.A4	Nagata, Mikihiko, 1887-1964 (Table P-PZ40)
834.A43	Nagayo, Yoshirō, 1888-1961 (Table P-PZ40)
834.A5	Nakagawa, Yoichi, 1897- (Table P-PZ40)
834.A59	Nakayama, Gishū, 1900-1969 (Table P-PZ40)
834.A594	Nakazato, Kaizan, 1885-1944 (Table P-PZ40)
	Nanjō, Norio, 1908- see PL832.O36

Japanese language and literature
Japanese literature
Individual authors and works
Showa period, 1926-1945
N -- Continued

834.A6	Naoki, Sanjūgo, 1891-1934 (Table P-PZ40)
834.I7524	Nishimoto, Saburō, 1907- (Table P-PZ40)
834.I8	Niwa, Fumio, 1904- (Table P-PZ40)
834.O4	Nogami, Yaeko, 1885- (Table P-PZ40)
	Nojiri, Kiyohiko, 1897-1973 see PL835.S3
834.O6	Noma, Hiroshi, 1915- (Table P-PZ40)
835	O

The author number is determined by the second letter of
the name
Subarrange each author by Table P-PZ40

835.O5	Ōoka, Shōhei, 1909- (Table P-PZ40)
835.S3	Osaragi, Jirō, 1897-1973 (Table P-PZ40)
835.T2	Ōta, Masao, 1885-1945 (Table P-PZ40)
	Ōtsubo, Noboru, 1911- see PL838.H5
835.Z3	Ozaki, Kazuo, 1899- (Table P-PZ40)
835.Z35	Ozaki, Shirō, 1898-1964 (Table P-PZ40)
836	P

The author number is determined by the second letter of
the name
Subarrange each author by Table P-PZ40

837	R

The author number is determined by the second letter of
the name
Subarrange each author by Table P-PZ40

838	S

The author number is determined by the second letter of
the name
Subarrange each author by Table P-PZ40

838.A5	Sakaguchi, Ango, 1906-1955 (Table P-PZ40)
838.A8	Sata, Ineko, 1904- (Table P-PZ40)
838.A86	Satō, Haruo, 1892-1964 (Table P-PZ40)
	Shibukawa, Gyō, 1905- see PL842.A54
838.H5	Shiina, Rinzō, 1911- (Table P-PZ40)
838.H55	Shimaki, Kensaku, pseud. (Table P-PZ40)
	Shimizu, Kinsaku, 1904-1968 see PL832.I828
	Shirai, Akira, 1903- see PL829.A85
	Shishi, Bunroku, 1893-1969 see PL830.W33
838.O38	Sōma, Gyofū, 1883-1950 (Table P-PZ40)
	Sōma, Masaharu, 1883-1950 see PL838.O38
	Suetomi, Tōsaku, 1901-1977 see PL832.A5

Japanese language and literature
Japanese literature
Individual authors and works
Showa period, 1926-1945 -- Continued

839   T

> The author number is determined by the second letter of the name
>
> Subarrange each author by Table P-PZ40
>
> Takama, Yoshio, 1907-1965 see PL839.A53

839.A53   Takami, Jun, 1907-1965 (Table P-PZ40)
839.A54   Takata, Tamotsu, 1895-1952 (Table P-PZ40)
839.A55   Takebayashi, Musōan, 1880-1962 (Table P-PZ40)

> Also called: Takebayashi, Seiichi
>
> Tamai, Katsunori, 1907-1960 see PL829.I5

839.A68   Tamura, Taijirō, 1911- (Table P-PZ40)

> Tanaka, Tomio, 1912- see PL828.E5

839.A7   Tanizaki, Jun'ichirō, 1886-1965 (Table P-PZ40)
839.O5   Tokunaga, Sunao, 1899-1958 (Table P-PZ40)
839.O55   Tonomura, Shigeru, 1902-1961 (Table P-PZ40)
839.S8   Tsuboi, Sakae, 1900-1967 (Table P-PZ40)

> Tsushima, Shūji, 1909-1948 see PL825.A8

840   U

> The author number is determined by the second letter of the name
>
> Subarrange each author by Table P-PZ40
>
> Ueda, Shigehiko, 1910- see PL830.S64
>
> Uemura, Sōichi, 1891-1934 see PL834.A6

840.N6   Uno, Kōji, 1891-1961 (Table P-PZ40)
841   Wa

> The author number is determined by the third letter of the name
>
> Subarrange each author by Table P-PZ40

841.5   Wu

> The author number is determined by the next portion of the author's name
>
> Subarrange each author by Table P-PZ40

841.5.C5   Wu, Cho-liu, 1900-1976 (Table P-PZ40)

> Wu, Zhuoliu, 1900-1976 see PL841.5.C5

842   Y

> The author number is determined by the second letter of the name
>
> Subarrange each author by Table P-PZ40

842.A43   Yamada, Yoshihiko, 1894-1975 (Table P-PZ40)
842.A4326   Yamaguchi, Kichirō, 1892- (Table P-PZ40)

> Yamaguchi, Seison, 1892- see PL842.A4326

842.A439   Yamamoto, Yūzō, 1887-1974 (Table P-PZ40)
842.A54   Yamasaki, Takeo, 1905- (Table P-PZ40)

Japanese language and literature
Japanese literature
Individual authors and works
Showa period, 1926-1945
Y -- Continued

842.O5	Yokomitsu, Riichi, 1898-1947 (Table P-PZ40)
842.O7	Yoshii, Isamu, 1886-1960 (Table P-PZ40)
842.O75	Yoshikawa, Eiji, 1892-1962 (Table P-PZ40)
843	Z

            The author number is determined by the second letter of the name

            Subarrange each author by Table P-PZ40

Shōwa period, 1945-1989

844.A-Z	Anonymous works. By title, A-Z

            Subarrange each by Table P-PZ43

845	A

            The author number is determined by the second letter of the name

            Subarrange each author by Table P-PZ40

845.K33	Akasegawa, Genpei (Table P-PZ40)
	Aono, Satoshi, 1943- see PL845.O5
845.O5	Aono, Sō, 1943- (Table P-PZ40)
	Asada, Tetsuya see PL853.R64
846	B

            The author number is determined by the second letter of the name

            Subarrange each author by Table P-PZ40

847	Ch

            The author number is determined by the third letter of the name

            Subarrange each author by Table P-PZ40

847.I9	Ch'iu, Ping-nan, 1924- (Table P-PZ40)
848	D

            The author number is determined by the second letter of the name

            Subarrange each author by Table P-PZ40

            Deguchi, Yasuaki, 1930- see PL862.O85

849	E

            The author number is determined by the second letter of the name

            Subarrange each author by Table P-PZ40

850	Fu

            The author number is determined by the third letter of the name

            Subarrange each author by Table P-PZ40

            Fujiwara, Hiroto, 1912- see PL857.I8

Japanese language and literature
Japanese literature
Individual authors and works
Shōwa period, 1945-1989 -- Continued
851   G
The author number is determined by the second letter of
the name
Subarrange each author by Table P-PZ40
852   H
The author number is determined by the second letter of
the name
Subarrange each author by Table P-PZ40
852.E45   Hemmi, Jun (Table P-PZ40)
Henmi, Jun see PL852.E45
853   I
The author number is determined by the second letter of
the name
Subarrange each author by Table P-PZ40
Ikeguchi, Kotarō, 1935- see PL861.A4793
853.R64   Irokawa, Takehiro (Table P-PZ40)
854   J
The author number is determined by the second letter of
the name
Subarrange each author by Table P-PZ40
855   K
The author number is determined by the second letter of
the name
Subarrange each author by Table P-PZ40
855.A35   Kajiyama, Toshiyuki, 1930-1975 (Table P-PZ40)
855.A877   Kawano, Yūko, 1946- (Table P-PZ40)
855.I65   Kita, Morio, 1927- (Table P-PZ40)
Kobayashi, Nobuhiko, 1932- see PL857.A3815
Kyū, Eikan, 1924- see PL847.I9
855.5   L
The author number is determined by the second letter of
the name
Subarrange each author by Table P-PZ40
855.5.I67   Lippit, Noriko Mizuta (Table P-PZ40)
856   M
The author number is determined by the second letter of
the name
Subarrange each author by Table P-PZ40
Maruya, Hiroshi, 1925- see PL856.I62
Misan, Kyeji, 1930-1975 see PL855.A35
856.I62   Mishō, Hiromi, 1925- (Table P-PZ40)
Mizuta, Muneko see PL855.5.I67
Mizuta, Noriko see PL855.5.I67

Japanese language and literature
Japanese literature
Individual authors and works
Shōwa period, 1945-1989 -- Continued

857	N

The author number is determined by the second letter of
the name
Subarrange each author by Table P-PZ40
Nagata, Yūko, 1946- see PL855.A877

857.A3815	Nakahara, Yumihiko, 1932- (Table P-PZ40)
857.I8	Nitta, Jirō (Table P-PZ40)
858	O

The author number is determined by the second letter of
the name
Subarrange each author by Table P-PZ40
Otsuji, Katsuhiko, 1937- see PL845.K33

859	P

The author number is determined by the second letter of
the name
Subarrange each author by Table P-PZ40

860	R

The author number is determined by the second letter of
the name
Subarrange each author by Table P-PZ40
Rei, Ra, 1924- see PL860.E36

860.E36	Reira, 1924- (Table P-PZ40)
861	S

The author number is determined by the second letter of
the name
Subarrange each author by Table P-PZ40
Saitō, Muneyoshi, 1927- see PL855.I65
Saito, Sōkichi, 1927-, see PL855.I65

861.A4793	Sakaiya, Taichi, 1935- (Table P-PZ40)
862	T

The author number is determined by the second letter of
the name
Subarrange each author by Table P-PZ40

862.A517	Tanaka, Kiyomitsu, 1931- (Table P-PZ40)

Tanaka, Kiyoteru, 1931- see PL862.A517
Tanaka, Seikō, 1931- see PL862.A517

862.O85	Towada, Ryū, 1930- (Table P-PZ40)
863	U

The author number is determined by the second letter of
the name
Subarrange each author by Table P-PZ40

Japanese language and literature
Japanese literature
Individual authors and works
Shōwa period, 1945-1989 -- Continued

864   Wa
                                     The author number is determined by the second letter of
                                        the name
                                     Subarrange each author by Table P-PZ40
864.5   Wu
                                     The author number is determined by the next portion of
                                        the author's name
                                     Subarrange each author by Table P-PZ40
864.5.C47   Wu, Chien-t'ang (Table P-PZ40)
                                     Wu, Jiantang see PL864.5.C47
865   Y
                                     The author number is determined by the second letter of
                                        the name
                                     Subarrange each author by Table P-PZ40
865.O674   Yoshida, Toshi, 1925- (Table P-PZ40)
866   Z
                                     The author number is determined by the second letter of
                                        the name
                                     Subarrange each author by Table P-PZ40
                             Heisei period, 1989-
867.A-Z   Anonymous works. By title, A-Z
                                     Subarrange each work by Table P-PZ43
867.5   A
                                     The author number is determined by the second letter of
                                        the name
                                     Subarrange each author by Table P-PZ40
                                     Aida, Mariko, 1961- see PL871.5.C54
868   B
                                     The author number is determined by the second letter of
                                        the name
                                     Subarrange each author by Table P-PZ40
                                     Binādo, Āsā see PL868.I55
868.I55   Binard, Arthur (Table P-PZ40)
868.5   Ch
                                     The author number is determined by the third letter of the
                                        name
                                     Subarrange each author by Table P-PZ40
869   D
                                     The author number is determined by the second letter of
                                        the name
                                     Subarrange each author by Table P-PZ40

Japanese language and literature
Japanese literature
Individual authors and works
Heisei period, 1989- -- Continued

869.5   E
> The author number is determined by the second letter of the name
> Subarrange each author by Table P-PZ40

870   Fu
> The author number is determined by the third letter of the name
> Subarrange each author by Table P-PZ40

870.5   G
> The author number is determined by the second letter of the name
> Subarrange each author by Table P-PZ40

871   H
> The author number is determined by the second letter of the name
> Subarrange each author by Table P-PZ40

871.5   I
> The author number is determined by the second letter of the name
> Subarrange each author by Table P-PZ40

871.5.C54   Ichihara, Mariko, 1961- (Table P-PZ40)

872   J
> The author number is determined by the second letter of the name
> Subarrange each author by Table P-PZ40

872.5   K
> The author number is determined by the second letter of the name
> Subarrange each author by Table P-PZ40

872.5.I55   Kimura, Takeshi, 1962- (Table P-PZ40)

873   M
> The author number is determined by the second letter of the name
> Subarrange each author by Table P-PZ40

873.5   N
> The author number is determined by the second letter of the name
> Subarrange each author by Table P-PZ40

874   O
> The author number is determined by the second letter of the name
> Subarrange each author by Table P-PZ40
> Ozaka, Gō see PL872.5.I55

Japanese language and literature
Japanese literature
Individual authors and works
Heisei period, 1989-
874.5   P
The author number is determined by the second letter of
the name
Subarrange each author by Table P-PZ40
875   R
The author number is determined by the second letter of
the name
Subarrange each author by Table P-PZ40

875.5   S
The author number is determined by the second letter of
the name
Subarrange each author by Table P-PZ40
876   T
The author number is determined by the second letter of
the name
Subarrange each author by Table P-PZ40
876.5   U
The author number is determined by the second letter of
the name
Subarrange each author by Table P-PZ40
877   Wa
The author number is determined by the third letter of the
name
Subarrange each author by Table P-PZ40
877.5   Y
The author number is determined by the second letter of
the name
Subarrange each author by Table P-PZ40
878   Z
The author number is determined by the second letter of
the name
Subarrange each author by Table P-PZ40
Local literature
Japan
885   Regional. General or several regions
886.A-Z   Special provinces, prefectures, regions, A-Z
Subarrange each by Table P-PZ26
887.A-Z   Special cities, etc., A-Z
Subarrange each by Table P-PZ26
Japanese literature outside Japan
888   General

	Japanese language and literature
	Japanese literature
	Local literature
	Japanese literature outside Japan -- Continued
889.A-Z	Special countries, A-Z

Under each:

.x	*History*
.x2	*Collections*
.x3A-.x3Z	*Individual authors, A-Z*

	Korean language and literature
	Korean language
901	Periodicals. Societies. Annuals. Yearbooks
901.5	Congresses
901.7	Societies
902	Collections (nonserial)
903	Encyclopedias
904	Philosophy. Theory. Method. Relations
	History of philology
	Cf. PL907 Study and teaching
	Cf. PL909+ History of the language
905	General works
	Biography, memoirs, etc.
906.A2	Collective
906.A5-Z	Individual, A-Z
	Subarrange each by Table P-PZ50
	Study and teaching. Research
907	General works
907.5.A-Z	By region or country, A-Z
907.6.A-Z	By school, A-Z
907.7.A-Z	By research institute, A-Z
	General works
908	Treatises (Philology, General)
908.4	Relation to other languages
908.5	Language data processing
908.8	Language standardization and variation
908.83	Political aspects
908.84	Social aspects
908.85	Spoken language
908.86	Language acquisition
	History of the language
	By region see PL941+
909	General works
909.2	Earliest
909.3	Middle Korean
909.4	1500-1894
909.43	1894-
909.5	Outlines

	Korean language and literature
	Korean language
	General works -- Continued
910	Popular works
910.5	Script
	Grammar
911	General works
912	General special
	Textbooks
913.A2	History and criticism
913.A3-Z	Textbooks
	Including conversation books, phrase books, and readers
913.4	Self-instructors
913.5	Audiovisual instructors
	Readers
913.6	History and criticism
913.63	Primers. Primary grade readers
913.65	Intermediate and advanced
913.7	Examinations, questions, etc.
914	Conversation. Phrase books
	Idioms. Errors. Usage see PL927.6
	Textbooks for foreign speakers
914.4	General works
914.6.A-Z	By language, A-Z
	Phonology
	Including phonemics and phonetics
	Cf. PL918+ Alphabet
915	General works
915.4	Pronunciation
915.6	Accent
915.8	Intonation
915.9	Transliteration
917	Orthography. Spelling
918-918.7	Alphabet
918	General works
918.6	Vowels
918.7	Consonants
918.8	Syllabication
918.9	Morphophonemics
	Morphology
919	General works
919.4	Word formation
919.6	Inflection
	Parts of speech (Morphology and Syntax)
921	General works
921.4	Noun
921.5	Adjective. Adverb. Comparison

	Korean language and literature
	Korean language
	Grammar
	Parts of speech (Morphology and Syntax) -- Continued
921.56	Negatives
921.6	Pronoun
921.7	Verb
921.8	Particle
923	Syntax
925.A-Z	Other aspects, A-Z
	For list of Cutter numbers, see Table P-PZ1 398.A+
(926)	Grammatical usage of particular authors
	see the author in classes PA-PT
	Style. Composition. Rhetoric
	For study and teaching see PL907
927	General works
927.4	Discourse analysis
927.6	Idioms. Errors. Usage
	Translating
	For special subjects, see classes B-Z, e.g. T11.5, Technology
928	General works
928.4	Machine translating
	Including research
929	Prosody. Metrics. Rhythmics
930	Lexicology
	Etymology
931	General treatises. Dictionaries
	Special elements
	Cf. PL936 Dictionaries
931.2.A2	Foreign elements (General)
931.2.A3-Z	By language, A-Z
932	Semantics
933	Synonyms. Antonyms. Paronyms. Homonyms
933.5	Onomatopoeic words
933.9.A-Z	Particular words, A-Z
	Lexicography
934	General works
	Dictionaries
935	Dictionaries with definitions in same language
935.5	Chinese character dictionaries
935.6	Chinese character glossaries, etc.
936	Dictionaries with definitions in two or more languages, or dictionaries of two or more languages with definitions in one language
937.A-Z	Dictionaries with definitions in English or other languages. By language, A-Z
	Dictionaries exclusively etymological see PL931

Korean language and literature
Korean language
Lexicography
Dictionaries -- Continued

938	Dictionaries of particular periods (other than periods separately specified elsewhere)
	Other special lists
	For special subjects, see classes A-N, Q-Z
939	Glossaries
939.7	Dictionaries of terms and phrases
	Linguistic geography. Dialects, etc.
941.A1	Linguistic geography
	Dialects, provincialsms, etc.
	For language standardization and variation see PL908.8
941.A2-.A29	Periodicals. Collections
941.A3	Collections of texts, etc.
941.A5-Z	General works. Grammar
943	Dictionaries
(945.A1)	Atlases. Maps
	see class G
945.A5-Z	Local. By region, place, etc., A-Z
	Slang. Argot
946	General works
946.6	Dictionaries. Lists
946.7.A-Z	Special topics, A-Z
	For list of Cutter numbers, see Table P-PZ2 421.A+
	Korean literature
	Including Korean literature written in Chinese characters (Hanmunhak)
	History and criticism
950.2	Periodicals. Serials
(950.4)	Yearbooks
	see PL950.2
950.6	Societies
950.8	Congresses
	Bibliography
	see Z3319.L5
	Collections
951	Serial
951.2.A-Z	In honor of an individual or institution, A-Z
951.4	By an individual author
951.6	Encyclopedias. Dictionaries. Indexes
951.8	Theory. Philosophy. Aesthetics. Psychology
	Study and teaching
952	General works
952.2.A-Z	By region or country, A-Z

Korean language and literature
  Korean literature
    History and criticism
      History
        Special aspects and topics
          Treatment of special subjects, A-Z -- Continued

957.5.C46	Ch'ŏndogyo
957.5.C464	Ch'ŏyong, 9th cent.
957.5.C47	Christianity
957.5.C54	Civil rights movements
957.5.C63	Coal mines and mining
957.5.C66	Confucianism
957.5.C68	Courts and courtiers
957.5.D43	Death
	Decolonization see PL957.5.P65
957.5.D48	Detective and mystery stories
957.5.D49	Devil
957.5.D65	Domestic life
957.5.D73	Dragons
957.5.D74	Dreams
957.5.D75	Drinking
957.5.E34	Ecology. Environment
	Environment see PL957.5.E34
957.5.E58	Entertainers
957.5.E76	Eroticism
957.5.E86	Ethics
957.5.F35	Family
957.5.F357	Fantasy
957.5.F36	Farewells
957.5.F37	Farm life
957.5.F38	Fascism
957.5.F45	Feminism
957.5.F46	Feng shui
957.5.F55	Flowers
957.5.G56	Ghosts
957.5.G83	Guerrillas
957.5.H47	Heroes
957.5.H57	History
957.5.H67	Horror
957.5.H86	Human body
957.5.I52	Imitation
957.5.I527	Individuality
957.5.I53	Industrial revolution
957.5.J34	Japan
957.5.J36	Japanese invasions, 1592-1598
957.5.K36	Kangwŏn-do (Korea)
957.5.K53	Kim, Kwang-nim, 1929-

Korean language and literature
Korean literature
History and criticism
History
Special aspects and topics
Treatment of special subjects, A-Z -- Continued

957.5.K55	Kim, P'ellich'ida
957.5.K56	Kim, Tŏng-nyŏng, 1568-1596
957.5.K565	Kim, Tong-sik, 1854-1910
957.5.K57	Kim, Yu-sin, 595-673
957.5.K64	Koguryŏ (Kingdom)
957.5.K67	Korean War, 1950-1953
957.5.K84	Kung, Ye, d. 918
957.5.K88	Kwangju Uprising, 1980
957.5.L68	Love
957.5.M36	Manners and customs
957.5.M37	Martial arts
957.5.M46	Memory
957.5.M63	Modernism
957.5.M68	Mountains
957.5.M87	Music
957.5.M95	Mysticism
	Mystery stories see PL957.5.D48
957.5.M98	Mythology
957.5.N38	Nationalism
957.5.N39	Naturalism
957.5.N4	Nature
957.5.N46	Neo-Confucianism
957.5.N67	Nostalgia
957.5.O43	Oedipus complex
	Older people see PL957.5.A35
957.5.P33	Paektu Mountain (Korea)
957.5.P37	Patriotism
	Peasantry see PL957.5.P42
957.5.P42	Peasants
957.5.P64	Politics
957.5.P65	Postcolonialism. Decolonization
957.5.P76	Proletariat
957.5.P77	Psychoanalysis
957.5.P78	Psychology
957.5.R43	Realism
957.5.R435	Regionalism
957.5.R44	Reincarnation
957.5.R45	Religion
957.5.R64	Roh, Moo Hyun, 1946-2009
957.5.S35	Science. Science fiction
957.5.S42	Sea

Korean language and literature
Korean literature
History and criticism
History
Special aspects and topics
Treatment of special subjects, A-Z -- Continued

957.5.S46	Seoul (Korea)
957.5.S47	Sequels
957.5.S48	Sex
957.5.S53	Shamanism
957.5.S55	Slavery
957.5.S65	Social realism
957.5.S66	Socialist realism
957.5.S68	Sound. Sounds
957.5.S69	Space and time
957.5.S694	Spies
957.5.S696	Sports
957.5.S74	Stepmothers
957.5.S96	Supernatural
957.5.S97	Symbolism
957.5.S98	Sympathy
957.5.T34	Taoism
957.5.T4	Tea
957.5.T464	Tok Island (Korea)
957.5.T65	Tonghak Incident, 1894
957.5.T72	Tragic, The
957.5.T73	Travel
957.5.U85	Utopias
957.5.W37	War
957.5.W38	Water
957.5.W5	Wit and humor. Satire
957.5.W65	Women
	Women heroes see PL957.5.W65
957.5.W68	Working class
(957.6)	Treatment of special classes, races, etc.
	see PL957.5
	Awards, prizes
957.64	General works
957.65.A-Z	Special, A-Z
	Biography of authors
957.7	Collective
	Including memoirs and letters
(957.71)	Individual
	see PL986.5+
957.8	Literary landmarks. Homes and haunts of authors
957.9	Women authors. Literary relations of women
957.95.A-Z	Other classes of authors, A-Z

Korean language and literature
Korean literature
History and criticism
History
Other classes of authors, A-Z -- Continued

957.95.C38	Catholic
957.95.W67	Working class
958-958.8	By period (Table PL2)

Special forms
Poetry
General works

959.A2	Early works through 1893
959.A3-Z	1894-
959.5	Addresses, essays, lectures, etc.

By form

960	Ballads
960.2	Changga
960.23	Epic poetry

Folk poetry

960.25	General
960.26	Arirang
960.3	Hyangga
960.4	Kasa
960.46	Narrative poetry
960.5	Sasŏl sijo
960.6	Sijo
960.7.A-Z	Other, A-Z
960.7.C45	Children's poetry
960.7.E44	Elegiac poetry
960.8.A-Z	Special topics, A-Z

For list of topics, see PL957.5.A+

961-961.8	By period (Table PL2 modified)
961	Through 1894
961.15	Chosŏn dynasty, 1392-1894
961.2	1392-1598
961.2.Y6	Yongbi ŏch'ŏn'ga

Drama
Cf. PN2930+ Korean theater
General works

962.A2	Early works through 1893
962.A3-Z	1894-
962.5	Addresses, essays, lectures

By form

963	Ch'anggŭk (Classical opera)
	Inhyŏnggŭk (Puppet plays) see PN1978.A+
963.3	Kamyŏn'gŭk (Mask plays)
	Motion picture plays see PN1993.5.A3+

PL

	Korean language and literature
	Korean literature
	History and criticism
	History
	Special forms
	Drama
	By form -- Continued
	Shadow plays see PN1979.S5
963.5.A-Z	Other, A-Z
963.5.A26	Arirang
963.5.R33	Radio plays
963.5.T44	Television plays
963.6.A-Z	Special topics, A-Z
	For list of topics, see PL957.5.A+
964-964.8	By period (Table PL2)
	Prose. Fiction
	General works
965.A2	Early works through 1893
965.A3-Z	1894-
965.5	Addresses, essays, lectures
965.6	Synopses, etc.
965.7.A-Z	Special topics, A-Z
	For list of topics, see PL957.5.A+
	By form
966.2	Diaries
966.3	Essay
	Fiction see PL965+
966.4	Letters
966.5	Romance (Iyaki)
966.6	Short story
966.7	Wit and humor. Satire
	Aphorisms, apothegms, etc. see PN6269+
	Maxims see PN6299+
	Fables, parables, etc. see PN989.A+
	Journalism see PN5411+
	Proverbs see PN6519.K6
967-967.8	By period (Table PL2)
	Folk literature
(968.2)	History and criticism
	see GR342+
(968.4)	Collections
	see GR342+
	Tales see GR342+
	Folk-songs see M1816; ML3752+
	Inscriptions
969.2	History and criticism
969.4	Collections

Korean language and literature
Korean literature
History and criticism
History
Special forms -- Continued
969.5　　　　　　　　Juvenile literature (General)
　　　　　　　　　　For special genres, see the genre
　　　　　　　　Collections
969.8　　　　　　　Periodicals. Societies. Serials
　　　　　　　　General (Comprehensive, not confined to any one period
　　　　　　　　or form)
970.A2　　　　　　　Published before 1894
970.A3-Z　　　　　　Published 1894-
971　　　　　　　Selections
972-972.8　　　　　By period (Table PL2)
　　　　　　　　Special classes of authors
973　　　　　　　Women
973.2.A-Z　　　　　Other, A-Z
973.2.C38　　　　　　Catholic authors
973.2.C45　　　　　　Children
　　　　　　　　　　Children with disabilities see PL973.2.P48
973.2.C47　　　　　　Christian authors
973.2.C64　　　　　　College students
973.2.H54　　　　　　High school students
973.2.L33　　　　　　Laboring class. Working class
973.2.P48　　　　　　Physical disabilities, Children with
973.2.S65　　　　　　Soldiers
973.2.T43　　　　　　Teachers
973.2.T45　　　　　　Teenagers
　　　　　　　　　　Working class. see PL973.2.L33
973.4.A-Z　　　　　Special topics, A-Z
　　　　　　　　　　For list of topics, see PL957.5.A+
　　　　　　　　Special forms
　　　　　　　　Poetry
974.A1　　　　　　Periodicals. Societies. Serials
　　　　　　　　General
974.A2　　　　　　　Early through 1893
974.A3-Z　　　　　　1894-
974.2　　　　　　Selections
　　　　　　　　By form
975　　　　　　　Ballads
975.2　　　　　　Changga
975.3　　　　　　Hyangga
975.4　　　　　　Kasa
975.46　　　　　　Narrative poetry
975.5　　　　　　Sasŏl sijo
975.6　　　　　　Sijo

PL

	Korean language and literature
	Korean literature
	Collections
	Special forms
	Poetry
	By form
	Sijo -- Continued
975.63	Ch'ŏnggu yŏngŏn
975.65	Haedong kayo
975.7.A-Z	Other, A-Z
975.7.C55	Children's poetry
975.7.D53	Dialect poetry
975.7.E44	Elegiac poetry
975.7.F64	Folk poetry
975.8.A-Z	Special classes of authors, A-Z
975.8.C55	Children
975.8.C64	College students
975.8.S62	Soldiers
975.8.S75	Students
975.8.W6	Women
975.8.W67	Working class
975.9.A-Z	Special topics, A-Z
	For list of topics, see PL957.5.A+
976-976.8	By period (Table PL2 modified)
976	Through 1894
976.15	Chosŏn dynasty, 1392 to 1894
976.2	1392-1598
976.2.Y6	Yongbi ŏch'ŏn'ga
	Drama
977.A1	Periodicals. Societies. Serials
	General
977.A2	Early works through 1893
977.A3-Z	1894-
977.2	Selections
	By form
978	Ch'anggŭk (Classical opera)
	Inhyŏnggŭk (Puppet plays) see PN1981
978.3	Kamyŏn'gŭk (Mask plays)
	Motion picture plays see PN1997.A1
	Shadow plays see PN6120.S5
978.5.A-Z	Other, A-Z
978.5.A4	Amateur drama. Juvenile drama
	Juvenile drama see PL978.5.A4
978.5.R33	Radio plays
978.5.T44	Television plays
978.6.A-Z	Special topics, A-Z
	For list of topics, see PL957.5.A+

          Korean language and literature
            Korean literature
              Collections
                Translations
                  From Korean into foreign languages
                    Chinese -- Continued

984.C3	Poetry
984.C5	Drama
984.C8	Prose. Prose fiction
	Japanese
984.J1	General
984.J3	Poetry
984.J5	Drama
984.J8	Prose. Prose fiction
	Individual authors and works
	Origins. Early to 935 A.D.
986.A-Z	Anonymous works. By title, A-Z
	Subarrange each by Table P-PZ43
986.5.A-Z	Individual authors, A-Z
986.5.C53	Chin, Hwa, 12th-13th cent. (Table P-PZ40)
986.5.C56	Ch'oe, Ch'i-wŏn, b. 857 (Table P-PZ40)
986.5.C59	Ch'ŏyong, 9th cent. (Table P-PZ40)
	Koryŏ period, 935-1392
987.A1A-.A1Z	Anonymous works. By title, A-Z
987.C52	Ch'oe, Hae, 1287-1340 (Table P-PZ40)
987.C53	Ch'oe, Kwŏn-hŭng (Table P-PZ40)
987.C535	Chŏng, I-o, 1347-1434 (Table P-PZ40)
987.C54	Chŏng, Mong-ju, 1337-1392 (Table P-PZ40)
987.C555	Chŏng, P'o, 1309-1345 (Table P-PZ40)
987.C56	Chŏng, Sŏ (Table P-PZ40)
987.C58	Chŏng, To-jŏn, d. 1398 (Table P-PZ40)
987.H339	Ha, Yun, 1347-1416 (Table P-PZ40)
987.H35	Han, Su, 1333-1384 (Table P-PZ40)
987.H94	Hyegŭn, 1320-1376 (Table P-PZ40)
987.I43	Im, Ch'un, 12th cent. (Table P-PZ40)
987.K564	Kim, Ku-yong, 1338-1384 (Table P-PZ40)
987.K57	Kim, Kŭk-ki (Table P-PZ40)
987.K92	Kwŏn, Kŭn, 1352-1409 (Table P-PZ40)
987.K95	Kyunyŏ, 923-973 (Table P-PZ40)
987.P35	Pak, Ik, 1332-1398 (Table P-PZ40)
987.T83	Tŭgo (Table P-PZ40)
987.Y5	Yi, Che-hyŏn, 1287-1367 (Table P-PZ40)
987.Y525	Yi, Chŏng-gan, 1360-1439 (Table P-PZ40)
987.Y53	Yi, Il-lo, 1152-1220 (Table P-PZ40)
987.Y536	Yi, Kang, 1333-1368 (Table P-PZ40)
987.Y54	Yi, Kok, 1298-1351 (Table P-PZ40)
987.Y56	Yi, Kyu-bo, 1168-1241 (Table P-PZ40)

Korean language and literature
Korean literature
Individual authors and works
Koryo period, 935-1392 -- Continued

987.Y58	Yi, Saek, 1328-1396 (Table P-PZ40)
987.Y588	Yi, Sung-in, 1349-1392 (Table P-PZ40)
987.Y59	Yi, Tal-ch'ung, 1309-1385 (Table P-PZ40)
	1392-1598
988.A1A-.A1Z	Anonymous works. By title, A-Z
988.C32	Ch'a, Ch'ŏl-lo, 1556-1615 (Table P-PZ40)
988.C37	Chang, Hyŏn-gwang, 1554-1637 (Table P-PZ40)
988.C4	Cho, Sik, 1501-1572 (Table P-PZ40)
988.C42	Cho, Sŏng-ga (Table P-PZ40)
988.C43	Cho, Sŏng, 1492-1555 (Table P-PZ40)
988.C44	Cho, Wi, 1454-1503 (Table P-PZ40)
988.C46	Ch'oe, Hang, 1409-1474 (Table P-PZ40)
988.C47	Ch'oe, Hŭi-ryang, 1560-1651 (Table P-PZ40)
988.C48	Ch'oe, Ip, 1539-1612 (Table P-PZ40)
988.C6	Chŏng, Ch'ŏl, 1536-1593 (Table P-PZ40)
988.C63	Chŏng, Kŭg-in, 1401-1481 (Table P-PZ40)
988.C636	Chŏng, Kwang-p'il, 1462-1538 (Table P-PZ40)
988.C64	Chŏng, Kyŏng-se, 1563-1633 (Table P-PZ40)
988.C65	Chŏng, Nyŏm, 1506-1549 (Table P-PZ40)
(988.C66)	Chŏng, To-jŏn, d. 1398
	see PL987.C58
988.C84	Chu, Se-bung, 1495-1554 (Table P-PZ40)
988.H3	Han, Hong, 1480-1543 (Table P-PZ40)
988.H62	Hŏ, Ch'e, b. 1563 (Table P-PZ40)
988.H63	Hŏ, Chin-dong, 1525-1610 (Table P-PZ40)
988.H64	Hŏ, Kyŏng-nan (Table P-PZ40)
988.H65	Hŏ, Nansŏrhŏn, 1563-1589 (Table P-PZ40)
988.H92	Hwang, Chin-i (Table P-PZ40)
988.H93	Hwang, Chul-lyang, 1517-1563 (Table P-PZ40)
988.I53	Im, Che, 1549-1587 (Table P-PZ40)
988.I54	Im, Chŏn, 1560-1611 (Table P-PZ40)
988.I56	Im, Ŏng-nyŏng, 1496-1568 (Table P-PZ40)
988.I57	Im, Sŏ, 1570-1624 (Table P-PZ40)
988.K35	Kang, Hŭi-maeng, 1424-1483 (Table P-PZ40)
988.K38	Ki, Pok-chae, 1492-1521 (Table P-PZ40)
988.K414	Kim, Chang-saeng, 1548-1631 (Table P-PZ40)
988.K42	Kim, Chong-jik, 1431-1492 (Table P-PZ40)
988.K44	Kim, Hak-pong, 1538-1593 (Table P-PZ40)
988.K448	Kim, Hŭn, b. 1448 (Table P-PZ40)
988.K45	Kim, In-hu, 1510-1560 (Table P-PZ40)
988.K48	Kim, Mun-gi, 1399-1456 (Table P-PZ40)
988.K52	Kim, Sang-hŏn, 1570-1622 (Table P-PZ40)
988.K54	Kim, Si-sŭp, 1435-1493 (Table P-PZ40)

Korean language and literature
Korean literature
Individual authors and works
1392-1598 -- Continued

988.K57	Kim, Su-on, 1409-1481 (Table P-PZ40)
988.K58	Kim, Tŭg-yŏn, 1555-1637 (Table P-PZ40)
988.K59	Kim, U-ong, 1540-1603 (Table P-PZ40)
988.K64	Ko, Kyŏng-myŏng, 1533-1592 (Table P-PZ40)
988.K67	Ko, Sang-an, 1553-1623 (Table P-PZ40)
988.K75	Ku, Pong-nyŏng, 1526-1586 (Table P-PZ40)
988.K92	Kwŏn, Mun-hae, 1534-1591 (Table P-PZ40)
988.K926	Kwŏn, O-bok, 1467-1498 (Table P-PZ40)
988.K93	Kwŏn, P'il, 1569-1612? (Table P-PZ40)
988.M55	Min, Che-in, 1493-1549. (Table P-PZ40)
988.N32	Na, Se-ch'an, 1498-1551 (Table P-PZ40)
988.N36	Nam, Hyo-on, 1454-1492 (Table P-PZ40)
988.N62	No, In, 1566-1622 (Table P-PZ40)
988.N65	Non'gae, d. 1593 (Table P-PZ40)
988.O23	Ŏ, Suk-kwŏn, 16th cent. (Table P-PZ40)
988.P28	Paek, Kwang-hong, 1522-1556 (Table P-PZ40)
988.P35	Pak, Ch'ung-wŏn, 1507-1581 (Table P-PZ40)
988.P36	Pak, Kwang-jŏn, 1526-1597 (Table P-PZ40)
988.P37	Pak, Sang, 1474-1530 (Table P-PZ40)
988.P38	Pak, Sun, 1523-1589 (Table P-PZ40)
988.P39	Pak, Sŭng-im, 1517-1586 (Table P-PZ40)
988.P48	Pak, Ŭn, 1479-1504 (Table P-PZ40)
988.P68	Pou, 1515-1565 (Table P-PZ40)
988.P95	P'yo, Yŏn-mal, 1449-1498 (Table P-PZ40)
988.P96	Pyŏn, Kye-ryang, 1369-1430. (Table P-PZ40)
	Sejong, King of Korea, 1396-1450 see PL988.Y58
988.S34	Sim, Ŏn-gwang, 1487-1540. (Table P-PZ40)
988.S35	Sim, Su-gyŏng, 1516-1599 (Table P-PZ40)
988.S38	Sin, Hŭl, 1550-1614 (Table P-PZ40)
988.S42	Sin, Hŭm, 1566-1628 (Table P-PZ40)
988.S43	Sin, Kae, 1374-1446 (Table P-PZ40)
988.S44	Sin, Kwang-han, 1484-1555 (Table P-PZ40)
988.S46	Sin, Suk-chu, 1417-1475 (Table P-PZ40)
988.S56	Sŏ, Kŏ-jŏng, 1420-1488 (Table P-PZ40)
988.S58	Sŏ, Kyŏng-dŭk, 1489-1546 (Table P-PZ40)
988.S59	Sŏ, Sa-wŏn, 1550-1615 (Table P-PZ40)
988.S6	Sŏng, Hyŏn, 1439-1504 (Table P-PZ40)
988.S615	Song, Ik-p'il, 1534-1599 (Table P-PZ40)
988.S62	Sŏng, Im, 1421-1484 (Table P-PZ40)
988.S63	Sŏng, Kan, 1427-1456 (Table P-PZ40)
988.S64	Song, Mong-in, 1582-1612 (Table P-PZ40)
988.S646	Sŏng, Sam-mun, 1418-1456 (Table P-PZ40)
988.S65	Song, Sun, 1493-1582 (Table P-PZ40)

Korean language and literature
Korean literature
Individual authors and works
1392-1598 -- Continued

988.S67	Sŏsan Taesa, 1520-1604 (Table P-PZ40)
988.Y23	Yang, Sŏng-ji, 1415-1482 (Table P-PZ40)
988.Y25	Yang, Ŭng-jŏng, 1519-1579 (Table P-PZ40)
988.Y33	Yi, An-nul, 1571-1637 (Table P-PZ40)
988.Y423	Yi, Cha, 1480-1533 (Table P-PZ40)
988.Y428	Yi, Chŏng-am, 1541-1600 (Table P-PZ40)
988.Y43	Yi, Chŏng-gwi, 1564-1635 (Table P-PZ40)
988.Y45	Yi, Haeng, 1478-1534 (Table P-PZ40)
988.Y46	Yi, Hwang, 1501-1570 (Table P-PZ40)
988.Y5	Yi, Hyŏn-bo, 1467-1555 (Table P-PZ40)
988.Y54	Yi, I, 1536-1584 (Table P-PZ40)
988.Y56	Yi, Maech'ang, 1573-1610 (Table P-PZ40)
988.Y57	Yi, Mok, 1471-1498 (Table P-PZ40)
988.Y58	Yi, Sejong, King of Korea, 1397-1450 (Table P-PZ40)
988.Y592	Yi, Su-gwang, 1563-1628 (Table P-PZ40)
988.Y5925	Yi, Sŭng-so, 1422-1484 (Table P-PZ40)
988.Y593	Yi, Tal, 1539-1612 (Table P-PZ40)
988.Y66	Yŏnsan Kan, King of Korea, 1476-1506 (Table P-PZ40)
988.Y82	Yu, Sŏng-nyong, 1542-1607 (Table P-PZ40)
988.Y84	Yujŏng, 1544-1610 (Table P-PZ40)
988.Y845	Yun, Ch'un-nyŏn, 1514-1567 (Table P-PZ40)
988.Y85	Yun, Sang, 1373-1455 (Table P-PZ40)
988.Y86	Yun, Tu-su, 1533-1601 (Table P-PZ40)
989-989.98	1598-1894 (Table PL3 modified)
989.A1A-.A1Z	Anonymous works. By title, A-Z
989.A1C55	Ch'unhyang chŏn
989.A1H32	Ha Chin yangmullok
989.A1H85	Hungbu chŏn
989.A1H89	Hwa ssi ch'unghyorok
989.A1N36	Nanch'o chaese kiyŏnnok
989.A1O49	Ogwŏn chunghoeyŏn
989.A1O525	Okp'o-dong kiwallok
989.A1O53	Ongnumong
989.A1P35	Pak T'ae-bo chŏn
989.A1P36	Pang Hallim chŏn
989.A1S27	Sasŏng kibong
989.A1S95	Sukhyang chŏn
989.A1T65	T'okki chŏn
989.12	Ch'a
989.12.C43	Ch'a, Chwa-il, 1753-1809 (Table P-PZ40)
989.13	Ch'ae
989.13.C44	Ch'ae, Che-gong, 1720-1799 (Table P-PZ40)
989.14	Chang

Korean language and literature
Korean literature
Individual authors and works
1598-1894
Chang -- Continued

989.14.Y8	Chang, Yu, 1587-1638 (Table P-PZ40)
989.155	Chin
989.155.S5	Chin, Si-ch'aek, 1831-1906 (Table P-PZ40)
989.17	Cho. Ch'o
989.17.C46	Cho, Chang-ha, 1847-1910 (Table P-PZ40)
989.17.H35	Cho, Hang (Table P-PZ40)
989.17.H96	Cho, Hyŏn-bŏm, 1716-1790 (Table P-PZ40)
989.17.I3	Cho, Ik, 1579-1655 (Table P-PZ40)
989.17.M96	Cho, Myŏn-ho, 1804-1887 (Table P-PZ40)
989.17.S66	Cho, Sŏng-gi, 1638-1689 (Table P-PZ40)
989.17.S87	Cho, Su-sam, 1762-1849 (Table P-PZ40)
989.17.T34	Cho, T'ae-ch'ae, 1660-1722 (Table P-PZ40)
989.17.W54	Cho, Wi-han, 1567-1649 (Table P-PZ40)
989.17.Y66	Cho, Yŏng-sŏk, 1686-1761 (Table P-PZ40)
989.18	Ch'oe
989.18.C48	Ch'oe, Che-u, 1824-1864 (Table P-PZ40)
989.18.H96	Ch'oe, Hyŏn-p'il, 1860-1937 (Table P-PZ40)
989.18.I53	Ch'oe, Ik-hyŏn, 1833-1906 (Table P-PZ40)
989.18.M36	Ch'oe, Man-sŏng (Table P-PZ40)
989.2	Chong. Chŏng
989.2.C46	Chŏng, Chong-no (Table P-PZ40)
989.2.C5	Chŏng, Hag-yu, 1786-1855 (Table P-PZ40)
989.2.K8	Chŏng, Ku, b. 1664 (Table P-PZ40)
989.2.S35	Chŏng, Sang-jŏm, 1693- (Table P-PZ40)
989.2.T33	Chŏng, T'ae-je, 1612-1669 (Table P-PZ40)
989.2.T38	Chŏng, T'ae-wŏn, 1824-1880 (Table P-PZ40)
989.2.W66	Chŏng, Wŏn-yong, 1783-1873 (Table P-PZ40)
989.2.Y24	Chŏng, Yag-yong, 1762-1836 (Table P-PZ40)
989.264.C48	Hansan Yi Ssi, Chŏnggyŏng Puin, 1659-1727 (Table P-PZ40)
989.27	Ho. Hŏ
989.27.K9	Hŏ, Kyun, 1569-1618 (Table P-PZ40)
989.27.M65	Hŏ, Mok, 1595-1682 (Table P-PZ40)
989.28	Hong
989.28.M35	Hong, Man-jong, 1643-1725 (Table P-PZ40)
989.28.S48	Hong, Se-t'ae, 1653-1725 (Table P-PZ40)
989.28.S6	Hong, Sŏ-bong, 1572-1645 (Table P-PZ40)
989.28.S8	Hong, Sun-hak (Table P-PZ40)
989.28.Y26	Hong, Yang-ho, 1724-1802 (Table P-PZ40)
989.29	Hwang
989.29.H9	Hwang, Hyŏn, 1855-1910 (Table P-PZ40)
989.33	Im

Korean language and literature
Korean literature
Individual authors and works
1598-1894
Im -- Continued

989.33.H66	Im, Hŏn-hoe, 1811-1876 (Table P-PZ40)
989.33.S66	Im, Sŏng-ju, 1711-1788 (Table P-PZ40)
989.33.Y85	Im, Yunjidang, d. 1721-1793 (Table P-PZ40)
989.38	Kang
989.38.S44	Kang, Se-hwang, 1713-1791 (Table P-PZ40)
989.38.T35	Kang, Tam-un (Table P-PZ40)
989.415	Kim
989.415.C45	Kim, Ch'ang-hyŏp, 1651-1708 (Table P-PZ40)
989.415.C46	Kim, Cho-sun, 1765-1832 (Table P-PZ40)
989.415.C466	Kim, Chŏng-hŭi, 1786-1856 (Table P-PZ40)
989.415.C47	Kim, Chŭng-jŏng, 1602-1689 (Table P-PZ40)
989.415.I5	Kim, In-gyŏm, 1707-1772. (Table P-PZ40)
989.415.M3	Kim, Man-jung, 1637-1692 (Table P-PZ40)
989.415.M86	Kim, Mun-bae, 1864-1925 (Table P-PZ40)
	Kim, Nip, 1807-1863 see PL989.415.S3
989.415.P89	Kim, Pu-yong (Table P-PZ40)
989.415.S26	Kim, Samŭidang, 1769-1823 (Table P-PZ40)
989.415.S3	Kim, Satkat, 1807-1863 (Table P-PZ40)
989.415.S64	Kim, So-haeng, 1765-1859 (Table P-PZ40)
989.415.S86	Kim, Su-min, 1734-1811 (Table P-PZ40)
989.415.Y5	Kim, Yŏ, 19th cent. (Table P-PZ40)
989.415.Y6	Kim, Yŏng-su, 1829-1899 (Table P-PZ40)
989.415.Y9	Kim, Yu, 1814-1884 (Table P-PZ40)
989.45	Kwak
989.45.C46	Kwak, Chong-sŏk, 1846-1925 (Table P-PZ40)
989.46	Kwŏn
989.46.K96	Kwŏn, Kyŏng-ha, 1828-1905 (Table P-PZ40)
989.46.S26	Kwŏn, Sang-il, 1679-1760 (Table P-PZ40)
989.46.S65	Kwŏn, Sŏp, 1671-1759 (Table P-PZ40)
989.56	Nam
989.56.K66	Nam, Kong-ch'ŏl, 1760-1840 (Table P-PZ40)
989.56.K86	Nam, Ku-man, 1629-1711 (Table P-PZ40)
989.58	O. Ŏ
989.58.T37	O, Tar-un, 1700-1747 (Table P-PZ40)
989.58.T65	O, To-il, 1645-1703 (Table P-PZ40)
989.6	Pae
989.6.S26	Pae, Sang-bok, 1728-1802 (Table P-PZ40)
989.62	Pak
989.62.C4	Pak, Che-ga, 1750-1815 (Table P-PZ40)
989.62.C5	Pak, Chi-wŏn, 1737-1805 (Table P-PZ40)
989.62.C52	Pak, Chuk-sŏ, 1817-1851 (Table P-PZ40)
989.62.I4	Pak, Il-lo, 1561-1642 (Table P-PZ40)

Korean language and literature
Korean literature
Individual authors and works
1598-1894
Pak -- Continued

989.62.P55	Pak, P'il-chu, 1665-1748 (Table P-PZ40)
989.62.S4	Pak, Se-dang, 1629-1703 (Table P-PZ40)
989.62.S66	Pak, Son-gyŏng, 1713-1782 (Table P-PZ40)
989.73	Sin
989.73.C48	Sin, Chae-hyo, 1812-1884 (Table P-PZ40)
989.73.K96	Sin, Kwang-su, 1712-1775 (Table P-PZ40)
989.73.W5	Sin, Wi, 1769-1845 (Table P-PZ40)
989.74	So. Sŏ
989.74.Y8	Sŏ, Yu-bon, 1762-1822 (Table P-PZ40)
989.74.Y89	Sŏ, Yu-yŏng, b. 1801 (Table P-PZ40)
989.78	Song. Sŏng
989.78.H83	Song, Hwan-gi, 1728-1807 (Table P-PZ40)
989.78.K56	Song, Ki-myŏn (Table P-PZ40)
989.78.M66	Song, Mong-in, 1582-1612 (Table P-PZ40)
989.78.T34	Sŏng, Tae-jung, 1732-1812 (Table P-PZ40)
989.834	Ŭisun, 1786-1866 (Table P-PZ39)
989.9	Yi
989.9.C43	Yi, Chae, 1657-1731 (Table P-PZ40)
989.9.C433	Yi, Chae, 1680-1746 (Table P-PZ40)
989.9.C45	Yi, Chin-sang, 1818-1886 (Table P-PZ40)
989.9.C48	Yi, Chŏng-jak, 1678-1758 (Table P-PZ40)
989.9.H32	Yi, Haeng-jin, 1597-1665 (Table P-PZ40)
989.9.H35	Yi, Hak-kyu, 1770-1835 (Table P-PZ40)
989.9.H4	Yi, Hang-bok, 1556-1618 (Table P-PZ40)
989.9.H96	Yi, Hyŏn-il, 1627-1704 (Table P-PZ40)
989.9.I4	Yi, Ik, 1681-1763 (Table P-PZ40)
989.9.K66	Yi, Kŏn-ch'ang, 1852-1898 (Table P-PZ40)
989.9.K67	Yi, Kyŏng-sŏk, 1595-1671 (Table P-PZ40)
989.9.N35	Yi, Nam-gyu, 1855-1907 (Table P-PZ40)
989.9.O4	Yi, Ok, 1760-1815 (Table P-PZ40)
989.9.O66	Yi, Ŏn-jin, 1740-1766 (Table P-PZ40)
989.9.S24	Yi, Sang-jŏk, 1803-1865 (Table P-PZ40)
989.9.S26	Yi, Sang-jŏng, 1710-1781 (Table P-PZ40)
989.9.S32	Yi, Se-bo, 1832-1895 (Table P-PZ40)
989.9.S323	Yi, Se-hwan, 1664-1752 (Table P-PZ40)
989.9.S64	Yi, Sŏ-gu, 1754-1825 (Table P-PZ40)
989.9.T36	Yi, Tan-sang, 1628-1669 (Table P-PZ40)
989.9.T6	Yi, Tŏk-hyŏng, 1561-1613 (Table P-PZ40)
989.9.T62	Yi, Tŏk-su, 1673-1744 (Table P-PZ40)
989.9.T65	Yi, Tong-jun, 1842-1897 (Table P-PZ40)
989.9.T66	Yi, Tŏng-mu, 1741?-1793 (Table P-PZ40)
989.9.U54	Yi, Ŭi-hyŏn, 1669-1745 (Table P-PZ40)

Korean language and literature
Korean literature
Individual authors and works
1598-1894
Yi -- Continued

989.9.W66	Yi, Wŏn-jo, 1792-1871 (Table P-PZ40)
989.9.Y65	Yi, Yong-hyu, 1708-1782 (Table P-PZ40)
989.94	Yu
989.94.H36	Yu, Han-jun, 1732-1811 (Table P-PZ40)
989.94.I54	Yu, In-mok, 1839-1900 (Table P-PZ40)
989.94.K86	Yu, Kŭm, 1741-1788 (Table P-PZ40)
989.94.M6	Yu, Mong-in, 1559-1623 (Table P-PZ40)
989.94.S66	Yu, Sŏng-nyong, 1542-1607 (Table P-PZ40)
989.94.T85	Yu, Tŭk-kong (Table P-PZ40)
989.96	Yun
989.96.C48	Yun, Chŭng, 1629-1714 (Table P-PZ40)
989.96.H8	Yun, Hŭi-gu, 1867-1927 (Table P-PZ40)
989.96.H96	Yun, Hyu, 1617-1680 (Table P-PZ40)
989.96.S6	Yun, Sŏn-do, 1587-1671 (Table P-PZ40)
989.96.S86	Yun, Sun-gŏ, 1596-1668 (Table P-PZ40)
989.96.Y35	Yun, Yang-nae, 1673-1751 (Table P-PZ40)
990-990.98	1894-1919 (Table PL3 modified)
	Subarrange each author by Table P-PZ40
990.A1A-.A1Z	Anonymous works. By title, A-Z
990.115	An
990.115.K8	An, Kuk-sŏn, 1854-1928 (Table P-PZ40)
990.17	Cho. Ch'o
990.17.P69	Cho, Po-yŏn, 1875-1934 (Table P-PZ40)
990.18	Ch'oe
990.18.C5	Ch'oe, Ch'an-sik, 1881-1951 (Table P-PZ40)
990.18.N3	Ch'oe, Nam-sŏn, 1890-1957 (Table P-PZ40)
990.18.S65	Ch'oe, Songsŏltang, 1855-1939 (Table P-PZ40)
990.2	Chong. Chŏng
990.2.C48	Chŏng, Chun-mo, 1860-1935 (Table P-PZ40)
990.2.H96	Chŏng, Hyŏng-gyu, 1880- (Table P-PZ40)
990.28	Hong
990.28.M9	Hong, Myŏng-hŭi, 1888- (Table P-PZ40)
990.415	Kim
990.415.T34	Kim, T'aeg-yŏng, 1850-1927 (Table P-PZ40)
990.415.Y55	Kim, Yŏng-gŭn, 1865-1934 (Table P-PZ40)
990.43	Ku
990.43.Y65	Ku, Yŏn-ho, 1861-1940 (Table P-PZ40)
990.58	O. Ŏ
990.58.C45	O, Chin-yŏng, 1868-1944 (Table P-PZ40)
990.62	Pak
990.62.U55	Pak, Ŭn-sik, 1859-1926 (Table P-PZ40)
990.73	Sin

Korean language and literature
Korean literature
Individual authors and works
1894-1919
Sin -- Continued

990.73.C5	Sin, Ch'ae-ho, 1880-1936 (Table P-PZ40)
990.78	Song. Sŏng
990.78.H96	Song, Hyŏn-sŏp, 1862-1938 (Table P-PZ40)
990.78.K86	Song, Kŭng-sŏp, 1873-1933 (Table P-PZ40)
990.7915.S94	Sunjong, King of Korea, 1874-1926 (Table P-PZ40)
990.9	Yi
990.9.H3	Yi, Hae-jo, 1869-1927 (Table P-PZ40)
990.9.I5	Yi, In-jik, 1862-1916 (Table P-PZ40)
990.9.K9	Yi, Kwang-su, 1892- (Table P-PZ40)
990.9.P36	Yi, Pang-hŏn, 1857-1923 (Table P-PZ40)
990.9.S36	Yi, Sang-nyong, 1858-1932 (Table P-PZ40)
990.9.T64	Yi, Tŏg-u, 1887-1960 (Table P-PZ40)
990.96	Yun
990.96.C36	Yun, Ch'ang-man, 1896-1967 (Table P-PZ40)
991-991.98	1919-1945 (Table PL3 modified)
	Subarrange each author by Table P-PZ40
991.A1A-.A1Z	Anonymous works. By title, A-Z
991.115	An
991.115.H63	An, Hoe-nam, 1910- (Table P-PZ40)
991.115.S78	An, Sŏk-chu, 1901-1950 (Table P-PZ40)
991.115.S8	An, Su-gil (Table P-PZ40)
991.13	Ch'ae
991.13.M3	Ch'ae, Man-sik, 1902-1950 (Table P-PZ40)
991.14	Chang. Ch'ang
991.14.C5	Chang, Chŏng-sim (Table P-PZ40)
991.14.M3	Chang, Man-yŏng, 1914- (Table P-PZ40)
991.14.S6	Chang, Sŏ-ŏn, 1912- (Table P-PZ40)
991.14.T6	Chang, Tŏk-cho, 1915- (Table P-PZ40)
991.17	Cho. Ch'o
991.17.M9	Cho, Myŏng-hŭi, 1894-1942 (Table P-PZ40)
991.17.Y6	Cho, Yong-man, 1909- (Table P-PZ40)
991.18	Ch'oe
991.18.C5	Ch'oe, Chŏng-hŭi, 1912- (Table P-PZ40)
991.18.H3	Ch'oe, Hak-song, 1901-1933 (Table P-PZ40)
991.19	Chon. Chŏn. Ch'ŏn
991.19.H3	Chŏn, Han-ch'on (Table P-PZ40)
991.2	Chong. Chŏng
991.2.C4	Chŏng, Chi-yong, 1903- (Table P-PZ40)
991.2.I45	Chŏng, In-bo, 1893- (Table P-PZ40)
991.2.P5	Chŏng, Pisŏk, 1911- (Table P-PZ40)
991.215	Chu. Ch'u
991.215.Y5	Chu, Yo-han, 1900- (Table P-PZ40)

Korean language and literature
Korean literature
Individual authors and works
1919-1945
Chu. Ch'u -- Continued

991.215.Y55	Chu, Yo-sŏp, 1902- (Table P-PZ40)
991.25	Ham
991.25.S4	Ham, Se-dŏk, 1915-1950 (Table P-PZ40)
991.25.T3	Ham, Tae-hun, 1907-1949 (Table P-PZ40)
991.26	Han
991.26.S6	Han, Sŏr-ya, 1900- (Table P-PZ40)
991.26.T3	Han, T'ae-ch'ŏn, 1906- (Table P-PZ40)
991.26.Y6	Han, Yong-un, 1879-1944 (Table P-PZ40)
991.28	Hong
991.28.H9	Hong, Hyomin, 1904- (Table P-PZ40)
991.28.S2	Hong, Sa-yong, 1900-1947 (Table P-PZ40)
991.29	Hwang
991.29.S9	Hwang, Sun-wŏn, 1915- (Table P-PZ40)
991.3	Hyon. Hyŏn
991.3.C5	Hyŏn, Chin-gŏn, 1900-1943 (Table P-PZ40)
991.3.T63	Hyŏn, Tŏk, 1912- (Table P-PZ40)
991.33	Im
991.33.H3	Im, Hak-su, 1911- (Table P-PZ40)
991.33.H8	Im, Hwa, 1908-1953 (Table P-PZ40)
991.33.O4	Im, Og-in (Table P-PZ40)
991.415	Kim
991.415.C4	Kim, Chin-su, 1909- (Table P-PZ40)
991.415.C5	Kim, Chŏng-sik, 1903-1934 (Table P-PZ40)
991.415.C56	Kim, Ch'un-dong, 1906-1982 (Table P-PZ40)
	Kim, Hae-gyŏng, 1910-1937 see PL991.9.S3
991.415.I2	Kim, I-sŏk, 1914-1964 (Table P-PZ40)
991.415.I7	Kim, Ir-yŏp, 1896-1971 (Table P-PZ40)
991.415.K5	Kim, Ki-jin (Table P-PZ40)
991.415.K54	Kim, Ki-rim, 1908- (Table P-PZ40)
991.415.K75	Kim, Kwang-gyun, 1914- (Table P-PZ40)
991.415.K85	Kim, Kwang-sŏp, 1905-1977 (Table P-PZ40)
991.415.M3	Kim, Mal-bong, 1901-1961 (Table P-PZ40)
991.415.N2	Kim, Nae-sŏng, 1909-1957 (Table P-PZ40)
991.415.N3	Kim, Namch'ŏn, 1911- (Table P-PZ40)
991.415.O4	Kim, Ŏk, 1896- (Table P-PZ40)
991.415.S23	Kim, Sa-ryang, 1914-1950 (Table P-PZ40)
991.415.S3	Kim, Sang-yong, 1902-1951 (Table P-PZ40)
(991.415.S4)	Kim, Si-ch'ang, 1914-1950 see PL991.415.S23
991.415.S5	Kim, So-un, 1907- (Table P-PZ40)
	Kim, So-wŏl, 1903-1934 see PL991.415.C5
991.415.S6	Kim, Song, 1907- (Table P-PZ40)

Korean language and literature
Korean literature
Individual authors and works
1919-1945
Kim -- Continued

991.415.T3	Kim, Tal-chin, 1907- (Table P-PZ40)
991.415.T6	Kim, Tong-hwan, 1901- (Table P-PZ40)
991.415.T63	Kim, Tong-in, 1900-1951 (Table P-PZ40)
991.415.T65	Kim, Tong-myŏng, 1901-1968 (Table P-PZ40)
991.415.T7	Kim, Tongni, 1913- (Table P-PZ40)
991.415.U18	Kim, U-jin, 1897-1926 (Table P-PZ40)
991.415.Y6	Kim, Yong-ho, 1912- (Table P-PZ40)
991.415.Y63	Kim, Yong-je, 1909- (Table P-PZ40)
991.415.Y77	Kim, Yu-jŏng, 1908-1937 (Table P-PZ40)
991.415.Y8	Kim, Yun-sik, 1903-1950 (Table P-PZ40)
991.42	Ko
991.42.T8	Ko, Tu-dong (Table P-PZ40)
991.47	Kye
991.47.Y6	Kye, Yong-muk, 1904-1961 (Table P-PZ40)
991.48	Lee
991.48.Y3	Lee, Yang Ha, 1904-1963 (Table P-PZ40)
991.49	Ma
991.49.H3	Ma, Haesong, 1905- (Table P-PZ40)
991.52	Mo
991.52.Y85	Mo, Yun-suk, 1910- (Table P-PZ40)
991.55	Na
991.55.H93	Na, Hye-sŏk (Table P-PZ40)
991.55.K9	Na, Kyŏng-son, 1902-1926 (Table P-PZ40)
991.57	No
991.57.C3	No, Cha-yŏng, 1898-1940 (Table P-PZ40)
991.57.C5	No, Ch'ŏn-myŏng, 1911-1957 (Table P-PZ40)
991.58	O. Ŏ
991.58.C4	O, Chang-hwan, 1916- (Table P-PZ40)
991.58.S3	O, Sang-sun, 1894-1963 (Table P-PZ40)
991.59	Ŏm
991.59.H75	Ŏm, Hŭng-sŏp, 1906- (Table P-PZ40)
991.613	Paek
991.613.S57	Paek, Sin-ae, 1908-1939 (Table P-PZ40)
991.613.S587	Paek, Sŏk, 1912- (Table P-PZ40)
991.62	Pak
991.62.C5	Pak, Chong-hwa, 1901- (Table P-PZ40)
991.62.H8	Pak, Hwa-sŏng, 1904- (Table P-PZ40)
991.62.I4	Pak, Il-gwŏn (Table P-PZ40)
991.62.K6	Pak, Kŏyŏng, 1911- (Table P-PZ40)
991.62.K9	Pak, Kye-ju, 1913- (Table P-PZ40)
991.62.N3	Pak, Nam-su, 1913- (Table P-PZ40)
991.62.N6	Pak, No-gap, 1905- (Table P-PZ40)

Korean language and literature
Korean literature
Individual authors and works
1919-1945
Pak -- Continued

991.62.P3	Pak, Pʻar-yang, 1905- (Table P-PZ40)
991.62.S89	Pak, Sŭng-hŭi, 1901-1964 (Table P-PZ40)
991.62.T3	Pak, Tʻae-wŏn, 1909- (Table P-PZ40)
991.62.Y6	Pak, Yong-chʻŏl, 1904-1938 (Table P-PZ40)
991.62.Y64	Pak, Yŏng-jun, 1911- (Table P-PZ40)
991.63	Pang. Pʻang
991.63.C5	Pang, Chong-hwan, 1899-1931 (Table P-PZ40)
991.63.I5	Pang, In-gŭn, 1899- (Table P-PZ40)
991.64	Pʻi
991.64.C5	Pʻi, Chʻŏn-dŭk, 1910- (Table P-PZ40)
991.67	Pyon. Pyŏn
991.67.Y6	Pyŏn, Yŏng-no, 1898-1961 (Table P-PZ40)
991.72	Sim
991.72.H8	Sim, Hun, 1901-1936 (Table P-PZ40)
991.72.U36	Sim, Ŭi-rin (Table P-PZ40)
991.73	Sin
991.73.S56	Sin, Sŏk-chʻo, 1909-1975 (Table P-PZ40)
991.74	So. Sŏ
991.74.C5	Sŏ, Chŏng-ju, 1915?- (Table P-PZ40)
991.78	Song. Sŏng
991.78.Y6	Song, Yŏng, 1903- (Table P-PZ40)
991.89	Yang
991.89.C5	Yang, Chu-dong, 1903- (Table P-PZ40)
991.89.S3	Yang, Sang-gyŏng, 1904- (Table P-PZ40)
991.9	Yi
991.9.C42	Yi, Chang-hŭi, 1900-1929 (Table P-PZ40)
991.9.C45	Yi, Chŏng-gu, 1911- (Table P-PZ40)
991.9.C5	Yi, Chu-hong, 1906- (Table P-PZ40)
991.9.H8	Yi, Hŭi-sŭng, 1896- (Table P-PZ40)
(991.9.H85)	Yi, Hwal, 1905-1944 see PL991.9.Y63
991.9.H9	Yi, Hyo-sŏk, 1907-1942 (Table P-PZ40)
991.9.K5	Yi, Ki-yŏng, 1894- (Table P-PZ40)
991.9.K85	Yi, Kŭn-yŏng, 1910- (Table P-PZ40)
991.9.K9	Yi, Kyŏng-son (Table P-PZ40)
991.9.M8	Yi, Muyŏng, 1908-1960 (Table P-PZ40)
991.9.P9	Yi, Pyŏng-gi, 1891- (Table P-PZ40)
991.9.S3	Yi, Sang, 1910-1937 (Table P-PZ40)
991.9.S4	Yi, Sang-hwa, 1901-1943 (Table P-PZ40)
991.9.S6	Yi, Sŏ-gu, 1899- (Table P-PZ40)
991.9.S64	Yi, Sŏk-hun, 1907- (Table P-PZ40)
991.9.T3	Yi, Tʻae-jun, 1904- (Table P-PZ40)

PL

	Korean language and literature
	Korean literature
	Individual authors and works
	1919-1945
	Yi -- Continued
991.9.T65	Yi, Tong-gyu (Table P-PZ40)
991.9.U5	Yi, Ŭn-sang, 1903- (Table P-PZ40)
	Yi, Yang-ha, 1904-1963 see PL991.48.Y3
991.9.Y6	Yi, Yong-su, 1908- (Table P-PZ40)
991.9.Y63	Yi, Yuk-sa, 1904-1944 (Table P-PZ40)
991.92	Yŏm
991.92.S3	Yŏm, Sang-sŏp, 1897-1963 (Table P-PZ40)
991.94	Yu
991.94.C4	Yu, Ch'i-hwan, 1908-1967 (Table P-PZ40)
991.94.C43	Yu, Ch'i-jin, 1905- (Table P-PZ40)
991.94.C5	Yu, Chin-o, 1906- (Table P-PZ40)
991.94.Y6	Yu, Yŏp, 1902- (Table P-PZ40)
991.96	Yun
991.96.K6	Yun, Kon'gang, 1911-1948 (Table P-PZ40)
991.96.P3	Yun, Paengnam, 1888-1954 (Table P-PZ40)
991.96.S64	Yun, Sok-chung, 1911- (Table P-PZ40)
991.96.T6	Yun, Tong-ju, 1917-1945 (Table P-PZ40)
991.96.Y6	Yun, Yŏng-ch'un, 1912- (Table P-PZ40)
992-992.98	1945-2000 (Table PL3 modified)
	Subarrange each author by Table P-PZ40 unless otherwise indicated
992.143	Ch'angmaengin (Table P-PZ39)
	Chŏng, Min see PL992.792
992.792	Syabet'ŭ (Table P-PZ39)
993.A-Z	Corporate authors, A-Z
994-994.98	2001- (Table PL3)
	Subarrange each author by Table P-PZ40
	Local literature
	Korea
997.A2	Regional. General or several regions
	North Korea (General)
	For local of North Korea see PL997.A3+
997.A25	History
997.A26	Collections
	South Korea (General) see PL950+
997.A3-Z	Special provinces, regions, A-Z
	Subarrange each by Table P-PZ26
997.5.A-Z	Special cities, etc., A-Z
	Subarrange each by Table P-PZ26
	Korean literature outside Korea
998.A2	General

	Korean language and literature
	Korean literature
	Local literature
	Korean literature outside Korea -- Continued
998.A3-Z	Special countries, A-Z
	Subarrange each by Table P-PZ26
	For individual authors, see PL986+
	Chinese language and literature
	Chinese language
	Periodicals
1001.A1-.A3	International
1001.A4-Z	English and American
1002	French
1003	German
1004	Chinese
1006	Japanese
1007	Korean
1009.A-Z	Other languages, A-Z
1010	Annuals. Yearbooks, etc.
	Societies
1011.A1-.A3	International
1011.A4-Z	English and American
1012	French
1013	German
1014	Chinese
1016	Japanese
1017	Korean
1019	Other
1021	Congresses
1023	Collected works (nonserial)
1031	Encyclopedias
(1033)	Atlases. Maps
	see class G
1035	Philosophy. Theory. Method. Relations
	History of philology
1051	General works
1060.A-Z	By region or country, A-Z
	Biography, memoirs, etc.
1063	Collective
1064.A-Z	Individual, A-Z
	Subarrange each by Table P-PZ50
	Study and teaching. Research
1065	General works
1068.A-Z	By region or country, A-Z
1069.A-Z	By school, research institute, etc., A-Z
1071	Treatises (Philology, General)
1074	Relation to other languages

	Chinese language and literature
	Chinese language -- Continued
1074.5	Language data processing
1074.7	Language standardization and variation
1074.8	Spoken language
1074.85	Language acquisition
	History of the language
1075	General works
1077	Early to 600. Proto-Chinese. Archaic Chinese
1079	Ancient Chinese, 600-1200
1081	Middle Chinese, 1200-1919
1083	Modern Chinese, 1919-
1093	Outlines, syllabi, tables, etc.
1095	Popular works
	Grammar
1099	Comparative (Two or more languages)
1101	Historical
	General works
1103	In eastern languages
1107	In western languages
	Textbooks
1109	In eastern languages
1111	In western languages
	Readers
1113	Series
1115	Primary
1117	Intermediate and advanced
1117.5.A-Z	By subject, A-Z
1117.5.A34	Agriculture
1117.5.A76	Art
1117.5.C6	China
1117.5.C65	Commerce
1117.5.E36	Economics
1117.5.F66	Food habits
1117.5.H57	History
1117.5.L38	Law
1117.5.L48	Letters
1117.5.M43	Medicine
1117.5.S56	Short stories
1117.5.T42	Technology
1117.5.T44	Television
	Travels see PL1117.5.V68
1117.5.V68	Voyages and travels
1118	Outlines, syllabi, tables, etc.
1119	Examinations, questions,etc.
1120	Manuals for special classes of students, A-Z
	Conversation. Phrase books

	Chinese language and literature
	Chinese language
	Grammar
	Conversation. Phrase books -- Continued
1121.A-Z	For eastern languages, A-Z
1125.A-Z	For western languages, A-Z
1125.E6	English
	Textbooks for foreign speakers
1128	General
1129.A-Z	By language, A-Z
	Script. Chinese characters
1171	General works
1175	Script reform. Simplified characters
	Transliteration
1181	Into eastern languages
1185	Into western languages
1188	From eastern languages
1189	From western languages
	Phonology
1201	General works
1205	Phonetics
1209	Pronunciation
1213	Tones
1215	Vowels
1219	Consonants
	Morphology
1230	General works
1231	Word formation
	Parts of speech
1231.5	General works
1232	Noun
1233	Adjective. Adverb. Comparison
1234	Pronoun
1235	Verb
1237	Particles
	Including individual particles
1238	Quantifiers. Numerals
1241	Syntax
1250.A-Z	Other aspects, A-Z
1250.H65	Honorific
	Style. Composition. Rhetoric
1271	General works
1272	Punctuation
1273	Idioms
1274	Report writing
1275	Letter writing

Chinese language and literature
Chinese language -- Continued
Translating
For special subjects, see classes B - Z, e.g. Technology,
T11.5

1277	General works
1278	Machine translating
1279	Prosody. Metrics. Rhythmics
1280	Lexicology
	Etymology
1281	Treatises
1287.A-Z	Special elements. By language, A-Z
1291	Semantics
1301	Synonyms. Antonyms
1303	Paronyms
1311	Homonyms
1312	Onomatopoeic words
1313	Heteronyms
1315.A-Z	Particular words, A-Z
1315.X56	Xin
	Lexicography
1401	Collections
1411	General works. History. Treatises
1417	Criticism of particular dictionaries
	Dictionaries
1420	Dictionaries in Chinese only
1423	Dictionaries with definitions in two or more languages
	Bilingual dictionaries
1451	Chinese-Latin; Latin-Chinese
1455	Chinese-English; English-Chinese
1459.A-Z	Other languages, A-Z
	Class with language less known
(1459.J3)	Japanese
	see PL681.C5
(1459.K6)	Korean
	see PL937.C5
	Dictionaries (exclusively etymological) see PL1281+
1465	Dictionaries of earlier periods
1469	Dictionaries of special styles
	Dictionaries of special dialects see PL1681+
	Mandarin see PL1420+
1481	Dictionaries of particular authors or works
	For literary authors see PL2661+
1481.B6	Glossaries of Chinese Bible or special parts
1483	Dictionaries of names
1485	Dictionaries of obsolete, archaic words
	Dictionaries of foreign words

	Chinese language and literature
	Chinese language
	Lexicography
	Dictionaries
	Dictionaries of foreign words -- Continued
1487	General
1488.A-Z	Special languages, A-Z
	Special words see PL1495
1489	Special lists (Technical, etc.)
1495	Special words, including translations of foreign words
1497	Dictionaries of terms and phrases
1498	Other
	Including word frequency, etc.
	Dialects
1501	Periodicals. Societies. Serials
1510	General works
	Grammar
	For the grammar of specific dialects, see PL1681+
1520	General works
1525	Phonology
1541	Syntax
1545	Other
1547	Dictionaries
	For dictionaries of specific dialects, see PL1681+
1621.A-Z	By place, A-Z
	Groups of dialects
1681-1690	Northern Min dialects (Table PL8 modified)
1690.A-Z	By place, A-Z
1690.F75	Fuqing Xian
1690.F8	Fuzhou Fu
1690.J52	Jian'ou Shi
1701-1710	Southern Min dialects (Table PL8 modified)
1710.A-Z	By place, A-Z
1710.C45	Chao'an Xian
1710.P87	Putian Xian
1710.S88	Swatow. Shantou
1710.T25	T'ai-nan shih
1710.T28	Taiwan
1710.T85	Tunchang Xian
1731-1740	Cantonese (Yue) dialects (Table PL8)
1851-1860	Hakka dialects (Table PL8)
1861-1870	Hsiang (Xiang, Hunanese) dialects (Table PL8 modified)
1870.A-Z	By place, A-Z
1870.A54	Anxiang
1870.C44	Chiang-yung hsien. Jiangyong Xian
1870.W46	Wenqiao Zhen, Guangxi Zhuangzu Zizhiqu

	Chinese language and literature
	Chinese language
	Dialects
	Groups of dialects -- Continued
1871-1880	Kan (Gan, Jiangxi) dialects (Table PL8)
1891-1900	Mandarin (Northern) dialects (Table PL8 modified)

> Class here works on dialects spoken north of the Yangtze River and also in large areas south of the river in Southwestern China
>
> For works in "guo yu", or "putonghua", see the general Chinese language schedule with period and/or form subdivisions

1900.A-Z	By name or place, A-Z
	Beijing see PL1900.P44
1900.C52	Ch'ang-chih shih. Changzhi Shi
1900.C532	Ch'ang-te shih. Changde Shi
	Deng Xian see PL1900.T45
1900.D85-.D8595	Dungan (Table P-PZ16)
1900.G85	Guizhou Sheng
1900.H37	Harbin
1900.H75	Hsi-ning shih. Xining
1900.H78	Hsü-chou shih. Xuzhou
1900.H8	Hsüan-hua hsien. Xuanhua Xian
1900.I66	Inner Mongolia
1900.J53	Jiangsu Sheng
1900.J57	Jishou Shi
1900.L37	Lanzhou Shi
1900.M37	Maoxing Zhen
1900.P44	Peking. Beijing

> Class here works on the dialects spoken by the natives of Peking (Beijing)

1900.P56	Pinggu Xian (Beijing)
	Qingdao see PL1900.T75
1900.S45	Shaanxi Sheng. Shensi Province
1900.S46	Shansi Province. Shanxi Sheng
1900.S5	Shantung Province. Shandong Sheng
1900.S94	Szechwan. Sichuan Sheng
1900.T45	Teng-hsien. Deng Xian
1900.T75	Tsingtao. Qingdao
1900.U78	Ürümqi
1900.W98	Wutun
	Xining see PL1900.H75
	Xuanhua Xian see PL1900.H8
	Xuzhou see PL1900.H78
1900.Y85	Yunnan
1900.Z44	Zhengzhou
1931-1940	Wu dialects (Table PL8 modified)

	Chinese language and literature
	Chinese language
	Dialects
	Groups of dialects
	Wu dialects -- Continued
1940.A-Z	By name or place, A-Z
1940.C54	Chou-shan Archipelago. Zhoushan Archipelago
1940.N54	Ningbo Shi
1940.S53	Shanghai
1940.S8	Suzhou
1940.T53	Tiantai Xian
1940.W44	Wenzhou
	Zhoushan Archipelago see PL1940.C54
	Slang. Argot
1952	General works
1954	Dictionaries. Lists
1956	Texts
1958.A-Z	Special topics, A-Z
1960.A-Z	Local, A-Z
	Chinese literature
	History and criticism
2250	Periodicals. Serials
(2251)	Yearbooks
	see PL2250
2252	Societies
2253	Congresses
2253.5	Museums. Exhibitions
	Bibliographies
	see Z3108.L5
	Collections
2254	Serial
2255.A-Z	In honor of a special individual or institution, A-Z
2256	By an individual author
2257	Encyclopedias. Dictionaries. Indexes
	Study and teaching
2258	General works
2259.A-Z	By region or country, A-Z
2260.A-Z	By school, A-Z
	Biography of historians, teachers, critics, and editors
2260.5	Collective
2260.52.A-Z	Individual, A-Z
	Subarrange each by Table P-PZ50
	Criticism
2261	Early works through 1911
2262	1912-
2262.2	Addresses, essays, lectures
	History

	Chinese language and literature
	Chinese literature
	History and criticism
	History -- Continued
	General works
	Chinese
2263	Early works through 1911
2264	1912-
2265	English
2266	French
2267	German
2268	Japanese
2269	Korean
2270	Russian
2271	Other
2272	Outlines, syllabi
2272.5	Addresses, essays, lectures
	Special aspects and topics
2273	Relation to history, civilization, culture, etc.
	Relation to other literatures
2274	General works
2274.2.A-Z	By country or language, A-Z
2274.5	Translations of foreign literature into Chinese
2275.A-Z	Special topics, A-Z
	Class here general works only; for history of a special form or period, see the form or period
2275.A87	Authorship
	Baishan shui dian zhan (Huadian Xian, China) see PL2275.P34
2275.B35	Bamboo
2275.B45	Beggars
	Beijing (China) see PL2275.P42
2275.B55	Birds
2275.B57	Birth control
2275.B65	Book collectors
2275.B74	Brigands and robbers
2275.B8	Buddhism
2275.C24	Calligraphy, Chinese
2275.C38	Characters
2275.C42	Chen San Wuniang
2275.C422	Chengde Diqu (China)
2275.C423	Chengdu (China)
2275.C426	Chien-ko hsien (China). Jian'ge Xian (China)
2275.C43	Ch'ih-pi (Huang-kang hsien, China). Red Cliffs
2275.C44	Chin-t'ien ts'un (China). Jintian cun (China)
2275.C45	China. Chinese
	Chongqing (China) see PL2275.C53

Chinese language and literature
Chinese literature
History and criticism
History
Special aspects and topics
Special topics, A-Z -- Continued

2275.C47	Chrysanthemums
2275.C49	Ch'ü, Yüan, ca. 343-ca. 277 B.C. Qu, Yuan, ca. 343-ca. 277 B.C.
2275.C5	Ch'ü-fu hsien (China). Qufu Xian (China)
2275.C53	Chung-ching shih (China). Chongqing (China)
2275.C56	Cinnamon tree
2275.C62	Commerce
2275.C65	Confucian ethics
2275.C67	Cosmology
	Dali Shi (China) see PL2275.T27
2275.D48	Detective and mystery stories
2275.D53	Didactic literature
2275.D74	Dreams
	Egoism see PL2275.S44
	Emei Mountain (China) see PL2275.O43
2275.E74	Erotic literature
2275.F32	Fa men si (Fufeng Xian, China)
2275.F33	Fairy tales
2275.F34	Family
2275.F35	Fantastic literature
2275.F36	Farewells
2275.F45	Feminism
2275.F47	Fengyang Xian (China)
2275.F53	Fisheries
	Flowering plums see PL2275.P55
2275.F56	Flowers
2275.F66	Food
2275.F67	Forests and forestry
2275.F73	Friendship
2275.F76	Frontier and pioneer life
2275.F84	Fujian Sheng (China)
2275.G5	Ghosts
2275.G73	Great Wall of China
	Guangyuan Shi (China) see PL2275.K83
	Guilin Shi (China) see PL2275.K85
2275.H34	Hainan Island (China). Hainan Sheng (China)
	Henan Sheng (China) see PL2275.H65
2275.H47	Heroes and heroines
2275.H57	History
2275.H63	Hong Kong
2275.H65	Honan Province (China). Henan Sheng (China)

Chinese language and literature
 Chinese literature
  History and criticism
   History
    Special aspects and topics
     Special topics, A-Z -- Continued

2275.H78	Hsü-chou shih (China). Xuzhou Shi (China)
2275.H82	Huang Mountains
2275.H83	Huang he lou (China)
2275.H86	Hunan Sheng (China)
2275.I57	Intellectuals
	Jinan (Shandong Sheng, China) see PL2275.T74
	Jian'ge Xian (China) see PL2275.C426
	Jiangxi Sheng (China) see PL2275.K53
	Jintian cun (China) see PL2275.C44
2275.K53	Kiangsi Province (China). Jiangxi Sheng (China)
2275.K83	Kuang yüan shih (China). Guangyuan Shi (China)
2275.K85	Kuei-lin shih (China). Guilin Shi (China)
2275.L38	Law. Legal novels
	Legal novels see PL2275.L38
2275.L63	Lo-yang shih (China). Luoyang Shi (China)
2275.L65	Loneliness
	Longmen Caves see PL2275.L85
2275.L68	Love
2275.L83	Lu Mountains (China)
2275.L85	Lung-men Caves. Longmen Caves
	Luoyang Shi (China) see PL2275.L63
2275.M37	Martial arts fiction
2275.M49	Merchants
2275.M52	Mianyang Shi (China)
2275.M54	Military. Militia
2275.M63	Moggallāna
2275.M65	Moon
2275.M68	Mountains
2275.M87	Music. Musical instruments. Musicians
	Mystery stories see PL2275.D48
2275.M94	Mythology
2275.N27	Nanjing (Jiansu Sheng, China)
2275.N3	Nature
2275.N67	Nostalgia
2275.O43	O-mei Mountain (China). Emei Mountain (China)
2275.P34	Pai-shan shui tien chan (Hua-tien hsien, China). Baishan shui dian zhan (Huadian Xian, China)
2275.P36	Pastoral literature
2275.P37	Patriotism
2275.P39	Peasants
2275.P42	Peking (China). Beijing (China)

Chinese language and literature
Chinese literature
History and criticism
History
Special aspects and topics
Special topics, A-Z -- Continued

2275.P43	Penglai ge (China)
2275.P44	Peonies
2275.P53	Pine tree
2275.P55	Plums. Flowering plums
2275.P64	Police
2275.P76	Prostitutes. Prostitution
	Prostitution see PL2275.P76
	Qinghai Sheng (China) see PL2275.T76
	Qu, Yuan, ca. 343-ca. 277 B.C. see PL2275.C49
	Qufu Xian (China) see PL2275.C5
	Red Cliffs see PL2275.C43
2275.R48	Revenge
2275.R58	Rivers
2275.S34	Science fiction
2275.S39	Seasons
2275.S44	Self. Self-knowledge. Self-perception. Egoism, etc.
	Sex see PL2275.E74
2275.S55	Shandong Sheng (China)
2275.S56	Shao hsing hsien (China). Shaoxing Xian (China)
2275.S57	Shao lin si (Dengfeng Xian, China)
	Shaoxing Xian (China) see PL2275.S56
	Sichuan Sheng (China) see PL2275.S95
2275.S6	Space and time
2275.S65	Sports
2275.S93	Suzhou (Jiangsu Sheng, China)
2275.S95	Szechwan Province (China). Sichuan Sheng (China)
2275.T27	Ta-li shih (China). Dali Shi (China)
2275.T33	Tai Mountains
2275.T34	Taiwan
2275.T36	Taoism
2275.T42	Tea
2275.T45	Teng wang ge (China)
2275.T53	Tiananmen Square Incident, 1989
2275.T74	Tsinan (China). Jinan (Shandong Sheng, China)
2275.T76	Tsinghai Province (China). Qinghai Sheng (China)
2275.T93	Typhoons
2275.V52	Vietnam. Vietnamese
2275.V53	Vietnam War, 1961-1975
2275.W37	War
2275.W47	West Lake (China)

Chinese language and literature
Chinese literature
History and criticism
History
Special aspects and topics
Special topics, A-Z -- Continued

2275.W55	Wine
2275.W65	Women
2275.W82	Wu-chih Mountains (China). Wuzhi Mountains (China)
2275.W83	Wu-hsi shih (China). Wuxi Shi (China)
2275.W84	Wu-i Mountains (China). Wuyi Mountains (China)
2275.W85	Wu-t'ai Mountains (China). Wutai Mountains (China)
2275.W87	Wu-tang Mountains (China). Wudang Mountains (China)
	Wudang Mountains (China) see PL2275.W87
	Wutai Mountains (China) see PL2275.W85
	Wuxi Shi (China) see PL2275.W83
	Wuyi Mountains (China) see PL2275.W84
	Wuzhi Mountains (China) see PL2275.W82
2275.X56	Xinjiang Uygur Zizhiqu
	Xuzhou Shi (China) see PL2275.H78
2275.Y35	Yang-chou shih (China). Yangzhou Shi (China)
2275.Y358	Yangtze River. Yangtze River Gorges
(2275.Y36)	Yangtze River Gorges
	see PL2275.Y358
	Yangzhou Shi (China) see PL2275.Y35
2275.Y45	Yellow River
2275.Y83	Yuan Ming Yuan (Beijing, China)
2275.Y85	Yunnan Sheng (China)
2275.Z75	Zhengzhou Shi (China)
2277	Biography (Collective)
	Special classes of authors
2278	Women
2278.5.A-Z	Other, A-Z
2278.5.B83	Buddhists
2278.5.C45	Children
2278.5.L33	Laboring class
2278.5.M55	Minorities
2278.5.M66	Mongolians
2278.5.M68	Muslims
2278.5.S65	Soldiers
2278.5.T72	Travelers
2278.5.Y68	Youth
2279.A-Z	Special families, A-Z
2280-2303	By period (Table PL6)

Chinese language and literature
Chinese literature
History and criticism
History -- Continued
Special forms
Poetry
General works

2306	Early works through 1911
2307	1912-
2308	Essays, etc.
2308.5.A-Z	Special topics, A-Z
	Prefer classification by form
	For list of topics see PL2275.A+
2309.A-Z	Special forms, A-Z
2309.C45	Children's poetry
2309.C48	Chüeh chü. Jue ju
2309.C68	Couplets
2309.D52	Didactic poetry
2309.E5	Elegiac poetry
2309.E6	Epic poetry
2309.F65	Folk poetry
2309.F8	Fu
	Jue ju see PL2309.C48
2309.L68	Love poetry
2309.L83	Lü shi
2309.N47	Narrative poetry
2309.P37	Pastorals
2309.P39	Patriotic poetry
2309.P76	Prose poetry
2309.R48	Revolutionary poetry
2309.Y8	Yue fu
2310-2333	By period (Table PL6)
	Ci (Tz'u)
2336	General works
2338	Addresses, essays, lectures
2341-2353	By period (Table PL6a)
	Qu (Ch'ü)
2354	General works
	Special forms
2354.4	San qu
	Including xiao ling and san tao
2354.6	Ju qu
	Including za ju, zhuan qi, kun qu, and duan ju
	By period
2355	Yuan dynasty, 1260-1368
2355.4	Ming dynasty, 1368-1644
2355.6	Qing dynasty, 1644-1912

Chinese language and literature
Chinese literature
History and criticism
History
Special forms
Qu (Ch'ü)
By period -- Continued
2355.8   1912-
Drama
General works
2356   Early works to 1800
2357   1800-
2358   Essays, etc.
2359.A-Z   Special topics, A-Z
Class here general works only
For history of a special form or period, see the form
or period
For list of topics see PL2275.A+
Special forms
Puppet shows see PN1978.A+
Shadow plays see PN1979.S5
Motion picture plays see PN1993+
2365   Bian wen (Buddhist song-tales)
2366   Tan ci (Southern song-tales)
2367   Gu ci (Northern song-tales)
2368.A-Z   Other, A-Z
2368.B34   Bao juan (Buddhist song-tales)
2368.D53   Dialogues
2368.H58   Historical plays
2368.H75   Hsiang sheng. Xiang sheng
2368.K77   Kuai shu
2368.O53   One-act plays
(2368.P36)   Pao chüan
see PL2368.B34
2368.P56   Ping ju (Folk dramas)
2368.P58   Ping shu
2368.R33   Radio plays
2368.T44   Television plays
2368.T7   Tragedy
Xiang sheng see PL2368.H75
2370-2393   By period (Table PL6)
Essay
2395   General works
2398.A-Z   Special topics, A-Z
Special forms
2399   Oratory
2400   Letters

	Chinese language and literature
	Chinese literature
	History and criticism
	History
	Special forms
	Essay
	Special forms -- Continued
2402	Pian wen
2403	Wit and humor
2404	Reportage literature
2405	Examination literature
	Aphorisms, apothegms, etc. see PN6277.A+
	Maxims see PN6307.A+
	Fables, parables, etc. see PN989.A+
	Proverbs see PN6519.C5
	By period
2408	Early to 221 B.C.
2409	221 B.C.-1368 A.D.
2410	Ming dynasty, 1368-1644
2411	Qing dynasty, 1644-1912
2412	1912-1949
2413	1949-
	Fiction
2415	General works
2416	Addresses, essays, lectures
2419.A-Z	Special topics, A-Z
	For list of topics see PL2275.A+
2420-2443	By period (Table PL6)
	Folk literature
(2445)	History and criticism
	see GR334+
(2446)	Collections
	see GR334+
	Folk poetry see PL2309.F65; PL2519.F6
	Tales see GR334+
	Folk-songs see ML3746+
	Inscriptions
2447	History and criticism
2448	Collections
	Cf. PL2456+ Oracle bones
	Cf. PL2458+ Confucian Canon
2449	Juvenile literature (General)
	For special genres, see the genre
	Collections
	General (Comprehensive, not confined to any one period or form)
2450	Published before 1644

Chinese language and literature
Chinese literature
Collections
General (Comprehensive, not confined to any one period
or form) -- Continued

2451	Published during the Qing dynasty (1644-1912)
2452	Published since 1912
2455	Selections
	Oracle bones
2456	General works
2457.A-Z	By place, A-Z
	Confucian Canon. The Chinese Classics
2458	Fragments on bamboo, wood, silk, etc.
	Stone inscriptions of the Canon. By editor or commentator
2459.A1-.A9	Han, 175 A.D.
2459.B1-.B9	Wei, 240-245
2459.C1-.C9	Tang, 837
2459.D1-.D9	Later Shu
2459.E1-.E9	Song, 1056
2459.F1-.F9	Jin, 1126
2459.G1-.G9	Qing, 1802
2459.Z6	Commentaries
2461-2476	Printed editions, including manuscript copies (Table PL4)
	Translations
2477.A-Z	Polyglot. By editor, A-Z
2478	English (Table PL5)
2479	French (Table PL5)
2480	Italian (Table PL5)
2481	Spanish (Table PL5)
2482	Portuguese (Table PL5)
2483	Dutch (Table PL5)
2484	German (Table PL5)
2485	Russian (Table PL5)
2486	Polish (Table PL5)
2487	Hebrew (Table PL5)
2488	Japanese (Table PL5)
2489	Korean (Table PL5)
2489.5	Mongolian (Table PL5)
2489.6.A-Z	Other languages, A-Z
2490-2513	By period (Table PL6)
	Special classes of authors
2515	Women authors
2515.5.A-Z	Other, A-Z
2515.5.B8	Buddhists
2515.5.C5	Children

	Chinese language and literature
	Chinese literature
	Collections
	Special classes of authors
	Other, A-Z -- Continued
2515.5.C64	College students
2515.5.L33	Laboring class
2515.5.M56	Minorities
2515.5.P45	People with disabilities
2515.5.P65	Prisoners
2515.5.S6	Soldiers
2515.5.T72	Travelers
2515.5.Y68	Youth
2516.A-Z	Special families, A-Z
2516.5.A-Z	Special topics, A-Z
	For list of topics see PL2275.A+
	Special forms
	Poetry
	General
2517	Published before 1912
2518	Published since 1912
2518.5	Concordances, dictionaries, indexes, etc.
2518.8.A-Z	Special topics, A-Z
	Prefer classification by form
	For list of topics see PL2275.A+
2519.A-Z	Special forms, A-Z
2519.B34	Ballads. Songs
2519.C45	Children's poetry
2519.C47	Chüeh chü. Jue ju
2519.C7	Couplets
2519.D52	Didactic poetry
2519.E43	Elegiac poetry
2519.E5	Epic poetry
2519.F6	Folk poetry
2519.F8	Fu
2519.H3	Haiku
2519.H8	Humorous poetry
	Jue ju see PL2519.C47
2519.L6	Love poetry
2519.L83	Lü shi
2519.L93	Lyric poetry
2519.N47	Narrative poetry
2519.P37	Pastorals
2519.P39	Patriotic poetry
2519.P76	Prose poetry
2519.R48	Revolutionary poetry
	Songs see PL2519.B34

	Chinese language and literature
	Chinese literature
	Collections
	Special forms
	Poetry
	Special forms, A-Z -- Continued
2519.Y8	Yue fu
2520-2543	By period (Table PL6)
	Ci (Tz'u)
2548	General works
2551-2563	By period (Table PL6a)
	Qu (Ch'ü)
2564	General works
	Special forms
2564.4	San qu
	Including xiao ling and san tao
2564.6	Ju qu
	Including za ju, zhuan qi, kun qu, and duan ju
	By period
2565	Yuan dynasty, 1260-1368
2565.4	Ming dynasty, 1368-1644
2565.6	Qing dynasty, 1644-1912
2565.8	1912-
	Drama
	General
2566	Published before 1912
2567	Published since 1912
	Special forms
2574	Bian wen (Buddhist song-tales)
2575	Tan ci (Southern song-tales)
2576	Gu ci (Northern song-tales)
2579.A-Z	Other, A-Z
2579.B34	Bao juan (Buddhist song-tales)
2579.C58	Children's plays
2579.C6	Comedy
2579.D53	Dialogues
2579.H58	Historical plays
2579.H8	Hsiang sheng. Xiang sheng
2579.K83	Kuai shu
2579.O53	One-act plays
(2579.P28)	Pao chüan
	see PL2579.B34
2579.P56	Ping ju (Folk dramas)
2579.P58	Ping shu
2579.R33	Radio plays
2579.T44	Television plays
2579.T7	Tragedy

	Chinese language and literature
	Chinese literature
	Collections
	Special forms
	Drama
	Special forms
	Other, A-Z -- Continued
2579.T73	Tragicomedy
	Xiang sheng see PL2579.H8
2580-2603	By period (Table PL6)
	Essays
	General
2606	Published before 1912
2607	Published since 1912
2608.A-Z	Special topics, A-Z
	Prefer classification by subject, classes B - Z
	Special forms
2609	Oratory
2610	Letters
2611	Diaries
2612	Pian wen
2613	Wit and humor. Satire
2614	Reportage literature
2615	Examination essays
	By period
2618	Early to 221 B.C.
2619	221 B.C.-1368 A.D.
2620	Ming Dynasty, 1368-1644
2621	Qing Dynasty, 1644-1912
2622	1912-1949
2623	1949-
	Fiction
2625	General works
2629.A-Z	Special topics, A-Z
	For list of topics see PL2275.A+
2630-2653	By period (Table PL6)
	Folk literature see GR334+
	Inscriptions see PL2448
	Translations
(2655-2657)	From foreign languages into Chinese
	For collections of translations, see the literature of the original language; for the collections from several languages, see PN
2658-2659	From Chinese into foreign languages (Table P-PZ30 modified)
	For translations of the Confucian Canon see PL2477+

Chinese language and literature
Chinese literature
Translations
From Chinese into foreign languages -- Continued
Japanese
2658.J1	General
2658.J3	Poetry
2658.J5	Drama
2658.J8	Prose. Prose fiction

Korean
2658.K1	General
2658.K3	Poetry
2658.K5	Drama
2658.K8	Prose. Prose fiction

Individual authors and works
Early to 221 B.C.
2661	Qu, Yuan, ca. 343-ca 277 B.C. 屈原 (Table P-PZ39)
2662.A-Z	Other, A-Z
2662.J82-.J823	Ju you cao (Table P-PZ43)
2663	Qin and Han dynasties, 221 B.C.-220 A.D.

Subarrange individual authors by Table P-PZ40
Subarrange individual works by Table P-PZ43

2663.B36	Ban, Gu, 32-92. 班 固 (Table P-PZ40)
	Cai, Wenji, ca. 177-ca. 239. 蔡文姬 see PL2663.T75
2663.C3	Chang, Heng, 78-139. 張衡; 张衡 (Table P-PZ40)
2663.C35	Chao, Yeh, fl. 40. 趙曄; 赵晔 (Table P-PZ40)
	Gu shi shi jiu shou. 古詩十九首; 古诗十九首 see PL2663.K8+
	Guo, Xian, 1st cent. 郭憲; 郭宪 see PL2663.K87
2663.H8	Hsü, Kan, 171-218. 徐幹; 徐干 (Table P-PZ40)
2663.K8-.K83	Ku shih shih chiu shou. 古詩十九首; 古诗十九首 (Table P-PZ43)
2663.K87	Kuo, Hsien, 1st cent. 郭憲; 郭宪 (Table P-PZ40)
2663.L5	Liu, Xiang, 77?-6? B.C. 劉向; 刘向 (Table P-PZ40)
2663.L8-.L83	Lü shi chun qiu. 呂氏春秋; 吕氏春秋 (Table P-PZ43)
2663.M3	Ma, Rong, 79-166. 馬融; 马融 (Table P-PZ40)
	Sima, Xiangru, ca. 180-117 B.C. 司馬相如; 司马相如 see PL2663.S8
2663.S8	Ssu-ma, Hsiang-ju, ca. 180-117 B.C. 司馬相如; 司马相如 (Table P-PZ40)
2663.T75	Ts'ai, Yen, ca. 177-ca. 239. 蔡琰 (Table P-PZ40)
2663.T77	Ts'ai, Yung, 133-192. 蔡邕 (Table P-PZ40)
	Wang, Can, 177-217. 王粲 see PL2663.W35
2663.W33	Wang, Fu, ca. 76-ca. 157. 王符 (Table P-PZ40)
2663.W35	Wang, Ts'an, 177-217. 王粲 (Table P-PZ40)
	Xu, Gan, 171-218. 徐幹; 徐干 see PL2663.H8

Chinese language and literature
Chinese literature
Individual authors and works
Qin and Han dynasties, 221 B.C.-220 A.D. -- Continued

2663.Y35	Yang, Xiong, 53 B.C.-18 A.D. 揚雄; 扬雄 (Table P-PZ40)
	Zhang, Heng, 78-139. 張衡; 张衡 see PL2663.C3
	Zhao, Ye, fl. 40. 趙曄; 赵晔 see PL2663.C35
2664	The Three Kingdoms, 220-265
	Subarrange individual authors by Table P-PZ40
	Subarrange individual works by Table P-PZ43
	Cao, Cao, 155-220. 曹操 see PL2664.T8
	Cao, Pi, 187-226. 曹丕 see PL2664.T78
	Cao, Zhi, 192-232. 曹植 see PL2664.T75
2664.C5	Chi, K'ang, 223-262. 嵇康 (Table P-PZ40)
	Ji, Kang, 223-262. 嵇康 see PL2664.C5
2664.J8	Juan, Chi, 210-263. 阮籍 (Table P-PZ40)
	Ruan, Ji, 210-263. 阮籍 see PL2664.J8
2664.T75	Ts'ao, Chih, 192-232. 曹植 (Table P-PZ40)
2664.T78	Ts'ao, P'i, 187-226. 曹丕 (Table P-PZ40)
2664.T8	Ts'ao, Ts'ao, 155-220. 曹操 (Table P-PZ40)
2665	Jin dynasty, 265-419
	Subarrange individual authors by Table P-PZ40
	Subarrange individual works by Table P-PZ43
	Cui, Bao, fl. 290-306. 崔豹 see PL2665.T8
	Guo, Pu, 276-324. 郭璞 see PL2665.K8
2665.K8	Kuo, P'u, 276-324. 郭璞 (Table P-PZ40)
2665.L8	Lu, Ji, 261-303. 陸機; 陆机 (Table P-PZ40)
2665.L84	Lu, Yun, 262-303. 陸雲; 陆云 (Table P-PZ40)
2665.P3	Pan, Yue, 247-300. 潘岳 (Table P-PZ40)
2665.S9	Su, Hui, 4th cent. 蘇蕙; 苏蕙 (Table P-PZ40)
2665.T3	Tao, Qian, 372?-427. 陶潛; 陶潜 (Table P-PZ40)
2665.T77	Tso, Ssu, ca. 250-ca. 305. 左思 (Table P-PZ40)
2665.T8	Ts'ui, Pao, fl. 290-306. 崔豹 (Table P-PZ40)
2665.W27	Wang, Jia, 4th cent. 王嘉 (Table P-PZ40)
2665.W3	Wang, Xizhi, 321-379. 王羲之 (Table P-PZ40)
	Zuo, Si, ca. 250-ca. 305. 左思 see PL2665.T77
2665.5	Five Hu and the Sixteen Kingdoms, 304-439
	Subarrange individual authors by Table P-PZ40
	Subarrange individual works by Table P-PZ43
	Northern and Southern dynasties, 386-589
2666	Liu Song dynasty (Former Song), 420-479
	Subarrange individual authors by Table P-PZ40
	Subarrange individual works by Table P-PZ43
	Bao, Zhao, 405-466. 鮑照; 鲍照 see PL2666.P3
2666.C45	Chiang, Yen, 444-505. 江淹 (Table P-PZ40)

Chinese language and literature
Chinese literature
Individual authors and works
Northern and Southern dynasties, 386-589
Liu Song dynasty (Former Song), 420-479 -- Continued

2666.H75	Hsieh, Ling-yün, 385-433. 謝靈運; 谢灵运 (Table P-PZ40)
	Jiang, Yan, 444-505. 江淹 see PL2666.C45
2666.K66-.K663	Kong que dong nan fei. 孔雀東南飛; 孔雀东南飞 (Table P-PZ43)
2666.L5	Liu, Jingshu, d. 468? 劉敬叔; 刘敬叔 (Table P-PZ40)
2666.L55	Liu, Yiqing, 403-444. 劉義慶; 刘义庆 (Table P-PZ40)
2666.P3	Pao, Chao, 405-466. 鮑照; 鲍照 (Table P-PZ40)
	Xie, Lingyun, 385-433. 謝靈運; 谢灵运 see PL2666.H75
2666.Y38	Yan, Yanzhi, 384-456. 顏延之; 颜延之 (Table P-PZ40)
2667	Qi dynasty, 479-502
	Subarrange individual authors by Table P-PZ40
	Subarrange individual works by Table P-PZ43
2667.H73	Hsieh, T'iao, 464-499. 謝朓; 谢朓 (Table P-PZ40)
	Xie, Tiao, 464-499. 謝朓; 谢朓 see PL2667.H73
2668	Liang dynasty, etc., 502-557. Chen dynasty, 557-589
	Subarrange individual authors by Table P-PZ40
	Subarrange individual works by Table P-PZ43
2668.H6	He, Xun, d. ca. 527. 何遜; 何逊 (Table P-PZ40)
2668.H7	Hsiao, Tung, 501-531. 蕭統; 萧统 (Table P-PZ40)
2668.L47	Liang Jianwendi, Emperor of China, 503-551. 梁簡文帝; 梁简文帝 (Table P-PZ40)
2668.L5	Liu, Chou, 514-565. 劉晝; 刘昼 (Table P-PZ40)
2668.L52	Liu, Xiaobiao, 462-521. 劉孝標; 刘孝标 (Table P-PZ40)
2668.L58	Liu, Xiaochuo, 481-539. 劉孝綽; 劉孝綽 (Table P-PZ40)
	Liu, Zhou, 514-565. 劉晝; 刘昼 see PL2668.L5
2668.M83-.M833	Mulan shi. 木蘭詩; 木兰诗 (Table P-PZ43)
2668.S54	Shen, Yue, 441-513. 沈約; 沈约 (Table P-PZ40)
	Xiao, Tong, 501-531. 蕭統; 萧统 see PL2668.H7
2668.X54	Xiao, Yan, 464-549. 蕭衍; 萧衍 (Table P-PZ40)
2668.Y4	Yan, Zhitui, 531-591. 顏之推; 颜之推 (Table P-PZ40)
2668.Y54	Yin, Yun, 471-529. 殷芸 (Table P-PZ40)
2668.Y8	Yu, Xin, 513-581. 庾信 (Table P-PZ40)

	Chinese language and literature
	Chinese literature
	Individual authors and works
	Northern and Southern dynasties, 386-589 -- Continued
2668.5	Northern Wei dynasty, 386-534. Eastern Wei dynasty, 534-550. Western Wei dynasty, 535-556. Northern Qi dynasty, 550-577. Northern Zhou dynasty, 557-581
	Subarrange individual authors by Table P-PZ40
	Subarrange individual works by Table P-PZ43
2669	Sui Dynasty, 581-618
	Subarrange individual authors by Table P-PZ40
	Subarrange individual works by Table P-PZ43
	Tang dynasty, 618-907
	Bai, Juyi, 772-846. 白居易 see PL2674
	Du, Fu, 712-770. 杜甫 see PL2675
2670	Han, Yu, 768-824. 韓愈; 韩愈 (Table P-PZ37)
2671	Li, Bai, 701-762. 李白 (Table P-PZ37)
2672	Li, Shangyin, 813-858. 李商隱; 李商隐 (Table P-PZ37)
2673	Liu, Zongyuan, 773-819. 柳宗元 (Table P-PZ39)
2674	Pai, Chu-i, 772-846. 白居易 (Table P-PZ37)
2675	Tu, Fu, 712-770. 杜甫 (Table P-PZ37)
2676	Wang, Wei, 701-761. 王維; 王维 (Table P-PZ37)
2677.A-Z	Other, A-Z
	Subarrange individual authors by Table P-PZ40
	Subarrange individual works by Table P-PZ43
	Bai, Xingjian, 776-826. 白行簡; 白行简 see PL2677.P35
	Bao, Rong, jin shi 809. 鮑溶; 鲍溶 see PL2677.P37
	Cao, Tang, fl. 847-873. 曹唐 see PL2677.T65
	Cao, Ye, jin shi 850. 曹鄴; 曹邺 see PL2677.T67
	Cen, Shen, 715-770. 岑參; 岑参 see PL2677.T7
2677.C33	Chan-Šan (Table P-PZ40)
2677.C35	Chang, Chi, ca. 765-ca. 830. 張籍; 张籍 (Table P-PZ40)
2677.C36	Chang, Chiu-ling, 678-740. 張九齡; 张九龄 (Table P-PZ40)
2677.C37	Chang, Cho, ca. 660-ca. 740. 張鷟; 张鷟 (Table P-PZ40)
2677.C373	Chang, Hu, d. ca. 853. 張祜; 张祜 (Table P-PZ40)
2677.C375	Chang, Jo-hsü, fl. 711. 張若虛; 张若虚 (Table P-PZ40)
(2677.C378)	Chang, Shuo, 667-730. 張說; 张说 (Table P-PZ40) see PL2677.C385
2677.C383	Chang, Wei, chin shih 743. 張謂; 张谓 (Table P-PZ40)
2677.C385	Chang, Yüeh, 667-730. 張說; 张说 (Table P-PZ40)

Chinese language and literature
Chinese literature
Individual authors and works
Tang dynasty, 618-907
Other, A-Z -- Continued

2677.C388	Chao, Ku, 9th cent. 趙嘏; 赵嘏 (Table P-PZ40)
2677.C4	Chen, Zi'ang, 661-702. 陳子昂; 陈子昂 (Table P-PZ40)
2677.C413	Cheng, Ku, ca. 851-ca. 910. 鄭谷; 郑谷 (Table P-PZ40)
2677.C42	Chia, Tao, 779-843. 賈島; 贾岛 (Table P-PZ40)
2677.C43	Chiao-jan, 8th cent. 皎然 (Table P-PZ40)
(2677.C44)	Ch'oe, Ch'i-wŏn, b. 857. 崔致遠 　　see PL986.5.C56
2677.C47	Chu, Guangxi, jin shi 726. 儲光羲; 储光羲 (Table P-PZ40)
2677.C49	Ch'üan, Te-yü, 759-818. 權德輿; 权德舆 (Table P-PZ40)
	Dai, Fu, jin shi 757. 戴孚 see PL2677.T35
	Dai, Shulun, 732-789. 戴叔倫; 戴叔伦 see PL2677.T36
	Damuqianlian ming jian jiu mu bian wen. 　　大目乾連冥間救母變文; 大目乾连冥间救母变文 　　see PL2677.T3+
	Decheng, Shi, 9th cent. 德誠; 德诚 see PL2677.T42
	Du, Mu, 803-853? 杜牧 see PL2677.T8
	Du, Shenyan, 648?-708. 杜審言; 杜审言 see PL2677.T83
	Du, Xunhe, 846-907. 杜荀鶴; 杜荀鹤 see PL2677.T75
	Duan, Chengshi, d. 863. 段成式 see PL2677.T87
	Dugu, Ji, 725-777. 獨孤及; 独孤及 see PL2677.T85
2677.F33	Fan, Zongshi, 8th/9th cent. 樊宗師; 樊宗师 (Table P-PZ40)
2677.F36	Fang, Gan, 809-873. 方干 (Table P-PZ40)
	Gao, Shi, 707-765. 高適; 高适 see PL2677.K32
	Gu, Kuang, jin shi 757. 顧況; 顾况 see PL2677.K7
	Gu, Shenzi, 9th cent. 谷神子 see PL2677.K74
	Guanxiu, 832-912. 貫休; 贯休 see PL2677.K8
2677.H25	Han, Hung, fl. 742-779. 韓翃; 韩翃 (Table P-PZ40)
2677.H27	Han, Wo, 844-923. 韓偓; 韩偓 (Table P-PZ40)
2677.H3	Hanshan, fl. 627-649. 寒山 (Table P-PZ40)
2677.H69	Hsiao, Ying-shih, 717-768. 蕭穎士; 萧颖士 (Table P-PZ40)
2677.H74	Hsü, Hun, chin shih 832. 許渾; 许浑 (Table P-PZ40)
2677.H76	Hsüeh, T'ao, 768-831. 薛濤; 薛涛 (Table P-PZ40)
2677.H78	Hu, Zeng, 9th/10th cent. 胡曾 (Table P-PZ40)
2677.H79	Huangfu, Ran, 714-767. 皇甫冉 (Table P-PZ40)

Chinese language and literature
Chinese literature
Individual authors and works
Tang dynasty, 618-907
Other, A-Z -- Continued

2677.H83	Huangfu, Shi, jin shi 806. 皇甫湜 (Table P-PZ40)
	Jia, Dao, 779-843. 賈島; 贾岛 see PL2677.C42
	Jiaoran, 8th cent. 皎然 see PL2677.C43
2677.J85	Jung, Yü, 8th cent. 戎昱 (Table P-PZ40)
2677.K32	Kao, Shih, 707-765. 高適; 高适 (Table P-PZ40)
2677.K7	Ku, K'uang, chin shih 757. 顧況; 顾况 (Table P-PZ40)
2677.K74	Ku, Shen-tzu, 9th cent. 谷神子 (Table P-PZ40)
2677.K8	Kuan-hsiu, 832-912. 貫休; 贯休 (Table P-PZ40)
2677.L4	Li, Ao, 772-841. 李翱 (Table P-PZ40)
2677.L42	Li, Ch'i, 690-751? 李頎; 李颀 (Table P-PZ40)
2677.L423	Li, Chiao, 644-713. 李嶠; 李峤 (Table P-PZ40)
2677.L43	Li, Chien-hsün, ca. 872-952. 李建勳; 李建勋 (Table P-PZ40)
2677.L435	Li, Ching, 571-649. 李靖 (Table P-PZ40)
2677.L45	Li, Ch'ün-yü, 9th cent. 李羣玉; 李群玉 (Table P-PZ40)
	Li, Deyu, 787-849. 李德裕 see PL2677.L5315
	Li, Guan, 766-794. 李觀; 李观 see PL2677.L523
2677.L5	Li, He, 790-816. 李賀; 李贺 (Table P-PZ40)
2677.L52	Li, I, 748-829. 李益 (Table P-PZ40)
	Li, Jianxun, ca. 872-952. 李建勳; 李建勋 see PL2677.L43
	Li, Jiao, 644-713. 李嶠; 李峤 see PL2677.L423
	Li, Jing, 571-649. 李靖 see PL2677.L435
2677.L523	Li, Kuan, 766-794. 李觀; 李观 (Table P-PZ40)
2677.L525	Li, Pin, jin shi 854. 李頻; 李频 (Table P-PZ40)
	Li, Qi, 690-751? 李頎; 李颀 see PL2677.L42
	Li, Qunyu, 9th cent. 李羣玉; 李群玉 see PL2677.L45
2677.L527	Li, Shen, 772-846. 李紳; 李绅 (Table P-PZ40)
2677.L5315	Li, Te-yü, 787-849. 李德裕 (Table P-PZ40)
	Li, Yi, 748-829. 李益 see PL2677.L52
2677.L535	Li, Yong, 678-747. 李邕 (Table P-PZ40)
2677.L544	Liu, Changqing, jin shi 733. 劉長卿; 刘长卿 (Table P-PZ40)
2677.L547	Liu, Xiyi, 7th cent. 劉希夷; 刘希夷 (Table P-PZ40)
2677.L56	Liu, Yuxi, 772-842. 劉禹錫; 刘禹锡 (Table P-PZ40)
2677.L6	Lo, Pin-wang, d. 684. 駱賓王; 骆宾王 (Table P-PZ40)
2677.L63	Lo, Yeh, b. 825? 羅鄴; 罗邺 (Table P-PZ40)
2677.L64	Lo, Yin, 833-910. 羅隱; 罗隐 (Table P-PZ40)
2677.L78	Lu, Chao-lin, ca. 635-ca. 689. 盧照鄰; 卢照邻 (Table P-PZ40)
2677.L8	Lu, Chih, 754-805. 陸贄; 陆贽 (Table P-PZ40)

Chinese language and literature
Chinese literature
Individual authors and works
Tang dynasty, 618-907
Other, A-Z -- Continued

	Lu, Guimeng, 9th cent. 陸龜蒙; 陆龟蒙 see PL2677.L84
(2677.L83)	Lü, Ho-shu, 772-811. 呂和叔; 吕和叔 (Table P-PZ40) see PL2677.L857
2677.L84	Lu, Kuei-meng, 9th cent. 陸龜蒙; 陆龟蒙 (Table P-PZ40)
2677.L85	Lu, Lun, 748?-798? 盧綸; 卢纶 (Table P-PZ40)
2677.L857	Lü, Wen, 772-811. 呂温 (Table P-PZ40)
2677.L86	Lu, Yu, d. 804. 陸羽; 陆羽 (Table P-PZ40)
	Lu, Zhaolin, ca. 635-ca. 689. 盧照鄰; 卢照邻 see PL2677.L78
	Lu, Zhi, 754-805. 陸贄; 陆贽 see PL2677.L8
	Luo, Binwang, d. 684. 駱賓王; 骆宾王 see PL2677.L6
	Luo, Ye, b. 825? 羅鄴; 罗邺 see PL2677.L63
	Luo, Yin, 833-910. 羅隱; 罗隐 see PL2677.L64
2677.M3	Ma, Dai, jin shi 844. 馬戴; 马戴 (Table P-PZ40)
2677.M4	Meng, Chiao, 751-814. 孟郊 (Table P-PZ40)
2677.M45	Meng, Haoran, 689-740. 孟浩然 (Table P-PZ40)
	Meng, Jiao, 751-814. 孟郊 see PL2677.M4
2677.M53-.M533	Miao fa lian hua jing bian wen. 妙法蓮華經變文; 妙法莲华经变 (Table P-PZ43)
2677.N53	Nie, Yizhong, b. 837. 聶夷中; 聂夷中 (Table P-PZ40)
2677.N58	Niu, Sengru, 779-847. 牛僧孺 (Table P-PZ40)
2677.O89	Ouyang, Zhan, 798-ca. 827. 歐陽詹; 欧阳詹 (Table P-PZ40)
2677.P35	Pai, Hsing-chien, 776-826. 白行簡; 白行简 (Table P-PZ40)
2677.P37	Pao, Jung, chin shih 809. 鮑溶; 鲍溶 (Table P-PZ40)
2677.P44	Pei, Xing, 9th cent. 裴鉶; 裴铏 (Table P-PZ40)
2677.P5	Pi, Rixiu, ca. 834-ca. 833. 皮日休 (Table P-PZ40)
	Quan, Deyu, 759-818. 權德輿; 权德舆 see PL2677.C49
	Rong, Yu, 8th cent. 戎昱 see PL2677.J85
2677.S45	Shen, Quanqi, ca. 656-713. 沈佺期 (Table P-PZ40)
2677.S47	Shen, Yazhi, jin shi 815. 沈亞之; 沈亚之 (Table P-PZ40)
	Sikong, Tu, 837-908. 司空圖; 司空图 see PL2677.S87
	Song, Zhiwen, ca. 656-712. 宋之問; 宋之问 see PL2677.S95
2677.S87	Ssu-k'ung, T'u, 837-908. 司空圖; 司空图 (Table P-PZ40)
2677.S92	Su, Weidao, 648-705. 蘇味道; 苏味道 (Table P-PZ40)

Chinese language and literature
Chinese literature
Individual authors and works
Tang dynasty, 618-907
Other, A-Z -- Continued

(2677.S94)	Sugawara, Michizane, 845-903. 菅原道真 see PL788.7
2677.S95	Sung, Chih-wen, ca. 656-712. 宋之問; 宋之问 (Table P-PZ40)
2677.T3-.T33	Ta-mu-ch'ien-lien ming chien chiu mu pien wen. 大目乾連冥間救母變文; 大目乾连冥间救母变文 (Table P-PZ43)
2677.T35	Tai, Fu, chin shih 757. 戴孚 (Table P-PZ40)
2677.T36	Tai, Shu-lun, 732-789. 戴叔倫; 戴叔伦 (Table P-PZ40)
2677.T37	Tang, Lin, b. 600. 唐臨; 唐临 (Table P-PZ40)
2677.T42	Te-ch'eng, Shih, 9th cent. 德誠; 德诚 (Table P-PZ40)
2677.T65	Ts'ao, T'ang, fl. 847-873. 曹唐 (Table P-PZ40)
2677.T67	Ts'ao, Yeh, chin shih 850. 曹鄴; 曹邺 (Table P-PZ40)
2677.T7	Ts'en, Shen, 715-770. 岑參; 岑参 (Table P-PZ40)
2677.T75	Tu, Hsün-ho, 846-907. 杜荀鶴; 杜荀鹤 (Table P-PZ40)
2677.T8	Tu, Mu, 803-853? 杜牧 (Table P-PZ40)
2677.T83	Tu, Shen-yen, 648?-708. 杜審言; 杜审言 (Table P-PZ40)
2677.T85	Tu-ku, Chi, 725-777. 獨孤及; 独孤及 (Table P-PZ40)
2677.T87	Tuan, Ch'eng-shih, d. 863. 段成式 (Table P-PZ40)
	Wang, Bo, 650-675. 王勃 see PL2677.W29
2677.W26	Wang, Changling, 698-757. 王昌齡; 王昌龄 (Table P-PZ40)
2677.W265	Wang, Chi, 585-644. 王績; 王绩 (Table P-PZ40)
2677.W267	Wang, Chien, chin shih 775. 王建 (Table P-PZ40)
2677.W27	Wang, Fanzhi, ca. 590-ca. 660. 王梵志 (Table P-PZ40)
	Wang, Ji, 585-644. 王績; 王绩 see PL2677.W265
	Wang, Jian, jin shi 775. 王建 see PL2677.W267
2677.W29	Wang, Po, 650-675. 王勃 (Table P-PZ40)
2677.W4	Wei, Chuang, chin shih 894. 韋莊; 韦庄 (Table P-PZ40)
2677.W43	Wei, Yingwu. 韋應物; 韦应物 (Table P-PZ40)
2677.W45	Wen, Tingyun, 812-ca. 870. 溫庭筠 (Table P-PZ40)
2677.W83	Wu, Rong, jin shi 889. 吳融; 吴融 (Table P-PZ40)
2677.W84	Wu, Yun, d. 778. 吳筠; 吴筠 (Table P-PZ40)
	Xiao, Yingshi, 717-768. 蕭穎士; 萧颖士 see PL2677.H69
	Xu, Hun, jin shi 832. 許渾; 许浑 see PL2677.H74
	Xue, Tao, 768-831. 薛濤; 薛涛 see PL2677.H76

Chinese language and literature
Chinese literature
Individual authors and works
Tang dynasty, 618-907
Other, A-Z -- Continued

Yan, Shigu, 581-645. 顏師古; 颜师古 see PL2677.Y4
Yan, Zhenqing, 709-785. 顏眞卿; 颜真卿 see PL2677.Y38

2677.Y34	Yang, Jiong, 650-ca. 693. 楊烱; 杨炯 (Table P-PZ40)
2677.Y36	Yao, He, 775-854? 姚合 (Table P-PZ40)
2677.Y38	Yen, Chen-ch'ing, 709-785. 顏眞卿; 颜真卿 (Table P-PZ40)
2677.Y4	Yen, Shih-ku, 581-645. 顏師古; 颜师古 (Table P-PZ40)

Yong, Tao, jin shi 834. 雍陶 see PL2677.Y86

2677.Y77	Yu, Xuanji, 842-872. 魚玄機; 鱼玄机 (Table P-PZ40)
2677.Y8	Yüan, Chen, 779-831. 元稹 (Table P-PZ40)
2677.Y84	Yuan, Jie, 719-772. 元結; 元结 (Table P-PZ40)

Yuan, Zhen, 779-831. 元稹 see PL2677.Y8

2677.Y86	Yung, T'ao, chin shih 834. 雍陶 (Table P-PZ40)

Zhang, Hu, d. ca. 853. 張祜; 张祜 see PL2677.C373
Zhang, Ji, ca. 765-ca. 830. 張籍; 张籍 see PL2677.C35
Zhang, Jiuling, 678-740. 張九齡; 张九龄 see PL2677.C36
Zhang, Ruoxu, fl. 711. 張若虛; 张若虚 see PL2677.C375
Zhang, Wei, jin shi 743. 張謂; 张谓 see PL2677.C383
Zhang, Yue, 667-730. 張說; 张说 see PL2677.C385
Zhang, Zhuo, ca. 660-ca. 740 see PL2677.C37
Zhao, Gu, 9th cent. 趙嘏; 赵嘏 see PL2677.C388
Zheng, Gu, ca. 851-ca. 910. 鄭谷; 郑谷 see PL2677.C413

2678	Five dynasties and the Ten Kingdoms, 907-979
	Subarrange individual authors by Table P-PZ40
	Subarrange individual works by Table P-PZ43
2678.F45	Feng, Yansi, 903-960. 馮延巳; 冯延巳 (Table P-PZ40)
2678.H8	Huaruifuren, fl. 935-964. 花蕊夫人 (Table P-PZ40)
2678.L45	Li, Jing, 916-961. 李璟 (Table P-PZ40)
2678.L48	Li, Yu, 937-978. 李煜 (Table P-PZ40)
	Song dynasty, 960-1279. Liao dynasty, 947-1125. Xi Xia dynasty, 1038-1227. Jin dynasty, 1115-1234
2679	Chu, Hsi, 1130-1200. 朱熹 (Table P-PZ39)
2680	Hsin, Ch'i-chi, 1140-1207. 辛棄疾; 辛弃疾 (Table P-PZ39)
2681	Huang, Tingjian, 1045-1105. 黄庭堅; 黄庭坚 (Table P-PZ39)

Chinese language and literature
  Chinese literature
    Individual authors and works
      Song dynasty, 960-1279. Liao dynasty, 947-1125. Xi Xia
        dynasty, 1038-1227. Jin dynasty, 1115-1234 --
        Continued

2682	Li, Qingzhao, 1081-ca. 1141. 李清照 (Table P-PZ39)
2683	Ouyang, Xiu, 1007-1072. 歐陽修; 欧阳修 (Table P-PZ39)
2684	Sima, Guang, 1019-1086. 司馬光; 司马光 (Table P-PZ39)
2685	Su, Shi (Su Dongpo), 1036-1101. 蘇軾; 苏轼 (Table P-PZ39)
2686	Wang, Anshi, 1021-1086. 王安石 (Table P-PZ39)
	Xin, Qiji, 1140-1207. 辛棄疾; 辛弃疾 see PL2680
	Zhu, Xi, 1130-1200. 朱熹 see PL2679
2687.A-Z	Other, A-Z
	Subarrange individual authors by Table P-PZ40
	Subarrange individual works by Table P-PZ43
2687.A35	Ai, Xingfu, 13th cent. 艾性夫 (Table P-PZ40)
2687.B5	Bi, Zhongyou, 1047-1121. 畢仲游; 毕仲游 (Table P-PZ40)
	Cai, Xiang, 1012-1067. 蔡襄 see PL2687.T6
2687.C33	Chai, Ju-wen, 1076-1141. 翟汝文 (Table P-PZ40)
2687.C35	Chang, Hao, fl. 1196-1225. 張淏; 张淏 (Table P-PZ40)
2687.C3534	Chang, Hsiao-hsiang, 1133-1170. 張孝祥; 张孝祥 (Table P-PZ40)
2687.C3535	Chang, Hsien, 990-1078. 張先; 张先 (Table P-PZ40)
2687.C354	Chang, K'an, 12th/13th cent. 張侃; 张侃 (Table P-PZ40)
2687.C355	Chang, K'uo, d. 1147. 張擴; 张扩 (Table P-PZ40)
2687.C359	Chang, Shih, 1133-1180. 張栻; 张栻 (Table P-PZ40)
2687.C36	Chang, Tuan-i, 1179-ca. 1235. 張端義; 张端义 (Table P-PZ40)
2687.C363	Chang, Yen, 1248-1320? 張炎; 张炎 (Table P-PZ40)
2687.C364	Chang, Yüan-Kan, 1091-1161? 張元幹; 张元干 (Table P-PZ40)
	Chao, Buzhi, 1053-1110. 晁補之; 晁补之 see PL2687.C37
2687.C366	Chao, Ju-t'eng, d. 1261. 趙汝騰; 赵汝腾 (Table P-PZ40)
2687.C368	Chao, Meng-chien, 1199-ca. 1264. 趙孟堅; 赵孟坚 (Table P-PZ40)
2687.C369	Chao, Pien, 1008-1084. 趙抃; 赵抃 (Table P-PZ40)
2687.C37	Ch'ao, Pu-chih, 1053-1110. 晁補之; 晁补之 (Table P-PZ40)

Chinese language and literature
　Chinese literature
　　Individual authors and works
　　　Song dynasty, 960-1279. Liao dynasty, 947-1125. Xi Xia
　　　　dynasty, 1038-1227. Jin dynasty, 1115-1234
　　　　Other, A-Z -- Continued

2687.C377	Chao, Ting-ch'en, b. 1070. 趙鼎臣; 赵鼎臣 (Table P-PZ40)
2687.C383	Chao, Yuezhi, 1059-1129. 晁說之; 晁说之 (Table P-PZ40)
2687.C39-.C393	Chao-chün ho fan. 昭君和番 (Table P-PZ43)
2687.C395	Chen, Changfang, 1108-1148. 陳長方; 陈长方 (Table P-PZ40)
2687.C4	Ch'en, Ch'i-ch'ing, chin shih 1214. 陳耆卿; 陈耆卿 (Table P-PZ40)
2687.C42	Chen, Liang, 1143-1194. 陈亮; 陈亮 (Table P-PZ40)
	Chen, Qiqing, jin shi 1214. 陳耆卿; 陈耆卿 see PL2687.C4
2687.C443	Chen, Shidao, 1053-1102. 陳師道; 陈师道 (Table P-PZ40)
2687.C444	Chen, Te-hsiu, 1178-1235. 真德秀 (Table P-PZ40)
2687.C477	Ch'en, Yü-i, 1090-1138. 陳與義; 陈与义 (Table P-PZ40)
2687.C48	Chen, Yuanjin, jin shi 1211. 陳元晉; 陈元晋 (Table P-PZ40)
	Chen, Yuyi, 1090-1138. 陳與義; 陈与义 see PL2687.C477
2687.C482	Cheng, Ch'iao, 1104-1162. 鄭樵; 郑樵 (Table P-PZ40)
	Cheng, Gongxu, jin shi 1211. 程公許; 程公许 see PL2687.C49
2687.C484	Cheng, Ju, 1078-1144. 程俱 (Table P-PZ40)
2687.C49	Ch'eng, Kung-hsü, chin shih 1211. 程公許; 程公许 (Table P-PZ40)
2687.C495	Chia, Hsüan-weng, b. 1213. 家鉉翁; 家铉翁 (Table P-PZ40)
2687.C496	Chiang, Chieh, chin shih 1276. 蔣捷; 蒋捷 (Table P-PZ40)
2687.C497	Ch'iang, Chih, 1022-1076. 強至; 强至 (Table P-PZ40)
2687.C5	Chiang, K'uei, ca. 1155-ca. 1235. 姜夔 (Table P-PZ40)
2687.C55	Ch'in, Kuan, 1049-1100. 秦觀; 秦观 (Table P-PZ40)
2687.C555	Chin, Lü-hsiang, 1232-1303. 金履祥 (Table P-PZ40)
2687.C635	Chou, Mi, 1232-1308. 周密 (Table P-PZ40)
2687.C64	Chou, Pang-yen, 1056-1121. 周邦彦 (Table P-PZ40)
2687.C687	Chou, Wen-p'u, 13th cent. 周文璞 (Table P-PZ40)

Chinese language and literature
Chinese literature
Individual authors and works
Song dynasty, 960-1279. Liao dynasty, 947-1125. Xi Xia
dynasty, 1038-1227. Jin dynasty, 1115-1234
Other, A-Z -- Continued

2687.C75	Chu, Hsi-yen, 1221-1279. 朱晞顏; 朱晞颜 (Table P-PZ40)
2687.C77	Chu, Shu-chen, fl. 1095-1131. 朱淑真 (Table P-PZ40)
2687.C8	Chu, Tun-ju, 1081-1159. 朱敦儒 (Table P-PZ40)
2687.C87	Chung, Ping, chin shih 1132. 仲并 (Table P-PZ40)
	Da Tang San Zang qu jing shi hua. 大唐三藏取經詩話; 大唐三藏取经诗话 see PL2687.T22+
	Dai, Fugu, b. 1167. 戴復古; 戴复古 see PL2687.T26
	Deng, Mu, 1247-1306. 鄧牧; 邓牧 see PL2687.T4
	Ding, Wei, 966-1037. 丁謂; 丁谓 see PL2687.T55
	Dong, Jieyuan, fl. 1189-1208. 董解元 see PL2687.T9
	Du, Zheng, jin shi 1190. 度正 see PL2687.T75
	Duan, Keji, 1196-1254. 段克己 see PL2687.T77
2687.F3	Fan, Chengda, 1126-1193. 范成大 (Table P-PZ40)
2687.F313	Fan, Jun, 12th cent. 范浚 (Table P-PZ40)
2687.F318	Fang, Feng, 1240-1321. 方鳳; 方凤 (Table P-PZ40)
2687.F325	Fang, Xinru, 1177-1220. 方信孺 (Table P-PZ40)
2687.F35	Fang, Yue, 1199-1262. 方岳 (Table P-PZ40)
2687.F46	Feng, Shixing, d. 1163. 馮時行; 冯时行 (Table P-PZ40)
2687.G86	Guo, Xiangzheng, 11th cent. 郭 祥正 (Table P-PZ40)
	Guo, Yin, 12th cent. 郭印 see PL2687.K8
2687.H23	Han, Qi, 1008-1075. 韓琦; 韩琦 (Table P-PZ40)
2687.H34	Han, Yuanji, b. 1118 (Table P-PZ40)
	He, Zhu, 1052-1125. 賀鑄; 贺铸 see PL2687.H55
2687.H55	Ho, Chu, 1052-1125. 賀鑄; 贺铸 (Table P-PZ40)
	Hong, Mai, 1123-1202. 洪邁; 洪迈 see PL2687.H887
	Hong, Peng, 1072-1109. 洪朋 see PL2687.H89
	Hong, Zikui, d. 1236. 洪咨夔 see PL2687.H93
2687.H578	Hsiang, Tzu-yin, 1085-1152. 向子諲 (Table P-PZ40)
2687.H583	Hsieh, Fang-te, 1226-1289. 謝枋得; 谢枋得 (Table P-PZ40)
2687.H594	Hsü, Fei, 13th cent. 許棐; 许棐 (Table P-PZ40)
2687.H595	Hsü, Hsüan, 916-991. 徐鉉; 徐铉 (Table P-PZ40)
2687.H6	Hsü, Ying-lung, 1168-1248. 許應龍; 许应龙 (Table P-PZ40)
2687.H68	Hu, Ch'üan, 1102-1180. 胡銓; 胡铨 (Table P-PZ40)
2687.H7	Hu, Chung-kung, 13th cent. 胡仲弓 (Table P-PZ40)
2687.H73	Hu, Hong, 1105-1155. 胡宏 (Table P-PZ40)
	Hu, Quan, 1102-1180. 胡銓; 胡铨 see PL2687.H68

Chinese language and literature
Chinese literature
Individual authors and works
Song dynasty, 960-1279. Liao dynasty, 947-1125. Xi Xia
dynasty, 1038-1227. Jin dynasty, 1115-1234
Other, A-Z -- Continued
Hu, Zhonggong, 13th cent. 胡仲弓 see PL2687.H7

2687.H76	Hua, Yue, 13th cent. 華岳; 华岳 (Table P-PZ40)
2687.H85	Huangdufengyuezhuren. 皇都風月主人; 皇都风月主人 (Table P-PZ40)
2687.H87	Huihong, 1071-1128. 惠洪 (Table P-PZ40)
2687.H887	Hung, Mai, 1123-1202. 洪邁; 洪迈 (Table P-PZ40)
2687.H89	Hung, P'eng, 1072-1109. 洪朋 (Table P-PZ40)
2687.H93	Hung, Tzu-k'uei, d. 1236. 洪咨夔 (Table P-PZ40)
(2687.I43)	Im, Ch'un, d. 12th cent. (Table P-PZ40)
	see PL987.I43
	Jia, Xuanweng, b. 1213. 家鉉翁; 家铉翁 see PL2687.C495
	Jiang, Jie, jin shi 1276. 蔣捷; 蒋捷 see PL2687.C496
	Jiang, Kui, ca. 1155-ca. 1235. 姜夔 see PL2687.C5
	Jin, Lüxiang, 1232-1303. 金履祥 see PL2687.C555
2687.K664	Kong, Wenzhong, 1038-1088. 孔文仲 (Table P-PZ40)
2687.K8	Kuo, Yin, 12th cent. 郭印 (Table P-PZ40)
	Li, Gang, 1083-1140. 李綱; 李纲 see PL2687.L474
2687.L474	Li, Kang, 1083-1140. 李綱; 李纲 (Table P-PZ40)
2687.L475	Li, Liu, fl. 1216. 李劉; 李刘 (Table P-PZ40)
	Lin, Bu, 967-1028. 林逋 see PL2687.L532
2687.L5	Lin, Jingxi, 1242-1310. 林景熙 (Table P-PZ40)
2687.L532	Lin, Pu, 967-1028. 林逋 (Table P-PZ40)
	Liu, Caishao, 1086-1158. 劉才邵; 刘才邵 see PL2687.L57
2687.L534	Liu, Changshi, jin shi 1205. 劉昌詩; 刘昌诗 (Table P-PZ40)
2687.L535	Liu, Chenweng, 1232-1297. 劉辰翁; 刘辰翁 (Table P-PZ40)
2687.L55	Liu, Fu, 11th cent. 劉斧; 刘斧 (Table P-PZ40)
	Liu, Guo, 1154-1206. 劉過; 刘过 see PL2687.L562
2687.L5616	Liu, Kezhuang, 1187-1269. 劉克莊; 刘克庄 (Table P-PZ40)
2687.L562	Liu, Kuo, 1154-1206. 劉過; 刘过 (Table P-PZ40)
2687.L57	Liu, Ts'ai-shao, 1086-1158. 劉才邵; 刘才邵 (Table P-PZ40)
2687.L586	Liu, Xueji, b. 1155?. 劉學箕; 刘学箕 (Table P-PZ40)
2687.L589	Liu, Yong, jin shi 1034. 柳永 (Table P-PZ40)
2687.L68	Lou, Yao, 1137-1213. 樓鑰; 楼钥 (Table P-PZ40)
	Lü, Benzhong, jin shi 1136. 陸九淵; 陆九渊 see PL2687.L793

Chinese language and literature
Chinese literature
Individual authors and works
Song dynasty, 960-1279. Liao dynasty, 947-1125. Xi Xia
dynasty, 1038-1227. Jin dynasty, 1115-1234
Other, A-Z -- Continued

2687.L78	Lu, Chiu-yüan, 1139-1193. 陸九淵; 陆九渊 (Table P-PZ40)
2687.L79	Lü, I-hao, 1071-1139. 呂頤浩; 吕颐浩 (Table P-PZ40)
	Lu, Jiuyuan, 1139-1193. 陸九淵; 陆九渊 see PL2687.L78
2687.L793	Lü, Pen-chung, chin shih 1136. 呂本中; 吕本中 (Table P-PZ40)
2687.L795	Lü, Tsu-ch'ien, 1137-1181. 呂祖謙; 吕祖谦 (Table P-PZ40)
	Lü, Yihao, 1071-1139. 呂頤浩; 吕颐浩 see PL2687.L79
2687.L8	Lu, You, 1125-1210. 陸游; 陆游 (Table P-PZ40)
	Lü, Zuqian, 1137-1181. 呂祖謙; 吕祖谦 see PL2687.L795
2687.M38	Mao, Pang, 1067-1120?. 毛滂 (Table P-PZ40)
2687.M4	Mei, Yaochen, 1002-1060. 梅堯臣; 梅尧臣 (Table P-PZ40)
2687.M5	Mi, Fu, 1051-1107. 米芾 (Table P-PZ40)
2687.M78	Mu-jung, Yen-feng, 1067?-1117. 慕容彥逢 (Table P-PZ40)
2687.P8	Pu, Shoucheng, 13th cent (Table P-PZ40)
	Qiang, Zhi, 1022-1076. 強至; 强至 see PL2687.C497
	Qin, Guan, 1049-1100. 秦觀; 秦观 see PL2687.C55
2687.S47	Shao, Yong, 1011-1077. 邵雍 (Table P-PZ40)
2687.S5	Shen, Kuo, 1031-1095. 沈括 (Table P-PZ40)
2687.S516	Shen, Yuqiu, 1086-1137. 沈與求; 沈与求 (Table P-PZ40)
	Shi, Dazu, fl. 1195. 史達祖; 史达祖 see PL2687.S545
	Shi, Jie, 1005-1045. 石介 see PL2687.S52
2687.S518	Shi, Mining, 13th cent. 史彌寧; 史弥宁 (Table P-PZ40)
2687.S5193	Shi, Yaobi, jin shi 1157. 史堯弼, 史尧弼 (Table P-PZ40)
2687.S52	Shih, Chieh, 1005-1045. 石介 (Table P-PZ40)
2687.S534	Shih, Rong, 12th/13th cent. 史容 (Table P-PZ40)
2687.S545	Shih, Ta-tsu, fl. 1195. 史達祖; 史达祖 (Table P-PZ40)
	Song, Boren. 宋伯仁 see PL2687.S94
2687.S565	Song, Qi, 998-1061. 宋祁 (Table P-PZ40)
	Song Taizong, Emperor of China, 939-997. 宋太宗 see PL2687.S965
2687.S72	Su, Che, 1039-1112. 蘇轍; 苏辙 (Table P-PZ40)

Chinese language and literature
  Chinese literature
    Individual authors and works
      Song dynasty, 960-1279. Liao dynasty, 947-1125. Xi Xia
        dynasty, 1038-1227. Jin dynasty, 1115-1234
        Other, A-Z -- Continued

2687.S75	Su, Chiung, 12th/13th cent. 蘇泂; 苏泂 (Table P-PZ40)
	Su, Guo, 1072-1123. 蘇過; 苏过 see PL2687.S79
2687.S78	Su, Hsün, 1009-1066. 蘇洵; 苏洵 (Table P-PZ40)
	Su, Jiong, 12th/13th cent. 蘇泂; 苏泂 see PL2687.S75
2687.S79	Su, Kuo, 1072-1123. 蘇過; 苏过 (Table P-PZ40)
2687.S8	Su, Shunqin, 1008-1048. 蘇舜欽; 苏舜钦 (Table P-PZ40)
2687.S85	Su, Song, 1020-1101. 蘇頌; 苏颂 (Table P-PZ40)
	Su, Xun, 1009-1066. 蘇洵; 苏洵 see PL2687.S78
	Su, Zhe, 1039-1112. 蘇轍; 苏辙 see PL2687.S72
2687.S94	Sung, Po-jen. 宋伯仁 (Table P-PZ40)
2687.S965	Sung T'ai-tsung, Emperor of China, 939-997. 宋太宗 (Table P-PZ40)
2687.T22-.T223	Ta T'ang San Tsang ch'ü ching shih hua. 大唐三藏取經詩話; 大唐三藏取经诗话 (Table P-PZ43)
2687.T26	Tai, Fu-ku, b. 1167. 戴復古; 戴复古 (Table P-PZ40)
2687.T35	Tang, Geng, 1071-1121. 唐庚 (Table P-PZ40)
2687.T4	Teng, Mu, 1247-1306. 鄧牧; 邓牧 (Table P-PZ40)
2687.T55	Ting, Wei, 966-1037. 丁謂; 丁谓 (Table P-PZ40)
2687.T6	Ts'ai, Hsiang, 1012-1067. 蔡襄 (Table P-PZ40)
2687.T679	Tseng, Kung, 1019-1083. 曾鞏; 曾巩 (Table P-PZ40)
2687.T687	Tsou, Hao, 1060-1111. 鄒浩; 邹浩 (Table P-PZ40)
2687.T7	Tsung, Tse, 1059-1128. 宗澤; 宗泽 (Table P-PZ40)
2687.T75	Tu, Cheng, chin shih 1190. 度正 (Table P-PZ40)
2687.T77	Tuan, K'o-chi, 1196-1254. 段克己 (Table P-PZ40)
2687.T9	Tung, Chieh-yüan, fl. 1189-1208. 董解元 (Table P-PZ40)
2687.W253	Wang, An'guo, 1028-1074. 王安國; 王安国 (Table P-PZ40)
2687.W265	Wang, Cho, 1162-1237. 汪晫 (Table P-PZ40)
	Wang, Guanguo, jin shi 1119. 王觀國; 王观国 see PL2687.W269
2687.W267	Wang, I-sun, d. ca. 1290. 王沂孫; 王沂孙 (Table P-PZ40)
2687.W269	Wang, Kuan-kuo, chin shih 1119. 王觀國; 王观国 (Table P-PZ40)
2687.W274	Wang, Ling, 1032-1059. 王令 (Table P-PZ40)

Chinese language and literature
Chinese literature
Individual authors and works
Song dynasty, 960-1279. Liao dynasty, 947-1125. Xi Xia
dynasty, 1038-1227. Jin dynasty, 1115-1234
Other, A-Z -- Continued

2687.W28	Wang, Mingqing, 1127-ca. 1215. 王明清 (Table P-PZ40)
2687.W285	Wang, Pizhi, jin shi 1067. 王闢之; 王辟之 (Table P-PZ40)
2687.W355	Wang, Yinglin, 1223-1296. 王應麟; 王应麟 (Table P-PZ40)
	Wang, Yisun, d. ca. 1290. 王沂孫; 王沂孙 see PL2687.W267
2687.W358	Wang, Yü-ch'eng, 954-1001. 王禹偁 (Table P-PZ40)
2687.W359	Wang, Yuanliang, 13th cent. 汪元量 (Table P-PZ40)
	Wang, Yucheng, 954-1001. 王禹偁 see PL2687.W358
	Wang, Zhuo, 1162-1237. 汪晫 see PL2687.W265
	Wei, Bo, 12th cent. 衛博; 卫博 see PL2687.W38
2687.W37	Wei, Chu, 1232-1292. 魏初 (Table P-PZ40)
2687.W38	Wei, Po, 12th cent. 衛博; 卫博 (Table P-PZ40)
2687.W39	Wei, Tsung-wu, d. 1289. 衛宗武; 卫宗武 (Table P-PZ40)
2687.W393	Wei, Ye, 960-1019. 魏野 (Table P-PZ40)
	Wei, Zongwu, d. 1289. 衛宗武; 卫宗武 see PL2687.W39
2687.W4	Wen, Tianxiang, 1236-1283. 文天祥 (Table P-PZ40)
2687.W43	Wen, Tong, 1018-1079. 文同 (Table P-PZ40)
2687.W465	Wenxiang, Shi, b. 1211. 文珦 (Table P-PZ40)
2687.W83	Wu, Wenying. 吳文英; 吴文英 (Table P-PZ40)
	Xiang, Ziyin, 1085-1152. 向子諲 see PL2687.H578
	Xie, Fangde, 1226-1289. 謝枋得; 谢枋得 see PL2687.H583
	Xu, Fei, 13th cent. 許棐; 许棐 see PL2687.H594
	Xu, Xuan, 916-991. 徐鉉; 徐铉 see PL2687.H595
	Xu, Yinglong, 1168-1248. 許應龍; 许应龙 see PL2687.H6
	Yan, Jidao, ca. 1030-ca. 1106. 晏幾道; 晏几道 see PL2687.Y426
	Yan, Shu, 991-1055. 晏殊 see PL2687.Y43
	Yan, Yu, 12th cent. 嚴羽; 严羽 see PL2687.Y434
2687.Y22	Yang, Chieh, chin shih 1059. 楊傑; 杨杰 (Table P-PZ40)
2687.Y23	Yang, Hsien-chih, fl. 1246. 楊顯之; 杨显之 (Table P-PZ40)
2687.Y24	Yang, I, 974-1020. 楊億; 杨亿 (Table P-PZ40)

Chinese language and literature
    Chinese literature
        Individual authors and works
                Song dynasty, 960-1279. Liao dynasty, 947-1125. Xi Xia
                    dynasty, 1038-1227. Jin dynasty, 1115-1234
                  Other, A-Z -- Continued

	Yang, Jie, jin shi 1059. 楊傑; 杨杰 see PL2687.Y22
2687.Y3	Yang, Wanli, 1127-1206. 楊萬里; 杨万里 (Table P-PZ40)
	Yang, Yi, 974-1020. 楊億; 杨亿 see PL2687.Y24
2687.Y4	Ye, Mengde, 1077-1148. 葉夢得; 叶梦得 (Table P-PZ40)
2687.Y42	Ye, Shi, 1150-1223. 葉適; 叶适 (Table P-PZ40)
2687.Y426	Yen, Chi-tao, ca. 1030-ca. 1106. 晏幾道; 晏几道 (Table P-PZ40)
2687.Y43	Yen, Shu, 991-1055. 晏殊 (Table P-PZ40)
2687.Y434	Yen, Yü, 12th cent. 嚴羽; 严羽 (Table P-PZ40)
(2687.Y5)	Yi, Kyu-bo, 1168-1241. 李奎報; 李圭报 see PL987.Y56
2687.Y55	Yin, Shun, 1061-1132. 尹焞 (Table P-PZ40)
2687.Y68	Yü, Ching, 1000-1064. 余靖 (Table P-PZ40)
2687.Y7	Yu, Chou, jin shi 1163. 虞儔; 虞俦 (Table P-PZ40)
	Yu, Jing, 1000-1064. 余靖 see PL2687.Y68
2687.Y725	Yü, Kuei. 俞桂 (Table P-PZ40)
2687.Y8	Yuan, Haowen, 1190-1257. 元好問; 元好问 (Table P-PZ40)
	Zeng, Gong, 1019-1083. 曾鞏; 曾巩 see PL2687.T679
	Zhai, Ruwen, 1076-1141. 翟汝文 see PL2687.C33
	Zhang, Duanyi, 1179-ca. 1235. 張端義; 张端义 see PL2687.C36
	Zhang, Hao, fl. 1196-1225. 張淏; 张淏 see PL2687.C35
	Zhang, Kan, 12th/13th cent. 張侃; 张侃 see PL2687.C354
	Zhang, Kuo, d. 1147. 張擴; 张扩 see PL2687.C355
	Zhang, Shi, 1133-1180. 張栻; 张栻 see PL2687.C359
	Zhang, Xian, 990-1078. 張先; 张先 see PL2687.C3535
	Zhang, Xiaoxiang, 1133-1170. 張孝祥; 张孝祥 see PL2687.C3534
	Zhang, Yan, 1248-1320? 張炎; 张炎 see PL2687.C363
	Zhang, Yuan'gan, 1091-1161? 張元幹; 张元干 see PL2687.C364
	Zhao, Bian, 1008-1084. 趙抃; 赵抃 see PL2687.C369

Chinese language and literature
Chinese literature
Individual authors and works
Song dynasty, 960-1279. Liao dynasty, 947-1125. Xi Xia
dynasty, 1038-1227. Jin dynasty, 1115-1234
Other, A-Z -- Continued
Zhao, Dingchen, b. 1070. 趙鼎臣; 赵鼎臣 see
PL2687.C377
Zhao, Ruteng, d. 1261. 趙汝騰; 赵汝腾 see
PL2687.C366
Zhaojun he fan. 昭君和番 see PL2687.C39+
Zhen, Dexiu, 1178-1235. 真德秀 see PL2687.C444
Zheng, Qiao, 1104-1162. 鄭樵; 郑樵 see
PL2687.C482
Zhong, Bing, jin shi 1132. 仲并 see PL2687.C87
Zhou, Bangyan, 1056-1121. 周邦彥 see PL2687.C64
Zhou, Mi, 1232-1308. 周密 see PL2687.C635
Zhu, Dunru, 1081-1159. 朱敦儒 see PL2687.C8
Zhu, Shuzhen, fl. 1095-1131. 朱淑真 see
PL2687.C77
Zhu, Xiyan, 1221-1279. 朱晞顏; 朱晞颜 see
PL2687.C75
Zong, Ze, 1059-1128. 宗澤; 宗泽 see PL2687.T7
Zou, Hao, 1060-1111. 鄒浩; 邹浩 see PL2687.T687
Yuan dynasty, 1260-1368

2687.5.A-Z	Anonymous works. By title, A-Z
	Subarrange each by Table P-PZ43
2687.5.H832-.H8323	Hua Guansuo ci hua. 花關索詞話; 花关索词话 (Table P-PZ43)
2688	Chao, Mêng-fu, 1254-1322. 趙孟頫; 赵孟頫 (Table P-PZ39)
2689	Guan, Hanqing, ca. 1210-ca. 1298. 關漢卿; 关汉卿 (Table P-PZ39)
2690	Luo, Guanzhong, ca. 1330-ca. 1400. 羅貫中;罗贯中 (Table P-PZ39)
2691	Ma, Zhiyuan, 1250?-1324? 馬致遠; 马致远 (Table P-PZ39)
2692	Shi, Nai'an, ca. 1290-ca. 1365. 施耐庵 (Table P-PZ39)
	Shui hu zhuan. 水滸傳; 水浒传 see PL2694.S5+
2693	Wang, Shifu, fl. 1295-1307. 王實甫; 王实甫 (Table P-PZ39)
	Zhao, Mengfu, 1254-1322. 趙孟頫; 赵孟頫 see PL2688
2694.A-Z	Other, A-Z
	Subarrange each author by Table P-PZ40
	Bai, Pu, b. 1226. 白樸; 白朴 see PL2694.P35
2694.C28	Chang, Chung-shen, 14th cent. 張仲深; 张仲深 (Table P-PZ40)

Chinese language and literature
Chinese literature
Individual authors and works
Yuan dynasty, 1260-1368
Other, A-Z -- Continued

2694.C286	Chang, K'o-chiu, ca. 1271-ca. 1346. 張可久 (Table P-PZ40)
2694.C29	Chang, Po-ch'un, 1243-1303. 張伯淳; 张伯淳 (Table P-PZ40)
2694.C294	Chang, Yang-hao, 1269-1329. 張養浩; 张养浩 (Table P-PZ40)
2694.C295	Chang, Yü, 1277-1348. 張雨; 张雨 (Table P-PZ40)
2694.C3	Chao, Wen, 1239-1315. 趙文; 赵文 (Table P-PZ40)
2694.C39	Ch'en, Chi, 1314-1370. 陳基; 陈基 (Table P-PZ40)
2694.C4	Ch'en, I-fu, 1255-1299. 陳宜甫; 陈宜甫 (Table P-PZ40)
	Chen, Ji, 1314-1370. 陳基; 陈基 see PL2694.C39
2694.C42	Chen, Lü, 1287-1342. 陳旅; 陈旅 (Table P-PZ40)
	Chen, Yifu, 1255-1299. 陳宜甫; 陈宜甫 see PL2694.C4
2694.C45	Cheng, Jufu, 1249-1318. 程鉅夫; 程钜夫 (Table P-PZ40)
2694.C453	Cheng, Kuang-tsu, fl. 1294. 鄭光祖; 郑光祖 (Table P-PZ40)
2694.C455	Cheng, Ssu-hsiao, 1241-1318. 鄭思肖; 郑思肖 (Table P-PZ40)
2694.C47	Cheng, Yüan-yu, 1292-1364. 鄭元祐; 郑元祐 (Table P-PZ40)
2694.C52	Ch'iao, Chi, d. 1345. 喬吉; 乔吉 (Table P-PZ40)
2694.C56	Chieh, Hsi-ssu, 1274-1344. 揭傒斯 (Table P-PZ40)
2694.C57	Ch'ing-kung, 1272-1352. 清珙 (Table P-PZ40)
2694.C58	Ch'iu, Yüan, b. 1247. 仇遠; 仇远 (Table P-PZ40)
2694.C78	Chu, Te-jun, 1294-1365. 朱德潤; 朱德润 (Table P-PZ40)
2694.D35	Daichi, 1290-1366. 大智 (Table P-PZ40)
	Du, Ben, 1276-1350. 杜本 see PL2694.T86
2694.F3	Fang, Hui, 1227-1307. 方回 (Table P-PZ40)
	Gao, Ming, ca. 1306-1359. 高明 see PL2694.K36
	Gao, Qi, 1336-1374. 高啓; 高启 see PL2694.K3
(2694.G54)	Gidō Shūshin, 1325?-1388. 義堂周信; 义堂周信 see PL792.G54
	Gu, Ying, 1310-1369. 顧瑛; 顾瑛 see PL2694.K78
	Guan, Yunshi, 1286-1324. 貫雲石; 贯云石 see PL2694.K783
	Guo, Bi, ca. 1268-ca. 1339. 郭畀 see PL2694.K8
	Guo, Yuheng, 13th/14th cent. 郭豫亨 see PL2694.K86

Chinese language and literature
Chinese literature
Individual authors and works
Yuan dynasty, 1260-1368
Other, A-Z -- Continued

2694.H72	Hsieh, Ying-fang, 1296-1392. 謝應芳; 谢应芳 (Table P-PZ40)
2694.H733	Hsü, Tsai-ssu, fl. 1320. 徐再思 (Table P-PZ40)
2694.H823	Hu, Zuanzong, 1480-1560. 胡纘宗; 胡缵宗 (Table P-PZ40)
(2694.H89)	Hyegŭn, 1320-1376. 慧勤 see PL987.H94
	Jie, Xisi, 1274-1344. 揭傒斯 see PL2694.C56
2694.K3	Kao, Ch'i, 1336-1374. 高啓; 高启 (Table P-PZ40)
2694.K36	Kao, Ming, ca. 1306-1359. 高明 (Table P-PZ40)
	Ke, Danqiu. 柯丹丘 see PL2694.K65
2694.K65	K'o, Tan-ch'iu. 柯丹丘 (Table P-PZ40)
2694.K78	Ku, Ying, 1310-1369. 顧瑛; 顾瑛 (Table P-PZ40)
2694.K783	Kuan, Yün-shih, 1286-1324. 貫雲石; 贯云石 (Table P-PZ40)
2694.K8	Kuo, Pi, ca. 1268-ca. 1339. 郭畀 (Table P-PZ40)
2694.K86	Kuo, Yü-heng, 13th/14th cent. 郭豫亨 (Table P-PZ40)
2694.L463	Li, Hsing-tao. 李行道 (Table P-PZ40)
2694.L467	Li, Shouqing, 13th cent. 李壽卿; 李寿卿 (Table P-PZ40)
2694.L47	Li, Xiaoguang, 1297-1348. 李孝光 (Table P-PZ40)
	Li, Xingdao. 李行道 see PL2694.L463
2694.L476	Liu, Guan, 1270-1342. 柳貫 (Table P-PZ40)
2694.L48	Liu, Ji, 1311-1375. 劉基; 刘基 (Table P-PZ40)
2694.L5	Liu, Yueshen, 1260-1346. 劉岳申; 刘岳申 (Table P-PZ40)
	Long tu gong an. 龍圖公案; 龙图公案 see PL2694.L75+
2694.L65	Lu, Zhi, 1242?-1314? 盧摯; 卢挚 (Table P-PZ40)
2694.L75-.L753	Lung t'u kung an. 龍圖公案; 龙图公案 (Table P-PZ43)
2694.M27	Ma, Zhen, fl. 1302. 馬臻; 马臻 (Table P-PZ40)
2694.M37	Ma, Zuchang, 1279-1338. 馬祖常; 马祖常 (Table P-PZ40)
2694.M46	Meng, Hanqing, 13th cent. 孟漢卿; 孟汉卿 (Table P-PZ40)
(2694.M87)	Musō Soseki, 1275-1351. 夢窓疎石 see PL792.M87
2694.N32	Na, Yan, b. 1309. 納延; 纳延 (Table P-PZ40)
2694.N5	Ni, Zan, 1301-1374. 倪瓚; 倪瓒 (Table P-PZ40)
2694.P35	Pai, P'u, b. 1226. 白樸; 白朴 (Table P-PZ40)
2694.P8	Pu, Daoyuan, 1260-1336. 蒲道源 (Table P-PZ40)
	Qiao, Ji, d. 1345. 喬吉; 乔吉 see PL2694.C52

130

Chinese language and literature
  Chinese literature
    Individual authors and works
      Yuan dynasty, 1260-1368
        Other, A-Z -- Continued

	Qinggong, 1272-1352. 清珙 see PL2694.C57
	Qiu, Yuan, b. 1247. 仇遠; 仇远 see PL2694.C58
2694.S24	Sa, Dula, b. 1272. 薩都剌; 萨都剌 (Table P-PZ40)
2694.S46	Shang, Zhongxian, 13th cent. 尚仲賢; 尚仲贤 (Table P-PZ40)
2694.S5-.S53	Shui hu zhuan. 水滸傳; 水浒传 (Table P-PZ43)
2694.T3	Tao, Zongyi, fl. 1360-1368. 陶宗儀; 陶宗仪 (Table P-PZ40)
2694.T4	Teng, Anshang, 1242-1295. 滕安上 (Table P-PZ40)
2694.T86	Tu, Pen, 1276-1350. 杜本 (Table P-PZ40)
2694.W3	Wang, Chieh, 1275-1336. 王結; 王结 (Table P-PZ40)
	Wang, Jie, 1275-1336. 王結; 王结 see PL2694.W3
2694.W36	Wang, Mian, 1287-1359. 王結; 王结 (Table P-PZ40)
2694.W77	Wu, Cheng, 1249-1333. 吳澄; 吴澄 (Table P-PZ40)
2694.W8	Wu, Hanchen, 13th cent. 武漢臣; 武汉臣 (Table P-PZ40)
2694.W84	Wu, Shidao, 1283-1344. 吳師道; 吴师道 (Table P-PZ40)
	Xie, Yingfang, 1296-1392. 謝應芳; 谢应芳 see PL2694.H72
	Xu, Zaisi, fl. 1320. 徐再思 see PL2694.H733
2694.Y33	Yang, Weizhen, 1296-1370. 楊維楨; 杨维桢 (Table P-PZ40)
(2694.Y5)	Yi, Che-hyŏn, 1287-1367. 李齊賢 see PL987.Y5
2694.Y8	Yu, Ji, 1272-1348. 虞集 (Table P-PZ40)
	Zhang, Bochun, 1243-1303. 張伯淳; 张伯淳 see PL2694.C29
	Zhang, Kejiu, ca. 1271-ca. 1346. 張可久 see PL2694.C286
	Zhang, Yanghao, 1269-1329. 張養浩; 张养浩 see PL2694.C294
	Zhang, Yu, 1277-1348. 張雨; 张雨 see PL2694.C295
	Zhang, Zhongshen, 14th cent. 張仲深; 张仲深 see PL2694.C28
	Zhao, Wen, 1239-1315. 趙文; 赵文 see PL2694.C3
	Zheng, Guangzu, fl. 1294. 鄭光祖; 郑光祖 see PL2694.C453
	Zheng, Sixiao, 1241-1318. 鄭思肖; 郑思肖 see PL2694.C455
	Zheng, Yuanyou, 1292-1364. 鄭元祐; 郑元祐 see PL2694.C47

Chinese language and literature
Chinese literature
Individual authors and works
Yuan dynasty, 1260-1368
Other, A-Z -- Continued
Zhu, Derun, 1294-1365. 朱德潤; 朱德润 see
PL2694.C78
Ming Dynasty, 1368-1644

2694.5.A-Z	Anonymous works. By title, A-Z
	Subarrange each by Table P-PZ43
	Bai tu ji. 白兔記; 白兔记 see PL2694.5.P34+
	Bei you ji. 北遊記; 北游记 see PL2694.5.P45+
2694.5.C45-.C453	Chao shih ku erh chi. 趙氏孤兒記; 赵氏孤儿记 (Table P-PZ43)
2694.5.C47-.C473	Ch'i shih erh ch'ao jen wu yen i. 七十二朝人物演義; 七十二朝人物演义 (Table P-PZ43)
	Dong Xi Jin yan yi. 東西晉演義; 东西晋演义 see PL2694.5.T84+
2694.5.H68-.H683	Hou Xi you ji. 後西遊記; 后西游记 (Table P-PZ43)
2694.5.H76-.H763	Hsü hsi yu chi. 續西遊記; 续西游记 (Table P-PZ43)
2694.5.H78-.H783	Hsuan-ho i shih. 宣和遺事; 宣和遗事 (Table P-PZ43)
2694.5.H8-.H83	Hsüan-te hsieh pen chin Ch'ai chi. 宣德寫本金釵記; 宣德写本金钗记 (Table P-PZ43)
2694.5.L54-.L543	Li jing ji. 荔鏡記; 荔镜记 (Table P-PZ43)
2694.5.L56-.L563	Liang Han kai guo zhong xing zhuan zhi. 两汉开国中兴传志 (Table P-PZ43)
2694.5.P34-.P343	Pai t'u chi. 白兔記; 白兔记 (Table P-PZ43)
2694.5.P45-.P453	Pei yu chi. 北遊記; 北游记 (Table P-PZ43)
2694.5.P86-.P863	Puming bao juan. 普明寶卷 (Table P-PZ43)
	Qi shi er chao ren wu yan yi. 七十二朝人物演義; 七十二朝人物 演义 see PL2694.5.C47+
2694.5.R89-.R893	Ruyijun zhuan. 如意君傳; 如意君传 (Table P-PZ43)
2694.5.T54-.T543	Tian bao tu. 天寶圖; 天宝图 (Table P-PZ43)
2694.5.T84-.T843	Tung-hsi chin yen i. 東西晉演義; 东西晋演义 (Table P-PZ43)
	Xu Xi you ji. 續西遊記; 续西游记 see PL2694.5.H76+
	Xuande xie ben jin chai ji. 宣德寫本金釵記; 宣德写本金钗记 see PL2694.5.H8+
	Xuanhe yi shi. 宣和遺事; 宣和遗事 see PL2694.5.H78+
2694.5.Y35-.Y353	Yang jia fu yan yi. 楊家府演義; 杨家府演义 (Table P-PZ43)
2694.5.Y54-.Y543	Ying lie zhuan. 英烈傳; 英烈传 (Table P-PZ43)
	Zhao shi gu er ji. 趙氏孤兒記; 赵氏孤儿记 see PL2694.5.C45+
2695	Tang, Xianzu, 1550-1616. 湯顯祖; 汤显祖 (Table P-PZ39)

Chinese language and literature
Chinese literature
Individual authors and works
Ming Dynasty, 1368-1644 -- Continued

2696	Wang, Yangming, 1472-1529. 王陽明; 王阳明 (Table P-PZ39)
2697	Wu, Cheng'en, ca. 1500-ca. 1582. 吳承恩; 吴承恩 (Table P-PZ39)
2698.A-Z	Other, A-Z
	Subarrange each author by Table P-PZ40
	Bi, Zhenji, jin shi 1646. 畢振姬; 毕振姬 see PL2698.P45
	Bian, Gong, 1476-1532. 邊貢; 边贡 see PL2698.P54
	Cai, Qing, 1453-1509. 蔡清 see PL2698.T72
	Cao, Duan, 1376-1434. 曹端 see PL2698.T764
(2698.C22)	Ch'a, Ch'ŏl-lo, 1556-1615. 車天輅; 车天辂 see PL988.C32
2698.C25	Chang, Chia-yü, 1616-1647. 張家玉; 张家玉 (Table P-PZ40)
2698.C27	Chang, Feng-i, 1527-1613. 張鳳翼; 张凤翼 (Table P-PZ40)
2698.C3	Chang, Huang-yen, 1620-1664. 張煌言; 张煌言 (Table P-PZ40)
2698.C312	Chang, Mao, 1437-1522. 章懋 (Table P-PZ40)
2698.C313	Chang, Mao-hsiu. 張懋修; 张懋修 (Table P-PZ40)
2698.C316	Chang, P'u, 1602-1641. 張溥; 张溥 (Table P-PZ40)
2698.C32	Chang, Shen-yen, 1577-1645. 張慎言; 张慎言 (Table P-PZ40)
2698.C33	Chang, Tai, 1597-1679. 張岱; 张岱 (Table P-PZ40)
2698.C332	Chang, Yü, 1333-1385. 張羽; 张羽 (Table P-PZ40)
2698.C348	Chao, Nan-hsing, 1550-1627. 趙南星; 赵南星 (Table P-PZ40)
2698.C35	Chao, Pi, chin shih 1481. 趙弼; 赵弼 (Table P-PZ40)
	Chen, Bi, b. 1605. 陳璧; 陈璧 see PL2698.C4545
2698.C38	Chen, Chen, b. ca. 1608. 陳忱; 陈忱 (Table P-PZ40)
2698.C385	Ch'en, Chi-t'ai, 1573-1640. 陳際泰; 陈际泰 (Table P-PZ40)
2698.C39	Chen, Chun, 1483-1544. 陳淳; 陈淳 (Table P-PZ40)
2698.C45	Ch'en, Hsien-chang, 1428-1500. 陳獻章; 陈献章 (Table P-PZ40)
2698.C453	Chen, Jiru, 1558-1639. 陳繼儒; 陈继儒 (Table P-PZ40)
	Chen, Jitai, 1573-1640. 陳際泰; 陈际泰 see PL2698.C385
2698.C4545	Ch'en, Pi, b. 1605. 陳璧; 陈璧 (Table P-PZ40)
2698.C4556	Ch'en, Tzu-lung, 1608-1647. 陳子龍; 陈子龙 (Table P-PZ40)

Chinese language and literature
Chinese literature
Individual authors and works
Ming Dynasty, 1368-1644
Other, A-Z -- Continued

2698.C4557	Ch'en, Tzu-sheng, 17th cent. 陳子升; 陈子升 (Table P-PZ40)
2698.C4559	Chen, Wei, 16th/17th cent. 甄偉; 甄伟 (Table P-PZ40)
	Chen, Xianzhang, 1428-1500. 陳獻章; 陈献章 see PL2698.C45
	Chen, Zilong, 1608-1647. 陳子龍; 陈子龙 see PL2698.C4556
2698.C456	Cheng, Jiasui, 1565-1643. 程嘉燧 (Table P-PZ40)
2698.C457	Cheng, Shan-fu, 1485-1523. 鄭善夫; 郑善夫 (Table P-PZ40)
2698.C458	Cheng, Yüeh, 1468-1539. 鄭岳; 郑岳 (Table P-PZ40)
2698.C52	Ch'i-tung-yeh-jen. 齋東野人; 齐东野人 (Table P-PZ40)
2698.C53	Chia, Ying-ch'ung, ca. 1589-ca. 1671. 賈應寵; 贾应宠 (Table P-PZ40)
2698.C532	Chiang, Tung-wei, chü jen 1606. 江东伟; 江東偉 (Table P-PZ40)
2698.C5325	Chiang, Ying-k'o, 1553-1605. 江盈科 (Table P-PZ40)
2698.C533	Chiao, Hung, 1541-1620. 焦竑 (Table P-PZ40)
(2698.C534)	Ch'iao-yün-shan-jen. 樵雲山人; 樵云山人 see PL2705.I268
2698.C54	Ch'ien, Ch'eng-chih, 1612-1693. 錢澄之; 钱澄之 (Table P-PZ40)
2698.C5444	Chin, Lüan, ca. 1495-ca. 1584. 金鑾; 金銮 (Table P-PZ40)
2698.C545	Chin, Shan, 1368-1431. 金善 (Table P-PZ40)
2698.C548	Ch'in-huai-mo-k'o. 秦淮墨客 (Table P-PZ40)
2698.C552	Chin-mu-san-jen. 金木散人 (Table P-PZ40)
(2698.C553)	Ch'ing-hsi-tao-jen, 17th cent. 清溪道人 (Table P-PZ40) see PL2698.F34
2698.C554	Ch'ing-lien-shih-chu-jen. 青蓮室主人; 青莲室主人 (Table P-PZ40)
2698.C558	Ch'iu, Chün, 1421-1495. 邱濬; 丘濬 (Table P-PZ40)
(2698.C562)	Chŏng, Ch'ŏl, 1536-1593. 鄭澈; 郑澈 see PL988.C6
2698.C5626	Chou, Ch'ao-chün, 16th/17th cent. 周朝俊 (Table P-PZ40)
2698.C5628	Chou, Ch'ing-yüan, 16th/17th cent. 周清源 (Table P-PZ40)
2698.C5636	Chou, Shih-hsiu, 1354-1402. 周是脩; 周是修 (Table P-PZ40)

Chinese language and literature
Chinese literature
Individual authors and works
Ming Dynasty, 1368-1644
Other, A-Z -- Continued

2698.C65	Chou, Yu, 17th cent. 周游 (Table P-PZ40)
2698.C75	Chu, Chih-yü, 1600-1682. 朱之瑜 (Table P-PZ40)
2698.C754	Chu, Ch'üan, 1378-1448. 朱權; 朱权 (Table P-PZ40)
(2698.C77)	Chu, Se-bung, 1495-1554. 周世鵬; 周世鵬 see PL988.C84
2698.C78	Chu, Sheng-lin, 16th/17th cent. 諸聖隣; 诸圣邻 (Table P-PZ40)
2698.C783	Ch'ü, Shih-ssu, 1590-1651. 瞿式耜 (Table P-PZ40)
2698.C79	Chu, Su-ch'en, fl. 1644. 朱素臣 (Table P-PZ40)
2698.C793	Ch'ü, Ta-chün, 1630-1696. 屈大均 (Table P-PZ40)
2698.C794	Chu, Ting-ch'en, 16th cent. 朱鼎臣 (Table P-PZ40)
2698.C795	Chu, Ts'un-li, 1444-1513. 朱存理 (Table P-PZ40)
2698.C798	Chu, Yu, 1314-1376. 朱右 (Table P-PZ40)
2698.C8	Ch'ü, Yu, 1341-1427. 瞿佑 (Table P-PZ40)
2698.C82	Chu, Yu-tun, 1379-1439. 朱有燉 (Table P-PZ40)
2698.C83	Chu, Yün-ming, 1460-1526. 祝允明 (Table P-PZ40)
2698.C89	Chung, Hsing, 1574-1625. 鍾惺; 钟惺 (Table P-PZ40)
	Dong, Yue, 1620-1686. 董說; 董说 see PL2698.T83
	Duche, Shi, 1588-1656. 讀徹; 读彻 see PL2698.T813
2698.F3	Fan, Yunlin, 1558-1641. 范允臨; 范允临 (Table P-PZ40)
	Fang, Gongqian, 1596-1666. 方拱乾 see PL2698.F36
2698.F33	Fang, I-chih, 1611-1671. 方以智 (Table P-PZ40)
2698.F34	Fang, Ju-hao, 17th cent. 清溪道人 (Table P-PZ40)
2698.F36	Fang, Kung-ch'ien, 1596-1666. 方拱乾 (Table P-PZ40)
	Fang, Yizhi, 1611-1671. 方以智 see PL2698.F33
2698.F385	Feng, Fang, jin shi 1523. 豐坊; 丰坊 (Table P-PZ40)
2698.F4	Feng, Menglong, 1574-1646. 馮夢龍; 冯梦龙 (Table P-PZ40)
2698.F42	Feng, Weimin, 1511-1580? 馮惟敏; 冯惟敏 (Table P-PZ40)
2698.F428-.F4283	Feng shen yan yi. 封神演義; 封神演义 (Table P-PZ43)
2698.F8	Fucijiaozhu, 17th cent. 伏雌教主 (Table P-PZ40)
	Gao, Lian, 16th cent. 高濂 see PL2698.K27
	Gu, Tianjun, jin shi 1592. 顧天埈; 顾天埈 see PL2698.K82
	Gu, Xiancheng, 1550-1612. 顧憲成; 顾宪成 see PL2698.K785
	Gui, Youguang, 1507-1571. 歸有光; 归有光 see PL2698.K856

Chinese language and literature
Chinese literature
Individual authors and works
Ming Dynasty, 1368-1644
Other, A-Z -- Continued

	Gui, Zhuang, 1613-1673. 歸莊; 归庄 see PL2698.K85
	Guo, Xun, 1475-1542. 郭勳; 郭勋 see PL2698.K87
2698.H34	Han, Bangqi, 1479-1555. 韓邦奇; 韩邦奇 (Table P-PZ40)
2698.H35	Han, Shanggui, d. 1644. 韓上桂; 韩上桂 (Table P-PZ40)
2698.H38	Hanshi, 1608-1685. 函是 (Table P-PZ40)
	He, Jingming, 1483-1521. 何景明 see PL2698.H524
	He, Liangjun, 1506-1573. 何良俊 see PL2698.H6
2698.H44	He, Mengchun, 1474-1536. 何孟春 (Table P-PZ40)
	He, Qiaoxin, 1427-1502. 何喬新; 何乔新 see PL2698.H52
	He, Tang, 1474-1543. 何瑭 see PL2698.H64
	He, Xinyin, 1517-1579. 何心隱; 何心隐 see PL2698.H56
	He, Yisun, 1605-1688 or 9. 賀貽孫; 贺贻孙 see PL2698.H58
(2698.H47)	Hŏ, Ch'e, b. 1563. 許褅
	see PL988.H62
2698.H52	Ho, Ch'iao-hsin, 1427-1502. 何喬新; 何乔新 (Table P-PZ40)
2698.H524	Ho, Ching-ming, 1483-1521. 何景明 (Table P-PZ40)
2698.H56	Ho, Hsin-yin, 1517-1579. 何心隱; 何心隐 (Table P-PZ40)
2698.H58	Ho, I-sun, 1605-1688 or 9. 賀貽孫; 贺贻孙 (Table P-PZ40)
(2698.H59)	Hŏ, Kyun, 1569-1618. 許筠
	see PL989.27.K9
2698.H6	Ho, Liang-chün, 1506-1573. 何良俊 (Table P-PZ40)
(2698.H63)	Hŏ, Nansŏrhŏn, 1563-1589. 許蘭雪軒
	see PL988.H65
2698.H64	Ho, Tang, 1474-1543. 何瑭 (Table P-PZ40)
	Hong, Pian, 16th cent. 洪楩 see PL2698.H84
2698.H7	Hsia, Wan-ch'un, 1631-1647. 夏完淳 (Table P-PZ40)
2698.H724-.H7243	Hsia Hsi-yang tsa chü. 下西洋雜劇; 下西洋杂剧 (Table P-PZ43)
2698.H73	Hsiao-hsiao-sheng. 笑笑生 (Table P-PZ40)
2698.H734	Hsieh, Chen, 1495-1575. 謝榛; 谢榛 (Table P-PZ40)
2698.H736	Hsieh, Ch'ien, 1449-1531. 謝遷; 谢迁 (Table P-PZ40)
2698.H74	Hsieh, Chin, 1369-1415. 解縉; 解缙 (Table P-PZ40)
2698.H755	Hsiung, Lung-feng. 熊龍峯; 熊龙峰 (Table P-PZ40)
2698.H76	Hsiung, Ta-mu, 16th cent. 熊大木 (Table P-PZ40)

Chinese language and literature
Chinese literature
Individual authors and works
Ming Dynasty, 1368-1644
Other, A-Z -- Continued

2698.H77	Hsü, Chen, fl. 1377. 徐[田臣] (Table P-PZ40)
2698.H7713	Hsü, Chung-hsing, 1517-1578. 徐中行 (Table P-PZ40)
2698.H7716	Hsü, Fang, 1622-1694. 徐枋 (Table P-PZ40)
2698.H774	Hsü, Tao, 17th cent. 徐道 (Table P-PZ40)
2698.H775	Hsü, Wei, 1521-1593. 徐渭 (Table P-PZ40)
2698.H776	Hsü, Yeh, 1614-1685. 徐夜 (Table P-PZ40)
2698.H777	Hsü, Yu-chen, 1407-1472. 徐有貞; 徐有贞 (Table P-PZ40)
2698.H7777	Hsüeh, Hsüan, 1392-1464. 薛瑄 (Table P-PZ40)
2698.H7785	Hsüeh, Shih-heng, 1617-1686. 薛始亨 (Table P-PZ40)
2698.H7794	Hu, Han, 1307-1381. 胡翰 (Table P-PZ40)
2698.H79	Hu, Yinglin, 1551-1602. 胡應麟; 胡应麟 (Table P-PZ40)
	Huang, Daozhou, 1585-1646. 黄道周 see PL2698.H82
2698.H814	Huang, Fangyin. 黄方胤; 黄方胤 (Table P-PZ40)
2698.H816	Huang, Hui, chin shih 1589. 黄輝; 黄辉 (Table P-PZ40)
2698.H82	Huang, Tao-chou, 1585-1646. 黄道周 (Table P-PZ40)
2698.H84	Hung, P'ien, 16th cent. 洪楩 (Table P-PZ40)
(2698.H88)	Hwang, Chul-lyang, 1517-1563. 黃俊良 see PL988.H93
(2698.I35)	Ikkyū, 1394-1481. 一休 see PL792.I35
(2698.I4)	Im, Che, 1549-1587. 林悌 see PL988.I53
(2698.I43)	Im, Chŏn, 1560-1611. 任錪 see PL988.I54
(2698.I44)	Im, Ŏng-nyŏng, 1496-1568. 林億齡 see PL988.I56
(2698.I45)	Im, Sŏ, 1570-1624. 林忄胥 see PL988.I57
	Jia, Yingchong, ca. 1589-ca. 1671. 賈應寵; 贾应宠 see PL2698.C53
	Jiang, Dongwei, ju ren 1606. 江东伟; 江東偉 see PL2698.C532
	Jiang, Yingke, 1553-1605. 江盈科 see PL2698.C5325
	Jiao, Hong, 1541-1620. 焦竑 see PL2698.C533
	Jin, Luan, ca. 1495-ca. 1584. 金鑾; 金銮 see PL2698.C5444

Chinese language and literature
Chinese literature
Individual authors and works
Ming Dynasty, 1368-1644
Other, A-Z -- Continued
Jin, Shan, 1368-1431. 金善 see PL2698.C545
Jinmusanren. 金木散人 see PL2698.C552

2698.J8	Juan, Ta-ch'eng, 1587-1646. 阮大鋮; 阮大铖 (Table P-PZ40)
2698.K25	Kang, Hai, 1475-1540. 康海 (Table P-PZ40)
(2698.K26)	Kao, Ch'i, 1336-1374. 高啓; 高启 see PL2694.K3
2698.K27	Kao, Lien, 16th cent. 高濂 (Table P-PZ40)
(2698.K44)	Keijo Shūrin, 1440-1518. 景徐周麟 see PL792.K42
(2698.K46)	Kim, Chong-jik, 1431-1492. 金宗直 see PL988.K42
(2698.K48)	Kim, In-hu, 1510-1560. 金麟厚 see PL988.K45
(2698.K49)	Kim, Sang-hŏn, 1570-1652. 金尚憲 see PL988.K52
(2698.K5)	Kim, Si-sŭp, 1435-1493. 金時習 see PL988.K54
(2698.K52)	Kim, Tŭg-yŏn, 1555-1637. 金得研 see PL988.K58
(2698.K59)	Ko, Kyŏng-myŏng, 1533-1592. 高敬命 see PL988.K64
	Konggulaoren, 16th/17th cent. 空谷老人 see PL2698.K864
2698.K785	Ku, Hsien-ch'eng, 1550-1612. 顧憲成; 顾宪成 (Table P-PZ40)
(2698.K816)	Ku, Pong-nyŏng, 1526-1586. 具鳳齡 see PL988.K75
2698.K82	Ku, T'ien-chün, chin shih 1592. 顧天埈; 顾天埈 (Table P-PZ40)
2698.K84	Kuang, Lu, 1604-1650 or 51. 鄺露; 邝露 (Table P-PZ40)
2698.K85	Kuei, Chuang, 1613-1673. 歸莊; 归庄 (Table P-PZ40)
2698.K856	Kuei, Yu-kuang, 1507-1571. 歸有光; 归有光 (Table P-PZ40)
2698.K864	K'ung-ku-lao-jen, 16th/17th cent. 空谷老人 (Table P-PZ40)
2698.K87	Kuo, Hsün, 1475-1542. 郭勳; 郭勋 (Table P-PZ40)
(2698.K94)	Kwŏn, Kŭn, 1352-1409. 權近; 权近 see PL987.K92
(2698.K95)	Kwŏn, P'il, 1569-1612? 權韠 see PL988.K93

PL

Chinese language and literature
Chinese literature
Individual authors and works
Ming Dynasty, 1368-1644
Other, A-Z -- Continued

2698.L36	Lan, Mao, 1397-1476. 蘭茂; 兰茂 (Table P-PZ40)
2698.L45	Li, Chih, 1527-1602. 李贄; 李贽 (Table P-PZ40)
	Li, Dongyang, 1447-1516. 李東陽; 李东阳 see PL2698.L49
2698.L465	Li, Jih-hua, 1565-1635. 李日華; 李日华 (Table P-PZ40)
2698.L468	Li, Kai, ju ren 1624. 李楷 (Table P-PZ40)
2698.L47	Li, Kaixian, 1502-1568. 李開先; 李开先 (Table P-PZ40)
2698.L475	Li, Liufang, 1575-1629. 李流芳 (Table P-PZ40)
2698.L477	Li, Mengyang, 1472-1529. 李夢陽; 李梦阳 (Table P-PZ40)
2698.L478	Li, Minbiao, ju ren 1534. 黎民表 (Table P-PZ40)
2698.L48	Li, Panlong, 1514-1570. 李攀龍; 李攀龙 (Table P-PZ40)
	Li, Rihua, 1565-1635. 李日華; 李日华 see PL2698.L465
2698.L487	Li, Suiqiu, 1602-1646. 黎遂球 (Table P-PZ40)
2698.L49	Li, Tung-yang, 1447-1516. 李東陽; 李东阳 (Table P-PZ40)
2698.L497	Li, Yu, 14th cent. 李昱 (Table P-PZ40)
2698.L5	Li, Yu, ca. 1590-ca. 1660. 李玉 (Table P-PZ40)
2698.L52	Li, Yu, 1611-1680? 李漁; 李渔 (Table P-PZ40)
	Li, Zhi, 1527-1602. 李贄; 李贽 see PL2698.L45
	Lian, Zining, jin shi 1385. 練子寧; 练子宁 see PL2698.L538
2698.L53	Liang, Chenyu, 1519?-1591? 梁辰魚; 梁辰鱼 (Table P-PZ40)
2698.L537	Liang, Yu-yü, chin shih 1550. 梁有譽; 梁有誉 (Table P-PZ40)
2698.L538	Lien, Tzu-ning, chin shih 1385. 練子寧; 练子宁 (Table P-PZ40)
	Lin, Bi, 1324 or 5-1381. 林弼 see PL2698.L545
2698.L54	Lin, Chün, 1452-1527. 林俊 (Table P-PZ40)
	Lin, Dachun, 1523-1588. 林大春 see PL2698.L546
2698.L543	Lin, Hong, 14th cent. 林鴻; 林鸿 (Table P-PZ40)
	Lin, Jun, 1452-1527. 林俊 see PL2698.L54
2698.L545	Lin, Pi, 1324 or 5-1381. 林弼 (Table P-PZ40)
2698.L546	Lin, Ta-ch'un, 1523-1588. 林大春 (Table P-PZ40)
2698.L55	Ling, Mengchu, 1580-1644. 凌濛初 (Table P-PZ40)
2698.L5838	Liu, Liangchen, 1482-ca. 1551. 劉良臣; 刘良臣 (Table P-PZ40)

Chinese language and literature
Chinese literature
Individual authors and works
Ming Dynasty, 1368-1644
Other, A-Z -- Continued

2698.L59	Liu, Zongzhou, 1578-1645. 劉宗周; 刘宗周 (Table P-PZ40)
2698.L62	Lo, Ch'i, d. ca. 1519. 羅玘; 罗玘 (Table P-PZ40)
2698.L63	Lo, Ch'in-shun, 1465-1547. 羅欽順; 罗钦顺 (Table P-PZ40)
2698.L67	Lo, Mao-teng, 16th/17th cent. 羅懋登; 罗懋登 (Table P-PZ40)
2698.L68	Lou, Jian, 1567-1631. 婁堅; 娄坚 (Table P-PZ40)
	Lu, Can, 1494-1551. 陸粲; 陆粲 see PL2698.L86
2698.L77	Lu, Jen-lung, 17th cent. 陸人龍; 陆人龙 (Table P-PZ40)
	Lu, Renlong, 17th cent. 陸人龍; 陆人龙 see PL2698.L77
2698.L85	Lu, Shen, 1477-1544. 陸深; 陆深 (Table P-PZ40)
2698.L853	Lü, Tiancheng, 1580-1618. 呂天成 (Table P-PZ40)
2698.L86	Lu, Ts'an, 1494-1551. 陸粲; 陆粲 (Table P-PZ40)
2698.L865	Luo, Hongxian, 1504-1564. 羅洪先 (Table P-PZ40)
	Luo, Maodeng, 16th/17th cent. 羅懋登; 罗懋登 see PL2698.L67
	Luo, Qi, d. ca. 1519. 羅玘; 罗玘 see PL2698.L62
	Luo, Qinshun, 1465-1547. 羅欽順; 罗钦顺 see PL2698.L63
2698.M44	Meng, Chengshun, 17th cent. 孟稱舜; 孟称舜 (Table P-PZ40)
2698.M564	Mingquyikuang, 16th/17th cent. 名衢逸狂 (Table P-PZ40)
(2698.N35)	Nam, Hyo-on, 1454-1492. 南孝溫 see PL988.N36
2698.N52	Ni, Yuanlu, 1593-1644. 倪元璐 (Table P-PZ40)
2698.N54	Ni, Yue, jin shi 1464. 倪岳 (Table P-PZ40)
2698.N6	No, Su-sin, 1515-1590. 盧守愼 (Table P-PZ40)
(2698.O55)	Ŏ, Suk-kwŏn, 16th cent. 魚叔權 see PL988.O23
(2698.P33)	Pak, Sang, 1474-1530. 朴祥 see PL988.P37
(2698.P332)	Pak, Sun, 1523-1589. 朴淳 see PL988.P38
(2698.P3324)	Pak, Sŭng-im, 1517-1586. 朴承任 see PL988.P39
(2698.P333)	Pak, Ŭn, 1479-1504. 朴誾 see PL988.P48

Chinese language and literature
Chinese literature
Individual authors and works
Ming Dynasty, 1368-1644
Other, A-Z -- Continued

2698.P45	Pi, Chen-chi, chin shih 1646. 畢振姬; 毕振姬 (Table P-PZ40)
2698.P54	Pien, Kung, 1476-1532. 邊貢; 边贡 (Table P-PZ40)
2698.Q25	Qi, Jiguang, 1528-1587. 戚繼光; 戚继光 (Table P-PZ40)
	Qian, Chengzhi, 1612-1693. 錢澄之; 钱澄之 see PL2698.C54
	Qidongyeren. 齋東野人; 齐东野人 see PL2698.C52
	Qinglianshizhuren. 青蓮室主人; 青莲室主人 see PL2698.C554
	Qingxidaoren, 17th cent. 清溪道人 see PL2698.F34
	Qinhuaimoke. 秦淮墨客 see PL2698.C548
	Qiu, Jun, 1421-1495. 邱濬; 丘濬 see PL2698.C558
	Qu, Dajun, 1630-1696. 屈大均 see PL2698.C793
	Qu, Shisi, 1590-1651. 瞿式耜 see PL2698.C783
	Qu, You, 1341-1427. 瞿佑 see PL2698.C8
	Ruan, Dacheng, 1587-1646. 阮大鋮; 阮大铖 see PL2698.J8
2698.S37	Shao, Bao, 1460-1527. 邵寶; 邵宝 (Table P-PZ40)
2698.S45	She, Xiang, ju ren 1558. 佘翔 (Table P-PZ40)
2698.S47	Shen, Ching, 1553-1610. 沈璟 (Table P-PZ40)
	Shen, Guangwen, 1612?-1688. 沈光文 see PL2698.S477
	Shen, Jing, 1553-1610. 沈璟 see PL2698.S47
2698.S477	Shen, Kuang-wen, 1612?-1688. 沈光文 (Table P-PZ40)
2698.S48	Shen, Lian, 1507-1557. 沈鍊; 沈炼 (Table P-PZ40)
2698.S49	Shen, Zijin, 1583-1665. 沈自晉; 沈自晋 (Table P-PZ40)
2698.S495	Shengrenheshang, 1612-1660. 剩人和尚 (Table P-PZ40)
2698.S52	Shi, Shaoshen, b. 1588. 施紹莘; 施绍莘 (Table P-PZ40)
(2698.S543)	Sim, Su-gyŏng, 1516-1599. 沈守慶 see PL988.S35
(2698.S55)	Sin, Suk-chu, 1417-1475. 申叔舟 see PL988.S46
(2698.S56)	Sŏ, Kŏ-jŏng, 1420-1488. 徐居正 see PL988.S56
(2698.S6)	Song, Ik-p'il, 1534-1599. 宋翼弼 see PL988.S615
	Song, Lian, 1310-1381. 宋濂 see PL2698.S84

Chinese language and literature
Chinese literature
Individual authors and works
Ming Dynasty, 1368-1644
Other, A-Z -- Continued
Song, Maocheng, ju ren 1612. 宋懋澄 see
PL2698.S85

(2698.S64)	Sŏsan Taesa, 1520-1604. 西山大師 see PL988.S67
2698.S793	Sun, Gaoliang, 16th cent. 孫高亮; 孙高亮 (Table P-PZ40)
2698.S797	Sun, Qifeng, 1585-1675. 孫奇逢; 孙奇逢 (Table P-PZ40)
2698.S83	Sun, Zhonglin, 16th/17th cent. 孫鍾齡; 孙钟龄 (Table P-PZ40)
2698.S84	Sung, Lien, 1310-1381. 宋濂 (Table P-PZ40)
2698.S85	Sung, Mao-ch'eng, chü jen 1612. 宋懋澄 (Table P-PZ40)
2698.T24	Tan, Yuanchun, 1586-1637. 譚元春; 谭元春 (Table P-PZ40)
2698.T27	Tang, Shisheng, 1551-1636. 唐時升; 唐时升 (Table P-PZ40)
2698.T28	Tang, Shunzhi, 1507-1560. 唐順之; 唐顺之 (Table P-PZ40)
2698.T3	Tang, Yin, 1470-1524. 唐寅 (Table P-PZ40)
2698.T34	Tao, Wangling, b. 1562. 陶望齡; 陶望龄 (Table P-PZ40)
2698.T54	Tianranchisou. 天然癡叟; 天然痴叟 (Table P-PZ40) Tianranheshang, 1608-1685. 函是 see PL2698.H38
2698.T72	Ts'ai, Ch'ing, 1453-1509. 蔡清 (Table P-PZ40)
2698.T76	Tsang, Mao-hsün, 1550-1620. 臧懋循 (Table P-PZ40)
2698.T764	Ts'ao, Tuan, 1376-1434. 曹端 (Table P-PZ40)
2698.T767	Tso-hua-san-jen. 坐花散人 (Table P-PZ40)
2698.T78	Tsou, Yüan-piao, 1551-1624. 鄒元標; 邹元标 (Table P-PZ40)
2698.T784	Tsui-chu-chü-shih. 醉竹居士 (Table P-PZ40)
2698.T786	Tsui-Hsi-hu-hsin-yüeh-chu-jen. 醉西湖心月主人 (Table P-PZ40)
2698.T79	Tsung, Ch'en, 1525-1560. 宗臣 (Table P-PZ40)
2698.T812	Tu, Long, 1542-1605 (Table P-PZ40)
2698.T813	Tu-ch'e, Shih, 1588-1656. 讀徹; 读彻 (Table P-PZ40)
2698.T83	Tung, Yüeh, 1620-1686. 董說; 董说 (Table P-PZ40)
2698.W238	Wang, Cheng, 1370-1415. 王偁 (Table P-PZ40)
2698.W24	Wang, Chi, 1498-1583. 王畿 (Table P-PZ40)
(2698.W2415)	Wang, Chi-chung, 1575-1646. 王季重 see PL2698.W322
2698.W242	Wang, Chih, 1379-1462. 王直 (Table P-PZ40)

Chinese language and literature
    Chinese literature
        Individual authors and works
            Ming Dynasty, 1368-1644
                Other, A-Z -- Continued

2698.W243	Wang, Chih-teng, 1535-1612. 王穉登 (Table P-PZ40)
2698.W247	Wang, Chiu-ssu, 1468-1551. 王九思 (Table P-PZ40)
	Wang, Guangyang, d. 1380. 汪廣洋; 汪广洋 see PL2698.W275
2698.W267	Wang, Heng, 1564-1607. 王衡 (Table P-PZ40)
2698.W268	Wang, Hongru, jin shi 1487. 王鴻儒; 王鸿儒 (Table P-PZ40)
	Wang, Ji, 1498-1583. 王畿 see PL2698.W24
	Wang, Jiusi, 1468-1551. 王九思 see PL2698.W247
2698.W275	Wang, Kuang-yang, d. 1380. 汪廣洋; 汪广洋 (Table P-PZ40)
2698.W28	Wang, Mian, 1335-1407. 王冕 (Table P-PZ40)
2698.W294	Wang, Shenzhong, 1509-1559. 王慎中 (Table P-PZ40)
2698.W3	Wang, Shizhen, 1526-1590. 王世貞; 王世贞 (Table P-PZ40)
2698.W322	Wang, Siren, 1575-1646. 王思任 (Table P-PZ40)
2698.W325	Wang, Tingxiang, 1474-1544. 王廷相 (Table P-PZ40)
2698.W33	Wang, Tongxiang, 1420-1505. 王桐鄉; 王桐乡 (Table P-PZ40)
2698.W36	Wang, Yanhong, 16th cent. 王彥泓 (Table P-PZ40)
	Wang, Zhi, 1379-1462. 王直 see PL2698.W242
	Wang, Zhideng, 1535-1612. 王穉登 see PL2698.W243
2698.W39	Wei, Geng, d. 1663. 魏畊; 魏耕 (Table P-PZ40)
2698.W4	Wen, Zhengming, 1470-1559. 文徵明; 文征明 (Table P-PZ40)
	Wu, Bing, jin shi 1619. 吳炳 see PL2698.W79
2698.W78	Wu, Kuo-lun, 1524-1593. 吳國倫; 吴国伦 (Table P-PZ40)
2698.W79	Wu, Ping, chin shih 1619. 吳炳 (Table P-PZ40)
2698.W84	Wu, Yuantai, fl. 1566. 吳元泰; 吴元泰 (Table P-PZ40)
2698.W86	Wugenzi, fl. 1573. 無根子; 无根子 (Table P-PZ40)
2698.W89	Wumenxiaoke. 吳門嘯客; 吴门啸客 (Table P-PZ40)
	Xia, Wanchun, 1631-1647. 夏完淳 see PL2698.H7
	Xia xi yang za ju. 下西洋雜劇; 下西洋杂剧 see PL2698.H724+
	Xiaoxiaosheng. 笑笑生 see PL2698.H73
	Xie, Jin, 1369-1415. 解縉; 解缙 see PL2698.H74
	Xie, Qian, 1449-1531. 謝遷; 谢迁 see PL2698.H736
2698.X538	Xie, Zhao, jin shi 1574 謝昭; 谢昭 (Table P-PZ40)
2698.X54	Xie, Zhaozhe, 1567-1624. 謝肇淛 (Table P-PZ40)

Chinese language and literature
Chinese literature
Individual authors and works
Ming Dynasty, 1368-1644
Other, A-Z -- Continued

	Xie, Zhen, 1495-1575. 謝榛; 谢榛 see PL2698.H734
	Xiong, Damu, 16th cent. 熊大木 see PL2698.H76
	Xiong, Longfeng. 熊龍峯; 熊龙峰 see PL2698.H755
	Xu, Dao, 17th cent. 徐道 see PL2698.H774
	Xu, Fang, 1622-1694. 徐枋 see PL2698.H7716
2698.X827	Xu, Tong, ju ren 1618. 徐 熥 (Table P-PZ40)
	Xu, Wei, 1521-1593. 徐渭 see PL2698.H775
	Xu, Ye, 1614-1685. 徐夜 see PL2698.H776
	Xu, Youzhen, 1407-1472. 徐有貞; 徐有贞 see PL2698.H777
	Xu, Zhen, fl. 1377. 徐[田臣] see PL2698.H77
	Xue, Xuan, 1392-1464. 薛瑄 see PL2698.H7777
2698.Y24	Yang, Chüeh, 1493-1549. 楊爵; 杨爵 (Table P-PZ40)
2698.Y26	Yang, Erzeng, 17th cent. 楊爾曾; 杨尔曾 (Table P-PZ40)
2698.Y27	Yang, Hsün-chi, 1456-1544. 楊循吉; 杨循吉 (Table P-PZ40)
	Yang, Jue, 1493-1549. 楊爵; 杨爵 see PL2698.Y24
2698.Y273	Yang, Jung, 1371-1440. 楊榮; 杨荣 (Table P-PZ40)
	Yang, Rong, 1371-1440. 楊榮; 杨荣 see PL2698.Y273
2698.Y274	Yang, Shen, 1488-1559. 楊慎; 杨慎 (Table P-PZ40)
2698.Y275	Yang, Shiqi, 1365-1444. 楊士奇; 杨士奇 (Table P-PZ40)
2698.Y277	Yang, Wencong, 1596-1646. 楊文驄; 杨文骢 (Table P-PZ40)
	Yang, Xunji, 1456-1544. 楊循吉; 杨循吉 see PL2698.Y27
	Yanxiayishi. 烟霞逸士 see PL2698.Y417
2698.Y32	Yao, Shou, 1423-1495. 姚綬; 姚绶 (Table P-PZ40)
2698.Y417	Yen-hsia-i-shih. 烟霞逸士 (Table P-PZ40)
(2698.Y42)	Yi, An-nul, 1571-1637. 李安訥 see PL988.Y33
(2698.Y428)	Yi, Chŏng-am, 1541-1600. 李廷馣 see PL988.Y428
(2698.Y43)	Yi, Chŏng-gwi, 1564-1635. 李廷龜 see PL988.Y43
(2698.Y45)	Yi, Haeng, 1478-1534. 李荇 see PL988.Y45
(2698.Y47)	Yi, Hwang, 1501-1570. 李滉 see PL988.Y46

Chinese language and literature
Chinese literature
Individual authors and works
Ming Dynasty, 1368-1644
Other, A-Z -- Continued

(2698.Y48)	Yi, Hyŏn-bo, 1467-1555. 李賢輔 see PL988.Y5
(2698.Y484)	Yi, Kyŏng-sŏk, 1595-1671. 李景奭 see PL989.9.K67
(2698.Y486)	Yi, Maech'ang, 1573-1610. 李梅窓 see PL988.Y56
(2698.Y493)	Yi, Saek, 1328-1396. 李穡 see PL987.Y58
(2698.Y53)	Yi, Tal, 1539-1612. 李達 see PL988.Y593
(2698.Y66)	Yŏnsan Kun, 1476-1506. 燕山君 see PL988.Y66
	You gui ji. 幽閨記; 幽闺记 see PL2698.Y83+
2698.Y8	Yü, Ch'ien, 1398-1457. 于謙; 于谦 (Table P-PZ40)
2698.Y816	Yu, Mong-in, 1559-1623. 柳夢寅 (Table P-PZ40)
	Yu, Qian, 1398-1457. 于謙; 于谦 see PL2698.Y8
2698.Y818	Yu, Shaoyu, 16th cent. 余邵魚; 余邵鱼 (Table P-PZ40)
2698.Y83-.Y833	Yu kuei chi. 幽閨記; 幽闺记 (Table P-PZ43)
2698.Y84	Yüan, Chung-tao, 1570-1623. 袁中道 (Table P-PZ40)
2698.Y85	Yuan, Hongdao, 1568-1610. 袁宏道 (Table P-PZ40)
2698.Y86	Yüan, Tsung-tao, 1560-1600. 袁宗道 (Table P-PZ40)
2698.Y87	Yuan, Yuling, 1592-1674. 袁于令 (Table P-PZ40)
	Yuan, Zhongdao, 1570-1623. 袁中道 see PL2698.Y84
	Yuan, Zongdao, 1560-1600. 袁宗道 see PL2698.Y86
(2698.Y93)	Yun, Sun-gŏ, 1596-1668. 尹舜擧 see PL989.96.S86
	Zang, Maoxun, 1550-1620. 臧懋循 see PL2698.T76
(2698.Z44)	Zekkai Chūshin, 1336-1405. 絶海中津 see PL792.Z44
	Zhang, Dai, 1597-1679. 張岱; 张岱 see PL2698.C33
	Zhang, Fengyi, 1527-1613. 張鳳翼; 张凤翼 see PL2698.C27
	Zhang, Huangyan, 1620-1664. 張煌言; 张煌言 see PL2698.C3
	Zhang, Jiayu, 1616-1647. 張家玉; 张家玉 see PL2698.C25
	Zhang, Mao, 1437-1522. 章懋 see PL2698.C312
	Zhang, Maoxiu. 張懋修; 张懋修 see PL2698.C313
	Zhang, Pu, 1602-1641. 張溥; 张溥 see PL2698.C316

Chinese language and literature
Chinese literature
Individual authors and works
Ming Dynasty, 1368-1644
Other, A-Z -- Continued
Zhang, Shenyan, 1577-1645. 張愼言; 张慎言 see PL2698.C32
Zhang, Yu, 1333-1385. 張羽; 张羽 see PL2698.C332
Zhao, Bi, jin shi 1481. 趙弼; 赵弼 see PL2698.C35
Zhao, Nanxing, 1550-1627. 趙南星; 赵南星 see PL2698.C348
Zhen, Wei, 16th/17th cent. 甄偉; 甄伟 see PL2698.C4559
Zheng, Shanfu, 1485-1523. 鄭善夫; 郑善夫 see PL2698.C457
Zheng, Yue, 1468-1539. 鄭岳; 郑岳 see PL2698.C458
Zhong, Xing, 1574-1625. 鍾惺; 钟惺 see PL2698.C89
Zhou, Chaojun, 16th/17th cent. 周朝俊 see PL2698.C5626
Zhou, Qingyuan, 16th/17th cent. 周清源 see PL2698.C5628
Zhou, Shixiu, 1354-1402. 周是脩; 周是修 see PL2698.C5636
Zhou, You, 17th cent. 周游 see PL2698.C65
Zhu, Cunli, 1444-1513. 朱存理 see PL2698.C795
Zhu, Dingchen, 16th cent. 朱鼎臣 see PL2698.C794
Zhu, Quan, 1378-1448. 朱權; 朱权 see PL2698.C754
Zhu, Shenglin, 16th/17th cent. 諸聖隣; 诸圣邻 see PL2698.C78
Zhu, Shunshui, 1600-1682. 朱之瑜 see PL2698.C75
Zhu, Suchen, fl. 1644. 朱素臣 see PL2698.C79
Zhu, You, 1314-1376. 朱右 see PL2698.C798
Zhu, Youdun, 1379-1439. 朱有燉 see PL2698.C82
Zhu, Yunming, 1460-1526. 祝允明 see PL2698.C83
Zong, Chen, 1525-1560. 宗臣 see PL2698.T79
Zou, Yuanbiao, 1551-1624. 鄒元標; 邹元标 see PL2698.T78
Zuixihuxinyuezhuren. 醉西湖心月主人 see PL2698.T786
Zuizhujushi. 醉竹居士 see PL2698.T784
Zuohuasanren. 坐花散人 see PL2698.T767
Qing dynasty, 1644-1912

2699.A-Z	Anonymous works. By title, A-Z
	Subarrange each by Table P-PZ43
2699.C456-.C4563	Cheng ch'un yüan. 爭春園; 争春园 (Table P-PZ43)

Chinese language and literature
Chinese literature
Individual authors and works
Qing dynasty, 1644-1912
Anonymous works. By title, A-Z -- Continued

2699.C473-.C4733	Ch'ien-lung hsün hsing Chiang nan chi. 乾隆巡幸江南記; 乾隆巡幸江南记 (Table P-PZ43)
2699.C5-.C53	Chu lin yeh shih. 株林野史 (Table P-PZ43)
2699.F45-.F453	Feng seng dian mi. 瘋僧點迷; 疯僧点迷 (Table P-PZ43)
	Fo Dao dou fa. 佛道鬥法; 佛道斗法 see PL2699.F67+
2699.F64-.F643	Fo mo zhui zong. 佛魔追踪 (Table P-PZ43)
2699.F67-.F673	Fo Tao tou fa. 佛道鬥法; 佛道斗法 (Table P-PZ43)
2699.F69-.F693	Fo ying xia zong. 佛影俠踪 (Table P-PZ43)
2699.H26-.H263	Hai chiao i pien. 海角遺編; 海角遗编 (Table P-PZ43)
	Hai gong da hong pao quan zhuan. 海公大紅袍全傳; 海公大红袍全传 see PL2699.H34+
	Hai jiao yi bian. 海角遺編; 海角遗编 see PL2699.H26+
2699.H34-.H343	Hai kung ta hung p'ao ch'üan chuan. 海公大紅袍全傳; 海公大红袍全传 (Table P-PZ43)
2699.H57-.H573	Hou Hsi yu chi. 後西遊記; 后西游记 (Table P-PZ43)
	Hou Xi you ji. 後西遊記; 后西游记 see PL2699.H57+
2699.H65-.H653	Hsiang yao fu mo. 降妖伏魔 (Table P-PZ43)
2699.H67-.H673	Hsiao wu i. 小五義; 小五义 (Table P-PZ43)
2699.H677-.H6773	Hsien fa ch'ü mo. 仙法驅魔; 仙法驱魔 (Table P-PZ43)
2699.H68-.H683	Hsien mo cheng hsiung. 仙魔爭雄; 仙魔争雄 (Table P-PZ43)
(2699.H7)	Hsü Chi-kung chuan. 續濟公傳; 续济公传 see PL2699.X82+
2699.H73-.H733	Hsü Hsiao wu i. 續小五義; 续小五义 (Table P-PZ43)
2699.H74-.H743	Hua tian jin yu yuan. 花田金玉緣; 花田金玉缘 (Table P-PZ43)
2699.L45-.L453	Lei feng ta qi zhuan. 雷峰塔奇傳; 雷峰塔奇传 (Table P-PZ43)
2699.L55-.L553	Lin er bao. 麟兒報; 麟儿报 (Table P-PZ43)
2699.P56-.P563	Ping Shan Leng Yan. 平山冷燕 (Table P-PZ43)
	Qianlong xun xing Jiang nan ji. 乾隆巡幸江南記; 乾隆巡幸江南记 see PL2699.C473+
2699.S43-.S433	Shan shui qing. 山水情 (Table P-PZ43)
2699.S482-.S4823	Shen tong xian hua. 神通顯化; 神通显化 (Table P-PZ43)
2699.S484-.S4843	Sheng seng xian wei. 聖僧顯威; 圣僧显威 (Table P-PZ43)
2699.S5-.S53	Shuang chu feng. 雙珠鳳; 双珠凤 (Table P-PZ43)
2699.S55-.S553	Shuo Tang. 說唐; 说唐 (Table P-PZ43)

Chinese language and literature
Chinese literature
Individual authors and works
Qing dynasty, 1644-1912
Anonymous works. By title, A-Z -- Continued

2699.S57-.S573	Shuo Tang Xue Gang zhuan. 說唐薛剛傳; 说唐薛刚传 (Table P-PZ43)
2699.T35-.T353	Tao wu xian ping. 檮杌閒評; 梼杌闲评 (Table P-PZ43)
2699.T53-.T533	Tian xian di guai. 天仙地怪 (Table P-PZ43)
2699.W78-.W783	Wu hu p'ing hsi. 五虎平西 (Table P-PZ43)
2699.W79-.W793	Wu hu ping nan yan yi. 五虎平南演義; 五虎平南演义 (Table P-PZ43)
	Wu hu ping xi yan yi. 五虎平西演義; 五虎平西演义 see PL2699.W78+
2699.W8-.W83	Wu Zetian si da qi an. 武則天四大奇案; 武则天四大奇案 (Table P-PZ43)
	Xian fa qu mo. 仙法驅魔; 仙法驱魔 see PL2699.H677+
	Xian mo zheng xiong. 仙魔爭雄; 仙魔争雄 see PL2699.H68+
	Xiang yao fu mo. 降妖伏魔 see PL2699.H65+
	Xiao wu yi. 小五義; 小五义 see PL2699.H67+
2699.X82-.X823	Xu Ji gong zhuan. 續濟公傳; 续济公传 (Table P-PZ43)
	Xu Xiao wu yi. 續小五義; 续小五义 see PL2699.H73+
2699.Y55-.Y553	Yin ping mei. 銀瓶梅; 银瓶梅 (Table P-PZ43)
	Zheng chun yuan. 爭春園; 争春园 see PL2699.C456+
2699.Z46-.Z463	Zhong lie quan zhuan. 忠烈 全傳; 忠烈 全传 (Table P-PZ43)
	Zhu lin ye shi. 株林野史 see PL2699.C5+
2700	A - B
	Subarrange each author by Table P-PZ40
(2700.A59)	Aizawa, Nanjō, 1792-1860. 藍沢南城 see PL799.A32
	Bao, Dongli, 19th cent. 鮑東里; 鮑东里 see PL2722.A6
	Baoting, 1840-1890. 寶廷; 宝廷 see PL2722.A64
2700.B53	Bian, Lianbao, 1701-1773. 邊連寶; 边连宝 (Table P-PZ40)
2700.3	Ca - Ce
	The author number is determined by the second letter of the name
	Subarrange each author by Table P-PZ40
	Cai, Yuanfang, fl. 1736-1770. 蔡元放 see PL2727.S14
2700.3.A62	Cao, Qujing. 曹去晶 (Table P-PZ40)

Chinese language and literature
Chinese literature
Individual authors and works
Qing dynasty, 1644-1912
Ca - Ce -- Continued

Cao, Wugang, 19th cent. 曹梧冈; 曹梧冈 see
PL2727.S28

Cao, Xueqin, ca. 1717-1763. 曹雪芹 see PL2727.S2+

Cao, Yin, 1658-1712. 曹寅 see PL2727.S29

Cao, Yuanbi, b. 1879. 曹元弼 see PL2727.S3

2701	Ch'ien, Ch'ien-i, 1582-1664. 錢謙益; 钱谦益 (Table P-PZ39)
2702	Ch'ing Kao-tsung, Emperor, 1711-1799. 清高宗 (Table P-PZ39)
2703	Chu, I-tsun, 1629-1709. 朱彝尊 (Table P-PZ39)
2704	Ch'üan, Tsu-wang, 1705-1755. 全祖望 (Table P-PZ39)
2705	Other names beginning with Ch

The author number is determined by the letter or letters
following "Ch"

Subarrange each author by Table P-PZ40

(2705.A413)	Ch'a Chwa-il, 1753-1809. 車佐一 see PL989.12.C43
2705.A415	Cha, Shen-hsing, 1650-1727. 查慎行 (Table P-PZ40)
2705.A42	Chai, Jingping, ju ren 1832. 柴景平 (Table P-PZ40)
2705.A45	Chang, Ch'i-kan, b. 1859. 張其淦; 张其淦 (Table P-PZ40)
2705.A454	Chang, Chien, 1768-1850. 張鑑; 张鉴 (Table P-PZ40)
2705.A455	Chang, Chien, 1853-1926. 張謇; 张謇 (Table P-PZ40)
2705.A46	Chang, Ch'in, 1828-1883. 章嶔; 章嵚 (Table P-PZ40)
2705.A48	Chang, Chu-p'o, 1670-1698. 張竹坡; 张竹坡 (Table P-PZ40)
2705.A49	Chang, Erh-ch'i, 1612-1677. 張爾岐; 张尔岐 (Table P-PZ40)
2705.A52	Chang, Hui-yen, 1761-1802. 張惠言; 张惠言 (Table P-PZ40)
(2705.A55)	Chang, Ping-lin, 1868-1936. 章炳麟 see PL2740.P5
2705.A574	Chang, Shu, ca. 1776-1847. 張澍; 张澍 (Table P-PZ40)
2705.A576	Chang, Wei-p'ing, 1780-1859. 張維屏; 张维屏 (Table P-PZ40)
2705.A578	Chang, Wen-t'ao, 1764-1814. 張問陶; 张问陶 (Table P-PZ40)
2705.A586	Chang, Yü, 1865-1937. 章鈺; 章钰 (Table P-PZ40)
2705.A587	Chang, Yü-chao, 1823-1894. 張裕釗; 张裕钊 (Table P-PZ40)
2705.A588	Chang, Yün. 張勻; 张匀 (Table P-PZ40)

Chinese language and literature
Chinese literature
Individual authors and works
Qing dynasty, 1644-1912
Other names beginning with Ch -- Continued

2705.A5883	Changbaihaogezi. 長白浩歌子; 长白浩歌子 (Table P-PZ40)
2705.A5887	Chao, Chih-hsin, 1662-1744. 趙執信; 赵执信 (Table P-PZ40)
2705.A59	Chao, I, 1727-1814. 趙翼; 赵翼 (Table P-PZ40)
2705.A6	Chao, Lieh-wen, 1832-1893. 趙烈文; 赵烈文 (Table P-PZ40)
2705.A64	Chao, Sung, d. 1900. 趙崧; 赵崧 (Table P-PZ40)
2705.E43	Chen, Baochen, 1848-1935. 陳寶琛 (Table P-PZ40)
2705.E47	Ch'en, Chao-hsing, fl. 1852-1863. 陳肇興; 陈肇兴 (Table P-PZ40)
2705.E522	Ch'en, Ch'iu, fl. 1808. 陳球; 陈球 (Table P-PZ40)
2705.E524	Ch'en, Ch'üeh, 1604-1677. 陳確; 陈确 (Table P-PZ40)
	Chen, Duansheng, 1751-ca. 1796. 陳端生; 陈端生 see PL2705.E55
2705.E526	Chen, Hang, 1785-1826. 陳沆; 陈沆 (Table P-PZ40)
2705.E527	Chen, He, 1757-1811. 陳鶴; 陈鹤 (Table P-PZ40)
2705.E5276	Ch'en, Hsi-tseng, 1767-1816. 陳希曾; 陈希曾 (Table P-PZ40)
2705.E529	Chen, Kuilong, b. 1857. 陳夔龍; 陈夔龙 (Table P-PZ40)
2705.E533	Chen, Lang, 18th cent. 陈朗; 陈朗 (Table P-PZ40)
2705.E54	Chen, Li, 1810-1882. 陳澧; 陈澧 (Table P-PZ40)
2705.E544	Chen, Liangyu, 19th cent. 陳良玉; 陈良玉 (Table P-PZ40)
2705.E5443	Chen, Menglei, b. 1651. 陳夢雷; 陈梦雷 (Table P-PZ40)
	Chen, Qiu, fl. 1808. 陳球; 陈球 see PL2705.E522
	Chen, Que, 1604-1677. 陳確; 陈确 see PL2705.E524
2705.E5448	Chen, Sen, fl. 1823-1849. 陳森; 陈森 (Table P-PZ40)
2705.E54486	Chen, Shaohai. 陳少海; 陈少海 (Table P-PZ40)
2705.E5449	Chen, Shihe, 1887-1955. 陳士和; 陈士和 (Table P-PZ40)
2705.E54495	Chen, Shuji, 18th/19th cent. 陳樹基; 陈树基 (Table P-PZ40)
2705.E548	Chen, Tingjing, 1639-1712. 陳廷敬; 陈廷敬 (Table P-PZ40)
2705.E55	Ch'en, Tuan-sheng, 1751-ca. 1796. 陳端生; 陈端生 (Table P-PZ40)
2705.E564	Chen, Weisong, 1626-1682. 陳維崧; 陈维崧 (Table P-PZ40)

Chinese language and literature
Chinese literature
Individual authors and works
Qing dynasty, 1644-1912
Other names beginning with Ch -- Continued

2705.E568	Chen, Weiying, 1811-1866. 陳維英; 陈维英 (Table P-PZ40)
	Chen, Xizeng, 1767-1816. 陳希曾; 陈希曾 see PL2705.E5276
2705.E57	Chen, Yan, 1856-1937. 陳衍; 陈衍 (Table P-PZ40)
2705.E586	Chen-sung, Shih, 1794-1868. 真嵩 (Table P-PZ40)
2705.E59	Cheng, Chen, 1806-1864. 鄭珍; 郑珍 (Table P-PZ40)
2705.E595	Cheng, Hsiao-hsü, 1860-1938. 鄭孝胥; 郑孝胥 (Table P-PZ40)
2705.E6	Cheng, Hsieh, 1693-1765. 鄭燮; 郑燮 (Table P-PZ40)
2705.E613	Ch'eng, Hsien-chen, 1607-1673. 程先貞; 程先贞 (Table P-PZ40)
2705.E617	Cheng, Huiying. 程蕙英 (Table P-PZ40)
2705.E62	Cheng, Shengxiu, jin shi 1730. 程盛修 (Table P-PZ40)
2705.E63	Cheng, Tingzuo, 1691-1767. 程廷祚 (Table P-PZ40)
	Cheng, Xianzhen, 1607-1673. 程先貞; 程先贞 see PL2705.E613
2705.E64	Cheng, Ying, 18th/19th cent. 程燨 (Table P-PZ40)
2705.I13	Ch'i, Chou-hua, 1698-1767. 齊周華; 齐周华 (Table P-PZ40)
2705.I14	Ch'i, Chün-tsao, 1793-1866. 祁寯藻 (Table P-PZ40)
2705.I17	Chi, Yün, 1724-1805. 紀昀; 纪昀 (Table P-PZ40)
2705.I23	Chiang, Ch'ao-po, chin shih 1845. 蔣超伯; 蒋超伯 (Table P-PZ40)
2705.I24	Chiang, Chen-ming, 19th cent. 姜振名 (Table P-PZ40)
2705.I25	Chiang, Ch'un-lin, 1818-1868. 蔣春霖; 蒋春霖 (Table P-PZ40)
2705.I255	Chiang, Hung, 18th/19th cent. 江洪 (Table P-PZ40)
2705.I256	Chiang, Jih-sheng, fl. 1692. 江日昇; 江日升 (Table P-PZ40)
2705.I26	Chiang, Shih-ch'üan, 1725-1785. 蔣士銓; 蒋士铨 (Table P-PZ40)
2705.I264	Chiang-shang-lao-sou. 江上老叟 (Table P-PZ40)
2705.I266	Chiao, Hsün, 1763-1820. 焦循 (Table P-PZ40)
2705.I268	Ch'iao-yün-shan-jen. 樵雲山人; 樵云山人 (Table P-PZ40)
2705.I277	Ch'ien, Ta-hsin, 1728-1804. 錢大昕; 钱大昕 (Table P-PZ40)
2705.I28	Ch'ien, T'ai-chi, 1791-1863. 錢泰吉; 钱泰吉 (Table P-PZ40)

Chinese language and literature
Chinese literature
Individual authors and works
Qing dynasty, 1644-1912
Other names beginning with Ch -- Continued

2705.I3	Ch'ien, Ts'ai, fl. 1729. 錢彩; 钱彩 (Table P-PZ40)
2705.I32	Ch'ien, Tseng, 1629-1701. 錢曾; 钱曾 (Table P-PZ40)
2705.I34	Ch'ien, Yung, 1759-1844. 錢泳; 钱泳 (Table P-PZ40)
(2705.I35)	Ch'ien-lung, Emperor of China, 1711-1799. 乾隆 see PL2702
2705.I5	Chin, Jen-jui, 1608-1661. 金人瑞 (Table P-PZ40)
2705.I535	Chin, Nung, 1687-1764. 金農; 金农 (Table P-PZ40)
	Chin, Sheng-t'an, 1608-1661. 金聖嘆; 金圣叹 see PL2705.I5
2705.I538	Ch'in, Tzu-ch'en, fl. 1795. 秦子忱 (Table P-PZ40)
2705.I54	Chin, Yung-chüeh, 1802-1868. 金永爵 (Table P-PZ40)
2705.I546	Ching-an, Shih, 1851-1912. 敬安 (Table P-PZ40)
2705.I548	Ch'ing-hsin-ts'ai-tzu. 青心才子 (Table P-PZ40)
2705.I55	Ch'ing Jen-tsung, Emperor of China, 1760-1820. 清仁宗 (Table P-PZ40)
2705.I58	Ching-shih-shan-min. 荆石山民 (Table P-PZ40)
2705.I8	Ch'iu, Chin, 1875-1907. 秋瑾 (Table P-PZ40)
2705.I83	Ch'iu, Feng-chia, 1864-1912. 丘逢甲 (Table P-PZ40)
2705.I85	Ch'iu, Hsin-ju, fl. 1857. 邱心如 (Table P-PZ40)
(2705.O16)	Cho, Sŏng-ga. 趙性家 see PL988.C42
(2705.O17)	Cho, Sŏng-gi, 1638-1689. 趙聖期 see PL989.17.S66
(2705.O2)	Cho, Su-sam, 1762-1849. 趙秀三 see PL989.17.S87
(2705.O22)	Cho, T'ae-ch'ae, 1660-1722. 趙泰采 see PL989.17.T34
(2705.O23)	Cho, Yŏng-sŏk, 1686-1761. 趙榮祏 see PL989.17.Y66
2705.O27	Cho-yüan-t'ing-chu-jen, 17th cent. 酌元亭主人 (Table P-PZ40)
(2705.O42)	Ch'oe, Hyŏn-p'il, 1860-1937. 崔鉉弼 see PL989.18.H96
(2705.O67)	Chŏng, Chong-no. 鄭宗魯 see PL989.2.C46
(2705.O69)	Chŏng, Chun-mo, 1869-1935. 鄭駿謨 see PL990.2.C48
(2705.O72)	Chŏng, Hyŏng-gyu, 1880- 鄭衡圭 see PL990.2.H96
(2705.O74)	Chŏng, T'ae-won, 1824-1880. 鄭泰元 see PL989.2.T38

Chinese language and literature
Chinese literature
Individual authors and works
Qing dynasty, 1644-1912
Other names beginning with Ch -- Continued

(2705.O75)	Chŏng, Un-o, 1846-1920. 鄭雲五 see PL989.2.U66
(2705.O76)	Chŏng, Yag-yong, 1762-1836. 丁若鏞 see PL989.2.Y24
2705.O77	Chou, Ch'i-wei, 1666-1714. 周起渭 (Table P-PZ40)
2705.O772	Chou, Chih-ch'i, 1782-1862. 周之琦 (Table P-PZ40)
2705.O8	Chou, Liang-kung, 1612-1672. 周亮工 (Table P-PZ40)
2705.O83	Chou, Shou-ch'ang, 1814-1884. 周壽昌; 周寿昌 (Table P-PZ40)
2705.O85	Chou, T'ung-yü, d. 1916. 周同愈 (Table P-PZ40)
2705.U12	Chu, Ch'i-lien, d. 1899. 朱啟連; 朱启连 (Table P-PZ40)
2705.U13	Chü-ch'i-tzu, 17th cent. 菊畦子 (Table P-PZ40)
(2705.U14)	Chu-ch'iu-shih. 竹秋氏 see PL2710.S47
2705.U18	Chu, Ho-ling, 1606-1683. 朱鶴齡; 朱鹤龄 (Table P-PZ40)
2705.U19	Chu, I-ch'ing, b. 1795. 朱翊清 (Table P-PZ40)
2705.U2	Chu, Renhu, fl. 1675-1695. 褚人穫; 褚人获 (Table P-PZ40)
2705.U22	Chu, Shu, 1654-1707. 朱書; 朱书 (Table P-PZ40)
2705.U23	Chu, Ta, 1626-ca. 1705. 朱耷 (Table P-PZ40)
2705.U24	Chu, Tsu-mou, 1857-1931. 朱祖謀; 朱祖谋 (Table P-PZ40)
2705.U28	Chu, Yung-ch'un, 1617-1689. 朱用純; 朱用纯 (Table P-PZ40)
2705.U8	Ch'ü-yüan. 蘧園; 蘧园 (Table P-PZ40)
2705.U83	Chuyueshanren. 鋤月山人; 锄月山人 (Table P-PZ40)
2705.5	Ci - Cz
	The author number is determined by the second letter of the name
	Subarrange each author by Table P-PZ40
	Cui, Xiangchuan, fl. 1836. 崔象川 see PL2729.S79
2705.5.U52	Cui, Yuquan, b. 1876 崔 毓荃 (Table P-PZ40)
2706	D
	The author number is determined by the second letter of the name
	Subarrange each author by Table P-PZ40
	Dafulaoren, ju ren 1885. 大浮老人 see PL2725.A68
	Dai, Mingshi, 1653-1713. 戴名世 see PL2727.A3
	Dai, Yanru, 1864-1916. 戴延儒 see PL2727.A38

Chinese language and literature
Chinese literature
Individual authors and works
Qing dynasty, 1644-1912
D -- Continued
Dai, Zhen, 1724-1777. 戴震 see PL2726
Dansou. 誕叟; 诞叟 see PL2727.A57
Deng, Tingzhen, 1775-1846. 鄧廷楨; 邓廷桢 see
PL2727.E54
Ding, Yaokang, 1599-1669. 丁耀亢 see PL2727.I59
Ding, Zhitang, 1837-1902. 丁治棠 see PL2727.I56
Dong, Han, 17th cent. 董含 see PL2729.U478
Dongguo, Zi, 19th cent. 東郭子; 东郭子 see
PL2729.U49
Donglugukuangsheng, 17th cent. 東魯古狂生;
东鲁古狂生 see PL2729.U5
Du, Gang, fl. 1775. 杜綱; 杜纲 see PL2729.U2
Duan, Yucai, 1735-1815. 段玉裁 see PL2729.U3
Duncheng, 1734-1792. 敦誠; 敦诚 see PL2729.U43
Dunmin, 1729-1796. 敦敏 see PL2729.U47

2707	E
	The author number is determined by the second letter of the name
	Subarrange each author by Table P-PZ40
(2707.M3)	Ema, Saikō, 1787-1861. 江馬細香 see PL799.E52
2707.N2	Enxi, fl. 1864-1871 (Table P-PZ40)
2708	F
	The author number is determined by the second letter of the name
	Subarrange each author by Table P-PZ40
2708.A2	Fa, Shishan, 1753-1813. 法式善 (Table P-PZ40)
2708.A247	Fan, Tseng-hsiang, 1846-1931. 樊增祥 (Table P-PZ40)
2708.A248	Fan, Xingrong, 1786-1848. 范興榮; 范兴荣 (Table P-PZ40)
	Fan, Zengxiang, 1846-1931. 樊增祥 see PL2708.A247
2708.A249	Fang, Bao, 1668-1749. 方苞 (Table P-PZ40)
2708.A25	Fang, Dongshu, 1772-1851. 方東樹; 方东树 (Table P-PZ40)
2708.A27	Fang, Wen, 1612-1669. 方文 (Table P-PZ40)
2708.A28	Fang, Xiaobiao, 1618-1649. 方孝標 (Table P-PZ40)
2708.U2	Fu, Shan, 1606-1684. 傅山 (Table P-PZ40)
2708.U25	Fu, Yutian. 傅 于天 (Table P-PZ40)
2708.U3	Fu, Zeng, b. 1688. 符曾 (Table P-PZ40)

Chinese language and literature
  Chinese literature
    Individual authors and works
      Qing dynasty, 1644-1912 -- Continued

2709   G

The author number is determined by the second letter of the name

Subarrange each author by Table P-PZ40

Gan, Pengyun, b. 1861. 甘鵬雲; 甘鹏云 see PL2715.A46

Gao, E, ca. 1738-ca. 1815. 高鶚; 高鹗 see PL2715.A53

Gao, Fenghan, 1683-1748. 高鳳翰; 高凤翰 see PL2715.A54

Gao, Shuran, 1774-1841. 高澍然 see PL2715.A57

2709.O54   Gong, Dingzi, 1616-1673. 龔鼎孳 (Table P-PZ40)

Gong, Zizhen, 1792-1841. 龔自珍; 龚自珍 see PL2717.U5

Gu, Guangqi, 1776-1835. 顧廣圻; 顾广圻 see PL2715.U6

Gu, Qian, 1646-1712. 顧汧; 顾汧 see PL2715.U27

2709.U27   Gu, Taiqing, 1799-1877. 顧太清; 顾太清 (Table P-PZ40)

Gu, Yanwu, 1613-1682. 顧炎武; 顾炎武 see PL2716

Gu, Yun, 1845-1906. 顧雲; 顾云 see PL2717.U23

Gu, Zhen'guan, b. 1637. 顧貞觀; 顾贞观 see PL2715.U23

Guan, Shiming, 1738-1798. 管世銘; 管世铭 see PL2717.U33

Guan, Tingfen, 1797-1880. 管庭芬 see PL2717.U335

Guichuzi, 18th/19th cent. 歸鋤子; 归锄子 see PL2717.U35

Guo, Ermin, 1834-1900. 果爾敏; 果尔敏 see PL2717.U57

Guo, Songtao, 1818-1891. 郭嵩燾; 郭嵩焘 see PL2717.U6

Guo, Xiaoting, 18th cent. 郭小亭 see PL2717.U575

Guo, Zeyun, b. 1884. 郭則澐; 郭则沄 see PL2717.U63

2710   H - Huang

The author number is determined by the second letter of the name

Subarrange each author by Table P-PZ40

2710.A47   Haishangsoushisheng, 1863-1939. 海上漱石生 (Table P-PZ40)

2710.A58   Han, Bangqing, 1856-1894. 韓邦慶; 韩邦庆 (Table P-PZ40)

Chinese language and literature
Chinese literature
Individual authors and works
Qing dynasty, 1644-1912
H - Huang -- Continued

2710.A59	Hanshangmengren, 19th cent. 邗上蒙人 (Table P-PZ40)
(2710.A62)	Hattori, Nankaku, 1683-1759. 服部南郭 see PL795.H35
	He, Shaoji, 1799-1873. 何紹基; 何绍基 see PL2710.O12
	He, Shuangqing, b. 1712. 賀雙卿; 贺双卿 see PL2710.O125
	Hebang'e, b. 1736. 和邦額; 和邦额 see PL2710.S58
	Heshidaoren. 鶴市道人; 鹤市道人 see PL2710.O16
(2710.I76)	Hirose, Kyokusō, 1807-1863. 廣瀬旭莊; 広瀬旭荘 see PL799.H48
2710.O115	Ho, Chiang, 1627-1712. 何絳; 何绛 (Table P-PZ40)
2710.O12	Ho, Shao-chi, 1799-1873. 何紹基; 何绍基 (Table P-PZ40)
2710.O125	Ho, Shuang-ch'ing, b. 1712. 賀雙卿; 贺双卿
2710.O16	Ho-shih-tao-jen. 鶴市道人; 鹤市道人 (Table P-PZ40)
	Hong, Liangji, 1746-1809. 洪亮吉 see PL2712.U47
(2710.O47)	Hong, Se-t'ae, 1653-1725. 洪世泰 see PL989.28.S48
	Hong, Sheng, 1645-1704. 洪昇; 洪升 see PL2712.U5
(2710.O53)	Hong, Yang-ho, 1724-1802. 洪良浩 see PL989.28.Y26
2710.O55	Hou, Fangyu, 1618-1654. 侯方域 (Table P-PZ40)
2710.S44	Hsi-hung-chü-shih. 惜紅居士; 惜红居士 (Table P-PZ40)
2710.S47	Hsi-leng-yeh-ch'iao. 西泠野樵 (Table P-PZ40)
2710.S48	Hsi-yin-t'ang-chu-jen. 惜陰堂主人; 惜阴堂主人 (Table P-PZ40)
2710.S5	Hsia, Ching-ch'ü. 夏敬渠 (Table P-PZ40)
2710.S5124	Hsia, Tseng-yu, 1861-1924. 夏曾佑 (Table P-PZ40)
(2710.S515)	Hsiao wu i. 小五義; 小五义 see PL2699.H67+
2710.S517	Hsiao-yao-tzu, 18th/19th cent. 逍遙子 (Table P-PZ40)
2710.S53	Hsieh, Ch'i-k'un, 1737-1802. 謝啓昆; 谢启昆 (Table P-PZ40)
2710.S55	Hsieh, Hsü-min, 1845-1890. 謝緒民; 谢绪民 (Table P-PZ40)
2710.S58	Hsien-chai-shih, b. 1736. 和邦額; 和邦额 (Table P-PZ40)
2710.S62	Hsin-yüan-chu-jen, 17th/18th cent. 心遠主人; 心远主人 (Table P-PZ40)

156

Chinese language and literature
Chinese literature
Individual authors and works
Qing dynasty, 1644-1912
H - Huang -- Continued

2710.S822	Hsü, Ch'eng-tsu, 18th cent. 許承祖; 许承祖 (Table P-PZ40)
2710.S823	Hsü, Ch'ien-hsüeh, 1631-1694. 徐乾學; 徐乾学 (Table P-PZ40)
2710.S824	Hsü, Ch'iu, 1636-1708. 徐釚 (Table P-PZ40)
2710.S83	Hsü, Chüeh, 1843-1916. 許珏; 许珏 (Table P-PZ40)
2710.S8335	Hsü, Feng-en, d. 1887. 許奉恩; 许奉恩 (Table P-PZ40)
2710.S834	Hsü, Hsi-shen. 許禧身; 许禧身 (Table P-PZ40)
2710.S84	Hsü, Nan-ying, 1855-1917. 許南英; 许南英 (Table P-PZ40)
2710.S85	Hsü, Tso-su, 1616-1684. 徐作肅; 徐作肃 (Table P-PZ40)
2710.S86	Hsü, Tsung-kan, 1796-1866. 徐宗幹; 徐宗干 (Table P-PZ40)
2710.S864	Hsü, Wen-ching, 1667-1756? 徐文靖 (Table P-PZ40)
2710.S88	Hsüan, Ting, 1832-1880? 宣鼎 (Table P-PZ40)
2710.U1624	Hu, Chün, chin shih 1903. 胡駿; 胡骏 (Table P-PZ40)
2710.U163	Hu, Fang, 1654-1727. 胡方 (Table P-PZ40)
	Hu, Jun, jin shi 1903. 胡駿; 胡骏 see PL2710.U1624
2710.U2	Hu, Yü-chin, 1859-1940. 胡玉縉; 胡玉缙 (Table P-PZ40)
2710.U22	Hu, Yuanzuo. 胡源祚 (Table P-PZ40)
	Hu, Yujin, 1859-1940. 胡玉縉; 胡玉缙 see PL2710.U2
2710.U24	Hua-yang-san-jen, ca. 1610-ca. 1675. 華陽散人; 华阳散人 (Table P-PZ40)
2710.U26	Hua-yüeh-ch'ih-jen, 19th cent. 花月痴人 (Table P-PZ40)
2710.U27	Huan-ming, 1771-1831. 煥明; 焕明 (Table P-PZ40)
2710.U2714	Huang, Chan'gui, 18th cent. 黄蟾桂 (Table P-PZ40)
2710.U2716	Huang, Chih-chün, 1668-1748. 黄之雋; 黄之隽 (Table P-PZ40)
2710.U272	Huang, Ching-jen, 1749-1783. 黄景仁 (Table P-PZ40)
2710.U273	Huang, Cho-lai, b. 1649. 黄鷟來; 黄鷟来 (Table P-PZ40)
2710.U275	Huang, Ch'ün, 1883-1945. 黄羣; 黄群 (Table P-PZ40)
	Huang, Daorang, 1814-1868. 黄道讓; 黄道让 see PL2710.U285
2710.U2773	Huang, Jen, 1866-1913. 黄人 (Table P-PZ40)
	Huang, Jingren, 1749-1783. 黄景仁 see PL2710.U272

Chinese language and literature
Chinese literature
Individual authors and works
Qing dynasty, 1644-1912
H - Huang -- Continued

2710.U278	Huang, Ju-ch'eng, 1799-1837. 黄汝成 (Table P-PZ40)
	Huang, Qun, 1883-1945. 黄羣; 黄群 see PL2710.U275
	Huang, Ren, 1866-1913. 黄人 see PL2710.U2773
	Huang, Rucheng, 1799-1837. 黄汝成 see PL2710.U278
2710.U279	Huang, Shaotong. 黄紹統; 黄绍统 (Table P-PZ40)
2710.U2794	Huang, Shizhong, 1872-1912. 黄世仲 (Table P-PZ40)
2710.U285	Huang, Tao-jang, 1814-1868. 黄道讓; 黄道让 (Table P-PZ40)
2710.U29	Huang, T'i-fang, 1832-1899. 黄體芳; 黃体芳 (Table P-PZ40)
2710.U3	Huang, Tsun-hsien, 1848-1905. 黄遵憲; 黄遵宪 (Table P-PZ40)
2711	Huang, Tsung-hsi, 1610-1695. 黄宗羲 (Table P-PZ39)
2712	Huang - Hz
	The author number is determined by the second letter of the name
	Subarrange each author by Table P-PZ40
2712.U15	Huang, Tsung-hui, 17th cent. 黄宗會; 黄宗会 (Table P-PZ40)
2712.U18	Huang, Yuanzhi, 17th cent. 黄元治 (Table P-PZ40)
2712.U19	Huang, Yue, 1750-1841. 黄鉞; 黄钺 (Table P-PZ40)
	Huang, Zhijun, 1668-1748. 黄之雋; 黄之隽 see PL2710.U2716
	Huang, Zhuolai, b. 1649. 黄鷟來; 黄鷟来 see PL2710.U273
	Huang, Zonghui, 17th cent. 黄宗會; 黄宗会 see PL2712.U15
	Huang, Zongxi, 1610-1695. 黄宗羲 see PL2711
2712.U25	Huang, Zongyang, 1865-1921. 黄宗仰 (Table P-PZ40)
	Huang, Zunxian, 1848-1905. 黄遵憲; 黄遵宪 see PL2710.U3
	Huanming, 1771-1831. 煥明; 焕明 see PL2710.U27
	Huayangsanren, ca. 1610-ca. 1675. 華陽散人; 华阳散人 see PL2710.U24
2712.U46	Hui, Dong, 1697-1758. 惠棟; 惠栋 (Table P-PZ40)
2712.U47	Hung, Liang-chi, 1746-1809. 洪亮吉 (Table P-PZ40)
2712.U5	Hung, Sheng, 1645-1704. 洪昇; 洪升 (Table P-PZ40)

Chinese language and literature
Chinese literature
Individual authors and works
Ch'ing Dynasty, 1644-1912

2713	I

Subarrange each author by Table P-PZ40
Class here authors whose names begin with the single letter I
The author number is determined by the next portion of the author's name

2713.S59	I, Shun-ting, 1858-1920. 易順鼎; 易顺鼎 (Table P-PZ40)
2713.Y85	I-yün-shih. 倚雲氏; 倚云氏 (Table P-PZ40)
2713.5	Ia - Iz

The author number is determined by the second letter of the name
Subarrange each author by Table P-PZ40

(2713.5.M25)	Im, Hŏn-hoe, 1811-1876. 任憲晦 see PL989.33.H66
	Injannasi, 1837-1892. 尹湛納希; 尹湛纳希 see PL2733.I53
(2713.5.R74)	Irie, Jakusu, 1671-1729. 入江若水 see PL795.I68
(2713.5.T62)	Itō, Jinsai, 1627-1705. 伊藤仁斎 see PL795.I78
(2713.5.T63)	Itō, Kanpō, 1717-1787. 伊藤冠峰 see PL795.I79
2714	J

The author number is determined by the second letter of the name
Subarrange each author by Table P-PZ40

2714.E62	Jen, Hsüan, chü jen 1788. 任璇 (Table P-PZ40)
	Ji, Yun, 1724-1805. 紀昀; 纪昀 see PL2705.I17
	Jiang, Chaobo, jin shi 1845. 蔣超伯; 蒋超伯 see PL2705.I23
	Jiang, Chunlin, 1818-1868. 蔣春霖; 蒋春霖 see PL2705.I25
	Jiang, Hong, 18th/19th cent. 江洪 see PL2705.I255
	Jiang, Risheng, fl. 1692. 江日昇; 江日升 see PL2705.I256
	Jiang, Shiquan, 1725-1785. 蔣士銓; 蒋士铨 see PL2705.I26
	Jiang, Zhenming, 19th cent. 姜振名 see PL2705.I24
	Jiangshanglaosou. 江上老叟 see PL2705.I264
	Jiao, Xun, 1763-1820. 焦循 see PL2705.I266
	Jiaqing, Emperor of China, 1760-1820. 嘉慶; 嘉庆 see PL2705.I55

Chinese language and literature
Chinese literature
Individual authors and works
Qing dynasty, 1644-1912
J -- Continued
Jin, Nong, 1687-1764. 金農; 金农 see PL2705.I535
Jin, Shengtan, 1608-1661. 金聖嘆; 金圣叹 see
PL2705.I5
Jin, Yongjue, 1802-1868. 金永爵 see PL2705.I54
Jing'an, Shi, 1851-1912. 敬安 see PL2705.I546
Jingshishanmin. 荊石山民 see PL2705.I58

2714.U27	Ju-lien-chü-shih, 18th cent. 如蓮居士; 如莲居士 (Table P-PZ40)
2714.U3	Juan, K'uei-sheng, 1727-1789. 阮葵生 (Table P-PZ40)
2714.U35	Juan, Yüan, 1764-1849. 阮元 (Table P-PZ40)
	Juqizi, 17th cent. 菊畦子 see PL2705.U13
2715	K - Ku
	The author number is determined by the second letter of the name
	Subarrange each author by Table P-PZ40
2715.A46	Kan, P'eng-yün, b. 1861. 甘鵬雲; 甘鹏云 (Table P-PZ40)
(2715.A47)	Kan, Sazan, 1748-1827. 菅茶山 see PL799.K27
(2715.A49)	Kang, Se-hwang, 1713-1791. 姜世晃 see PL989.38.S44
2715.A5	Kang, Youwei, 1858-1927. 康有為; 康有为 (Table P-PZ40)
2715.A52	Kangxi, Emperor of China, 1654-1722. 康熙 (Table P-PZ40)
2715.A53	Kao, E, ca. 1738-ca. 1815. 高鶚; 高鹗 (Table P-PZ40)
2715.A54	Kao, Feng-han, 1683-1748. 高鳳翰; 高凤翰 (Table P-PZ40)
2715.A57	Kao, Shu-jan, 1774-1841. 高澍然 (Table P-PZ40)
(2715.I55)	Kikuchi, Gozan, 1769?-1853? 菊池五山 see PL799.K53
(2715.I558)	Kim, Mun-bae, 1864-1925. 金文培 see PL989.415.M86
(2715.I56)	Kim, Samŭidang, 1769-1823. 金三宜堂 see PL989.415.S26
(2715.I564)	Kim, Su-min, 1734-1811. 金壽民 see PL989.415.S86
(2715.I567)	Kim, Yŏng-gŭn, 1865-1934. 金永根 see PL990.415.Y55
(2715.I57)	Kinoshita, Jun'an, 1621-1699. 木下順庵 see PL795.K55

        Chinese language and literature
          Chinese literature
            Individual authors and works
              Qing dynasty, 1644-1912
                Ku - Kz

	Kong, Jiheng. 孔繼鑅; 孔继鑅 see PL2717.U43
	Kong, Shangren, 1648-1718. 孔尚任 see PL2717.U47
(2715.O76)	Kōtoku, Shūsui, 1871-1911. 幸徳秋水 see PL810.O85
2715.U23	Ku, Chen-kuan, b. 1637. 顧貞觀; 顾贞观 (Table P-PZ40)
2715.U27	Ku, Ch'ien, 1646-1712. 顧汧; 顾汧 (Table P-PZ40)
2715.U6	Ku, Kuang-ch'i, 1776-1835. 顧廣圻; 顾广圻 (Table P-PZ40)
2716	Ku, Yen-wu, 1613-1682. 顧炎武; 顾炎武 (Table P-PZ39)
2717	Ku - Kz
	The author number is determined by the second letter of the name
	Subarrange each author by Table P-PZ40
2717.U23	Ku, Yün, 1845-1906. 顧雲; 顾云 (Table P-PZ40)
2717.U33	Kuan, Shih-ming, 1738-1798. 管世銘; 管世铭 (Table P-PZ40)
2717.U335	Kuan, T'ing-fen, 1797-1880. 管庭芬 (Table P-PZ40)
2717.U35	Kuei-ch'u-tzu, 18th/19th cent. 歸鋤子; 归锄子 (Table P-PZ40)
(2717.U37)	Kuga, Katsunan, 1857-1907. 陸羯南 see PL810.U35
2717.U43	K'ung, Chi-heng. 孔繼鑅; 孔继鑅 (Table P-PZ40)
2717.U46	K'ung, Hsien-i, 19th cent. 孔憲彝; 孔宪彝 (Table P-PZ40)
2717.U47	K'ung, Shang-jen, 1648-1718. 孔尚任 (Table P-PZ40)
2717.U5	Kung, Tzu-chen, 1792-1841. 龔自珍; 龚自珍 (Table P-PZ40)
2717.U57	Kuo, Erh-Min, 1834-1900. 果爾敏; 果尔敏 (Table P-PZ40)
2717.U575	Kuo, Hsiao-t'ing, 18th cent. 郭小亭 (Table P-PZ40)
2717.U6	Kuo, Sung-t'ao, 1818-1891. 郭嵩燾; 郭嵩焘 (Table P-PZ40)
2717.U63	Kuo, Tse-yün, b. 1884. 郭則澐; 郭则沄 (Table P-PZ40)
(2717.W34)	Kwak, Chong-sŏk, 1846-1925. 郭鍾錫 see PL989.45.C46
(2717.W36)	Kwŏn, Sang-il, 1679-1760. 權相一 see PL989.46.S26

Chinese language and literature
  Chinese literature
    Individual authors and works
      Qing dynasty, 1644-1912 -- Continued

2718	L
	The author number is determined by the second letter of the name
	Subarrange each author by Table P-PZ40
2718.A4	Lai, Chi-hsi, 1865-1937. 賴際熙; 赖际熙 (Table P-PZ40)
2718.A5	Lan, Dingyuan, 1680-1733. 藍鼎元; 蓝鼎元 (Table P-PZ40)
2718.A54	Lan'gaozhuren, 18th/19th cent. 蘭皋主人; 兰皋主人 (Table P-PZ40)
2718.A57	Langhuanshanqiao, 18th/19th cent. 嫏嬛山樵 (Table P-PZ40)
	Li, Baichuan, 18th cent. 李百川 see PL2718.I19
	Li, Boyuan, 1867-1906. 李伯元 see PL2718.I2
2718.I117	Li, Chien, 1747-1799. 黎簡; 黎简 (Table P-PZ40)
2718.I118	Li, Chunfang, 17th cent. 李春芳 (Table P-PZ40)
2718.I119	Li, Chunrong, 18th cent. 李春榮; 李春荣 (Table P-PZ40)
	Li, Ciming, 1830-1894. 李慈銘; 李慈铭 see PL2718.I24
	Li, E, 1692-1752. 厲鶚; 厉鹗 see PL2718.I18
2718.I122	Li, Fengshi, 1829-1876. 李逢時; 李逢时 (Table P-PZ40)
2718.I123	Li, Fu, 1666-1749. 李馥 (Table P-PZ40)
2718.I125	Li, Fuping, 1770-1833. 李黼平 (Table P-PZ40)
	Li, Gong, 1659-1733. 李塨 see PL2718.I17
	Li, Guiyu, 19th cent. 李桂玉 see PL2718.I166
	Li, Jian, 1747-1799. 黎簡; 黎简 see PL2718.I117
2718.I15	Li, Ju-chen, ca. 1763-ca. 1830. 李汝珍 (Table P-PZ40)
2718.I16	Li, Jui-ch'ing, 1867-1920. 李瑞清 (Table P-PZ40)
2718.I166	Li, Kuei-yü, 19th cent. 李桂玉 (Table P-PZ40)
2718.I17	Li, Kung, 1659-1733. 李塨 (Table P-PZ40)
2718.I175	Li, Lüyuan, 1707-1790. 李綠園; 李绿园 (Table P-PZ40)
2718.I18	Li, O, 1692-1752. 厲鶚; 厉鹗 (Table P-PZ40)
2718.I19	Li, Pai-ch'uan, 18th cent. 李百川 (Table P-PZ40)
2718.I2	Li, Po-yüan, 1867-1906. 李伯元 (Table P-PZ40)
	Li, Ruiqing, 1867-1920. 李瑞清 see PL2718.I16
	Li, Ruzhen, ca. 1763-ca. 1830. 李汝珍 see PL2718.I15
2718.I215	Li, Shenchan, b. 1824. 黎申產; 黎申产 (Table P-PZ40)

Chinese language and literature
Chinese literature
Individual authors and works
Qing dynasty, 1644-1912
L -- Continued

2718.I22	Li, Tiaoyuan, 1734-1803. 李調元; 李调元 (Table P-PZ40)
2718.I24	Li, Tz'u-ming, 1830-1894. 李慈銘; 李慈铭 (Table P-PZ40)
2718.I243	Li, Yang, 1759-1791. 李暘; 李旸 (Table P-PZ40)
2718.I246	Li, Yesi, 1622-1680. 李鄴嗣; 李邺嗣 (Table P-PZ40)
	Li, Yong, 1627-1705. 李顒; 李颙 see PL2718.I26
	Li, Yongqing, 1829-1898. 李用清 see PL2718.I27
2718.I25	Li, Yü-t'ang, fl. 1835. 李雨堂 (Table P-PZ40)
2718.I26	Li, Yung, 1627-1705. 李顒; 李颙 (Table P-PZ40)
2718.I27	Li, Yung-ch'ing, 1829-1898. 李用清 (Table P-PZ40)
	Li, Yutang, fl. 1835. 李雨堂 see PL2718.I25
2718.I29	Liang, Chang-chü, 1775-1849. 梁章鉅; 梁章钜 (Table P-PZ40)
	Liang, Dingfen, 1859-1919. 梁鼎芬 see PL2718.I35
2718.I33	Liang, Fen, 1641-1729. 梁份 (Table P-PZ40)
2718.I35	Liang, Ting-fen, 1859-1919. 梁鼎芬 (Table P-PZ40)
2718.I37	Liang, Tingnan, 1796-1861. 梁廷柟 (梁廷枏); 梁廷枏 (Table P-PZ40)
	Liang, Zhangju, 1775-1849. 梁章鉅; 梁章钜 see PL2718.I29
2718.I45	Lin, Changyi, 1803-1876. 林昌彝 (Table P-PZ40)
2718.I5	Lin, Shu, 1852-1924. 林紓; 林纾 (Table P-PZ40)
2718.I52	Lin, Sijin, 1873-1953. 林思進; 林思进 (Table P-PZ40)
2718.I53	Lin, Weichao, 1868-1934. 林維朝 (Table P-PZ40)
2718.I538	Lin, Zexu, 1785-1850. 林则徐 (Table P-PZ40)
2718.I56	Lin-ho-shan-jen. 臨鶴山人; 临鹤山人 (Table P-PZ40)
2718.I58	Ling, Tingkan, 1757-1809. 凌廷堪 (Table P-PZ40)
	Linheshanren. 臨鶴山人; 临鹤山人 see PL2718.I56
2718.I674	Lirenheqiu, 18th century 里人何求 (Table P-PZ40)
	Liu, Dakui, 1698-1779. 劉大櫆; 刘大櫆 see PL2718.I895
2718.I8	Liu, E, 1857-1909. 劉鶚; 刘鹗 (Table P-PZ40)
2718.I84	Liu, Hsien-t'ing, 1648-1695. 劉獻廷; 刘献廷 (Table P-PZ40)
2718.I853	Liu, Ju-shih, 1617-1664. 柳如是 (Table P-PZ40)
	Liu, Rushi, 1617-1664. 柳如是 see PL2718.I853
2718.I89	Liu, Shipei, 1884-1919. 劉師培; 刘师培 (Table P-PZ40)
2718.I895	Liu, Ta-k'uei, 1698-1779. 劉大櫆; 刘大櫆 (Table P-PZ40)

Chinese language and literature
Chinese literature
Individual authors and works
Qing dynasty, 1644-1912
L -- Continued

2718.I9	Liu, Tiren, jin shi 1655. 劉體仁; 刘体仁 (Table P-PZ40)
2718.I94	Liu, Tung-hsü, 19th cent. 劉東序; 刘东序 (Table P-PZ40)
	Liu, Xianting, 1648-1695. 劉獻廷; 刘献廷 see PL2718.I84
2718.I96	Liu, Xingsan, 19th cent. 劉省三; 刘省三 (Table P-PZ40)
2718.I97	Liu, Yusong, 1818-1867. 劉毓崧; 刘毓崧 (Table P-PZ40)
2718.U2	Lü, Fu, fl. 1722-1732. 呂撫; 吕抚 (Table P-PZ40)
2718.U22	Lü, Hsiung, ca. 1640-ca. 1722. 呂熊; 吕熊 (Table P-PZ40)
2718.U23	Lü, Liuliang, 1629-1683. 呂留良; 吕留良 (Table P-PZ40)
2718.U235	Lu, Longqi, 1630-1693. 陸隴其; 陆陇其 (Table P-PZ40)
	Lü, Xiong, ca. 1640-ca. 1722. 呂熊; 吕熊 see PL2718.U22
2718.U245	Lu, Yingyang, ca. 1572-ca. 1658. 陸應暘; 陆应旸 (Table P-PZ40)
2718.U5	Lung, Chi-tung, 1845-1900. 龍繼棟; 龙继栋 (Table P-PZ40)
2719	M
	The author number is determined by the second letter of the name
	Subarrange each author by Table P-PZ40
2719.A17	Ma, Changhai, 1667-1744. 馬長海; 马长海 (Table P-PZ40)
2719.A2	Ma, Chien-chung, 1844-1900. 馬建忠; 马建忠 (Table P-PZ40)
2719.A225	Ma, Shitao, 1809-1875. 馬世燾; 马世焘 (Table P-PZ40)
	Ma, Jianzhong, 1844-1900. 馬建忠; 马建忠 see PL2719.A2
2719.A29	Mantuoluoshizhuren. 曼陀羅室主人; 曼陀罗室主人 (Table P-PZ40)
2719.A34	Mao, Xianglin, b. ca. 1815. 毛祥麟 (Table P-PZ40)
(2719.A38)	Masaoka, Shiki, 1867-1902. 正岡子規 see PL811.A83
2719.E33	Mei, Dingzuo, 1549-1615. 梅鼎祚 (Table P-PZ40)
	Mengmengxiansheng see PL2718.I56

Chinese language and literature
Chinese literature
Individual authors and works
Qing dynasty, 1644-1912
M

2719.I17   Miao, Quansun, 1844-1919. 繆荃孫; 缪荃孙 (Table P-PZ40)
(2719.I56)   Minagawa, Kien, 1734-1807. 皆川淇園
                        see PL799.M47
2719.I6   Mingjiaozhongren. 名教中人 (Table P-PZ40)
2720   N
                    The author number is determined by the second letter of
                        the name
                    Subarrange each author by Table P-PZ40
2720.A2   Na-lan, Hsing-te, 1655-1685. 納蘭性德; 纳兰性德
                        (Table P-PZ40)
2720.A213   Na-yin-chü-shih. 訥音居士; 讷音居士 (Table P-PZ40)
(2720.A215)   Nakajima, Sōin, 1799?-1855. 中島棕隠
                        see PL799.N233
                    Nalan, Xingde, 1655-1685. 納蘭性德; 纳兰性德 see
                        PL2720.A2
(2720.A22)   Nam, Ku-man, 1629-1711. 南九萬
                        see PL989.56.K86
2720.A23   Nanbidunsou. 南鄙遯叟 (Table P-PZ40)
(2720.A24)   Natsume, Sōseki, 1867-1916. 夏目漱石
                        see PL812.A8
                    Nayinjushi. 訥音居士; 讷音居士 see PL2720.A213
(2720.I25)   Nichisei, 1623-1668. 日政
                        see PL795.N53
2721   O
                    The author number is determined by the second letter of
                        the name
                    Subarrange each author by Table P-PZ40
(2721.A24)   O, Chin-yŏng, 1868-1944. 吳震泳
                        see PL990.58.C45
(2721.A27)   O, To-il, 1645-1703. 吳道一
                        see PL989.58.T65
(2721.K56)   Okkotsu, Taiken, 1806-1859. 乙骨耐軒
                        see PL799.O35
2722   P
                    The author number is determined by the second letter of
                        the name
                    Subarrange each author by Table P-PZ40
2722.A34   Pai-i-chü-shih. 百一居士 (Table P-PZ40)
(2722.A38)   Pak, Che-ga, 1750-1815. 朴齊家
                        see PL989.62.C4

Chinese language and literature
Chinese literature
Individual authors and works
Qing dynasty, 1644-1912
P -- Continued

(2722.A4)	Pak, Chi-wǒn, 1737-1805. 朴趾源 see PL989.62.C5
(2722.A43)	Pak, P'il-chu, 1665-1748. 朴弼周 see PL989.62.P55
(2722.A44)	Pak, Son-gyŏng, 1713-1782. 朴孫慶 see PL989.62.S66
2722.A57	P'an, Fei-sheng. 潘飛聲; 潘飞声 (Table P-PZ40)
2722.A58	Pan, Lun'en, ca. 1796-ca. 1855. 潘綸恩; 潘纶恩 (Table P-PZ40)
2722.A593	Pan, Zutong, 1829-1902. 潘祖同 (Table P-PZ40)
2722.A6	Pao, Tung-li, 19th cent. 鮑東里; 鲍东里 (Table P-PZ40)
2722.A64	Pao-t'ing, 1840-1890. 寶廷; 宝廷 (Table P-PZ40)
2722.E44	Pei, Hengzi, 17th cent. 佩蘅子 (Table P-PZ40)
2722.E45	P'eng, Chao-sun, 1769-1821. 彭兆蓀; 彭兆荪 (Table P-PZ40)
2722.E464	Peng, Shaosheng, 1740-1796. 彭紹升; 彭绍升 (Table P-PZ40)
2722.E47	Peng, Sunyi, 1615-1673. 彭孫貽; 彭孙贻 (Table P-PZ40)
2722.E478	Peng, Sunyu, 1631-1700. 彭孫遹; 彭孙遹 (Table P-PZ40)
	Peng, Zhaosun, 1769-1821. 彭兆蓀; 彭兆荪 see PL2722.E45
2722.U15	Pu, Lin, 18th/19th cent. 浦琳 (Table P-PZ40)
2722.U2	Pu, Songling, 1640-1715. 蒲松齡; 蒲松龄 (Table P-PZ40)
2722.5	Q

	The author number is determined by the second letter of
	        the name
	    Subarrange each author by Table P-PZ40
	    Qi, Junzao, 1793-1866. 祁寯藻 see PL2705.I14
	    Qi, Zhouhua, 1698-1767. 齊周華; 齐周华 see
	        PL2705.I13
	    Qian, Cai, fl. 1729. 錢彩; 钱彩 see PL2705.I3
	    Qian, Daxin, 1728-1804. 錢大昕; 钱大昕 see
	        PL2705.I277

2722.5.I52	Qian, Guisen, jih shi 1850. 錢桂森; 钱桂森 (Table P-PZ40)
	Qian, Qianyi, 1582-1664. 錢謙益; 钱谦益 see PL2701 Qian, Taiji, 1791-1863. 錢泰吉; 钱泰吉 see PL2705.I28

Chinese language and literature
Chinese literature
Individual authors and works
Qing dynasty, 1644-1912
Q -- Continued

Qian, Yong, 1759-1844. 錢泳; 钱泳 see PL2705.I34
Qian, Zeng, 1629-1701. 錢曾; 钱曾 see PL2705.I32
Qianlong, Emperor of China, 1711-1799 see PL2702
Qiaoyunshanren. 樵雲山人; 樵云山人 see
    PL2705.I268
Qin, Zichen, fl. 1795. 秦子忱 see PL2705.I538
Qingxincaizi. 青心才子 see PL2705.I548
Qiu, Fengjia, 1864-1912. 丘逢甲 see PL2705.I83
Qiu, Jin, 1875-1907. 秋瑾 see PL2705.I8
Qiu, Xinru, fl. 1857. 邱心如 see PL2705.I85

2722.5.U35   Qu, Bingyun, 1767-1810. 屈秉筠 (Table P-PZ40)
                    Quan, Zuwang, 1705-1755. 全祖望 see PL2704
                    Quyuan. 蘧園; 蘧园 see PL2705.U8
2723   R
                    The author number is determined by the second letter of
                        the name
                    Subarrange each author by Table P-PZ40
(2723.A5)   Rai, San'yo, 1780-1832. 賴山陽
                      see PL799.R34
                    Ren, Xuan, ju ren 1788. 任璇 see PL2714.E62
(2723.I48)   Rikunyo, 1734?-1801. 六如
                      see PL799.R55
                    Ruan, Kuisheng, 1727-1789. 阮葵生 see PL2714.U3
                    Ruan, Yuan, 1764-1849. 阮元 see PL2714.U35
                    Rulianjushi, 18th cent. 如蓮居士; 如莲居士 see
                      PL2714.U27
(2723.Y64)   Ryōkan, 1758-1831. 良寛
                      see PL797.6
2724   S
                    The author number is determined by the second letter of
                        the name
                    Subarrange each author by Table P-PZ40
(2724.A32)   Sai, Taitei, b. 1823?. 蔡大鼎
                      see PL799.S15
(2724.A35)   Saigō, Takamori, 1828-1877. 西鄉隆盛
                      see PL799.S16
(2724.A38)   Sato, Issai, 1772-1859. 佐藤一齋
                      see PL799.S28
2724.H27   Sha, Yüan-ping, 1855-1927. 沙元炳 (Table P-PZ40)
2724.H3   Shao, Tingcai, 1648-1711. 邵廷采 (Table P-PZ40)
2724.H36   Shen, Ch'eng-chang, 1859-1898. 沈成章 (Table P-
                    PZ40)

Chinese language and literature
Chinese literature
Individual authors and works
Qing dynasty, 1644-1912
S -- Continued

2724.H37	Shen, Ch'i-feng, b. 1741. 沈起鳳; 沈起凤 (Table P-PZ40)
2724.H372	Shen, Chia-pen, 1840-1913. 沈家本 (Table P-PZ40)
2724.H38	Shen, Ch'ien, 1620-1670. 沈謙; 沈谦 (Table P-PZ40)
	Shen, Deqian, 1673-1769. 沈德潛; 沈德潜 see PL2724.H47
2724.H4	Shen, Fu, 1763-ca. 1808. 沈復; 沈复 (Table P-PZ40)
	Shen, Jiaben, 1840-1913. 沈家本 see PL2724.H372
	Shen, Qian, 1620-1670. 沈謙; 沈谦 see PL2724.H38
	Shen, Qifeng, b. 1741. 沈起鳳; 沈起凤 see PL2724.H37
2724.H467	Shen, Tao, ju ren 1810. 沈濤; 沈涛 (Table P-PZ40)
2724.H47	Shen, Te-ch'ien, 1673-1769. 沈德潛; 沈德潜 (Table P-PZ40)
2724.H475	Shen, Tseng-chih, 1850-1922. 沈曾植; 沈曾植 (Table P-PZ40)
	Shi, Menglan, 1813-1898. 史夢蘭; 史梦兰 see PL2724.H487
2724.H4825	Shi, Runzhang, 1619-1683. 施閏章 (Table P-PZ40)
	Shi, Shiji, 1855-1922. 施士洁 see PL2724.H49
	Shi, Yukun, 19th cent. 石玉崑; 石玉昆 see PL2724.H5
	Shen, Zengzhi, 1850-1922. 沈曾植 see PL2724.H475
	Shi, Zhenlin, 1692-1778. 史震林 see PL2724.H485
2724.H485	Shih, Chen-lin, 1692-1778. 史震林 (Table P-PZ40)
2724.H487	Shih, Meng-lan, 1813-1898. 史夢蘭; 史梦兰 (Table P-PZ40)
2724.H49	Shih, Shih-chi, 1855-1922. 施士洁 (Table P-PZ40)
2724.H5	Shih, Yü-k'un, 19th cent. 石玉崑; 石玉昆 (Table P-PZ40)
2724.H58	Shu, Wei, 1765-1815. 舒位 (Table P-PZ40)
(2724.I53)	Sin, Kwang-su, 1712-1775. 申光洙 see PL989.73.K96
(2724.I55)	Sin, Wi, 1769-1845. 申緯 see PL989.73.W5
	Siqiaojushi. 四橋居士; 四桥居士 see PL2724.S8
(2724.O25)	Sŏ, Yu-yŏng, b. 1801. 徐有英 see PL989.74.Y89
(2724.O53)	Song, Hyŏn-sŏp, 1862-1938. 宋賢燮 see PL990.78.H96
(2724.O54)	Song, Ki-myŏn. 宋基冕 see PL989.78.K56

Chinese language and literature
Chinese literature
Individual authors and works
Qing dynasty, 1644-1912
S -- Continued

(2724.O55)	Song, Kŭng-sŏp, 1873-1933 see PL990.78.K86
(2724.O57)	Sŏng, Tae-jung, 1732-1812. 成大中 see PL989.78.T34
2724.O6	Song, Wan, 1614-1673. 宋琬 (Table P-PZ40)
2724.O64	Song, Xiangfeng, 1776-1860. 宋翔鳳; 宋翔凤 (Table P-PZ40)
	Song, Xiang, 1757-1826. 宋湘 see PL2724.U537
	Song, Yun. 松雲; 松云 see PL2724.U56
	Songyun, 1752-1835. 松筠 see PL2724.U57
2724.S8	Ssu-ch'iao-chü-shih. 四橋居士; 四桥居士 (Table P-PZ40)
2724.U2	Su, Manshu, 1884-1918. 蘇曼殊; 苏曼殊 (Table P-PZ40)
2724.U22	Su'anzhuren, 18th cent. 蘇庵主人; 苏庵主人 (Table P-PZ40)
2724.U45	Suiyuanxiashi. 隨緣下士; 隨緣下士 (Table P-PZ40)
2724.U46	Sun, Chih-wei, 1620-1687. 孫枝蔚; 孙枝蔚 (Table P-PZ40)
2724.U48	Sun, Jan, ca. 1684-ca. 1774. 孫髯; 孙髯 (Table P-PZ40)
2724.U495	Sun, Qutian. 孫蒅田; 孙蒅田 (Table P-PZ40)
	Sun, Ran, ca. 1684-ca. 1774. 孫髯; 孙髯 see PL2724.U48
2724.U5	Sun, Yuanheng, fl. 1705-1708. 孫元衡; 孙元衡 (Table P-PZ40)
2724.U52	Sun, Yuanxiang, 1760-1829. 孫原湘 (Table P-PZ40)
	Sun, Zhiwei, 1620-1687. 孫枝蔚; 孙枝蔚 see PL2724.U46
2724.U537	Sung, Hsiang, 1757-1826. 宋湘 (Table P-PZ40)
2724.U56	Sung, Yün. 松雲; 松云 (Table P-PZ40)
2724.U57	Sung-yün, 1752-1835. 松筠 (Table P-PZ40)
2725	T - Tai The author number is determined by the second letter of the name Subarrange each author by Table P-PZ40
2725.A68	Ta-fu-lao-jen, chü jen 1885. 大浮老人 (Table P-PZ40)
2726	Tai, Chen, 1724-1777. 戴震 (Table P-PZ39)

	Chinese language and literature
	Chinese literature
	Individual authors and works
	Qing dynasty, 1644-1912 -- Continued
2727	Tai - Tseng
	The author number is determined by the second letter of the name
	Subarrange each author by Table P-PZ40 unless otherwise specified
2727.A3	Tai, Ming-shih, 1653-1713. 戴名世 (Table P-PZ40)
2727.A38	Tai, Yen-ju, 1864-1916. 戴延儒 (Table P-PZ40)
2727.A52	Tan, Renfeng, 1860-1920. 譚人鳳; 谭人凤 (Table P-PZ40)
2727.A55	Tan, Sitong, 1865-1898. 譚嗣同; 谭嗣同 (Table P-PZ40)
2727.A56	Tan, Xian, 1830-1901. 譚獻; 谭献 (Table P-PZ40)
2727.A57	Tan-sou. 誕叟; 诞叟 (Table P-PZ40)
2727.A6	T'ang, Chen, 1630-1704. 唐甄 (Table P-PZ40)
2727.A62	T'ang, I-fen, 1778-1853. 湯貽汾; 汤贻汾 (Table P-PZ40)
2727.A67	Tang, Sunhua, 1634-1723. 唐孫華; 唐孙华 (Table P-PZ40)
	Tang, Yifen, 1778-1853. 湯貽汾; 汤贻汾 see PL2727.A62
2727.A69	Tang, Ying, 1682-1756. 唐英 (Table P-PZ40)
	Tang, Zhen, 1630-1704. 唐甄 see PL2727.A6
2727.A75	Tao, Zhenhuai, 17th cent. 陶貞懷; 陶贞怀 (Table P-PZ40)
2727.E54	Teng, T'ing-chen, 1775-1846. 鄧廷楨; 邓廷桢 (Table P-PZ40)
2727.I38	Tian, Wen, 1635-1704. 田雯 (Table P-PZ40)
	Tianhuacaizi. 天花才子 see PL2727.I43
	Tianhuazangzhuren. 天花藏主人 see PL2727.I44
	Tianzhuisheng. 天贅生; 天赘生 see PL2727.I42
2727.I42	T'ien-chui-sheng. 天贅生; 天赘生 (Table P-PZ40)
2727.I43	T'ien-hua-ts'ai-tzu. 天花才子 (Table P-PZ40)
2727.I44	T'ien-hua-tsang-chu-jen. 天花藏主人 (Table P-PZ40)
2727.I56	Ting, Chih-t'ang, 1837-1902. 丁治棠 (Table P-PZ40)
2727.I59	Ting, Yao-k'ang, 1599-1669. 丁耀亢 (Table P-PZ40)
2727.S14	Ts'ai, Yüan-fang, fl. 1736-1770. 蔡元放 (Table P-PZ40)
2727.S17	Tsang, Hsüeh-lou, 1864-1932. 臧雪樓; 臧雪楼 (Table P-PZ40)
	Ts'ao, Hsüeh-ch'in, ca. 1717-1763. 曹雪芹 (Table P-PZ38 modified)
	Hong lou meng
2727.S2 date	Editions. By date

Chinese language and literature
Chinese literature
Individual authors and works
Qing dynasty, 1644-1912
Tai - Tseng
Ts'ao, Hsüeh-ch'in, ca. 1717-1763. 曹雪芹
Hong lou meng -- Continued

2727.S2A11-.S2A19	Editions. By editor, if given
2727.S2A2-.S2A59	Translations of Hong lou meng
2727.S2A6	Selections from Hong lou meng. By date
(2727.S2A61-.S2A78)	Separate works see PL2727.S2+
2727.S2A79-.S2Z	Biography and criticism Including criticism of Hong lou meng
2727.S28	Ts'ao, Wu-kang, 19th cent. 曹梧岡; 曹梧冈 (Table P-PZ40)
2727.S29	Ts'ao, Yin, 1658-1712. 曹寅 (Table P-PZ40)
2727.S3	Ts'ao, Yüan-pi, b. 1879. 曹元弼 (Table P-PZ40)
2727.S4	Tseng, Chi-tse, 1839-1890. 曾紀澤; 曾紀泽 (Table P-PZ40)
2728	Tseng, Kuo-fan, 1811-1872. 曾國藩; 曾国藩 (Table P-PZ39)

2729	Tseng - Tz
	    The author number is determined by the second letter of
	      the name
	    Subarrange each author by Table P-PZ40

2729.S4	Tseng, P'u, 1872-1935. 曾樸; 曾朴 (Table P-PZ40)
2729.S413	Tseng, Yen-tung, 1750-1825? 曾衍東; 曾衍东 (Table P-PZ40)
2729.S55	Tsou, Chung, ca. 1827-ca. 1886. 鄒鍾; 邹钟 (Table P-PZ40)
2729.S58	Tsou, T'ao, 19th cent. 鄒弢; 邹弢 (Table P-PZ40)
2729.S76	Tsubouchi, Shōyō, 1859-1935. 坪內逍遥 (Table P-PZ40)
2729.S79	Ts'ui, Hsiang-ch'uan, fl. 1836. 崔象川 (Table P-PZ40)
2729.S794	Tsui-yüeh-shan-jen, fl. 1804-1876. 醉月山人 (Table P-PZ40)
2729.U2	Tu, Kang, fl. 1775. 杜綱; 杜纲 (Table P-PZ40)
2729.U25	Tu, Shen, 1744-1801. 屠紳; 屠绅 (Table P-PZ40)
2729.U3	Tuan, Yü-ts'ai, 1735-1815. 段玉裁 (Table P-PZ40)
2729.U43	Tun-ch'eng, 1734-1792. 敦誠; 敦诚 (Table P-PZ40)
2729.U47	Tun-min, 1729-1796. 敦敏 (Table P-PZ40)
2729.U478	Tung, Han, 17th cent. 董含 (Table P-PZ40)
2729.U49	Tung-kuo, Tzu, 19th cent. 東郭子; 东郭子 (Table P-PZ40)
2729.U5	Tung-lu-ku-k'uang-sheng, 17th cent. 東魯古狂生; 东鲁古狂生 (Table P-PZ40)

Chinese language and literature
Chinese literature
Individual authors and works
Qing dynasty, 1644-1912 -- Continued

2730	U
	The author number is determined by the second letter of the name
	Subarrange each author by Table P-PZ40
2731	V
	The author number is determined by the second letter of the name
	Subarrange each author by Table P-PZ40
2732	W
	The author number is determined by the second letter of the name
	Subarrange each author by Table P-PZ40
2732.A3	Wan, Shu, fl. 1680-1692. 萬樹; 万树 (Table P-PZ40)
2732.A34	Wang, Chao, 1859?-1935? 王照 (Table P-PZ40)
2732.A35	Wang, Chao-yung, 1861-1939. 汪兆鏞; 王兆镛 (Table P-PZ40)
2732.A37	Wang, Chi, d. ca. 1796. 汪寄 (Table P-PZ40)
2732.A373	Wang, Chih-ch'ang, 1837-1895. 汪之昌 (Table P-PZ40)
2732.A4	Wang, Chung, 1745-1794. 汪中 (Table P-PZ40)
	Wang, Duo, 1592-1652. 王鐸; 王铎 see PL2732.A59
2732.A44	Wang, Fuzhi, 1619-1692. 王夫之 (Table P-PZ40)
	Wang, Guowei, 1877-1927. 王國維; 王国维 see PL2732.A5
	Wang, Hongxu, 1645-1723. 王鴻緒; 王鸿绪 see PL2732.A463
2732.A444	Wang, Hsi-sun, 1786-1847. 汪喜孫; 汪喜孙 (Table P-PZ40)
2732.A463	Wang, Hung-hsü, 1645-1723. 王鴻緒; 王鸿绪 (Table P-PZ40)
2732.A466	Wang, Ju-pi, d. 1806. 王汝璧 (Table P-PZ40)
2732.A5	Wang, Kuo-wei, 1877-1927. 王國維; 王国维 (Table P-PZ40)
2732.A53	Wang, Maohong, 1668-1741. 王懋竑 (Table P-PZ40)
2732.A534	Wang, Maolin, 1640-1688. 汪懋麟 (Table P-PZ40)
2732.A535	Wang, Mengji, 17th cent. 王夢吉; 王梦吉 (Table P-PZ40)
2732.A54	Wang, Niansun, 1744-1832. 王念孫; 王念孙 (Table P-PZ40)
2732.A547	Wang, Pao-yung, b. 1827. 王寶庸; 王宝庸 (Table P-PZ40)
2732.A55	Wang, Pengyun, 1849-1904. 王鵬運; 王鹏运 (Table P-PZ40)

Chinese language and literature
Chinese literature
Individual authors and works
Qing dynasty, 1644-1912
W -- Continued

	Wang, Rubi, d. 1806. 王汝璧 see PL2732.A466
2732.A56	Wang, Shizhen, 1634-1711. 王士禛; 王士禎 (Table P-PZ40)
2732.A563	Wang, Shouxun, 1864- 王守恂 (Table P-PZ40)
2732.A564	Wang, Shu, 1636-1699. 王據; 王摅 (Table P-PZ40)
2732.A58	Wang, Tao, 1828-1897. 王韜; 王韬 (Table P-PZ40)
2732.A59	Wang, To, 1592-1652. 王鐸; 王铎 (Table P-PZ40)
	Wang, Tongyu, 1855-1941. 王同愈 see PL2732.A62
2732.A62	Wang, T'ung-yü, 1855-1941. 王同愈 (Table P-PZ40)
2732.A65	Wang, Wenzhi, 1730-1802. 王文治 (Table P-PZ40)
	Wang, Xisun, 1786-1847. 汪喜孫; 汪喜孙 see PL2732.A444
2732.A68	Wang, Yin-chih, 1766-1834. 王引之 (Table P-PZ40)
2732.A683	Wang, Yingkui, 1683-ca. 1760. 王應奎; 王应奎 (Table P-PZ40)
	Wang, Yinzhi, 1766-1834. 王引之 see PL2732.A68
2732.A73	Wang, Yun, 1749-1819. 王筠 (Table P-PZ40)
2732.A74	Wang, Yun, 1784-1854. 王筠 (Table P-PZ40)
2732.A75	Wang, Yün, b. 1816. 汪鋆 (Table P-PZ40)
	Wang, Zhao, 1859?-1935? 王照 see PL2732.A34
	Wang, Zhaoyong, 1861-1939. 汪兆鏞; 王兆镛 see PL2732.A35
	Wang, Zhichang, 1837-1895. 汪之昌 see PL2732.A373
	Wang, Zhong, 1745-1794. 汪中 see PL2732.A4
2732.E52	Wei, Hsi, 1624-1681. 魏禧 (Table P-PZ40)
2732.E525	Wei, Hsiang-shu, 1617-1687. 魏象樞; 魏象枢 (Table P-PZ40)
2732.E537	Wei, Tzu-an, 1819-1874. 魏子安 (Table P-PZ40)
	Wei, Xi, 1624-1681. 魏禧 see PL2732.E52
	Wei, Xiangshu, 1617-1687. 魏象樞; 魏象枢 see PL2732.E525
2732.E538	Wei, Xiumeng, 1856-1929. 韋綉孟 ; 韦绣孟 (Table P-PZ40)
2732.E54	Wei, Yuan, 1794-1857. 魏源 (Table P-PZ40)
	Wei, Zi'an, 1819-1874. 魏子安 see PL2732.E537
2732.E57	Wen-k'ang, fl. 1842-1851. 文康 (Table P-PZ40)
2732.E59	Weng, Fanggang, 1733-1818. 翁方綱; 翁方纲 (Table P-PZ40)
2732.E63	Weng, Tao, jin shi 1890. 翁燾; 翁焘 (Table P-PZ40)
	Wenkang, fl. 1842-1851. 文康 see PL2732.E57

Chinese language and literature
Chinese literature
Individual authors and works
Qing dynasty, 1644-1912
W -- Continued

2732.U16	Wu, Changshuo, 1844-1927. 吳昌碩; 吴昌硕 (Table P-PZ40)
2732.U184	Wu, Chao-ch'ien, 1631-1684. 吳兆騫; 吴兆骞 (Table P-PZ40)
2732.U19	Wu, Chia-chi, 1618-1684. 吳嘉紀; 吴嘉紀 (Table P-PZ40)
2732.U2	Wu, Ching-heng, 1864-1953. 呉敬恒; 吴敬恒 (Table P-PZ40)
2732.U22	Wu, Ching-tzu, 1701-1754. 吳敬梓; 吴敬梓 (Table P-PZ40)
2732.U226	Wu, Hsiang, chin shih 1713. 吳襄; 吴襄 (Table P-PZ40)
2732.U227	Wu, Hsüan, 18th cent. 吳璿; 吴璿 (Table P-PZ40)
2732.U228	Wu, I-feng, 1742-1819. 吳翌鳳; 吴翌凤 (Table P-PZ40)
	Wu, Jiaji, 1618-1684. 吳嘉紀; 吴嘉紀 see PL2732.U19
	Wu, Jianren, 1866-1910. 吳趼人; 吴趼人 see PL2732.U24
	Wu, Jingheng, 1864-1953. 呉敬恒; 吴敬恒 see PL2732.U2
	Wu, Jingzi, 1701-1754. 吳敬梓; 吴敬梓 see PL2732.U22
2732.U23	Wu, Ju-lun, 1840-1903. 吳汝綸; 吴汝纶 (Table P-PZ40)
2732.U233	Wu, K'o-tu, 1812-1879. 吳可讀; 吴可读 (Table P-PZ40)
2732.U2337	Wu, Li, 1632-1718. 吳歷; 吴历 (Table P-PZ40)
2732.U234	Wu, Lu, 1845-1912. 吳魯; 吴鲁 (Table P-PZ40)
	Wu, Rulun, 1840-1903. 吳汝綸; 吴汝纶 see PL2732.U23
2732.U236	Wu, Tzu-kuang, b. 1819. 吳子光; 吴子光 (Table P-PZ40)
2732.U238	Wu, Weiye, 1609-1672. 吳偉業; 吴伟业 (Table P-PZ40)
2732.U24	Wu, Woyao, 1866-1910. 吳沃堯; 吴沃尧 (Table P-PZ40)
	Wu, Xiang, jin shi 1713. 吳襄; 吴襄 see PL2732.U226
	Wu, Xuan, 18th cent. 吳璿; 吴璿 see PL2732.U227
	Wu, Yifeng, 1742-1819. 吳翌鳳; 吴翌凤 see PL2732.U228

Chinese language and literature
Chinese literature
Individual authors and works
Qing dynasty, 1644-1912
W -- Continued

2732.U26   Wu, Yuchang, 18th/19th cent. 吳毓昌; 吴毓昌 (Table P-PZ40)

Wu, Zhaoqian, 1631-1684. 吳兆騫; 吴兆骞 see PL2732.U184

Wu, Ziguang, b. 1819. 吳子光; 吴子光 see PL2732.U236

2732.U267   Wumingzi, 18th/19th cent. 無名子; 无名子 (Table P-PZ40)

2732.U27   Wuseshizhuren, ju ren 1738. 五色石主人 (Table P-PZ40)

2732.5   X

The author number is determined by the second letter of the name

Subarrange each author by Table P-PZ40

Xia, Jingqu. 夏敬渠 see PL2710.S5

Xia, Zengyou, 1861-1924. 夏曾佑 see PL2710.S5124

Xiaoyaozi, 18th/19th cent. 逍遙子 see PL2710.S517

Xie, Qikun, 1737-1802. 謝啓昆; 谢启昆 see PL2710.S53

Xie, Xumin, 1845-1890. 謝緒民; 谢绪民 see PL2710.S55

Xihongjushi. 惜紅居士; 惜红居士 see PL2710.S44

Xilengyeqiao. 西冷野樵 see PL2710.S47

Xinyuanzhuren, 17th/18th cent. 心遠主人; 心远主人 see PL2710.S62

Xiyintangzhuren. 惜陰堂主人; 惜阴堂主人 see PL2710.S48

Xu, Chengzu, 18th cent. 許承祖; 许承祖 see PL2710.S822

Xu, Feng'en, d. 1887. 許奉恩; 许奉恩 see PL2710.S8335

Xu, Jue, 1843-1916. 許珏; 许珏 see PL2710.S83

Xu, Nanying, 1855-1917. 許南英; 许南英 see PL2710.S84

Xu, Qianxue, 1631-1694. 徐乾學; 徐乾学 see PL2710.S823

Xu, Qiu, 1636-1708. 徐釚 see PL2710.S824

Xu, Wenjing, 1667-1756? 徐文靖 see PL2710.S864

Xu, Xishen. 許禧身; 许禧身 see PL2710.S834

Xu, Zonggan, 1796-1866. 徐宗幹; 徐宗干 see PL2710.S86

Chinese language and literature
 Chinese literature
  Individual authors and works
   Qing dynasty, 1644-1912
    X -- Continued
     Xu, Zuosu, 1616-1684. 徐作肅; 徐作肅 see
      PL2710.S85
     Xuan, Ding, 1832-1880? 宣鼎 see PL2710.S88

2733	Y - Yu

     The author number is determined by the second letter of
      the name
     Subarrange each author by Table P-PZ40

(2733.A48)	Yanada, Zeigan, 1672-1757. 梁田蛻巖 see PL795.Y357
(2733.A52)	Yanagawa, Seigan, 1789-1858. 梁川星巖 see PL799.Y34
2733.A55	Yang, Chaoguan, 1710-1788. 楊潮觀; 杨潮观 (Table P-PZ40)
2733.A552	Yang, Chung-hsi, 1865-1940. 楊鐘羲; 杨钟羲 (Table P-PZ40)
	Yang, Daheng. 楊大脝 see PL2733.A56
2733.A553	Yang, Enshou, 1835-1891. 楊恩壽; 杨恩寿 (Table P- PZ40)
2733.A56	Yang, Ta-heng. 楊大脝 (Table P-PZ40)
	Yang, Zhongxi, 1865-1940. 楊鐘羲; 杨钟羲 see PL2733.A552
	Yanxiasanren. 煙霞散人; 烟霞散人 see PL2733.E56
	Yanxiazhuren, 18th cent. 煙霞主人; 烟霞主人 see PL2733.E55
2733.A565	Yao, Chen-tsung, 1843-1906. 姚振宗 (Table P-PZ40)
2733.A567	Yao, Hsieh, 1805-1864. 姚燮 (Table P-PZ40)
2733.A57	Yao, Nai, 1732-1815. 姚鼐 (Table P-PZ40)
	Yao, Xie, 1805-1864. 姚燮 see PL2733.A567
2733.A6	Yao, Ying, 1785-1853. 姚瑩; 姚莹 (Table P-PZ40)
	Yao, Zhenzong, 1843-1906. 姚振宗 see PL2733.A565
	Ye, Changchi, 1847?-1917. 葉昌熾; 叶昌炽 see PL2733.E35
	Ye, Jingkui, 1874-1949. 葉景葵; 叶景葵 see PL2733.E354
	Ye, Tingguan, b. 1791. 葉廷琯; 叶廷琯 see PL2733.E4
	Ye, Xie, 1627-1703. 葉燮; 叶燮 see PL2733.E36
2733.E35	Yeh, Ch'ang-ch'ih, 1847?-1917. 葉昌熾; 叶昌炽 (Table P-PZ40)
2733.E354	Yeh, Ching-k'uei, 1874-1949. 葉景葵; 叶景葵 (Table P-PZ40)

Chinese language and literature
Chinese literature
Individual authors and works
Qing dynasty, 1644-1912
Y - Yu -- Continued

2733.E36	Yeh, Hsieh, 1627-1703. 葉燮; 叶燮 (Table P-PZ40)
2733.E4	Yeh, T'ing-kuan, b. 1791. 葉廷琯; 叶廷琯 (Table P-PZ40)
2733.E55	Yen-hsia-chu-jen, 18th cent. 煙霞主人; 烟霞主人 (Table P-PZ40)
2733.E56	Yen-hsia-san-jen. 煙霞散人; 烟霞散人 (Table P-PZ40)
(2733.I128)	Yi, Chae, 1657-1731. 李裁 see PL989.9.C43
(2733.I13)	Yi, Chae, 1680-1746. 李縡 see PL989.9.C433
(2733.I16)	Yi, Chin-sang, 1818-1886. 李震相 see PL989.9.C45
(2733.I18)	Yi, Hak-kyu, 1770-1835. 李學逵 see PL989.9.H35
(2733.I19)	Yi, Hyŏn-il, 1627-1704. 李玄逸 see PL989.9.H96
(2733.I23)	Yi, Kŏn-ch'ang, 1852-1898. 李建昌 see PL989.9.K66
(2733.I28)	Yi, Ŏn-jin, 1740-1766. 李彦瑱 see PL989.9.O66
(2733.I317)	Yi, Sang-jŏk, 1803-1865. 李尚迪 see PL989.9.S24
(2733.I318)	Yi, Sang-jŏng, 1710-1781. 李象靖 see PL989.9.S26
(2733.I32)	Yi, Sŏ-gu, 1754-1825. 李書九 see PL989.9.S64
(2733.I33)	Yi, Tan-sang, 1628-1669. 李端相 see PL989.9.T36
(2733.I34)	Yi, Tong-jun, 1842-1897. 李東浚 see PL989.9.T65
(2733.I36)	Yi, Ŭi-hyŏn, 1669-1745. 李宜顯 see PL989.9.U54
(2733.I37)	Yi, Wŏn-jo, 1792-1871. 李源祚 see PL989.9.W66
2733.I53	Yin-chan-na-hsi, 1837-1892. 尹湛納希; 尹湛纳希 (Table P-PZ40)
2733.I55	Yin-mei-shan-jen. 吟梅山人 (Table P-PZ40)
2733.I56	Yinghe, 1771-1839. 英和 (Table P-PZ40)
	Yinmeishanren. 吟梅山人 see PL2733.I55
	Yiyunshi. 倚雲氏; 倚云氏 see PL2713.Y85
	Yongzheng, Emperor of China, 1677-1735. 雍正 see PL2735.N24

Chinese language and literature
Chinese literature
Individual authors and works
Qing dynasty, 1644-1912
Y - Yu -- Continued
Yongzhong, 1735-1793. 永忠 see PL2735.N26

2733.O83	Yoshida, Shōin, 1830-1859. 吉田松陰 (Table P-PZ40)
	You, Tong, 1618-1704. 尤侗 see PL2733.U16
	Yu, Binshi. 余賓碩; 余宾硕 see PL2733.U152
2733.U14	Yü, Chiao, 18th/19th cent. 俞蛟 (Table P-PZ40)
	Yu, Da, d. 1884. 俞達; 俞达 see PL2733.U153
2733.U144	Yu, Huai, 1616-1696. 余懷 (Table P-PZ40)
	Yu, Jiao, 18th/19th cent. 俞蛟 see PL2733.U14
2733.U152	Yü, Pin-shih. 余賓碩; 余宾硕 (Table P-PZ40)
2733.U153	Yü, Ta, d. 1884. 俞達; 俞达 (Table P-PZ40)
(2733.U155)	Yu, Tŭk-kong, b. 1748?. 柳得恭 see PL989.94.T85
2733.U16	Yu, T'ung, 1618-1704. 尤侗 (Table P-PZ40)
2733.U27	Yu, Wanchun, d. 1849. 俞萬春; 俞万春 (Table P-PZ40)
2734	Yu, Yue, 1821-1906. 俞樾 (Table P-PZ39)
2735	Yu - Yuz
	The author number is determined by the third letter of the name
	Subarrange each author by Table P-PZ40
2735.A25	Yü-an-shih. 遇安氏 (Table P-PZ40)
2735.A44	Yuan, Chang, 1846-1900. 袁昶 (Table P-PZ40)
2735.A45	Yüan, Chia, d. 1853. 袁嘉 (Table P-PZ40)
2735.A5	Yuan, Mei, 1716-1798. 袁枚 (Table P-PZ40)
2735.A56	Yuanhuyanshuisanren, 17th/18th cent. 鴛湖煙水散人; 鸳湖烟水散人 (Table P-PZ40)
2735.E48	Yue, Jun, 1766-1814. 樂鈞; 乐钧 (Table P-PZ40)
2735.L55	Yulinglaoren, 18th cent. 庾嶺勞人; 庾岭劳人 (Table P-PZ40)
2735.N19	Yün-ch'a-wai-shih, 19th cent. 雲槎外史; 云槎外史 (Table P-PZ40)
2735.N2	Yün-chung-tao-jen. 雲中道人; 云中道人 (Table P-PZ40)
	Yunchawaishi, 19th cent. 雲槎外史; 云槎外史 see PL2735.N19
2735.N23	Yunduan, 1671-1704. 蘊端; 蕴端 (Table P-PZ40)
2735.N24	Yung-cheng, Emperor of China, 1677-1735. 雍正 (Table P-PZ40)
2735.N26	Yung-chung, 1735-1793. 永忠 (Table P-PZ40)
	Yunzhongdaoren. 雲中道人; 云中道人 see PL2735.N2

Chinese language and literature
  Chinese literature
   Individual authors and works
    Qing dynasty, 1644-1912 -- Continued

2735.3   Z

      The author number is determined by the second letter of
       the name
      Subarrange each author by Table P-PZ40

      Zang, Xuelou, 1864-1932. 臧雪樓; 臧雪楼 see
       PL2727.S17

      Zeng, Guofan, 1811-1872. 曾國藩; 曾国藩 see
       PL2728

      Zeng, Jize, 1839-1890. 曾紀澤; 曾紀泽 see
       PL2727.S4

      Zeng, Pu, 1872-1935. 曾樸; 曾朴 see PL2729.S4

      Zeng, Yandong, 1750-1825? 曾衍東; 曾衍东 see
       PL2729.S413

      Zha, Shenxing, 1650-1727. 查慎行 see PL2705.A415

2735.3.H36   Zhang, Diaoyuan, 1784-1853. 張調元; 张调元 (Table
       P-PZ40)

      Zhang, Erqi, 1612-1677. 張爾岐; 张尔岐 see
       PL2705.A49

      Zhang, Huiyan, 1761-1802. 張惠言; 张惠言 see
       PL2705.A52

      Zhang, Jian, 1768-1850. 張鑑; 张鉴 see
       PL2705.A454

      Zhang, Jian, 1853-1926. 張謇; 张謇 see
       PL2705.A455

      Zhang, Qigan, b. 1859. 張其淦; 张其淦 see
       PL2705.A45

      Zhang, Qin, 1828-1883. 章嶔; 章嵚 see PL2705.A46

2735.3.H52   Zhang, Shaoxian, fl. 1850. 張紹賢; 张绍贤 (Table P-
       PZ40)

      Zhang, Shu, ca. 1776-1847. 張澍; 张澍 see
       PL2705.A574

      Zhang, Weiping, 1780-1859. 張維屏; 张维屏 see
       PL2705.A576

      Zhang, Wentao, 1764-1814. 張問陶; 张问陶 see
       PL2705.A578

      Zhang, Yu, 1865-1937. 章鈺; 章钰 see PL2705.A586

      Zhang, Yun. 張勻; 张匀 see PL2705.A588

      Zhang, Yuzhao, 1823-1894. 張裕釗; 张裕钊 see
       PL2705.A587

      Zhang, Zhupo, 1670-1698. 張竹坡; 张竹坡 see
       PL2705.A48

      Zhao, Liewen, 1832-1893. 趙烈文; 赵烈文 see
       PL2705.A6

Chinese language and literature
Chinese literature
Individual authors and works
Qing dynasty, 1644-1912
Z -- Continued
Zhao, Song, d. 1900. 趙崧; 赵崧 see PL2705.A64
Zhao, Yi, 1727-1814. 趙翼; 赵翼 see PL2705.A59
Zhao, Zhixin, 1662-1744. 趙執信; 赵执信 see
PL2705.A5887
Zheng, Xiaoxu, 1860-1938. 鄭孝胥; 郑孝胥 see
PL2705.E595
Zheng, Xie, 1693-1765. 鄭燮; 郑燮 see PL2705.E6
Zheng, Zhen, 1806-1864. 鄭珍; 郑珍 see PL2705.E59
Zhensong, Shi, 1794-1868. 真嵩 see PL2705.E586
Zhou, Lianggong, 1612-1672. 周亮工 see PL2705.O8
Zhou, Qiwei, 1666-1714. 周起渭 see PL2705.O77
Zhou, Shouchang, 1814-1884. 周壽昌; 周寿昌 see
PL2705.O83
Zhou, Tongyu, d. 1916. 周同愈 see PL2705.O85
Zhou, Zhiqi, 1782-1862. 周之琦 see PL2705.O772
Zhu, Da, 1626-ca. 1705. 朱耷 see PL2705.U23
Zhu, Heling, 1606-1683. 朱鶴齡; 朱鹤龄 see
PL2705.U18
Zhu, Qilian, d. 1899. 朱啟連; 朱启连 see PL2705.U12
Zhu, Shu, 1654-1707. 朱書; 朱书 see PL2705.U22
Zhu, Yiqing, b. 1795. 朱翊清 see PL2705.U19
Zhu, Yizun, 1629-1709. 朱彝尊 see PL2703
Zhu, Yongchun, 1617-1689. 朱用純; 朱用纯 see
PL2705.U28
Zhu, Zumou, 1857-1931. 朱祖謀; 朱祖谋 see
PL2705.U24
2735.3.H86   Zhuo, Erkan, b. 1653. 卓爾堪; 卓尔堪 (Table P-PZ40)
Zhuoyuantingzhuren, 17th cent. 酌元亭主人 see
PL2705.O27
Zou, Tao, 19th cent. 鄒弢; 邹弢 see PL2729.S58
Zou, Zhong, ca. 1827-ca. 1886. 鄒鍾; 邹钟 see
PL2729.S55
Zuiyueshanren, fl. 1804-1876. 醉月山人 see
PL2729.S794
1912-1949
2735.5.A-Z   Anonymous works. By title, A-Z
Subarrange each by Table P-PZ43
2736   A
The author number is determined by the second letter of
the name
Subarrange each author by Table P-PZ40
Aying, 1900-1977. 阿英 see PL2749.H7

Chinese language and literature
Chinese literature
Individual authors and works
1912-1949 -- Continued

2736.5	B

> The author number is determined by the second letter of
> the name
> Subarrange each author by Table P-PZ40
> Ba, Jin, 1904-2005. 巴金 see PL2780.F4
> Ba, Ren, b. 1897. 巴人 see PL2822.J4
> Bingxin, 1900- 冰心 see PL2765.I49

2736.8	C - Cg

> The author number is determined by the second letter of
> the name
> Subarrange each author by Table P-PZ40

2737	Cha

> Subarrange each author by Table P-PZ40
> Class here authors whose names begin with this word
> The author number is determined by the next portion of
> the author's name

2738	Chai

> Subarrange each author by Table P-PZ40
> Class here authors whose names begin with this word
> The author number is determined by the next portion of
> the author's name

2739	Chan

> The author number is determined by the next portion of
> the author's name
> Subarrange each author by Table P-PZ40
> Class here authors whose names begin with this word

2740	Chang

> The author number is determined by the next portion of
> the author's name
> Subarrange each author by Table P-PZ40
> Class here authors whose names begin with this word

2740.K8	Chang, Kuang-jen, 1902-1985. 張光人; 张光人 (Table P-PZ40)
2740.N3	Chang, Nai-ying, 1911-1942. 張廼瑩; 张廼莹 (Table P-PZ40)
2740.P5	Chang, Ping-lin, 1868-1936. 章炳麟 (Table P-PZ40)
2741	Chao

> The author number is determined by the next portion of
> the author's name
> Subarrange each author by Table P-PZ40
> Class here authors whose names begin with this word

2741.Y36	Chao, Yao-sheng, 1867-1948. 趙堯生; 赵尧生 (Table P-PZ40)

Chinese language and literature
Chinese literature
Individual authors and works
1912-1949
Chao -- Continued

2741.Y82   Chao, Yü-sen, 1868-1945. 趙玉森; 赵玉森 (Table P-PZ40)

2742   Che
The author number is determined by the next portion of the author's name
Subarrange each author by Table P-PZ40
Class here authors whose names begin with this word

2743   Chen
The author number is determined by the next portion of the author's name
Subarrange each author by Table P-PZ40
Class here authors whose names begin with this word
Chen, Hengzhe, 1890-1976. 陳衡哲; 陈衡哲 see PL2832.3.E5

2744   Cheng
The author number is determined by the next portion of the author's name
Subarrange each author by Table P-PZ40
Class here authors whose names begin with this word

2745   Chi
The author number is determined by the next portion of the author's name
Subarrange each author by Table P-PZ40
Class here authors whose names begin with this word

2746   Chia
The author number is determined by the next portion of the author's name
Subarrange each author by Table P-PZ40
Class here authors whose names begin with this word

2747   Chiang
The author number is determined by the next portion of the author's name
Subarrange each author by Table P-PZ40
Class here authors whose names begin with this word

2747.P5   Chiang, Ping-chih, 1904- 蔣冰之; 蒋冰之 (Table P-PZ40)

2748   Chiao
The author number is determined by the next portion of the author's name
Subarrange each author by Table P-PZ40
Class here authors whose names begin with this word

Chinese language and literature
Chinese literature
Individual authors and works
1912-1949 -- Continued

2748.5	Chiap - Chiem
	The author number is determined by the fourth letter of the name
	Subarrange each author by Table P-PZ40
2749	Chien
	The author number is determined by the next portion of the author's name
	Subarrange each author by Table P-PZ40
	Class here authors whose names begin with this word
2749.H7	Ch'ien, Hsing-ts'un, 1900-1977. 錢杏邨; 钱杏邨 (Table P-PZ40)
2750	Chih
	The author number is determined by the next portion of the author's name
	Subarrange each author by Table P-PZ40
	Class here authors whose names begin with this word
2751	Chin
	The author number is determined by the next portion of the author's name
	Subarrange each author by Table P-PZ40
	Class here authors whose names begin with this word
2751.C3	Chin, Chao-fan, 1868-1950. 金兆蕃 (Table P-PZ40)
2752	Ching
	The author number is determined by the next portion of the author's name
	Subarrange each author by Table P-PZ40
	Class here authors whose names begin with this word
2752.5	Chio - Chiu
	The author number is determined by the fourth letter of the name
	Subarrange each author by Table P-PZ40
2753	Cho
	The author number is determined by the next portion of the author's name
	Subarrange each author by Table P-PZ40
	Class here authors whose names begin with this word
(2753.P62)	Cho, Po-yŏn, 1875-1934. 趙甫衍
	see PL990.17.P69
2753.5	Choa - Chot
	The author number is determined by the fourth letter of the name
	Subarrange each author by Table P-PZ40

Chinese language and literature
Chinese literature
Individual authors and works
1912-1949 -- Continued

2754   Chou
The author number is determined by the next portion of
the author's name
Subarrange each author by Table P-PZ40
Class here authors whose names begin with this word

2754.S5   Chou, Shu-jen, 1881-1936. 周樹人; 周树人 (Table P-
PZ40)

2755   Chu
The author number is determined by the next portion of
the author's name
Subarrange each author by Table P-PZ40
Class here authors whose names begin with this word

2755.5   Chua - Chum
The author number is determined by the fourth letter of
the name
Subarrange each author by Table P-PZ40

2756   Chun
The author number is determined by the next portion of
the author's name
Subarrange each author by Table P-PZ40
Class here authors whose names begin with this word

2757   Chung
Subarrange each author by Table P-PZ40
Class here authors whose names begin with this word
The author number is determined by the next portion of
the author's name

2757.W3   Chung, Wang-yang. 鍾望陽; 钟望阳 (Table P-PZ40)
2757.5   Chunga - Cz
The author number is determined by the second letter of
the name
Subarrange each author by Table P-PZ40

2758   D
The author number is determined by the second letter of
the name
Subarrange each author by Table P-PZ40
Ding, Ling, 1904- 丁玲 see PL2747.P5
Dong, Lu'an, 1896-1953. 董魯安; 董鲁安 see
PL2817.N2
Duanmu, Hongliang, 1912- 端木蕻良 see
PL2815.A636

Chinese language and literature
Chinese literature
Individual authors and works
1912-1949 -- Continued

2759	E
	The author number is determined by the second letter of the name
	Subarrange each author by Table P-PZ40
2760	Fa - Ft
	The author number is determined by the second letter of the name
	Subarrange each author by Table P-PZ40
2761	Fu
	Subarrange each author by Table P-PZ40
	Class here authors whose names begin with this word
	The author number is determined by the next portion of the author's name
2761.T74	Fu, Tseng-hsiang, 1872-1949. 傅增湘 (Table P-PZ40)
	Fu, Zengxiang, 1872-1949. 傅增湘 see PL2761.T74
2762	Fua - Fuz
	The author number is determined by the third letter of the name
	Subarrange each author by Table P-PZ40
2763	G
	The author number is determined by the second letter of the name
	Subarrange each author by Table P-PZ40
	Gu, Yiqiao, 1902- 顧一樵; 顾一樵 see PL2777.Y8
	Guo, Moruo, 1892-1978. 郭沫若 see PL2778.O2
2764	Ha - Hr
	The author number is determined by the second letter of the name
	Subarrange each author by Table P-PZ40
2765	Hs
	The author number is determined by the third letter of the name
	Subarrange each author by Table P-PZ40
	Hsiao, Hung, 1911-1942. 蕭紅; 萧红 see PL2740.N3
2765.I49	Hsieh, Wan-ying, 1902- 謝婉瑩; 谢婉莹 (Table P-PZ40)
2765.U174	Hsü, Ch'eng-yao. 許承堯; 許承尧 (Table P-PZ40)
2765.U2	Hsü, Chih-mo, 1896-1931. 徐志摩 (Table P-PZ40)
2766	Hu
	Subarrange each author by Table P-PZ40
	Class here authors whose names begin with this word
	The author number is determined by the next portion of the author's name

Chinese literature
   Individual authors and works
      1912-1949
         1912-1949
           Hu
              Hu, Feng, 1902-1985. 胡風; 胡风 see PL2740.K8

2766.S5	Hu, Shi, 1891-1962. 胡適; 胡适 (Table P-PZ40)
2766.5	Hua

              The author number is determined by the next portion of
                the author's name
              Subarrange each author by Table P-PZ40
              Class here authors whose names begin with this word

2767	Huaa - Huan

              The author number is determined by the fourth letter of
                the name
              Subarrange each author by Table P-PZ40

2768	Huang

              Subarrange each author by Table P-PZ40
               Class here authors whose names begin with this word
              The author number is determined by the next portion of
                the author's name

2768.Y5	Huang, Ying, 1898-1934. 黄英 (Table P-PZ40)
2769	Hue - Huz

              The author number is determined by the third letter of the
                name
              Subarrange each author by Table P-PZ40

2770	I

              Subarrange each author by Table P-PZ40
              Class here authors whose names begin with the single
                letter I
              The author number is determined by the next portion of
                the author's name

2770.5	Ia - Iz

              The author number is determined by the second letter of
                the name
              Subarrange each author by Table P-PZ40

2771	J

              The author number is determined by the second letter of
                the name
              Subarrange each author by Table P-PZ40

2772	Kaa - Kaz

              The author number is determined by the third letter of the
                name
              Subarrange each author by Table P-PZ40

Chinese language and literature
Chinese literature
Individual authors and works
1912-1949 -- Continued

2773	Kea - Kez
	The author number is determined by the third letter of the name
	Subarrange each author by Table P-PZ40
2774	Kia - Kiz
	The author number is determined by the third letter of the name
	Subarrange each author by Table P-PZ40
2775	Ko
	Subarrange each author by Table P-PZ40
	Class here authors whose names begin with this word
	The author number is determined by the next portion of the author's name
2776	Koa - Koz
	The author number is determined by the third letter of the name
	Subarrange each author by Table P-PZ40
2777	Ku
	Subarrange each author by Table P-PZ40
	Class here authors whose names begin with this word
	The author number is determined by the next portion of the author's name
	Ku, I-ch'iao, 1902- 顧一樵; 顾一樵 see PL2777.Y8
2777.Y8	Ku, Yü-hsiu, 1902- 顧毓琇; 顾毓琇 (Table P-PZ40)
2778	Kua - Kuz
	The author number is determined by the third letter of the name
	Subarrange each author by Table P-PZ40
2778.O2	Kuo, Mo-jo, 1892-1978. 郭沫若 (Table P-PZ40)
2778.5	Kv - Kz
	The author number is determined by the second letter of the name
	Subarrange each author by Table P-PZ40
2779	La - Lh
	The author number is determined by the second letter of the name
	Subarrange each author by Table P-PZ40
	Lao, She, 1898-1966. 老舍 see PL2804.C5
2780	Li
	Subarrange each author by Table P-PZ40
	Class here authors whose names begin with this word
	The author number is determined by the next portion of the author's name

	Chinese language and literature
	Chinese literature
	Individual authors and works
	1912-1949
	Li -- Continued
2780.F4	Li, Fei-kan, 1904-2005. 李芾甘 (Table P-PZ40)
2781	Lia - Lit
	The author number is determined by the third letter of the name
	Subarrange each author by Table P-PZ40
2781.A5	Liang, Ch'i-ch'ao, 1873-1929. 梁啟超; 梁启超 (Table P-PZ40)
	Liang, Qichao, 1873-1929. 梁啟超; 梁启超 see PL2781.A5
2782	Liu
	Subarrange each author by Table P-PZ40
	Class here authors whose names begin with this word
	The author number is determined by the next portion of the author's name
	Liu, Datong, 1865-1952. 劉大同; 刘大同 see PL2782.T29
2782.S42	Liu, Shanze, 1885-1949. 劉善澤; 刘善泽 (Table P-PZ40)
2782.T29	Liu, Ta-t'ung, 1865-1952. 劉大同; 刘大同 (Table P-PZ40)
2783	Lo - Ly
	The author number is determined by the second letter of the name
	Subarrange each author by Table P-PZ40
	Lo, Shu, 1903-1938. 羅淑; 罗淑 see PL2784.S5
	Lu, Xun, 1881-1936. 魯迅; 鲁迅 see PL2754.S5
	Lu, Yin, 1898-1934. 廬隱; 庐隐 see PL2768.Y5
	Luo, Shu, 1903-1938. 羅淑; 罗淑 see PL2784.S5
2784	Ma
	Subarrange each author by Table P-PZ40
	Class here authors whose names begin with this word
	The author number is determined by the next portion of the author's name
2784.S5	Ma, Shih-mi (Lo), 1903-1938. 馬世彌 (羅); 马世弥(罗) (Table P-PZ40)
2785	Maa - Maz
	The author number is determined by the third letter of the name
	Subarrange each author by Table P-PZ40
	Mao, Dun, 1896- 茅盾 see PL2801.N2

Chinese language and literature
Chinese literature
Individual authors and works
1912-1949

2786	Mea - Mez
	The author number is determined by the third letter of the name
	Subarrange each author by Table P-PZ40
2787	Mi
	Subarrange each author by Table P-PZ40
	Class here authors whose names begin with this word
	The author number is determined by the next portion of the author's name
2788	Mia - Miz
	The author number is determined by the third letter of the name
	Subarrange each author by Table P-PZ40
2789	Mo - Mz
	The author number is determined by the second letter of the name
	Subarrange each author by Table P-PZ40
2789.5	Na
	The author number is determined by the next portion of the author's name
	Subarrange each author by Table P-PZ40
	Class here authors whose names begin with this word
2790	Naa - Naz
	The author number is determined by the third letter of the name
	Subarrange each author by Table P-PZ40
2791	Ni
	Subarrange each author by Table P-PZ40
	Class here authors whose names begin with this word
	The author number is determined by the next portion of the author's name
2792	Nia - Niz
	The author number is determined by the third letter of the name
	Subarrange each author by Table P-PZ40
2793	No - Nz
	The author number is determined by the second letter of the name
	Subarrange each author by Table P-PZ40
2794	O
	The author number is determined by the second letter of the name
	Subarrange each author by Table P-PZ40

Chinese language and literature
Chinese literature
Individual authors and works
1912-1949
O -- Continued

2794.U29	Ou-yang, Chi-hsiu, 1902- 歐陽繼修; 欧阳继修 (Table P-PZ40)
2795	P

The author number is determined by the second letter of the name
Subarrange each author by Table P-PZ40
Pa, Chin, 1904-2005. 巴金 see PL2780.F4
Ping-hsin, 1902- 冰心 see PL2765.I49
Pa, Jen, b. 1897. 巴人 see PL2822.J4

2795.5	Q

The author number is determined by the second letter of the name
Subarrange each author by Table P-PZ40

2795.5.I84	Qiu, Dongping, 1910-1941. 丘東平; 丘东平 (Table P-PZ40)
2796	R

The author number is determined by the second letter of the name
Subarrange each author by Table P-PZ40

2797	Sa - Sg

The author number is determined by the second letter of the name
Subarrange each author by Table P-PZ40

2798	Sha

Subarrange each author by Table P-PZ40
Class here authors whose names begin with this word
The author number is determined by the next portion of the author's name

2799	Shaa - Shaz

The author number is determined by the fourth letter of the name
Subarrange each author by Table P-PZ40

2800	She

Subarrange each author by Table P-PZ40
Class here authors whose names begin with this word
The author number is determined by the next portion of the author's name

2801	Shea - Shez

The author number is determined by the fourth letter of the name
Subarrange each author by Table P-PZ40

2801.N2	Shen, Yen-ping, 1896- 沈雁冰 (Table P-PZ40)

Chinese language and literature
Chinese literature
Individual authors and works
1912-1949 -- Continued

2801.5   Shi

> The author number is determined by the next portion of the author's name
>
> Subarrange each author by Table P-PZ40
>
> Class here authors whose names begin with this word

2802   Shia - Shiz

> The author number is determined by the fourth letter of the name
>
> Subarrange each author by Table P-PZ40

2803   Shoa - Shoz

> The author number is determined by the fourth letter of the name
>
> Subarrange each author by Table P-PZ40

2804   Shu

> Subarrange each author by Table P-PZ40
>
> Class here authors whose names begin with this word
>
> The author number is determined by the next portion of the author's name

2804.C5   Shu, Chʻing-chʻun, 1898-1966. 舒慶春; 舒庆春 (Table P-PZ40)

2805   Shua - Shuz

> The author number is determined by the fourth letter of the name
>
> Subarrange each author by Table P-PZ40

2806   Si - St

> The author number is determined by the second letter of the name
>
> Subarrange each author by Table P-PZ40

2807   Su

> Subarrange each author by Table P-PZ40
>
> Class here authors whose names begin with this word
>
> The author number is determined by the next portion of the author's name

> Su, Su. 蘇蘇; 苏苏 see PL2757.W3

2808   Sua - Suz

> The author number is determined by the third letter of the name
>
> Subarrange each author by Table P-PZ40

2809   Sz

> The author number is determined by the third letter of the name
>
> Subarrange each author by Table P-PZ40

Chinese language and literature
Chinese literature
Individual authors and works
1912-1949 -- Continued

2810	Ta
	Subarrange each author by Table P-PZ40
	Class here authors whose names begin with this word
	The author number is determined by the next portion of the author's name
2811	Taa - Taz
	The author number is determined by the third letter of the name
	Subarrange each author by Table P-PZ40
2812	Te - Ti
	The author number is determined by the second letter of the name
	Subarrange each author by Table P-PZ40
	Ting, Ling, 1904- 丁玲 see PL2747.P5
2813	To
	Subarrange each author by Table P-PZ40
	Class here authors whose names begin with this word
	The author number is determined by the next portion of the author's name
2814	Toa - Toz
	The author number is determined by the third letter of the name
	Subarrange each author by Table P-PZ40
2815	Tsa - Tsz
	The author number is determined by the third letter of the name
	Subarrange each author by Table P-PZ40
2815.A636	Ts'ao, Chia-ching, 1912- 曹家京 (Table P-PZ40)
2816	Tu
	Subarrange each author by Table P-PZ40
	Class here authors whose names begin with this word
	The author number is determined by the next portion of the author's name
2817	Tua - Tuz
	The author number is determined by the third letter of the name
	Subarrange each author by Table P-PZ40
	Tuan-mu, Hung-liang, 1912- 端木蕻良 see PL2815.A636
2817.N2	Tung, Fan, 1896-1953. 董璠 (Table P-PZ40)
	Tung, Lu-an, 1896-1953. 董魯安; 董鲁安 see PL2817.N2

Chinese language and literature
Chinese literature
Individual authors and works
1912-1949

2818	Tzu
	Subarrange each author by Table P-PZ40
	Class here authors whose names begin with this word
	The author number is determined by the next portion of the author's name
2819	U
	The author number is determined by the second letter of the name
	Subarrange each author by Table P-PZ40
2820	V
	The author number is determined by the second letter of the name
	Subarrange each author by Table P-PZ40
2821	Waa - Wan
	The author number is determined by the third letter of the name
	Subarrange each author by Table P-PZ40
2822	Wang
	Subarrange each author by Table P-PZ40
	Class here authors whose names begin with this word
	The author number is determined by the next portion of the author's name
2822.J4	Wang, Jen-shu, b. 1897. 王任叔 (Table P-PZ40)
2822.S5	Wang, Shu-nan, 1851-1936. 王樹枏; 王樹枏 (Table P-PZ40)
2823	Wanga - Wo
	The author number is determined by the second letter of the name
	Subarrange each author by Table P-PZ40
2824	Wu
	Subarrange each author by Table P-PZ40
	Class here authors whose names begin with this word
	The author number is determined by the next portion of the author's name
2824.Y9	Wu, Yu, b. 1872. 吳虞; 吳虞 (Table P-PZ40)
2824.3	X
	The author number is determined by the second letter of the name
	Subarrange each author by Table P-PZ40
	Xu, Chengyao. 許承堯; 許承尧 see PL2765.U174
	Xu, Zhimo, 1896-1931. 徐志摩 see PL2765.U2

Chinese language and literature
Chinese literature
Individual authors and works
1912-1949 -- Continued

2824.5	Ya

      Subarrange each author by Table P-PZ40
      Class here authors whose names begin with this word
      The author number is determined by the next portion of
         the author's name

2824.7	Yaa - Yanf

      The author number is determined by the third letter of the
         name
      Subarrange each author by Table P-PZ40
      Yan, Fu, 1853-1921. 嚴復; 严复 see PL2828.F8

2825	Yang

      Subarrange each author by Table P-PZ40
      Class here authors whose names begin with this word
      The author number is determined by the next portion of
         the author's name
      Yang, Hansheng, 1902- 陽翰笙; 阳翰笙 see
         PL2794.U29

2826	Yao

      Subarrange each author by Table P-PZ40
      Class here authors whose names begin with this word
      The author number is determined by the next portion of
         the author's name

2826.7	Ye

      The author number is determined by the next portion of
         the author's name
      Subarrange each author by Table P-PZ40
      Class here authors whose names begin with this word
      Ye, Shengtao, b. 1893. 葉聖陶; 叶圣陶 see
         PL2827.S4
      Ye, Zi, 1912-1939. 葉紫; 叶紫 see PL2831.H6

2827	Yeh

      Subarrange each author by Table P-PZ40
      Class here authors whose names begin with this word
      The author number is determined by the next portion of
         the author's name

2827.S4	Yeh, Shao-chün, b. 1893. 葉紹鈞; 叶绍钧 (Table P-PZ40)

      Yeh, Sheng-t'ao, b. 1893. 葉聖陶; 叶圣陶 see
         PL2827.S4
      Yeh, Tzu, 1912-1939. 葉紫; 叶紫 see PL2831.H6

	Chinese language and literature
	Chinese literature
	Individual authors and works
	1912-1949
2828	Yen

          Subarrange each author by Table P-PZ40
          Class here authors whose names begin with this word
          The author number is determined by the next portion of
              the author's name

2828.F8   Yen, Fu, 1853-1921. 嚴復; 严复 (Table P-PZ40)

2828.5   Yi

          Subarrange each author by Table P-PZ40
          Class here authors whose names begin with this word
          The author number is determined by the next portion of
              the author's name

(2828.5.S26)   Yi, Sang-nyong, 1858-1932. 李相龍
              see PL990.9.S36

(2828.5.T63)   Yi, Tŏg-u, 1887-1960
              see PL990.9.T64

2829   Yia - Yiz

          The author number is determined by the third letter of the
              name
          Subarrange each author by Table P-PZ40

2830   Yo

          Subarrange each author by Table P-PZ40
          Class here authors whose names begin with this word
          The author number is determined by the next portion of
              the author's name

2831   Yu

          Subarrange each author by Table P-PZ40
          Class here authors whose names begin with this word
          The author number is determined by the next portion of
              the author's name

2831.H6   Yü, Ho-lin, 1912-1939. 余鶴林; 余鹤林 (Table P-
              PZ40)

2832   Yua - Yuz

          The author number is determined by the third letter of the
               name
          Subarrange each author by Table P-PZ40

2832.3   Z

          The author number is determined by the second letter of
              the name
          Subarrange each author by Table P-PZ40

2832.3.E5   Zen, Sophia H. Chen, 1890-1976. 陳衡哲; 陈衡哲
              (Table P-PZ40)
          Zhao, Yaosheng, 1867-1948. 趙堯生; 赵尧生 see
              PL2741.Y36

                         Chinese language and literature
                          Chinese literature
                             Individual authors and works
                                 1912-1949
                                       Z -- Continued
                                           Zhao, Yusen, 1868-1945. 趙玉森; 赵玉森 see
                                             PL2741.Y82
                                   1949-2000

2832.5.A-Z	Anonymous works. By title, A-Z
	Subarrange each work by Table P-PZ43
2833	A
	The author number is determined by the second letter of
	the name
	Subarrange each author by Table P-PZ40
2833.5	B
	The author number is determined by the second letter of
	the name
	Subarrange each author by Table P-PZ40
	Boyang, 1920- 柏楊; 柏杨 see PL2875.O17
2833.7	Ca - Ce
	The author number is determined by the second letter of
	the name
	Subarrange each author by Table P-PZ40
2834	Cha
	Subarrange each author by Table P-PZ40
	Class here authors whose names begin with this word
	The author number is determined by the next portion of
	the author's name
2835	Chai
	Subarrange each author by Table P-PZ40
	Class here authors whose names begin with this word
	The author number is determined by the next portion of
	the author's name
2836	Chan
	Subarrange each author by Table P-PZ40
	Class here authors whose names begin with this word
	The author number is determined by the next portion of
	the author's name
2837	Chang
	Subarrange each author by Table P-PZ40
	Class here authors whose names begin with this word
	The author number is determined by the next portion of
	the author's name
	Chang, Ai-ling. 張愛玲; 张爱玲 see PL2837.E35
2837.E35	Chang, Eileen (Table P-PZ40)
	Chang, Min, 1949- 張敏; 张敏 see PL2861.A575

Chinese language and literature
Chinese literature
Individual authors and works
1949-2000 -- Continued

2838   Chao
Subarrange each author by Table P-PZ40
Class here authors whose names begin with this word
The author number is determined by the next portion of
the author's name

2839   Che
Subarrange each author by Table P-PZ40
Class here authors whose names begin with this word
The author number is determined by the next portion of
the author's name

2840   Chen
Subarrange each author by Table P-PZ40
Class here authors whose names begin with this word
The author number is determined by the next portion of
the author's name

2840.C35   Ch'en, Che, 1938- 陳喆; 陈喆 (Table P-PZ40)
2840.J8   Ch'en, Jung, 1936- 諶容; 谌容 (Table P-PZ40)
2841   Cheng
Subarrange each author by Table P-PZ40
Class here authors whose names begin with this word
The author number is determined by the next portion of
the author's name

2841.5   Chenh - Chenz
The author number is determined by the fifth letter of the
name
Subarrange each author by Table P-PZ40

2842   Chi
Subarrange each author by Table P-PZ40
Class here authors whose names begin with this word
The author number is determined by the next portion of
the author's name
Ch'i-chün, 1918- 琦君 see PL2892.A54

2843   Chia
Subarrange each author by Table P-PZ40
Class here authors whose names begin with this word
The author number is determined by the next portion of
the author's name

2844   Chiang
Subarrange each author by Table P-PZ40
Class here authors whose names begin with this word
The author number is determined by the next portion of
the author's name

Chinese language and literature
Chinese literature
Individual authors and works
1949-2000 -- Continued

2845	Chiao
	Subarrange each author by Table P-PZ40
	Class here authors whose names begin with this word
	The author number is determined by the next portion of the author's name
2846	Chiea - Chien
	The author number is determined by the fifth letter of the name
	Subarrange each author by Table P-PZ40
2847	Chih
	Subarrange each author by Table P-PZ40
	Class here authors whose names begin with this word
	The author number is determined by the next portion of the author's name
2848	Chin
	Subarrange each author by Table P-PZ40
	Class here authors whose names begin with this word
	The author number is determined by the next portion of the author's name
2848.P4	Chin, P'ei-fen. 靳佩芬 (Table P-PZ40)
	Chin-yün, 1938- 錦雲; 锦云 see PL2879.C497
2848.5	China - Chinf
	The author number is determined by the fifth letter of the name
	Subarrange each author by Table P-PZ40
2849	Ching - Chiu
	The author number is determined by the fourth letter of the name
	Subarrange each author by Table P-PZ40
	Ch'iung-yao, 1938- 瓊瑤; 琼瑶 see PL2840.C35
2850	Cho
	Subarrange each author by Table P-PZ40
	Class here authors whose names begin with this word
	The author number is determined by the next portion of the author's name
2850.5	Choa - Chot
	The author number is determined by the fourth letter of the name
	Subarrange each author by Table P-PZ40

Chinese language and literature
Chinese literature
Individual authors and works
1949-2000 -- Continued

2851   Chou
                    Subarrange each author by Table P-PZ40
                    Class here authors whose names begin with this word
                    The author number is determined by the next portion of
                        the author's name
2852   Chu
                    Subarrange each author by Table P-PZ40
                    Class here authors whose names begin with this word
                    The author number is determined by the next portion of
                        the author's name
2852.5   Chua - Chum
                    The author number is determined by the fourth letter of
                        the name
                    Subarrange each author by Table P-PZ40
2853   Chun
                    Subarrange each author by Table P-PZ40
                    Class here authors whose names begin with this word
                    The author number is determined by the next portion of
                        the author's name
2854   Chung
                    Subarrange each author by Table P-PZ40
                    Class here authors whose names begin with this word
                    The author number is determined by the next portion of
                        the author's name
2854.3   Chuo
                    The author number is determined by the next portion of
                        the author's name
                    Subarrange each author by Table P-PZ40
                    Class here authors whose names begin with this word
2854.5   Ci - Cu
                    The author number is determined by the second letter of
                        the name
                    Subarrange each author by Table P-PZ40
2855   D
                    The author number is determined by the second letter of
                        the name
                    Subarrange each author by Table P-PZ40
2856   E
                    The author number is determined by the second letter of
                        the name
                    Subarrange each author by Table P-PZ40
2856.N4   Engle, Hua-ling Nieh, 1926- (Table P-PZ40)

Chinese language and literature
Chinese literature
Individual authors and works
1949-2000 -- Continued

2857	Fa - Ft
	The author number is determined by the second letter of the name
	Subarrange each author by Table P-PZ40
	Fang, Si. 方思 see PL2865.S5
	Fang, Ssu. 方思 see PL2865.S5
	Fei, Meng. 費蒙; 费蒙 see PL2877.F385
2858	Fu
	Subarrange each author by Table P-PZ40
	Class here authors whose names begin with this word
	The author number is determined by the next portion of the author's name
	Fu, Shisen, 1933- 宓世森 see PL2874.T8
2859	Fua - Fuz
	The author number is determined by the third letter of the name
	Subarrange each author by Table P-PZ40
2860	G
	The author number is determined by the second letter of the name
	Subarrange each author by Table P-PZ40
	Gu, Du, 1933- 古渡 see PL2874.T8
2861	Ha - Hr
	The author number is determined by the second letter of the name
	Subarrange each author by Table P-PZ40
2861.A575	Hai, Wen, 1949- 海汶 (Table P-PZ40)
2861.A85	Hartzell, Richard W., 1951- (Table P-PZ40)
	He, Ruiyuan, 1951- 何瑞元 see PL2861.A85
	He, Suo. 何索 see PL2922.W373
	Ho, Jui-yüan, 1951- 何瑞元 see PL2861.A85
	Ho, So. 何索 see PL2922.W373
2862	Hs
	The author number is determined by the third letter of the name
	Subarrange each author by Table P-PZ40
	Hsin, Yü, 1933- 辛鬱 see PL2874.T8
	Hsing-lin-tzu, 1942- 杏林子 see PL2879.H654
2862.U1495	Hsü, En-mei, 1934- 徐恩楣 (Table P-PZ40)
	Hsü, I-lan, 1934- 徐蕙藍; 徐蕙蓝 see PL2862.U1495

Chinese language and literature
Chinese literature
Individual authors and works
1949-2000 -- Continued

2863	Hu
	Subarrange each author by Table P-PZ40
	Class here authors whose names begin with this word
	The author number is determined by the next portion of the author's name
	Hu, Naiqiu. 胡耐秋 see PL2922.M5
2863.5	Hua
	Subarrange each author by Table P-PZ40
	Class here authors whose names begin with this word
	The author number is determined by the next portion of the author's name
2863.5.L86	Hua, Lung-ying, 1952- (Table P-PZ40)
	Hua, Nongying, 1952- 花弄影 see PL2863.5.L86
	Hua, Yan, 1926- 華嚴; 华严 see PL2925.T5
2864	Huaa - Huan
	The author number is determined by the fourth letter of the name
	Subarrange each author by Table P-PZ40
2865	Huang
	Subarrange each author by Table P-PZ40
	Class here authors whose names begin with this word
	The author number is determined by the next portion of the author's name
2865.M3	Huang, Mao, 1948- 黃毛 (Table P-PZ40)
2865.S5	Huang, Shih-shu. 黃時樞; 黄时枢 (Table P-PZ40)
2865.5	Huanga - Huangz
	The author number is determined by the sixth letter of the name
	Subarrange each author by Table P-PZ40
2866	Hue - Huz
	The author number is determined by the third letter of the name
	Subarrange each author by Table P-PZ40
2867	I
	Subarrange each author by Table P-PZ40
	Class here authors whose names begin with the single letter I
	The author number is determined by the next portion of the author's name
2867.T3	I, Ta. 依達; 依达 (Table P-PZ40)
	I-ta. 依達; 依达 see PL2867.T3

Chinese language and literature
Chinese literature
Individual authors and works
1949-2000 -- Continued

2867.5	Ia - Iz
	The author number is determined by the second letter of the name
	Subarrange each author by Table P-PZ40
2868	J
	The author number is determined by the second letter of the name
	Subarrange each author by Table P-PZ40
	Jinyun, 1938- 錦雲; 锦云 see PL2879.C497
2868.5	Ka
	The author number is determined by the next portion of the author's name
	Subarrange each author by Table P-PZ40
	Class here authors whose names begin with this word
2869	Kaa - Kaz
	The author number is determined by the third letter of the name
	Subarrange each author by Table P-PZ40
2869.5	Ke
	The author number is determined by the next portion of the author's name
	Subarrange each author by Table P-PZ40
	Class here authors whose names begin with this word
2870	Kea - Kez
	The author number is determined by the third letter of the name
	Subarrange each author by Table P-PZ40
2871	Kia - Kiz
	The author number is determined by the third letter of the name
	Subarrange each author by Table P-PZ40
2872	Ko
	Subarrange each author by Table P-PZ40
	Class here authors whose names begin with this word
	The author number is determined by the next portion of the author's name
2873	Koa - Koz
	The author number is determined by the third letter of the name
	Subarrange each author by Table P-PZ40

Chinese language and literature
Chinese literature
Individual authors and works
1949-2000 -- Continued

2874	Ku
	Subarrange each author by Table P-PZ40
	Class here authors whose names begin with this word
	The author number is determined by the next portion of the author's name
2874.T8	Ku, Tu, 1933- 古渡 (Table P-PZ40)
	K'u-ling, 1955- 苦苓 see PL2919.Y775
2875	Kua - Kuz
	The author number is determined by the third letter of the name
	Subarrange each author by Table P-PZ40
	Kuling, 1955- 苦苓 see PL2919.Y775
2875.O17	Kuo, I-tung, 1920- 郭衣洞 (Table P-PZ40)
2876	La - Lh
	The author number is determined by the second letter of the name
	Subarrange each author by Table P-PZ40
2877	Li
	Subarrange each author by Table P-PZ40
	Class here authors whose names begin with this word
	The author number is determined by the next portion of the author's name
2877.C83	Li, Chung-t'ien. 黎中天 (Table P-PZ40)
2877.F385	Li, Fei-meng. 李費蒙; 李费蒙 (Table P-PZ40)
	Li, Zhongtian. 黎中天 see PL2877.C83
2878	Lia - Lit
	The author number is determined by the third letter of the name
	Subarrange each author by Table P-PZ40
2878.N1479	Lin, Shih-ts'un, 1915- 林適存; 林适存 (Table P-PZ40)
2879	Liu
	Subarrange each author by Table P-PZ40
	Class here authors whose names begin with this word
	The author number is determined by the next portion of the author's name
2879.C497	Liu, Chin-yün, 1938- 劉錦雲; 刘锦云 (Table P-PZ40)
2879.H654	Liu, Hsia, 1942- 劉俠; 刘侠 (Table P-PZ40)
2880	Lo - Ly
	The author number is determined by the second letter of the name
	Subarrange each author by Table P-PZ40
	Luo, Lan. 羅蘭; 罗兰 see PL2848.P4

Chinese language and literature
Chinese literature
Individual authors and works
1949-2000 -- Continued

2881   Ma
Subarrange each author by Table P-PZ40
Class here authors whose names begin with this word
The author number is determined by the next portion of
the author's name
Ma, Bin. 馬彬; 马彬 see PL2881.P5

2881.P5   Ma, Pin. 馬彬; 马彬 (Table P-PZ40)

2882   Maa - Maz
The author number is determined by the third letter of the
name
Subarrange each author by Table P-PZ40

2883   Mea - Mez
The author number is determined by the third letter of the
name
Subarrange each author by Table P-PZ40
Meng, Yao, 1919- 孟瑤 see PL2922.T78

2884   Mi
Subarrange each author by Table P-PZ40
Class here authors whose names begin with this word
The author number is determined by the next portion of
the author's name

2885   Mia - Miz
The author number is determined by the third letter of the
name
Subarrange each author by Table P-PZ40

2886   Mo - Mz
The author number is determined by the second letter of
the name
Subarrange each author by Table P-PZ40

2886.5   Na
The author number is determined by the next portion of
the author's name
Subarrange each author by Table P-PZ40
Class here authors whose names begin with this word

2887   Naa - Naz
The author number is determined by the third letter of the
name
Subarrange each author by Table P-PZ40
Nan, Guo. 南郭 see PL2878.N1479
Nan'gong, Bo. 南宮博 see PL2881.P5

Chinese language and literature
Chinese literature
Individual authors and works
1949-2000 -- Continued

2887.5   Nei - Nen
The author number is determined by the third letter of the name
Subarrange each author by Table P-PZ40

2888   Ni
Subarrange each author by Table P-PZ40
Class here authors whose names begin with this word
The author number is determined by the next portion of the author's name

2888.K8   Ni, Kuang. 倪匡 (Table P-PZ40)

2889   Nia - Niz
The author number is determined by the third letter of the name
Subarrange each author by Table P-PZ40
Nie, Hualing, 1926- 聶華苓; 聂华苓 see PL2856.N4

2890   No - Nz
The author number is determined by the second letter of the name
Subarrange each author by Table P-PZ40

2891   O
The author number is determined by the second letter of the name
Subarrange each author by Table P-PZ40
Ouyang, Shan, 1907- 歐陽山; 欧阳山 see PL2922.I3

2892   P
The author number is determined by the second letter of the name
Subarrange each author by Table P-PZ40

2892.A54   P'an, Hsi-chen, 1918- 潘希珍 (Table P-PZ40)
Peng, Ge, 1926- 彭歌 see PL2923.P4
Po-yang, 1920- 柏楊; 柏杨 see PL2875.O17

2892.3   Qi
The author number is determined by the next portion of the author's name
Subarrange each author by Table P-PZ40
Class here authors whose names begin with this word

2892.5   Qia - Qiu
The author number is determined by the third letter of the name
Subarrange each author by Table P-PZ40
Qijun, 1918- see PL2892.A54
Qiongyao, 1938- 瓊瑤; 琼瑶 see PL2840.C35

Chinese language and literature
Chinese literature
Individual authors and works
1949-2000 -- Continued

2892.7   Qu
Subarrange each author by Table P-PZ40
Class here authors whose names begin with this word
The author number is determined by the next portion of
the author's name

2892.8   Qua - Qun
The author number is determined by the third letter of the
name
Subarrange each author by Table P-PZ40

2893   R
The author number is determined by the second letter of
the name
Subarrange each author by Table P-PZ40

2894   Sa - Sg
The author number is determined by the second letter of
the name
Subarrange each author by Table P-PZ40

2895   Sha
Subarrange each author by Table P-PZ40
Class here authors whose names begin with this word
The author number is determined by the next portion of
the author's name
Sha, Ting, 1905- 沙汀 see PL2922.T8

2896   Shaa - Shaz
The author number is determined by the fourth letter of
the name
Subarrange each author by Table P-PZ40
Shangguan, Yu, 1928- 上官予 see PL2919.C482

2897   She
Subarrange each author by Table P-PZ40
Class here authors whose names begin with this word
The author number is determined by the next portion of
the author's name

2898   Shea - Shez
The author number is determined by the fourth letter of
the name
Subarrange each author by Table P-PZ40
Shen, Jung, 1936- 諶容; 谌容 see PL2840.J8
Shen, Rong, 1936- 諶容; 谌容 see PL2840.J8

Chinese language and literature
Chinese literature
Individual authors and works
1949-2000 -- Continued

2898.5 Shi
The author number is determined by the next portion of
the author's name
Subarrange each author by Table P-PZ40
Class here authors whose names begin with this word
Shi, Tuo. 師陀; 师陀 see PL2919.C42

2899 Shia - Shiz
The author number is determined by the fourth letter of
the name
Subarrange each author by Table P-PZ40
Shih, T'o. 師陀; 师陀 see PL2919.C42

2900 Shoa - Shoz
The author number is determined by the fourth letter of
the name
Subarrange each author by Table P-PZ40

2901 Shu
Subarrange each author by Table P-PZ40
Class here authors whose names begin with this word
The author number is determined by the next portion of
the author's name

2902 Shua - Shuz
The author number is determined by the fourth letter of
the name
Subarrange each author by Table P-PZ40

2903 Si - St
The author number is determined by the second letter of
the name
Subarrange each author by Table P-PZ40
Sima, Zhongyuan, 1933- 司馬中原; 司马中原 see
PL2921.Y4
Ssu-ma, Chung-yüan, 1933- 司馬中原; 司马中原 see
PL2921.Y4

2904 Su
Subarrange each author by Table P-PZ40
Class here authors whose names begin with this word
The author number is determined by the next portion of
the author's name

2905 Sua - Suz
The author number is determined by the third letter of the
name
Subarrange each author by Table P-PZ40

Chinese language and literature
Chinese literature
Individual authors and works
1949-2000 -- Continued

2906   Sz
> The author number is determined by the third letter of the name
> Subarrange each author by Table P-PZ40

2907   Ta
> Subarrange each author by Table P-PZ40
> Class here authors whose names begin with this word
> The author number is determined by the next portion of the author's name

2908   Taa - Taz
> The author number is determined by the third letter of the name
> Subarrange each author by Table P-PZ40
> T'ao, Jan. 陶然 see PL2913.T3

2909   Te - Ti
> The author number is determined by the second letter of the name
> Subarrange each author by Table P-PZ40
> Tian, Jian, 1916- 田間; 田间 see PL2914.N57
> T'ien, Chien, 1916- 田間; 田间 see PL2914.N57

2910   To
> Subarrange each author by Table P-PZ40
> Class here authors whose names begin with this word
> The author number is determined by the next portion of the author's name

2911   Toa - Toz
> The author number is determined by the third letter of the name
> Subarrange each author by Table P-PZ40

2912   Tsa - Tsz
> The author number is determined by the third letter of the name
> Subarrange each author by Table P-PZ40
> Ts'ai, Chao-ming, 1948- 蔡昭明 see PL2865.M3

2913   Tu
> Subarrange each author by Table P-PZ40
> Class here authors whose names begin with this word
> The author number is determined by the next portion of the author's name

2913.T3   Tu, Taoran. 涂陶然 (Table P-PZ40)

Chinese language and literature
Chinese literature
Individual authors and works
1949-2000 -- Continued

2914   Tua - Tuz
         The author number is determined by the third letter of the name
         Subarrange each author by Table P-PZ40

2914.N57   T'ung, T'ien-chien, 1916- 童天鑑; 童天鉴 (Table P-PZ40)

2915   Tzu
         Subarrange each author by Table P-PZ40
         Class here authors whose names begin with this word
         The author number is determined by the next portion of the author's name

2916   U
         The author number is determined by the second letter of the name
         Subarrange each author by Table P-PZ40

2917   V
         The author number is determined by the second letter of the name
         Subarrange each author by Table P-PZ40

2917.5   Wa
         The author number is determined by the next portion of the author's name
         Subarrange each author by Table P-PZ40
         Class here authors whose names begin with this word

2918   Waa - Wan
         The author number is determined by the third letter of the name
         Subarrange each author by Table P-PZ40

2919   Wang
         Subarrange each author by Table P-PZ40
         Class here authors whose names begin with this word
         The author number is determined by the next portion of the author's name

2919.C42   Wang, Ch'ang-chien. 王長簡; 王长简 (Table P-PZ40)
2919.C482   Wang, Chih-chien. 王志健 (Table P-PZ40)
2919.Y77   Wang, Yü-chün,1919- 王聿均 (Table P-PZ40)
2919.Y775   Wang, Yü-jen, 1955- 王裕仁 (Table P-PZ40)
         Wang, Zhijian, 1928- 王志健 see PL2919.C482

2920   Wanga - Wo
         The author number is determined by the second letter of the name
         Subarrange each author by Table P-PZ40
         Wei, Sili. 衞斯理; 卫斯理 see PL2888.K8

	Chinese language and literature
	Chinese literature
	Individual authors and works
	1949-2000 -- Continued
2921	Wu

Subarrange each author by Table P-PZ40
Class here authors whose names begin with this word
The author number is determined by the next portion of
the author's name

| 2921.Y4 | Wu, Yen-mei, 1933- 吳延玫; 吴延玫 (Table P-PZ40) |
| 2921.2 | Xi |

The author number is determined by the next portion of
the author's name
Subarrange each author by Table P-PZ40
Class here authors whose names begin with this word

| 2921.3 | Xia |

The author number is determined by the next portion of
the author's name
Subarrange each author by Table P-PZ40
Class here authors whose names begin with this word

| 2921.4 | Xian - Xiao |

The author number is determined by the fourth letter of
the name
Subarrange each author by Table P-PZ40

| 2921.5 | Xie - Xiu |

The author number is determined by the third letter of the
name
Subarrange each author by Table P-PZ40
Xin, Yu, 1933- 辛鬱 see PL2874.T8
Xinglinzi, 1942- 杏林子 see PL2879.H654

| 2921.6 | Xu |

The author number is determined by the next portion of
the author's name
Subarrange each author by Table P-PZ40
Class here authors whose names begin with this word
Xu, Yilan, 1934- see PL2862.U1495

| 2921.7 | Xua - Xun |

The author number is determined by the third letter of the
name
Subarrange each author by Table P-PZ40

| 2921.8 | Ya |

The author number is determined by the next portion of
the author's name
Subarrange each author by Table P-PZ40
Class here authors whose names begin with this word

Chinese language and literature
Chinese literature
Individual authors and works
1949-2000 -- Continued

2921.9	Yai - Yan
	The author number is determined by the third letter of the name
	Subarrange each author by Table P-PZ40
2922	Yang
	Subarrange each author by Table P-PZ40
	Class here authors whose names begin with this word
	The author number is determined by the next portion of the author's name
2922.I3	Yang, I, 1907- 楊儀; 杨仪 (Table P-PZ40)
2922.M5	Yang, Ming. 楊明; 杨明 (Table P-PZ40)
	Yang, Mu, 1940- 楊牧; 杨牧 see PL2924.S47
2922.T78	Yang, Tsung-chen, 1919- 楊宗珍; 杨宗珍 (Table P-PZ40)
2922.T8	Yang, T'ung-fang, 1905- 楊同芳; 杨同芳 (Table P-PZ40)
2922.W373	Yang, Wei, fl. 1973- 楊蔚; 杨蔚 (Table P-PZ40)
2922.5	Yanga - Yanz
	The author number is determined by the fourth letter of the name
	Subarrange each author by Table P-PZ40
	Yangliuqingqing. 楊柳青青; 杨柳青青 see PL2877.C83
	Yanhuo, 1947- 彦火 see PL2925.H84
	Yanran, 1919- 燕然 see PL2919.Y77
	Yanyi, 1927- 雁翼 see PL2925.I2
2923	Yao
	Subarrange each author by Table P-PZ40
	Class here authors whose names begin with this word
	The author number is determined by the next portion of the author's name
2923.H73	Yao, Hsin-nung, 1904- 姚莘農; 姚莘农 (Table P-PZ40)
	Yao, Ke, 1904- 姚克 see PL2923.H73
2923.P4	Yao, P'eng, 1926- 姚朋 (Table P-PZ40)
2923.5	Ye
	The author number is determined by the next portion of the author's name
	Subarrange each author by Table P-PZ40
	Class here authors whose names begin with this word
	Ye, Shan. 葉珊; 叶珊 see PL2924.S47

Chinese language and literature
Chinese literature
Individual authors and works
1949-2000 -- Continued

2924	Yeh
	Subarrange each author by Table P-PZ40
	Class here authors whose names begin with this word
	The author number is determined by the next portion of the author's name
2924.S47	Yeh, Shan. 葉珊; 叶珊 (Table P-PZ40)
2925	Yen
	Subarrange each author by Table P-PZ40
	Class here authors whose names begin with this word
	The author number is determined by the next portion of the author's name
2925.H84	Yen, Huo, 1947- 彥火 (Table P-PZ40)
2925.I2	Yen, I, 1927- 雁翼 (Table P-PZ40)
2925.T5	Yen, T'ing-yün, 1926- 嚴停雲; 严停云 (Table P-PZ40)
	Yen-jan, 1919- 燕然 see PL2919.Y77
2925.5	Yi
	Subarrange each author by Table P-PZ40
	Class here authors whose names begin with this word
	The author number is determined by the next portion of the author's name
2926	Yia - Yiz
	The author number is determined by the third letter of the name
	Subarrange each author by Table P-PZ40
	Yida. 依達; 依达 see PL2867.T3
2927	Yo
	Subarrange each author by Table P-PZ40
	Class here authors whose names begin with this word
	The author number is determined by the next portion of the author's name
2927.5	Yon - You
	The author number is determined by the third letter of the name
	Subarrange each author by Table P-PZ40
2928	Yu
	Subarrange each author by Table P-PZ40
	Class here authors whose names begin with this word
	The author number is determined by the next portion of the author's name
2929	Yua - Yuz
	The author number is determined by the third letter of the name
	Subarrange each author by Table P-PZ40

Chinese language and literature
Chinese literature
Individual authors and works
1949-2000 -- Continued

2929.3   Za - Ze
The author number is determined by the second letter of
the name
Subarrange each author by Table P-PZ40

2929.4   Zha
The author number is determined by the next portion of
the author's name
Subarrange each author by Table P-PZ40
Class here authors whose names begin with this word

2929.5   Zhai - Zhan
The author number is determined by the fourth letter of
the name
Subarrange each author by Table P-PZ40
Zhang, Ailing. 張愛玲; 张爱玲 see PL2837.E35
Zhang, Min, 1949- 張敏; 张敏 see PL2861.A575

2929.6   Zhao
The author number is determined by the next portion of
the author's name
Subarrange each author by Table P-PZ40
Class here authors whose names begin with this word

2929.7   Zhe - Zhu
The author number is determined by the third letter of the
name
Subarrange each author by Table P-PZ40

2929.8   Zhua - Zhuo
The author number is determined by the fourth letter of
the name
Subarrange each author by Table P-PZ40

2929.9   Zi - Zu
The author number is determined by the second letter of
the name
Subarrange each author by Table P-PZ40

2001-
2930.A-Z   Anonymous works. By title, A-Z
Subarrange each work by Table P-PZ43

2930.5   A
The author number is determined by the second letter of
the name
Subarrange each author by Table P-PZ40

2931   Ba - Be
The author number is determined by the second letter of
the name
Subarrange each author by Table P-PZ40

Chinese language and literature
Chinese literature
Individual authors and works
2001- -- Continued

2931.5	Bi - Bu
	The author number is determined by the second letter of the name
	Subarrange each author by Table P-PZ40
2932	Ca - Ce
	The author number is determined by the second letter of the name
	Subarrange each author by Table P-PZ40
2932.5	Cha
	The author number is determined by the next portion of the author's name
	Subarrange each author by Table P-PZ40
	Class here authors whose names begin with this word
2932.7	Chaa - Chao
	The author number is determined by the fourth letter of the name
	Subarrange each author by Table P-PZ40
2933	Che - Chu
	The author number is determined by the third letter of the name
	Subarrange each author by Table P-PZ40
2934.3	Ci - Cu
	The author number is determined by the second letter of the name
	Subarrange each author by Table P-PZ40
2935	Da - Di
	The author number is determined by the second letter of the name
	Subarrange each author by Table P-PZ40
2936.3	Do - Du
	The author number is determined by the second letter of the name
	Subarrange each author by Table P-PZ40
2937	Fa - Fe
	The author number is determined by the second letter of the name
	Subarrange each author by Table P-PZ40
2937.5	Fo - Fu
	The author number is determined by the second letter of the name
	Subarrange each author by Table P-PZ40

Chinese language and literature
Chinese literature
Individual authors and works
2001- -- Continued

2938	Ga - Gu
	The author number is determined by the second letter of the name
	Subarrange each author by Table P-PZ40
2938.5	Gua - Guz
	The author number is determined by the third letter of the name
	Subarrange each author by Table P-PZ40
2939	Ha - Hs
	The author number is determined by the second letter of the name
	Subarrange each author by Table P-PZ40
2939.5	Hu
	The author number is determined by the next portion of the author's name
	Subarrange each author by Table P-PZ40
	Class here authors whose names begin with this word
2940	Hua
	The author number is determined by the next portion of the author's name
	Subarrange each author by Table P-PZ40
	Class here authors whose names begin with this word
2940.5	Huaa - Huan
	The author number is determined by the fourth letter of the name
	Subarrange each author by Table P-PZ40
2941	Huang
	The author number is determined by the next portion of the author's name
	Subarrange each author by Table P-PZ40
	Class here authors whose names begin with this word
2941.3	Huba - Huhu
	The author number is determined by the third letter of the name
	Subarrange each author by Table P-PZ40
2941.5	Hui - Huo
	The author number is determined by the third letter of the name
	Subarrange each author by Table P-PZ40
2941.7	I
	The author number is determined by the second letter of the name
	Subarrange each author by Table P-PZ40

PL

Chinese language and literature
Chinese literature
Individual authors and works
2001- -- Continued

2942	Ji

The author number is determined by the next portion of the author's name

Subarrange each author by Table P-PZ40

Class here authors whose names begin with this word

2942.3	Jia - Jie

The author number is determined by the third letter of the name

Subarrange each author by Table P-PZ40

2942.5	Jin - Jiu

The author number is determined by the third letter of the name

Subarrange each author by Table P-PZ40

2942.7	Ju

The author number is determined by the next portion of the author's name

Subarrange each author by Table P-PZ40

Class here authors whose names begin with this word

2942.8	Jua - Jun

The author number is determined by the third letter of the name

Subarrange each author by Table P-PZ40

2943	Ka - Ke

The author number is determined by the second letter of the name

Subarrange each author by Table P-PZ40

2944	Ko - Ku

The author number is determined by the second letter of the name

Subarrange each author by Table P-PZ40

2945	La - Le

The author number is determined by the second letter of the name

Subarrange each author by Table P-PZ40

2946	Li

The author number is determined by the next portion of the author's name

Subarrange each author by Table P-PZ40

Class here authors whose names begin with this word

2946.3	Lian - Lie

The author number is determined by the third letter of the name

Subarrange each author by Table P-PZ40

Chinese language and literature
Chinese literature
Individual authors and works
2001- -- Continued

2946.5   Lin
The author number is determined by the next portion of the author's name
Subarrange each author by Table P-PZ40
Class here authors whose names begin with this word

2946.7   Ling
The author number is determined by the next portion of the author's name
Subarrange each author by Table P-PZ40
Class here authors whose names begin with this word

2946.8   Linga - Lingz
Subarrange each author by Table P-PZ40
The author number is determined by the fifth letter of the name

2946.9   Linh - Lit
The author number is determined by the third letter of the name
Subarrange each author by Table P-PZ40

2947   Liu
The author number is determined by the next portion of the author's name
Subarrange each author by Table P-PZ40
Class here authors whose names begin with this word
Liu, Yan. 劉燕; 刘燕 see PL2971.3.Z52

2947.3   Liua - Liuz
The author number is determined by the fourth letter of the name
Subarrange each author by Table P-PZ40

2947.5   Lo - Lu
The author number is determined by the second letter of the name
Subarrange each author by Table P-PZ40

2948.3   Ma
The author number is determined by the next portion of the author's name
Subarrange each author by Table P-PZ40
Class here authors whose names begin with this word

2948.5   Maa - Mao
The author number is determined by the third letter of the name
Subarrange each author by Table P-PZ40

Chinese language and literature
Chinese literature
Individual authors and works
2001- -- Continued

2948.7	Mei - Men
	The author number is determined by the third letter of the name
	Subarrange each author by Table P-PZ40
2949	Mi
	The author number is determined by the next portion of the author's name
	Subarrange each author by Table P-PZ40
	Class here authors whose names begin with this word
2949.5	Mia - Miu
	The author number is determined by the third letter of the name
	Subarrange each author by Table P-PZ40
2949.7	Mo - Mu
	The author number is determined by the second letter of the name
	Subarrange each author by Table P-PZ40
2950	Na - Ne
	The author number is determined by the second letter of the name
	Subarrange each author by Table P-PZ40
2950.5	Ni
	The author number is determined by the next portion of the author's name
	Subarrange each author by Table P-PZ40
	Class here authors whose names begin with this word
2950.7	Nia - Niu
	The author number is determined by the third letter of the name
	Subarrange each author by Table P-PZ40
2951	No - Nu
	The author number is determined by the second letter of the name
	Subarrange each author by Table P-PZ40
2951.5	Ou
	The author number is determined by the third letter of the name
	Subarrange each author by Table P-PZ40
2952	Pa - Pe
	The author number is determined by the second letter of the name
	Subarrange each author by Table P-PZ40

Chinese language and literature
Chinese literature
Individual authors and works
2001- -- Continued

2953	Pi - Pu
	The author number is determined by the second letter of the name
	Subarrange each author by Table P-PZ40
2954	Qi
	The author number is determined by the next portion of the author's name
	Subarrange each author by Table P-PZ40
	Class here authors whose names begin with this word
2954.3	Qia - Qiu
	The author number is determined by the third letter of the name
	Subarrange each author by Table P-PZ40
2954.5	Qu
	The author number is determined by the next portion of the author's name
	Subarrange each author by Table P-PZ40
	Class here authors whose names begin with this word
2954.7	Qua - Qun
	The author number is determined by the third letter of the name
	Subarrange each author by Table P-PZ40
2955	Ra - Ri
	The author number is determined by the second letter of the name
	Subarrange each author by Table P-PZ40
2956	Ro - Ru
	The author number is determined by the second letter of the name
	Subarrange each author by Table P-PZ40
2957	Sa - Sg
	The author number is determined by the second letter of the name
	Subarrange each author by Table P-PZ40
2958	Sha - Sho
	The author number is determined by the third letter of the name
	Subarrange each author by Table P-PZ40
2959	Shu
	The author number is determined by the next portion of the author's name
	Subarrange each author by Table P-PZ40
	Class here authors whose names begin with this word

Chinese language and literature
Chinese literature
Individual authors and works
2001- -- Continued

2959.5	Shua - Shuo
	The author number is determined by the fourth letter of the name
	Subarrange each author by Table P-PZ40
2960	Si - Su
	The author number is determined by the second letter of the name
	Subarrange each author by Table P-PZ40
2961	Ta - Te
	The author number is determined by the second letter of the name
	Subarrange each author by Table P-PZ40
2962	Ti - Tu
	The author number is determined by the second letter of the name
	Subarrange each author by Table P-PZ40
2963	U
	The author number is determined by the second letter of the name
	Subarrange each author by Table P-PZ40
2963.5	V
	The author number is determined by the second letter of the name
	Subarrange each author by Table P-PZ40
2964	Wa
	The author number is determined by the next portion of the author's name
	Subarrange each author by Table P-PZ40
	Class here authors whose names begin with this word
2964.5	Waa - Wan
	The author number is determined by the third letter of the name
	Subarrange each author by Table P-PZ40
2965	Wang
	The author number is determined by the next portion of the author's name
	Subarrange each author by Table P-PZ40
	Class here authors whose names begin with this word
2965.5	Wanga-Wangz
	Subarrange each author by Table P-PZ40
	The author number is determined by the fifth letter of the name

Chinese language and literature
Chinese literature
Individual authors and works
2001- -- Continued

2966   We - Wu
                    The author number is determined by the second letter of
                        the name
                    Subarrange each author by Table P-PZ40

2967   Xi
                    The author number is determined by the next portion of
                        the author's name
                    Subarrange each author by Table P-PZ40
                    Class here authors whose names begin with this word

2967.5   Xia
                    The author number is determined by the next portion of
                        the author's name
                    Subarrange each author by Table P-PZ40
                    Class here authors whose names begin with this word

2967.7   Xian - Xiao
                    The author number is determined by the fourth letter of
                        the name
                    Subarrange each author by Table P-PZ40

2968   Xie
                    The author number is determined by the next portion of
                        the author's name
                    Subarrange each author by Table P-PZ40
                    Class here authors whose names begin with this word

2968.5   Xin - Xiz
                    The author number is determined by the third letter of the
                        name
                    Subarrange each author by Table P-PZ40

2969   Xu
                    The author number is determined by the next portion of
                        the author's name
                    Subarrange each author by Table P-PZ40
                    Class here authors whose names begin with this word

2969.5   Xua - Xun
                    The author number is determined by the third letter of the
                        name
                    Subarrange each author by Table P-PZ40

2970   Ya
                    The author number is determined by the next portion of
                        the author's name
                    Subarrange each author by Table P-PZ40
                    Class here authors whose names begin with this word

Chinese language and literature
Chinese literature
Individual authors and works
2001- -- Continued

2970.5	Yai - Yan
	The author number is determined by the third letter of the name
	Subarrange each author by Table P-PZ40
2971	Yang
	The author number is determined by the next portion of the author's name
	Subarrange each author by Table P-PZ40
	Class here authors whose names begin with this word
2971.3	Yanh - Yanz
	The author number is determined by the fourth letter of the name
	Subarrange each author by Table P-PZ40
2971.3.Z52	Yanzi. 燕子 (Table P-PZ40)
2971.5	Yao
	The author number is determined by the next portion of the author's name
	Subarrange each author by Table P-PZ40
	Class here authors whose names begin with this word
2972	Ye
	The author number is determined by the next portion of the author's name
	Subarrange each author by Table P-PZ40
	Class here authors whose names begin with this word
2972.3	Yea - Yez
	The author number is determined by the third letter of the name
	Subarrange each author by Table P-PZ40
2972.5	Yi - Yo
	The author number is determined by the second letter of the name
	Subarrange each author by Table P-PZ40
2973	Yu
	The author number is determined by the next portion of the author's name
	Subarrange each author by Table P-PZ40
	Class here authors whose names begin with this word
2973.5	Yua - Yun
	The author number is determined by the third letter of the name
	Subarrange each author by Table P-PZ40

Chinese language and literature
Chinese literature
Individual authors and works
2001- -- Continued

2973.7   Yuo - Yuz
The author number is determined by the third letter of the name
Subarrange each author by Table P-PZ40

2974   Za - Ze
The author number is determined by the second letter of the name
Subarrange each author by Table P-PZ40

2975   Zha
The author number is determined by the next portion of the author's name
Subarrange each author by Table P-PZ40
Class here authors whose names begin with this word

2975.5   Zhai - Zhan
The author number is determined by the fourth letter of the name
Subarrange each author by Table P-PZ40

2976   Zhang
The author number is determined by the next portion of the author's name
Subarrange each author by Table P-PZ40
Class here authors whose names begin with this word

2977   Zhao
The author number is determined by the next portion of the author's name
Subarrange each author by Table P-PZ40
Class here authors whose names begin with this word

2977.5   Zhe - Zhi
The author number is determined by the third letter of the name
Subarrange each author by Table P-PZ40

2977.7   Zhong
Subarrange each author by Table P-PZ40
Class here authors whose names begin with this word
The author number is determined by the next portion of the author's name

2978   Zhou
The author number is determined by the next portion of the author's name
Subarrange each author by Table P-PZ40
Class here authors whose names begin with this word

Chinese language and literature
Chinese literature
Individual authors and works
2001- -- Continued

2978.3   Zhoua - Zhouz
The author number is determined by the fifth letter of the name
Subarrange each author by Table P-PZ40

2978.5   Zhu
The author number is determined by the next portion of the author's name
Subarrange each author by Table P-PZ40
Class here authors whose names begin with this word

2978.7   Zhua - Zhuo
The author number is determined by the fourth letter of the name
Subarrange each author by Table P-PZ40

2979   Zi - Zu
The author number is determined by the second letter of the name
Subarrange each author by Table P-PZ40

Provincial, local, colonial, etc.
China

3030   Regional. General or several regions
3031.A-Z   Special provinces, regions, etc., A-Z
Subarrange each place by Table P-PZ26
3032.A-Z   Special cities, etc., A-Z
Subarrange each place by Table P-PZ26

Chinese literature outside China
3033   General
Special
For individual authors and works see PL2661+
Asia
3038   General
3040-3057   Japan (Table P-PZ23 modified)
Class here works of Chinese literature created in Japan
For Japanese literature written in Chinese characters (Kanbungaku), see PL719.79+ ; PL731.89+ ; PL754.69+ ; PL761.89+ ; etc.
Individual authors or works see PL2661+
3060-3077   Korea (Table P-PZ23 modified)
Class here works of Chinese literature created in Korea
For Korean literature written in Chinese characters (Hanmunhak) see PL950+
Individual authors or works see PL2661+
3080-3097   Southeast Asia (Table P-PZ23 modified)

Chinese language and literature
Chinese literature
Chinese literature outside China
Special
Asia
Southeast Asia -- Continued
3097.A-Z   Local. By country, A-Z
Subarrange each by Table P-PZ26
Individual authors or works see PL2661+
3119.A-Z   Other Asian countries, A-Z
Subarrange each by Table P-PZ26
3120-3137   Australia. New Zealand (Table P-PZ23 modified)
Individual authors or works see PL2661+
Europe
3145   General
3148.A-Z   By region or country, A-Z
Subarrange each by Table P-PZ26
The Americas
3149   General
3150-3167   United States (Table P-PZ23 modified)
Individual authors or works see PL2661+
3170-3187   Canada (Table P-PZ23 modified)
Individual authors or works see PL2661+
3189.5.A-Z   Other, A-Z
Subarrange each by Table P-PZ26
3190-3207   Africa (Table P-PZ23 modified)
Individual authors or works see PL2661+
Non-Chinese languages of China
3301   General
3311.A-Z   Special, A-Z
(3311.C5)   Ching-p'o
see PL4001.K32+
Hmong see PL4072+
3311.K45   Khitan
Lahu see PL4001.L18+
Lolo. Yi see PL3311.Y5
Miao, see PL4072+
(3311.M7)   Moso
see PL4001.N35+
(3311.P34)   Pai
see PL4001.B16
Pai-Miao see PL4072.95.W45
Pho see PL4072.95.B53
3311.S4   Shani
3311.S44   She
Tai Nüa see PL4251.T27
3311.T68   Tosu

	Non-Chinese languages of China
	Special, A-Z -- Continued
(3311.W3)	Wa
	see PL4470
	White Miao see PL4072.95.W45
	Xiandao see PL4001.X53+
	Yao see PL4074+
3311.Y5	Yi
	Cf. PL3916+ Lolo
3501-3509.5	Non-Aryan languages of India and Southeast Asia in general
	(Table P-PZ8a)
3512-3512.9	Malaysian literature (Table P-PZ25)
3515-3515.9	Singapore literature (Table P-PZ25)
3518-3518.95	Languages of the Montagnards (Table P-PZ15a)
	Sino-Tibetan languages
3521-3529.5	General (Table P-PZ8a)
	Tibeto-Burman languages
3551-3559.5	General (Table P-PZ8a)
	Tibeto-Himalayan languages
3561-3569.5	General (Table P-PZ8a)
	Tibetan (Bhōṭiā, Tangutan, Bhotanta)
3601-3646	Tibetan language (Table P-PZ5)
	For groups of dialects see PL3641+
	For particular dialects see PL3651.A+
3651.A-Z	Particular dialects, A-Z
3651.A6-.A695	Amdo (Table P-PZ16)
3651.B2-.B295	Balti (Table P-PZ16)
3651.D2	Dänjong-kä or Bhōṭiā of Sikkim (Table P-PZ40)
3651.D96-.D9695	Dzongkha (Table P-PZ16)
3651.G3	Gaṛhwāl dialect
3651.G9-.G995	Gyarung (Table P-PZ16)
3651.J2	Jaḍ dialect
3651.K3	Kāgate
3651.K5	Khams
3651.K95	Kyirong
3651.L3-.L395	Ladakhī (Table P-PZ16)
3651.L43-.L4395	Lahuli (Table P-PZ16)
3651.L45-.L4595	Lhasa (Table P-PZ16)
(3651.L5)	Lhoke (Bhōṭiā of Bhutan)
	see PL3651.D96+
3651.L65	Lopa (Nepal)
3651.M6	Monpa
3651.N8	Nyamkat
3651.P8	Purik
3651.S38	Sherdukpen
3651.S4	Sherpa
3651.S7	Spiti dialect

Sino-Tibetan languages
Tibeto-Burman languages
Tibeto-Himalayan languages
Tibetan (Bhōtiā, Tangutan, Bhotanta)
Tibetan language
Particular dialects, A-Z -- Continued

3651.T7	Tromowa (Chumbi Valley)
3651.T84	Tshangla
3651.U7	Ü Kā'
3701-3748	Literature (Table P-PZ22 modified)
3748.A-Z	Individual authors or works, A-Z

Subarrange individual authors by Table P-PZ40 unless
otherwise specified
Subarrange individual works by Table P-PZ43 unless
otherwise specified
e.g.

3748.B554	Blo-bzaṅ-chos-kyi-ñi-ma, Thu'u-bkwan III, 1737-1802 (Table P-PZ40)
3748.B56	Blo-bzaṅ-ye-śes, Panchen Lama II, 1663-1737 (Table P-PZ40)
3748.C47	Chos-dbaṅ-grags-pa, Źaṅ-źuṅ-pa (Table P-PZ40)
3748.G4-.G43	Gesar
3748.G4	Texts
3748.G4A-.G4Z	Translations. By language
3748.G425A-.G425Z	Individual episodes. By title
3748.G43	Criticism
3748.G8	Guṅ-thaṅ Dkon-mchog-bstan-pa'i-sgron-me, 1762-1823 (Table P-PZ40)
3748.M38	Mdo-mkhar Tshe-riṅ-dbaṅ-rgyal, 1697-1763 (Table P-PZ40)
3748.M54	Mi-pham-rgya-mtsho, 'Jam-mgon 'Ju, 1846-1912 (Table P-PZ40)
3748.P33	Padma-rig-'dzin, Rdzogs-chen Sprul-sku I, 1625-1697 (Table P-PZ40)
3748.R55	Rin-spuṅs-pa Ṅag-dbaṅ-'jig-rten-dbaṅ-phyug-grags-pa (Table P-PZ40)
3748.S2	Sa-skya Paṇḍi-ta Kun-dga'-rgyal-mtshan, 1182-1251 (Table P-PZ40)
3748.S35	Sdiṅ-chen-nas, Tshe-riṅ-dbaṅ-'dus, 18th cent. (Table P-PZ40)
3748.S55	Skal-ldan-rgya-mtsho, Roṅ-po Grub-chen, 1607-1677 (Table P-PZ40)
3748.T75	Tshaṅs-dbyaṅs-rgya-mtsho, Dalai Lama VI, 1683-1706 (Table P-PZ40)
	Tshe-riṅ-dbaṅ-rgyal, Mdo-mkhar Źabs-druṅ, 1697-1763 see PL3748.M38
	Translations

	Sino-Tibetan languages
	Tibeto-Burman languages
	Tibeto-Himalayan languages
	Tibetan (Bhōtiā, Tangutan, Bhotanta)
	Literature
	Translations -- Continued
(3751-3755)	From foreign languages into Tibetan
	see the original language
3771-3772	From Tibetan into other languages (Table P-PZ30)
	Himalayan languages
3781	General works
3791	Non-pronominalized languages
	For particular languages or dialects see PL3801.A+
3795	Pronominalized languages
	For particular languages or dialects see PL3801.A+
3801.A-Z	Particular languages or dialects, A-Z
3801.A64-.A6495	Athpare (Table P-PZ16)
3801.B2-.B295	Bāhing (Table P-PZ16)
3801.B297-.B29795	Baima (Table P-PZ16)
(3801.B3)	Bālālī
	see PL3801.L7
3801.B34-.B3495	Bantawa (Table P-PZ16)
3801.B4-.B495	Baram (Table P-PZ16)
3801.B8-.B895	Bunán (Table P-PZ16)
3801.B9-.B995	Byāngsī (Table P-PZ16)
3801.C4-.C495	Chamba Lāhulī (Table P-PZ16)
3801.C415-.C41595	Chamling (Table P-PZ16)
3801.C418-.C41895	Chantel (Table P-PZ16)
3801.C42-.C4295	Chaudāngsi (Table P-PZ16)
(3801.C44-.C4495)	Chaurāsya
	see PL3801.W43+
3801.C5-.C595	Chēpāng (Table P-PZ16)
3801.C55-.C5595	Chhingtāng (Table P-PZ16)
3801.C58-.C5895	Chitkhuli (Table P-PZ16)
3801.D3-.D395	Dārmiyā (Table P-PZ16)
3801.D5-.D595	Dhīmāl (Table P-PZ16)
3801.D8-.D895	Dūmī (Table P-PZ16)
	Gōndlā see PL3801.R4+
3801.G8-.G895	Gūrung (Table P-PZ16)
3801.H45	Helambu Sherpa (Table P-PZ16)
	Hāyū see PL3801.W45+
3801.I38-.I3895	Idu (Table P-PZ16)
3801.J2-.J295	Janggalī (Table P-PZ16)
3801.J37-.J3795	Jero (Table P-PZ16)
3801.J5-.J595	Jimdār (Table P-PZ16)
3801.J55-.J5595	Jirel (Table P-PZ16)
3801.K18-.K1895	Kaike (Table P-PZ16)

Sino-Tibetan languages
Tibeto-Burman languages
Tibeto-Himalayan languages
Himalayan languages
Particular languages or dialects, A-Z -- Continued

3801.K2-.K295	Kāmī (Table P-PZ16)
3801.K25-.K2595	Kanāshī (Table P-PZ16)
3801.K3-.K395	Kanauri. Kinnauri (Table P-PZ16)
3801.K4-.K495	Khāling (Table P-PZ16)
3801.K497-.K49795	Kham (Table P-PZ16)
3801.K5-.K595	Khambū (Table P-PZ16)
3801.K8-.K895	Kūlung (Table P-PZ16)
3801.K9-.K995	Kusūndā (Table P-PZ16)
3801.L2-.L295	Lāmbichhōng (Table P-PZ16)
3801.L4-.L495	Lepcha or Rong (Table P-PZ16)
3801.L54-.L5495	Lhomi (Table P-PZ16)
3801.L57-.L5795	Limbu (Table P-PZ16)
3801.L7-.L795	Lōhorōng (Table P-PZ16)
3801.M15-.M1595	Magar (Table P-PZ16)
3801.M2-.M295	Manchātī, or Patnī (Table P-PZ16)
3801.M4-.M495	Mānjhī (Table P-PZ16)
	Multhānī see PL3801.K3+
	Murmi see PL3801.T24+
3801.N3-.N395	Nāchherēng (Table P-PZ16)
3801.N4-.N495	Nam (Table P-PZ16)
3801.N5-.N595	Nēwārī (Table P-PZ16)
3801.P34-.P3495	Pahri (Table P-PZ16)
	Patnī see PL3801.M2+
3801.R3-.R395	Rangkas, or Saukiyā Khun (Table P-PZ16)
3801.R4-.R495	Ranglōī (Table P-PZ16)
3801.R6-.R695	Rōdōng (Table P-PZ16)
	Rong see PL3801.L4+
3801.R8-.R895	Rūngchhēnbūng (Table P-PZ16)
3801.S3-.S395	Sāngpāng (Table P-PZ16)
	Saukiyā Khuh see PL3801.R3+
3801.S5-.S595	Si-hia. Tangut (Table P-PZ16)
3801.S77-.S7795	Sulung (Table P-PZ16)
3801.S8-.S895	Sunwār (Table P-PZ16)
3801.T24-.T2495	Tamang. Murmi (Table P-PZ16)
	Tangut see PL3801.S5+
3801.T3-.T395	Thāksyā. Thakali (Table P-PZ16)
3801.T4-.T495	Thāmī (Table P-PZ16)
3801.T5-.T595	Thūlung (Table P-PZ16)
	Tinūn see PL3801.R4+
3801.T7-.T795	Tōtō (Table P-PZ16)
3801.T85-.T8595	Tulung (Table P-PZ16)

	Sino-Tibetan languages
	Tibeto-Burman languages
	Tibeto-Himalayan languages
	Himalayan languages
	Particular languages or dialects, A-Z -- Continued
(3801.V2-.V295)	Vāyū, or Hāyū (Table P-PZ16)
	see PL3801.W45+
3801.W3-.W395	Wāling (Table P-PZ16)
3801.W43-.W4395	Wambule (Table P-PZ16)
3801.W45-.W4595	Wayu (Table P-PZ16)
3801.Y3-.Y395	Yākhā (Table P-PZ16)
3801.Y43-.Y4395	Yamphu (Table P-PZ16)
3801.Z3-.Z395	Zhangzhung (Table P-PZ16)
	Assam and Burma
	Assamese see PK1550+
3851-3854	North Assam dialects (Table P-PZ11a)
	Assam Burmese dialects
3861-3864	General (Table P-PZ11a)
	Special groups
3871-3874	Bodo group (Table P-PZ11a)
3881-3884	Nāgā group (Table P-PZ11a)
3891-3894	Kuki-Chin group (Table P-PZ11a)
3911-3914	Burma group (Table P-PZ11a)
3916-3919	Lolo group (Table P-PZ11a)
	Cf. PL3311.Y5 Yi
	Special languages and dialects
	Burmese
3921-3966	Language (Table P-PZ5)
3970-3988	Literature (Table P-PZ23 modified)
3988.A-Z	Individual authors or works, A-Z
	Subarrange individual authors by Table P-PZ40
	unless otherwise indicated
	Subarrange individual works by Table P-PZ43
	unless otherwise specified
	e.g.
3988.A39	Aggadhammālaṅkāra, Sayadaw, 1851-1886
	(Table P-PZ40)
3988.A4	Aggasamādhi, Shin, 1478-1557 (Table P-PZ40)
3988.A52	Anantathuriya, d. 1173 (Table P-PZ40)
3988.B36	Bānmaw, Sayadaw, 1806-1877 (Table P-PZ40)
3988.B38	Banyā Dala, ca. 1518-ca. 1572 (Table P-PZ40)
	Bhun'" Nuiṅ', Takkasuil', 1930- see PL3988.T25
	Candā, Ma see PL3988.S258
	Cvam'" Raññ', Moṅ' see PL3988.S85
	Da gun' Tārā see PL3988.D3
3988.D3	Dagon Taya (Table P-PZ40)
3988.G3	Gaung, U. (Table P-PZ40)

Sino-Tibetan languages
    Tibeto-Burman languages
      Assam and Burma
        Assam Burmese dialects
          Special languages and dialects
            Burmese
              Literature
                Individual authors or works, A-Z -- Continued

3988.H487	Hkin Hnīn Yu (Table P-PZ40)
3988.H49	Hkin Kyī Pyaw, Sayadaw, 1725-1762 (Table P-PZ40)
3988.H513	Hla, U, Ludu (Table P-PZ40)
3988.H52	Hlaing Hteik Hkaung Tin, 1833-1875 (Table P-PZ40)
3988.H53	Hle, Sayadaw U, fl. 1882- (Table P-PZ40)
3988.H546	Hpei, Saya, 1838-1894 (Table P-PZ40)
3988.H8	Hsameikkhon Ywazā, b. 1783 (Table P-PZ40)
3988.H839	Htin, Maung (Table P-PZ40)
	Htin Fatt, U. see PL3988.H839
3988.H854	Htin Lin, 1919- (Table P-PZ40)
	Jo'gyī, 1908- see PL3988.T52
3988.K33	Kaṅ'" Van' Maṅ'" krī" , 1822-1908 (Table P-PZ40)
3988.K34	Kandaw Mingyaung, Sayadaw, fl. 1480 (Table P-PZ40)
	Khaṅ' Nhan'" Yu see PL3988.H487
	Krū Krū Saṅ'" see PL3988.K98
3988.K88	Kyaw, U, fl. 1842-1889 (Table P-PZ40)
3988.K884	Kyaw Aung San Htā, Sayadaw (Table P-PZ40)
3988.K8843	Kyaw Hla, U, 1841-1919 (Table P-PZ40)
3988.K98	Kyu Kyu Thīn (Table P-PZ40)
3988.L3	Lat, U, 1866 or 7-1921 (Table P-PZ40)
	Le" Lum, Ma, 1935-1991 see PL3988.L37
3988.L37	Lēi Lon, Ma, 1935-1991 (Table P-PZ40)
3988.L42	Letwethondara, b. 1736 or 7 (Table P-PZ40)
	Lha, Lū thu Ū" see PL3988.H513
3988.L55	Linkarathara, Shin, b. 1726 (Table P-PZ40)
3988.M273	Mahāsīlavaṁsa, Thera, fl. 1492 (Table P-PZ40)
3988.M28	Manle, Sayadaw, 1841-1919 (Table P-PZ40)
3988.M65	Monywe, Sayadaw, 1767-1835 (Table P-PZ40)
3988.M8	Munindābhiddhaja, 1818-1895 or 6 (Table P-PZ40)
3988.N27	Nandadhaja, Shin, 1757-1824 (Table P-PZ40)
3988.N35	Nat Shin Naung, King of Toungoo, 1577-1613 (Table P-PZ40)
3988.N37	Nawade, 1755-1840 (Table P-PZ40)
3988.N38	Nawadegyi, fl. 1532 (Table P-PZ40)

Sino-Tibetan languages
Tibeto-Burman languages
Assam and Burma
Assam Burmese dialects
Special languages and dialects
Burmese
Literature
Individual authors or works, A-Z -- Continued

3988.N6	Nō, U, fl. 1776-1786 (Table P-PZ40)
3988.O2	Ōbhāsa, U, fl. 1762-1826 (Table P-PZ40)
3988.O35	Okhpo, Sayadaw, 1817-1905 (Table P-PZ40)
3988.P3	Padeithayaza, 1684-1754 (Table P-PZ40)
3988.P345	Pandita, U, 1806- (Table P-PZ40)
3988.P35	Paññā, U. (Table P-PZ40)
3988.P4	Pe Thein, U, 1889-1973 (Table P-PZ40)
	Phe, 'A khyup' taṅ'" Cha rā, 1838-1894 see PL3988.H546
3988.P6	Puñña, Ca le Ū", 1802 or 3-1866 or 7 (Table P-PZ40)
	Rāma vatthu see PL3988.Y33+
	Ran' 'Oṅ', 1904- see PL3988.Y34
3988.R3	Raṭṭhasāra, 1468-1520 (Table P-PZ40)
	Rvhe U Doṅ'" , 1889-1973 see PL3988.P4
3988.S258	Sanda, Ma (Table P-PZ40)
3988.S4	Seinda Kyawthu, fl. 1737-1782 (Table P-PZ40)
3988.S425	Shin Htwe Nyo, fl. 1442. (Table P-PZ40)
3988.S435	Shin Ōn Nyo, 15th cent. (Table P-PZ40)
3988.S437	Shin Than Hko, b. 1598 (Table P-PZ40)
3988.S44	Shin Thu Y, fl. 1477 (Table P-PZ40)
3988.S46	Shwedaung Nandathu (Table P-PZ40)
3988.S47	Shwedaung Thihathu (Table P-PZ40)
	Sin'" Phe Mraṇ", 1914-1978 see PL3988.T57
3988.S57	Sithu Kyawhtin, fl. 1470-14820 (Table P-PZ40)
	So'tā Chve see PL3988.T514
3988.S85	Sūn Yi, Maung (Table P-PZ40)
3988.T25	Takkatho Bōn Naing, 1930- (Table P-PZ40)
3988.T44	Teizāwthara, Shin, fl. 1509 (Table P-PZ40)
	Thaṅ' Laṅ" , 1919- see PL3988.H854
3988.T514	Thawta Hswei (Table P-PZ40)
3988.T517	Thein Gyi, Hmawbi Saya, 1862-1953 (Table P-PZ40)
3988.T52	Thein Han, U, 1908- (Table P-PZ40)
3988.T57	Thein Pe Myint, 1914-1978 (Table P-PZ40)
3988.T9	Twīnthīn Taikwun Maha Sithu, 1727-1810 (Table P-PZ40)
3988.U85	Uttamakyaw, Shin, 1453-1542 (Table P-PZ40)

Sino-Tibetan languages
Tibeto-Burman languages
Assam and Burma
Assam Burmese dialects
Special languages and dialects
Burmese
Literature
Individual authors or works, A-Z -- Continued

3988.W3	Warabịthingạnahtạ, Sayadaw, fl. 1605 (Table P-PZ40)
3988.W44	Wet Mạ Sut Myọ Sā Mīn, 1845-1930 (Table P-PZ40)
3988.W55	Winzin Min Yaza, fl. 1338 (Table P-PZ40)
3988.Y3	Yā, U, ca. 1729-1786 or 7 (Table P-PZ40)
3988.Y33-.Y333	Yamạ wathtụ (Table P-PZ43)
3988.Y34	Yan Aung, 1904- (Table P-PZ40)
3988.Z48	Zeya Yantameik, fl. 1579-1610 (Table P-PZ40)
(3989.A-Z)	Individual authors or works, A-Z see PL3988.A+
4001.A-Z	Other languages and dialects, A-Z
4001.A2-.A295	Abor-Miri (Table P-PZ16)
4001.A58-.A5895	Anal (Table P-PZ16)
4001.A6	Andro
4001.A65-.A6595	Angāmi (Table P-PZ16)
4001.A68	Anu
4001.A69-.A6995	Ao (Table P-PZ16)
4001.A75-.A7595	Apatani (Table P-PZ16)
4001.A83-.A8395	Arakanese (Table P-PZ16)
4001.B16	Bai
4001.B2	Banjōgī
4001.B3-.B395	Bara. Bodo. Mech (Table P-PZ16)
	Baungsh see PL4001.L2
4001.B65-.B6595	Bokar (Table P-PZ16)
4001.B77-.B7795	Bori (Table P-PZ16)
4001.C35-.C3595	Chakhesang (Table P-PZ16)
4001.C37-.C3795	Chang (Table P-PZ16)
4001.C4	Chaw
4001.C5	Chin Cf. PL4001.K6 Khyang Chingpaw see PL4001.K32+
4001.C53	Chino
4001.C7	Chutiyā
4001.D2	Daflā Deori see PL4001.C7
4001.D53	Digaro. Taraon. Taying
4001.D55-.D5595	Dimasa (Table P-PZ16) Dulien see PL4001.L8+

Sino-Tibetan languages
Tibeto-Burman languages
Assam and Burma
Assam Burmese dialects
Special languages and dialects
Other language and dialects, A-Z

4001.E6	Empēo, or Kachchā Nāgā
4001.G16-.G1695	Gallong (Table P-PZ16)
4001.G17-.G1795	Gangte (Table P-PZ16)
4001.G2-.G295	Gārō (Table P-PZ16)
4001.G35-.G3595	Geman Deng (Table P-PZ16)
4001.H27	Haka
4001.H3	Hallām
4001.H35-.H3595	Hani (Table P-PZ16)
4001.H55-.H5595	Hmar (Table P-PZ16)
	Jangshēn see PL4001.T4+
	Jingpo see PL4001.K32+
4001.K2-.K295	Kabui (Table P-PZ16)
	Kāchārī, Plains see PL4001.B3+
	Kachchā Nāgā see PL4001.E6
4001.K32-.K3295	Kachin. Jingpo (Table P-PZ16)
4001.K334-.K33495	Kadu (Table P-PZ16)
4001.K336-.K33695	Kaduo (Table P-PZ16)
4001.K34-.K3495	Karko (Table P-PZ16)
	Kathē see PL4001.M31+
4001.K35-.K3595	Kaw (Table P-PZ16)
(4001.K5)	Khami, or Khweymi
	see PL4001.K57+
4001.K54-.K5495	Khezha (Table P-PZ16)
4001.K55-.K5595	Khiamniungan (Table P-PZ16)
4001.K57-.K5795	Khumi (Table P-PZ16)
4001.K6	Khyang
4001.K72-.K7295	Kok Borok (Table P-PZ16)
4001.K73-.K7395	Kom (Table P-PZ16)
4001.K75-.K7595	Konyak (Table P-PZ16)
4001.K8-.K895	Kuki (Table P-PZ16)
4001.L18-.L1895	Lahu (Table P-PZ16)
4001.L2	Lai
4001.L28	Lakher
4001.L3	Lālung
4001.L4-.L495	Lashi (Table P-PZ16)
4001.L5	Lhota. Tsōntsü
4001.L6-.L695	Lisu (Table P-PZ16)
4001.L73-.L7395	Liyang. Liangmai Naga (Table P-PZ16)
4001.L8-.L895	Lushai (Table P-PZ16)
4001.M2	Maingtha
4001.M31-.M3195	Manipurī (Table P-PZ16)

Sino-Tibetan languages
Tibeto-Burman languages
Assam and Burma
Assam Burmese dialects
Special languages and dialects
Other language and dialects, A-Z -- Continued

4001.M32-.M3295	Mao (Table P-PZ16)
4001.M34-.M3495	Maram (Table P-PZ16)
4001.M35	Maru
	Mech see PL4001.B3+
	Meithei see PL4001.M31+
4001.M37-.M3795	Memba (Table P-PZ16)
4001.M49-.M4995	Miji (Table P-PZ16)
4001.M52-.M5295	Mikir (Table P-PZ16)
4001.M53-.M5395	Milang (Table P-PZ16)
4001.M55-.M5595	Mishmi (Table P-PZ16)
	Mojung see PL4001.C37+
4001.M64-.M6495	Moklum (Table P-PZ16)
4001.M7	Mōran
4001.M8	Mrū
4001.N24-.N2495	Naga Chothe (Table P-PZ16)
(4001.N3)	Namsangiā
	see PL4001.N63+
4001.N35-.N3595	Naxi (Table P-PZ16)
4001.N63-.N6395	Nocte (Table P-PZ16)
4001.N8	Nung
4001.P23	Padam
4001.P28-.P2895	Paite (Table P-PZ16)
4001.P3	Pānkhū
4001.P45-.P4595	Phom (Table P-PZ16)
	Plains Kachārī see PL4001.B3+
4001.P63-.P6395	Pochury (Table P-PZ16)
	Pōnnā see PL4001.M31+
4001.R2	Rābhā
4001.R3	Rāngkhōl
4001.R35-.R3595	Rawang (Table P-PZ16)
4001.R4-.R495	Rengmā (Table P-PZ16)
4001.S3	Sairang
4001.S34-.S3495	Sangtam (Table P-PZ16)
4001.S52-.S5295	Semā (Table P-PZ16)
4001.S56-.S5695	Simte (Table P-PZ16)
4001.S6	Siyin
4001.S8	Szi Lepai
4001.T2	Tableng
4001.T24-.T2495	Tagin (Table P-PZ16)
4001.T25	Tamlu
4001.T28-.T2895	Tangkhul (Table P-PZ16)

	Sino-Tibetan languages
	Tibeto-Burman languages
	Assam and Burma
	Assam Burmese dialects
	Special languages and dialects
	Other language and dialects, A-Z -- Continued
4001.T32-.T3295	Tangsa (Table P-PZ16)
	Taraon see PL4001.D53
	Taying see PL4001.D53
4001.T4-.T495	Thādo, or Jangshēn (Table P-PZ16)
4001.T5	That
4001.T6	Thukumi
4001.T65	Tiddim Chin
(4001.T7)	Tipura
	see PL4001.K7
	Tsōntsü see PL4001.L5
4001.V34-.V3495	Vaiphei (Table P-PZ16)
4001.W35-.W3595	Wancho (Table P-PZ16)
4001.X53-.X5395	Xiandao (Table P-PZ16)
(4001.Y3)	Yachumi
	see PL4001.Y38+
4001.Y38-.Y3895	Yimchungru (Table P-PZ16)
4001.Y4	Yindu
4001.Y63-.Y6395	Yogli (Table P-PZ16)
4001.Z3	Zahao
4001.Z33	Zakhring
4001.Z44-.Z4495	Zeliang (Table P-PZ16)
4001.Z68-.Z6895	Zou (Table P-PZ16)
4051-4054	Karen languages (Table P-PZ11a modified)
	Regarded for the present as an independent group of dialects
4054.Z8-.Z9	Dialects
4054.Z9A-.Z9Z	Local. By dialect name or place, A-Z
4054.Z9P8	Pwo Karen
4054.Z9S5	Sgaw Karen
	Miao-Yao languages
4070	General
4072-4072.95	Hmong language. Miao. Mao (Table P-PZ15a modified)
	Dialects
4072.94	General works
4072.95.A-Z	Special. By name or place, A-Z
4072.95.B53	Black Hmong. Black Miao. Pho. Hei-Miao
	Black Miao see PL4072.95.B53
	Blue Meo see PL4072.95.H56
	Green Miao see PL4072.95.H56
	Hei-Miāo, see PL4072.95.B53
	Hmong Daw see PL4072.95.W45
4072.95.H56	Hmong Njua. Blue Meo. Green Miao

	Miao-Yao languages
	Hmong language. Miao. Mao
	Dialects
	Special -- Continued
	Pai-Miao see PL4072.95.W45
	Pho see PL4072.95.B53
4072.95.W45	White Hmong. Hmong Daw. White Meo.
	White Meo see PL4072.95.W45
	White Miao see PL4072.95.W45
4074-4074.95	Yao language. Yao-Min (Table P-PZ15a)
	Tai-Kadai languages. Tai languages
4111-4119.5	General (Table P-PZ8a)
	Thai. Siamese
4151-4196	Language (Table P-PZ5)
4200-4209	Literature (Table P-PZ24 modified)
4209.A-Z	Individual authors or works, A-Z
	Subarrange individual authors by Table P-PZ40 unless otherwise specified
	Subarrange individual works by Table P-PZ43 unless otherwise specified
	e.g.
4209.C45	Chai Bangkok, 1931- (Table P-PZ40)
	Khwanchai, 1931- see PL4209.C45
4209.N27	Naritsarănuwattiwong, Prince, 1863-1947 (Table P-PZ40)
	Phet Chomphu, 1931- see PL4209.C45
4209.P537	Phromsomphatsŏn (Mĭ), Mŭn, ca. 1796-ca. 1856 (Table P-PZ40)
4209.P548	Phutthaloetlă Naphălai, King of Siam, 1768-1824 (Table P-PZ40)
4209.P5484	Phutthayotfa Chulalok, King of Siam, 1737-1809 (Table P-PZ40)
	Prasoet Phichansophon, 1931- see PL4209.C45
4209.S82	Sunthon Phŭ, 1786-1855 (Table P-PZ40)
4209.T4785	Thanmāphimon (ThƯk), Lŭang (Table P-PZ40)
4209.W335	Warōdom (Table P-PZ40)
	Wōrakān Čharōendī see PL4209.W335
4236-4236.95	Lao (Table P-PZ15a modified)
	Literature
4236.9.A-Z	Individual authors or works, A-Z
	Subarrange individual authors by Table P-PZ40 unless otherwise specified
	Subarrange individual works by Table P-PZ43 unless otherwise specified
	e. g.
4236.9.S48	Sieosavat (Table P-PZ40)
4251.A-Z	Other special languages and dialects, A-Z

	Tai languages
	Other special languages and dialects, A-Z -- Continued
4251.A4	Āhom
4251.A5	Aiton
4251.B4-.B495	Be. Ongbe (Table P-PZ16)
4251.B57-.B5795	Black Tai (Table P-PZ16)
	Bouyei see PL4251.P85+
4251.C27-.C2795	Cao Lan (Table P-PZ16)
4251.C4-.C495	Chuang. Zhuang (Table P-PZ16)
(4251.D5)	Dioi
	see PL4251.P85+
	Dong see PL4251.T85
	Karen see PL4051+
4251.K4	Khāmtī
4251.K5	Khün
4251.L27	Laha
	Lao see PL4236+
4251.L5	Li
4251.L8	Lü
4251.L85	Lungming
4251.M36	Maonan
4251.M85	Mulao
4251.N6	Norā
4251.N63-.N6395	Northern Thai (Table P-PZ16)
4251.P4	Phākial
4251.P48-.P4895	Phu Thai (Table P-PZ16)
4251.P85-.P8595	Pu-i. Bouyei (Table P-PZ16)
4251.S23	Saek
4251.S6-.S695	Shan (Table P-PZ16)
4251.S95-.S9595	Sui (Table P-PZ16)
4251.T27	Tai Nüa
4251.T3	Tai-rong
4251.T38-.T3895	Tay-Nung (Table P-PZ16)
4251.T5-.T595	Tho (Table P-PZ16)
4251.T85	Tung. Dong
4251.W55-.W5595	White Tai (Table P-PZ16)
4251.Y32	Ya
(4251.Y38)	Yay
	see PL4251.P85+
	Zhuang see PL4251.C4+
	Austroasiatic languages
4281-4289.5	General (Table P-PZ8a)
	Mon-Khmer (Mon-Anam) languages
4301	General works
4303	Grammar
4306	Dictionaries
4308-4308.9	Literature (Table P-PZ25)

Austroasiatic languages
Mon-Khmer (Mon-Anam) languages -- Continued

4309	Other special
	e.g. Etymology
4310.A-Z	Special groups, A-Z
4310.B34	Bahnaric
4310.K38	Katuic
4310.S45	Senoic languages
	Individual languages
4311-4314	Bahnar (Table P-PZ11)
4321-4329.5	Khmer (Cambodian) (Table P-PZ8a)
4331-4339.5	Mon (Talaing or Peguan) (Table P-PZ8a)
4341-4344	Stieng (Table P-PZ11)
4371-4379.5	Vietnamese. Annamese (Table P-PZ8a modified)
4378-4378.9	Literature (Table P-PZ25 modified)
4378.9.A-Z	Individual authors or works, A-Z
	Subarrange individual authors by Table P-PZ40 unless otherwise specified
	Subarrange individual works by Table P-PZ43 unless otherwise specified
	e.g.
4378.9.B844	Bùi, Hữu Nghĩa, 1807-1872 (Table P-PZ40)
4378.9.B845	Bùi, Huy Bích, 1744-1818 (Table P-PZ40)
4378.9.C37	Cao, Bá Quát, 1808-1855 (Table P-PZ40)
4378.9.C487	Chu, Văn An, 1292-1370 (Table P-PZ40)
4378.9.D33	Đặng, Trần Côn, b. 1715? (Table P-PZ40)
4378.9.D3379	Đào, Tấn, 1845-1907 (Table P-PZ40)
4378.9.D593	Đoàn, Hữu Trưng, 1844-1866 (Table P-PZ40)
4378.9.H53	Hồ Dzếnh, 1916- (Table P-PZ40)
4378.9.H5415	Hồ, Huyên Qui, 15th cent. (Table P-PZ40)
4378.9.H5425	Hồ, Xuân Hương (Table P-PZ40)
4378.9.H615	Học Lạc, 1842-1915 (Table P-PZ40)
4378.9.L363	Lê, Ngô Cát, 1827-1876 (Table P-PZ40)
4378.9.L369	Lê, Quý Đôn, 1726-1784 (Table P-PZ40)
4378.9.L373	Lê, Thánh Tông, King of Vietnam, 1442-1497 (Table P-PZ40)
4378.9.L927	Lý, Tế Xuyên, 14th cent. (Table P-PZ40)
4378.9.N4434	Ngô, Thì Nhậm, 1746-1803 (Table P-PZ40)
4378.9.N4435	Ngô, Thì Sĩ, 1726-1780 (Table P-PZ40)
4378.9.N4484	Nguyễn, Bỉnh Khiêm, 1491-1585 (Table P-PZ40)
4378.9.N452	Nguyễn, Công Trứ, 1778-1858 (Table P-PZ40)
4378.9.N46	Nguyễn, Đình Chiểu, 1822-1888 (Table P-PZ40)
4378.9.N5	Nguyễn, Du, 1765-1820 (Table P-PZ40)
4378.9.N516	Nguyễn, Hữu Hào, d. 1733 (Table P-PZ40)
4378.9.N5169	Nguyễn, Huy Tự, 1743-1790 (Table P-PZ40)
4378.9.N5236	Nguyễn, Khuyến, 1835-1909 (Table P-PZ40)
4378.9.N534	Nguyễn, Nhược Thị, 1830-1909 (Table P-PZ40)

Austroasiatic languages
Mon-Khmer (Mon-Anam) languages
Individual languages
Vietnamese. Annamese
Literature
Individual authors or works, A-Z -- Continued

4378.9.N5475	Nguyễn, Thông, 1827-1884 (Table P-PZ40)
4378.9.N54776	Nguyễn, Trãi, 1380-1442 (Table P-PZ40)
4378.9.N5486	Nguyễn, Xuân Ôn, 1825-1889 (Table P-PZ40)
4378.9.O5	Ôn Như Hầu, 1741-1798 (Table P-PZ40)
4378.9.P524	Phạm, Văn Nghị, 1805-1881 (Table P-PZ40)
4378.9.P53	Phan, Bội Châu, 1867-1940 (Table P-PZ40)
4378.9.P536	Phan, Chu Trinh, 1872-1926 (Table P-PZ40)
4378.9.P546	Phan, Huy Ích, 1750-1822 (Table P-PZ40)
4378.9.P583	Phan, Văn Trị, 1830-1910 (Table P-PZ40)
4378.9.P62	Phùng, Khắc Khoan, 1528-1613 (Table P-PZ40)
4378.9.T667	Trần, Tế Xương, 1870-1907 (Table P-PZ40)
4378.9.T818	Tùng Thiện Vương, 1819-1870 (Table P-PZ40)
4378.9.T819	Tương An Quận Vương, 1820-1854 (Table P-PZ40)
4420	Besisi
4423	Bru
4429	Chrau
4433	Cua
4439	Hrê
	Huei see PL4461
4443	Jeh
4444	Jehai
4447	Katu
4451-4451.95	Khasi (Table P-PZ15a modified)
	Literature
4451.9.A-Z	Individual authors or works, A-Z
	Subarrange individual authors by Table P-PZ40 unless otherwise specified
	Subarrange individual works by Table P-PZ43 unless otherwise specified
	e.g.
4451.9.R68	Roy, Jeebon, 1838-1903 (Table P-PZ40)
4451.9.T46	Tham, Soso, 1873-1940 (Table P-PZ40)
4452	Khmu
4453	Koho
	Including Srê
4454	Kui
4454.5	Laqua
4454.7	Laven
4455	Lawa
4456	Mang
4457	Mnong, Eastern

Austroasiatic languages
Mon-Khmer (Mon-Anam) languages
Individual languages -- Continued

4459-4459.95	Muong (Table P-PZ15a)
4459.97	Nguon
4460	Nyah Kur
4461	Oi. Huei
4462	Pacoh
4463	Palaung
4464	Pear
4464.5	Puoc
4465	Rengao
4466	Riang
4466.5	Ruc
4466.7	Sapuan
4467	Sedang
4467.5	Semai
4467.6	Semelai
	Srê see PL4453
4468	Temiar
4469	T'in
4470	Wa
	Nicobarese
4471	General works
4471.5	Nancowry language
	Chamic languages
4490	General (Table P-PZ15)
4491-4491.95	Cham (Table P-PZ15a)
4498.A-Z	Other, A-Z
	Djarai see PL4498.J3
4498.H37	Haroi
4498.J3	Jarai
4498.R3-.R395	Rade (Table P-PZ16)
4498.R63-.R6395	Roglai (Table P-PZ16)
4498.X3	Xinca (Jinca)
	Munda languages (Kolarian languages)
	Chiefly of Southern India
4501-4509	General (Table P-PZ8)
	Kherwārī languages
4511-4519.5	General (Table P-PZ8a)
4531	Agariā
4535	Asurī
4539	Bhumij
4543-4543.95	Birhor (Table P-PZ15a)
4545	Gata'
4547-4547.95	Hō (Table P-PZ15a)
4551	Kōdā

	Austroasiatic languages
	Munda languages (Kolarian languages)
	Kherwārī languages -- Continued
	Kol (or Kolh) see PL4559+
4555-4555.95	Korwa (Table P-PZ15a)
4559-4559.95	Muṇḍārī (Table P-PZ15a modified)
	Dialects spoken by the Mankipatti Bund and Tamar
	Literature
4559.9.A-Z	Individual authors or works, A-Z
	Subarrange individual authors by Table P-PZ40 unless otherwise specified
	Subarrange individual works by Table P-PZ43 unless otherwise specified
	e.g.
4559.9.B85	Budu Bābū, 19th cent. (Table P-PZ40)
4563-4563.95	Santali (Table P-PZ15a)
4571-4571.95	Tūrī (Table P-PZ15a)
	Other Munda languages
4572	Bonda
4573	Gadabā
4575	Juāṅg
4579-4579.95	Kharia (Table P-PZ15a)
4583-4583.95	Kūrkū (Table P-PZ15a)
4583.9.A-Z	Individual authors or works, A-Z
	Subarrange individual authors by Table P-PZ40
	Subarrange individual works by Table P-PZ43
4583.9.D46-.D463	Ḍholā Kuṁvara (Table P-PZ43)
4585-4585.95	Nahali. Nihali (Table P-PZ15a)
4586	Parengi
4587-4587.95	Savara. Sora (Table P-PZ15a)
	Dravidian languages
4601-4609.5	General (Table P-PZ8a)
4617-4617.95	Alu Kurumba (Table P-PZ15a)
	Baḍaga see PL4641+
4621-4624	Brāhūī (Table P-PZ11)
	Carnataca see PL4641+
4627-4627.95	Gadabā (Table P-PZ15a)
	Gentoo see PL4771+
4631-4634	Gōṇḍī (Table P-PZ11)
4636-4636.95	Irula (Table P-PZ15a)
	Kandh see PL4695+
4641-4649.5	Kannada. Kanarese (including Baḍaga dialect) (Table P-PZ8a modified)
(4648-4648.9)	Literature
	see PL4650+
4650-4659	Literature (Table P-PZ24 modified)

Dravidian languages
   Kannada. Kanarese (including Baḍaga dialect)
     Literature -- Continued
4659.A-Z   Individual authors or works, A-Z
          Subarrange individual authors by Table P-PZ40 unless
            otherwise specified
          Subarrange individual works by Table P-PZ43 unless
            otherwise specified
          e.g.

4659.A16	Abhinavacandra, 15th cent. (Table P-PZ40)
4659.A2	Ācārya, Pā. Veṃ., 1915-1991 (Table P-PZ40)
4659.A24	Ādidēva, fl. 1500-1546 (Table P-PZ40)
4659.A315	Aggaḷadēva, 12th cent. (Table P-PZ40)
4659.A34	Akkamahādēvi, fl. 1160 (Table P-PZ40)
4659.A35	Akkanāgamma, 12th cent. (Table P-PZ40)
4659.A42	Aliya Liṅgarāja, 1823-1874 (Table P-PZ40)
4659.A43	Allamaprabhu, fl. 1160 (Table P-PZ40)
4659.A43727	Ambalige, Cannamalla, b. 1700? (Table P-PZ40)
4659.A4373	Ambigara Caudayya, 12th cent. (Table P-PZ40)
4659.A469	Anantādrīśa, 1776-1840 (Table P-PZ40)
4659.A53	Āṇḍayya, 13th cent. (Table P-PZ40)
4659.A67	Aparāḷa Timmaṇṇa, 19th cent. (Table P-PZ40)
4659.A88	Attigēri Māstara, 19th cent. (Table P-PZ40)
4659.A93	Āydakki Lakkamma, 12th cent. (Table P-PZ40)
4659.A95	Ayyappa, 19th cent. (Table P-PZ40)
4659.B15	Bahubali, 16th cent. (Table P-PZ40)
4659.B16	Bālabhāskara, 18th cent. (Table P-PZ40)
4659.B18	Bālagōpāla, Kavi, 1830-1930 (Table P-PZ40)
4659.B34	Basava, fl. 1160 (Table P-PZ40)
4659.B3435	Basavāṅka, 16th cent. (Table P-PZ40)
4659.B3445	Basavappaɪsāstri, 1843-1891 (Table P-PZ40)
4659.B347	Battaleśvara, fl. 1500 (Table P-PZ40)
4659.B35	Beḷagali, Du. Nim. (Duranduṇḍēśvara Niṅgappa), 1931-
	(Table P-PZ40)
4659.B433	Bhadrēśvara, 1832-1902 (Table P-PZ40)
4659.B462	Bhāskara, fl. 1424 (Table P-PZ40)
4659.B486	Bhat, V. G., 1923- (Table P-PZ40)
	Bhaṭṭa, Vi, Ji., 1923- see PL4659.B486
4659.B52	Bhīmakavi, fl. 1369 (Table P-PZ40)
	Bhīmasēnarāya, Rayasaṃ, 1912- see PL4659.B556
4659.B556	Bīci, 1912- (Table P-PZ40)
4659.B568-.B5683	Biḷigiri Raṅgana kāvya (Table P-PZ43)
4659.B63	Bommaṇa, 18th cent. (Table P-PZ40)
4659.B65	Boppaṇa, Paṇḍita (Table P-PZ40)
4659.B74	Brahmaśiva, fl. 1125-1190 (Table P-PZ40)
4659.C315	Cadura Candrama, 17th cent. (Table P-PZ40)
4659.C35	Cāmarasa, 15th cent. (Table P-PZ40)

Dravidian languages
  Kannada. Kanarese (including Badaga dialect)
    Literature
      Individual authors or works, A-Z -- Continued

4659.C415	Cannabasavāṅka (Table P-PZ40)
4659.C417	Cannavīrāṅka, 15th cent. (Table P-PZ40)
4659.C43	Cauṇḍarasa, fl. 1185-1240 (Table P-PZ40)
4659.C44	Celuvāmbe, 18th cent. (Table P-PZ40)
	Cennabasavaṇṇa, 12th cent. see PL4659.C515
4659.C454	Cennayya, 17th cent. (Table P-PZ40)
4659.C515	Channabasava, 12th cent. (Table P-PZ40)
4659.C52	Chennabasavaraja Desikendra Shivacharya, 1911- (Table P-PZ40)
4659.C525	Chittal, Gangadhar, 1923-1987 (Table P-PZ40)
4659.C5273	Cidānandāvadhūta, 18th cent. (Table P-PZ40)
4659.C5274	Cikkamallaṇa, 16th cent. (Table P-PZ40)
4659.C528	Cikkamallikārjuna (Table P-PZ40)
4659.C529	Cikupādhyāya, fl. 1672-1704 (Table P-PZ40)
4659.C533	Cilāḷaprabhusvāmi, b. 1615 (Table P-PZ40)
4659.D37	Dēparāja, 15th cent. (Table P-PZ40)
4659.D463	Dēvacandra, 1770-1841 (Table P-PZ40)
4659.D4635	Dēvakavi, 13th cent. (Table P-PZ40)
4659.D464	Dēvakavi, 16th cent. (Table P-PZ40)
4659.D472	Dēvappa, fl. 1540 (Table P-PZ40)
4659.D473	Dēvaradāsimayya, fl. 1008-1050 (Table P-PZ40)
4659.D474	Dēvidāsa, 17th cent. (Table P-PZ40)
4659.D475	Dhāravāḍa, Cennabasavappa, 1833-1881 (Table P-PZ40)
4659.D494	Dhūpadahaḷḷi Śānta, fl. 1678-1728 (Table P-PZ40)
4659.D593	Doḍḍayya, 17th cent. (Table P-PZ40)
4659.D78	Durgasiṃha, fl. 1139-1150 (Table P-PZ40)
4659.G33	Gajēśa Masaṇayya, 12th cent. (Table P-PZ40)
4659.G338	Galagali Avva, ca. 1670-ca. 1760 (Table P-PZ40)
4659.G34	Galaganātha, V.T. Kulakarni, 1869-1942 (Table P-PZ40)
4659.G373	Gangadhara, 16th/17th cent. (Table P-PZ40)
4659.G374	Garaniya Basavaliṅga, 15th cent. (Table P-PZ40)
4659.G672	Gōpāladāsa, 1721-1762 (Table P-PZ40)
4659.G692	Gōvindadāsa, 19th cent. (Table P-PZ40)
4659.G693	Gōvindakavi, 18th cent. (Table P-PZ40)
4659.G695	Gōvindavaidya, 17th cent. (Table P-PZ40)
4659.G72	Gubbiya Mallaṇārya, fl. 1509-1529 (Table P-PZ40)
4659.G764	Guṇavarma (Table P-PZ40)
4659.G766	Guṇḍabrahmayya, 17th cent. (Table P-PZ40)
4659.G797	Guñjāḷa, Es. Ār., 1932- (Table P-PZ40)
4659.G83	Gurubasavārya, 15th cent. (Table P-PZ40)
4659.G834	Gurubasavēśa, fl. 1730-1740 (Table P-PZ40)

Dravidian languages
Kannada. Kanarese (including Badaga dialect)
Literature
Individual authors or works, A-Z -- Continued

4659.G84	Gurulingasiddha, 1870-1928 (Table P-PZ40)
4659.G87	Gururāmaviṭhala, ca. 1850-1915 (Table P-PZ40)
4659.H16	Haḍapada Appaṇṇa, 12th cent. (Table P-PZ40)
4659.H276	Haradanahaḷḷi Nañjaṇārya, 17th cent. (Table P-PZ40)
4659.H278-.H2783	Haraḷayyana carite (poem) (Table P-PZ43)
4659.H2784	Harapanahaḷḷi Bhīmavva, 1823-1903 (Table P-PZ40)
4659.H29	Harihara, Hampeya (Table P-PZ40)
4659.H424	Heḷavanakaṭṭe, Giriyamma, 18th cent. (Table P-PZ40)
4659.H433	Hērambakavi, 16th cent. (Table P-PZ40)
4659.H6	Honnamma, Sañciya, 17th cent. (Table P-PZ40)
	Indirā, Em. Ke., 1917 see PL4659.I5
4659.I5	Indirā, M.K. (Table P-PZ40)
4659.I56	Indra Dēvarasa, 17th cent. (Table P-PZ40)
	Ja. Ca. Ni., 1911- see PL4659.C52
4659.J184	Jagannāthadāsa, 1728-1809 (Table P-PZ40)
4659.J187	Jālavādiya Mallaṇṇa, 15th cent. (Table P-PZ40)
4659.J2	Janna (Table P-PZ40)
4659.J45	Jiguni Maruḷadēva, 16th cent. (Table P-PZ40)
4659.K17	Kaḍakoḷa Maḍivāḷēśvara, 1780-1855 (Table P-PZ40)
4659.K235	Kākemāni (Table P-PZ40)
4659.K253	Kallarasa, 15th cent. (Table P-PZ40)
4659.K257	Kalyāṇakīrti, fl. 1400-1460 (Table P-PZ40)
	Kamalā Hampanā, 1935- see PL4659.K272
4659.K268	Kamalabhava, 13th cent. (Table P-PZ40)
4659.K272	Kamalamma Hampana, C. R., 1935- (Table P-PZ40)
4659.K29	Kanakadāsa, 1509-1607 (Table P-PZ40)
4659.K2967-.K29673	Kannīrāmbiya kathe (Table P-PZ43)
4659.K314	Karibasavārya, 1745-1840 (Table P-PZ40)
4659.K317	Karināḍa Karibasavēndraru, fl. 12th cent. (Table P-PZ40)
4659.K32	Karki, Di. Es., 1907-1984 (Table P-PZ40)
4659.K334	Karṇapārya, 12th cent. (Table P-PZ40)
4659.K364	Kavicenna (Table P-PZ40)
4659.K369	Keḷadi Veṅkaṇṇa, 18th cent. (Table P-PZ40)
4659.K3692	Kellaṅgere Timmappadāsa, 1834-1926 (Table P-PZ40)
4659.K378	Kereya Padmarasa, fl. 1165-1200 (Table P-PZ40)
4659.K6833	Krishnakumar, C. P., 1939- (Table P-PZ40)
4659.K685	Krishnasharma, Betageri Shrinivasarao, 1900- (Table P-PZ40)
	Kṛṣṇakumār, Si. Pi., 1939- see PL4659.K6833
	Kṛṣṇaśarmā, Beṭagēri, 1900- see PL4659.K685
4659.K755	Kūḍalūru Basavalingaśaraṇa, 18th cent. (Table P-PZ40)

Dravidian languages
   Kannada. Kanarese (including Badaga dialect)
     Literature
      Individual authors or works, A-Z -- Continued

4659.K832	Kumāra Padmarasa, 13th cent. (Table P-PZ40)
4659.K837	Kumāra Vālmīki, fl. 1500 (Table P-PZ40)
4659.K84	Kumāravyāsa, fl. 1419-1446 (Table P-PZ40)
4659.K842	Kumbaḷe Pārti Subba, 17th cent. (Table P-PZ40)
4659.K847	Kumudēndu, 8th cent. (Table P-PZ40)
4659.K848	Kumudēndu, 13th cent. (Table P-PZ40)
4659.K86	Kurtakōṭi, Ke. Di., 1928- (Table P-PZ40)
	Kuvempu, 1904- see PL4659.P797
4659.L22	Lakkannadaṇḍēśa, 15th cent. (Table P-PZ40)
4659.L25	Lakshmana Rao, Birur Rajarao, 1946- (Table P-PZ40)
4659.L276	Lakṣmakavi, 18th cent. (Table P-PZ40)
	Lakṣmaṇarāv, Bi., Ār, 1946- see PL4659.L25
4659.L278	Lakṣmīdēvamma, Ōrabayi, 1865-1950 (Table P-PZ40)
4659.L28	Lakṣmīśa (Table P-PZ40)
	Lāngūlācārya, 1915-1991 see PL4659.A2
4659.L33	Laṅkēś, Pi., 1935-2000 (Table P-PZ40)
4659.L45	Ligāde, Jayadēvitāyi, 1912- (Table P-PZ40)
	Liṅgaṇṇa, Simpi, 1905- see PL4659.S555
4659.M13	Mādāra Cennayya, 11th cent. (Table P-PZ40)
4659.M2165	Maggeya Māyidēva, fl. 1419-1446 (Table P-PZ40)
4659.M2169	Mahādēva, fl. 1863-1870 (Table P-PZ40)
4659.M21694	Mahādēva, Dēvanūra, 1949- (Table P-PZ40)
4659.M2175	Mahāliṅgadēva, 15th cent. (Table P-PZ40)
4659.M2176	Mahāliṅgasvāmi, Hampeya (Table P-PZ40)
4659.M2187	Mahipatidāsa, 1611-1681 (Table P-PZ40)
4659.M2243-.M22433	Māliṅgarāyana kāvya (Table P-PZ43)
4659.M2246	Mallaṇa, 19th cent. (Table P-PZ40)
	Mallikā, 1920- see PL4659.M282
4659.M227	Mallikārjuna, 16th cent. (Table P-PZ40)
4659.M263	Maṅgarasa, fl. 1508 (Table P-PZ40)
4659.M27	Mangesha Rao, Panje (Table P-PZ40)
4659.M282	Manjappa, Laxmi Devi Kadidal, 1920- (Table P-PZ40)
4659.M294	Maruḷu Śaṅkaradēva, 12th cent. (Table P-PZ40)
4659.M38	Mēdāra Kētayya, 12th cent. (Table P-PZ40)
4659.M57	Mogasāle, Nā., 1944- (Table P-PZ40)
4659.M76	Muddana, 1870-1901 (Table P-PZ40)
4659.M77	Mudgalanātha, fl. 1700- (Table P-PZ40)
4659.M784	Mukhabōḷu Siddharāma, 16th cent. (Table P-PZ40)
4659.N187	Nadig, Sumatheendra, 1935- (Table P-PZ40)
	Nāḍiga, Sumatīndra, 1935- see PL4659.N187
	Nāgacandra, fl. 1100-1140 see PL4659.P26
4659.N218	Nāgarājakavi, 14th cent. (Table P-PZ40)
4659.N225	Nāgava, 18th cent. (Table P-PZ40)

Dravidian languages
  Kannada. Kanarese (including Badaga dialect)
    Literature
      Individual authors or works, A-Z -- Continued

4659.N226	Nāgavarma, 10th cent. (Table P-PZ40)
4659.N227	Nāgavarma, 12th cent. (Table P-PZ40)
4659.N2849	Nañjuṇda, 19th cent. (Table P-PZ40)
4659.N29	Narasiṃha Śāstri, Dēvuḍu, 1896-1963 (Table P-PZ40)
4659.N2925	Narasiṃhācārya, Es. Ji., 1862-1907 (Table P-PZ40)
	Narasiṃhaśāstri, Dēvudu, 1896-1963 see PL4659.N29
4659.N297	Narasiṃhasvāmi, Ke. Es., 1915- (Table P-PZ40)
4659.N344	Navanīra, 16th cent. (Table P-PZ40)
4659.N395	Nayasēna, 12th cent. (Table P-PZ40)
4659.N42	Nēmaṇṇa, 16th cent. (Table P-PZ40)
4659.N43	Nēmicandra, fl. 1170 (Table P-PZ40)
4659.N47	Nijaguṇa Śivayogi, fl. 1500 (Table P-PZ40)
4659.N48	Nījaliṅgārādhya (Table P-PZ40)
4659.N516	Nīlakaṇṭhācārya, 15th cent. (Table P-PZ40)
	Nīlu, 1935-2000 see PL4659.L33
	Niranjana, 1923- see PL4659.S54
4659.N594	Niścintātma, 18th cent. (Table P-PZ40)
4659.O38	Ōduva Giriya, 16th cent. (Table P-PZ40)
4659.P236	Padma Kavi, fl. 1509-1529 (Table P-PZ40)
4659.P2536	Padmasāle Timmaṇṇa, 18th/19th cent. (Table P-PZ40)
4659.P258	Pampa, b. 902 (Table P-PZ40)
4659.P26	Pampa, fl. 1100 (Table P-PZ40)
4659.P2647	Paramadēva, 18th cent. (Table P-PZ40)
4659.P2696	Pārśvakavi, 17th cent. (Table P-PZ40)
4659.P2698	Partisubba (Table P-PZ40)
4659.P26985	Parvatadēva, 16th cent. (Table P-PZ40)
4659.P36	Pattāra, Rāyappa, fl. 1860-1950 (Table P-PZ40)
4659.P58	Ponna, 10th cent. (Table P-PZ40)
4659.P67	Prabhākar, Bi. Es., 1933- (Table P-PZ40)
4659.P7244	Prāṇēśadāsa, 1736-1822 (Table P-PZ40)
4659.P728	Prasannavenkaṭadāsa, 1680-1752 (Table P-PZ40)
4659.P769	Puṇḍarīkaviṭṭhala, 16th cent. (Table P-PZ40)
	Purandaradāsa see PL4659.S685
4659.P795	Puṭṭaṇṇa, Eṃ. Es., 1854-1930 (Table P-PZ40)
4659.P797	Puttapa, K. Venkatappa Gowda, 1904- (Table P-PZ40)
4659.R25	Rāghavāṅka (Table P-PZ40)
4659.R316	Rama Raya, Samethana Halli, 1917- (Table P-PZ40)
4659.R3185	Ramadasa, 18th cent. (Table P-PZ40)
4659.R34275	Rāmapura Bakkappayya, 1660-1730 (Table P-PZ40)
	Rāmarāya, Sameētanahaḷḷi, 1917- see PL4659.R316
4659.R35	Rangacharya, Adya, 1904- (Table P-PZ40)
4659.R39	Ranna, fl. 993 (Table P-PZ40)
4659.R42	Ratnākaravarni, 16th cent. (Table P-PZ40)

Dravidian languages
  Kannada. Kanarese (including Badaga dialect)
    Literature
      Individual authors or works, A-Z -- Continued

4659.R8	Rudrabhatta, fl. 1173-1220 (Table P-PZ40)
4659.R83	Rudrakavi, 17th cent. (Table P-PZ40)
4659.R84	Rudramūrtiśāstri, Su. (Sugganahaḷḷi), 1948- (Table P-PZ40)
4659.S22	Saḍaksaradēva, fl. 1655 (Table P-PZ40)
	Sadaksarisa, 17th cent. see PL4659.S22
4659.S245	Sāḷva, fl. 1550 (Table P-PZ40)
4659.S2614	Śaṅkaradēva, 17th cent. (Table P-PZ40)
4659.S262	Śaṅkha, 17th cent. (Table P-PZ40)
4659.S27215	Śāntaniranjaña, 17th cent. (Table P-PZ40)
4659.S27218	Śāntavīra (Table P-PZ40)
4659.S2722	Śāntavīra Dēśika, fl. 1650 (Table P-PZ40)
4659.S2725	Santikirtimuni, 18th cent. (Table P-PZ40)
	Śarma, Rāmacandra see PL4659.S526
4659.S286	Sarpabhūṣaṇa Śivayōgi, 1794-1839 (Table P-PZ40)
4659.S287	Sarvajña, fl. 1600 (Table P-PZ40)
4659.S3487	Sejjeya Siddhaliṅga, 17th cent. (Table P-PZ40)
4659.S5	Shankar, Anusuya, 1928-1963 (Table P-PZ40)
4659.S52	Shanker Bhat, Kadengodlu, 1904-1968 (Table P-PZ40)
4659.S526	Sharma, Ramachandra, 1925- (Table P-PZ40)
4659.S54	Shiva Rao, Kulkunda, 1923- (Table P-PZ40)
4659.S5525	Siddhakavi, 17th/18th cent. (Table P-PZ40)
4659.S5527	Siddhaliṅga (Table P-PZ40)
4659.S5528-.S55283	Siddhamaṅka carite (Table P-PZ43)
4659.S5533	Siddhanañjēśa, fl. 1600-1678 (Table P-PZ40)
4659.S5534	Siddhārama, 12th cent. (Table P-PZ40)
4659.S555	Simpi Linganna, Shivayogappa, 1905- (Table P-PZ40)
4659.S559	Siṅgarārya, fl. 1672-1704 (Table P-PZ40)
4659.S566	Śiśunāla Śarīpha, 19th cent. (Table P-PZ40)
4659.S5826	Śivānanda, 1873?-1953? (Table P-PZ40)
4659.S598	Sōmanātha, fl. 1600 (Table P-PZ40)
4659.S612-.S6123	Sōmēśvara sātaka (Table P-PZ43)
4659.S637	Śrīdaviṭhaladāsa, 1740?-1820 (Table P-PZ40)
4659.S6464	Srikanthesha Gowda, M.L., 1852-1926 (Table P-PZ40)
4659.S685	Śrīnivāsanāyaka, 1484-1564 (Table P-PZ40)
4659.S74	Śrīpādarāja, 1404-1502 (Table P-PZ40)
	Śrīraṅga, 1904- see PL4659.R35
4659.S79	Śrutakīrti, 16th cent. (Table P-PZ40)
	Subbarāv, Taḷakina Rāmasvāmayya, 1923- see PL4659.T23
4659.S873	Subbarāya, Kerōḍi, 1863-1928 (Table P-PZ40)
	Svāmi, Bi. Es. see PL4659.S96
4659.S955	Svatantra Siddhaliṅgeśvara, fl. 1480 (Table P-PZ40)

Dravidian languages
  Kannada. Kanarese (including Badaga dialect)
    Literature
      Individual authors or works, A-Z -- Continued

4659.S96	Swamy, B.S., 1942- (Table P-PZ40)
4659.T23	Ta.Ra.Su. (Taḷakina Rāmasvāmayya Subbarāv), 1923- (Table P-PZ40)
4659.T414	Terakanambi Bommarasa (Table P-PZ40)
4659.T4157	Timmakavi, 18th cent. (Table P-PZ40)
4659.T416	Timmaṇṇakavi, fl. 1510-1529 (Table P-PZ40)
4659.T417	Timmappadāsa, 1770?-1860? (Table P-PZ40)
4659.T418	Tinthaṇi Maunēśvara, fl. 1540-1650 (Table P-PZ40)
4659.T45	Thrivikrama, 1920- (Table P-PZ40)
4659.T526	Tirumalārya, fl. 1672-1704 (Table P-PZ40)
	Trivēṇi see PL4659.S5
	Trivikrama, 1920- see PL4659.T45
4659.T796	Tuḷasirāmadāsaru, 1847-1903 (Table P-PZ40)
4659.T83	Tupāki Veṅkaṭaramaṇācārya, fl. 1810-1893 (Table P-PZ40)
4659.T84	Turamari, Gaṅgādhara Maḍivaḷēśvara, 1827-1877 (Table P-PZ40)
4659.U74	Uriliṅgipeddi (Table P-PZ40)
4659.V17	Vādirāja, 16th cent. (Table P-PZ40)
4659.V26	Varadācārya, E. Vi., 1869-1926 (Table P-PZ40)
4659.V35	Vāsudēvācārya, Ke., 1866-1921 (Table P-PZ40)
4659.V353	Vāsudēvayya, ca. 1852-1943 (Table P-PZ40)
4659.V377	Venkat Rao, Alur, 1880-1964 (Table P-PZ40)
4659.V41529	Veṅkaṭarāv, Gulvāḍi, 1844-1913 (Table P-PZ40)
	Veṅkaṭarāva, Ālura, 1880-1964 see PL4659.V377
4659.V4872	Vijayadāsa, 18th cent. (Table P-PZ40)
4659.V489	Vijayaṇṇa, 15th cent. (Table P-PZ40)
4659.V515	Viśālākṣi Dakṣiṇāmūrti, 1935- (Table P-PZ40)
4659.V77	Vṛttavilāsa, 14th cent. (Table P-PZ40)
4659.V93	Vyāsatīrtha, 1460-1539 (Table P-PZ40)
4659.Y24	Yādavārya, 1541-1646 (Table P-PZ40)
4659.Y248	Yadugiriyamma, 1828-1908 (Table P-PZ40)
	Kandhī see PL4695+
	Khondi see PL4695+
4665	Kisan
4671-4671.95	Koḍagu (Table P-PZ15a modified)
	Literature
4671.9.A-Z	Individual authors or works, A-Z
	Subarrange individual authors by Table P-PZ40 unless otherwise specified
	Subarrange individual works by Table P-PZ43 unless otherwise specified
	e.g.

Dravidian languages
    Koḍagu
        Literature
            Individual authors or works, A-Z -- Continued

4671.9.A65	Appaccu Kavi, Haradāsa, 1868-1944 (Table P-PZ40)
4681	Kolāmī
4684-4684.95	Konda. Kūbi (Table P-PZ15a)
4687	Koraga
4691	Kōta
4693	Koya
4695-4695.95	Kui (Table P-PZ15a)
4701-4704	Kurukh (Table P-PZ11)
	Cf. PL4665 Kisan
4706	Kuvi
	Malabar see PL4711+
4711-4719.5	Malayāḷam (Malabar) (Table P-PZ8a modified)
	Cf. PL4751+ Tamil
4718-4718.9	Literature (Table P-PZ25 modified)
4718.9.A-Z	Individual authors or works, A-Z

            Subarrange individual authors by Table P-PZ40 unless
                otherwise specified
            Subarrange individual works by Table P-PZ43 unless
                otherwise specified
            e.g.

4718.9.A32	Achyuthan Namboodiri, Akkitham, 1926- (Table P-PZ40)
4718.9.A324	Acyutan, Māvēlikkara, 1926- (Table P-PZ40)
	Akkittaṃ see PL4718.9.A32
4718.9.A512-.A5123	Anantapuravarṇanaṃ (Table P-PZ43)
	Āṇtaṇi, Puḷiṅkunnà, 1938- see PL4718.9.A583
4718.9.A583	Antony, Pulincunnoo, 1938- (Table P-PZ40)
4718.9.A614	Appu Neṭuṅṅāṭi, 1862-1933 (Table P-PZ40)
4718.9.A74	Arjjunan, Veḷḷāyaṇi, 1933- (Table P-PZ40)
4718.9.A75	Arṇṇōs Pādṛi, d. 1732 (Table P-PZ40)
	Asīs, Vi. E. E., 1932- see PL4718.9.A97
4718.9.A9	Ayyappan, V. V., 1923- (Table P-PZ40)
4718.9.A97	Azeez, V. A. A., 1932- (Table P-PZ40)
4718.9.B328-.B3283	Bāṇayuddhaṃ (Table P-PZ43)
4718.9.B4	Bhaskara Menon, Puttelattu (Table P-PZ40)
	Bhāskaramēnōn, Puttēḷattu see PL4718.9.B4
4718.9.B53	Bhattathiripad, M. P., 1908- (Table P-PZ40)
4718.9.B6	Biccu Tirumala (Table P-PZ40)
	Candran, Pi. Ār.,1929- see PL4718.9.C414
	Candranpilla, Katavūr Ji., 1939- see PL4718.9.C417
4718.9.C324	Cāvara, Kuryākkōs Ēliyāsaccan, 1805-1871 (Table P-PZ40)

PL

	Dravidian languages
	Malayalam (Malabar)
	Literature
	Individual authors or works, A-Z -- Continued
4718.9.C343	Ceriyān Māppila, Kaṭṭallayattil, 1859-1936 (Table P-PZ40)
4718.9.C35	Ceruśśēri, 15th cent. (Table P-PZ40)
4718.9.C414	Chandran, P.R., 1929- (Table P-PZ40)
4718.9.C417	Chandran Pillai, Kadavoor G. (Table P-PZ40)
4718.9.C427	Chānthu Menon, Oyyarattu, 1846-1899 (Table P-PZ40)
4718.9.C4276	Chathukkutty Mannadiar, 1857-1905 (Table P-PZ40)
4718.9.C459	Chinnangath, Rajan D., 1943- (Table P-PZ40)
	Cinnaṅṅatt, Rājan, 1943- see PL4718.9.C459
4718.9.C54	Cīrāman (Table P-PZ40)
4718.9.D27	Dāmōdaraccākyār, 14th cent. (Table P-PZ40)
4718.9.D325	Dāmōdaran Nampūtiri, Pūntōṭṭattu, 1815-1865 (Table P-PZ40)
	Das, Kamala see PL4718.9.M24
4718.9.E46	Ēkalavyan, 1933- (Table P-PZ40)
4718.9.E5	Eluttaccan, 16th cent. (Table P-PZ40)
	Eluttacchan, Ke. En., 1911- see PL4718.9.E94
4718.9.E94	Ezhuthachan, K. N., 1911- (Table P-PZ40)
4718.9.G45	George, Thomas, 1935- (Table P-PZ40)
4718.9.H24	Haneef, Nooranad, 1935- (Table P-PZ40)
	Hanīph, Nūranāṭ, 1935- see PL4718.9.H24
4718.9.I7	Irayimmantampi, 1783-1856 (Table P-PZ40)
4718.9.J183	Jacob, Chalil, 1921- (Table P-PZ40)
4718.9.J28	Jamāl, Iṭavā, 1920- (Table P-PZ40)
	Jēkkab, Cālil, 1921- see PL4718.9.J183
	Jōrj, Paravūr, 1936- see PL4718.9.P363
	Jōs, Ti. El. see PL4718.9.J584
4718.9.J584	Jose, T.L. (Table P-PZ40)
4718.9.J7	Joy Muttar, 1929- (Table P-PZ40)
	Jōyi Muṭṭār, 1929- see PL4718.9.J7
4718.9.K386	Kēccēri, Yūsaphali, 1934- (Table P-PZ40)
4718.9.K396	Kēraḷavarmma, 1844-1917 (Table P-PZ40)
4718.9.K397	Kēraḷavarmma, Kōṭṭayam, 1645-1696 (Table P-PZ40)
4718.9.K398	Kēraḷavarmmatampurān, Anilaṃṇāḷ, 1853-1907 (Table P-PZ40)
4718.9.K399	Kēsari Nāyanār, 1860-1914 (Table P-PZ40)
4718.9.K423	Kesava Pillai, K.C., 1868-1913 (Table P-PZ40)
4718.9.K465	Kēśavannampūtiri, V. A., 1923- (Table P-PZ40)
4718.9.K57	Koccīppan Tarakan, Pōḷacciraykkal, 1861-1940 (Table P-PZ40)
4718.9.K615	Kōṭṭārakkarattampurān (Table P-PZ40)
4718.9.K62	Kōṭṭayattu Tampurān (Table P-PZ40)
	Kōvilan, 1923- see PL4718.9.A9

Dravidian languages
Malayāḷam (Malabar)
Literature
Individual authors or works, A-Z -- Continued
Kōyittampurān, Kiḷimānūr see PL4718.9.R234

4718.9.K675	Krishna Pillai, Kuttipuzha, 1900-1971 (Table P-PZ40)
4718.9.K677	Krishna Pillai, Neelakanta Pillai, 1916- (Table P-PZ40)
4718.9.K6815	Krishna Warrior, N.V., 1917- (Table P-PZ40)
4718.9.K713	Krishnan Nair, C., 1922- (Table P-PZ40)
4718.9.K765	Krishnankutty, Veloor, 1933- (Table P-PZ40)
	Kr̥ṣṇankutti, Vēḷūr, 1933- see PL4718.9.K765
	Kr̥ṣṇannāyar, Si., 1922- see PL4718.9.K713
	Kr̥ṣṇapiḷḷa, En., 1916- see PL4718.9.K677
	Kr̥ṣṇapiḷḷa, Kuttippuḷa, 1900-1971 see PL4718.9.K675
	Kr̥ṣṇavāriyar, En. Vi., 1917- see PL4718.9.K6815
4718.9.K787	Kumaran, Moorkothu, 1873-1940 (Table P-PZ40)
4718.9.K7876	Kumaran Asan, 1873-1924 (Table P-PZ40)
4718.9.K789	Kuñcannampyār, 18th cent. (Table P-PZ40)
4718.9.K8	Kunjiraman Nair, P., 1905-1978 (Table P-PZ40)
4718.9.K8533	Kuññāyin Muslyār, b. ca. 1700 (Table P-PZ40)
4718.9.K8537	Kuññikkuttantampurān, 1864-1912 (Table P-PZ40)
	Kunniramannayar, Pi., 1905-1978 see PL4718.9.K8
4718.9.K855	Kunttikkuññutankacci, 1820-1904 (Table P-PZ40)
4718.9.K8946- .K89463	Kuśalavacaritam kiḷippāṭṭ (Table P-PZ43)
4718.9.M14	Maccāttu Nārāyaṇaneḷayatā, 1750-1843 (Table P-PZ40)
4718.9.M24	Mādhavadas, Kamala, 1932- (Table P-PZ40)
4718.9.M25	Mādhavan, Vallacira, ‡d 1934- (Table P-PZ40)
4718.9.M2665	Mādhavi Amma, Kaṭattanāṭṭ, 1909- (Table P-PZ40)
4718.9.M2712	Maṇalikkara, Ke. Vi. (Table P-PZ40)
4718.9.M3	Mathai, K. Easo, 1925- (Table P-PZ40)
4718.9.M319	Mathew, Mattam, 1953- (Table P-PZ40)
4718.9.M33	Māttantarakan, Puttankāvȧ, 1903- (Table P-PZ40)
	Mātyu Mattam, 1953- see PL4718.9.M319
	Mēnōn, Em. Em., 1935- see PL4718.9.M397
4718.9.M397	Menon, Manakkaparambil Madhava, 1935- (Table P-PZ40)
4718.9.M59	Mōhanavarmma, Ke. El., 1936- (Table P-PZ40)
	Muhammad, En. Pi., 1928- see PL4718.9.M72
4718.9.M72	Muhammad, N.P., 1928- (Table P-PZ40)
4718.9.M84	Mundassery, Joseph, 1903-1977 (Table P-PZ40)
	Muntaśśeri, Jōsaph, 1903-1977 see PL4718.9.M84
4718.9.M855	Muraleedharan Nair, Nellickal, 1948- (Table P-PZ40)
	Muralīdharan, Nellikkal, 1948- see PL4718.9.M855
	Muttār, Jōyi, 1929-, see PL4718.9.J7
4718.9.N295	Nārāyaṇa, 16th cent. (Table P-PZ40)

	Dravidian languages
	Malayāḷam (Malabar)
	Literature
	Individual authors or works, A-Z
	Narayana Guru, 1856-1928 see PL4718.9.S64
4718.9.N298	Narayana Menon, Nalapat, 1888-1955 (Table P-PZ40)
4718.9.N3	Narayana Menon, Vallathol, 1878-1958 (Table P-PZ40)
4718.9.N323	Narayana Pillai, P.K., 1878-1938 (Table P-PZ40)
	Nārāyaṇamēnōn, Nālappātt, 1888-1955 see PL4718.9.N298
4718.9.N326	Nārāyaṇamēnōr, Kuṇṭūr, 1861-1936 (Table P-PZ40)
4718.9.N329	Narayanan Kutty, Velanthoda Koottala (Table P-PZ40)
4718.9.N33	Narayanan Nair, Palai, 1911- (Table P-PZ40)
	Nārāyaṇannāyar, Pālā, 1911- see PL4718.9.N33
	Nārāyaṇapilḷa, Pi. Ke., 1878-1938 see PL4718.9.N323
4718.9.N5	Nilakanta Pillai, Karoor, 1898- (Table P-PZ40)
4718.9.N52	Nīlakaṇṭhakavi (Table P-PZ40)
	Nīlakaṇṭhapilḷa, Kārūr see PL4718.9.N5
4718.9.P267	Padmanabha Panikkar, Mulur S., 1869-1931 (Table P-PZ40)
4718.9.P278	Padmanabhan, Thinakkal, 1931- (Table P-PZ40)
4718.9.P29458	Palathumkal, Joykutty, 1943- (Table P-PZ40)
	Pālattuṇkal, Jōyikkuṭṭi, 1943- see PL4718.9.P29458
	Pamman, 1922- see PL4718.9.P339
	Paramēśvaran, Ēvūr, 1927- see PL4718.9.P3396
4718.9.P33	Paramēśvarayyar, Uḷḷūr Es., 1877-1949 (Table P-PZ40)
4718.9.P339	Parameswara Menon, R., 1922- (Table P-PZ40)
4718.9.P3396	Parameswaran, Evoor, 1927- (Table P-PZ40)
4718.9.P358	Parappaḷḷi, Kṛṣṇan, 1921- (Table P-PZ40)
	Pārappurattā, 1925- see PL4718.9.M3
4718.9.P363	Parur, George, 1936- (Table P-PZ40)
	Patmanābhan, Ṭi., 1931- see PL4718.9.P278
	Prēmji, 1908- see PL4718.9.B53
4718.9.P374	Punaṃnampūtiri, 15th cent. (Table P-PZ40)
4718.9.P737	Pūntānam Nampūtiri (Table P-PZ40)
4718.9.P88	Puthussery, A.K., 1935- (Table P-PZ40)
	Putusseri, E.Ke., 1938- see PL4718.9.P88
4718.9.P886-.P8863	Puttariyaṅkam (Table P-PZ43)
4718.9.R2	Radhakrishnan, C., 1939- (Table P-PZ40)
4718.9.R21134	Radhakrishnan, Methil, 1946- (Table P-PZ40)
	Rādhākṛṣṇan, Mētil, 1946- see PL4718.9.R21134
	Rādhākṛṣṇan, Si., 1939- see PL4718.9.R2
4718.9.R2126	Rahimān Vāṭānappaḷḷi, 1940- (Table P-PZ40)
4718.9.R213	Rājā, Ke. Ke., 1890-1968 (Table P-PZ40)
4718.9.R23	Rajaraja Varma, A.R., 1863-1918 (Table P-PZ40)
4718.9.R234	Rājarājavarmma Kōyittampurān, Kiḷimānūr (Table P-PZ40)

Dravidian languages
Malayalam (Malabar)
Literature
Individual authors or works, A-Z -- Continued

4718.9.R2443	Rama Menon, Puthezheth, 1889-1973 (Table P-PZ40)
4718.9.R2445	Rama Varma, Vayalar, 1928-1975 (Table P-PZ40)
4718.9.R247	Ramakrishnan, K. V., 1935- (Table P-PZ40)
	Rāmakṛṣṇan, Ke. Vi., 1935- see PL4718.9.R247
	Rāmamēnōn, Puttēḻattu, 1889-1973 see PL4718.9.R2443
4718.9.R249	Raman Pillai, C.V. (Table P-PZ40)
4718.9.R2496	Rāmappaṇikkar, 14th cent. (Table P-PZ40)
	Rāmavarmma, Vayalār, 1928-1975 see PL4718.9.R2445
4718.9.R28	Ramēśan Nāyar, Es., 1948- (Table P-PZ40)
4718.9.R378	Ravivarmmakōyittampurān, Caṅṅanāśśēri, 1862-1900 (Table P-PZ40)
	Sakkariya, 1945- see PL4718.9.Z3
4718.9.S3138	Sanātananpiḷḷa, Ār., 1929- (Table P-PZ40)
4718.9.S315	Śaṅkarakkuruppǎ, Ji, 1901-1978 (Table P-PZ40)
4718.9.S3216	Śaṅkaran (Table P-PZ40)
	Śaṅkarappaṇikkar see PL4718.9.S3216
4718.9.S334	Śaṅkuṇṇi, Koṭṭārattil, 1855-1937 (Table P-PZ40)
4718.9.S3393	Śarmmā, Vi. Es., 1936- (Table P-PZ40)
4718.9.S37	Satyavratan, Āranmuḷa, 1927- (Table P-PZ40)
	Sharma, Vasudeva Subramonia, 1936- see PL4718.9.S3393
4718.9.S42	Sethu, 1942- (Table P-PZ40)
	Sētu, 1942- see PL4718.9.S42
4718.9.S57	Śivaśaṅkarapiḷḷa, Takaḻi, 1912-1999 (Table P-PZ40)
4718.9.S64	Sree Narayanan, Swami, 1856-1928 (Table P-PZ40)
4718.9.S665	Sreeman Namboothiri, D., 1921- (Table P-PZ40)
4718.9.S734-.S7343	Śrīkṛṣṇacaritam Maṇipravāḷam (Table P-PZ43)
	Śrīmān Nampūtiri, Di., 1921- see PL4718.9.S665
4718.9.S765	Subayyāpiḷḷa, Pi., 1924- (Table P-PZ40)
4718.9.S83	Sugatakumāri, 1934- (Table P-PZ40)
	Sugathakumāri, 1934- see PL4718.9.S83
4718.9.S93	Śyāmaḷa, Pi. Ār., 1932- (Table P-PZ40)
	Tarakan, Ke. Em., 1930- see PL4718.9.T473
4718.9.T473	Tharakan, Kizhakkethalakkal Mathan Tharakan, 1930- (Table P-PZ40)
4718.9.T499	Thomas, C.J., 1918-1960 (Table P-PZ40)
	Tōmas, Jōrj, 1935- see PL4718.9.G45
	Tōmas, Si. Je., 1918-1960 see PL4718.9.T499
4718.9.U47	Uṇṇāyivāriyar (Table P-PZ40)
4718.9.U533	Unnikrishnan, Puthoor, 1933- (Table P-PZ40)
4718.9.U535	Unnikrishnan, Thiruvazhiyode (Table P-PZ40)

	Dravidian languages
	Malayāḷam (Malabar)
	Literature
	Individual authors or works, A-Z
	Uṇṇikṛṣṇan, Putūr, 1933- see PL4718.9.U533
	Uṇṇikṛṣṇan, Tiruvāḷoyōṭa, 1942- see PL4718.9.U535
	Vaḷḷattōl, 1878-1958 see PL4718.9.N3
4718.9.V284	Varkey, Ponkunnam, 1910- (Table P-PZ40)
4718.9.V2844	Varkey, T.V., 1938- (Table P-PZ40)
	Varkki, Ponkunnaṃ, 1908- see PL4718.9.V284
	Varkki, Ti. Vi. 1938- see PL4718.9.V2844
4718.9.V2864	Varugīsumāppiḷa, Kaṇṭattil, 1857-1904 (Table P-PZ40)
4718.9.V2882	Vasu Pradhip, 1930- (Table P-PZ40)
	Vāsupradīp, 1930- see PL4718.9.V2882
4718.9.V365	Veeyyoth, N.M., 1925- (Table P-PZ40)
	Viśvanāthakkuṟupp, Kāvālaṃ, 1927- see
	PL4718.9.V495
4718.9.V495	Viswanatha Kurup, Kavalam, 1927- (Table P-PZ40)
	Vi. Ke. En. 1933- see PL4718.9.N329
	Vīyyōtt, En. Eṃ., 1925- see PL4718.9.V365
4718.9.Z3	Zachariah, 1945- (Table P-PZ40)
4719.4	Dialects
4719.5.A-Z	Special. By name or place, A-Z
4719.5.E94	Ezhava
4719.5.M65	Moplah
4719.5.Y47	Yerava
4731-4731.95	Malto (Table P-PZ15a)
4741-4741.95	Parji (Table P-PZ15a)
4745	Pengo
4751-4759.5	Tamil (or Tamul) (Table P-PZ8a modified)
	Cf. PL4711+ Malayāḷam
4758-4758.9	Literature (Table P-PZ25 modified)
4758.9.A-Z	Individual authors or works, A-Z
	Subarrange individual authors by Table P-PZ40 unless
	otherwise specified
	Subarrange individual works by Table P-PZ43 unless
	otherwise specified
	e.g.
4758.9.A226	Abdul Rahman, 1937- (Table P-PZ40)
4758.9.A294	Agastya (Table P-PZ40)
4758.9.A333	Akilēcapiḷḷai, Vē., b. 1853 (Table P-PZ40)
4758.9.A35	Alagiriswami, G., 1923-1970 (Table P-PZ40)
4758.9.A353	Alagumuthu, V., 1927- (Table P-PZ40)
	Alakiricāmi, Ku. (Kurucāmi), 1923-1970 see
	PL4758.9.A35
4758.9.A356	Alakiya Maṇavāḷapperumāḷ Nāyanā (Table P-PZ40)

Dravidian languages
Tamil (or Tamul)
Literature
Individual authors or works, A-Z -- Continued

4758.9.A3629- .A36293	Āmaiyar ammānai (Table P-PZ43)
4758.9.A376	Ammūvanar (Table P-PZ40)
4758.9.A38	Ampai, 1944- (Table P-PZ40)
4758.9.A385	Ampalavāna Tēcikar (Table P-PZ40)
4758.9.A386	Ampalavānak Kavirāyar (Table P-PZ40)
4758.9.A4	Amudan, Poovai (Table P-PZ40)
4758.9.A42	Amutā Kanēcan, 1940- (Table P-PZ40)
	Amutan, Pūvai, 1932- see PL4758.9.A4
4758.9.A44	Anandam, 1925- (Table P-PZ40)
4758.9.A573	Annāmalai Rettiyār, 1860-1891 (Table P-PZ40)
4758.9.A58	Āntāl (Table P-PZ40)
4758.9.A5835	Āntān Kavirāyan, 18th/19th cent. (Table P-PZ40)
	Anuttamā, 1922- see PL4758.9.P23
4758.9.A6	Apirāmi Pattar, 18th cent. (Table P-PZ40)
4758.9.A627	Appāccāmi Aiyar, Kā., 1845-1925 (Table P-PZ40)
4758.9.A65	Appar, 7th cent. (Table P-PZ40)
4758.9.A656	Aptul Kātir Nayinār, 19th cent. (Table P-PZ40)
	Aptul Rakumān, 1937- see PL4758.9.A226
4758.9.A664-.A6643	Ara Marikarutammāl ammānai (Table P-PZ43)
4758.9.A6646	Aracakēcari, 16th cent. (Table P-PZ40)
4758.9.A665	Aracañcanmukanār, 1868-1915 (Table P-PZ40)
4758.9.A682	Aravazhi, Mari, 1935- (Table P-PZ40)
4758.9.A723-.A7233	Ārkolō caturar (Table P-PZ43)
4758.9.A76	Arumuga Navalar, 1822-1879 (Table P-PZ40)
4758.9.A7825	Ārumukam, Pa., 18th cent. (Table P-PZ40)
4758.9.A7856	Ārumukapperumāl Ciravān (Table P-PZ40)
4758.9.A788	Arunācalakkavirāyar, M.R., 1852-1939 (Table P-PZ40)
4758.9.A794	Arunagirinātha, 15th cent. (Table P-PZ40)
	Arunakirinātar, 15th cent. see PL4758.9.A794
4758.9.A79746	Arutanakkutti Atikalār, 1575-1675 (Table P-PZ40)
4758.9.A82	Ativīrarāma Pāntiyar, fl. 1564-1610 (Table P-PZ40)
4758.9.A8216	Ātiyappa Pulavar, 18th cent. (Table P-PZ40)
4758.9.A822	Atiyārkkunallār (Table P-PZ40)
4758.9.A827	Attaṅki Tātāriyar Tontan (Table P-PZ40)
4758.9.A83	Auvaiyār (Table P-PZ40)
4758.9.B276	Balamanoharan, A., 1942- (Table P-PZ40)
4758.9.B3	Balasubrahmanyam, T.K. (Table P-PZ40)
4758.9.B32	Balasubramaniam, Ponnuswamy, 1936- (Table P-PZ40)
4758.9.B35	Beschi, Constantino Giuseppe, 1680-1747 (Table P-PZ40)

Dravidian languages
Tamil (or Tamul)
Literature
Individual authors or works, A-Z -- Continued

(4758.9.C143)	Cāminātaiyar, U. Vē., 1855-1942
	see PL4758.9.S89
4758.9.C15	Campantar, 7th cent. (Table P-PZ40)
4758.9.C1638	Caṅkara Cuppiramaṇiya Kavirāya Cāstirikaḷ (Table P-PZ40)
4758.9.C164	Caṅkara Irāmēcar, 18th cent. (Table P-PZ40)
	Caṇmukam, Kuruvikkarampai, 1943- see PL4758.9.S465
4758.9.C185	Cāntalinka, Swami (Table P-PZ40)
	Cantamiku Tamilmarai see PL4758.9.N289+
	Cāntilyan, 1910-1987 see PL4758.9.C457
	Cārāṇā Kaiyūm, 1938- see PL4758.9.S17
4758.9.C269	Caravaṇaiyā, 14th cent. (Table P-PZ40)
4758.9.C3	Cāttaṉār (Table P-PZ40)
4758.9.C317	Cāttiram Cāminātamuṉivar, 18th cent. (Table P-PZ40)
4758.9.C349	Cavarāyalu Nāyakar, 1829-1911 (Table P-PZ40)
4758.9.C37	Cayankoṇṭār (Table P-PZ40)
	Cekatīcaṉ, Na. (Naṭarācañ), 1933- see PL4758.9.J23
4758.9.C384	Cēkātinayiṉāp Pulavar (Table P-PZ40)
4758.9.C385	Cēkkilār, 12th cent. (Table P-PZ40)
4758.9.C3886	Celvakkēcavarāya Mutaliyār, T., 1864-1921 (Table P-PZ40)
	Ceṅkai Āliyaṉ, 1941- see PL4758.9.K787
4758.9.C437	Centinātaiyar, Kācivāci C., 1848-1924 (Table P-PZ40)
4758.9.C443	Cēraik Kavirāca Piḷḷai, 16th cent. (Table P-PZ40)
4758.9.C445	Cēramāṉ Perumāḷ Nāyaṉār, 9th cent. (Table P-PZ40)
4758.9.C4513	Ceturāmaṉ, Vā. Mu., 1935- (Table P-PZ40)
4758.9.C4564	Ceyyitu Mukammatu Aṇṇāviyār, 1857-1934 (Table P-PZ40)
4758.9.C457	Chandilyan, 1910-1987 (Table P-PZ40)
4758.9.C4915	Chidambara Subramanian, N., 1912- (Table P-PZ40)
4758.9.C49162	Chidambaram Pillai, V.U., 1872-1936 (Table P-PZ40)
	Cīṉivācaṉ, Ti. Kō. (Tiruccirāppaḷḷi Kōtaṇṭapāṇi), 1922-1989 see PL4758.9.S74
4758.9.C499	Ciṉṉattampip Pulavar, Nallūr, 1716-1780 (Table P-PZ40)
	Cirpi, 1936- see PL4758.9.B32
4758.9.C515	Cirrampalak Kavirāyar (Table P-PZ40)
4758.9.C5153	Cirrampalak Kavirāyar, 17th cent. (Table P-PZ40)
4758.9.C516	Cirrampalanātikal, 14th cent. (Table P-PZ40)
4758.9.C5176	Cītakkāti, fl. 1657-1720 (Table P-PZ40)
	Citampara Cupramaṇiyaṉ, Na., b. 1912- see PL4758.9.C4915

Dravidian languages
Tamil (or Tamul)
Literature
Individual authors or works, A-Z -- Continued

4758.9.C5185	Citamparanāta Kavi, Vicayanāraṇam, fl. 1575-1600 (Table P-PZ40)
4758.9.C5228-.C52283	Cittūr Taḷavāy Māṭaṉ katai (Table P-PZ43)
4758.9.C5257	Civañāṉa Muṉivar, 18th cent. (Table P-PZ40)
	Civaṉēcaṉ, Ciṉṉaiyā, 1939- see PL4758.9.S567
4758.9.C5287	Civapperumāḷ Kavirācaṉ, 17th cent. (Table P-PZ40)
4758.9.C53	Civappirakācar, 17th cent. (Table P-PZ40)
	Co, 1934- see PL4758.9.R3527
	Cokkan, 1930- see PL4758.9.S577
4758.9.C58	Cokkanāta Piḷḷai, Palapaṭṭaṭai, 18th cent. (Table P-PZ40)
4758.9.C59	Cokkappap Pulavar (Table P-PZ40)
	Cōmu, 1921- see PL4758.9.S6
	Cujātā see PL4758.9.S8758
	Cukicuppiramaniyaṉ, Ṭi. Eṉ., 1917- see PL4758.9.S876
	Cuntara Rāmacami, 1931- see PL4758.9.R353
	Cuntaram Piḷḷai, Pe., 1855-1897 see PL4758.9.S8834
4758.9.C786	Cuntarar (Table P-PZ40)
4758.9.C78914-.C789143	Cuntari ammāṉai (Table P-PZ43)
4758.9.C7924	Cuppaiyaṉ, fl. 18th cent. (Table P-PZ40)
4758.9.C7927	Cuppiramaṇi (Table P-PZ40)
4758.9.C79386	Cuppiramaṇiyam (Table P-PZ40)
	Cuppulaṭcumi see PL4758.9.C7988
4758.9.C7988	Cupra (Table P-PZ40)
4758.9.C8	Cupramaniyam, Kōmati, 1925- (Table P-PZ40)
4758.9.C85	Cupratīpak Kavirāyar, 18th cent. (Table P-PZ40)
	Curatā, 1921- see PL4758.9.S8848
4758.9.C89	Cuvāmināta Tēcikar, Tiruvārur (Table P-PZ40)
4758.9.D29	Dasan, N. R., 1933- (Table P-PZ40)
4758.9.D49	Devan, 1913-1957 (Table P-PZ40)
4758.9.E44	Ellappa Nāvalar (Table P-PZ40)
	Es. Vi Vi. see PL4758.9.V49
4758.9.G3	Ganapati, Ra., 1935- (Table P-PZ40)
4758.9.G33	Ganesalingan, S., 1928- (Table P-PZ40)
4758.9.I27	Īcuvarapākkiya Īcākku, R., 1858-1932 (Table P-PZ40)
4758.9.I4	Ilaṅkōvaṭikal (Table P-PZ40)
4758.9.I418	Ịlattup Pūtan Tēvaṉār (Table P-PZ40)
4758.9.I72	Irācēntiraṉ, M. (Table P-PZ40)
4758.9.I72536	Irāmacāmik Kavirāyar, Vālakavi, 17th cent. (Table P-PZ40)

Dravidian languages
  Tamil (or Tamul)
    Literature
      Individual authors or works, A-Z -- Continued

	Irāmaliṅkam Piḷḷai, Ve., 1888-1972 see PL4758.9.R324
	Irāmaliṅkam, Mā. see PL4758.9.R32366
4758.9.I72555	Irāmanāta Kavirāyar, 19th cent. (Table P-PZ40)
4758.9.I742-.I7423	Irāvaṇēsvaraṉ pūjai (Table P-PZ43)
4758.9.I748	Ireṭṭiyapaṭṭi, Swami, 1856-1923 (Table P-PZ40)
	Irukūrāṉ, 1937- see PL4758.9.S877
4758.9.I85	Iṭaikkaḻināṭṭu Nallūr Nattattaṉār (Table P-PZ40)
4758.9.J23	Jagadeesan, Jatarajan, 1933- (Table P-PZ40)
4758.9.J25	Jagasirpian, P. 1925- (Table P-PZ40)
	Jekacirpiyaṉ, 1925-1978 see PL4758.9.J25
4758.9.J54	Jivaram Pirumil, Tarmo, 1939- (Table P-PZ40)
4758.9.J62	Jotirlatā Kirijā, 1935- (Table P-PZ40)
4758.9.K12	Kacciyappa Civācāriyar, 12th cent. (Table P-PZ40)
4758.9.K13	Kacciyappa Muṉivar, d., 1788 (Table P-PZ40)
	Kailācanātaṉ, P. see PL4758.9.K383768
4758.9.K19	Kāḷamēkam, 15th cent. (Table P-PZ40)
	Kalki see PL4758.9.K68
4758.9.K27	Kampar, 9th cent. (Table P-PZ40)
	Kampatācaṉ, 1916-1973 see PL4758.9.R28
	Kaṇapati, Rā. 1935- see PL4758.9.G3
	Kaṇēcaliṅkan, Ce., 1928- see PL4758.9.G33
4758.9.K345	Kantacāmi, Cā., (Cāntappaṉ), 1940- (Table P-PZ40)
4758.9.K34555	Kantacāmi Mutaliyār (Table P-PZ40)
4758.9.K3472	Kantappa Munivar, 18th cent. (Table P-PZ40)
4758.9.K37	Kapilar (Table P-PZ40)
4758.9.K3732	Kāraikkālammai, 6th cent. (Table P-PZ40)
4758.9.K3736	Kariccāṉ Kuñcu, 1919- (Table P-PZ40)
4758.9.K3738	Kārmēkak Kaviñar, fl. 1672-1699 (Table P-PZ40)
4758.9.K3745- .K37453	Kaṟpakavalli Nāyaki mālai (Table P-PZ43)
	Karuṇāṉantam, 1925- see PL4758.9.A44
4758.9.K3776	Karuppaṉēntiraṉ, Veṅkiṭācala (Table P-PZ40)
4758.9.K3777	Karuvūrttēvar, 9th cent. (Table P-PZ40)
4758.9.K38374- .K383743	Kāttavarāya nāṭakam (Table P-PZ43)
4758.9.K383768	Kautama Nīlāmparaṉ (Table P-PZ40)
(4758.9.K48)	Kirijā, Jōtirlatā, 1935- see PL4758.9.J54
4758.9.K52	Kirupāṉantavāriyār, 1906- (Table P-PZ40)
4758.9.K5253- .K52533	Kiruṣṇa līlai (Table P-PZ43)
	Kiruṣṇaṉ, Nākarkōvil, 1933- see PL4758.9.K69
	Kōmati Cupramaṇiyam, 1925- see PL4758.9.C8

Dravidian languages
Tamil (or Tamul)
Literature
Individual authors or works, A-Z -- Continued

4758.9.K567	Kōṇaṅki (Table P-PZ40)
4758.9.K57	Koṅkuvēḷir (Table P-PZ40)
4758.9.K66	Krishna Pillai, Henry Albert, 1827-1900 (Table P-PZ40)
4758.9.K68	Krishnamurthy, Ramaswami, 1899-1954 (Table P-PZ40)
4758.9.K69	Krishnan, Nagercoil Kesava Iyer Venkata, 1933- (Table P-PZ40)
4758.9.K75	Krishnaswamy, R.S., 1920- (Table P-PZ40)
4758.9.K755-.K7553	Kucalavaṉ katai (Table P-PZ43)
4758.9.K767	Kulacēkara Pāṇṭiyaṉ, 16th cent. (Table P-PZ40)
4758.9.K7745	Kulōttuṅkaṉ, 1929- (Table P-PZ40)
4758.9.K7747	Kumāracāmik Kavirācaṉ (Table P-PZ40)
4758.9.K775	Kumaragurudasa Swamigal, Pompen, 1853-1929 (Table P-PZ40)
4758.9.K777	Kumarakurupara Aṭikaḷ, 17th cent. (Table P-PZ40)
	Kumarakurutāca Cuvāmikaḷ, Pāmpaṉ see PL4758.9.K775
4758.9.K7843	Kumaraswamy Pillai, A., 1854-1922 (Table P-PZ40)
4758.9.K787	Kunarasah, K., 1941- (Table P-PZ40)
4758.9.K793	Kuruñāṉacampantar (Table P-PZ40)
4758.9.K797	Kūṭalūr Kiḷar (Table P-PZ40)
	Lakshmi, C.S. see PL4758.9.A38
4758.9.L33	Lakshmi Subramaniam, Swaminathan, 1932- (Table P-PZ40)
	Lakṣmi, 1921- see PL4758.9.T37
	Laṭcumi Cuppiramaṇiyam, Es., 1932- see PL4758.9.L33
4758.9.L5	Lila, Es., 1939- (Table P-PZ40)
4758.9.M213	Madhaviah, A., 1872-1925 (Table P-PZ40)
	Mahalingam, Vairavam Ramia, 1930- see PL4758.9.S15
	Makariṣi, 1932- see PL4758.9.B3
4758.9.M2382	Māmpaḷak Kavicciṅka Nāvalar, 1836-1884 (Table P-PZ40)
4758.9.M242	Maṇavāḷa Māmuṉi, 1370-1444 (Table P-PZ40)
	Maṇi, Ar. Es., 1934- see PL4758.9.M26
4758.9.M26	Mani, R. S., 1934- (Table P-PZ40)
4758.9.M262	Manian, S.V.S., 1933- (Table P-PZ40)
	Maṇicēkaraṉ, Kōvi, 1927- see PL4758.9.M27
4758.9.M266	Māṇikkāvacakar, 9th cent. (Table P-PZ40)
4758.9.M27	Manisekaran, Kovi, 1927- (Table P-PZ40)
4758.9.M29	Maṇivēntaṉ, 1939- (Table P-PZ40)
	Maṇiyaṉ, 1933- see PL4758.9.M262

Dravidian languages
 Tamil (or Tamul)
  Literature
   Individual authors or works, A-Z -- Continued
    Maraimalaiyaṭikaḷ, 1876-1950 see PL4758.9.V384
    Māri Aravāli, 1935- see PL4758.9.A682

4758.9.M345	Mārimuttup Piḷḷai, Tillaiviṭaṅkan, 18th cent. (Table P-PZ40)
4758.9.M373	Mastan Cāhipu, Kuṇankuṭi, 1788-1835 (Table P-PZ40)
4758.9.M3925	Maturakavi, d. 1863 (Table P-PZ40)
4758.9.M394	Mauni, 1907-1985 (Table P-PZ40)
4758.9.M43	Meykaṇṭatēvar (Table P-PZ40)
4758.9.M45	Minakshisundaram Pillai, 1815-1867 (Table P-PZ40)
4758.9.M458	Mīnāṭcī Tācan, 18th-19th cent. (Table P-PZ40)
(4758.9.M459)	Mīnāṭcicuntaram Piḷḷai
	see PL4758.9.M45
	Mīrā, 1838- see PL4758.9.I72
4758.9.M742-.M7423	Mukkūṭar paḷḷu (Table P-PZ43)
4758.9.M755-.M7553	Mullaippaṭṭu (Table P-PZ43)
4758.9.M76	Muṇaippāṭiyār, 13th cent. (Table P-PZ40)
4758.9.M765	Munruraiyaraiyānar (Table P-PZ40)
4758.9.M79	Murugesan, Murugaiyan Sivanandam Paramasivam, 1939- (Table P-PZ40)
4758.9.M796	Muṭattāmak Kaṇṇiyar (Table P-PZ40)
4758.9.M7993	Muttampala Vāttiyār, 18th cent. (Table P-PZ40)
4758.9.M79935	Muttānantar, 18th cent. (Table P-PZ40)
4758.9.M7994	Muttāṇtip Pulavar (Table P-PZ40)
4758.9.M79977	Muttucāmi Aiyar, Pavāni, 19th cent. (Table P-PZ40)
4758.9.M79983	Muttukkaviñar, 17th/18th cent. (Table P-PZ40)
4758.9.M79985	Muttukkumaran, 19th cent. (Table P-PZ40)
4758.9.M79986	Muttukkumāru, 19th cent. (Table P-PZ40)
4758.9.N2515- .N25153	Naccuppoykai vilācam (Table P-PZ43)
4758.9.N272	Nagarajan, Ganesan, 1929- (Table P-PZ40)
4758.9.N275-.N2752	Nākakumāra kāviyam (Table P-PZ43a)
4758.9.N2753	Nākaliṅkap Piḷḷai, Tirunelvēli (Table P-PZ40)
	Nākarājan, Ji., 1929- see PL4758.9.N272
4758.9.N28	Nakkīrar (Table P-PZ40)
4758.9.N2855- .N28553	Naḷaccakkaravarttik katai (Table P-PZ43)
4758.9.N289-.N2893	Nālāyirat tivviyap pirapantam (Table P-PZ43)
4758.9.N294	Nallantuvanār (Table P-PZ40)
4758.9.N3155	Nammālvār (Table P-PZ40)
4758.9.N31758- .N317583	Nānavarōtaya Paṇṭāram (Table P-PZ43)
4758.9.N31778- .N317783	Nannakar veṇpā (Table P-PZ43)

Dravidian languages
Tamil (or Tamul)
Literature
Individual authors or works, A-Z -- Continued

(4758.9.N33)	Nāraṇa Turaikkaṇṇaṉ, 1906-1996
	see PL4758.9.T7825
4758.9.N344	Nārāyaṇa Tīkṣitar, 18th cent. (Table P-PZ40)
4758.9.N363	Natanogopala Nayaki, 1843-1914 (Table P-PZ40)
4758.9.N389	Natesa Sastri, S.M., 1859-1906 (Table P-PZ40)
4758.9.N3934	Nattattaṉār, Iṭaikkaḻiṉāṭṭu Nallūr (Table P-PZ40)
4758.9.N399-.N3993	Nāvāy cāttiram (Table P-PZ43)
4758.9.N4783- .N47833	Nīlakēci (Table P-PZ43)
(4758.9.N4814)	Nīlāmparaṉ, Kautama
	see PL4758.9.K383768
	Nīlāmpikai, Tiruvaraṅka, 1903- see PL4758.9.N4815
4758.9.N4815	Nīlāmpikai Ammaiyār, Tiruvaraṅka, 1903-1945 (Table P-PZ40)
4758.9.N485	Nirampa Aḻakiya Tēcikar, 16th cent. (Table P-PZ40)
4758.9.O8	Oṭṭakkūttar, 12th cent. (Table P-PZ40)
4758.9.P218	Padmanabhan, Neela, 1938- (Table P-PZ40)
4758.9.P23	Padmanabhar, Rajeswari, 1922- (Table P-PZ40)
4758.9.P236	Pakshirajan, T. 1929- (Table P-PZ40)
	Pālacuppiramaṇiyaṉ, Mu., Pi., 1939- see PL4758.9.M29
(4758.9.P239)	Pālaipāṭiya Peruṅkaṭuṅkō
	see PL4758.9.P418
	Pālamaṉōkaraṉ, Nilakkiḷi see PL4758.9.B276
4758.9.P257	Pāmpāṭṭic Cittar (Table P-PZ40)
4758.9.P2754	Pāṇṭitturaittēvar, 1867-1910 (Table P-PZ40)
4758.9.P283	Paraṇar (Table P-PZ40)
4758.9.P287-.P2873	Pārata ammāṉai (Table P-PZ43)
	Pāratitācan, 1891-1964 see PL4758.9.S84
	Pāratiyār, 1882-1921 see PL4758.9.S8437
4758.9.P2932	Pārīcuvaṉātaṉ (Table P-PZ40)
	Paṭcirājaṉ, Ti., 1929- see PL4758.9.P236
	Patmanāpaṉ, Nila see PL4758.9.P218
4758.9.P33	Paṭṭiṇattār, 10th cent. (Table P-PZ40)
4758.9.P344	Paturuttīṉ Pulavar, 19th cent. (Table P-PZ40)
4758.9.P354	Pāṭuvār Muttappar, fl. 1690-1763 (Table P-PZ40)
4758.9.P3812	Periyāḻvār (Table P-PZ40)
4758.9.P425	Peruṅkaṭuṅkō (Table P-PZ40)
4758.9.P43	Peruntēvaṉār, 9th cent. (Table P-PZ40)
4758.9.P45	Pēyāḻvār (Table P-PZ40)
	Pi. Vi. Ar., 1927- see PL4758.9.R32
4758.9.P519	Piḷḷaipperumāl Ciṟaimīttāṉ, 17th cent. (Table P-PZ40)
4758.9.P52	Piḷḷaipperumāḷaiyaṅkār, 17th cent. (Table P-PZ40)

Dravidian languages
 Tamil (or Tamul)
  Literature
   Individual authors or works, A-Z -- Continued

4758.9.P525	Pīrmukammatu Valiyullā, 17th cent. (Table P-PZ40)
4758.9.P527	Poṉcuvāmi Ceṭṭiyār, Cu., 1869-1929 (Table P-PZ40)
4758.9.P53	Ponnadiyan, 1940- (Table P-PZ40)
4758.9.P535	Ponnampalappiḷḷai, P., 1845-1890 (Table P-PZ40)
	Poṉṉaṭiyāṉ, 1940- see PL4758.9.P53
4758.9.P55	Poṉṉutturai, Ē. Ri., 1928- (Table P-PZ40)
4758.9.P57	Poṉrattiṉam, Es., 1914- (Table P-PZ40)
	Premil, 1939- see PL4758.9.J54
4758.9.P695-.P6953	Pūcciyammaṉ villuppāṭṭu (Table P-PZ43)
4758.9.P8	Pukalēntip Pulavar, 12th cent. (Table P-PZ40)
4758.9.P813	Pulamaippittaṉ, 1935- (Table P-PZ40)
	Puṉitaṉ, 1928- see PL4758.9.S52
4758.9.R28	Rajappa, C.C., 1916- (Table P-PZ40)
4758.9.R293	Ramachandran, Poornam, 1915- (Table P-PZ40)
4758.9.R32	Ramakrishnan, P.V., 1927- (Table P-PZ40)
4758.9.R323	Ramalinga, Swami, 1823-1874 (Table P-PZ40)
4758.9.R32366	Ramalingam, M., 1940- (Table P-PZ40)
4758.9.R324	Ramalingam Pillai, Venkatarama, 1888-1972 (Table P-PZ40)
4758.9.R34	Ramanathan, Lakshmanan, 1926-1977 (Table P-PZ40)
4758.9.R3527	Ramaswamy, Srinivasan, 1934- (Table P-PZ40)
4758.9.R353	Ramaswamy, Sundara, 1931- (Table P-PZ40)
	Rāmprēmil, Ajit, 1939- see PL4758.9.J54
4758.9.R43	Reṅkañata Upāttiyāyar, d. 1849 (Table P-PZ40)
4758.9.S15	Saalai Ilanthiraian, 1930- (Table P-PZ40)
4758.9.S17	Saaranaa Kaiyoom, 1938- (Table P-PZ40)
4758.9.S2288	Sambanda Mudaliar, Pammal (Table P-PZ40)
4758.9.S2635	Sankaradas, Swami, 1867-1922 (Table P-PZ40)
	Saṇmukacuntaram, Ār., 1918-1977 see PL4758.9.S523
	Satakopan, Bhashyam, 1910-1987, see PL4758.9.C457
	Serīp, Kavi Kā. Mu., 1914- see PL4758.9.S53
	Sethuraman, V.M., 1938- see PL4758.9.C4513
4758.9.S448	Ṣeyku Muhammatu, V.A., 1855-1920 (Table P-PZ40)
4758.9.S465	Shanmugam, Kuruvikkarambai Eakambaram, 1943- (Table P-PZ40)
4758.9.S52	Shanmugasundaram, Palanisamy, 1928- (Table P-PZ40)
4758.9.S523	Shanmugasundaram, R., 1918-1977 (Table P-PZ40)
4758.9.S53	Sharif, K.M., 1914- (Table P-PZ40)
4758.9.S54116	Ṣiddi Lebbe, M.C., 1838-1898 (Table P-PZ40)
4758.9.S567	Sivanesan, Chinniah, 1939- (Table P-PZ40)
4758.9.S577	Sokkan, 1930- (Table P-PZ40)

Dravidian languages
Tamil (or Tamul)
Literature
Individual authors or works, A-Z -- Continued

4758.9.S6	Somasundaram, M.P., 1921- (Table P-PZ40)
4758.9.S676	Sree Narayanan, Swami, 1856-1928 (Table P-PZ40)
4758.9.S74	Srinivasan, T. K., 1922- (Table P-PZ40)
4758.9.S84	Subburathnam, Kanaga, 1891-1964 (Table P-PZ40)
4758.9.S8437	Subrahmanya Bharati, C., 1882-1921 (Table P-PZ40)
4758.9.S853	Subramania Mudaliar, V.P., 1857- (Table P-PZ40)
4758.9.S8758	Sujatha, 1935-2008 (Table P-PZ40)
4758.9.S876	Suki Subramaniam, T.N., 1917- (Table P-PZ40)
4758.9.S877	Sultan, I.M., 1937- (Table P-PZ40)
4758.9.S8834	Sundaram Pillai, P., 1855-1897 (Table P-PZ40)
4758.9.S8848	Suradha, 1921- (Table P-PZ40)
4758.9.S89	Swaminathaiyar, Uttamadanapuram Venkata Subba Ayyar, 1855-1942 (Table P-PZ40)
	Tācaṉ, Eṉ. Ār., 1933- see PL4758.9.D29
	Tāmaraikkaṇṇaṉ, 1934- see PL4758.9.T34
	Tamilanpan, 1933- see PL4758.9.J23
	Tamiḻvāṉaṉ, 1926-1977 see PL4758.9.R34
4758.9.T31638	Tāmōtarampiḷḷai, Ci. Vai., 1832-1901 (Table P-PZ40)
4758.9.T323	Taṇṭapāṇi, Swami, 1839-1898 (Table P-PZ40)
4758.9.T324	Tāṇṭavārāya Cuvāmikaḷ, 1408-1534 (Table P-PZ40)
4758.9.T33	Tāyumāṉavar, 1705-1742 (Table P-PZ40)
	Tēvaṉ, 1913-1957 see PL4758.9.D49
4758.9.T3379	Teyvarāyaṉ, 19th cent. (Table P-PZ40)
4758.9.T34	Thamaraikkannan, 1934- (Table P-PZ40)
4758.9.T37	Thirupurasundari, S., 1921- (Table P-PZ40)
4758.9.T45	Tirikūṭarācappak Kavirāyar, 18th cent. (Table P-PZ40)
4758.9.T459	Tirukkurukaip Perumāḷ Kavirāyar (Table P-PZ40)
4758.9.T47	Tirumaṅkaiyāḷvār (Table P-PZ40)
4758.9.T474	Tirumēṉi Kāri Irattiṉa Kavirāyar, fl. 1550-1575 (Table P-PZ40)
4758.9.T475	Tirumūlar (Table P-PZ40)
4758.9.T48	Tirumuṟai (Table P-PZ40)
4758.9.T49	Tiruttakkatēvar (Table P-PZ40)
4758.9.T5	Tiruvaḷḷuvar (Table P-PZ40)
4758.9.T572	Tiruvāṉantam (Table P-PZ40)
4758.9.T5738	Tiruvaraṅkattamutaṉār (Table P-PZ40)
4758.9.T57397	Tiruveṇṇey Nallūr Irācappa Upāttiyāyar, 19th cent. (Table P-PZ40)
	Tiṭṭūrt Tēcikar, 1858-1932 see PL4758.9.I27
4758.9.T59	Tōlāmoḻittēvar (Table P-PZ40)
4758.9.T66	Toṇṭaraṭippoṭi Āḷvār (Table P-PZ40)
4758.9.T774	Turaicāmi, Ṭi. Es., b. 1869 (Table P-PZ40)
4758.9.T7825	Turaikkaṇṇaṉ, Nāraṇa., 1906-1996 (Table P-PZ40)

Dravidian languages
  Tamil (or Tamul)
    Literature
      Individual authors or works, A-Z -- Continued

4758.9.T786	Turaiyappāpillai, T.A., 1872-1929 (Table P-PZ40)
4758.9.U387	Ulōccanār (Table P-PZ40)
	Umācantiran, 1915- see PL4758.9.R293
4758.9.U39	Umāpati Civācāriyār, 14th cent. (Table P-PZ40)
4758.9.U4	Umarup Pulavar, 18th cent. (Table P-PZ40)
4758.9.U47	Unnāyivāriyar (Table P-PZ40)
4758.9.U7	Uruttiraṅ Kaṇṇanār (Table P-PZ40)
4758.9.U867	Uttaṇṭan Kōvai (Table P-PZ40)
4758.9.V26	Vaalee, 1931- (Table P-PZ40)
4758.9.V29	Vācavan, 1927- (Table P-PZ40)
4758.9.V313	Vācutēvakavi, 17th/18th cent. (Table P-PZ40)
4758.9.V325	Vaidheeswaran, S., 1935- (Table P-PZ40)
	Vaitīsvaran, Es., 1935- see PL4758.9.V325
4758.9.V337	Vaittiyanāta Tēcikar (Table P-PZ40)
4758.9.V339	Vaiyapūri Aiyar, 15th/16th cent. (Table P-PZ40)
4758.9.V3412	Vaiyāpuric Cittar, 19th cent. (Table P-PZ40)
	Vaiyavan, 1939- see PL4758.9.M79
4758.9.V342	Vālacuntarak Kaviñar, 12th cent. (Table P-PZ40)
4758.9.V34426	Valaṅkai vālttu (Table P-PZ43)
	Vāli, 1931- see PL4758.9.V26
4758.9.V345	Valliappa, Alagappa, 1922-1989 (Table P-PZ40)
	Vallikkaṇṇan, 1920- see PL4758.9.K75
	Valḷiyappā, Ala, 1922-1989 see PL4758.9.V345
4758.9.V3453	Vāmana, Muni, 14th cent. (Table P-PZ40)
4758.9.V347	Vaṇṇakkaḷañciyap Pulavar, 18th cent. (Table P-PZ40)
4758.9.V384	Vedachalam Pillai, Nagapattinam R.S., 1876-1950 (Table P-PZ40)
4758.9.V388	Vedanayaga Shastriar, 1774-1864 (Table P-PZ40)
4758.9.V39	Vedanayakam Pillai, Samuel, 1826-1889 (Table P-PZ40)
4758.9.V395	Veeragathy, Kantar, 1922- (Table P-PZ40)
4758.9.V4186	Vēluppiḷḷai, Kallaṭi, 1860-1944 (Table P-PZ40)
4758.9.V42	Vembu, Suyodanan, 1928- (Table P-PZ40)
4758.9.V445	Veṅkaṭrām, Em. Vi., 1920- (Table P-PZ40)
4758.9.V4657	Vētanāyakam, Ji. Cē. (Table P-PZ40)
	Vētanāyakam Piḷḷai, 1826-1889 see PL4758.9.V39
	Vi, Ē. Em., 1927- see PL4758.9.A353
4758.9.V49	Vijiaraghavachari, S.V. (Table P-PZ40)
	Vikkiraman, 1928- see PL4758.9.V42
4758.9.V492	Villiputtūrālvār (Table P-PZ40)
4758.9.V49425	Viṇaitīrttān (Table P-PZ40)
4758.9.V495	Vipulānanta, 1892-1947 (Table P-PZ40)
4758.9.V4959	Vīrākamam (Table P-PZ43)

Dravidian languages
Tamil (or Tamul)
Literature
Individual authors or works, A-Z -- Continued
Vīrakatti, Ka. (Kantar), 1922- see PL4758.9.V395

4758.9.V4966	Vīramāra<u>n</u> katai (Table P-PZ43)
4758.9.V4985	Vīrarākava Mutaliyār, 17th cent. (Table P-PZ40)
4758.9.V534	Viṭṭalrāv, 1942- (Table P-PZ40)
4758.9.Y56	Yogaswami (Table P-PZ40)

Telinga see PL4771+
Telugu (Gentoo)

4771-4779.5	Language (Table P-PZ8a modified)
(4778-4778.9)	Literature
	see PL4780+
	Dialects
4779.4	General works
4779.5.A-Z	Special. By name or place, A-Z
4779.5.K66	Konda-Reddi
4780-4780.9	Literature (Table P-PZ25 modified)
4780.9.A-Z	Individual authors or works, A-Z

Subarrange individual authors by Table P-PZ40 unless
otherwise specified
Subarrange individual works by Table P-PZ43 unless
otherwise specified
e.g.

4780.9.A3415	Addaṅki Gaṅgādharakavi (Table P-PZ40)
4780.9.A415	Ajantā (Table P-PZ40)
4780.9.A428	Allāḍu Narasiṃhakavi, 17th cent. (Table P-PZ40)
4780.9.A43	Allasāni Peddana, 16th cent. (Table P-PZ40)
4780.9.A475	Anantāmātyuḍu, 15th cent. (Table P-PZ40)
4780.9.A484	Andhra-Bilhaṇīyamu (Table P-PZ40)
4780.9.A487	Aniseṭṭi, 1922-1979 (Table P-PZ40)
4780.9.A5957	Apparao, Gurujada Venkata, 1861-1915 (Table P-PZ40)
4780.9.A59573	Apparao, P.S.R (Ponangi Sri Rama), 1923- (Table P-PZ40)
4780.9.A718	Āratīmūrti (Table P-PZ40)
	Arudra, 1925- see PL4780.9.S3163
4780.9.A783	Āśārāju (Table P-PZ40)
4780.9.A97	Ayyalarāju Nārāyaṇāmātya, 19th cent. (Table P-PZ40)
4780.9.B445	Bhagvān (Table P-PZ40)
4780.9.B452	Bhairavakavi, 15th cent. (Table P-PZ40)
4780.9.B5116	Bhāratīdēvi (Table P-PZ40)
	Bīnādēvi, 1935- see PL4780.9.T7
	Calaṃ, 1894-1979 see PL4780.9.V4
4780.9.C4	Cēmakūra Vēnkaṭakavi, fl. 1630-1640 (Table P-PZ40)
4780.9.C413	Cennamarāju, 1600-1675 (Table P-PZ40)

Dravidian languages
　Telugu (Gentoo)
　　Literature
　　　Individual authors or works, A-Z -- Continued
　　　　Chalam, 1894-1979, see PL4780.9.V4

4780.9.C4634	Chāyā Bhāskar, 1940- (Table P-PZ40)
4780.9.C55	Chiranjeevi, K. (Table P-PZ40)
4780.9.C554	Chittibabu, Parimisetti, 1943- (Table P-PZ40)
4780.9.C5684	Cintalapūdi Ellanārya, 16th cent. (Table P-PZ40)
	Cirañjivi, Ke., 1935- see PL4780.9.C55
	Ciṭṭibābu, 1943- see PL4780.9.C554
4780.9.D23	Daggupalli Duggana, 15th cent. (Table P-PZ40)
4780.9.D28	Dantulūribāpakavi, 17th cent. (Table P-PZ40)
4780.9.D6	Dhūrjati, 16th cent. (Table P-PZ40)
4780.9.D8	Dūbaguṇta Nārāyana Kavi, 15th cent. (Table P-PZ40)
4780.9.D945	Dvārakā (Table P-PZ40)
4780.9.E45	Ellūri Narasingakavi, 19th cent. (Table P-PZ40)
4780.9.E48	Eṃesār, 1969-1992 (Table P-PZ40)
4780.9.E65	Eraguḍipāṭi Vēṅkaṭācalamu Pantulu, 1801-1874 (Table P-PZ40)
4780.9.G18	Gaddar (Table P-PZ40)
4780.9.G29	Gaṇapānāradhya, 1323-1345 (Table P-PZ40)
4780.9.G3	Ganapati Sastri, P., 1911- (Table P-PZ40)
	Gaṇapatiśastri, Pilakā, 1911- see PL4780.9.G3
4780.9.G35	Gaurana, 15th cent. (Table P-PZ40)
4780.9.G358	Gaurīśaṅkar (Table P-PZ40)
4780.9.G43	Ghaṭṭuprabhu, fl. 1730-1780 (Table P-PZ40)
4780.9.G494	Girijā Nārāyan, 1957- (Table P-PZ40)
4780.9.G495	Girijaśrībhagavān, 1943- (Table P-PZ40)
4780.9.G5615	Gōpālacakravarti (Table P-PZ40)
	Gōpīcand, 1910-1962 see PL4780.9.G6
4780.9.G6	Gopichand, Tripuraneni, 1910-1962 (Table P-PZ40)
4780.9.G63	Gōpīnāthamu Vēṅkaṭakavi, 1820-1892 (Table P-PZ40)
4780.9.G778	Gurramu Cinakapōtayya, fl. 1750-1800. (Table P-PZ40)
4780.9.H45	Hēmalatālavaṇaṃ (Table P-PZ40)
4780.9.H83	Huḷakki Bhāskaruḍu, 14th cent. (Table P-PZ40)
4780.9.I79	Īśvari, 1959-1988 (Table P-PZ40)
	Jānakījāni, 1932- see PL4780.9.J33
4780.9.J33	Jānakirāmasāstri, Sāmāvēdam, 1932- (Table P-PZ40)
4780.9.K248	Kaivāra Nārēyaṇa, 18th/19th cent. (Table P-PZ40)
4780.9.K253	Kaḷāsāgar (Table P-PZ40)
4780.9.K265	Kamalāsanuḍu, 1935- (Table P-PZ40)
4780.9.K2694	Kāmēśvari, Ḍi., 1935- (Table P-PZ40)
	Kameswari, D., 1935- see PL4780.9.K2694
4780.9.K2767	Kānādam Peddana Sōmayāji, 18th cent. (Table P-PZ40)
4780.9.K283	Kandukūri Rudrakavi, 16th cent. (Table P-PZ40)

Dravidian languages
Telugu (Gentoo)
Literature
Individual authors or works, A-Z -- Continued

4780.9.K285	Kankanti Paparaju, 17th cent. (Table P-PZ40)
4780.9.K35	Kāsula Purusōttamakavi, 18th cent. (Table P-PZ40)
4780.9.K3836	Kavi Samyamīndra (Table P-PZ40)
4780.9.K433	Kēśavācāryulu, Nambūri (Table P-PZ40)
4780.9.K578	Kondaiah, Utla, 1918- (Table P-PZ40)
4780.9.K58	Koṇḍalarāvu, Rāvi, 1932- (Table P-PZ40)
	Koṇḍayya, Ūṭla, 1918- see PL4780.9.K578
4780.9.K588	Koravi Goparāju, 15th cent. (Table P-PZ40)
4780.9.K657	Krishnadeva Raya, King of Vijayanagar, 1529 or 30 (Table P-PZ40)
4780.9.K732	Kṛṣṇamūrti, Piḷḷā, 1937- (Table P-PZ40)
4780.9.K747	Kṛṣṇamūrtiśāstri, Srīpāda, 1866-1960 (Table P-PZ40)
4780.9.K78	Kṣētrayya, 17th cent. (Table P-PZ40)
4780.9.K785	Kūcimañci Jaggakavi, 1700-1760 (Table P-PZ40)
4780.9.K798	Kundurti, 1922- (Table P-PZ40)
4780.9.L247	Lakshmi Narasimha Rao, Panuganti, 1865-1940 (Table P-PZ40)
4780.9.L275	Lakshmikantham, Pingali, 1894-1972 (Table P-PZ40)
4780.9.L286	Lakshminarasimham, Chilakamarti, 1867-1945 (Table P-PZ40)
4780.9.L2872	Lakṣmaṇadēśikulu, Āsūri Maringaṇṭi, 1864-1930 (Table P-PZ40)
4780.9.L2938	Lakṣmi, 1942- (Table P-PZ40)
	Lakṣmīkāntaṃ, Piṅgaḷi, 1894-1972 see PL4780.9.L275
4780.9.M233	Mādayagāri Mallana, 16th cent. (Table P-PZ40)
4780.9.M234	Maddipatla Appanaśāstri, 18th cent. (Table P-PZ40)
4780.9.M245	Madhubābu (Table P-PZ40)
4780.9.M2516	Madhuśrī (Table P-PZ40)
4780.9.M2533	Maḍiki Siṅgana, 15th cent. (Table P-PZ40)
4780.9.M2537	Māgaṇṭi (Table P-PZ40)
4780.9.M2614	Maithilī Veṅkaṭēśvararāvu (Table P-PZ40)
	Mallaiah, Dongari, 1941- see PL4780.9.N42
4780.9.M268	Mallanna, 15th cent. (Table P-PZ40)
	Māllayya, Doṅgari, 1941-, see PL4780.9.N42
4780.9.M2747	Mallik, 1945- (Table P-PZ40)
4780.9.M2757	Mallikārjuna Bhaṭṭu, fl. 1280-1330 (Table P-PZ40)
4780.9.M276	Mallikārjuna Paṇḍita, 12th cent. (Table P-PZ40)
4780.9.M295	Maṅgaḷagiri Ānandakavi, 18th cent. (Table P-PZ40)
4780.9.M315	Mānsu (Table P-PZ40)
4780.9.M328	Marana (Table P-PZ40)
4780.9.M3295	Maṛiṅgaṇṭi Jagannāthācāryulu, 16th cent. (Table P-PZ40)
4780.9.M33	Mariṅgaṇṭi Singarācārya, 16th cent. (Table P-PZ40)

Dravidian languages
Telugu (Gentoo)
Literature
Individual authors or works, A-Z -- Continued

4780.9.M42	Maṭla Anantarāju, 16th cent. (Table P-PZ40)
4780.9.M613	Mohanangi, 16th cent. (Table P-PZ40)
4780.9.M82	Mūlaghaṭika Kētana, 13th cent. (Table P-PZ40)
4780.9.M825	Mulugu Pāpayārādhyulu, 1756-1852 (Table P-PZ40)
	Munisundaram, Yas., 1937- see PL4780.9.S245
4780.9.M836	Muppirāla Subbarāyakavi (Table P-PZ40)
4780.9.N24	Nācana Sōmana, 14th cent. (Table P-PZ40)
4780.9.N2923	Nallakālvavarakavi Sītāpati, fl. 1620-1670 (Table P-PZ40)
4780.9.N2925	Namberumāḷḷa Puruṣakāri Keśavayya, 1734-1819 (Table P-PZ40)
4780.9.N292553	Nambūri Kēśavācāryulu, 19th cent. (Table P-PZ40)
4780.9.N2939	Nandi Mallaya, 15th cent. (Table P-PZ40)
4780.9.N294	Nandi Timmana, 16th cent. (Table P-PZ40)
4780.9.N295	Nannaya, 11th cent. (Table P-PZ40)
4780.9.N296	Nannecōḍa, fl. 1100 (Table P-PZ40)
4780.9.N318	Narasimha Rao, Munimanikyam, 1898- (Table P-PZ40)
4780.9.N34	Narasiṃha Sastri, Nori, 1900- (Table P-PZ40)
4780.9.N3413	Narasiṃhācāryulu, Nallāncakravartula, 1809-1881 (Table P-PZ40)
	Narasimharavu, Munimanikyam, 1898- see PL4780.9.N318
	Narasiṃhareḍḍi, Cīnīpalli see PL4780.9.K253
	Narasimhásāstri, Nōri, 1900- see PL4780.9.N34
4780.9.N34493	Narasiṅgakavi, Vellūru, fl. 1860-1920 (Table P-PZ40)
4780.9.N3465	Narayana Das, Azzada Adibhatla, 1864-1945 (Table P-PZ40)
4780.9.N39	Nārāyaṇarāvu, Kāḷḷakūri, 1871-1927 (Table P-PZ40)
4780.9.N396	Nārāyaṇasvāmi (Table P-PZ40)
4780.9.N42	Navīn, 1941- (Table P-PZ40)
4780.9.N47	Nēmānibhairavakavi (Table P-PZ40)
4780.9.O43	Ōlgā (Table P-PZ40)
4780.9.P237	Palakuriki Somanatha, 13th cent. (Table P-PZ40)
4780.9.P238	Pālavēkari Kadirīpati, 17th cent. (Table P-PZ40)
4780.9.P268	Pānugaṇṭi (Table P-PZ40)
4780.9.P277	Paraśurāma Pantula Liṅgamūrti Gurumūrti, 18th cent. (Table P-PZ40)
4780.9.P28	Pardha Saradhi, Nandury, 1938- (Table P-PZ40)
	Pārthasārathi, Naṇḍuri, 1938- , see PL4780.9.P28
4780.9.P48	Pillalamarri Pinavīrabhadra, 1450-1480 (Table P-PZ40)
4780.9.P49	Piṅgaḷi Sūrana (Table P-PZ40)
4780.9.P62	Pōtana, 15th cent. (Table P-PZ40)
4780.9.P68	Prabhākararāvu, Ādipūḍi, 1871-1933 (Table P-PZ40)

Dravidian languages
Telugu (Gentoo)
Literature
Individual authors or works, A-Z -- Continued

4780.9.P7428	Pulakaṇḍamu Vēṅkaṭa Kṛṣṇakavi, 17th/18th cent. (Table P-PZ40)
4780.9.R22	Radhakrishna Sarma, Challa, 1929- (Table P-PZ40)
	Rādhākṛṣṇaśarma, Callā, 1929- see PL4780.9.R22
4780.9.R2394	Rādhēya (Table P-PZ40)
4780.9.R26273	Raghunatha Nayaka, Ruler of Tanjore, fl. 1600-1634 (Table P-PZ40)
4780.9.R2652	Rājamannāru, Kāryamupūḍi, 1846-1916 (Table P-PZ40)
4780.9.R2719	Rākamacarla Vēṅkaṭadāsu, 1834-1882 (Table P-PZ40)
4780.9.R2729	Rāmabhadra, Ayyalarāju (Table P-PZ40)
4780.9.R274	Rāmacandrarāvu, C. (Table P-PZ40)
	Rāmacandrarāvu, Si. see PL4780.9.R274
4780.9.R2744	Rāmacandraśāstri, Mārēpalli, 1874-1951 (Table P-PZ40)
4780.9.R2877	Ramakrishna Sastri, Malladi, 1905-1965 (Table P-PZ40)
4780.9.R28845	Rāmakṛṣṇamācāryulu, Dharmavaraṃ, 1853-1912 (Table P-PZ40)
4780.9.R29	Ramalingeswara Rao, T. (Tummalapalli), 1921- (Table P-PZ40)
	Rāmakṛṣṇaśāstri, Mallādi, 1905-1965 see PL4780.9.R2877
4780.9.R316	Rāmarāja Bhūshana (Table P-PZ40)
4780.9.R3177	Ramarao, Arige (Table P-PZ40)
	Rāmārāvu, Arigē see PL4780.9.R3177
4780.9.R3326	Ranga Rao, Madiraju, 1936- (Table P-PZ40)
	Raṅgārāvu, Mādirāju, 1936- see PL4780.9.R3326
4780.9.R347	Rāṇimōhanrāv (Table P-PZ40)
4780.9.R3747	Rāvūri Sañjīvarāya, fl. 1730-1786 (Table P-PZ40)
4780.9.S242	Śāhajī, King of Tanjore, fl. 1684-1712 (Table P-PZ40)
4780.9.S245	Śākyamuni, 1937- (Table P-PZ40)
4780.9.S26	Sambasiva Rao, Potukuchi, 1929- (Table P-PZ40)
	Sāmbaśivarāvu, Pōtukūci,1929- see PL4780.9.S26
4780.9.S3136	Samudruḍu, d. 1991 (Table P-PZ40)
4780.9.S314	Samukha Vēṅkaṭakṛṣṇappanāyaka (Table P-PZ40)
4780.9.S31547	Sāndhyaśrī (Table P-PZ40)
4780.9.S3159	Śaṅkarakavi (Table P-PZ40)
4780.9.S3163	Sankarasastry, Bhagavatula, 1925- (Table P-PZ40)
4780.9.S31635	Saṅkusāla Nṛsiṃhakavi, 16th cent. (Table P-PZ40)
4780.9.S342	Satyanārāyaṇa, Suṅkara, 1909-1975 (Table P-PZ40)
	Satyanārāyaṇaśarma, Maddāli see PL4780.9.M315

Dravidian languages
Telugu (Gentoo)
Literature
Individual authors or works, A-Z -- Continued

4780.9.S3892	Sāyapanēni Veṅkaṭadrināyakuḍu, 17th cent. (Table P-PZ40)
4780.9.S398	Śēṣappakavi, 10th cent. (Table P-PZ40)
4780.9.S417	Sesham Venkatapati (Table P-PZ40)
4780.9.S484	Siripragaḍa Dharmaya, 17th/18th cent. (Table P-PZ40)
4780.9.S494	Sītārāmamūrti, Tummala, 1901- (Table P-PZ40)
4780.9.S517	Śivanāgu (Table P-PZ40)
4780.9.S528	Śivanām (Table P-PZ40)
4780.9.S6134	Sōmbābu, Candu (Table P-PZ40)
4780.9.S6212	Sreeramulu, Dasu, 1846-1908 (Table P-PZ40)
	Śrī Śrī, 1910-1983 see PL4780.9.S653
4780.9.S6217-.S62173	Śrī Veṅkaṭēśvara suprabhātam (Table P-PZ43)
	Śri Viriñci, 1935- see PL4780.9.K265
4780.9.S64	Śrīnātha, fl. 1400-1440 (Table P-PZ40)
4780.9.S6514	Srinivasa Rao, Kolachalam, 1854-1919 (Table P-PZ40)
4780.9.S653	Srinivasa Rao, Srirangam, 1910-1983 (Table P-PZ40)
	Śrīnivāsācārya, Tirumala see PL4780.9.S6543
4780.9.S6543	Śrīnivāsācāryulu, Tirumala (Table P-PZ40)
4780.9.S745	Subba Rao, Rayaprolu, 1892- (Table P-PZ40)
	Subbārāvu, Rāyaprōlu, 1892- see PL4780.9.S745
4780.9.S79	Surya Prakasa Deekshitulu, Puranapanda, 1928- (Table P-PZ40)
4780.9.S7935	Sūryadēvara, 1958- (Table P-PZ40)
4780.9.T25	Tallapaka Annamacharya, 1408-1503 (Table P-PZ40)
4780.9.T253	Tāḷḷapāka Cina Tirumalācārya, fl. 1493-1553 (Table P-PZ40)
4780.9.T26	Tāḷḷapāka Peda Tirumalācāryulu, 1493-1553 (Table P-PZ40)
4780.9.T33	Tarigoṇḍa Veṅgamāmba, 19th cent. (Table P-PZ40)
4780.9.T427	Tenāli Rāmabhadrakavi (Table P-PZ40)
4780.9.T43	Tenāli Rāmakṛṣṇa (Table P-PZ40)
4780.9.T445	Tikkana, 1220-1300 (Table P-PZ40)
4780.9.T474	Timmaya, 16th cent. (Table P-PZ40)
4780.9.T49	Tirupati Shastri, 1871-1919 (Table P-PZ40)
4780.9.T7	Tripura Sundaramma, Bhagavatula, 1935- (Table P-PZ40)
4780.9.T9	Tyāgarāja, Swami, 1767-1847 (Table P-PZ40)
	Uṣaśrī see PL4780.9.S79
4780.9.V253	Varadarāmadāsu (Table P-PZ40)
4780.9.V2735	Varma, Vikramadēva, 1869-1951 (Table P-PZ40)
4780.9.V38	Vēmana (Table P-PZ40)
4780.9.V39483	Venkata Rao, Vasanta Rao, 1909- (Table P-PZ40)

Dravidian languages
Telugu (Gentoo)
Literature
Individual authors or works, A-Z -- Continued

4780.9.V4	Venkatachalam, Gudipati, 1894-1979 (Table P-PZ40)
	Vēnkaṭa Kavula, Tirupati, 1871-1919 see PL4780.9.T49
4780.9.V412524	Vēṅkaṭanaraṣimhācārya, Āsūri Mariṅgaṇṭi, 1817-1880 (Table P-PZ40)
4780.9.V41258	Vēnkaṭappayyaśāstri, Tāḍēpalli, 1867-1934 (Table P-PZ40)
4780.9.V41266	Veṅkaṭarāmamūrti, Giḍugu, 1863-1940 (Table P-PZ40)
4780.9.V41388	Vēnkatarāmayya, Janamanci, 1872-1933 (Table P-PZ40)
	Venkataravu, Vasantaravu, 1909- see PL4780.9.V39483
	Veṅkaṭēśvarlu, Pullābhoṭla see PL4780.9.V41993
4780.9.V414648	Venkataraya Shastri, Vedam, 1853-1929 (Table P-PZ40)
4780.9.V414916	Venkatasubbarayakavi, Kesiraju, 1858-1889 (Table P-PZ40)
4780.9.V41492	Vēṅkaṭasubbarāyakavi, Sōmarāju, b. 1868 (Table P-PZ40)
4780.9.V415	Venkatesvararavu, Sitamraju, 1924- (Table P-PZ40)
4780.9.V41993	Venkateswarlu, Pullabhotla (Table P-PZ40)
4780.9.V4846	Vindhyārāṇi (Table P-PZ40)
4780.9.V485	Vinukonda Vallabharāya, 15th cent. (Table P-PZ40)
	Vīrājī, 1937- see PL4780.9.K732
4780.9.V4895	Vīrēśaliṅgaṃ, Kandukūri, 1848-1919 (Table P-PZ40)
4780.9.V4963	Viśvabhagavān (Table P-PZ40)
4780.9.V497	Visvanatham, Tenneti, 1895-1979 (Table P-PZ40)
4780.9.V498	Visvaprasad, 1932- (Table P-PZ40)
	Visvanathareddi, Ketu, 1939- see PL4780.9.V4996
4780.9.V4996	Viswanatha Reddy, Ketu, 1939- (Table P-PZ40)
	Volga see PL4780.9.O43
4780.9.Y3	Yagnanna Sastry, Somanchi, 1913- (Table P-PZ40)
	Yajñannaśātri, Sōmañci, 1913- see PL4780.9.Y3
4780.9.Y4	Yerrapragada, 14th cent. (Table P-PZ40)
4785	Toda
4791-4794	Tulu (Table P-PZ11 modified)
	Literature
4794.A3-.Z5	Individual authors or works, A-Z
	Subarrange individual authors by Table P-PZ40 unless otherwise specified
	Subarrange individual works by Table P-PZ43 unless otherwise specified
	e.g.

	Dravidian languages
	Tulu
	Literature
	Individual authors or works, A-Z -- Continued
4794.A78	Aruṇābja, 14/15th cent. (Table P-PZ40)
4794.K38	Kāvēri (Table P-PZ40)
4794.V57	Viṣṇu Tuṅga, b. 1636 (Table P-PZ40)
4797-4797.95	Yerukala (Table P-PZ15a)
(4890)	Romany (Gipsy, Gypsy)
	see PK2896+
	Languages of Oceania
	Austronesian, Papuan, and Australian languages
5001-5009.5	General (Table P-PZ8a)
	Austronesian
5021-5049	General (Table P-PZ6)
	Malayan (Indonesian) languages
5051-5059.5	General (Table P-PZ8a modified)
(5058-5058.9)	Literature
	see PL5060+
5060-5069	Malayan literature (Table P-PZ24)
	Special. By language or region
	Indonesian
5071-5079.5	Language (Table P-PZ8a modified)
(5078-5078.9)	Literature
	see PL5080+
5080-5089	Literature (Table P-PZ24 modified)
5089.A-Z	Individual authors or works, A-Z
	Subarrange individual authors by Table P-PZ40
	unless otherwise specified
	Subarrange individual works by Table P-PZ43
	unless otherwise specified
	e.g.
	Toer, Pramoeda Ananta see PL5089.T8
5089.T8	Tur, Pramudya Ananta, 1925- (Table P-PZ40)
	Malay
5101-5129	Language (Table P-PZ6 modified)
5103	General works. History
	Grammar
5106	Treatises in Oriental languages
	Treatises in Western languages
5107	General works
5108	Exercises, chrestomathies, phrasebooks, etc.
5109	Phonology. Phonetics
5111	Alphabet
5113	Morphology. Inflection. Accidence
5115	Syntax
	Dialects

Languages of Oceania
   Austronesian, Papuan, and Australian languages
   Austronesian
     Malayan (Indonesian) languages
      Special. By language or region
       Malay
        Language
         Dialects -- Continued

5127	General works
5128.A-Z	Special. By name or place, A-Z
5128.A37	Akit
5128.A43	Ambonese Malay
5128.B4	Besemah
5128.B46	Betawi
5128.B65	Bonai
5128.B78	Brunei
5128.D4	Deli
5128.J34	Jakarta
5128.K45	Kelantan
5128.L36	Langkat
5128.L4	Lembak Bilide
5128.L54	Lintang
5128.M47	Meratus
5128.M87	Musi
5128.O33	Ogan
5128.P35	Paku
5128.P368	Pasir
5128.P39	Pattani
5128.R39	Rawas
5128.S46	Semendo
5128.S55	Siladang
5128.S72	Sri Lanka
5128.S85	Sulawesi Tengah
5128.S94	Sumatera Utara
5128.U48	Ulu Terengganu
5130-5139	Literature (Table P-PZ24 modified)
5139.A-Z	Individual authors or works, A-Z
	Subarrange individual authors by Table P-PZ40 unless otherwise specified
	Subarrange individual works by Table P-PZ43 unless otherwise specified
	e.g.
5139.A3747	Ali al-Haji Riau, Raja, 1809-1870 (Table P-PZ40)

	Languages of Oceania
	Austronesian, Papuan, and Australian languages
	Austronesian
	Malayan (Indonesian) languages
	Special. By language or region
	Malay
	Literature
	Individual authors or works, A-Z -- Continued
5139.H3	Hamzah Fansuri, 16th/17th cent. (Table P-PZ40)
	For Hamzah Fansuri's religious life see BP80.H279
5139.H478-.H4783	Hikayat Bakhtiar (Table P-PZ43)
5139.L85	Lukman, Khatib (Table P-PZ40)
5139.O65	Ophuijsen, Ch. A. van, 1856-1917 (Table P-PZ40)
	P. Ramlee, 1928-1973 see PL5139.R3
5139.R3	Ramlee, P., 1928-1973 (Table P-PZ40)
5151-5179	Javanese and Kawi
5151-5159.5	Kawi (Old Javanese) (Table P-PZ8a modified)
5158-5158.9	Literature (Table P-PZ25 modified)
5158.9.A-Z	Individual authors or works, A-Z
	Subarrange individual authors by Table P-PZ40 unless otherwise specified
	Subarrange individual works by Table P-PZ43 unless otherwise specified
	e.g.
5158.9.K35	Kanwa, Empu, 11th cent. (Table P-PZ40)
5158.9.P35	Panuluh, Mpu, 12th cent. (Table P-PZ40)
5158.9.T26	Tantular, Mpu (Table P-PZ40)
5161-5179	Javanese
5161-5169.5	Language (Table P-PZ8a modified)
(5168-5168.9)	Literature
	see PL5170+
5170-5179	Literature (Table P-PZ24 modified)
5179.A-Z	Individual authors or works, A-Z
	Subarrange individual authors by Table P-PZ40 unless otherwise specified
	Subarrange individual works by Table P-PZ43 unless otherwise specified
	e.g.
5179.M36	Mangkunegara IV, Prince of Surakarta, 1809-1881 (Table P-PZ40)
5179.P27	Paku Buwana IV, Sunan of Surakarta, d. 1820 (Table P-PZ40)
5179.P87	Purwasastra, 18th cent. (Table P-PZ40)

Languages of Oceania
 Austronesian, Papuan, and Australian languages
  Austronesian
   Malayan (Indonesian) languages
    Special. By language or region
     Javanese and Kawi
      Javanese
       Literature
        Individual authors or works, A-Z -- Continued

5179.R32	Ranggawarsita, Raden Ngabei, 1802-1874 (Table P-PZ40)
5179.S29	Sasradipraja, Raden Ngabehi (Table P-PZ40)
5179.Y35	Yasadipura I, Radèn Ngabèhi, 1729-1803 (Table P-PZ40)
	Other (alphabetically)
5191-5194	Achinese (Table P-PZ11)
5201-5204	Alfurese (Table P-PZ11)
5205	Alune (Table P-PZ15)
5206-5209	Amboinese (Table P-PZ11)
5210-5210.95	Angkola (Table P-PZ15a)
5211-5211.95	Asilulu (Table P-PZ15)
5212-5212.95	Atinggola (Table P-PZ15a)
(5213-5213.95)	Atoni
	see PL5465+
5214-5214.95	Bada (Table P-PZ15a)
5215-5215.95	Bajau (Table P-PZ15a)
5219-5219.95	Balaesang (Table P-PZ15a)
5220-5220.95	Balantak (Table P-PZ15a)
5221-5224	Balinese (Table P-PZ11)
5225-5225.95	Banda (Table P-PZ15a)
5226-5226.95	Banjarese (Table P-PZ15a)
5229-5229.95	Barangas (Table P-PZ15a)
5231-5234	Bareë dialect (Table P-PZ11)
	Batak see PL5241+
5241-5244	Batta (Table P-PZ11)
	For Karo see PL5334+
	Cf. PL5401+ Mandailing
	Cf. PL5471+ Toba-Batak
5246-5246.95	Bayan (Table P-PZ15a)
5247-5247.95	Bekati' (Table P-PZ15a)
5248-5248.95	Biak (Table P-PZ15a)
	Bidayuh see PL5301+
5251-5251.95	Bimanese (Table P-PZ15a)
5254-5254.95	Bintauna (Table P-PZ15a)
5256-5256.95	Bolaang Mongondow (Table P-PZ15a)

	Languages of Oceania
	Austronesian, Papuan, and Australian languages
	Austronesian
	Malayan (Indonesian) languages
	Special. By language or region
	Other (alphabetically) -- Continued
5261	Borneo (Table P-PZ15)
	Cf. PL5101+ Malay
	Cf. PL5301+ Dyak
5271-5271.95	Bugis (Table P-PZ15a)
5276-5276.95	Bukar Sadong (Table P-PZ15a)
5277-5277.95	Bunak (Table P-PZ15a)
5278-5278.95	Bune Bonda (Table P-PZ15a)
5278.973-.97395	Bungku (Table P-PZ15b)
5279-5279.95	Buol (Table P-PZ15a)
5281	Buru (Table P-PZ15)
5291	Celebes (Table P-PZ15)
5295-5295.95	Chamorro (Table P-PZ15a)
5296-5296.95	Cia-cia (Table P-PZ15a)
5297-5297.95	Dairi Pakpak (Table P-PZ15a)
5298.5-.595	Dampelas (Table P-PZ15b)
	Dayak see PL5301+
5298.7-.795	Dayak Kantuk (Table P-PZ15b)
5298.93-.9395	Dayak Krio (Table P-PZ15b)
5298.95-.9595	Dedua (Table P-PZ15b)
5298.97-.9795	Donggo (Table P-PZ15b)
5299-5299.95	Dusun (Table P-PZ15a)
5301-5304	Dyak. Dayak (Table P-PZ11)
5307	Enggano (Table P-PZ15)
5318-5318.95	Fordata (Table P-PZ15a)
	Formosan. Taiwan see PL6145+
5323	Galelarese (Table P-PZ15)
5324-5324.95	Galoli (Table P-PZ15a)
5325-5325.95	Gayo (Table P-PZ15a)
5327-5327.95	Gorontalo (Table P-PZ15a)
	Guam see PL5295+
	Holontalo see PL5327+
5333-5333.95	Iban (Table P-PZ15a)
5333.953-.95395	Ida'an (Table P-PZ15b modified)
	Dialects
5333.95394	General works
5333.95395.A-Z	Special. By name or place, A-Z
5333.95395.B44	Begak
5333.955-.95595	Idaté (Table P-PZ15b)
5333.96-.9695	Jamee (Table P-PZ15b)
5333.965-.96595	Kahayan (Table P-PZ15b)
5333.9667	Kaidipang (Table P-PZ15)

Languages of Oceania
  Austronesian, Papuan, and Australian languages
    Austronesian
      Malayan (Indonesian) languages
        Special. By language or region
          Other (alphabetically) -- Continued

5333.97	Kaili
5334-5334.95	Karo-Batak (Table P-PZ15a)
5334.975	Katingan
5335	Kaure (Table P-PZ15)
5336-5336.95	Kayan (Table P-PZ15a)
5337-5337.95	Kedang (Table P-PZ15a)
5337.96-.9695	Kemak (Table P-PZ15b)
(5338)	Kendayan
	see PL5301+
5338.97	Kerinci
5338.974	Kisar
5338.975	Kluet
5339-5339.95	Kubu (Table P-PZ15a)
5339.96-.9695	Kutai (Table P-PZ15b)
5339.98-.9895	Lamaholot (Table P-PZ15b)
5340-5340.95	Lamandau (Table P-PZ15a)
5341-5341.95	Lampung (Table P-PZ15a)
5342	Larike-Wakasihu
5342.9	Lawangan (Table P-PZ15)
5342.93	Lematang (Table P-PZ15)
5342.98	Lolak (Table P-PZ15)
5343	Lombok (Island) (Table P-PZ15)
5345-5345.95	Lundayeh (Table P-PZ15a)
5347-5347.95	Maanyan (Table P-PZ15a)
5351-5354	Madurese (Table P-PZ11)
5365-5368	Makasar (Table P-PZ11)
5371-5379.5	Malagasy (Table P-PZ8a modified)
5378-5378.9	Literature (Table P-PZ25 modified)
5378.9.A-Z	Individual authors or works, A-Z
	Subarrange individual authors by Table P-PZ40
	unless otherwise specified
	Subarrange individual works by Table P-PZ43
	unless otherwise specified
	e.g.
5378.9.D6	Dox, 1913-, (Table P-PZ40)
5378.9.F28	Faralahy, 1946- (Table P-PZ40)
5378.9.H39	Havoana (Table P-PZ40)
5378.9.I3	Idealy-Soa, 1911- (Table P-PZ40)
	Idealy-Soa, Zanany, 1946- see PL5378.9.F28
	Rapatsalahy, Faralahy, 1946-, see
	PL5378.9.F28

Languages of Oceania
　　Austronesian, Papuan, and Australian languages
　　　Austronesian
　　　　Malayan (Indonesian) languages
　　　　　Special. By language or region
　　　　　　Other (alphabetically)
　　　　　　　Malagasy
　　　　　　　　Literature
　　　　　　　　　Individual authors or works, A-Z -- Continued
　　　　　　　　　　Rapatsalahy, Paul, 1911- see PL5378.9.I3
　　　　　　　　　　Razakandrainy, Jean Verdi Salomon, 1913-
　　　　　　　　　　　see PL5378.9.D6
　　　　　　　　　　Razanamasy, Yvonne see PL5378.9.H39

5378.9.T74	Tselatra, 1863-1931 (Table P-PZ40)
	Dialects
5379.4	General works
5379.5.A-Z	Special. By name or place, A-Z
5379.5.A37	Antaisaka
5379.5.A38	Antandroy
5379.5.B37	Bara
5379.5.B47	Betsileo
5379.5.S25	Sakalava
5379.5.T35	Taimoro
5379.5.T75	Tsimihety
5391	Malacca (Table P-PZ15)
5395-5395.95	Mambai (Table P-PZ15a)
5401-5401.95	Mandailing (Table P-PZ15a modified)
	Literature
5401.9.A-Z	Individual authors, A-Z
	Subarrange individual authors by Table P-PZ40
	unless otherwise specified
	Subarrange individual works by Table P-PZ43
	unless otherwise specified
	e.g.
5401.9.I84	Iskandar, Willem, 1840-1876 (Table P-PZ40)
5402-5402.95	Mandar (Table P-PZ15a)
5404-5404.95	Manggarai (Table P-PZ15a)
5406-5406.95	Manui (Table P-PZ15a)
5408-5408.95	Masenrempulu (Table P-PZ15a)
5410	Ma'ya (Indonesian)
5410.5	Mekongga
5411-5411.95	Mentawai (Table P-PZ15a)
5415-5415.95	Minangkabau (Table P-PZ15a)
5417.4-.495	Moken (Table P-PZ15b)
5417.5-.595	Moklen (Table P-PZ15b)
5418-5418.95	Mori (Table P-PZ15a)
5421-5421.95	Moronene (Table P-PZ15a)

Languages of Oceania
Austronesian, Papuan, and Australian languages
Austronesian
Malayan (Indonesian) languages
Special. By language or region
Other (alphabetically) -- Continued

5423-5423.95	Mualang (Table P-PZ15a)
5425-5425.95	Muna (Table P-PZ15a)
5429-5429.95	Napu (Table P-PZ15a)
5431	Nenusa-Miangas
5432.2-.295	Ngada (Table P-PZ15b)
5432.5	Ngaju (Table P-PZ15)
5433	Nias (Table P-PZ15)
5433.3	Ormu (Table P-PZ15)
5433.6-.695	Ot Danum (Table P-PZ15b)
5434	Palauan (Table P-PZ15)
5434.3-.395	Pamona (Table P-PZ15b)
5434.34-.3495	Pendau (Table P-PZ15b)
	Philippine languages see PL5501+
5434.45-.4595	Ponosakan (Table P-PZ15b)
5434.467-.46795	Ranau (Table P-PZ15b)
5434.47-.4795	Ratahan (Table P-PZ15b)
5434.5-.595	Rejang (Sumatra) (Table P-PZ15b)
5434.63-.6395	Rembong (Table P-PZ15b)
5434.7-.795	Roma (Table P-PZ15b)
5435	Rottinese (Table P-PZ15)
5435.36-.3695	Rungus (Table P-PZ15b)
5435.5-.595	Saluan (Table P-PZ15b)
5436-5436.95	Sangen (Table P-PZ15a)
5437-5437.95	Sangil (Table P-PZ15a)
5438-5438.95	Sangir (Table P-PZ15a)
5439.13-.1395	Sasak (Table P-PZ15b)
5439.17-.1795	Serawai (Table P-PZ15b)
5439.183-.18395	Seruyan (Table P-PZ15b)
5439.19-.1995	Sikka (Table P-PZ15b)
5439.2-.295	Simelungun (Table P-PZ15b)
5439.3-.395	Simeulue (Table P-PZ15b)
5439.4-.495	Sindang Kelingi (Table P-PZ15b)
5439.5	Sobojo
	Soembawa see PL5445+
5439.8-.895	Sokop (Table P-PZ15b)
5441	Sumatra (Table P-PZ15)
	Cf. PL5101+ Malay
	Cf. PL5241+ Batta
	Cf. PL5415+ Menangkabau
5443-5443.95	Sumba (Table P-PZ15a)
5445-5445.95	Sumbawa (Table P-PZ15a)

	Languages of Oceania
	Austronesian, Papuan, and Australian languages
	Austronesian
	Malayan (Indonesian) languages
	Special. By language or region
	Other (alphabetically) -- Continued
5451-5454	Sundanese (Table P-PZ11 modified)
	Literature
5454.A3-.Z5	Individual authors or works, A-Z
	Subarrange individual authors by Table P-PZ40
	unless otherwise specified
	Subarrange individual works by Table P-PZ43
	unless otherwise specified
	e.g.
5454.A7	Ardiwinata, Daeng Kanduran, 1866-1947
	(Table P-PZ40)
5454.M37	Martanagara, Raden Adipati Aria, 1845-1920
	(Table P-PZ40)
5455-5455.95	Suwawa (Table P-PZ15a)
	Tae' see PL5487+
	Taiwan see PL6145+
5456.6	Talaud
5456.72-.7295	Taman (Table P-PZ15b)
5456.82-.8295	Tamiang (Table P-PZ15b)
5456.84-.8495	Tamuan (Table P-PZ15b)
5456.86-.8695	Tarangan (Table P-PZ15b)
5456.88-.8895	Tatana (Table P-PZ15b)
5456.92-.9295	Tawoyan (Table P-PZ15b)
5457-5457.95	Tetum (Table P-PZ15a)
5461	Tidong (Table P-PZ15)
5463	Tidore (Table P-PZ15)
5465-5465.95	Timorese (Table P-PZ15a)
5467-5467.95	Timugon (Table P-PZ15a)
5471-5471.95	Toba-Batak (Table P-PZ15a)
5474	Tolaki (Table P-PZ15)
5474.2-.295	Tolitoli (Table P-PZ15b)
5475-5475.95	Tombonuwo (Table P-PZ15a)
5478-5478.95	Tombulu (Table P-PZ15a)
5480-5480.95	Tompembuni (Table P-PZ15a)
5483-5485.95	Tondano (Table P-PZ15a)
5483.97-.9795	Tonsea (Table P-PZ15b)
5484	Tontemboan
5486	Toraja
5487-5487.95	Toraja Sa'dan (Table P-PZ15a)
5488.3-.395	Tukangbesi (Table P-PZ15b)
5488.43-.4395	Tutong (Table P-PZ15b)
5488.5-.595	Uma (Table P-PZ15b)

	Languages of Oceania
	Austronesian, Papuan, and Australian languages
	Austronesian
	Malayan (Indonesian) languages
	Special. By language or region
	Other (alphabetically) -- Continued
5488.63-.6395	Una (Table P-PZ15b)
5489.5	Wandamen
5490-5490.95	Wolio (Table P-PZ15a)
5495-5495.95	Yamdena (Table P-PZ15a)
5497-5497.95	Yawa (Table P-PZ15a)
	Philippine languages
	General
5501	Periodicals. Societies. Serials. Collections (nonserial)
5502	Congresses
5503	History of philology
5505	Study and teaching
5506	General works
5507	History of the language
5508	Script. Writing. Alphabet
	Grammar
5509	General works
5511	Phonology
5512	Transliteration
5513	Morphology
5514	Parts of speech
5515	Syntax
5517	Style. Composition. Rhetoric
5518	Translating
5519	Prosody. Metrics. Rhythmics
5520	Lexicology
5521	Etymology
	Lexicography
5523	Dictionaries with definitions in Philippine languages
5525	Dictionaries with definitions in English and other languages
5529.A-Z	Local, A-Z
	e. g.
5529.L9	Luzon
5530-5547	Philippine literature (General) (Table P-PZ23 modified)
	Individual authors or works
	see the specific language, e.g. PL6058.9 Tagalog; PR9550.9 English
	Special languages
5550	Agta (Table P-PZ15)
5551	Aklanon (Table P-PZ15)
5552-5552.95	Bagobo (Table P-PZ15a)

	Languages of Oceania
	Austronesian, Papuan, and Australian languages
	Austronesian
	Philippine languages
	Special languages -- Continued
5561	Balangao (Table P-PZ15)
5563-5563.95	Balangingi dialect (Table P-PZ15a)
5565	Banawi (Banaue) (Table P-PZ15)
5571	Batan (Ivatan) (Table P-PZ15)
5581-5584	Bikol (Bicol, Vicol, Bicolano) (Table P-PZ11)
5595	Bilan (Table P-PZ15)
5621-5629.5	Bisaya (Visaya) (Table P-PZ8a)
	Cf. PL5649+ Cebuano
	Cf. PL5711+ Hiligaynon
	Cf. PL6110+ Waray
5641	Bontok (Bontoc) (Table P-PZ15)
5644-5644.95	Botolan Sambal (Table P-PZ15a)
	Calamian see PL5841
5649-5649.95	Cebuano (Table P-PZ15a)
5650	Central Sama (Table P-PZ15)
5651-5651.95	Chabacano (Table P-PZ15a)
5654	Cuyunon (Table P-PZ15)
5661-5661.95	Dumagat (Casiguran) (Table P-PZ15a)
5665-5665.95	Filipino (Table P-PZ15a)
(5666.2)	Filipino (Tagalog)
	see PL6051+
5671-5671.95	Gaddang (Table P-PZ15a)
5685	Gianga (Guianga) (Table P-PZ15)
5691	Ginaan (Table P-PZ15)
5711-5711.95	Hiligaynon (Table P-PZ15a)
5719	Ibaloi (Table P-PZ15)
5721	Ibanag (Table P-PZ15)
5725-5725.95	Ifugao (Table P-PZ15a)
5731-5734	Igorot. Central Cordilleran languages (Table P-PZ11a)
	Cf. PL5641 Bontok
5751-5754	Iloko (Ilocano) (Table P-PZ11)
5771	Ilongot (Ilongoto) (Table P-PZ15)
(5785)	Inibaloi (Table P-PZ15)
	see PL5719
5801	Isinai dialect (Table P-PZ15)
5805	Isneg (Table P-PZ15)
5815	Itawi (Itaves, Itaues) (Table P-PZ15)
	Ivatan see PL5571
5821	Jama Mapun (Table P-PZ15)
	Joloano see PL6041+
5831-5831.95	Kalagan. Muslim Kalagan (Table P-PZ15a)

Languages of Oceania
Austronesian, Papuan, and Australian languages
Austronesian
Philippine languages
Special languages -- Continued

5841	Kalamian (Calamian) (Table P-PZ15)
5851	Kalinga (Calinga) (Table P-PZ15)
5865	Kankanay (Cancanay) (Table P-PZ15)
5867-5867.95	Karao (Table P-PZ15a)
5869	Kayapa Kallahan (Table P-PZ15)
5879	Keley-i Kallahan (Table P-PZ15)
5884	Lanao-Moro dialect (Table P-PZ15)
5895	Lutau (Lutao) (Table P-PZ15)
5911-5914	Magindanao (Table P-PZ11)
5923	Mamanwa (Table P-PZ15)
5925	Mandaya (Table P-PZ15)
5935	Mangwanga (Manguanga) (Table P-PZ15)
5946	Mangyan (Manguian) (Table P-PZ15)
5955	Manobo languages (Table P-PZ15)
5956	Mansaka (Table P-PZ15)
5957-5957.95	Maranao (Table P-PZ15a)
5958-5958.95	Masbateno (Table P-PZ15a)
	Moro see PL5911+
(5981)	Nabaloi
	see PL5719
5985	Palawanic languages (Table P-PZ15)
5987-5987.95	Palawano (Table P-PZ15a)
5991-5994	Pampanga (Table P-PZ11 modified)
5993.5-5994.Z5	Literature
5994.A3-.Z5	Individual authors, A-Z
	Subarrange individual authors by Table P-PZ40
	unless otherwise specified
	Subarrange individual works by Table P-PZ43
	unless otherwise specified
	e.g.
5994.S68	Soto, Juan Cristostomo, 1867-1918 (Table P-PZ40)
	Panayan see PL5711+
6015	Pangasinan (Table P-PZ15)
6018	Sama languages
6019-6019.95	Sama Sibutu (Table P-PZ15a)
(6023)	Samaro-Leytean
	see PL6110-PL6110.95
	Cf. PL5621+ Bisaya
6024.5-.595	Sambal (Table P-PZ15b modified)
	Dialects
6024.594	General works

Languages of Oceania
Austronesian, Papuan, and Australian languages
Austronesian
Philippine languages
Special languages
Sambal
Dialects -- Continued

6024.595.A-Z	Special, A-Z
6024.595.A93	Ayta Anchi Sambal
6024.595.A95	Ayta Mag Indi
6024.595.B64	Bolinao
6024.595.B66	Botolan Sambal
6024.595.T54	Tina Sambal
(6025)	Sangir
	see PL5438+
6029	Sarangani Manobo
6035-6035.95	Subanun (Table P-PZ15a)
6041-6044	Sulu (Joloano) (Table P-PZ11)
6051-6059.5	Tagalog (Table P-PZ8a modified)
6058-6058.9	Literature (Table P-PZ25 modified)
6058.9.A-Z	Individual authors or works, A-Z

Subarrange individual authors by Table P-PZ40
unless otherwise specified
Subarrange individual works by Table P-PZ43
unless otherwise specified
e.g.

6058.9.B3	Balagtas, Francisco, 1788-1862 (Table P-PZ40)
	De Jesus, Jose Corazon see PL6058.9.J4
	Huseng Batute, see PL6058.9.J4
6058.9.J4	Jesus, Jose Corazon de, 1894-1932 (Table P-PZ40)
6064	Tagabawa Manobo (Table P-PZ15)
6065	Tagakaolo (Tagacaola) (Table P-PZ15)
6071	Tagbanwa (Tagbana) (Table P-PZ15)
6075-6075.95	Tausug (Table P-PZ15a)
6078-6078.95	Tboli (Table P-PZ15a)
6085	Tinggian (Tinguian) (Table P-PZ15)
6101-6104	Tirurai (Table P-PZ11)
	Tolaki see PL5474
6110-6110.95	Waray (Table P-PZ15a)
6113	Western Bukidnon Manobo (Table P-PZ15)
6115	Yakan (Table P-PZ15)
6120	Yami (Table P-PZ15)
6135	Yogad (Table P-PZ15)

Taiwan languages. Formosan languages

6145-6145.95	General (Table P-PZ15a)

Special languages and groups of languages

	Languages of Oceania
	Austronesian, Papuan, and Australian languages
	Austronesian
	Taiwan languages. Formosan languages
	Special languages and groups of languages -- Continued
6149-6149.95	Amis. Ami (Table P-PZ15a)
6151-6151.95	Atayal (Table P-PZ15a)
6153-6153.95	Bunun (Table P-PZ15a)
6154-6154.95	Favorlang (Table P-PZ15a)
6157-6157.95	Paiwan (Table P-PZ15a)
6158.5-.595	Pazeh (Table P-PZ15b)
6159-6159.95	Rukai (Table P-PZ15a)
6161-6161.95	Sedik (Table P-PZ15a)
(6163)	Tayal
	see PL6151+
6164-6164.95	Thao (Table P-PZ15a)
6166-6166.95	Tsou (Table P-PZ15a)
6167-6167.95	Tsouic languages (Table P-PZ15a)
	Oceanic languages. Eastern Austronesian
6171-6175	General (Table P-PZ9)
	Micronesian and Melanesian languages
6191-6195	Micronesian languages (General) (Table P-PZ9)
	Melanesian languages (General)
6201	General works
6202	General special (Script)
6203	Grammar
6206	Dictionaries
6208-6208.9	Literature (Table P-PZ25)
6209	Other special
	e.g. Etymology
6211.A-Z	Special regions, A-Z
	Special languages
6213	Ajie (Table P-PZ15)
6215	Ambrym (Table P-PZ15)
6217	Aneityum (Table P-PZ15)
6218	Anesu. Kanala. Xaracuu (Table P-PZ15)
6218.5	Apma (Table P-PZ15)
	Aragure see PL6340
6219	Areare (Table P-PZ15)
6221	Arosi (Table P-PZ15)
6222	Arosi - Atsera
6222.A82-.A8295	Atchin (Table P-PZ16)
6223	Atsera (Table P-PZ15)
6224	Atsera - Bugotu
6224.A83-.A8395	Avava (Table P-PZ16)
6224.B37-.B3795	Bariai (Table P-PZ16)

PL

Languages of Oceania
   Austronesian, Papuan, and Australian languages
    Austronesian
     Oceanic languages. Eastern Austronesian
      Micronesian and Melanesian languages
       Special languages
        Atsera - Bugotu -- Continued

6224.B54-.B5495	Big Nambas (Table P-PZ16)
6224.B8-.B895	Buang (Table P-PZ16)
6225	Bugotu (Table P-PZ15)
6225.5	Bukawa (Table P-PZ15)
6226	Bwatoo (Table P-PZ15)
6227	Camuhi (Table P-PZ15)
6228	Carolinian (Table P-PZ15)
	Chamorro see PL5295+
6228.3	Cheke Holo (Table P-PZ15)
	Chuukese see PL6318
6229	Dehu (Table P-PZ15)
6230	Dehu - Efate
6230.D6-.D695	Dobu (Table P-PZ16)
6230.D85-.D8595	Dumbea (Table P-PZ16)
6230.E37-.E3795	East Makian (Table P-PZ16)
6231	Efate (Table P-PZ15)
6233	Eromanga (Table P-PZ15)
6235-6235.95	Fijian (Table P-PZ15a)
6240	Florida (Table P-PZ15)
	Futuna see PL6435
6243	Gapapaiwa (Table P-PZ15)
6245	Gilbertese (Table P-PZ15)
6247	Halia (Table P-PZ15)
6248	Halia - Iai
6248.H36-.H3695	Hano (Table P-PZ16)
6248.H84-.H8495	Hula (Table P-PZ16)
6249	Iai (Table P-PZ15)
6251	Jabim (Table P-PZ15)
6252	Jabim - Kz
	Kanala see PL6218
	Kapingamarangi see PL6452
6252.K35-.K3595	Kapone. Numee (Table P-PZ16)
6252.K37-.K3795	Kara (Table P-PZ16)
6252.K5-.K595	Kiriwinian (Table P-PZ16)
6252.K64-.K6495	Kitava (Table P-PZ16)
6252.K67-.K6795	Kokota (Table P-PZ16)
6252.K68-.K6895	Koluwawa (Table P-PZ16)
	Kuanua see PL6296.R34+
6252.K78-.K7895	Kumak. Nenema (Table P-PZ16)
6252.K82-.K8295	Kurada (Table P-PZ16)

Languages of Oceania
  Austronesian, Papuan, and Australian languages
  Austronesian
    Oceanic languages. Eastern Austronesian
     Micronesian and Melanesian languages
      Special languages
       Jabim - Kz -- Continued

6252.K86-.K8695	Kosraean. Kusaie (Table P-PZ16)
6252.K92-.K9295	Kwaio (Table P-PZ16)
6253	La - Lz
6253.L34-.L3495	Lamenu (Table P-PZ16)
6253.L38-.L3895	Lau (Table P-PZ16)
6253.L42-.L4295	Lavongai (Table P-PZ16)
6253.L58-.L5895	Lewo (Table P-PZ16)
6253.L65-.L6595	Loniu (Table P-PZ16)
6253.L85-.L8595	Lusi (Table P-PZ16)
6254	Ma - Marshall
6254.M27-.M2795	Malu (Table P-PZ16)
6254.M29-.M2995	Manam (Table P-PZ16)
6254.M35-.M3595	Mandegusu (Table P-PZ16)
6254.M36-.M3695	Mangseng (Table P-PZ16)
6254.M39-.M3995	Markham (Table P-PZ16)
6255	Marshall (Table P-PZ15)
6256	Marshall - Motu
6256.M56-.M5695	Minaveha (Table P-PZ16)
6256.M58-.M5895	Misima (Table P-PZ16)
6256.M83-.M8395	Mokilese (Table P-PZ16)
6256.M843-.M84395	Molima (Table P-PZ16)
6256.M845-.M84595	Mono-Alu (Table P-PZ16)
6256.M85-.M8595	Mortlock (Table P-PZ16)
6256.M87-.M8795	Mota (Table P-PZ16)
6257	Motu (Table P-PZ15)
6257.3	Muduapa (Table P-PZ15)
6257.5	Mukawa (Table P-PZ15)
6258	Muyuw (Table P-PZ15)
6262	Nakanai (Table P-PZ15)
6264	Nalik (Table P-PZ15)
6265	Naman (Table P-PZ15)
6267	Nemi (Table P-PZ15)
	Nenema see PL6252.K78+
6268	Nengone (Table P-PZ15)
6269	Nese (Table P-PZ15)
6271	Nguna (Table P-PZ15)
6279	Nufor (Table P-PZ15)
6280	Nufor - Pala
	Nukuoro see PL6485
	Numee see PL6252.K35+

Languages of Oceania
Austronesian, Papuan, and Australian languages
Austronesian
Oceanic languages. Eastern Austronesian
Micronesian and Melanesian languages
Special languages
Nufor - Pala

6280.N93-.N9395	Nyalayu (Table P-PZ16)
6280.P32-.P3295	Paama (Table P-PZ16)
6280.P35-.P3595	Paici (Table P-PZ16)
6281	Pala (Table P-PZ15)
6285	Patep (Table P-PZ15)
6295	Pohnpeian. Ponape (Table P-PZ15)
6296	Ponape - Rotuman
6296.P66-.P6695	Port Sandwich (Table P-PZ16)
6296.P84-.P8495	Puluwat (Table P-PZ16)
6296.R34-.R3495	Raluana (Table P-PZ16)
6297	Rotuman (Table P-PZ15)
6298	Roviana (Table P-PZ15)
6301	Saa (Table P-PZ15)
6303	Sakau (Table P-PZ15)
6303.5	Satawalese (Table P-PZ15)
6304	Seimat (Table P-PZ15)
6304.5	Siar-Lak (Table P-PZ15)
6305	Sinagoro (Table P-PZ15)
6308	Sissano (Table P-PZ15)
6313	Sonsorol-Tobi (Table P-PZ15)
6315	Tanga (Table P-PZ15)
6316	Tanga - Thz
6316.T35-.T3595	Tanna (Table P-PZ16)
6316.T37-.T3795	Tape (Table P-PZ16)
6317	Ti - Truk
6317.T53-.T5395	Tigak (Table P-PZ16)
	To'abaita see PL6254.M27+
	Tolai see PL6296.R34+
6318	Truk. Chuukese (Table P-PZ15)
6319	Tumleo (Table P-PZ15)
	Uea (Uvea) see PL6551
6321	Ulawa (Table P-PZ15)
6327	Ulithi (Table P-PZ15)
	Wagap see PL6227
6337	Wedau (Table P-PZ15)
6337.5	Wogeo (Table P-PZ15)
6338	Woleai (Table P-PZ15)
6339	Wuvulu (Table P-PZ15)
	Xaracuu see PL6218
6340	Xaragure. Aragure (Table P-PZ15)

Languages of Oceania
Austronesian, Papuan, and Australian languages
Austronesian
Oceanic languages. Eastern Austronesian
Micronesian and Melanesian languages
Special languages -- Continued

6341	Yap (Table P-PZ15)
	Polynesian languages
6401	General works
6402	Study and teaching
6403	Grammar
6405	Exercises. Readers. Phrase books, etc.
6406	Dictionaries
6408-6408.9	Literature (Table P-PZ25)
6409	Other special
	e.g. Etymology
6417.A-Z	Special regions, A-Z
	Special languages
6425	Anuta (Table P-PZ15)
	Easter Island see PL6498
6435	Futuna (Table P-PZ15)
6436	Futuna-Aniwa. West Futuna (Table P-PZ15)
6441-6449.5	Hawaiian (Table P-PZ8a)
6452	Kapingamarangi (Table P-PZ15)
6459	Leuangiua (Table P-PZ15)
6463	Mangaian (Table P-PZ15)
6464	Mangareva (Table P-PZ15)
6465	Maori (Table P-PZ15)
	Cf. PL6515 Tahitian
6471	Marquesan. Nukahiva (Table P-PZ15)
6475	Mele-Fila (Table P-PZ15)
6481	Niuean (Table P-PZ15)
6485	Nukuoro (Table P-PZ15)
6488	Pileni (Table P-PZ15)
6498	Rapanui (Table P-PZ15)
6499	Rarotongan (Table P-PZ15)
6500	Rarotongan - Samoan (Table P-PZ15)
6500.R4-.R495	Rennellese (Table P-PZ16)
6501-6501.95	Samoan (Table P-PZ15a)
6515	Tahitian (Table P-PZ15)
	Cf. PM7895.P5+ Pitcairnese
6516	Takuu (Table P-PZ15)
6517	Talise. Tolo (Table P-PZ15)
6520-6520.95	Tikopia (Table P-PZ15a)
6527-6527.95	Tokelau (Table P-PZ15a)
6531	Tonga (Table P-PZ15)
6535	Tuamotuan (Table P-PZ15)

	Languages of Oceania
	Austronesian, Papuan, and Australian languages
	Austronesian
	Oceanic languages. Eastern Austronesian
	Polynesian languages
	Special languages -- Continued
6541	Tuvaluan (Table P-PZ15)
6551	Uea (Uvea) (Table P-PZ15)
	West Futuna see PL6436
6571.A-Z	Doubtful or mixed Malayo-Polynesian languages, A-Z
	Papuan languages
	Including general works on language and literature of Papua New Guinea
6601	General works
6603	Grammar
6606	Dictionaries
6608-6608.9	Literature (Table P-PZ25)
6609	Other special
	e.g. Etymology
6621.A-Z	Special languages, A-Z
6621.A23	Abau
6621.A25	Abui (Table Table P-PZ15)
6621.A26	Abulas
6621.A29	Abun
6621.A34	Agarabe
6621.A35	Amanab
6621.A37	Amele
6621.A4	Ampale
6621.A46	Anem
6621.A65	Aomie
6621.A7	Arapesh
	Arorai see PL6245
6621.A8	Asmat
6621.A85	Auyana
6621.A9	Awa
6621.B3	Bahinemo
6621.B35	Barai
6621.B38	Baruya
6621.B39	Bauzi
6621.B44	Benabena
6621.B47	Berik
6621.B52	Bilua
6621.B53	Bimin
6621.B55	Blagar
6621.B66	Bom
6621.B7	Bongu
6621.B85	Buin

Languages of Oceania
Austronesian, Papuan, and Australian languages
Papuan languages
Special languages, A-Z -- Continued

6621.B86	Bukawa
6621.B87	Burum
6621.C38	Chambri
6621.C4	Chimbu
6621.D32	Daga
6621.D35	Dani
	Cf. PL6621.W48 Western Dani
(6621.D55)	Dimuga
	see PL6621.D32
6621.D65	Dom dialects
6621.E36	Eipo
6621.E5	Enga
6621.E74	Ese
6621.F3	Faiwol
6621.F54	Folopa
6621.F6	Fore
6621.F8	Fuyuge
6621.G3	Gadsup
6621.G33	Gahuku
6621.G73	Gresi
6621.H37	Hatam
6621.I35	Iha
6621.K117	Kalabra
6621.K1175	Kalam
6621.K118	Kaluli
6621.K12	Kamano
6621.K14	Kamoro
6621.K15	Kamtuk
6621.K154	Kamula
6621.K16	Kapau
6621.K2	Kapauku
6621.K28	Kasua
6621.K3	Kate
6621.K37	Ketengban
6621.K4	Kewa
6621.K5	Kiwai languages
	Including Kiwai proper
6621.K62	Kobon
6621.K65	Koiari
6621.K68	Korowai
6621.K7	Kosarek
6621.K75	Krisa
6621.K78	Kukukuku languages

Languages of Oceania
Austronesian, Papuan, and Australian languages
Papuan languages
Special languages, A-Z -- Continued

6621.K8	Kunimaipa
6621.K82	Kwerba
6621.L38	Lavukaleve
6621.M18	Magi (Southern Highlands Province)
6621.M19	Mai Brat
6621.M2	Mailu
6621.M215	Makasai
6621.M22	Maku'a (Indonesia)
(6621.M24)	Managalasi
	see PL6621.E74
6621.M25	Manambu
6621.M3	Marindinese
6621.M4	Mende
6621.M54	Migabac
6621.M6	Monumbo
6621.M8	Murray Island
6621.N34	Namia
6621.N345	Nankina
6621.N35	Narak
6621.N36	Nasioi
6621.N4	Ndu languages
6621.N45	Nek
6621.N55	Nimboran
6621.O44	Olo
6621.O76	Orokolo
	Pasa see PL6621.S55
6621.P55	Pinai-Hagahai
6621.P85	Purari
6621.R34	Rai Coast languages
6621.R36	Rao
6621.R38	Rawa
6621.S22	Saberi
6621.S24	Sahu
6621.S25	Samo (Western Province)
6621.S3	Savo
6621.S4	Selepet
6621.S44	Sentani
6621.S5	Siane
6621.S53	Sinagoro
6621.S55	Siroi
6621.S59	Siwai
6621.S68	Southern Arapesh
6621.S92	Suena

	Languages of Oceania
	Austronesian, Papuan, and Australian languages
	Papuan languages
	Special languages, A-Z -- Continued
6621.S94	Sulka
6621.T24	Tabla
6621.T28	Tagula
(6621.T33)	Tanah merah (Northeast Irian Jaya)
	see PL6621.T24
6621.T35	Tauya
6621.T38	Telefol
6621.T4	Telei
6621.T47	Ternate
6621.T6	Toaripi
6621.T65	Tobelo
6621.T67	Toror
6621.U77	Usan
6621.U8	Usurufa
6621.V3	Valman
6621.W25	Wahgi
6621.W26	Wambon
6621.W28	Warembori
6621.W29	Waris
6621.W3	Washkuk
6621.W33	Wasi
6621.W35	Waskia
6621.W45	West Makian
6621.W48	Western Dani
6621.W55	Wiru
6621.W65	Woisika
6621.Y27	Yagaria
6621.Y29	Yaqay
6621.Y3	Yareba
6621.Y35	Yele
6621.Y4	Yessan-Mayo
6621.Y55	Yimas
6621.Y65	Yongkom
6621.Y8	Yui
	Australian languages
7001	General works
7002	General special
7003	Grammar
7006	Dictionaries
7008-7008.9	Literature (Table P-PZ25)
7009	Other special
	e.g. Etymology

	Languages of Oceania
	Austronesian, Papuan, and Australian languages
	Australian languages -- Continued
7091.A-Z	By region, A-Z
	e.g.
7091.V5	Victoria
7091.W5	Western Australia
7101.A-Z	Special languages, A-Z
	For Papuan languages of Australia see PL6601+
7101.A33	Adnyamathanha
7101.A4	Alawa
7101.A48	Alyawarra
7101.A53	Arabana
(7101.A6)	Aranda (Aranta)
	see PL7101.E37 (Eastern Arrernte); PL7101.W398
	(Western Arrernte)
7101.A7	Awabakal
7101.B3	Bandjalang
	Including dialects
7101.B35	Bardi
7101.B38	Bayungu
7101.B53	Bidjara
7101.B57	Biri
7101.B87	Burarra
7101.B88	Butchulla
7101.D25	Daly languages
7101.D3	Dargari
7101.D33	Darling River dialects
7101.D34	Dhalandji
7101.D46	Dharawal
7101.D47	Diyari
7101.D475	Djaru
7101.D477	Djinang
7101.D48	Djingili
7101.D5	Djirbal
7101.E37	Eastern Arrernte language
7101.G34	Gagadu
7101.G37	Garawa
7101.G76	Gugada
7101.G77	Gugu Yalanji
7101.G79	Gumatj
(7101.G8)	Gumbáingar
	see PL7101.K85
7101.G82	Gundjun
7101.G824	Gunian
7101.G83	Gunwinggu
7101.G87	Gupapuyngu

PL

Languages of Oceania
Austronesian, Papuan, and Australian languages
Australian languages
Special languages, A-Z -- Continued

7101.G874	Gureng Gureng
7101.I93	Iwaidji
(7101.J55)	Jindjibandji
	see PL7101.Y54
7101.K3	Kalkatungu
7101.K35	Kamilaroi
7101.K37	Kattang
7101.K38	Kaurna
7101.K39	Kaytetye
7101.K6	Kogai
7101.K65	Koko-yimidir
7101.K85	Kumbainggar
	Kunjen see PL7101.G82
7101.K86	Kurnai
7101.K89	Kurung
	Including dialects
7101.L54	Limilngan
7101.M22	Malgana
7101.M23	Mangala
7101.M24	Mangarayi
7101.M26	Mara
7101.M28	Maranungku
7101.M284	Martuyhunira
7101.M3	Maung
7101.M37	Mayapic languages
7101.M77	Mullukmulluk
7101.M8	Murundi
7101.M84	Muruwari
7101.N25	Nakara
7101.N27	Narangga
7101.N3	Narrinyeri
7101.N43	Ngaanyatjarra
7101.N44	Ngadju
7101.N447	Ngalakan
7101.N45	Ngandi
7101.N46	Ngarinjin
7101.N48	Ngarluma
7101.N5	Nggerikudi
7101.N55	Nhanda
	Nufor see PL6279
7101.N75	Nukunu
7101.N8	Nunggubuyu
7101.N9	Nyangumata

                Languages of Oceania
                  Austronesian, Papuan, and Australian languages
                    Australian languages
                      Special languages, A-Z -- Continued

7101.N97	Nyunga dialects
7101.P5	Pitjandjara
7101.R58	Ritharrngu
7101.T57	Tiwi
7101.W26	Wageman
7101.W3	Walbiri
7101.W33	Walmajarri
7101.W336	Wandarang
7101.W34	Wangkumara (Galali)
7101.W36	Wardaman
7101.W38	Wariyangga
7101.W384	Warumungu
7101.W39	Wembawemba
7101.W398	Western Arrernte
7101.W4	Western desert language
7101.W5	Wik-Munkan
7101.W55	Wirangu
7101.W64	Wongaibon
7101.W67	Wororan languages
7101.W85	Wulguru
7101.Y34	Yandruwandha
7101.Y39	Yawuru
7101.Y53	Yidiny
7101.Y54	Yindjibarndi
7101.Y55	Yinggarda
7101.Y57	Yir-Yoront
7101.Y65	Yorta Yorta
7101.Y83	Yualyai
7501	Unclassed languages of Asia
7501.A6	Andamanese
7501.B8	Burushaski
7501.J37	Jarawa
7501.O53	Önge
7511.A-Z	Unclassed languages of the Pacific, A-Z

                African languages and literature
                  Languages

8000	Periodicals. Societies. Serials
8002	Congresses
8003	Collections of monographs, studies, etc.
8004	Study and teaching. Research
8005	General works
8007	Miscellaneous
8008	Grammar

	African languages and literature
	Languages -- Continued
8009	Vocabularies, glossaries, etc.
	Literature
8009.5	Periodicals. Societies. Serials
	Study and teaching. Research
8009.8	General works
8009.82.A-Z	By region or country, A-Z
8009.83.A-Z	By school, A-Z
	History and criticism
8010	General works
8010.2	Biography (Collective)
	Special forms
8010.4	Poetry
8010.5	Drama
8010.6	Prose. Fiction
8011	Collections
8013.A-Z	Translations of literature, folklore, etc. By language, A-Z
	e. g.
8013.E5	English
8014.A-Z	By region or country, A-Z

Under each country:

	.x	History
	.x2	Collections

	Languages. By region or country
	Special regions
8015	North
8016	East
8017	West
8018	Central
8019	South
8021.A-Z	Special countries, A-Z
	e. g.
8021.C6	Comoros
8021.C7	Congo (Democratic Republic). Zaire
	Côte d'Ivoire see PL8021.I8
8021.I8	Ivory Coast. Côte d'Ivoire
8021.L5	Liberia
8021.N5	Nigeria
8021.S4	Senegal
8021.S5	Sierra Leone
8021.S8	Sudan
	Cf. PL8027 Sudanian languages
	Zaire see PL8021.C7
	Special families of languages
8024	A - Bantu
8024.A333	Adamawa-Eastern

African languages and literature
  Special families of languages
    A - Bantu
      Afroasiatic see PJ991+
    Bantu

8025	General works
8025.1	Grammar
8025.2	Conversation and phrase books
8025.3	Phonology
	Literature
8025.5	History and criticism
8025.6	Collections
	Dialects
8025.94	General works
8025.95.A-Z	By place, A-Z
8026	Bantu - Sudanian
	Benue-Congo
8026.B4	General works
8026.B41	Grammar
8026.B44	Dictionaries
	Bushman see PL8026.K45
	Chadic
8026.C53	General works
8026.C531	Grammar
8026.C533	Etymology
8026.C534	Dictionaries
	Hamitic see PJ991+
8026.K45	Khoisan
8026.N44	Niger-Congo
8026.N47	Nilo-Hamitic
8026.N49	Nilo-Saharan
8026.N5	Nilotic
	Semitic
	see subclass PJ
8027	Sudanian
	Cf. PL8021.S8 Languages of Sudan
	Special languages (alphabetically)
8035-8035.95	Ababua (Table P-PZ15a)
8036	Ababua - Abua-Ogbia
8036.A55-.A5595	Abidji (Table P-PZ16)
8036.A62-.A6295	Abo (Cameroon) (Table P-PZ16)
8036.A66-.A6695	Abron (Table P-PZ16)
8036.A85-.A8595	Abua (Table P-PZ16)
8037	Abua-Ogbia languages (Table P-PZ15)
8039-8039.95	Abure (Table P-PZ15a)
	Accra see PL8191+
8041-8041.95	Acoli (Table P-PZ15a)

	African languages and literature
	Special languages (alphabetically) -- Continued
8043	Acoli - Aduma
8043.A3-.A395	Adangme (Table P-PZ16)
8045-8045.95	Aduma (Table P-PZ15a)
8046	Aduma - Angas
8046.A22-.A2295	Adyukru (Table P-PZ16)
8046.A23-.A2395	Afade (Table P-PZ16)
	Afar see PJ2465+
	Agau see PJ2425+
	Agni see PL8047.3.A6+
8046.A43-.A4395	Ahanta (Table P-PZ16)
8046.A44-.A4495	Ahizi (Table P-PZ16)
8046.A59-.A5995	Aka (Central African Republic) (Table P-PZ16)
8046.A63-.A6395	Akan (Table P-PZ16)
	Akarimojong see PL8373+
	Akra see PL8191+
8046.A67-.A6795	Akwa (Table P-PZ16)
	Akwapin see PL8751+
8046.A725-.A72595	Aladian. Alladian (Table P-PZ16)
8046.A73-.A7395	Alur (Table P-PZ16)
8047	Angas (Table P-PZ15)
8047.15	Angas languages (Table P-PZ15)
8047.3	Angas - Az
	Angola see PL8381+
8047.3.A57-.A5795	Anuak (Table P-PZ16)
8047.3.A58-.A5895	Anufo (Table P-PZ16)
8047.3.A597-.A59795	Anyang (Table P-PZ16)
8047.3.A6-.A695	Anyi (Table P-PZ16)
	Ashanti see PL8751+
8047.3.A77-.A7795	Asu (Table P-PZ16)
8047.3.A83-.A8395	Atisa (Table P-PZ16)
8047.3.A86-.A8695	Attie (Table P-PZ16)
8047.3.A94-.A9495	Avikam (Table P-PZ16)
8047.3.A96-.A9695	Awutu (Table P-PZ16)
8047.5	Ba - Bag
8047.5.B27-.B2795	Bade (Table P-PZ16)
8047.5.B33-.B3395	Badyaranke (Table P-PZ16)
8047.5.B42-.B4295	Bafia (Table P-PZ16)
8047.5.B45-.B4595	Bafut (Table P-PZ16)
8047.5.B47-.B4795	Bagirmi (Table P-PZ16)
8047.6	Bajele (Table P-PZ15)
8047.65	Baka (Cameroon and Gabon) (Table P-PZ15)
	Bakele see PL8377+
8047.7	Bakwé (Table P-PZ15)
8047.8	Balante (Table P-PZ15)
8048-8048.95	Balese (Table P-PZ15a)

African languages and literature
Special languages (alphabetically) -- Continued

8049	Balese - Bamun
8049.B3-.B395	Bambara (Table P-PZ16)
8049.B4-.B495	Bamileke (Table P-PZ16)
8050-8050.95	Bamun (Table P-PZ15a)
8051	Banda (Table P-PZ15)
8052	Banda languages (Table P-PZ15)
8052.5	Bandjoun (Table P-PZ15)
8053-8053.95	Banen (Table P-PZ15a)
	Bangala see PL8456+
8056	Bangala - Bao
8056.B25-.B2595	Bangubangu (Table P-PZ16)
8056.B26-.B2695	Bangwa (Table P-PZ16)
8056.B275-.B27595	Banziri (Table P-PZ16)
8056.B3-.B395	Baoulé. Baule (Table P-PZ16)
8057	Bap - Barambu
8058-8058.95	Barambu (Table P-PZ15a)
8061-8061.95	Bari (Table P-PZ15a)
8062-8062.95	Baria (Table P-PZ15a)
8063-8063.95	Bariba (Table P-PZ15a)
8065-8065.95	Basa (Table P-PZ15a)
8066	Basa - Bati
8066.B28-.B2895	Bassa (Liberia and Sierra Leone) (Table P-PZ16)
8066.B3-.B395	Bassari (Table P-PZ16)
8067-8067.95	Bati (Table P-PZ15a)
8068	Bati - Bemba
8068.B37	Bauchi languages, Southern
	Baule see PL8056.B3+
8068.B38-.B3895	Bebele (Table P-PZ16)
	Bechuana see PL8747+
8068.B39-.B3995	Bedik (Table P-PZ16)
8068.B4-.B495	Bekwarra (Table P-PZ16)
8069-8069.95	Bemba (Table P-PZ15a)
8070	Bemba - Benga
8070.B45-.B4595	Bembe (Congo (Brazzaville)) (Table P-PZ16)
8070.B54-.B5495	Bende (Table P-PZ16)
8070.B57-.B5795	Beng (Table P-PZ16)
8071-8074	Benga (Table P-PZ11)
8075	Benga - Bh
8075.B4-.B495	Benge (Table P-PZ16)
	Berber language see PJ2340+
8075.B57-.B5795	Bete (Ivory Coast) (Table P-PZ16)
8076	Bi - Bini
8076.B33-.B3395	Biali (Table P-PZ16)
8076.B53-.B5395	Bidiyo (Table P-PZ16)
8076.B55-.B5595	Bijago (Table P-PZ16)

African languages and literature
Special languages (alphabetically)
Bi - Bini -- Continued
Bilin see PJ2340+

8077-8077.95	Bini (Table P-PZ15a)
8078	Bini - Bobangi
8078.B34-.B3495	Birifor (Table P-PZ16)
8078.B36-.B3695	Birom (Table P-PZ16)
8078.B37-.B3795	Birri (Table P-PZ16)
8078.B4-.B495	Bisa (Table P-PZ16)
	Bishari see PJ2455
8078.B5-.B595	Bisio (Table P-PZ16)
8079-8079.95	Bobangi (Table P-PZ15a)
8080	Bobangi - Bongo
8080.B57-.B5795	Bobo. Bwamu (Table P-PZ16)
8080.B58-.B5895	Bobo Fing (Table P-PZ16)
	Bogos see PJ2430
8080.B62-.B6295	Bole (Table P-PZ16)
8080.B63	Bolewa languages
8080.B64-.B6495	Bolia (Table P-PZ16)
8080.B65-.B6595	Boma (Table P-PZ16)
8080.B68-.B6895	Bomitaba (Table P-PZ16)
8080.B75-.B7595	Bondei (Table P-PZ16)
8085-8085.95	Bongo (Table P-PZ15a)
8086	Bongo - Bozo
8086.B12	Bongo-Bagirmi languages
	Bornu see PL8361+
8087-8087.95	Bozo (Table P-PZ15a)
8089-8089.95	Brissa (Table P-PZ15a)
8090	Brissa - Bube
8090.B83	Bua languages
8091-8091.95	Bube (Table P-PZ15a)
8092	Bube - Bullom
8092.B84-.B8495	Bubi (Gabon) (Table P-PZ16)
8092.B86-.B8695	Budu (Table P-PZ16)
8092.B87-.B8795	Bukusu (Table P-PZ16)
8092.B88-.B8895	Buli (Table P-PZ16)
8093-8093.95	Bullom, Northern (Table P-PZ15a)
	Bullom, Southern see PL8668+
8095-8095.95	Bulu (Table P-PZ15a)
8096	Bulu - Bun
	Buluba-Lulua see PL8461+
	Bunda see PL8381+
8099-8099.95	Busa (Table P-PZ15a)
(8101-8104)	Bushman languages
	see PL8026.K45
8106-8106.95	Bushoong. Bushongo (Table P-PZ15a)

African languages and literature
   Special languages (alphabetically) -- Continued
      Bwamu see PL8080.B57+
      Caga see PL8110.C3+

8108	Cangin languages
8110.C25-.C2595	Cerma (Table P-PZ16)
8110.C3-.C395	Chaga (Bantu) (Table P-PZ16)
	Chagga see PL8110.C3+
8110.C398-.C39895	Chamba Daka (Table P-PZ16)
8110.C4-.C495	Chassu (Table P-PZ16)
8110.C5-.C595	Chewa (Table P-PZ16)
	Chi-Tonga see PL8740+
	Chikaranga see PL8681+
	Chitonga see PL8740+
8113-8113.95	Chokwe (Table P-PZ15a)
8115-8115.95	Chopi (Table P-PZ15a)
8115.97-.9795	Chuwabo (Table P-PZ15b)
8116-8116.95	Comorian (Table P-PZ15a modified)
	Dialects
8116.94	General works
8116.95.A-Z	Special. By name or place, A-Z
8116.95.S54	Shimaore
	Congo see PL8401+
	Cuanhama see PL8417+
8117-8117.95	Daba (Musgoy) (Table P-PZ15a)
8118	Daba - Dagomba
8118.D35-.D3595	Dagaare (Table P-PZ16)
8119-8119.95	Dagomba. Dagbane (Table P-PZ15a)
(8121)	Dahoman
	see PL8178+
8123-8123.95	Dan (Table P-PZ15a)
8125-8125.95	Dangaleat (Table P-PZ15a)
8126	Dangaleat - Daza
	Dankali see PJ2465+
8126.D39-.D3995	Day (Chad) (Table P-PZ16)
8127-8127.95	Dazaga (Table P-PZ15a)
8128-8128.95	Degema (Table P-PZ15a)
8129-8129.95	Dengese (Table P-PZ15a)
8130-8130.95	Digo (Table P-PZ15a)
8130.96-.9695	Dii (Table P-PZ15a)
	Dikele see PL8377+
8131-8131.95	Dinka (Table P-PZ15a)
8134-8134.95	Diola (Table P-PZ15a)
8134.97-.9795	Diola Kasa (Table P-PZ15b modified)
	Dialects
8134.9794	General works
8134.9795.A-Z	Special. By name or place, A-Z

African languages and literature
Special languages (alphabetically)
Diola Kasa
Dialects
Special. By name or place, A-Z -- Continued

8134.9795.E78	Esuulaalu
8135-8135.95	Diriku (Table P-PZ15a)
8139-8139.95	Dogon (Table P-PZ15a)
8140.1-.195	Doko (Table P-PZ15b)
8140.8-.895	Doyayo (Table P-PZ15b)
8141-8141.95	Duala (Table P-PZ15a)
8142	Duala - Dyur
8142.D87-.D8795	Duruma (Table P-PZ16)
8142.D94-.D9495	Dyula (Table P-PZ16)
8143-8143.95	Dyur (Table P-PZ15a)
	Edo see PL8077+
8147-8147.95	Efik (Table P-PZ15a)
8148-8148.95	Eggon (Table P-PZ15a)
8149	Eggon - Ekajuk
8149.E43-.E4395	Ejagham (Table P-PZ16)
8150-8150.95	Ekajuk (Table P-PZ15a)
8152-8152.95	Ekoi (Table P-PZ15a)
8153	Eloi - Engenni
8153.E3-.E395	Ekpeye (Table P-PZ16)
8153.E54-.E5495	Endo (Table P-PZ16)
8154-8154.95	Engenni (Table P-PZ15a)
8156-8156.95	Enya (Table P-PZ15a)
8158-8158.95	Eton (Table P-PZ15a)
8159-8159.95	Etsako (Table P-PZ15a)
8161-8164	Ewe (Table P-PZ11 modified)
	Dialects
8164.Z8	General works
8164.Z9A-.Z9Z	Individual. By name or place, A-Z
8164.Z9A4	Aja
(8164.Z9F55-.Z9F75)	Fon
	see PL8178+
8164.Z9M38	Maxi
8165	Ewe - Ey
8165.E9-.E995	Ewondo (Table P-PZ16)
8166	Ezaa (Table P-PZ15)
8166.5-.595	Falor (Table P-PZ15b)
8167.F3-.F395	Fang (Table P-PZ16)
8167.F4-.F495	Fanti (Table P-PZ16)
8168-8168.95	Farefare (Table P-PZ15a)
8169-8169.95	Fe'fe' (Table P-PZ15a)
	Fernandian see PL8091+
8171	Feroge (Table P-PZ15)

African languages and literature
Special languages (alphabetically) -- Continued

8178-8178.95	Fon. Dahoman (Table P-PZ15a)
	Frafra see PL8168+
8181-8184	Fula (Ful, Fulani, Fulbe, Fulfulde) (Table P-PZ11)
8185-8185.95	Fuliru (Table P-PZ15a)
8186-8186.95	Fur (Table P-PZ15a)
8187-8187.95	Furu (Table P-PZ15a)
8189-8189.95	Fyam (Table P-PZ15a)
8191-8191.95	Gã (Table P-PZ15a)
8192-8192.95	Gade (Table P-PZ15a)
8193-8193.95	Gagu (Table P-PZ15a)
	Galla see PJ2471+
8197-8197.95	Gambai (Table P-PZ15a)
8201-8201.95	Ganda (Table P-PZ15a)
8202-8202.95	Ganguela (Table P-PZ15a)
8203	Ganguela - Gbandi
8203.G35-.G3595	Gbagyi (Table P-PZ16)
8204-8204.95	Gbandi (Table P-PZ15a)
8205-8205.95	Gbaya. Gbea (Table P-PZ15a)
8206	Gbea - Gh
8206.G48-.G4895	Geviya (Table P-PZ16)
8207	Gi - Gogo
	Gi-Tonga see PL8739+
8207.G45-.G4595	Gikyode (Table P-PZ16)
8207.G47-.G4795	Giryama (Table P-PZ16)
8207.G53-.G5395	Gisiga (Table P-PZ16)
8207.G55-.G5595	Gisu (Table P-PZ16)
8207.G6-.G695	Glavda (Table P-PZ16)
8207.G7-.G795	Godié (Table P-PZ16)
8208-8208.95	Gogo (Table P-PZ15a)
8211-8211.95	Gola (Table P-PZ15a)
8215-8215.95	Gonja (Table P-PZ15a)
8219	Grassfields Bantu. Grasslands Bantu
8221	Grebo (Table P-PZ15)
8221.4	Gude (Table P-PZ15)
8221.57-.5795	Gun-Gbe (Table P-PZ15b)
8221.6	Gunu (Table P-PZ15)
8222	Gur languages
8223	Gur - Gusii
8223.G8-.G895	Gurma (Table P-PZ16)
8223.G9-.G995	Gurunsi. Grusi (Table P-PZ16)
8224-8224.95	Gusii (Table P-PZ15a)
8226-8226.95	Gwandara (Table P-PZ15a)
8227-8227.95	Gwari (Table P-PZ15a)
8228.2-.295	Gweno (Table P-PZ15b)
8228.3-.395	Gwere (Table P-PZ15b)

	African languages and literature
	Special languages (alphabetically) -- Continued
8228.6-.695	Ha (Table P-PZ15b)
8229-8229.95	Hanga (Table P-PZ15a)
8230.3-.395	Hangaza (Table P-PZ15b)
8231-8234	Hausa (Table P-PZ11 modified)
	Literature
8234.A3-.Z5	Individual authors or works, A-Z
	Subarrange individual authors by Table P-PZ40 unless otherwise specified
	Subarrange individual works by Table P-PZ43 unless otherwise specified
	e.g.
8234.A85	Asma'u, Nana, 1793-1865 (Table P-PZ40)
8234.U45	Umaru, Alhaji, 1858-1954 (Table P-PZ40)
8237-8237.95	Haya (Table P-PZ15a)
8239-8239.95	Hedi (Table P-PZ15a)
8241-8241.95	Herero (Table P-PZ15a)
8247-8247.95	Holoholo (Table P-PZ15a)
8251-8254	Hottentot. Khoikhoi (Table P-PZ11)
	Cf. PL8541+ Nama
8255-8255.95	Huba (Table P-PZ15a)
(8257-8257.95)	Humba
	see PL8417+
8258	Hunde - Ibibio
8258.H85-.H8595	Hunde (Table P-PZ16)
8259-8259.95	Ibibio (Table P-PZ15a)
8261-8261.95	Ibo (Table P-PZ15a)
8262-8263.95	Idaca (Table P-PZ15a)
8263-8263.95	Idoma (Table P-PZ15a)
	Idzo see PL8276+
8271-8271.95	Ifumu (Table P-PZ15a)
8272.5-.595	Igala (Table P-PZ15b)
8273-8273.95	Igbira (Table P-PZ15a)
	Igbo see PL8261+
8274-8274.95	Igede (Table P-PZ15a)
8275-8275.95	Igo (Table P-PZ15a)
8276-8276.95	Ijo (Table P-PZ15a)
8278.16-.1695	Ik (Table P-PZ15b)
8278.5-.595	Ikizu (Table P-PZ15b)
8279-8279.95	Ikwo (Table P-PZ15a)
8281-8281.95	Ila (Table P-PZ15a)
8282	Ila - Iraqw
	Incran see PL8191+
8282.I55-.I5595	Ingassana (Table P-PZ16)
	Iraqw see PJ2556
8285-8285.95	Isubu (Table P-PZ15a)

	African languages and literature
	Special languages (alphabetically) -- Continued
8286	Isubu - Jabo
8286.I9-.I995	Izi (Table P-PZ16)
8287-8287.95	Jabo (Gweabo) (Table P-PZ15a)
	Jagga see PL8110.C3+
(8291)	Jaunde
	see PL8165.E9+
8293-8293.95	Jeli (Table P-PZ15a)
8295-8295.95	Jita (Table P-PZ15a)
8301-8301.95	Jukun (Table P-PZ15a)
8302	Jukunoid languages
8308-8308.95	Kaba (Central Sudanic) (Table P-PZ15a)
8311-8311.95	Kabinda (Table P-PZ15a)
8313-8313.95	Kabiye (Table P-PZ15a)
	Kabyle see PJ2373+
(8321-8324)	Kafir
	see PL8795+
8338-8338.95	Kagoro (Mali) (Table P-PZ15a)
8341-8341.95	Kaguru (Table P-PZ15a)
8343-8343.95	Kahe (Table P-PZ15a)
8345-8345.95	Kaje (Table P-PZ15a)
8347-8347.95	Kako (Table P-PZ15a)
	Kakongo see PL8311+
8348.5-.595	Kalanga (Botswana and Zimbabwe) (Table P-PZ15b
	modified)
	Dialects
8348.594	General works
8348.595.A-Z	Special. By name or place, A-Z
8348.595.L55	Lilima
8349-8349.95	Kalenjin (Table P-PZ15a)
8351-8351.95	Kamba (Table P-PZ15a)
8357-8357.95	Kana (Table P-PZ15a)
8358-8358.95	Kanakuru (Table P-PZ15a)
8359-8359.95	Kanembu (Table P-PZ15a)
8361-8361.95	Kanuri (Table P-PZ15a)
8371-8371.95	Kaonde (Table P-PZ15a)
8372.5-.595	Kara (Sudan and Central African Republic) (Table P-PZ15b)
8373-8373.95	Karamojong (Table P-PZ15a)
8374	Karamojong - Kavirondo
8374.K32-.K3295	Karang (Cameroon) (Table P-PZ16)
8374.K33-.K3395	Kare (Table P-PZ16)
8374.K3397-.K339795	Karekare (Table P-PZ16)
8374.K34-.K3495	Kassonke (Table P-PZ16)
8374.K36-.K3695	Katab (Table P-PZ16 modified)

African languages and literature
Special languages (alphabetically)
Karamojong - Kavirondo
Katab -- Continued
Dialects

8374.K3695A- .K3695Z	Special. By name or place, A-Z
8374.K3695K33	Kagoro
8375-8375.95	Kavirondo. Luo (Kenya and Tanzania) (Table P-PZ15a)
8376	Kavirondo - Kele
	Kavirondo, Bantu see PL8779+
8376.K45-.K4595	Kela (Table P-PZ16)
8377-8377.95	Kele (Table P-PZ15a)
8378	Kele - Kikuyu
8378.K27-.K2795	Kelwel (Table P-PZ16)
8378.K31-.K3195	Kenga (Table P-PZ16)
8378.K37-.K3795	Kerebe (Table P-PZ16)
8378.K44-.KK4495	Kete (Table P-PZ16)
8378.K46-.K4695	Kgalagadi (Table P-PZ16 modified)
	Dialects
8378.K4694	General works
8378.K4695A- .K4695Z	Special. By name or place, A-Z
8378.K4695N48	Ngologa
8378.K48-.K4895	Kham (Table P-PZ16)
	Khoikhoi see PL8251+
8379-8379.95	Kikuyu (Table P-PZ15a)
8380	Kikuyu - Kimbundu
8380.K5-.K595	Kilega (Table P-PZ16)
8381-8381.95	Kimbundu (Table P-PZ15a)
8385-8385.95	Kinga (Table P-PZ15a)
8387-8387.95	Kingwana (Table P-PZ15a)
	Kinyaruanda see PL8608+
	Kioko see PL8113+
	Kirundi see PL8611+
8391-8391.95	Kitabwe (Table P-PZ15a)
	Kituba see PL8401+
8393-8393.95	Koalib (Table P-PZ15a)
8395-8395.95	Kom (Table P-PZ15a)
8396-8396.95	Kombe (Table P-PZ15a)
8397-8397.95	Komo (Congo) (Table P-PZ15a)
	Konde see PL8482.M8+
	Konde see PL8549+
8401-8404	Kongo. Congo (Table P-PZ11)
8405	Kongo - Kono
8405.K64-.K6495	Konjo language (Table P-PZ16)
8405.K65-.K6595	Konkomba (Table P-PZ16)

African languages and literature
Special languages (alphabetically)
Kongo - Kono -- Continued

8405.K67-.K6795	Konni (Table P-PZ16)
8406	Kono (Table P-PZ15)
8406.5-.595	Koonzime (Table P-PZ15b)
8407-8407.95	Korana (Table P-PZ15a)
8410	Korana - Kpelle
8410.K68-.K6895	Koti (Table P-PZ16)
8411-8411.95	Kpelle (Table P-PZ15a)
8412	Kpelle - Kreish
8412.K66-.K6695	Kposo (Table P-PZ16)
8413-8413.95	Kreish (Table P-PZ15a)
8414	Kreish - Kru
8414.K76-.K7695	Krongo (Table P-PZ16)
8415-8415.95	Kru (Table P-PZ15a)
8416	Kru languages (Table P-PZ15)
8417-8417.95	Kuanyama (Table P-PZ15a)
8418	Kuanyama - Kùláál
8418.K84-.K8495	Kukwa (Table P-PZ16)
8419-8419.95	Kùláál (Table P-PZ15a)
8420-8420.95	Kulango (Table P-PZ15a)
8421-8421.95	Kunama (Table P-PZ15a)
8422	Kunama - Kusaal
8422.K82-.K8295	Kuria (Table P-PZ16)
8422.K85-.K8595	Kurumba (Table P-PZ16)
8423-8423.95	Kusaal (Table P-PZ15a)
8424	Kwa languages (Table P-PZ15)
8425-8425.95	Kwafi (Table P-PZ15a)
8426.3-.395	Kwami (Table P-PZ15b)
8427-8427.95	Kwangali (Table P-PZ15a)
8428-8428.95	Kwanja (Table P-PZ15a)
	Kwanyama see PL8417+
8429-8429.95	Kweni (Table P-PZ15a)
8430	Kweni - Lamba
8430.K84-.K8495	Kwese (Table P-PZ16)
8430.K86-.K8695	Kwiri (Table P-PZ16)
8430.K89-.K8995	Kxoe (Table P-PZ16)
8430.L318-.L31895	Laal (Table P-PZ16)
8430.L32-.L3295	Laamang (Table P-PZ16)
8430.L33	Lagoon languages
8430.L35-.L3595	Lala (Table P-PZ16)
8431-8431.95	Lamba (Table P-PZ15a)
8433-8433.95	Lamé (Cameroon) (Table P-PZ15a)
8437-8437.95	Lango (Table P-PZ15a)
8441-8441.95	Latuka (Table P-PZ15a)
8447-8447.95	Lefana (Table P-PZ15a)

African languages and literature
Special languages (alphabetically) -- Continued

(8452)	Lele (Burkina Faso)
	see PL8474.L92+
8453.15-.1595	Lele (Chad) (Table P-PZ15b)
8453.18-.1895	Lendu (Table P-PZ15b)
8453.2-.295	Lenje (Table P-PZ15b)
8453.8-.895	Ligbi (Table P-PZ15b)
(8454)	Lilima
	see PL8348.595.L55
8455	Limba (Table P-PZ15)
8455.7-.795	Limbum (Table P-PZ15b)
8456-8456.95	Lingala (Table P-PZ15a)
8458-8458.95	Logbara (Table P-PZ15a)
8459	Logbara - Lozi
8459.L26-.L2695	Logo (Zaire-Sudan) (Table P-PZ16)
8459.L3-.L395	Logooli (Table P-PZ16)
8459.L52-.L5295	Loma (Table P-PZ16)
8459.L534-.L53495	Lomwe (Malawi) (Table P-PZ16)
8459.L55-.L5595	Longuda (Table P-PZ16)
8459.L63-.L6395	Lonkengo (Table P-PZ16)
8459.L66-.L6695	Losengo (Table P-PZ16)
8460-8460.95	Lozi (Table P-PZ15a)
	Lu-ganda see PL8201+
8461-8461.95	Luba (Table P-PZ15a)
8462-8462.95	Lucazi (Table P-PZ15a)
8465-8465.95	Lunda (Table P-PZ15a)
(8467-8467.95)	Lunkundu. Nkundu
	see PL8518+
	Luo (Kenya and Tanzania) see PL8375+
	Luragoli see PL8459.L3+
8473-8473.95	Luvale (Table P-PZ15a)
8474	Luvale - Maba
8474.L78-.L7895	Luyana (Table P-PZ16)
8474.L8-.L895	Luyia (Table P-PZ16)
8474.L92-.L9295	Lyele (Table P-PZ16)
8474.M3-.M395	Ma (Amadi) (Table P-PZ16)
8475-8475.95	Maba (Table P-PZ15a)
8477-8477.95	Maban (Table P-PZ15a)
8478.8-.895	Mada (Cameroon) (Table P-PZ15b)
8479-8479.95	Ma'di (Table P-PZ15a)
8481-8481.95	Madschame (Table P-PZ15a)
8482	Madschame - Makua
8482.M55-.M5595	Mafa (Table P-PZ16)
	Majingai see PL8644.95.M34+
8482.M795-.M79595	Maka (Table P-PZ16)
8482.M8-.M895	Makonde (Table P-PZ16)

African languages and literature
Special languages (alphabetically) -- Continued

8483-8483.95	Makua (Table P-PZ15a modified)
	Dialects
8483.94	General works
8483.95.A-Z	Individual. By name or place, A-Z
8483.95.E53	Enahara
8484	Makua - Mampruli
8484.M2-.M295	Makwe (Table P-PZ16)
8484.M23-.M2395	Mamara (Table P-PZ16)
8484.M25-.M2595	Mambila (Table P-PZ16)
8484.M3-.M395	Mambwe-Lungu (Table P-PZ16)
8485-8485.95	Mampruli (Table P-PZ15a)
8487-8487.95	Mamvu (Table P-PZ15a)
8489-8489.95	Mandara. Wandala (Table P-PZ15a)
8490	Mandara - Mandingo
	Mande languages
8490.M35	General works
8490.M3595S68	Southern Mande languages
8490.M3595W47	Western Mande languages
8490.M36	Mandekan languages
8491-8491.95	Mandingo (Table P-PZ15a)
8493-8493.95	Mandjak (Table P-PZ15a)
	Mang'anja see PL8593+
8495-8495.95	Mangbetu (Table P-PZ15a)
8496	Mangbetu - Margi
8496.M33-.M3395	Mankanya (Table P-PZ16)
8496.M35-.M3595	Mankon (Table P-PZ16)
8496.M37-.M3795	Mano (Table P-PZ16)
8497-8497.95	Margi (Marghi) (Table P-PZ15a)
8499-8499.95	Masa (Chadic) (Table P-PZ15a)
8501-8501.95	Masai (Table P-PZ15a)
8502	Masai - Maz
	Mashona see PL8681+
8502.M38-.M3895	Matumbi (Table P-PZ16)
8502.M42-.M4295	Mayogo (Table P-PZ16)
	Mbai see PL8648+
8503.3-.395	Mbala (Table P-PZ15b)
8503.7-.795	Mbili (Table P-PZ15b)
8504-8504.95	Mbinsa (Table P-PZ15a)
8505	Mbinsa - Mbn
8506	Mbo - Mbukushu
8506.M36-.M3695	Mbo (Cameroon) (Table P-PZ16)
8506.M38-.M3895	Mbuko (Table P-PZ16)
8507-8507.95	Mbukushu (Table P-PZ15a)
8508-8508.95	Mbum (Table P-PZ15a modified)
	Dialects

African languages and literature
Special languages (alphabetically)
Mbum
Dialects -- Continued

8508.95.A-Z	Special. By name or place, A-Z
8508.95.G38	Gbete
8509	Mbum - Md
8509.M28-.M2895	Mbunda (Angola and Zambia) (Table P-PZ16)
	Mbundu see PL8381+
8510	Me - Mende
8510.M42-.M4295	Medumba (Table P-PZ16)
	Megi see PL8625+
8511-8511.95	Mende (Table P-PZ15a)
8512	Mende - Meru
8512.M45-.M4595	Meroitic (Table P-PZ16)
8513-8513.95	Meru (Table P-PZ15a)
8514	Meru - Mi
8514.M47-.M4795	Meta (Table P-PZ16)
8515	Mi - Moba
8515.M45-.M4595	Mi Gangam (Table P-PZ16)
	Michi see PL8738
8515.M48-.M4895	Midob (Table P-PZ16)
8515.M52-.M5295	Migama (Table P-PZ16)
8515.M53-.M5395	Migili (Table P-PZ16)
8515.M54	Mijikenda languages
8515.M554-.M55495	Mina (Table P-PZ16)
8515.M56-.M5695	Mituku (Table P-PZ16)
8515.M58-.M5895	Miya (Table P-PZ16)
8515.M62-.M6295	Mo (Ghana and Ivory Coast) (Table P-PZ16)
8516-8516.95	Moba (Table P-PZ15a)
8516.97-.9795	Mochi (Table P-PZ15b)
8517	Mofu-Gudur. Southern Mofu (Table P-PZ15)
8517.5-.595	Mokulu (Table P-PZ15b)
8518-8518.95	Mongo (Table P-PZ15a)
8521-8521.95	Mooré. Mossi (Table P-PZ15a)
8523-8523.95	Moro (Table P-PZ15a)
8525-8525.95	Moru (Table P-PZ15a)
8529-8529.95	Mpiemo (Table P-PZ15a)
8531-8531.95	Mpongwe (Table P-PZ15a)
8532	Mpongwe - Musei
8532.M65-.M6595	Muana (Table P-PZ16)
8532.M73-.M7395	Mumuye (Table P-PZ16)
8532.M7397- .M739795	Mundang (Table P-PZ16)
8532.M74-.M7495	Mundani (Table P-PZ16)
8532.M76-.M7695	Mundu (Sudan and Zaire) (Table P-PZ16)
8532.M8-.M895	Murle (Table P-PZ16)

African languages and literature
Special languages (alphabetically) -- Continued

8533-8533.95	Musei (Table P-PZ15a)
8535-8535.95	Musgu (Table P-PZ15a modified)
	Dialects
8535.95.A-Z	Special. By name or place, A-Z
8535.95.V8	Vulum
8536-8536.95	Mwaghavul (Table P-PZ15a)
8538-8538.95	Mwamba (Table P-PZ15a)
8538.97-.9795	Mwenyi (Table P-PZ15b)
8539-8539.95	Mwera (Table P-PZ15a)
8540.4-.495	Nafaanra (Table P-PZ15b)
8541-8541.95	Nama (Table P-PZ15a)
	Cf. PL8251+ Hottentot
8544-8544.95	Nande (Table P-PZ15a)
8545-8545.95	Nandi (Table P-PZ15a)
8545.97	Nandi languages (Table P-PZ15)
(8546-8546.95)	Nankanse
	see PL8168+
8547	Nankanse - Nembe
8547.N21-.N2195	Nateni (Table P-PZ16)
8547.N22-.N2295	Nawdm (Table P-PZ16)
8547.N25-.N2595	Nchumburu (Table P-PZ16)
8547.N26-.N2695	Ndali (Table P-PZ16)
8547.N27-.N2795	Ndebele (South Africa) (Table P-PZ16)
8547.N28-.N2895	Ndebele (Zimbabwe) (Table P-PZ16)
8547.N3	Ndogo-Sere languages
8547.N4-.N495	Ndonga (Table P-PZ16)
8547.N5-.N595	Ndumu (Table P-PZ16)
8548	Nembe (Table P-PZ15)
	Ng'anga see PL8593+
8548.45-.4595	Ngamo (Table P-PZ15b)
8548.5-.595	Ngbaka ma'bo (Table P-PZ15b)
8548.55-.5595	Ngbandi (Table P-PZ15b)
8548.65-.6595	Ngiemboon (Ngyemboon) (Table P-PZ15b)
8548.663	Ngiri languages
8548.665-.66595	Ngiti (Table P-PZ15b)
8548.67-.6795	Ngizim (Table P-PZ15b)
8548.68-.6895	Ngo (Table P-PZ15b)
8548.7-.795	Ngombe (Table P-PZ15b)
8549-8549.95	Ngonde (Table P-PZ15a)
8550	Ngonde - Nika
8550.N44	Nguni languages
	Ngyemboon see PL8548.65+
8550.N49-.N4995	Nharo (Table P-PZ16)
8550.N53-.N5395	Nielim (Table P-PZ16)

African languages and literature
Special languages (alphabetically) -- Continued

(8551)	Nika
	see PL8515.M54
8555-8555.95	Nilamba (Table P-PZ15a)
8561-8561.95	Nkosi (Table P-PZ15a)
8562-8562.95	Nkoya (Table P-PZ15a)
8563-8563.95	Nkunya (Table P-PZ15a)
8564-8564.95	Nomaante (Table P-PZ15a)
8566.4-.495	Noon (Table P-PZ15b)
8566.5-.595	Noone (Table P-PZ15b)
	Northern Bullom see PL8093+
	Northern Sotho see PL8690+
	Nsenga see PL8656+
8568-8568.95	Ntomba (Table P-PZ15a)
8571-8574	Nubian languages (Table P-PZ11a)
(8575)	Nubian literature
	see PL8573.5+
8576	Nubian - Nupe
8576.N4-.N495	Nuer (Table P-PZ16)
	Nufi see PL8169+
8576.N57-.N5795	Nunuma (Table P-PZ16)
8577-8577.95	Nupe (Table P-PZ15a)
8579-8579.95	Nyabwa (Table P-PZ15a)
	Nyai see PL8727+
(8581-8581.95)	Nyakyusa
	see PL8549+
	Nyam-Nyam see PL8828+
8587-8587.95	Nyambo (Table P-PZ15a)
8591-8591.95	Nyamwezi (Table P-PZ15a)
8592	Nyamwezi - Nyanja
	Nyandja see PL8593+
8592.N3-.N395	Nyaneka (Table P-PZ16)
8592.N43-.N4395	Nyanga (Table P-PZ16)
8593-8593.95	Nyanja (Table P-PZ15a)
8594	Nyanja - Nyor
8594.N3-.N395	Nyankole (Table P-PZ16)
8594.N45-.N4595	Nyankore-Kiga (Table P-PZ16)
8595-8595.95	Nyoro (Table P-PZ15a)
8596	Nyoro - Nzima
8596.N9-.N995	Nyoro-Tooro (Table P-PZ16)
	Nyungwe see PL8727+
8596.N996-.N99695	Nzebi (Table P-PZ16)
8597-8597.95	Nzima (Table P-PZ15a)
8598	O - Oz
8598.O27-.O2795	Obolo (Table P-PZ16)
8598.O29-.O2995	Odual (Table P-PZ16)

African languages and literature
Special languages (alphabetically)
O - Oz -- Continued
Oji see PL8751+
8598.O32-.O3295	Ogba (Table P-PZ16)
8598.O33-.O3395	Ogbronuagum (Table P-PZ16)
8598.O355-.O35595	Okefani (Table P-PZ16)
8598.O357-.O35795	Okpe (Table P-PZ16)
8598.O4-.O495	Ombo (Table P-PZ16)
	Oromo see PJ2471+
8598.O8-.O895	Orungu (Table P-PZ16)
	Ovambo see PL8417+
8599	P - Ph
8599.P28-.P2895	Paduko (Table P-PZ16)
8599.P33-.P3395	Pangwa (Table P-PZ16)
8599.P35-.P3595	Päri (Sudan) (Table P-PZ16)
8599.P47-.P4795	Pero (Table P-PZ16)
8600	Pi - Pogoro
8600.P52-.P5295	Pinyin (Table P-PZ16)
8600.P55	Plateau languages (Benue-Congo)
8601-8601.95	Pogoro (Table P-PZ15a)
8603-8603.95	Pokomo (Table P-PZ15a)
8605-8605.95	Punu (Table P-PZ15a)
8606	Punu - Qz
8607	Ra - Ruanda
8607.R35-.R3595	Rangi (Table P-PZ16)
8607.R6-.R695	Ron (Table P-PZ16)
8607.R73-.R7395	Ronga (Table P-PZ16)
8608-8608.95	Ruanda. Kinyaruanda (Table P-PZ15a)
8611-8611.95	Rundi (Table P-PZ15a)
8613-8613.95	Runga (Table P-PZ15a)
8615-8615.95	Ruri (Table P-PZ15a)
8618-8618.95	Ruund (Table P-PZ15a)
8621-8621.95	Sabaot (Table P-PZ15a)
8624-8624.95	Safaliba (Table P-PZ15a)
8625-8625.95	Sagara (Table P-PZ15a)
8627-8627.95	Sakata (Table P-PZ15a)
8629-8629.95	Samburu (Table P-PZ15a)
8631-8631.95	Sandawe (Table P-PZ15a)
8641-8641.95	Sango (Table P-PZ15a)
8642-8642.95	Sangu (Gabon) (Table P-PZ15a)
8644-8644.95	Sara (Table P-PZ15a modified)
8644.94	Dialects
8644.95.A-Z	Special. By name or place, A-Z
8644.95.M34-.M3495	Majingai (Table P-PZ16)
8644.95.N45-.N4595	Ngama (Table P-PZ16)
8645	Sara languages (Table P-PZ15)

African languages and literature
Special languages (alphabetically) -- Continued

8648-8648.95	Sara mbai (Table P-PZ15a)
	Sechuana see PL8747+
8653-8653.95	Sembla (Table P-PZ15a)
8655-8655.95	Sena (Table P-PZ15a)
8656-8656.95	Senga. Nsenga (Table P-PZ15a)
8658-8658.95	Senufo (Table P-PZ15a)
8662-8662.95	Serer (Table P-PZ15a)
	Sesuto see PL8689+
8666-8666.95	Shambala (Table P-PZ15a)
8668-8668.95	Sherbro. Southern Bullom (Table P-PZ15a)
8670-8670.95	Shi (Table P-PZ15a)
	Shilha see PJ2379+
8671-8671.95	Shilluk (Table P-PZ15a)
8675-8675.95	Shira. Sira (Table P-PZ15a)
	Shironga see PL8607.R73+
8681-8681.95	Shona (Table P-PZ15a modified)
	Dialects
8681.94	General works
8681.95.A-Z	Special. By name or place, A-Z
8681.95.K67-.K6795	Korekore (Table P-PZ16)
8682	Shona - Songe
	Sira see PL8675+
8682.S55-.S5595	Sissala (Table P-PZ16)
	Siwah see PJ2361+
8682.S58-.S5895	So (Uganda) (Table P-PZ16)
8682.S62-.S6295	Soga (Table P-PZ16)
	Somali see PJ2531+
8682.S64-.S6495	Somba (Table P-PZ16)
8683-8683.95	Songe. Songye (Table P-PZ15a)
8685-8685.95	Songhai (Table P-PZ15a modified)
	Dialects
8685.95.A-Z	Special. By name or place, A-Z
8685.95.D45	Dendi
8685.95.K68	Koyraboro Senni
8685.95.T68	Tondi Songway Kiini
8685.95.Z35	Zarma
	Songye see PL8683+
8686-8686.95	Soninke (Table P-PZ15a)
8689-8689.95	Sotho. Southern Sotho (Table P-PZ15a)
8690-8690.95	Sotho, Northern (Table P-PZ15a)
8691	Sotho-Tswana languages (Table P-PZ15)
8692	Sotho-Tswana - Suku
	Southern Bauchi languages see PL8068.B37
	Southern Bullom see PL8668+
	Southern Mande languages see PL8490.M3595S68

African languages and literature
Special languages (alphabetically)
Sotho-Tswana - Suku -- Continued
Southern Mofu see PL8517

8692.S86-.S8695	Subiya (Table P-PZ16)
8692.S9-.S995	Suk (Table P-PZ16)
8693-8693.95	Suku (Table P-PZ15a)
8694	Suku - Susu
8694.S94-.S9495	Sukuma (Table P-PZ16)
8694.S95-.S9595	Sumbwa (Table P-PZ16)
8694.S96-.S9695	Suppire (Table P-PZ16)
8694.S97	Surmic languages
8695-8695.95	Susu (Table P-PZ15a)
8701-8704	Swahili (Table P-PZ11 modified)
	Literature
8704.A3-.Z5	Individual authors or works, A-Z
	Subarrange individual authors by Table P-PZ40 unless otherwise specified
	Subarrange individual works by Table P-PZ43 unless otherwise specified
8704.U76	Utendi wa kutawafu Nabii (Table P-PZ43)
	Dialects
8704.Z8	General works
8704.Z9A-.Z9Z	Local. By dialect name or place, A-Z
	e. g.
8704.Z9F85	Fundi
8704.Z9K33	Kae
8704.Z9M34	Mtang'ata
8705-8705.95	Swazi (Table P-PZ15a)
8706	Swazi - Taita
8706.T34-.T3495	Tagoi (Table P-PZ16)
8707-9707.95	Taita (Table P-PZ15a)
8709-8709.95	Talinga-Bwisi (Table P-PZ15a)
	Tamashek see PJ2381+
8711-8711.95	Tarok (Table P-PZ15a)
	Tamboka see PL8749+
8715-8715.95	Taveta (Table P-PZ15a)
	Tebele see PL8547.N28+
8724-8724.95	Tedaga (Table P-PZ15a)
8725	Teke (Table P-PZ15)
8725.15	Tem (Table P-PZ15)
8725.2	Tembo (Kivu, Zaire) (Table P-PZ15)
8725.3	Tepo (Table P-PZ15)
8725.5	Tera (Table P-PZ15)
8726-8726.95	Teso (Table P-PZ15a)
8727-8727.95	Tete. Nyungwe (Table P-PZ15a)
8728-8728.95	Tetela (Table P-PZ15a)

African languages and literature
Special languages (alphabetically) -- Continued

8731	Teuso languages (Table P-PZ15)
8732.5-.595	Tharaka (Table P-PZ15b)
	Tigrai see PJ9111+
	Tigré see PJ9131
	Tigriña see PJ9111+
8733-8733.95	Tikar (Table P-PZ15a)
8735-8735.95	Timne or Temne (Table P-PZ15a)
8738	Tivi, Tiv (Table P-PZ15)
8738.5	Tobote (Table P-PZ15)
8739-8739.95	Tonga of Inhambane (Gi-Tonga) (Table P-PZ15a)
8740-8740.95	Tonga of Lake Nyasa (Chi-Tonga) (Table P-PZ15a)
8741-8741.95	Tonga of Rhodesia, Zambesi (Ci-Tonga) (Table P-PZ15a)
8743-8743.95	Tooro (Table P-PZ15a)
8744.7-.795	Tsogo (Table P-PZ15b)
8745-8745.95	Tsonga (Table P-PZ15a)
8746	Tsonga - Tswana
8746.T85-.T8595	Tswa (Table P-PZ16)
8747-8747.95	Tswana (Table P-PZ15a)
8748	Tswana - Tumbuka
	Tuareg see PJ2381+
8748.T82-.T8295	Tuburi (Table P-PZ16)
8748.T84-.T8495	Tumak (Table P-PZ16)
8749-8749.95	Tumbuka (Table P-PZ15a)
8750	Tumbuka - Twi
8750.T82-.T8295	Tura (Table P-PZ16)
8750.T8298-.T829895	Turka (Table P-PZ16)
8750.T83-.T8395	Turkana (Table P-PZ16)
8750.T85-.T8595	Tusia (Table P-PZ16)
8751-8751.95	Twi (Table P-PZ15a)
8753	Uduk (Table P-PZ15)
8753.5	Uldeme (Table P-PZ15)
8755-8755.95	Umbundu (Table P-PZ15a)
8757-8757.95	Urhobo (Table P-PZ15a)
8758-8758.95	Uwana (Table P-PZ15a)
8759-8759.95	Vagala (Table P-PZ15a)
8761-8761.95	Vai (Table P-PZ15a)
8771-8771.95	Venda (Table P-PZ15a)
8772	Venda - Vh
8773	Vi - Vili
8773.V43-.V4395	Vige (Table P-PZ16)
8774-8774.95	Vili (Table P-PZ15a)
8775.7-.795	Vunjo (Table P-PZ15b)
8775.9-.995	Vute (Table P-PZ15b)
8776-8776.95	Waama (Table P-PZ15a)
8778-8778.95	Waja (Table P-PZ15a)

African languages and literature
Special languages (alphabetically) -- Continued

	Wandala see PL8489+
8779-8779.95	Wanga (Table P-PZ15a)
	Wemba see PL8069+
8783-8783.95	Wobe (Table P-PZ15a)
8785-8785.95	Wolof (Table P-PZ15a)
(8791-8791.95)	Wute
	see PL8775.9+
8795-8795.95	Xhosa (Table P-PZ15a)
8796.6-.695	!Xu (Table P-PZ15b)
8796.8-.895	Yaka (Congo and Angola) (Table P-PZ15b)
8797-8797.95	Yakö (Table P-PZ15a)
8799-8799.95	Yakoma (Table P-PZ15a)
8800	Yakoma - Yao
8800.Y25-.Y2595	Yala (Table P-PZ16)
8800.Y29-.Y2995	Yalunka (Table P-PZ16)
8800.Y33-.Y3395	Yamba (Table P-PZ16)
8800.Y35-.Y3595	Yambeta (Table P-PZ16)
8800.Y4-.Y495	Yanzi (Table P-PZ16)
8801-8804	Yao (Table P-PZ11)
8805-8805.95	Yaouré (Table P-PZ15a)
8807	Yaunde-Fang languages
8811-8811.95	Yebu (Table P-PZ15a)
8813-8813.95	Yemba (Table P-PZ15a)
8814.4-.495	Yeyi (Table P-PZ15b)
8814.8-.895	Yom (Table P-PZ15b)
8815-8815.95	Yombe (Congo and Angola) (Table P-PZ15a)
8821-8824	Yoruba (Table P-PZ11)
8826-8826.95	Yulu (Table P-PZ15a)
8828-8828.95	Zande (Table P-PZ15a)
8831-8831.95	Zeguha, or Zigula (Table P-PZ15a)
(8834)	Ziba
	see PL8237+
	Zigula see PL8831+
8835-8835.95	Zinza (Table P-PZ15a)
8839-8839.95	Zulgo (Table P-PZ15a)
8841-8844	Zulu (Table P-PZ11)

	Hyperborean, Indian, and artificial languages
	Hyperborean languages of Arctic Asia and America
1	General works
3	Grammar
6	Dictionaries
	Literature
8	History and criticism
8.5	Collections
9	Other special
	Asian. Paleosiberian languages
10	General works
10.5	Alutor
11-14	Chukchi (Table P-PZ11)
15	Gilyak (Table P-PZ15)
16	Kamchadal (Table P-PZ15)
17	Ket. Yenisei-Ostyak (Table P-PZ15)
18-18.95	Koryak (Table P-PZ15a)
19	Kott
19.5	Yugh
20-20.95	Yukagir (Table P-PZ15a)
	Eskimo-Aleut languages
	For Eskimo-Aleut and American Indian languages treated collectively see PM101+
30	General works
31-34	Aleut (Table P-PZ11)
	Cf. PM92 Eskimo Aleut
	Eskimo languages
50	General works (Table P-PZ15)
	Including general works on Inuit
	Inuit dialects
53	Inupiaq (Table P-PZ15)
55	Inuktitut (Table P-PZ15)
57	Inuvialuktun (Table P-PZ15)
61-64	Kalatdlisut. Greenlandic (Table P-PZ11)
	Yupik languages
80	General works
85	Aglemiut
87	Central Alaskan Yupik (Table P-PZ15)
92	Pacific Gulf Yupik. Eskimo Aleut (Table P-PZ15)
94	Yuit. Siberian Yupik (Table P-PZ15)
96	Sirinek (Table P-PZ15)
	Indian languages
	Including American Indian and Eskimo-Aleut languages treated collectively
101-146	Languages (General) (Table P-PZ5)
	Sign language see E98.S5

PM

	Indian languages -- Continued
	Literature
	History and criticism
151	Periodicals. Societies. Serials. Collected works (nonserial)
152	Encyclopedias. Dictionaries
153	Study and teaching
	History
155	General works
157	Relation to history, civilization, culture, etc.
	Relation to other literatures
158	General works
159	Translations (as subject)
160.A-Z	Treatment of special subjects, classes, etc., A-Z
163	Biography (Collective)
167	Poetry
171	Drama
173	Prose. Fiction
178	Other forms (not A-Z)
	For folk literature, see class E
	Collections
181	General collections
184	Poetry
187	Drama
189	Prose. Fiction
195	Other forms (not A-Z)
	For folk literature, see class E
197-198	Translations into other languages (Table P-PZ30)
	Languages north of Mexico
201	Periodicals. Societies. Serials. Collections (nonserial)
202	Congresses
203	History of philology
205	Study and teaching
206	General works
207	History of the languages
	Grammar
209	General works
211	Phonology
213	Morphology
214	Parts of speech
215	Syntax
217	Style. Composition. Rhetoric
218	Translating
219	Prosody. Metrics. Rhythmics
220	Lexicology
221	Etymology

	Indian languages
	Languages north of Mexico -- Continued
223	Dictionaries
	Languages of Canada
231	General works
232	General special
233	Grammar
236	Dictionaries
	Literature
238	History and criticism
238.5	Collections
238.65.A-Z	Translations. By language, A-Z
239	Other special
	By district, province, etc.
251	Alberta
261	Assiniboia
271	Athabasca
281-284	British Columbia (Table P-PZ11)
291	Keewatin
301	Manitoba
311	New Brunswick
321	Newfoundland
331	Nova Scotia
341	Ontario
351	Quebec
355.A-Z	Other special, A-Z
	e.g.
355.L3	Labrador
	Languages of United States
(401-409)	General
	see PM201+ ; Literature, see PM151+
	By region
421	Northeastern (New England) (Table P-PZ15)
431	Atlantic (Table P-PZ15)
441	South (Gulf, etc.) (Table P-PZ15)
451-454	Mississippi Valley (Table P-PZ11a)
456-459	Missouri Valley (Table P-PZ11a)
461-464	Southwest (Table P-PZ11a)
471	Northwest (Rocky Mountains) (Table P-PZ15)
481-484	Pacific coast (Table P-PZ11a)
501.A-Z	By state, A-Z
	Special languages and groups of languages
549.A2-.A295	Abitibi (Table P-PZ16)
551	Abnaki (Abenaki, Wabnaki) (Table P-PZ15)
	Cf. PM1791+ Micmac
	Cf. PM2147 Penobscot

	Indian languages
	Languages north of Mexico
	Special languages and groups of languages -- Continued
561	Achomawi (Table P-PZ15)
	Cf. PM2305 Shastan languages
	Acoma see PM1511
565	Acubadao (Florida) (Table P-PZ15)
571	Adaizan (Table P-PZ15)
(575)	Agnie
	see PM1881+
	Cf. PM1366 Huron
	Aht see PM2031
580	Ahtena (Table P-PZ15)
(585)	Akansa
	see PM2213
592	Alabama (Table P-PZ15)
599	Algonkin (Table P-PZ15)
	Cf. PM601+ Algonquian languages
601-609	Algonquian languages (Table P-PZ8)
610.A3-.A395	Alsea (Table P-PZ16)
610.A6-.A695	Amikwa (Table P-PZ16)
611	Anaddakkas (Table P-PZ15)
631	Apache (Table P-PZ15)
	Cf. PM858 Chiricahua
	Cf. PM1771 Mescalero
	Apache, Western see PM2583
633	Apalachee (Table P-PZ15)
635	Arapaho (Table P-PZ15)
	Cf. PM653 Atsina. Gros Ventre (Algonquian)
636.A7-.A795	Arikara (Table P-PZ16)
638	Assiniboin (Table P-PZ15)
(639)	Atayo
	see PM571
641	Athapascan languages (Table P-PZ15)
	Atnah (Alaska) see PM580
653	Atsina language. Gros Ventre language (Algonquian)
	(Table P-PZ15)
	Cf. PM635 Arapaho
655	Atsugewi (Table P-PZ15)
	Cf. PM2305 Shastan languages
661	Attacapa (Louisiana) (Table P-PZ15)
663.A7-.A795	Attikamek (Table P-PZ16)
	Cf. PM599 Algonkin
663.A8-.A895	Avavare (Table P-PZ16)
664	Babine (Table P-PZ15)

PM

	Indian languages
	Languages north of Mexico
	Special languages and groups of languages -- Continued
(665.B5-.B595)	Batem-da-Kai-Ee
	see PM1481
	Beaver Indians (Athapascan tribe) see PM2493
675	Bella Coola (Table P-PZ15)
685	Bemarino (Table P-PZ15)
695	Beothuk (Table P-PZ15)
702	Biloxi (Table P-PZ15)
	Blackfoot see PM2341+
(710.B6-.B695)	Bodega
	see PM1845
721	Caddoan languages (Table P-PZ15)
	Including Caddo
731	Cahuilla (Table P-PZ15)
735.C3-.C395	Caigua (Table P-PZ16)
735.C5-.C595	Cajueche (Table P-PZ16)
	Calapooya see PM1421
741	Cameole (Table P-PZ15)
745.C3-.C395	Caniba (Table P-PZ16)
745.C5-.C595	Caoque (Table P-PZ16)
	Carrier see PM2411
751	Catawba (Table P-PZ15)
753	Cathlamet (Table P-PZ15)
755.C3-.C395	Cathlascon (Table P-PZ16)
757	Cayuga (Table P-PZ15)
(759.C5-.C595)	Ceris (Gulf of California)
	see PM4251
761	Chastacosta (Table P-PZ15)
	Cf. PM641 Athapascan languages
(765.C3-.C395)	Chata
	see PM871+
765.C5-.C595	Chegakou (Table P-PZ16)
	Cf. PM599 Algonkin
	Chehalis see PM2513
	Chemegue see PM765.C8+
765.C8-.C895	Chemehuevi (Colorado River) (Table P-PZ16)
	Chepewyan see PM851+
781-784	Cherokee (Table P-PZ11)
	Chetemacha see PM861
795	Cheyenne (Table P-PZ15)
801	Chickasaw (Table P-PZ15)
803	Chilliwack dialect (Table P-PZ15)
805	Chilula (Table P-PZ15)
811	Chimakuan languages (Table P-PZ15)

Indian languages
Languages north of Mexico
Special languages and groups of languages -- Continued

821	Chimariko (Table P-PZ15)
(831)	Chimmesyan
	see PM2494
841-844	Chinook (Table P-PZ11)
846-849	Chinook jargon (Table P-PZ11)
850.C2-.C295	Chipewyan (Table P-PZ16)
851-854	Chippewa (Ojibway; Otchipwe) (Table P-PZ11)
858	Chiricahua (Table P-PZ15)
861	Chitimacha (Louisiana) (Table P-PZ15)
871-874	Choctaw (Table P-PZ11)
881	Chorruco (Table P-PZ15)
885.C3-.C395	Chorruto (Table P-PZ16)
885.C5-.C595	Chow-e-shak (Table P-PZ16)
891	Chumash (Table P-PZ15)
895	Clallam (Table P-PZ15)
	Coahuiltecan languages see PM4158
	Coahuilteco see PM3681
(911)	Cocomaricopa
	see PM1711
(915.C6)	Cocopa
	see PM3696
916	Coeur d'Alene (Table P-PZ15)
921	Comanche (Table P-PZ15)
931	Como (Table P-PZ15)
941	Comox (Table P-PZ15)
	Cookkoo-oose language see PM1611
	Coos see PM1611
	Cora see PM3711+
(971)	Costanoan
	see PM2053
981	Cowichan languages (Table P-PZ15)
982	Cowlitz (Table P-PZ15)
986-989	Cree (Table P-PZ11)
	For French Cree see PM7895.M53
991	Creek (Muskogee) (Table P-PZ15)
	Cf. PM1971+ Muskhogean languages
1001	Crow (Table P-PZ15)
1003	Cupan languages (Table P-PZ15)
1004	Cupeño (Table P-PZ15)
1005	Cushna (Table P-PZ15)
1011	Cutalchich (Table P-PZ15)
1015	Cutguane (Table P-PZ15)

	Indian languages
	Languages north of Mexico
	Special languages and groups of languages -- Continued
1021-1024	Dakota (Table P-PZ11)
	Including the Santee, Teton, and Yankton dialects
1031-1034	Delaware (Lenape) (Table P-PZ11)
	Dena'ina see PM2412
1041	Desnedekenade (Table P-PZ15)
1051	Dhatada (Table P-PZ15)
1058	Dhegiha (Table P-PZ15)
	Cf. PM2351 Siouan languages
1061	Dhigida (Table P-PZ15)
1071	Diegueño (Table P-PZ15)
1081	Ditsakana (Table P-PZ15)
1091	Dogrib (Table P-PZ15)
1101	Doguene (Table P-PZ15)
	Echemin (Etchemin) see PM2135
1125	Ehnek (N. California) (Table P-PZ15)
1131	Erie (Table P-PZ15)
	Eskelen see PM1137
	Eslene see PM1137
1137	Esselenian (Table P-PZ15)
	Etchoattine see PM2365
	Etchareottine see PM2365
	Etchemin see PM2135
1141	Etheneldeli (Table P-PZ15)
1151	Etiwaw (Table P-PZ15)
(1171)	Eudeve
	see PM3766
1181	Ewawoo (Table P-PZ15)
1191	Eyeish (Table P-PZ15)
	Flathead see PM1431; PM2261+
1195	Fox (Table P-PZ15)
	French Cree see PM7895.M53
1201	Gabrieleño (Table P-PZ15)
1205.G5-.G595	Geioguen (Table P-PZ16)
	Gitksan see PM1541
1211	Goasile (Table P-PZ15)
1221	Gosiute (Table P-PZ15)
	Gros Ventre (Algonquian) see PM653
	Gros Ventre (Siouan) see PM1331
1225	Guaicone (Florida) (Table P-PZ15)
1231	Guauaenok (Table P-PZ15)
	Gwich'in see PM1621
	Haeltzuk see PM1321
1261	Hahuamis (Table P-PZ15)

Indian languages
    Languages north of Mexico
        Special languages and groups of languages -- Continued

1271-1274	Haida (Table P-PZ11)
1281	Hainai (Table P-PZ15)
1282	Haisla (Table P-PZ15)
1285	Hane (Table P-PZ15)
1291	Hankutchin (Table P-PZ15)
	Hare see PM2365.Z9K39
1301	Hatawekela (Table P-PZ15)
1311	Havasupai (Table P-PZ15)
1321	Heiltsuk (Table P-PZ15)
1325.H3-.H395	Henaggi (Table P-PZ16)
1325.H4-.H495	Henya (Table P-PZ16)
1325.H5-.H595	Hesquiat (Table P-PZ16)
1325.H6-.H695	Heuchi (Table P-PZ16)
1331	Hidatsa (Table P-PZ15)
1341	Hitchiti (Table P-PZ15)
1343	Hokan-Coahuiltecan languages (Table P-PZ15)
	Including Hokan languages (General)
1345.H6-.H95	Holmiuk (Table P-PZ16)
	Hoo-pah see PM1361+
1351	Hopi (Table P-PZ15)
1356	Hualapai (Table P-PZ15)
1357.H3-.H395	Hudson's Bay Indians (Table P-PZ16)
1357.H7-.H795	Huma (Table P-PZ16)
1357.H9-.H995	Huna (Table P-PZ16)
1361-1364	Hupa (Table P-PZ11)
1366	Huron (Table P-PZ15)
	Cf. PM1381+ Iroquoian languages
1367.H5-.H595	Hutsnuevu (Table P-PZ16)
1367.H7-.H795	Hwotsoteune (Table P-PZ16)
(1367.I2-.I295)	Iakonan languages
	see PM2621
1367.I4-.I495	Iguaze (Table P-PZ16)
1371	Illinois (Table P-PZ15)
1373	Ingalik (Table P-PZ15)
1376	Iowa (Table P-PZ15)
1381-1384	Iroquoian (including Iroquois) (Table P-PZ11)
1386.I7-.I795	Iruwaitsu (Table P-PZ16)
1387	Isleta (Table P-PZ15)
1388.J3-.J395	Janos (Table P-PZ16)
1389	Jicarilla (Xicarolles) (Table P-PZ15)
1390.J8-.J895	Jumano (Table P-PZ16)
(1391)	Kadohadacho
	see PM721

Indian languages
    Languages north of Mexico
        Special languages and groups of languages -- Continued
1393   Kaigani (Table P-PZ15)
1395   Kainah (Table P-PZ15)
1401   Kaiyuhkhotana (Table P-PZ15)
1411   Kake (Table P-PZ15)
1421   Kalapuya (Kalapooiah) (Table P-PZ15)
1431   Kalispel (Flathead Indians) (Table P-PZ15)
1441   Kansa (Table P-PZ15)
1451   Karankawan (Table P-PZ15)
1461   Karok (Karuk) (Table P-PZ15)
1463   Kashaya (Table P-PZ15)
1465   Kaskaskia (Table P-PZ15)
                Kathlamet see PM753
1475   Katlaminimin (Table P-PZ15)
1481   Kato (Table P-PZ15)
                Kaus see PM1611
1487   Kawaiisu (Table P-PZ15)
                    Cf. PM2321 Shoshonean languages
(1489)   Kawchottine
                    see PM2365.Z9K39
                Kawia see PM2681
                Kenai see PM2412
1511   Keres (New Mexico) (Table P-PZ15)
1521   Kichai (Table P-PZ15)
1526   Kickapoo (Table P-PZ15)
1531   Kiowa (Table P-PZ15)
                Kitamat see PM1282
1541   Kitksan (Table P-PZ15)
                Kitunahan see PM1587
1551   Klamath (Table P-PZ15)
1555   Klikitat (Table P-PZ15)
                Knaiakhotana see PM2412
1571   Koasati (Table P-PZ15)
                Kolushan see PM2455
1585   Konomihu (Table P-PZ15)
                    Cf. PM2305 Shastan languages
1587   Kootenai (Table P-PZ15)
1591   Koskimo (Table P-PZ15)
1594   Koyukon (Table P-PZ15)
                Ksanka see PM1587
1598   Kuitsh (Lower Umpqua) (Table P-PZ15)
1601   Kulanapan languages. Pomo languages (Table P-PZ15)
                Kumiai see PM1071
1611   Kusan languages (including Coos) (Table P-PZ15)

Indian languages
  Languages north of Mexico
    Special languages and groups of languages -- Continued
(1615)   Kutchakutchin
                    see PM1621
1621   Kutchin (Table P-PZ15)
                    Cf. PM641 Athapascan
(1631)   Kutenai (Cootenay)
                    see PM1587
1641   Kwakiutl (Table P-PZ15)
                    Cf. PM2031 Nootka
                    Cf. PM2531 Wakashan languages
                  Kwokwoos language see PM1611
1645   Laguna (Table P-PZ15)
1646   Lag - Lip
                    Lahcotah see PM1021+
                    Lenape see PM1031+
1646.L7-.L795   Lillovet, or Lilowat (Table P-PZ16)
1647   Lipan (Table P-PZ15)
                  Lower Umpqua see PM1598
1651   Luiseño (Table P-PZ15)
1656   Lummi (Table P-PZ15)
1661   Lutuamian languages (Table P-PZ15)
                    Cf. PM1551 Klamath
                    Cf. PM1861 Modoc
1671   Mahican (Table P-PZ15)
1681   Maidu (Table P-PZ15)
1691   Makah (Table P-PZ15)
                  Malecite (Maliseet) see PM2135
1701   Mandan (Table P-PZ15)
1705.M3-.M395   Manso (Table P-PZ16)
1705.M5-.M595   Manta (Table P-PZ16)
1711   Maricopa (Table P-PZ15)
                  Mariposan see PM2681
(1731)   Maskegon
                    see PM986+
1736-1739   Massachuset (Table P-PZ11)
1745.M3-.M395   Mattole (Table P-PZ16)
1751   Mdewakanton (Table P-PZ15)
1761   Menominee (Table P-PZ15)
1771   Mescalero (Table P-PZ15)
1781   Miami (Table P-PZ15)
                  Michif see PM7895.M53
1791-1794   Micmac (Table P-PZ11)
1801   Miniconjou (Table P-PZ15)
1811   Minisink (Table P-PZ15)

PM

	Indian languages
	Languages north of Mexico
	Special languages and groups of languages -- Continued
1821	Mission Indians of California (Table P-PZ15)
1831	Missisauga (Table P-PZ15)
1841	Missouri (Table P-PZ15)
1845	Miwok (Table P-PZ15)
	Including all Miwok languages
1851	Moache (Table P-PZ15)
1855	Mobilian trade language (Table P-PZ15)
1861	Modoc (Table P-PZ15)
1871	Mohave (Mojave) (Table P-PZ15)
1881-1884	Mohawk (Table P-PZ11)
1885	Mohegan (including Pequot) (Table P-PZ15)
	Mohican see PM1885
1891	Molala (Table P-PZ15)
1901	Mono-Paviotso languages (Table P-PZ15)
1911	Monsoni (Table P-PZ15)
1921-1924	Montagnais (Algonquian) (Table P-PZ11)
	Montagnais (Athapascan) see PM850.C2+
1931	Montauk (Table P-PZ15)
	Moose Indians see PM1911
	Moquelumnan see PM1845
1961	Munsee (Table P-PZ15)
1971-1974	Muskhogean languages (Table P-PZ11a)
	Cf. PM991 Creek
	Muskogee see PM991
1976-1979	Mutsun (Table P-PZ11)
1980	Na-Dene languages (Table P-PZ15)
1981	Nachitoches (Table P-PZ15)
1991	Nahaunies (Nehaumis) (Table P-PZ15)
2001	Nanticoke (Table P-PZ15)
2003	Narraganset (Table P-PZ15)
2004.N3-.N395	Nascape (Table P-PZ16)
	Nasgá (Nasqua) see PM2026.N3+
	Natakos see PM611
2004.N4-.N495	Natchez (Table P-PZ16)
	Natick see PM1736+
2006-2009	Navaho (Table P-PZ11)
	Neklakapamuk see PM2045
2015	Netele (Table P-PZ15)
	Netlakapamuk see PM2045
2017.N8-.N895	New River (Table P-PZ16)
	Cf. PM2305 Shastan languages
2019	Nez Percé (Table P-PZ15)
2025	Nipissing (Table P-PZ15)

	Indian languages
	Languages north of Mexico
	Special languages and groups of languages -- Continued
2026.N25-.N2595	Nisenan (Table P-PZ16)
2026.N3-.N395	Niska (Nishga) (Table P-PZ16)
2026.N5-.N595	Nisqually (Table P-PZ16)
	Nitlakapamuk see PM2045
	Nocké (Noka, Nokes, Nokets) see PM2041
2031	Nootka (Table P-PZ15)
	Cf. PM2531 Wakashan languages
2041	Noquet (Nocké, Noka, Nokes, Nokets) (Table P-PZ15)
	Northern Paiute see PM2094
2043	Northern Pomo (Table P-PZ15)
	Nozi see PM2641
2045	Ntlakyapamuk (Table P-PZ15)
	Numipu see PM2019
	Nutka see PM2031
2049.O3-.O395	Ofogoula (Table P-PZ16)
2051	Ogallala (Table P-PZ15)
2053	Ohlone (Table P-PZ15)
	Ojibway see PM851+
2066	Okanagan (Table P-PZ15)
2071	Omaha (Table P-PZ15)
2073	Oneida (Table P-PZ15)
2076	Onondaga (Table P-PZ15)
2078	Opelousas (Table P-PZ15)
2081	Osage (Table P-PZ15)
	Cf. PM2351 Siouan languages
2082.O8-.O895	Oto (Table P-PZ16)
2083	Ottawa (Table P-PZ15)
	Cf. PM601+ Algonquian languages
	Otto, Ottoas see PM2082.O8+
	Pacao see PM2097
2091.P3-.P395	Pachalaque (Table P-PZ16)
2091.P5-.P595	Paduba (Table P-PZ16)
2094	Paiute. Northern Paiute. Southern Paiute (Table P-PZ15)
2097	Pakawa (Texas) (Table P-PZ15)
	Cf. PM4158 Mexican Indian languages
2101	Palaihnihan languages (Table P-PZ15)
	Cf. PM561 Achomawi
	Cf. PM2305 Shastan languages
2111	Pamptikokes (Table P-PZ15)
2115	Panamint (Table P-PZ15)
2121	Panistock (Table P-PZ15)
2123	Papago (Table P-PZ15)
2125.P3-.P395	Papinacho (Table P-PZ16)

Indian languages
  Languages north of Mexico
    Special languages and groups of languages -- Continued

2125.P5-.P595	Pascagoulas (Table P-PZ16)
2135	Passamaquoddy (Table P-PZ15)
2137	Pawnee (Table P-PZ15)
	Peaux-de-Lièvre see PM2365.Z9K39
2141	Pecuri (Table P-PZ15)
2147	Penobscot (Table P-PZ15)
	Cf. PM551 Abnaki (Abenaki)
	Pequot see PM1885
2151	Pericu (Table P-PZ15)
2161	Piankishaw (Table P-PZ15)
2165	Piegan (Table P-PZ15)
2171-2174	Pima (Table P-PZ11)
2175	Piman languages (Table P-PZ15)
2176	Piro (Tanoan) (Table P-PZ15)
	Piute see PM2094
	Pomo, Northern see PM2043
	Pomo languages see PM1601
2181	Ponca (Table P-PZ15)
2191	Potawatomi (Table P-PZ15)
2194	Powhatan (Table P-PZ15)
2201	Pueblo Indians (Table P-PZ15)
	Pujunan see PM1681
2211.Q3-.Q395	Quabaug (Table P-PZ16)
2211.Q5-.Q595	Quahatika (Table P-PZ16)
	Quaisla see PM1282
2213	Quapaw (Table P-PZ15)
	Queres see PM1511
2215	Quesene (Table P-PZ15)
2219	Quileute (Table P-PZ15)
2220	Quinault (Table P-PZ15)
2221	Quinnipiac (Quiripi) (Table P-PZ15)
2223	Quioucohanock (Tapehanek) (Table P-PZ15)
	Quiripi see PM2221
2225	Quitol (Table P-PZ15)
	Quoratean see PM1461
	Red Indians see PM695
2227	Roanoak (Table P-PZ15)
2235	Saanich (Table P-PZ15)
2243	Sahaptin (Table P-PZ15)
2245	Saki (Table P-PZ15)
2251	Salinan (Table P-PZ15)
2261-2264	Salishan (including Salish) (Table P-PZ11)
	Santee see PM1021+

	Indian languages
	Languages north of Mexico
	Special languages and groups of languages -- Continued
2275	Sarsi (Sarcee) (Table P-PZ15)
	Sastean, or Shasta see PM2305
	Sauteux see PM851+
2280	Sechelt (Table P-PZ15)
	Secoffee (Labrador) see PM2004.N3+
2285	Sekani (Table P-PZ15)
2291	Seminole (Table P-PZ15)
2296	Seneca (Table P-PZ15)
2301	Shahaptian languages (Table P-PZ15)
	Cf. PM2019 Nez Percé
	Cf. PM2243 Sahaptin
2305	Shastan languages (Table P-PZ15)
	Comprising the Sastean and Palaihnihan groups of Powell, and Shasta proper
2311	Shawnee (Table P-PZ15)
2321	Shoshonean languages (including Shoshoni) (Table P-PZ15)
2325	Shuswap (Table P-PZ15)
	Cf. PM2261+ Salishan languages
	Sicaunies see PM2285
2341-2344	Siksika (Blackfoot) (Table P-PZ11)
2351	Siouan languages (Table P-PZ15)
	Cf. PM1021+ Dakota
2357	Siuslaw (Table P-PZ15)
	Skidegate see PM1271+
	Skittagetan see PM1271+
	Skwamish see PM2381.S6+
2365	Slavey (Slavi, Slave) (Table P-PZ15 modified)
	Cf. PM641 Athapascan languages
2365.Z9A-.Z9Z	Local. By dialect name or place, A-Z
2365.Z9K39	Kawchottine
2371	Snohomish (Table P-PZ15)
	Southern Paiute see PM2094
	Southern Tutchone see PM2506
2376	Spokane (Table P-PZ15)
2381.S6-.S695	Squawmish (Table P-PZ16)
2381.S8-.S895	Stalo (Table P-PZ16)
	Tabitibi see PM549.A2+
2381.T3-.T395	Tachi (Table P-PZ16)
	Cf. PM2681 Yokuts
2391	Taensa (Table P-PZ15)
2401	Takelma (Table P-PZ15)
	Takudh see PM1621

	Indian languages
	Languages north of Mexico
	Special languages and groups of languages -- Continued
2411	Takulli (Carrier Indians) (Table P-PZ15)
	Cf. PM641 Athapascan
2411.5	Tanacross (Table P-PZ15)
2412	Tanai. Tanaina. Dena'ina (Table P-PZ15)
2412.5	Tanana (Table P-PZ15)
2413	Tanoan languages (Table P-PZ15)
2416	Taos Indians (Table P-PZ15)
	Tapehanek see PM2223
	Tatche see PM2381.T3+
2421	Tawakoni (Table P-PZ15)
	Tehua see PM2431
	Telame see PM2381.T3+
2425	Tenino (Table P-PZ15)
	Cf. PM2301 Shahaptian languages
	Teton see PM1021+
2431	Tewa (Table P-PZ15)
	Thompson River Indians see PM2045
(2441)	Tigua
	see PM2453.4
2446	Tillamook (Table P-PZ15)
2451	Timucuan languages (Table P-PZ15)
	Including Timucua
2453	Tinne languages (Table P-PZ15)
2453.4	Tiwa (Table P-PZ15)
2454	Tlakluit (Table P-PZ15)
2455	Tlingit (Kolushan) (Table P-PZ15)
2471	Tonikan (Table P-PZ15)
2481	Tonkawa (Table P-PZ15)
2491	Tontos (Table P-PZ15)
2493	Tsattine (Beaver Indians) (Table P-PZ15)
2494	Tsimshian. Chimmesyan (Table P-PZ15)
2495.T7-.T795	Tubatulabal (Table P-PZ16)
	Cf. PM2321 Shoshonean languages
(2496)	Tukkuthkutchin (Tukudh, Takudh)
	see PM1621
2497	Tul-Tunic (Table P-PZ15)
	Tul'bush see PM1745.M3+
2498	Tunica (Table P-PZ15)
	Tuolumne see PM1845
2501	Tuscarora (Table P-PZ15)
2506	Tutchone, Southern (Table P-PZ15)
2507	Tutelo (Table P-PZ15)

Indian languages
Languages north of Mexico
Special languages and groups of languages -- Continued

2511	Uchean languages (Table P-PZ15)
	Including Yuchi
	Umpqua, Lower see PM1598
2512	Unami jargon (Table P-PZ15)
	Unangan see PM31+
2513	Upper Chehalis (Table P-PZ15)
2515	Ute (Table P-PZ15)
	Cf. PM2321 Shoshonean languages
	Uto-Aztecan languages see PM4479
2521	Waiilatpuan (Table P-PZ15)
2531	Wakashan languages (Table P-PZ15)
	Cf. PM1641 Kwakiutl
	Cf. PM2031 Nootka
2541	Wallawalla (Table P-PZ15)
2544	Wampanoag (Table P-PZ15)
2547	Wappo (Table P-PZ15)
2551	Washoe. Washo. Washoa (Table P-PZ15)
2555	Wawenock (Table P-PZ15)
(2561)	Wayilatpu
	see PM2521
2571	Weas (Table P-PZ15)
2583	Western Apache (Table P-PZ15)
2586	Wichita (Table P-PZ15)
	Wikchamni see PM2681
2591	Winnebago (Table P-PZ15)
2595	Wintun (Table P-PZ15)
2605	Wiyot (Table P-PZ15)
2608	Woccon (Table P-PZ15)
2611	Yakima (Table P-PZ15)
2621	Yakonan languages (Table P-PZ15)
2631	Yamassee (Table P-PZ15)
2641	Yana (Table P-PZ15)
	Yankton see PM1021+
2661	Yatasse (Table P-PZ15)
2671	Yavapai, or Yavipai (Table P-PZ15)
2681	Yokuts (Table P-PZ15 modified)
2681.Z9A-.Z9Z	Local. By dialect name or place, A-Z
	Including Wikchamni and Yawelmani dialects
2691	Yukian languages (Table P-PZ15)
	Including Yuki
2701	Yuman languages (Table P-PZ15)
2703	Yurok (Table P-PZ15)
2711	Zuñi (Table P-PZ15)

PM

	Indian languages -- Continued
	Languages of Mexico and Central America
	Languages of Mexico belonging to one of the stocks of languages north of Mexico are classed with that stock even if dealt with from a purely local point of view, e.g. Shoshonean, Yuman, Athapascan, and other families.
3001-3046	Languages (Table P-PZ5 modified)
3010	Writing. Alphabet
	For Pre-Columbian writing systems, see the area or Indian group in class F
(3010.5)	Script
	see PM3010
	Literature
	History and criticism
3051	Periodicals. Societies. Serials. Collected works (nonserial)
3052	Encyclopedias. Dictionaries
3053	Study and teaching
	History
3055	General works
3057	Relation to history, civilization, culture, etc.
	Relation to other literatures
3058	General works
3059	Translations (as subject)
3060.A-Z	Treatment of special subjects, classes, etc., A-Z
3063	Biography (Collective)
3067	Poetry
3071	Drama
3073	Prose. Fiction
3078	Other forms (not A-Z)
	For folk literature, see class E
	Collections
3082	General collections
3084	Poetry
3087	Drama
3089	Prose. Fiction
3095	Other forms (not A-Z)
	For folk literature, see class E
3097-3098	Translations into other languages (Table P-PZ30)
	Languages of Mexico
	General see PM3001+
	By state
3100	Aguascalientes
3101	Baja California and Province of California to 1848
3111	Campeche
3115	Chiapas

Indian languages
Languages of Mexico and Central America
Languages of Mexico
By state -- Continued
3121	Chihuahua
3131	Coahuila
3135	Colima
3141	Durango
3151	Guanajuato
3155	Guerrero
3161	Hidalgo
3171	Jalisco
3175	Mexico (State)
3181	Michoacan
3185	Morelos
3191	Nuevo Leon
3195	Oaxaca
3197	Puebla
3199	Queretaro
3201	San Luis Potosi
3211	Sinaloa
3221	Sonora
3231	Tabasco
3241	Tamaulipas
3251	Tepic
3255	Tlaxcala
3261	Vera Cruz
3271	Yucatan
3281	Zacatecas

Languages of Central America
3301-3329	General (Table P-PZ6)

By country
3351	Costa Rica
3361	Guatemala
3371	Honduras
3381	Nicaragua
3391	Panama
3393	Salvador

Special languages and groups of languages
3501	Acaxee, or Topia (Table P-PZ15)
3506	Achi, or Ache (Table P-PZ15)
	Including Cubulco Achi and Rabinal Achi
3509	Aguacateca. Awakateko (Table P-PZ15)
3511	Ahualulco (Table P-PZ15)
3512	Akatek (Table P-PZ15)
3513	Alagüilac (Table P-PZ15)

	Indian languages
	Languages of Mexico and Central America
	Special languages and groups of languages -- Continued
3516	Amishgo (Amusgo, Amuzgo, Amuchco) (Table P-PZ15)
(3521)	Ateanaca
	see PM3711+
	Awakateko see PM3509
	Ayook see PM4011
	Aztec (Nahuatl, Mexican) see PM4061+
3526	Babispe (Table P-PZ15)
3531	Baimena (Table P-PZ15)
3536.B3-.B395	Basopa (Extinct) (Table P-PZ16)
	Batuca, Batuco see PM3766
3536.B5-.B595	Baturoque (Extinct) (Table P-PZ16)
	Bayano see PM3746
3539	Boruca (Table P-PZ15)
3541	Bribri (Table P-PZ15)
3546	Buasdaba (Table P-PZ15)
3549	Cabecar (Table P-PZ15)
3551	Cácari (Extinct) (Table P-PZ15)
	Cachiquel see PM3576
3561	Cahita (Table P-PZ15)
3566	Cahumeto (Table P-PZ15)
3571	Cajono (Table P-PZ15)
	Cakchi see PM3913
3576	Cakchikel (Cachiquel or Kacchiquel) (Table P-PZ15)
	Cf. PM5690 Cakchiquel
3581	Camoteco (Table P-PZ15)
	Carib see PM5756+
3586	Cascan, or Cazgan (Table P-PZ15)
3591	Cazdal (Table P-PZ15)
3596	Chacahuaxti (Table P-PZ15)
(3601)	Chañabal
	see PM4413
3606	Chantaleno (Extinct) (Table P-PZ15)
	Chapanec see PM3618
3616	Chatino (Table P-PZ15)
3618	Chiapanec (Table P-PZ15)
3619	Chicomucelteca (Table P-PZ15)
3621	Chihuahueño (Table P-PZ15)
3626	Chicorato (Extinct) (Table P-PZ15)
3630	Chinantecan languages (Table P-PZ15)
	Including individual dialects
	Chinarra see PM3706
	Chinipa see PM4481
3641	Chocho (Table P-PZ15)

               Indian languages
                 Languages of Mexico and Central America
                   Special languages and groups of languages -- Continued
                     Choloteca see PM3943

3649	Choltí (Table P-PZ15)
3651	Chontal (Table P-PZ15)
	Chora see PM3711+
	Chorotega see PM3943
3661	Chorti, or Chorte (Table P-PZ15)
	Chota see PM3711+
	Chuchon see PM3641
3668	Chuj (Table P-PZ15)
3671	Chumbia (Extinct) (Table P-PZ15)
3676	Chumula (Table P-PZ15)
	Cinantecan see PM3630
3681	Coahuilteco (Extinct) (Table P-PZ15)
	Cf. PM4158 Pakawan languages
3686	Coca (Extinct) (Table P-PZ15)
3688	Cochimi (Table P-PZ15)
3696	Cocopa (Table P-PZ15)
3701	Colotlan (Extinct) (Table P-PZ15)
3706	Concho, or Chinarra (Table P-PZ15)
3711-3711.95	Cora (Chora, Chota, Nayarita, or Nayaerita) (Table P-PZ15a)
3716	Coribici (Table P-PZ15)
3721	Coxoh (Extinct) (Table P-PZ15)
(3726)	Cuachichil (Extinct)
	see PM3774
3731	Cuicatec (Table P-PZ15)
3736	Cuilapa (Table P-PZ15)
3738	Cuitlateco, or Teco (Table P-PZ15)
3741	Cuixlahuac (Table P-PZ15)
3743-3743.95	Cuna (Table P-PZ15a)
3746	Darien, or Dariel (Table P-PZ15)
3751	Didú (Table P-PZ15)
	Dirian see PM3943
	Dohema (or Dohme) see PM3766
3753	Doraksean languages (Table P-PZ15)
	Including Dorask proper and the (extinct?) dialects
	Changuina, Chumula, Gualaca, and Teluskie
3756	Edú (Table P-PZ15)
3761	Etla (Table P-PZ15)
3766	Eudeve (Heve or Hegue, Dohema or Dohme, Batuco) (Table P-PZ15)
	Cf. PM4136 Opata
3774	Guachichile (Table P-PZ15)

Indian languages
   Languages of Mexico and Central America
      Special languages and groups of languages -- Continued

3786	Gualaca (Table P-PZ15)
3791	Guanuca (Table P-PZ15)
3793	Guarijío (Table P-PZ15)
	Guastec see PM3831
3796	Guatiquimane, or Huatiquimane (Table P-PZ15)
3798	Guatuso (Table P-PZ15)
3801	Guaxabana (lost) (Table P-PZ15)
3806	Guaymi. Guaymie (Table P-PZ15)
3811	Guazápere, or Guazapari (Table P-PZ15)
3816	Guazave, or Vacoregue (Table P-PZ15)
3818	Guetare (Table P-PZ15)
	Guichola see PM3841
	Hegue see PM3766
3821	Herisobocona (Table P-PZ15)
	Heve see PM3766
3826	Hualauise (Extinct) (Table P-PZ15)
3831	Huastec (Huaxteco) (Table P-PZ15)
3836	Huave (Huazonteco or Wabi) (Table P-PZ15)
3841	Huichol (Guichola) (Table P-PZ15)
3846	Huite (Table P-PZ15)
3851	Hume (Table P-PZ15)
3856	Ihio (Table P-PZ15)
3861	Intibucat (Table P-PZ15)
	Ipapana see PM4301
3866	Irritila (Table P-PZ15)
	Itzá see PM3969.5.I89
3876	Ixcateco (Table P-PZ15)
3881	Ixil (Table P-PZ15)
3886	Izcuco (Extinct) (Table P-PZ15)
3889	Jacalteca (Table P-PZ15)
3891	Jalisciense (Table P-PZ15)
	Janambre see PM4197
3893	Jicaque (Table P-PZ15)
	Jicarilla see PM1389
	Jinca see PM4498.X3+
3896	Joba, Joval, or Ova (Table P-PZ15)
	Jonaz see PM3993
3906	Jope, or Yope (Table P-PZ15)
3911	Julime (Extinct) (Table P-PZ15)
	Kacchiquel see PM3576
3912	Kanjobal (Table P-PZ15)
3913	Kekchi (Table P-PZ15)
	Kiché see PM4231

	Indian languages
	Languages of Mexico and Central America
	Special languages and groups of languages -- Continued
3914	Kiliwa (Table P-PZ15)
3916	Lacandon, or Xoquinoe (Table P-PZ15)
(3918)	Laguneros
	see PM3866
3921	Lenca (Table P-PZ15)
3926	Macoaque (Extinct) (Table P-PZ15)
3931	Macoyahuy (Extinct) (Table P-PZ15)
3936	Mam (Mame, Tapachulano, Zaklohpakap) (Table P-PZ15)
(3941)	Manche
	see PM3969.5.M65
3943	Mangue (Choloteca, Chorotega, Dirian, Masaya) (Table P-PZ15)
3946	Manzanillos (Table P-PZ15)
	Masaya see PM3943
3948	Matagalpa (Table P-PZ15)
	Matlaltzinca see PM4193
3951	Matlame (Extinct) (Table P-PZ15)
3961-3969.5	Mayan languages (Table P-PZ8a modified)
	Including Maya or Yucateco
(3962)	Mayan hieroglyphics
	see F1435.3.W75
	Dialects of Maya
3969.4	General works
3969.5.A-Z	Special. By name or place, A-Z
3969.5.I89	Itzá
3969.5.M65	Mopan
3972	Mayo (Piman) (Table P-PZ15)
3981	Mazahua (Mazahui or Matlazahua) (Table P-PZ15)
3986	Mazapili (Table P-PZ15)
3991	Mazateco (Table P-PZ15)
3993	Meco (Table P-PZ15)
3996	Mediotaguel (Extinct) (Table P-PZ15)
	Mexican see PM4061+
3998	Meztitlaneca (Table P-PZ15)
	Michoacan see PM4296+
4001	Mictlantongo (Table P-PZ15)
	Miskito see PM4036+
4011	Mixe, or Mije (Table P-PZ15)
4016	Mixtec (Table P-PZ15)
4017	Mixtecan languages (Table P-PZ15)
	Mopan see PM3969.5.M65
4026	Morocosi (Extinct) (Table P-PZ15)

PM

	Indian languages
	Languages of Mexico and Central America
	Special languages and groups of languages -- Continued
4031	Moroteco (Table P-PZ15)
4036-4039	Mosquito (Miskito) (Table P-PZ11)
4040.M6-.M695	Motozintleca (Table P-PZ16)
(4041)	Munzicat, Muntzicat, or Munzisiti
	see PM3711+
4051	Nagrandan (Table P-PZ15)
	Nahuatlan languages
4060	General works (Table P-PZ15)
4061-4070	Nahuatl (Aztec; Mexican) (Table P-PZ8a modified)
4068-4068.9	Literature (Table P-PZ25 modified)
4068.9.A-Z	Individual authors or works, A-Z
	Subarrange individual authors by Table P-PZ40
	Subarrange individual works by Table P-PZ43
4068.9.N49	Nezahualcóyotl (Table P-PZ40)
4070	Nahuatl-Spanish dialect (Table P-PZ15)
	Nayarita see PM3711+
4081	Nexitza, or Netizcho (Table P-PZ15)
4091	Nio (Extinct) (Table P-PZ15)
4096	Niquira, or Niquirán (Table P-PZ15)
4101	Nochistlan, or Nuchistlan (Table P-PZ15)
4106	Ocoroni (Table P-PZ15)
4111	Ocotlan (Table P-PZ15)
4116	Ocuiltec (Table P-PZ15)
4121	Ohuera (Table P-PZ15)
4126	Olive (Extinct) (Table P-PZ15)
4131	Olmeco (Table P-PZ15)
4136	Opata, Teguima or Tequima, Sonora or Sonorense
	(Table P-PZ15)
	Cf. PM3766 Eudeve
(4141)	Orotina
	see PM3943
4145	Otomanguean languages (Table P-PZ15)
4146-4149	Otomi, or Hia-Hiu (Table P-PZ11)
	Ova see PM3896
4151	Pachera (Table P-PZ15)
4157	Paipai (Table P-PZ15)
4158	Pakawan languages (including Pakawa) (Table P-PZ15)
	Cf. PM2097 Pakawa (Texas)
	Cf. PM3681 Coahuilteco
4161	Pame (Table P-PZ15)
4166	Panteca (Extinct) (Table P-PZ15)
4171	Papabuco (Table P-PZ15)
	Pápago, Papagol, or Papabicotam see PM2123

Indian languages

Languages of Mexico and Central America

Special languages and groups of languages -- Continued

4181	Parra (Table P-PZ15)
4183	Paya (Table P-PZ15)
	Perico see PM4489
(4186)	Peten Itza
	see PM3969.5.I89
	Pima see PM2171+
4187	Pima Bajo (Table P-PZ15)
	Piman languages see PM2175
4191	Pipil (Table P-PZ15)
4193	Pirinda, or Matlaltzinca (Table P-PZ15)
4197	Pisone and Janambre (Table P-PZ15)
4201	Pokonchi, or Pocoman (Table P-PZ15)
4206	Popolaca, or Popoloca (Table P-PZ15)
4207	Popoluca (Vera Cruz) (Table P-PZ15)
	Pueblo Indians see PM2201
4211	Punctunc (Table P-PZ15)
4216	Putima (Extinct) (Table P-PZ15)
4221	Quelen (Extinct) (Table P-PZ15)
4223	Quepo (Table P-PZ15)
4231	Quiché (Kiché, Quitzé, or Utlateca) (Table P-PZ15 modified)
4231.Z6	Popul vuh
	Class here original text and linguistics studies
	For translations and studies of the contents see F1465.P8+
4232	Quichean languages (Table P-PZ15)
4233	Rama (Table P-PZ15)
	Raramuri see PM4291
4241	Sabaibo (Table P-PZ15)
4246	Sabanero, or Savaneric (Table P-PZ15)
4248	Sacapulteco (Table P-PZ15)
4251	Seri (Table P-PZ15)
4256	Serrano de Ixtepexi (Table P-PZ15)
4258	Serrano de Miahutlan (Table P-PZ15)
4261	Similatón (Table P-PZ15)
4266	Sinaloense (Table P-PZ15)
4267	Sipacapense (Table P-PZ15)
4271	Sobaipure, or Sobaihipure (Table P-PZ15)
4281	Solteco (Table P-PZ15)
	Sonoran languages see PM2175
4285	Subinha (Table P-PZ15)
4286.S5-.S595	Subtiaban (Table P-PZ16)
4286.S7-.S795	Suerre (Table P-PZ16)

Indian languages
Languages of Mexico and Central America
Special languages and groups of languages -- Continued

4286.S8-.S895	Sumo (Table P-PZ16)
	Including Ulva dialect
4287	Tabasca (Table P-PZ15)
4288	Talamanca (Table P-PZ15)
	Cf. PM3541 Bribri dialect
4290.T3-.T395	Tamaulipeco (Table P-PZ16)
	Tapachulano see PM3936
4290.T4-.T495	Tapachulteca (Table P-PZ16)
4291	Tarahumare (Table P-PZ15)
4296-4299	Tarascan, or Michoacan (Table P-PZ11)
4301	Tatimolo, or Ipapana (Table P-PZ15)
4306	Tatiquilhati (Table P-PZ15)
(4311)	Teacucitzin, or Teacuacitzica
	see PM3711
4316	Tebaca (Table P-PZ15)
	Teco see PM3738
4319	Tectiteco (Table P-PZ15)
4321	Tecuexe (Table P-PZ15)
	Teguima see PM4136
4326	Tehuantepecano (Table P-PZ15)
4331	Tehueco (Table P-PZ15)
4336	Temori (Table P-PZ15)
4341	Tepahue (Table P-PZ15)
4346	Teparantana (Extinct) (Table P-PZ15)
4351	Tepecano (Extinct) (Table P-PZ15)
4356	Tepehuane, or Tepeguana (Table P-PZ15)
4361	Tepuzculano (Table P-PZ15)
4366	Tepuzteco (Table P-PZ15)
	Tequima see PM4136
	Tequistlateca see PM3651
4371	Terraba (Table P-PZ15)
4376.T3-.T395	Texome (Extinct) (Table P-PZ16)
4376.T4-.T495	Tezcateco (lost) (Table P-PZ16)
4376.T6-.T695	Tisteco (lost) (Table P-PZ16)
4376.T8-.T895	Tlacotepehue (lost) (Table P-PZ16)
4379	Tlapanec (Table P-PZ15)
4383	Tlascalteca (Table P-PZ15)
4396	Tlatzihuisteco (Extinct) (Table P-PZ15)
4401	Tlaxiaco (Table P-PZ15)
4406	Tlaxomulteco (Extinct) (Table P-PZ15)
4411	Toboso (Table P-PZ15)
4413	Tojolabal. Chañabal. Comiteco (Table P-PZ15)
4416	Tolimeca (Extinct) (Table P-PZ15)

	Indian languages
	Languages of Mexico and Central America
	Special languages and groups of languages -- Continued
	Tonaz see PM3993
	Topia see PM3501
4426	Totonac (Table P-PZ15)
4431	Trique. Triki (Table P-PZ15)
4436	Trokek (Extinct) (Table P-PZ15)
4441	Tubano (Table P-PZ15)
4446	Tubar (Table P-PZ15)
4456	Tuzteco (lost) (Table P-PZ15)
4461	Tzeltal (Tzental, Tzendal, Celdal) (Table P-PZ15)
4466	Tzotzil (Zotzil) (Table P-PZ15)
4471	Tzutuhil (Zutugil, Atiteca, or Zacapule) (Table P-PZ15)
(4473)	Ulva
	see PM4286.S8+
4476	Upanguaima (Table P-PZ15)
4478	Uspanteca (Table P-PZ15)
	Utlateca see PM4231
4479	Uto-Aztecan languages (Table P-PZ15)
4481	Varogio (Varohio or Chinipa) (Table P-PZ15)
4486	Vayema (Extinct) (Table P-PZ15)
4487.V6-.V695	Voto (Table P-PZ16)
	Wabi see PM3836
4489	Waïcuri and Perico (Table P-PZ15)
(4496)	Xanambre
	see PM4197
4498.X3-.X395	Xinca (Jinca) (Table P-PZ16)
4501	Xixime (Table P-PZ15)
4506	Xultepec, or Xaltepec (Table P-PZ15)
4521	Yanhuitlan (Table P-PZ15)
4526	Yaqui, or Hiaqui (Table P-PZ15)
(4531)	Ypapana
	see PM4301
4536	Zaachilla (Table P-PZ15)
4541	Zacateca (Table P-PZ15)
	Zaklohpakap see PM3936
4546-4549	Zapotec (Table P-PZ11)
	Zinantecan see PM3630
4551	Zoe (Table P-PZ15)
4556	Zoque (Table P-PZ15)
4561	Zotzlen (Extinct) (Table P-PZ15)
	Zuaque see PM4331
	Languages of South America and the West Indies
5001-5046	General (Table P-PZ5 modified)

PM

	Indian languages
	Languages of South America and the West Indies
	General -- Continued
5010	Writing. Alphabet
	For Pre-Columbian writing systems, see the area or Indian group in class F
	Languages of the West Indies
5071-5079	General (Table P-PZ8)
5081	Cuba
5085	Hispaniola
	Including Haiti and the Dominican Republic
5091	Jamaica
5095	Puerto Rico
5099.A-Z	Smaller islands, A-Z
	Languages of South America
	General see PM5001+
	By region or country
5099.8	Amazon River Region
5100	Andes Region
	Argentina
5101	General
5111.A-Z	By region, A-Z
5131	Bolivia
5151-5154	Brazil (Table P-PZ11)
5161	Chaco region
5171	Chile
5191	Colombia
5211	Ecuador
5231	Guiana
5251	Paraguay
5261	Patagonia
5271	Peru
5281	Uruguay
5291	Venezuela
5295.A-Z	Islands south of the 50th degree, A-Z
	Special languages and groups of languages
5301	Abipon (Table P-PZ15)
5306	Acarnaori (Table P-PZ15)
5308	Accawai (Table P-PZ15)
5311	Achagua (Table P-PZ15)
5316	Acherigota (Table P-PZ15)
5318	Achuar. Achuale (Table P-PZ15)
5321	Acroa (Table P-PZ15)
5326	Acroamirim (Table P-PZ15)
5331	Acúana (Table P-PZ15)

Indian languages
   Languages of South America and the West Indies
      Special languages and groups of languages -- Continued

5336	Agua
	see PM6686
5337.A5-.A595	Aguaruna dialect (Table P-PZ16)
5341	Ahunala (Table P-PZ15)
5346	Aicore (Table P-PZ15)
(5351)	Aimore
	see PM5641
5356	Airica (Table P-PZ15)
5361	Aisuari (Table P-PZ15)
5366	Akerecota, or Akiricota (Table P-PZ15)
	Akoniken see PM6691
	Akwẽ-Shavante see PM5809
5376	Alabona (Table P-PZ15)
5378	Alacaluf (Table P-PZ15)
5381	Alagoa (Table P-PZ15)
	Alikuluf see PM5378
5386	Allentiac (Table P-PZ15)
5388	Amahuaca (Table P-PZ15)
	Cf. PM6773 Panoan languages
5391	Amanipuque (Table P-PZ15)
5396	Amaono (Table P-PZ15)
5401	Amarizana (Table P-PZ15)
5406	Amasifuine (Table P-PZ15)
5411	Amjemhuaco (Table P-PZ15)
5413	Amuesha (Table P-PZ15)
5416	Anace (Table P-PZ15)
5421	Andaqui (Table P-PZ15)
5426	Andoa (Table P-PZ15)
5428	Andoque (Table P-PZ15)
	Anti see PM5716
	Aonik see PM6691
5430	Apalai (Table P-PZ15)
5431	Apiaca (Table P-PZ15)
5436	Apolista (Table P-PZ15)
5438	Arabela (Table P-PZ15)
5441	Araco (Table P-PZ15)
5446	Arane (Avane?) (Table P-PZ15)
5451	Aranhi or Arandi (Table P-PZ15)
5453	Araona (Table P-PZ15)
5456	Araro (Table P-PZ15)
5457	Arasa (Table P-PZ15)
5458	Arauca (Table P-PZ15)

Indian languages
Languages of South America and the West Indies
Special languages and groups of languages -- Continued

5461-5469.5	Araucanian. Mapuche (Table P-PZ8a)
	Cf. PM6541 Moluche
5471	Aravani (Table P-PZ15)
5476	Arawakan languages (Table P-PZ15)
	Including Arawak
	Arazo see PM7066
5486	Archidona (Table P-PZ15)
5491	Arda (Table P-PZ15)
5493	Arecuna (Table P-PZ15)
5496	Arenquepona (Table P-PZ15)
5501	Areveriano (Table P-PZ15)
5506	Aricari (Table P-PZ15)
5511	Arinacoto (Table P-PZ15)
5516	Aroa (Table P-PZ15)
5521	Atacameno (Table P-PZ15)
5524	Atahuate (Table P-PZ15)
5526	Atsahuaca (Table P-PZ15)
	Cf. PM7170 Tupi
	Cf. PM7171+ Tupian languages
5531	Atuara (Table P-PZ15)
5536	Aturari (Table P-PZ15)
5541	Ature (Table P-PZ15)
	Auca (Chile) see PM5461+
	Auca (Ecuador) see PM6165
5546	Avakiari (Table P-PZ15)
	Avane see PM5546
5551	Avaravaño (Table P-PZ15)
5561	Avaricota (Table P-PZ15)
5571-5579.5	Aymara (Table P-PZ8a)
5581	Bakairi (Table P-PZ15)
5581.5	Baniwa (Table P-PZ15)
5582	Barasana (Table P-PZ15)
	Including Barasana del Norte and Barasana del Sur
5583	Barbacoan languages (Table P-PZ15)
5586	Barbada (Table P-PZ15)
5591	Barbuda (Table P-PZ15)
5596	Barré (Table P-PZ15)
5601	Bataje (Table P-PZ15)
5606	Bauré (Table P-PZ15)
(5611)	Betoya
	see PM7164
	Bintukua see PM6179
5621	Bitocuru (Table P-PZ15)

Indian languages
  Languages of South America and the West Indies
    Special languages and groups of languages -- Continued
      Black Carib see PM6239

5626	Bobonazo (Table P-PZ15)
	Bohane see PM6126
5631	Bonari (Table P-PZ15)
5634	Bora. Boro (Table P-PZ15)
5636	Bororo (Table P-PZ15)
5641	Botocudo (Table P-PZ15)
5646	Bugre (Table P-PZ15)
5651	Caaiguá (Table P-PZ15)
5656	Cacabue (Table P-PZ15)
5658	Cacán (Table P-PZ15)
	Cachiquel see PM5690
5659	Caduveo (Table P-PZ15)
5661	Cahuaci (Table P-PZ15)
5666	Cahuapana (Table P-PZ15)
5671	Cahumari (Table P-PZ15)
5676	Caicai (Table P-PZ15)
5678	Caingua (Table P-PZ15)
5681	Caipotorade (Table P-PZ15)
5686	Caisina (Table P-PZ15)
5690	Cakchiquel (Table P-PZ15)
	Cf. PM3576 Cakchikel
	Calchaqui, or Tucumano see PM5658
5696	Calen (Table P-PZ15)
5701	Calicione (Table P-PZ15)
5703	Callahuaya (Table P-PZ15)
5706	Calza-blanca (Table P-PZ15)
5711	Camacori (Table P-PZ15)
	Camanacho see PM6386
5716	Campa, or Ande (Table P-PZ15)
	Including Pampa del Sacramento, Peru
	Cf. PM5476 Arawakan
5717	Campa (of Quito) (Table P-PZ15)
5718.C3-.C395	Camsa, or Sibondoy (Table P-PZ16)
5718.C45-.C4595	Canamari (Table P-PZ16)
5718.C5-.C595	Cañari (Table P-PZ16)
	Canchi see PM5571+
5718.C8-.C895	Candoshi (Table P-PZ16)
5719	Canella (Table P-PZ15)
5721	Canga (Table P-PZ15)
5723	Canichana (Table P-PZ15)
5726	Canisiá (Table P-PZ15)

	Indian languages
	Languages of South America and the West Indies
	Special languages and groups of languages -- Continued
(5731)	Canoeiro (Mato Grosso, Brazil)
	see PM7004
5735	Capanahua (Table P-PZ15)
5736	Capinjela (Table P-PZ15)
5739	Caquinte (Table P-PZ15)
5741	Caraja, or Caraya (Table P-PZ15)
5746	Caranca (Table P-PZ15)
5749	Carapana (Tucanoan) (Table P-PZ15)
5751	Carariu (Table P-PZ15)
	Carib, Island see PM6239
5756-5759	Cariban languages (including Carib) (Table P-PZ11a)
5761	Cariela (Table P-PZ15)
	Cariri see PM6286+
5763	Cashibo (Cacataibo, Comabo) (Table P-PZ15)
	Cashinawa see PM6290.K3+
5766	Casná (Table P-PZ15)
	Catamarca see PM5658
5773	Catapaturo (Table P-PZ15)
5776	Cateco (Table P-PZ15)
5778	Catio (Table P-PZ15)
5781	Catsipagoto (Table P-PZ15)
5786	Caucau (Table P-PZ15)
5788	Cauqui (Table P-PZ15)
	Cavinena (or Cavina) see PM7088
	Caxinaua see PM6290.K3+
5790	Cayapa (Table P-PZ15)
5791	Cayapo (Table P-PZ15)
(5793)	Caygua
	see PM5678
	Cf. PM7171+ Tupian languages
(5796)	Cayuá
	see PM5678
5801	Cayuvava (Table P-PZ15)
5804	Ceoqueyo (Table P-PZ15)
5804.5	Chacobo (Table P-PZ15)
5804.7	Chamí (Table P-PZ15)
5805	Chamicuro (Table P-PZ15)
	Chaná see PM6051
5806.C3-.C395	Chanese (Table P-PZ16)
5807	Changoan (Table P-PZ15)
5808.C4-.C495	Chapacuran (Table P-PZ16)
5808.C5-.C595	Charruan (Table P-PZ16)
5809	Chavante (Table P-PZ15)

Indian languages
Languages of South America and the West Indies
Special languages and groups of languages -- Continued

5809.5	Chayahuita (Table P-PZ15)
5810	Chechehet (Table P-PZ15)
5811	Chibcha (Muyska, Mosca) (Table P-PZ15)
5812	Chibchan languages (Table P-PZ15)
	Cf. PM4288 Talamanca
	Cf. PM4371 Terraba
	Chilupi see PM7246
5812.6	Chimane (Table P-PZ15)
5813	Chimu, or Muchic (Table P-PZ15)
5814.C3-.C395	Chinchasuyu (Table P-PZ16)
	Cf. PM6301+ Kechua
5814.C5-.C595	Chipaya (Table P-PZ16)
5816	Chiquito (Table P-PZ15)
5817.C2-.C295	Chiriguano (Table P-PZ16)
5817.C4-.C495	Choco (Table P-PZ16)
5817.C6-.C695	Cholon (Table P-PZ16)
5817.C7-.C795	Choroti (Table P-PZ16)
5817.C8-.C895	Chulupí (Table P-PZ16)
5818	Chuntaquiro (Chontaquiro, Piro) (Table P-PZ15)
	Cf. PM5476 Arawakan languages
5823	Cocama, Cocoma, or Ucayale (Table P-PZ15)
5824.C2-.C295	Cocina (Table P-PZ16)
5824.C3-.C395	Coconucan (Table P-PZ16)
5825	Cofane (Table P-PZ15)
5827	Colla, or Collagua (Table P-PZ15)
5829	Colorado (Table P-PZ15)
(5831)	Comabo
	see PM5763
(5833)	Conibo, or Kunibo
	see PM7073
5836	Corabé (Table P-PZ15)
5846	Coroado, or Coronado (?) (Table P-PZ15)
	The name has been applied to several unrelated tribes
	Cf. PM5636 Bororo
5851	Correguaje (Table P-PZ15)
5856	Coscoasoa (Table P-PZ15)
	Coto see PM6861
	Craho see PM5719
5861	Cuaca (Table P-PZ15)
5866	Cuacará (Table P-PZ15)
5868	Cuaiquer (Table P-PZ15)
	Cuariba see PM6018
5870	Cubeo (Table P-PZ15)

	Indian languages
	Languages of South America and the West Indies
	Special languages and groups of languages -- Continued
5871	Cuberé (Table P-PZ15)
5873	Cuiva (Table P-PZ15)
5875	Culina (Table P-PZ15)
5876	Cumana (Table P-PZ15)
5879	Cunan (Table P-PZ15)
5886	Cuoca (Table P-PZ15)
5891	Curano (Table P-PZ15)
5896	Curati (Table P-PZ15)
5901	Curomina (Table P-PZ15)
5902.C8-.C895	Curuahé (Table P-PZ16)
5906	Curucané (Table P-PZ15)
5911	Curumare (Table P-PZ15)
	Cururu see PM5911
5916	Cusitinavo (Table P-PZ15)
5921	Cutinana (Table P-PZ15)
5923	Damana (Table P-PZ15)
5924	Dâw (Table P-PZ15)
5926	Echibie (Table P-PZ15)
5931	Ecoboré (Table P-PZ15)
5936	Ele (Table P-PZ15)
5941	Enagua (Table P-PZ15)
5943	Enimagan (Table P-PZ15)
5946	Eparagota (Table P-PZ15)
	Epena Saija see PM7079
	Epera, Southern see PM7079
5951	Epuremeo (Table P-PZ15)
5956	Erascavina (Table P-PZ15)
5961	Eriteina (Table P-PZ15)
	Ese Ejja see PM7118
5963	Esmeraldan (Table P-PZ15)
5966	Evaiponomo (Table P-PZ15)
5971	Eyeye (Table P-PZ15)
5973	Fulnio (Table P-PZ15)
5974	Gae (Table P-PZ15)
(5976)	Galibi
	see PM5756
5978	Gavião language (Para, Brazil) (Table P-PZ15)
	Gê languages see PM7108
5981	Goajiro (Table P-PZ15)
5983	Goanase (Table P-PZ15)
5986	Goaregoare (Table P-PZ15)
5991	Gorgotoquiense (Table P-PZ15)
5996	Gotoguanchano (Table P-PZ15)

Indian languages
  Languages of South America and the West Indies
    Special languages and groups of languages -- Continued

6001	Goyana (Table P-PZ15)
6003	Goyatacan (Table P-PZ15)
6006	Grens (Table P-PZ15)
6011	Guachira, or Guaiqueria (Table P-PZ15)
6013	Guahibo (Table P-PZ15)
6016	Guaikirié (Guakirié) (Table P-PZ15)
	Guaiqueria see PM6011
6018	Guaiva, or Cuariba (Table P-PZ15)
	Guajajara see PM7115
6021	Guajiva (Table P-PZ15)
6026	Guajoyo (Table P-PZ15)
	Guakirié see PM6016
	Gualache see PM6056
6036	Guama (Table P-PZ15)
(6041)	Guamaka
	see PM5923
6046	Guambia, or Guambiano, or Moguex (Table P-PZ15)
6051	Guana, or Chaná (Table P-PZ15)
6056	Guañana (Guaniana or Gualache) (Table P-PZ15)
6058	Guanano (Table P-PZ15)
6061	Guanare (Table P-PZ15)
6066	Guanera (Table P-PZ15)
6071	Guañero (Table P-PZ15)
(6076)	Guaque
	see PM6714
6082	Guarani language (Table P-PZ15)
	For Tupi-Guarani languages see PM7171+
6086	Guarapuava (Table P-PZ15)
(6091)	Guaráuna
	see PM7253
6096	Guarayo (Table P-PZ15)
	Guarpe see PM5386
6106	Guató (Table P-PZ15)
6108	Guaxhica (Table P-PZ15)
6111	Guayana (Extinct) (Table P-PZ15)
	Closely related to or identical with Ingain
6113	Guayaqui (Table P-PZ15)
6116	Guaycuruan languages (Table P-PZ15)
6121	Guazago (Table P-PZ15)
6126	Guenoa (Table P-PZ15)
6131	Guencoyo (Table P-PZ15)
6136	Guentuse (Table P-PZ15)
6141	Guegue (Table P-PZ15)

Indian languages
  Languages of South America and the West Indies
    Special languages and groups of languages -- Continued

6146	Gujano (Table P-PZ15)
6151	Guypanave (Table P-PZ15)
6156	Haitian (Quizqueja or Itis) (Extinct) (Table P-PZ15)
6158	Hianakoto-Umáua (Table P-PZ15)
6161	Himuetaca (Table P-PZ15)
6163	Hixkaryâna (Table P-PZ15)
	Homagua see PM6686
6164.H83-.H8395	Huambisa (Table P-PZ16)
	Huanca (Wanka) see PM6301+
6165	Huao (Table P-PZ15)
6166	Humurano (Table P-PZ15)
	Hypurinan see PM7314
6171	Ibanoma (Extinct) (Table P-PZ15)
(6176)	Ibirayare
	see PM5791
6179	Ica (Table P-PZ15)
6181	Icahuate (Table P-PZ15)
6186	Iciba (Table P-PZ15)
6191	Ieico (Table P-PZ15)
	Ignaciano see PM6540
	Igneri see PM6239
6201	Ijinori (Table P-PZ15)
6206	Iltipo (Table P-PZ15)
6211	Imare (Table P-PZ15)
6213	Inapari (Table P-PZ15)
6216	Inemaga (Table P-PZ15)
6219	Ingain (Table P-PZ15)
	Cf. PM6111 Guayana
	Cf. PM6276 Kaingangue
6221	Ingano (Table P-PZ15)
6226	Inuaco (Table P-PZ15)
6229	Ipurina (Table P-PZ15)
6231	Iqueconejori (Table P-PZ15)
6236	Iquita-nanai (Table P-PZ15)
6238	Iranxe (Table P-PZ15)
6239	Island Carib. Igneri (Table P-PZ15)
	Including Black Carib
6240	Itene (Table P-PZ15)
	Itis see PM6156
6241	Itonama (Table P-PZ15)
(6246)	Itucale
	see PM7226
6251	Iurusme (Table P-PZ15)

	Indian languages
	Languages of South America and the West Indies
	Special languages and groups of languages -- Continued
	Jagane see PM7266
6253	Jaminaua (Table P-PZ15)
	Japoen see PM7296
6256	Jarabe (Table P-PZ15)
6258	Jaruára (Table P-PZ15)
6261	Jebero, or Xebero (Table P-PZ15)
	Cf. PM6273 Jivaran languages
6266	Jesarusu (Table P-PZ15)
	Jirara see PM7296
6273	Jivaran languages (Table P-PZ15)
	Including Shuar, Jivaro
	Cf. PM5337.A5+ Aguaruna dialect
6275.J8-.J895	Juiadge (Table P-PZ16)
6275.J92-.J9295	Jupda (Table P-PZ16)
	Kacchiquel see PM5690
6276	Kaingangue (Table P-PZ15)
	Cf. PM5846 Coroado
	Cf. PM6111 Guayana
	Cf. PM6219 Ingain
6281	Kaketan (Table P-PZ15)
6282	Kamaiurá (Table P-PZ15)
6283	Kamarakoto (Table P-PZ15)
	Karina, Kalina, or Kalinago see PM5756+
6286-6289	Kariri, or Kiriri (Table P-PZ14)
6290.K25-.K2595	Karo (Brazil) (Table P-PZ16)
6290.K3-.K395	Kashinaua (Caxinaua) (Table P-PZ16)
6291	Kavere, or Cavene (Table P-PZ15)
6294	Kayabi (Table P-PZ15)
6301-6309.5	Kechua (Quichua) (Table P-PZ8a)
	Including dialects, e.g. Huanca
6316	Kirikiripo (Table P-PZ15)
	Kiriri see PM6286+
6319	Koaia (Table P-PZ15)
6321	Koggaba (Table P-PZ15)
6326	Kunaguara (Table P-PZ15)
6331	Kupeno (Table P-PZ15)
6333	Lacheyel (Table P-PZ15)
6336	Lamano, or Lamisso (Table P-PZ15)
6341	Lamista (Extinct) (Table P-PZ15)
6348	Lecan (Table P-PZ15)
6351	Lengua (Lengua-Mascoi) (Table P-PZ15)
6356	Lluru (Table P-PZ15)

PM

Indian languages
   Languages of South America and the West Indies
      Special languages and groups of languages -- Continued

(6358)	Lorenzo
	see PM5413
6361	Lucumbia (Table P-PZ15)
6366	Lulé, or Lule-Tonocoté (Table P-PZ15)
6371	Lupaca (Table P-PZ15)
6373	Maca (Table P-PZ15)
6374	Macaguan (Table P-PZ15)
6376	Macaono (Table P-PZ15)
6381	Macarina (Table P-PZ15)
6386	Machacari (Table P-PZ15)
6388	Machiganga (Machiguenga) (Table P-PZ15)
	Maco see PM6906
6393	Macú (Table P-PZ15)
6394	Macuna (Table P-PZ15)
6396	Macuroto (Table P-PZ15)
6397	Macusi (Table P-PZ15)
	Maina see PM6476
6401	Maipure (Table P-PZ15)
	Maka see PM6373
6406	Makiritari (Table P-PZ15)
6411	Makoby (Table P-PZ15)
6413	Makuan (Table P-PZ15)
	Makusi see PM6397
6416	Manaci (Table P-PZ15)
6421	Manamabobo (Table P-PZ15)
6426	Manamabua (Table P-PZ15)
6428	Manao (Table P-PZ15)
6431	Manare (Table P-PZ15)
6436	Manatinavo (Table P-PZ15)
6441	Manuá (Table P-PZ15)
6446	Mapoye (Table P-PZ15)
	Mapuche see PM5461+
6451	Maramomisima, or Maramomi (Table P-PZ15)
6456	Maranshuaco (Table P-PZ15)
6461	Maropa (Table P-PZ15)
6462	Masacali (Table P-PZ15)
6463	Masamae (Table P-PZ15)
6464.M3-.M395	Mashco (Table P-PZ16)
6466	Mataco languages (Table P-PZ15)
	Cf. PM6676 Nocten
	Cf. PM7241 Vejoso
6471	Mataguaya (Table P-PZ15)
6473	Maue (Table P-PZ15)

Indian languages
    Languages of South America and the West Indies
        Special languages and groups of languages -- Continued

6476	Mayna (Table P-PZ15)
6479	Mayoruna (Table P-PZ15)
6485	Mbaya (Table P-PZ15)
6487	Mbya, or Mbya-Guarani (Table P-PZ15)
6491	Meepure (Table P-PZ15)
6496	Menhari (Table P-PZ15)
6501	Meque (Table P-PZ15)
	Michoacan see PM4296+
6506	Mighiana (Table P-PZ15)
6511	Millcayac (Table P-PZ15)
	Minuane see PM6216
6514	Miranhan (Table P-PZ15)
	Mobimi, or Mobima see PM6573
	Mochica see PM7316
6526	Mochono, or Muchojeone (Table P-PZ15)
6531	Mochova (Table P-PZ15)
6533	Mocoan (Table P-PZ15)
6536	Mocobi (Micoby, Micovi, Mocovito, Moscontica, Moscovik) (Table P-PZ15)
	Moguex see PM6046
6540	Mojo. Moxo. Ignaciano (Table P-PZ15)
6541	Moluche (Table P-PZ15)
6551	Mopecianá (Table P-PZ15)
6556	Moro (Morotoco, Ayoreo, Ayoreode, Coroino, Pyeta, Yova) (Table P-PZ15)
6558	Mosatenan (Table P-PZ15)
	Mosca see PM5811
6561	Moseteno (Table P-PZ15)
6566	Mosetie (Table P-PZ15)
6571	Motilon (Table P-PZ15)
6573	Movima (Mobima) (Table P-PZ15)
(6576)	Moxo
	see PM6540
	Muchic see PM5813
6581	Muchimo (Table P-PZ15)
	Muchojeone see PM6526
6586	Mucury (Table P-PZ15)
6589	Muinane (Table P-PZ15)
6591	Mukikero (Table P-PZ15)
6596	Mundurucú (Table P-PZ15)
6601	Muniche (Table P-PZ15)
6606	Mura (Table P-PZ15)
	Including Pirahá dialect

PM

Indian languages
Languages of South America and the West Indies
Special languages and groups of languages -- Continued

6616	Muraco (Table P-PZ15)
	Murato see PM5718.C8+
6626	Mure (Table P-PZ15)
6628	Murui (Table P-PZ15)
6631	Musima (Table P-PZ15)
	Muyska see PM5811
6641	Nahuapo (Table P-PZ15)
6643	Nambicuara (Table P-PZ15)
6646	Nanerua (Table P-PZ15)
6651	Napeano (Table P-PZ15)
6656	Napo, or Napotoa (Table P-PZ15)
6661	Nauon (Table P-PZ15)
6666	Neocoyo (Table P-PZ15)
6671	Nesahuaco (Table P-PZ15)
6673	Nevo (Table P-PZ15)
6676	Nocten (Table P-PZ15)
6678	Nomatsiguenga (Table P-PZ15)
6681	Oa (Table P-PZ15)
6682	Ocaina (Table P-PZ15)
6683	Ocorona (Table P-PZ15)
6686	Omagua, or Homagua (Table P-PZ15)
6691	Ona (Table P-PZ15)
6693	Ontoampa (Table P-PZ15)
6696	Orocotono (Table P-PZ15)
(6701)	Otanabe
	see PM6601
6703	Otomaco (Table P-PZ15)
	Otomagua see PM7296
	Otomaque see PM6703
	Ottomacque, Ottomaku see PM6703
6711	Otuque (Table P-PZ15)
6713	Oyampi (Table P-PZ15)
6714	Oyana, or Rucouyenne (Table P-PZ15)
6716	Oye (Table P-PZ15)
6721	Pabo (Table P-PZ15)
	Pacaguara see PM7073
6726	Pacasa (Table P-PZ15)
6731	Pacayu (Table P-PZ15)
6736	Páez, or Paes (Table P-PZ15)
6741	Paicone (Table P-PZ15)
6743	Pakaasnovos (Table P-PZ15)
6746	Palenke (Table P-PZ15)
6751	Pampa (Table P-PZ15)

Indian languages
　　Languages of South America and the West Indies
　　　Special languages and groups of languages -- Continued
6761	Panajori (Table P-PZ15)
6763	Panare (Table P-PZ15)
6766	Pandatoco (Table P-PZ15)
6771	Pandaveque (Table P-PZ15)
6772.P3-.P395	Paniquita (Table P-PZ16)
6773	Panoan languages (Table P-PZ15)
	Including Pano
6776	Papaya (Table P-PZ15)
6781	Parabá (Table P-PZ15)
6786	Paracati (Table P-PZ15)
6791	Paragoto (Table P-PZ15)
6796	Paranapuro (Table P-PZ15)
6801	Paratoa (Table P-PZ15)
6806	Paraviane (Table P-PZ15)
6811	Pareko (Table P-PZ15)
6816	Parene (Table P-PZ15)
6818	Parentintim (Table P-PZ15)
	Paresi see PM6831
6821	Paria (Table P-PZ15)
6826	Pariacota (Table P-PZ15)
6831	Parisi, or Paresi (Table P-PZ15)
6836	Passa, or Setaba (Table P-PZ15)
6838	Pasto (Table P-PZ15)
6841	Patacha (Table P-PZ15)
	Patagonian see PM7183
6851	Pativa (Table P-PZ15)
6856	Pauná (Table P-PZ15)
6859	Pauserna (Table P-PZ15)
6861	Payagua (Table P-PZ15)
6866	Payayace (Table P-PZ15)
6871	Payure (Table P-PZ15)
6873	Peban (Table P-PZ15)
6876	Pehuenche (Table P-PZ15)
6881	Pelado (Table P-PZ15)
6885	Pemón dialects (Table P-PZ15)
6891	Penoqui (Table P-PZ15)
6896	Pescheree, or Yakanaku (Table P-PZ15)
6901	Petiguaren (Table P-PZ15)
6903	Piapoco (Table P-PZ15)
6906	Piaroa, or Maco (Table P-PZ15)
6909	Pilaga (Table P-PZ15)
6916	Pinche (Table P-PZ15)
6921	Piñoco (Table P-PZ15)

Indian languages
  Languages of South America and the West Indies
    Special languages and groups of languages -- Continued
      Pirahá see PM6606
      Piro (Arawakan) see PM5818

6926	Polindara (Table P-PZ15)
6931	Potentu (Table P-PZ15)
	Potiguare see PM7170
6936	Poya (Table P-PZ15)
	Puelche see PM6751
6946	Puinabo (Table P-PZ15)
6947	Puinave (Table P-PZ15)
6951	Puizoca (Table P-PZ15)
6956	Puquina (Table P-PZ15)
6961	Purugoto (Table P-PZ15)
6963	Purupuru (Table P-PZ15)
6966	Putumayo (Table P-PZ15)
	Quechua see PM6301+
6971	Querandi (Table P-PZ15)
	Quiché see PM4231
	Quichua see PM6301+
6981	Quilivita (Table P-PZ15)
6986	Quirivina (Table P-PZ15)
6991	Quitu, or Soira (Table P-PZ15)
	Quizqueja see PM6156
6996	Ranquelche (Table P-PZ15)
7001	Rema (Table P-PZ15)
7003	Resigero (Table P-PZ15)
7004	Rikbaktsa (Table P-PZ15)
7006	Roamaino (Table P-PZ15)
7009	Rocotona (Table P-PZ15)
7016	Ruanababo (Table P-PZ15)
	Rucouyenne (Roucouyenne, etc.) see PM6714
	Sabela see PM7141
7021	Sabuja (Table P-PZ15)
7026	Sacacá (Table P-PZ15)
7031	Saliva (Table P-PZ15)
7036	Salmano (Table P-PZ15)
7038	Samagota (Table P-PZ15)
(7041)	Samucan see PM7329
7043	Sanavironan (Table P-PZ15)
7046	Sapibocono (Table P-PZ15)
	Sarura see PM7296
7049	Secoya (Table P-PZ15)
7051	Semigae (Table P-PZ15)

Indian languages
Languages of South America and the West Indies
Special languages and groups of languages -- Continued

7056	Sepaunabo (Table P-PZ15)
	Setaba see PM6836
7058	Sharanahua (Table P-PZ15)
7061	Shebago (Table P-PZ15)
	Shelknam see PM6691
	Shipibo see PM7073
	Shuar see PM6273
7063	Sicuane (Table P-PZ15)
7066	Simigaecurari (Table P-PZ15)
	Simirenchi see PM5818
7071	Singacuchuska (Table P-PZ15)
7072	Siona (Table P-PZ15)
7073	Sipibo (Pacaguara) (Table P-PZ15)
7074	Siriaño (Table P-PZ15)
7076	Situga, or Situsa (Table P-PZ15)
7079	Southern Epera. Epena Saija (Table P-PZ15)
7081	Suchichi (Table P-PZ15)
7086	Tabalosa (Table P-PZ15)
7088	Tacanan languages (Table P-PZ15)
	Including Cavineño and Tacana
	Cf. PM5453 Araona
	Cf. PM7321 Yuracare
7091	Taijataf (Table P-PZ15)
7093	Taino (Table P-PZ15)
(7096)	Tama
	see PM5851
7101	Tamanaco (Table P-PZ15)
7102	Tanimuca-Retuama (Table P-PZ15)
7104	Taparita (Table P-PZ15)
7105	Tapirapé (Table P-PZ15)
7106	Tapuri (Table P-PZ15)
7108	Tapuyan languages. Gê languages (Table P-PZ15)
7110	Tariana (Table P-PZ15)
7111	Tasio (Table P-PZ15)
7113	Taurepan (Table P-PZ15)
	Tehuelche (Tuelche) see PM7183
7115	Tenetehara (Table P-PZ15)
7116	Teremembre (Table P-PZ15)
7117	Terena. Tereno (Table P-PZ15)
7118	Tiatinagua (Table P-PZ15)
7121	Tibilo (Table P-PZ15)
7123	Ticuna (Table P-PZ15)
7126	Tikomeri (Table P-PZ15)

PM

	Indian languages
	Languages of South America and the West Indies
	Special languages and groups of languages -- Continued
7131	Timbire (Table P-PZ15)
7136	Timote (Table P-PZ15)
7141	Tiputini (Table P-PZ15)
(7143)	Tiriyó
	see PM7157
7146	Toba (Table P-PZ15)
7151	Tonocote (Table P-PZ15)
7156	Tremojori (Table P-PZ15)
7157	Trio (Table P-PZ15)
7158	Trumaian (Table P-PZ15)
	Tíntšay dialect see PM5814.C3+
	Tšintšaysuyu dialect see PM5814.C3+
	Tsoneca see PM7183
7161	Tuapoka (Table P-PZ15)
7164	Tucano (Table P-PZ15)
7165	Tucanoan languages (Table P-PZ15)
	Tucumaño see PM5658
	Tucuna see PM7123
	Tuelche see PM7183
7169	Tunebo (Table P-PZ15)
7170	Tupi language (Table P-PZ15)
7171-7179.5	Tupian languages (Table P-PZ8a)
	Including Tupi-Guarani languages and Old Tupi
7181	Tuyuca (Table P-PZ15)
7183	Tzoneca (Patagonian, Tehuelche, Tsoneca) (Table P-PZ15)
(7185)	Uaiuai
	see PM7252
7186	Uara-múcuru (Table P-PZ15)
7191	Uaraca-pachili (Table P-PZ15)
7196	Uarinacoto (Table P-PZ15)
	Ucayali see PM5823
7201	Ucoiña (Table P-PZ15)
	Uitoto see PM7254
(7203)	Umáua
	see PM6158
7204	Umotina (Table P-PZ15)
7206	Un buesa (Extinct) (Table P-PZ15)
7211	Uokeari (Table P-PZ15)
7216	Upatarinavo (Table P-PZ15)
7221	Urabo (Table P-PZ15)
(7223)	Uran
	see PM7228

Indian languages
   Languages of South America and the West Indies
      Special languages and groups of languages -- Continued

7226	Urarina (Table P-PZ15)
7228	Uru (Table P-PZ15)
7229	Urubu (Kaapor) (Table P-PZ15)
7231	Uspá (Extinct) (Table P-PZ15)
7236	Vaniva (Table P-PZ15)
7238	Vazevaco (Table P-PZ15)
7241	Vejoz (Vejoso) (Table P-PZ15)
7246	Vilela (Table P-PZ15)
7251	Villmoluche (Table P-PZ15)
7252	Waiwai (Table P-PZ15)
7253	Warao (Warrau) (Table P-PZ15)
7253.5	Waunana (Table P-PZ15)
	Wayampi see PM6713
	Wayana see PM6714
7254	Witotoan languages (Table P-PZ15)
	Including Witoto
7256	Xaquete (Table P-PZ15)
7261	Yacururé (Table P-PZ15)
7263	Yagua (Table P-PZ15)
7266	Yahgan (Table P-PZ15)
(7267)	Yahuna
	see PM7102
7269	Yamea (Table P-PZ15)
7270	Yanomamo (Table P-PZ15)
7271	Yaoi (Table P-PZ15)
(7281)	Yapitilaga
	see PM6909
7286	Yapua (Table P-PZ15)
	Yaro see PM6126
7296	Yarura (Sarura, Japoen, Jirara) (Table P-PZ15)
7301	Yativera (Table P-PZ15)
7306	Yekinahuer (Table P-PZ15)
7311	Yete (Table P-PZ15)
7314	Ypurinan (Hypurinan) (Table P-PZ15)
7314.5	Yucuna (Table P-PZ15)
	Yuguguarana see PM5983
7316	Yunca, or Yunga (Table P-PZ15)
7318	Yupa (Table P-PZ15)
7321	Yuracare (Table P-PZ15)
	Including Yucarari
7326	Yurimagua (Table P-PZ15)
7329	Zamucoan languages (Table P-PZ15)
	Zamucu see PM7329

PM

	Indian languages
	Languages of South America and the West Indies
	Special languages and groups of languages -- Continued
7336	Zapa (Table P-PZ15)
7341	Zaparo (Table P-PZ15)
7346	Zeona (Table P-PZ15)
7351	Zepo (Table P-PZ15)
7356	Ziecoya (Table P-PZ15)
	Mixed languages
	Including lingua francas, pidgin languages and Creole languages
	For Mixed Jewish dialects see PJ5061+
	Cf. PL6571.A+ Austronesian languages
7801-7805	General and miscellaneous (Table P-PZ9)
7807.A-Z	By region or country, A-Z
7811-7814	Sabir (Table P-PZ14)
	Creole languages
7831-7834	General and miscellaneous (Table P-PZ14)
7836-7839	Danish (Table P-PZ14)
7841-7844	Spanish (Table P-PZ14)
7846-7849	Portuguese (Table P-PZ14 modified)
7849.A-.Z9	Local. By dialect name or place, A-Z
7849.C37-.C3795	Cape Verde (Table P-PZ16 modified)
	Literature
7849.C379A-.C379Z	Individual authors or works, A-Z
	Carvalho Silva, Ramiro Alberto, 1978- see PM7849.C379Y44
7849.C379Y44	Ymez, 1978-
7849.C4	Ceylon
7849.D3	Daman
7849.D58	Diu (District)
7849.G6	Goa
7849.K75	Kristang language
	French (Table P-PZ14 modified)
7854.A-.Z9	Local. By dialect name or place, A-Z
7854.F7-.F795	French Guiana (Table P-PZ16)
7854.G8-.G895	Guadeloupe (Table P-PZ16)
7854.H3-.H395	Haiti (Table P-PZ16)
7854.M25-.M2595	Martinique (Table P-PZ16)
7854.M3-.M395	Mauritius (Table P-PZ16)
7854.R4-.R495	Réunion (Table P-PZ16)
7854.S4-.S495	Seychelles (Table P-PZ16)
7861-7864	Dutch (Table P-PZ14)
7871-7874	English (Table P-PZ14)
	Cf. PE3301+ English dialects in the West Indies
7875.A-Z	Special languages or dialects, A-Z
7875.D58	Djuka

	Mixed languages
	Creole languages
	Special languages or dialects, A-Z -- Continued
7875.G8	Gullah dialect. Sea Islands Creole
7875.K73	Krio
7875.K74	Kriol
7875.P55	Pijin
7875.S27	Saramaccan
	Sea Islands Creole see PM7875.G8
7875.S67-.S6795	Sranan (Table P-PZ16)
7891	Pidgeon English (Table P-PZ15)
7895.A-Z	Other dialects, trade jargons, etc., A-Z
7895.B4	Beach-la-mer
	Chinook jargon see PM846+
7895.F3	Fanakalo
7895.H5	Hiri Motu. Police Motu
7895.M53	Michif (French Cree)
	Mobilian trade language see PM1855
7895.N3	Naga Pidgin
7895.N83	Nubi (Arabic Creole)
7895.O3	Ochweśnicki jargon
7895.P3-.P395	Papiamento (Table P-PZ16)
7895.P5-.P595	Pitcairnese (Table P-PZ16)
	Sango see PL8641+
	Artificial languages. Universal languages
8001-8046	General (Table P-PZ5)
	For application of universal language to individual subjects, see the subject in classes A-N, Q-Z
	Special languages (alphabetically)
8060	Adam-man (Table P-PZ15)
8063	Afrihili (Table P-PZ15)
8072	Alwato (Table P-PZ15)
8077	American (Table P-PZ15)
8079	Ande (Table P-PZ15)
8079.7	Atélangue (Table P-PZ15)
8080	Antibabele (Table P-PZ15)
8085	Arulo (Table P-PZ15)
8090	Babm (Table P-PZ15)
8092	Balaibalan (Table P-PZ15)
	Basic English see PE1073.5.A1+
8095	Berendt (Table P-PZ15)
8101-8109.5	Blue language. Langue blue. Bolak (Table P-PZ8a)
8125	Cesges de damis (Langage des nombres) (Table P-PZ15)
8128	Chabé (Langue internationale naturelle) (Table P-PZ15)
8129	Code Ari (Table P-PZ15)
8133	Communis (Table P-PZ15)

Artificial languages. Universal languages
Special languages (alphabetically) -- Continued

8161-8164	Dilpok (Table P-PZ11)
8190	Ehmay ghee chah (Table P-PZ15)
8201-8298	Esperanto (Table P-PZ5 modified)
	Lexicography
	Dictionaries
8237.A-Z	English-Esperanto; Esperanto-English
	Subarrange by main entry
8238	Dictionaries with definitions in languages other than Esperanto or English
	Subarrange by language of definition
	e.g.
8238.A1	Polyglot
8238.F6	French
8238.I8	Italian
	Esperanto texts
8251	Polygraphy
8252	Philosophy
8253	Religion
	History
8254	Chronology. Diplomatics. Numismatics
8255	Biography. Genealogy
	General history
8256	General works
8257	Ancient
8258	Medieval
8259	Modern
	Europe
8260	General works
8261	Great Britain
8262	France
8263	Germany
8267.A-Z	Other European, A-Z
8268	Asia
8269	Africa
8270	Australia. Oceania
8271	United States
8272	British America. Canada
8273.A-Z	Other American, A-Z
8274	Geography. Anthropology
8275	Folklore. Manners and customs. Sports and games
	Social sciences
8276	General works
8277	Economics
8278	Sociology

	Artificial languages. Universal languages
	Special languages (alphabetically)
	Esperanto
	Esperanto texts -- Continued
8279	Political science
8280	Law
8281	Education
8282	Music
8283	Fine Arts
8284	Language
	Literature
8284.5	Literary history
	Collections
8285.A2	International
8285.A3A-.A3Z	Translations from individual languages, A-Z
8285.A5-Z	Individual authors
	Including translations
8286	Science. Mathematics. Astronomy. Physics. Chemistry
8287	Geology. Natural history. Botany. Zoology. Human anatomy. Physiology. Bacteriology
8288	Medicine
8289	Agriculture
8290	Technology. Manufactures. Trades
8291	Engineering and building
8292	Mineral industries. Chemical technology
8293	Photography
8294	Domestic science
8295	Military science
8296	Naval science
8298	Bibliography
8310	Eurolengo (Table P-PZ15)
8315	Europanto (Table P-PZ15)
8360.G2	Gab
8360.G4	Geoglot
	Germanic English see PM8862
8362	Glan-ik (Table P-PZ15)
	Gloro see PM8085
8365	Glosa (Table P-PZ15)
8368	Guosa (Table P-PZ15)
8370	Hom-idyomo (Table P-PZ15)
8371	HOOM-DIAL (Table P-PZ15)
8381-8384	Idiom neutral (Table P-PZ11)
8391-8394	Ido (Table P-PZ11)
	Modified Esperanto
8396	INO (Table P-PZ15)
8398	Interglossa (Table P-PZ15)

PM

Artificial languages. Universal languages
Special languages (alphabetically) -- Continued

8400	Interlingua (International Auxiliary Language Association) (Table P-PZ15)
8401	Interlingua (Latin without inflections) (Table P-PZ15)
8409	International auxiliari linguo (Table P-PZ15)
8412	Itza (Table P-PZ15)
8415	Klingon (Table P-PZ15)
8421	Kommunikationssprache (Shipfer, 1838) (Table P-PZ15)
8441	Kosmos (Table P-PZ15)
	Langue internationale naturelle see PM8128
8457	Langue internationale néo-latine (Table P-PZ15)
8501	Lengua catolica (Table P-PZ15)
8504	Lengua universal (L. Selbor) (Table P-PZ15)
8507	Leno gi-nasu (Table P-PZ15)
8508	Lincos (Table P-PZ15)
8509	Ling (Table P-PZ15)
8511	Lingu nov (Table P-PZ15)
8521	Lingu franca nuova (Table P-PZ15)
8531	Lingua internazional (Table P-PZ15)
8535	Lingua italiana infinitiva (Table P-PZ15)
8541	Lingua lumina (Table P-PZ15)
8551	Lingua moderna (Table P-PZ15)
8563	Lingua philosophica (Table P-PZ15)
8572	Lingua universal (of Sotos Ochando) (Table P-PZ15)
	Lingvo internacia of Zamenhof see PM8201+
8576-8579	Lingvo internaciona (Table P-PZ11)
8590	Loglan (Table P-PZ15)
8605	Manavabhasha (Table P-PZ15)
8612	Master language (Table P-PZ15)
8621	Mezzofanti language (Table P-PZ15)
8629	Mondi linguo (Table P-PZ15)
8630	Mondial (Table P-PZ15)
8633	Mondolingu (Table P-PZ15)
8637	Mundal (Table P-PZ15)
8643	Myrana (Table P-PZ15)
8651	Nal bino (Table P-PZ15)
8670	Neo (Table P-PZ15)
8673	Neoispano (Table P-PZ15)
8675	Neolatinus (Table P-PZ15)
	Neutral language see PM8381+
8679	North American (Table P-PZ15)
8682	Nov Latin (Table P-PZ15)
8685	Novial (Table P-PZ15)
8688	Novolingua (Table P-PZ15)
8693	Nula (Table P-PZ15)

Artificial languages. Universal languages
Special languages (alphabetically) -- Continued

8702	Occidental (Table P-PZ15)
8705	Oidapa (Table P-PZ15)
8706	Olingo (Table P-PZ15)
8707	Oz (Table P-PZ15)
8709	Panamane (Table P-PZ15)
8712	Pasilingua (Table P-PZ15)
8732	Pasilogia (Table P-PZ15)
8736	Pikto (Table P-PZ15)
8741	Qosmiani (Table P-PZ15)
8751	Ro (Table P-PZ15)
8753	Romanal (Table P-PZ15)
8753.5	Románica (Table P-PZ15)
8754	Romanid (Table P-PZ15)
8755	Rosaecrucian (Table P-PZ15)
8777	Salvador (Table P-PZ15)
8780	Sindarin (Table P-PZ15)
8790	Solresol (Table P-PZ15)
8795	Sona (Table P-PZ15)
8802	Spelin (Table P-PZ15)
8815	SPL (Table P-PZ15)
8822	Spokil (Table P-PZ15)
8840	Suma (Table P-PZ15)
8862	Teutonish (Tutonish) (Table P-PZ15)
8875	Tsolyáni (Table P-PZ15)
8900	Unilingua (Table P-PZ15)
8905	Universal language (J. Ruggles, 1829) (Table P-PZ15)
8912	Universal language (1869) (Table P-PZ15)
8922	Universala (Table P-PZ15)
8930	Vela (Table P-PZ15)
8933	Velt-Deutsch (Table P-PZ15)
8937	Veltlang (Table P-PZ15)
8942	Visona (Table P-PZ15)
8951-8959.5	Volapük (Table P-PZ8a)
8961	Voldu (Table P-PZ15)
8963	Wede (Table P-PZ15)
8971	Welt-Latein (Table P-PZ15)
8981	World English (Table P-PZ15)
8995	Zantum (Table P-PZ15)
8999	Picture languages
	Including Isotype
	Secret languages
	Cf. Slang and argot in special languages, e.g. PC3721+, French; PE3701+, English
9001	General works

                        Artificial languages--Universal languages
                              Secret languages
9021.A-Z   Special. By name, A-Z
9021.E55   Enochian
9021.O8   Ovano
9021.S5   Shelta

	Through 1867
0.1	General works
0.112.A-Z	Special topics, A-Z
	For list of topics, see PL721
0.113.A-Z	Treatment of special classes, races, etc., A-Z
	For list of special classes, races, etc., see PL722
	To 1600
0.115	General works
0.117.A-Z	Special topics, A-Z
	For list of topics, see PL721
0.118.A-Z	Treatment of special classes, races, etc., A-Z
	For list of special classes, races, etc., see PL722
	To 1185
0.1185	General works
0.1186.A-Z	Special topics, A-Z
	For list of topics, see PL721
	Origins. Early through 793 A.D.
0.12	General works
0.125.A-Z	Special topics, A-Z
	For list of topics, see PL721
0.126.A-Z	Treatment of special classes, races, etc., A-Z
	For list of special classes, races, etc., see PL722
	Heian period, 794-1185
0.2	General works
0.25.A-Z	Special topics, A-Z
	For list of topics, see PL721
0.26.A-Z	Treatment of special classes, races, etc., A-Z
	For list of special classes, races, etc., see PL722
	Kamakura through Momoyama periods, 1185-1600
0.3	General works
0.33.A-Z	Special topics, A-Z
	For list of topics, see PL721
0.34.A-Z	Treatment of special classes, races, etc., A-Z
	For list of special classes, races, etc., see PL722
	Edo period, 1600-1868
0.35	General works
0.37.A-Z	Special topics, A-Z
	For list of topics, see PL721
0.38.A-Z	Treatment of special classes, races, etc., A-Z
	For list of special classes, races, etc., see PL722
	Early Edo period, 1600-1788
0.4	General works
0.45.A-Z	Special topics, A-Z
	For list of topics, see PL721
	Late Edo period, 1789-1868
0.5	General works

TABLES

	Through 1867
	Edo period, 1600-1868
	Late Edo period, 1789-1868 -- Continued
0.53.A-Z	Special topics, A-Z
	For list of topics, see PL721
	1868-
0.55	General works
0.57.A-Z	Special topics, A-Z
	For list of topics, see PL721
0.58.A-Z	Treatment of special classes, races, etc., A-Z
	For list of special classes, races, etc., see PL722
	Meiji and Taishō periods, 1868-1926
0.6	General works
0.63.A-Z	Special topics, A-Z
	For list of topics, see PL721
0.64.A-Z	Treatment of special classes, races, etc., A-Z
	For list of special classes, races, etc., see PL722
	Shōwa period, 1926-1989
0.65	General works
0.67.A-Z	Special topics, A-Z
	For list of topics, see PL721
0.68.A-Z	Treatment of special classes, races, etc., A-Z
	For list of special classes, races, etc., see PL722
	1926-1945
0.7	General works
0.75.A-Z	Special topics, A-Z
	For list of topics, see PL721
0.77.A-Z	Treatment of special classes, races, etc., A-Z
	For list of special classes, races, etc., see PL722
	1945-1989
0.8	General works
0.82.A-Z	Special topics, A-Z
	For list of topics, see PL721
0.83.A-Z	Treatment of special classes, races, etc., A-Z
	For list of special classes, races, etc., see PL722
	Heisei period, 1989-
0.85	General works
0.87.A-Z	Special topics, A-Z
	For list of topics, see PL721
0.88.A-Z	Treatment of special classes, races, etc., A-Z
	For list of special classes, races, etc., see PL722

	Through 1867
.x1	General works
.x112.A-Z	Special topics, A-Z
	For list of topics, see PL721
.x113.A-Z	Treatment of special classes, races, etc., A-Z
	For list of special classes, races, etc., see PL722
	To 1600
.x115	General works
.x117.A-Z	Special topics, A-Z
	For list of topics, see PL721
.x118.A-Z	Treatment of special classes, races, etc., A-Z
	For list of special classes, races, etc., see PL722
	To 1185
.x1185	General works
.x1186.A-Z	Special topics, A-Z
	For list of topics, see PL721
	Origins. Early through 793 A.D.
.x12	General works
.x125.A-Z	Special topics, A-Z
	For list of topics, see PL721
.x126.A-Z	Treatment of special classes, races, etc., A-Z
	For list of special classes, races, etc., see PL722
	Heian period, 794-1185
.x2	General works
.x25.A-Z	Special topics, A-Z
	For list of topics, see PL721
.x26.A-Z	Treatment of special classes, races, etc., A-Z
	For list of special classes, races, etc., see PL722
	Kamakura through Momoyama periods, 1185-1600
.x3	General works
.x33.A-Z	Special topics, A-Z
	For list of topics, see PL721
.x34.A-Z	Treatment of special classes, races, etc., A-Z
	For list of special classes, races, etc., see PL722
	Edo period, 1600-1868
.x35	General works
.x37.A-Z	Special topics, A-Z
	For list of topics, see PL721
.x38.A-Z	Treatment of special classes, races, etc., A-Z
	For list of special classes, races, etc., see PL722
	Early Edo period, 1600-1788
.x4	General works
.x45.A-Z	Special topics, A-Z
	For list of topics, see PL721
	Late Edo period, 1789-1868
.x5	General works

TABLES

	Through 1867
	Edo period, 1600-1868
	Late Edo period, 1789-1868 -- Continued
.x53.A-Z	Special topics, A-Z
	For list of topics, see PL721
	1868-
.x55	General works
.x57.A-Z	Special topics, A-Z
	For list of topics, see PL721
.x58.A-Z	Treatment of special classes, races, etc., A-Z
	For list of special classes, races, etc., see PL722
	Meiji and Taishō periods, 1868-1926
.x6	General works
.x63.A-Z	Special topics, A-Z
	For list of topics, see PL721
.x64.A-Z	Treatment of special classes, races, etc., A-Z
	For list of special classes, races, etc., see PL722
	Shōwa period, 1926-1989
.x65	General works
.x67.A-Z	Special topics, A-Z
	For list of topics, see PL721
.x68.A-Z	Treatment of special classes, races, etc., A-Z
	For list of special classes, races, etc., see PL722
	1926-1945
.x7	General works
.x75.A-Z	Special topics, A-Z
	For list of topics, see PL721
.x77.A-Z	Treatment of special classes, races, etc., A-Z
	For list of special classes, races, etc., see PL722
	1945-1989
.x8	General works
.x82.A-Z	Special topics, A-Z
	For list of topics, see PL721
.x83.A-Z	Treatment of special classes, races, etc., A-Z
	For list of special classes, races, etc., see PL722
	Heisei period, 1989-
.x85	General works
.x87.A-Z	Special topics, A-Z
	For list of topics, see PL721
.x88.A-Z	Treatment of special classes, races, etc., A-Z
	For list of special classes, races, etc., see PL722

0	Through 1894
0.1	Origins. Early works to 935 A.D.
0.12	Koryo period, 935-1392
0.15	Chosŏn dynasty, 1392-1894
0.2	1392-1598
0.25	1598-1800
0.3	1800-1894
	20th century
0.4	General works
0.5	1894-1919
0.6	1919-1945
0.7	1945-2000
0.8	21st century

Since each decimal number represents an entire family name, the
author number is determined by the first letter of the given
name

Family names are arranged alphabetically according to
romanization, disregarding diacritical marks

0.A1A-.A1Z	Anonymous works. By title, A-Z
0.115	An
0.12	Ch'a
0.13	Ch'ae
0.14	Chang. Ch'ang
0.145	Che
0.148	Chegal
0.15	Chi
0.153	Chihyon
0.155	Chin
0.17	Cho. Ch'o
0.18	Ch'oe
0.181	Ch'ogye
0.182	Ch'oi
0.19	Chon. Chŏn. Ch'ŏn
0.2	Chong. Chŏng
0.2115	Chongsu
0.212	Choo
0.215	Chu. Ch'u
0.22	Chun
0.23	Chwa
0.235	Dyuna
0.24	Ha
0.25	Ham
0.26	Han
0.27	Ho. Hŏ
0.28	Hong
0.285	Hu
0.286	Hua
0.287	Hwa
0.29	Hwang
0.295	Hwangbo
0.296	Hyang
0.297	Hyok
0.3	Hyon. Hyŏn
0.313	Hyong. Hyŏng
0.32	I
0.33	Im
0.34	In
0.36	Ka
0.364	Kae
0.37	Kal

0.375	Kam
0.377	Kan
0.38	Kang
0.39	Ki
0.4	Kil
0.415	Kim
0.417	Kimsin
0.42	Ko
0.423	Kok
0.425	Kong
0.43	Ku
0.44	Kuk
0.445	Kum. Kŭm
0.447	Kun. Kŭn
0.448	Kung
0.45	Kwak
0.46	Kwŏn
0.47	Kye
0.474	Kyŏn
0.475	Kyong. Kyŏng
0.48	Lee
0.49	Ma
0.495	Mae
0.5	Maeng
0.513	Man
0.514	Mi
0.515	Min
0.52	Mo
0.53	Mok
0.534	Mu
0.535	Muk
0.54	Mun
0.545	Myong. Myŏng
0.55	Na
0.555	Nae
0.56	Nam
0.565	Namgung
0.568	Nang
0.57	No
0.573	Noe
0.58	O. Ŏ
0.582	Oh
0.585	Ok
0.59	Ŏm
0.592	Omiri
0.593	On
0.594	Ong

TABLES

0.595	Pa
0.6	Pae
0.613	Paek
0.615	Paeng. P'aeng
0.62	Pak
0.625	Pan. P'an
0.63	Pang. P'ang
0.632	Park
0.635	Pe
0.64	P'i
0.642	Pin
0.643	Ping
0.644	P'o
0.645	Poitras
0.65	Pok
0.6516	Pom. Pŏm
0.652	Pŏn
0.654	Pong
0.655	Pongmyŏnja
0.6552	Pŏpch'ŏl
0.656	Pu
0.658	Pulgŭn Suyŏm
0.659	P'ung
0.66	P'yo
0.67	Pyon. Pyŏn
0.68	P'yŏng
0.69	Ren
0.695	Rhee
0.7	Sa
0.712	Sagong
0.713	Sam
0.714	Sang
0.716	Si
0.72	Sim
0.73	Sin
0.74	So. Sŏ
0.742	Sodam
0.75	Sŏk
0.76	Sŏl
0.77	Son. Sŏn
0.78	Song. Sŏng
0.783	Sŏngu
0.785	Sŏnu
0.787	Sŏrin
0.7875	Su
0.788	Suan
0.789	Sun

0.79	Sung. Sŭng
0.793	Ta
0.796	T'ae
0.798	Taeu
0.8	T'ak
0.814	Tan. T'an
0.815	Tang
0.82	To
0.822	Tokko
0.824	Tong
0.8245	Tongbang
0.825	Tonyŏng
0.826	Tu
0.83	U
0.84	Uk
0.843	Ŭm
0.845	Ŭn
0.85	Ŭng
0.86	Wang
0.87	Wi
0.88	Wŏn
0.883	Wŏn'gwang
0.886	Ya
0.89	Yang
0.895	Ye
0.9	Yi
0.915	Yŏ
0.92	Yŏm
0.93	Yŏn
0.935	Yong. Yŏng
0.94	Yu
0.95	Yuk
0.96	Yun
0.98	Zong

TABLES

1	Comprehensive editions and selections. The 13, 12, 9, or 6 Classics (Table PL7)
2	Wu jing (The 5 Classics) (Table PL7) Includes Yi jing, Shu jing, Shi jing, Li ji, and Chun qiu
3	Si shu (The 4 books) (Table PL7) Includes Lun yu, Da xue, Zhong yong, Mengzi
	Individual classics
4	Yi jing (Book of changes) (Table PL7)
5	Shu jing (Book of history) (Table PL7)
6	Shi jing (Book of poetry) (Table PL7)
7	Li ji (Book of rites) (Table PL7)
8	Zhou li (Ritual of the Zhou Dynasty) (Table PL7)
9	Yi li (Ceremonial usages) (Table PL7)
10	Chun qiu (Spring and Autumn) (Table PL7)
11	Lun yu (The Analects) (Table PL7) For Confucius' philosophy, see B128.C8
12	Da xue (The Great learning) (Table PL7)
13	Zhong yong (Doctrine of the mean) (Table PL7)
14	Mengzi (Mencius' sayings and doings) (Table PL7) For Mencius' philosophy, see B128.M324
15	Er ya (Dictionary) (Table PL7)
16	Xiao jing (Book of filial piety) (Table PL7)

.A1-.A9	Comprehensive editions and selections. The 13, 12, 9, or 6 Classics
	Cutter numbers are arranged consecutively by name of translator, if given, or by date
.B1-.B9	Wu jing (The 5 Classics)
	Cutter numbers are arranged consecutively by name of translator, if given, or by date
	Includes Yi jing, Shu jing, Shi jing, Li ji, and Chun qiu
.C1-.C9	Si shu (The 4 books)
	Cutter numbers are arranged consecutively by name of translator, if given, or by date
	Includes Lun yu, Da xue, Zhong yong, Mengzi
	Individual classics
	Cutter numbers are arranged consecutively by name of translator, if given, or by date
.D1-.D9	Yi jing (Book of changes)
	Cutter numbers are arranged consecutively by name of translator, if given, or by date
.E1-.E9	Shu jing (Book of history)
	Cutter numbers are arranged consecutively by name of translator, if given, or by date
.F1-.F9	Shi jing (Book of poetry)
	Cutter numbers are arranged consecutively by name of translator, if given, or by date
.G1-.G9	Li ji (Book of rites)
	Cutter numbers are arranged consecutively by name of translator, if given, or by date
.H1-.H9	Zhou li (Ritual of the Zhou Dynasty)
	Cutter numbers are arranged consecutively by name of translator, if given, or by date
.J1-.J9	Yi li (Ceremonial usages)
	Cutter numbers are arranged consecutively by name of translator, if given, or by date
.K1-.K9	Chun qiu (Spring and Autumn)
	Cutter numbers are arranged consecutively by name of translator, if given, or by date
.L1-.L9	Lun yu (The Analects)
	Cutter numbers are arranged consecutively by name of translator, if given, or by date
	For Confucius' philosophy, see B128.C8
.M1-.M9	Da xue (The Great learning)
	Cutter numbers are arranged consecutively by name of translator, if given, or by date
.N1-.N9	Zhong yong (Doctrine of the mean)
	Cutter numbers are arranged consecutively by name of translator, if given, or by date

TABLES

	Individual classics -- Continued
.P1-.P9	Mengzi (Mencius' sayings and doings)
	Cutter numbers are arranged consecutively by name of translator, if given, or by date
	For Mencius' philosophy, see B128.M324
.Q1-.Q9	Er ya (Dictionary)
	Cutter numbers are arranged consecutively by name of translator, if given, or by date
.R1-.R9	Xiao jing (Book of filial piety)
	Cutter numbers are arranged consecutively by name of translator, if given, or by date

	Early to 221 B.C.
0	General
1	Zhou dynasty, 1122-221 B.C.
	For the Confucian canon and Chinese classics, see PL2458+
2	Spring and Autumn period, 722-481 B.C. Warring States, 403-221 B.C.
	221 B.C.-960 A.D.
3	General
4	Qin and Han dynasties, 221 B.C.-220 A.D.
	220-589 (Wei, Jin, Northern and Southern dynasties; or Six Dynasties)
4.5	General
5	The Three Kingdoms, 220-265
6	Jin dynasty, 265-419
8	Five Hu and the Sixteen Kingdoms, 303-439
9	Northern and Southern Dynasties, 386-589
	Including Northern Wei, Eastern Wei, Western Wei, Northern Qi, Northern Zhou, Liu Song (Former Song), Qi, Liang, Chen
10	Sui dynasty, 581-618
11	Tang dynasty, 618-907
12	Five Dynasties and the Ten Kingdoms, 907-979
	Including Later Liang, Later Tang, Later Jin, Later Han, Later Zhou, Wu, Southern Tang, Southern Ping, Earlier Shu, Qu, Later Shu, Wuyue, Min, Southern Han, Northern Han
	960-1644
12.5	General
13	Song dynasty, 960-1279. Liao dynasty, 947-1125. Xi Xia dynasty, 1038-1227. Jin dynasty, 1115-1234
14	Yuan dynasty, 1260-1368
16	Ming dynasty, 1368-1644
	Qing Dynasty, 1644-1912
17	General
18	Shunzhi, 1644-1661. Kangxi, 1662-1722. Yongzheng, 1723-1735
19	Qianlong, 1736-1795. Jiaqing, 1796-1820
20	Daoguang, 1820-1850. Xianfeng, 1850-1861
21	Tongzhi, 1861-1875. Guangxu, 1875-1908. Xuangtong, 1908-1912
22	Republic, 1912-1949
23	People's Republic, 1949-

TABLES

1	Tang dynasty, 618-907
2	Five Dynasties and the Ten Kingdoms, 907-979
	Including Later Liang, Later Tang, Later Jin, Later Han, Later Zhou, Wu, Southern Tang, Southern Ping, Earlier Shu, Qu, Later Shu, Wuyue, Min, Southern Han, Northern Han
	960-1644
2.5	General
3	Song dynasty, 960-1279. Liao dynasty, 947-1125. Xi Xia dynasty, 1038-1227. Jin dynasty, 1115-1234
4	Yuan dynasty, 1260-1368
6	Ming dynasty, 1368-1644
	Qing Dynasty, 1644-1912
7	General
8	Shunzhi, 1644-1661. Kangxi, 1662-1722. Yongzheng, 1723-1735
9	Qianlong, 1736-1795. Jiaqing, 1796-1820
10	Daoguang, 1820-1850. Xianfeng, 1850-1861
11	Tongzhi, 1861-1875. Guangxu, 1875-1908. Xuangtong, 1908-1912
12	Republic, 1912-1949
13	People's Republic, 1949-

.A1-.A9   Five Dynasties and the Ten Kingdoms, 907-979
                                    Cutter numbers are arranged consecutively by editor or
                                        commentator of the original edition
                                    Including Later Liang, Later Tang, Later Jin, Later Han, Later Zhou,
                                        Wu, Southern Tang, Southern Ping, Earlier Shu, Qu, Later Shu,
                                        Wuyue, Min, Southern Han, Northern Han
                           960-1644
.B1-.B9   Song dynasty, 960-1279. Liao dynasty, 947-1125. Xi Xia
                                dynasty, 1038-1227. Jin dynasty, 1115-1234
                                    Cutter numbers are arranged consecutively by editor or
                                        commentator of the original edition
.C1-.C9   Yuan dynasty, 1260-1368
                                    Cutter numbers are arranged consecutively by editor or
                                        commentator of the original edition
.D1-.D9   Ming dynasty, 1368-1644
                                    Cutter numbers are arranged consecutively by editor or
                                        commentator of the original edition
                           Qing Dynasty, 1644-1912
.E1-.E9   Shunzhi, 1644-1661
                                    Cutter numbers are arranged consecutively by editor or
                                        commentator of the original edition
.F1-.F9   Kangxi, 1662-1722
                                    Cutter numbers are arranged consecutively by editor or
                                        commentator of the original edition
.G1-.G9   Yongzheng, 1723-1735
                                    Cutter numbers are arranged consecutively by editor or
                                        commentator of the original edition
.H1-.H9   Qianlong, 1736-1795
                                    Cutter numbers are arranged consecutively by editor or
                                        commentator of the original edition
.J1-.J9   Jiaqing, 1796-1820
                                    Cutter numbers are arranged consecutively by editor or
                                        commentator of the original edition
.K1-.K9   Daoguang, 1820-1850
                                    Cutter numbers are arranged consecutively by editor or
                                        commentator of the original edition
.L1-.L9   Xianfeng, 1850-1861
                                    Cutter numbers are arranged consecutively by editor or
                                        commentator of the original edition
.M1-.M9   Tongzhi, 1861-1875
                                    Cutter numbers are arranged consecutively by editor or
                                        commentator of the original edition
.N1-.N9   Guangxu, 1875-1908
                                    Cutter numbers are arranged consecutively by editor or
                                        commentator of the original edition

TABLES

	Qing dynasty, 1644-1912 -- Continued
.P1-.P9	Xuantong, 1908-1912
	Cutter numbers are arranged consecutively by editor or commentator of the original edition
.Q1-.Q9	Republic, 1912-1949
	Cutter numbers are arranged consecutively by editor or commentator of the original edition
.R1-.R9	People's Republic, 1949-
	Cutter numbers are arranged consecutively by editor or commentator of the original edition
.Z5	Indexes
.Z6	Commentaries
.Z7	General treatises
.Z8	Treatises on special chapters or sections. By number or name
.Z9A-.Z9Z	Special topics, A-Z

1.A1-.A5	Periodicals. Societies. Serials. Collections (nonserial)
1.A6-Z	General works
2	General special (Script)
	Grammar. Treatises. Textbooks
3	Western
4	Oriental and other non-Western
5	Exercises. Readers. Phrase books, etc.
	Dictionaries
6	Western
7	Oriental and other non-Western
	Literature
8	History and criticism
8.5	Collections
9	Other special
	e.g. Etymology
10.A-Z	By place, A-Z

TABLES

.A11-.A2	Text. By editor
	Translations
.A3	English
.A35	French
.A36	German
.A4-.A59	Other languages (alphabetically)
.A6	Selections. By date

.xA11-.xA2	Text. By editor
	Translations
.xA3	English
.xA35	French
.xA36	German
.xA4-.xA59	Other languages (alphabetically)
.xA6	Selections. By date

TABLES

INDEX

Ayta Anchi Sambal dialect:
  PL6024.595.A93
Ayta Mag Indi dialect: PL6024.595.A95
Azerbaijani language: PL311+
Aztec language: PM4061+

B

Babine language: PM664
Babispe language: PM3526
Babm (Artificial language): PM8090
Bacteriology
  Esperanto texts: PM8287
Bada language (Indonesia): PL5214+
Baḍaga dialect: PL4641+
Bade language: PL8047.5.B27+
Badyaranke language: PL8047.5.B33+
Bafia language: PL8047.5.B42+
Bafut language: PL8047.5.B45+
Bagirmi language: PL8047.5.B47+
Bagobo language: PL5552+
Bahinemo language: PL6621.B3
Bāhing dialect: PL3801.B2+
Bahnar language: PL4311+
Bahnaric languages: PL4310.B34
Bai language (China): PL4001.B16
Baima language: PL3801.B297+
Baimena language: PM3531
Baishan shui dian zhan (Huadian Xian,
  China) in literature
  Chinese
    Literary history: PL2275.P34
Bajau language: PL5215+
Bajele language: PL8047.6
Baka language (Cameroon and Gabon):
  PL8047.65
Bakairi language: PM5581
Bakele language (Gabon): PL8377+
Bakwé language: PL8047.7
Balaesang language: PL5219+
Balaibalan (Artificial language):
  PM8092
Bālālī (Himalayan language):
  PL3801.B3
Balangao language: PL5561
Balangingi dialect: PL5563+
Balantak language: PL5220+

Balante language: PL8047.8
Balese language: PL8048+
Balinese language: PL5221+
Balkar literature: PL68.5+
Ballads
  Chinese poetry
    Collections: PL2519.B34
  Japanese poetry
    Collections: PL761+
    Literary history: PL731+
  Korean poetry
    Collections: PL975
    Literary history: PL960
Balti language: PL3651.B2+
Bambara language: PL8049.B3+
Bamboo in literature
  Chinese
    Literary history: PL2275.B35
Bamileke languages: PL8049.B4+
Bamun language: PL8050+
Banaue dialect: PL5565
Banawi dialect: PL5565
Banda language (Central Africa):
  PL8051
Banda language (Indonesia): PL5225+
Banda languages: PL8052
Bandjalang language: PL7101.B3
Bandjoun language: PL8052.5
Banen language: PL8053+
Bangala language (Congo): PL8456+
Bangubangu language: PL8056.B25+
Bangwa language: PL8056.B26+
Baniwa language: PM5581.5
Banjarese language: PL5226+
Banjōgī dialect: PL4001.B2
Bantawa language: PL3801.B34+
Bantu languages: PL8025+
Banziri language: PL8056.B275+
Bao juan (Buddhist song-tales)
  Chinese
    Collections: PL2579.B34
Bao juan (Buuddhist song-tales)
  Chinese drama
    Literary history: PL2368.B34
Baoulé language: PL8056.B3+
Bara dialect (Madagascar):
  PL5379.5.B37

394

Cahumari language: PM5671
Cahumeto language: PM3566
Caicai language: PM5676
Caigua language: PM735.C3+
Caingua language: PM5678
Caipotorade dialect: PM5681
Caisina language: PM5686
Cajono language: PM3571
Cajueche language: PM735.C5+
Cakchi language: PM3913
Cakchikel language (Guatemala):
   PM3576
Cakchiquel (Indian language of Mexico/
   Central America): PM5690
Calamian language: PL5841
Calapooya language: PM1421
Calchaqui language: PM5658
Calen language: PM5696
Calicione language: PM5701
Calinga languages: PL5851
Callahuaya language: PM5703
Calligraphy, Chinese, in literature
   Chinese
      Literary history: PL2275.C24
Calza-blanca language: PM5706
Camacori dialect: PM5711
Camanacho language: PM6386
Cambodian language: PL4321+
Cameole language: PM741
Camoteco language: PM3581
Campa language (Ecuador): PM5717
Campa language (Peru): PM5716
Camsa language: PM5718.C3+
Camuhi language: PL6227
Canamari language (Tucanoan):
   PM5718.C45+
Cañari language: PM5718.C5+
Cancanay language: PL5865
Canchi language: PM5571+
Candoshi language: PM5718.C8+
Canella language: PM5719
Canga dialect: PM5721
Cangin languages: PL8108
Caniba dialect (Abenaki): PM745.C3+
Canichana language: PM5723
Canisiná language: PM5726
Cantonese dialects: PL1731+

Cao Lan language: PL4251.C27+
Caoque language: PM745.C5+
Capanahua language: PM5735
Capinjela language: PM5736
Caquinte language: PM5739
Caraja language: PM5741
Caranca dialect: PM5746
Carapana language (Tucanoan):
   PM5749
Carariu language: PM5751
Caraya language: PM5741
Carib language: PM5756+
Carib language, Island: PM6239
Cariban languages: PM5756+
Cariela language: PM5761
Cariri language: PM6286+
Carnataca language: PL4641+
Carolinian language (Micronesia):
   PL6228
Carrier language: PM2411
Cascan language: PM3586
Cashibo language: PM5763
Cashinawa language: PM6290.K3+
Casiguran language: PL5661+
Casná dialect: PM5766
Castles in literature
   Japanese
      Literary history: PL721.C3
Catapaturo dialect: PM5773
Catawba language: PM751
Cateco dialect: PM5776
Cathlamet dialect: PM753
Cathlascon language: PM755.C3+
Catholic authors
   Korean
      Collections: PL973.2.C38
      Literary history: PL957.95.C38
Catholics in literature
   Korean
      Literary history: PL957.5.C36
Catio language: PM5778
Catsipagoto dialect: PM5781
Caucau language: PM5786
Cauqui language: PM5788
Cavene dialect: PM6291
Cavineño language: PM7088
Caxinaua language: PM6290.K3+

Chinarra language: PM3706
Chinchasuyu dialect: PM5814.C3+
Chinese characters
  Grammar: PL1171+
Chinese characters, Korean literature
  written in: PL950+
Chinese Classics (Literature)
  Collections: PL2458+
Chinese in literature
  Chinese
    Literary history: PL2275.C45
Chinese language: PL1001+
Chinese language and literature:
  PL1001+
Chinese language data processing:
  PL1074.5
Chinese literature: PL2250+
  Provincial, local, colonial, etc:
    PL3030+
Chinese literature outside China:
  PL3033+
Ching-p'o language: PL4001.K32+
Chinipa language: PM4481
Chinju-si (Korea) in literature
  Korean
    Literary history: PL957.5.C455
Chino language: PL4001.C53
Chinook jargon: PM846+
Chinook language: PM841+
Chipaya language: PM5814.C5+
Chipewyan language: PM850.C2+
Chippewa language: PM851+
Chiquito language: PM5816
Chirichahua language: PM858
Chiriguano language: PM5817.C2+
Chitimacha language: PM861
Chitkhuli language: PL3801.C58+
Chocho language (Popolucan):
  PM3641
Choco languages: PM5817.C4+
Choctaw language: PM871+
Chokwe language: PL8113+
Cholon language: PM5817.C6+
Choloteca language: PM3943
Choltí language (Guatemala and
  Mexico): PM3649

Ch'ŏndogyo in literature
  Korean
    Literary history: PL957.5.C46
Ch'ŏnggu yŏngŏn
  Korean poetry
    Collections: PL975.63
Chongqing (China) in literature
  Chinese
    Literary history: PL2275.C53
Chontal language: PM3651
Chontaquiro language: PM5818
Chopi language: PL8115+
Chora language: PM3711+
Chorotega language: PM3943
Choroti language: PM5817.C7+
Chorruco language: PM881
Chorruto language: PM885.C3+
Chorte language (Guatemala and
  Honduras): PM3661
Chorti language (Guatemala and
  Honduras): PM3661
Chota language: PM3711+
Chow-e-shak language: PM885.C5+
Ch'ŏyong, 9th cent., in literature
  Korean
    Literary history: PL957.5.C464
Chrau language: PL4429
Christian authors
  Japanese literature
    Literary history: PL725.2.C47
  Korean
    Collections: PL973.2.C47
Christianity in literature
  Japanese
    Literary history: PL721.C45
  Korean
    Literary history: PL957.5.C47
Chrysanthemums in literature
  Chinese
    Literary history: PL2275.C47
Ch'ü
  Chinese literature
    Literary history: PL2354+
Ch'ü-fu hsien (China) in literature
  Chinese
    Literary history: PL2275.C5

Ch'ü, Yüan, ca. 343-ca. 277 B.C., in
  literature
  Chinese
    Literary history: PL2275.C49
Chuang language: PL4251.C4+
Chuchon language: PM3641
Chüeh chü
  Chinese poetry
    Collections: PL2519.C47
    Literary history: PL2309.C48
Chuj language: PM3668
Chūjō-hime, 8th cent. in literature
  Japanese
    Literary history: PL721.C46
Chukchi language: PM11+
Chulupí language: PM5817.C8+
Chulym language: PL45.C48+
Chumash language: PM891
Chumbi Valley dialect (Tibetan):
  PL3651.T7
Chumbia language: PM3671
Chumula language: PM3676
Chung-ching shih (China) in literature
  Chinese
    Literary history: PL2275.C53
Chuntaquiro language: PM5818
Chutiyā language: PL4001.C7
Chuukese language: PL6318
Chuvash language: PL381+
Chuwabo language: PL8115.97+
Ci-Tonga language: PL8741+
Ci (Tz'u)
  Chinese literature
    Collections: PL2548+
    Literary history: PL2336+
Cia-cia language: PL5296+
Cinantecan languages: PM3630
Cinnamon tree in literature
  Chinese
    Literary history: PL2275.C56
Cities in literature
  Japanese
    Literary history: PL721.C5
Civil rights movements in literature
  Korean
    Literary history: PL957.5.C54

Civilization and Chinese literature:
  PL2273
Civilization and Japanese literature:
  PL720
Civilization and Korean literature:
  PL957.3
Clallam language: PM895
Coahuilteco language: PM3681
Coal mines and mining in literature
  Korean
    Literary history: PL957.5.C63
Coca language: PM3686
Cocama language: PM5823
Cochimi language: PM3688
Cocina dialect: PM5824.C2+
Cocoma language: PM5823
Coconucan language: PM5824.C3+
Cocopa language: PM3696
Code Ari (Artificial language): PM8129
Coeur d'Alene language: PM916
Cofane language: PM5825
Colla dialect: PM5827
Collagua dialect: PM5827
College students as authors
  Chinese
    Collections: PL2515.5.C64
  Korean
    Collections: PL973.2.C64
      Poetry: PL975.8.C64
      Prose: PL980.13.C64
Color in literature
  Japanese
    Literary history: PL721.C6
Colorado language: PM5829
Colotlan language: PM3701
Comabo language: PM5763
Comanche language: PM921
Comedy
  Chinese drama
    Collections: PL2579.C6
  Japanese drama
    Collections: PL764.7
    Literary history: PL738.C64
Comic poetry
  Japanese
    Collections: PL762.K9

Comic, The, in literature
  Japanese
    Literary history: PL721.C64
Commerce
  Chinese readers: PL1117.5.C65
Commerce in literature
  Chinese
    Literary history: PL2275.C62
Communis (Artificial language):
  PM8133
Como language (America): PM931
Comorian language: PL8116+
Comox language: PM941
Comparison
  Chinese: PL1233
  Korean: PL921.5
Composition
  Chinese language: PL1271+
  Korean language: PL927+
Concho language: PM3706
Confession in literature
  Japanese
    Literary history: PL721.C645
Confucian Canon
  Chinese literature
    Collections: PL2458+
Confucian ethics in literature
  Chinese
    Literary history: PL2275.C65
Congo language: PL8401+
Consonants
  Chinese: PL1219
  Korean: PL918.7
Conversation
  Korean grammar: PL914
Cookkoo-oose language: PM1611
Coos language: PM1611
Cora language: PM3711+
Corabé language: PM5836
Coribici language: PM3716
Coroado language: PM5846
Coroino language: PM6556
Correguaje language: PM5851
Coscoasoa language: PM5856
Cosmetics in literature
  Japanese
    Literary history: PL721.C65

Cosmology in literature
  Chinese
    Literary history: PL2275.C67
  Japanese
    Literary history: PL721.C66
Costanoan language: PM2053
Coto language: PM6861
Country life in literature
  Japanese
    Literary history: PL721.C68
Couplets
  Chinese poetry
    Collections: PL2519.C7
    Literary history: PL2309.C68
Courts and courtiers in literature
  Japanese
    Literary history: PL721.C7
  Korean
    Literary history: PL957.5.C68
Coversation
  Chinese grammar: PL1121+
Cowichan languages: PM981
Cowlitz language: PM982
Coxoh language: PM3721
Craho language: PM5719
Cree language: PM986+
Creek language: PM991
Creole languages: PM7831+
Crime in literature
  Japanese
    Literary history: PL721.C74
Crimean Tatar language: PL66+
Criticism
  Chinese literature: PL2261+
  Japanese literature: PL714+
  Korean literature: PL954+
Crow language: PM1001
Cua language: PL4433
Cuaca dialect: PM5861
Cuacará dialect: PM5866
Cuaiquer language: PM5868
Cuanhama language: PL8417+
Cuariba language: PM6018
Cubeo language: PM5870
Cuberé language: PM5871
Cubulco Achi language: PM3506
Cuicatec language: PM3731

Dōjōji (Kawabe-chō, Wakayama-ken, Japan) in literature
  Japanese
    Literary history: PL721.D64
Doko language (Congo): PL8140.1+
Dom dialects: PL6621.D65
Domestic life in literature
  Korean
    Literary history: PL957.5.D65
Domestic science
  Esperanto texts: PM8294
Dong language (China): PL4251.T85
Donggo language: PL5298.97+
Dongxiang language: PL431.D64+
Doraksean languages: PM3753
Doyayo language: PL8140.8+
Dragons in literature
  Korean
    Literary history: PL957.5.D73
Drama
  African
    Literary history: PL8010.5
  Chinese
    Collections: PL2566+
    Literary history: PL2356+
  Japanese
    Collections: PL764+
    Literary history: PL734+
  Korean
    Collections: PL977+
    Literary history: PL962+
Dravidian languages: PL4601+
Dreams in literature
  Chinese
    Literary history: PL2275.D74
  Japanese
    Literary history: PL721.D7
  Korean
    Literary history: PL957.5.D74
Drinking in literature
  Korean
    Literary history: PL957.5.D75
Duala language: PL8141+
Dulien language: PL4001.L8+
Dumagat language (Casiguran): PL5661+
Dumbea language: PL6230.D85+

Dūmī language: PL3801.D8+
Duruma language: PL8142.D87+
Dusun language: PL5299+
Dwellings in literature
  Japanese
    Literary history: PL721.D85
Dyak language: PL5301+
Dyula language: PL8142.D94+
Dyur language: PL8143+
Dzongkha language: PL3651.D96+

E

East Makian language: PL6230.E37+
Easter Island language: PL6498
Eastern Arrernte language: PL7101.E37
Eastern Austronesian languages: PL6171+
Eastern Mnong language: PL4457
Eastern Yugur language: PL431.E28+
Echemin language: PM2135
Echibie language: PM5926
Ecoboré language: PM5931
Ecology in literature
  Japanese
    Literary history: PL721.E32
  Korean
    Literary history: PL957.5.E34
Economics
  Chinese readers: PL1117.5.E36
  Esperanto texts: PM8277
Edo language: PL8077+
Edú dialect: PM3756
Education
  Esperanto texts: PM8281
Efate language: PL6231
Efik language: PL8147+
Eggon language: PL8148+
Egoism in literature
  Chinese
    Literary history: PL2275.S44
  Japanese
    Literary history: PL721.S45
Ehime-ken (Japan) in literature
  Japanese
    Literary history: PL721.E35

Ehnek language: PM1125
Eipo language: PL6621.E36
Ejagham language: PL8149.E43+
Ekajuk language: PL8150+
Ekoi languages: PL8152+
Ekpeye language: PL8153.E3+
Elderly people, Killing of, in literature
  Japanese
    Literary history: PL721.K44
Ele dialect (South America): PM5936
Elegiac poetry
  Chinese
    Collections: PL2519.E43
    Literary history: PL2309.E5
  Korean
    Collections: PL975.7.E44
    Literary history: PL960.7.E44
Emei Mountain (China) in literature
  Chinese
    Literary history: PL2275.O43
Empēo language: PL4001.E6
Emperors and empresses
  Japanese literature
    Literary history: PL725.2.E46
Enagua dialect: PM5941
Endo language: PL8153.E54+
Enga language: PL6621.E5
Engenni language: PL8154+
Enggano language: PL5307
Engineering and building
  Esperanto texts: PM8291
Enhara dialect: PL8483.95.E53
Enimagan language: PM5943
Enmay ghee chah (Artificial language):
  PM8190
Enochian language: PM9021.E55
Entertainers in literature
  Korean
    Literary history: PL957.5.E58
Environment in literature
  Korean
    Literary history: PL957.5.E34
Enya language: PL8156+
Eparagota dialect: PM5946
Epena Saija language: PM7079
Epera language, Southern: PM7079

Epic poetry
  Chinese
    Collections: PL2519.E5
    Literary history: PL2309.E6
  Korean
    Literary history: PL960.23
Epuremeo dialect: PM5951
Erascavina language: PM5956
Eremitic life in literature
  Japanese
    Literary history: PL721.E7
Erie language: PM1131
Eriteina language: PM5961
Eromanga language: PL6233
Erotic literature
  Chinese
    Literary history: PL2275.E74
  Japanese
    Literary history: PL721.E74
Eroticism in literature
  Korean
    Literary history: PL957.5.E76
Errors
  Korean: PL927.6
Ese Ejja language: PM7118
Ese language: PL6621.E74
Eskelen language: PM1137
Eskimo Aleut language: PM92
Eskimo-Aleut languages: PM30+
Eskimo languages: PM50+
Eslene language: PM1137
Esmeraldan language: PM5963
Esperanto (Artificial language):
  PM8201+
Esperanto texts: PM8251+
Essays
  Chinese
    Collections: PL2606+
    Literary history: PL2395+
  Japanese
    Collections: PL772+
    Literary history: PL742+
  Korean
    Collections: PL980.3
    Literary history: PL966.3
Esselenian language: PM1137
Esuulaalu dialect: PL8134.9795.E78

Fore language: PL6621.F6
Forests and forestry in literature
  Chinese
    Literary history: PL2275.F67
Formosan languages: PL6145+
Fortune-telling in literature
  Japanese
    Literary history: PL721.F66
Forty-seven Ronin in literature
  Japanese
    Literary history: PL721.F67
Fox language: PM1195
Foxes in literature
  Japanese
    Literary history: PL721.F69
French Cree language: PM7895.M53
Friendship in literature
  Chinese
    Literary history: PL2275.F73
Frontier and pioneer life in literature
  Chinese
    Literary history: PL2275.F76
Fruit in literature
  Japanese
    Literary history: PL721.F75
Fu
  Chinese poetry
    Collections: PL2519.F8
    Literary history: PL2309.F8
Fuji, Mount (Japan), in literature
  Japanese
    Literary history: PL721.F85
Fujian Sheng (China) in literature
  Chinese
    Literary history: PL2275.F84
Ful language: PL8181+
Fula language: PL8181+
Fulani language: PL8181+
Fulbe language: PL8181+
Fulfulde language: PL8181+
Fuliru language: PL8185+
Fulnio language: PM5973
Fundi dialect: PL8704.Z9F85
Fur language: PL8186+
Furu language: PL8187+
Futuna-Aniwa language: PL6436
Futuna language: PL6435

Fuyuge language: PL6621.F8
Fyam language: PL8189+

G

Gã language: PL8191+
Gab (Artificial language): PM8360.G2
Gabrieleño language: PM1201
Gadabā language (Dravidian): PL4627+
Gadabā language (Munda): PL4573
Gaddang language: PL5671+
Gade language: PL8192+
Gadsup language: PL6621.G3
Gae dialect: PM5974
Gagadu language: PL7101.G34
Gagauz language: PL316+
Gagu language: PL8193+
Gahuku language: PL6621.G33
Galali dialect: PL7101.W34
Galelarese language: PL5323
Gallong language: PL4001.G16+
Galoli language: PL5324+
Gambai dialect: PL8197+
Ganda language: PL8201+
Gangte language: PL4001.G17+
Ganguela language: PL8202+
Gapapaiwa language: PL6243
Garawa language: PL7101.G37
Gardens in literature
  Japanese
    Literary history: PL721.G37
Garhwāl dialect (Tibetan): PL3651.G3
Gārō language: PL4001.G2+
Gata' language: PL4545
Gavião language (Pará, Brazil):
  PM5978
Gayo language: PL5325+
Gbagyi language: PL8203.G35+
Gbandi language (Liberia): PL8204+
Gbaya language: PL8205+
Gbea language: PL8205+
Gbete dialect: PL8508.95.G38
Gê languages: PM7108
Geioguen language: PM1205.G5+
Geman Deng language: PL4001.G35+

Haedong kayo
  Korean poetry
    Collections: PL975.65
Haeeltzuk language: PM1321
Hahuamis dialect: PM1261
Haibun
  Japanese literature
    Collections: PL754.5
Haida language: PM1271+
Haikai
  Japanese poetry
    Collections: PL762.H3
    Literary history: PL732.H3
Haiku
  Chinese
    Collections: PL2519.H3
  Japanese poetry
    Collections: PL759+
    Literary history: PL729+
Hainai language: PM1281
Hainan Island (China) in literature
  Chinese
    Literary history: PL2275.H34
Hainan Sheng (China) in literature
  Chinese
    Literary history: PL2275.H34
Haisla language: PM1282
Haitian language (Indian): PM6156
Haka Chin language: PL4001.H27
Hakka dialects: PL1851+
Halia language: PL6247
Hallām Chin language: PL4001.H3
Hane language: PM1285
Hanga language (Ghana): PL8229+
Hangaza language: PL8230.3+
Hani language: PL4001.H35+
Hankutchin language: PM1291
Hanmunhak (Chinese characters),
  Korean literature written in: PL950+
Hano language: PL6248.H36+
Hare dialect: PM2365.Z9K39
Haroi language: PL4498.H37
Hatam language: PL6621.H37
Hatawekela language: PM1301
Hausa language: PL8231+
Hausa literature: PL8234.A3+
Havasupai language: PM1311

Hawaiian language: PL6441+
Haya language: PL8237+
Hedi language: PL8239+
Hegue language: PM3766
Hei-Miao dialect: PL4072.95.B53
Heiltsuk language: PM1321
Helambu Sherpa language:
  PL3801.H45
Hell in literature
  Japanese
    Literary history: PL721.H4
Henaggi language: PM1325.H3+
Henan Sheng (China) in literature
  Chinese
    Literary history: PL2275.H65
Henya language: PM1325.H4+
Herero language: PL8241+
Herisobocona language: PM3821
Hermits in literature
  Japanese
    Literary history: PL721.E7
Heroes and heroines in literature
  Chinese
    Literary history: PL2275.H47
Heroes in literature
  Korean
    Literary history: PL957.5.H47
Heroines in literature
  Chinese
    Literary history: PL2275.H47
Hesquiat language: PM1325.H5+
Heteronyms
  Chinese: PL1313
Heuchi language: PM1325.H6+
Heve language: PM3766
Hia-Hiu language: PM4146+
Hianakoto-Umáua language: PM6158
Hiaqui language: PM4526
Hidatsa language: PM1331
High school students as authors
  Korean
    Collections: PL973.2.H54
Hiligaynon language: PL5711+
Himalayan languages: PL3781+
Himeji-shi (Japan) in literature
  Japanese
    Literary history: PL721.H45

Himuetaca language: PM6161
Hiri Motu language: PM7895.H5
Hiroshima Bombardment, 1945, in
  literature
  Japanese
    Literary history: PL721.H52
Hiroshima in literature
  Japanese
    Literary history: PL721.H5
Historical plays
  Chinese
    Collections: PL2579.H58
    Literary history: PL2368.H58
History
  Chinese readers: PL1117.5.H57
  Esperanto texts: PM8254+
History and Chinese literature: PL2273
History and Japanese literature: PL720
History and Korean literature: PL957.3
History in literature
  Chinese
    Literary history: PL2275.H57
  Japanese
    Literary history: PL721.H54
  Korean
    Literary history: PL957.5.H57
History of Chinese language: PL1075+
History of Chinese philology: PL1051+
History of Korean language: PL909+
History of Korean literature: PL950.2+
History of literary criticism
  Japanese literature: PL712
  Korean literature: PL952.6
Hitchiti language: PM1341
Hixkaryâna language: PM6163
Hmar language: PL4001.H55+
Hmong Daw dialect: PL4072.95.W45
Hmong language: PL4072+
Hmong Njua dialect: PL4072.95.H56
Hō language (Munda): PL4547+
Hokan-Coahuiltecan languages:
  PM1343
Hokan languages: PM1343
Hokkaido (Japan) in literature
  Japanese
    Literary history: PL721.H57

Hollies in literature
  Japanese
    Literary history: PL721.H575
Holmiuk language: PM1345.H6+
Holoholo language: PL8247+
Holontalo language: PL5327+
Hom-idyomo (Artificial language):
  PM8370
Homagua language: PM6686
Homeland in literature
  Japanese
    Literary history: PL721.H58
Homes and haunts of authors
  Japanese literature: PL724+
  Korean literature: PL957.8
Homonyms
  Chinese: PL1311
  Korean: PL933
Homosexuality in literature
  Japanese
    Literary history: PL721.H59
Honan Province in literature
  Chinese
    Literary history: PL2275.H65
Hong Kong in literature
  Chinese
    Literary history: PL2275.H63
Hoo-pah language: PM1361+
HOOM-DIAL (Artificial language):
  PM8371
Hopi language: PM1351
Horror in literature
  Korean
    Literary history: PL957.5.H67
Hot springs in literature
  Japanese
    Literary history: PL721.H595
Hotels, taverns, etc. in literature
  Japanese
    Literary history: PL721.H6
Hottentot language: PL8251+
Hrê language: PL4439
Hsiang dialects: PL1861+
Hsiang sheng
  Chinese
    Collections: PL2579.H8
    Literary history: PL2368.H75

Icahuate language: PM6181
Ichikawa-shi (Japan) in literature
  Japanese
    Literary history: PL721.I24
Iciba language: PM6186
Ida'an language: PL5333.953+
Idaca language: PL8262+
Idaté language: PL5333.955+
Ide-chō (Japan) in literature
  Japanese
    Literary history: PL721.I3
Identity (Psychology) in literature
  Japanese
    Literary history: PL721.I34
Idiom neutral (Artificial language):
  PM8381+
Idioms
  Chinese: PL1273
  Korean: PL927.6
Ido (Artificial language): PM8391+
Idoma language: PL8263+
Idu language: PL3801.I38+
Idzo language: PL8276+
Ieico language: PM6191
Ifugao language: PL5725+
Ifumu language: PL8271+
Igala language: PL8272.5+
Igbira language: PL8273+
Igbo language: PL8261+
Igede language: PL8274+
Ignaciano language: PM6540
Igneri language: PM6239
Igo language: PL8275+
Igorot languages: PL5731+
Iguaze language: PM1367.I4+
Iha language: PL6621.I35
Ihio language: PM3856
Ijinori dialect: PM6201
Ijo language: PL8276+
Ik language: PL8278.16+
Ikizu language: PL8278.5+
Ikwo language: PL8279+
Ila language: PL8281+
Illinois language: PM1371
Ilocano language: PL5751+
Iloko language: PL5751+
Ilongot language: PL5771

Ilongoto language: PL5771
Iltipo dialect: PM6206
Imare language: PM6211
Imitation in literature
  Japanese
    Literary history: PL721.I42
  Korean
    Literary history: PL957.5.I52
Imperial anthologies
  Japanese poetry
    Collections: PL758.2+
    Waka
      Literary history: PL728.2+
Impermanence (Buddhism) in literature
  Japanese
    Literary history: PL721.I45
Inapari language: PM6213
Incense ceremony, Japanese, in
  literature
  Japanese
    Literary history: PL721.J335
Incran language: PL8191+
Indian languages, American: PM101+
Indian literature, American: PM151+
Individuality in literature
  Korean
    Literary history: PL957.5.I527
Indonesian language: PL5071+
Indonesian languages: PL5051+
Indonesian literature: PL5080+
Industrial revolution in literature
  Korean
    Literary history: PL957.5.I53
Inemaga language: PM6216
Inflection
  Korean: PL919.6
  Malay: PL5113
Ingain language: PM6219
Ingalik language: PM1373
Ingano language: PM6221
Ingassana language: PL8282.I55+
Inland Sea region in literature
  Japanese
    Literary history: PL721.I54
INO (Artificial language): PM8396
Inscriptions
  Chinese literature: PL2447+

Inscriptions
  Japanese literature
    Literary history: PL750+
  Korean literature
    Literary history: PL969.2+
Intellectuals in literature
  Chinese
    Literary history: PL2275.I57
Interglossa (Artificial language):
  PM8398
Interlingua (International Auxiliary
  Language Association): PM8400
Interlingua (Latin without inflections):
  PM8401
International auxiliari linguo (Artificial
  language): PM8409
Intibucat dialect: PM3861
Intonation
  Korean: PL915.8
Inuaco dialect: PM6226
Inuit language: PM50
Inuktitut dialect: PM55
Inupiaq dialect: PM53
Inuvialuktun dialect: PM57
Iowa language: PM1376
Ipapana dialect: PM4301
Ipurina language: PM6229
Iqueconejori dialect: PM6231
Iquita-nanai language: PM6236
Iranxe language: PM6238
Iroquoian languages: PM1381+
Iroquois language: PM1381+
Irritila language: PM3866
Irula language: PL4636+
Iruwaitsu language: PM1386.I7+
Ise-shi (Japan) in literature
  Japanese
    Literary history: PL721.I8
Ishikawa-ken (Japan) in literature
  Japanese
    Literary history: PL721.I82
Isinai dialect: PL5801
Island Carib language: PM6239
Isleta language: PM1387
Isneg language: PL5805
Isotype (Picture language): PM8999
Isubu language: PL8285+

Itaues language: PL5815
Itaves language: PL5815
Itawi language: PL5815
Itene language: PM6240
Itis language: PM6156
Itonama language: PM6241
Itucale (Indian language of South
  America/West Indies): PM6246
Itza (Artificial language): PM8412
Itzá dialect (Mayan): PM3969.5.I89
Iurusme language: PM6251
Ivatan language: PL5571
Iwaidji language: PL7101.I93
Ixcateco language: PM3876
Ixil language: PM3881
Iyaki
  Korean
    Collections
      Prose: PL980.5
    Literary history
      Prose: PL966.5
Izcuco language: PM3886
Izi language: PL8286.I9+
Izu Peninsula (Japan) in literature
  Japanese
    Literary history: PL721.I94

J

Jabim language: PL6251
Jabo language: PL8287+
Jacalteca language: PM3889
Jaḍ dialect: PL3651.J2
Jagan language: PM7266
Jagga language: PL8110.C3+
Jalisciense language: PM3891
Jama Mapun language: PL5821
Jamee language: PL5333.96+
Jaminaua language: PM6253
Janambre language: PM4197
Janggalī language: PL3801.J2+
Jangshēn language: PL4001.T4+
Janos language: PM1388.J3+
Japan in literature
  Japanese
    Literary history: PL721.J3

417

Japan in literature
Korean
Literary history: PL957.5.J34
Japanene invasions of Korea, 1592-1598 in literature
Korean
Literary history: PL957.5.J36
Japanese American authors
Japanese literature
Collections: PL756.J36
Japanese flowering cherry in literature
Japanese
Literary history: PL721.J33
Japanese incense ceremony in literature
Japanese
Literary history: PL721.J335
Japanese language: PL501+
Japanese literature: PL700+
Japanese tea ceremony in literature
Japanese
Literary history: PL721.J34
Jarabe language: PM6256
Jarai language: PL4498.J3
Jarawa language: PL7501.J37
Jaruára language: PM6258
Jaunde language: PL8165.E9+
Javanese language: PL5161+
Javanese literature: PL5170+
Jebero language: PM6261
Jeh language: PL4443
Jehai language: PL4444
Jeli language: PL8293+
Jero language: PL3801.J37+
Jesarusu language: PM6266
Jian'ge Xian (China) in literature
Chinese
Literary history: PL2275.C426
Jiangxi Sheng (China) in literature
Chinese
Literary history: PL2275.K53
Jicaque language: PM3893
Jicarilla language: PM1389
Jimdār language: PL3801.J5+
Jinan (Shandong Sheng, China) in literature
Chinese
Literary history: PL2275.T74

Jinca language: PL4498.X3, PM4498.X3+
Jingpo language: PL4001.K32+
Jintian cun (China) in literature
Chinese
Literary history: PL2275.C44
Jirara language: PM7296
Jirel language: PL3801.J55+
Jita language: PL8295+
Jivaran languages: PM6273
Joba language (Mexico): PM3896
Joloano language: PL6041+
Jonaz language: PM3993
Jope language: PM3906
Jōruri
Japanese drama
Collections: PL768.J6
Literary history: PL738.J6
Joval language: PM3896
Ju qu
Chinese literature
Collections: PL2564.6
Literary history: PL2354.6
Juāṅg language: PL4575
Jue ju
Chinese poetry
Collections: PL2519.C47
Literary history: PL2309.C48
Juiadge language: PM6275.J8+
Jukun language: PL8301+
Jukunoid languages: PL8302
Julime language: PM3911
Jumano language: PM1390.J8+
Jupda language: PM6275.J92+
Jurchen language: PL481.J8+
Juvenile drama
Japanese
Collections: PL768.A35
Literary history: PL738.A44
Korean
Collections: PL978.5.A4
Juvenile literature
Chinese
Literary history: PL2449
Japanese
Literary history: PL751.5

INDEX

Laamang language: PL8430.L32+
Labor in literature
  Japanese
    Literary history: PL722.L32
Laboring class authors
  Chinese
    Collections: PL2515.5.L33
    Literary history: PL2278.5.L33
  Japanese literature
    Collections: PL756.L33
      Poetry: PL757.4.W67
    Literary history: PL725.2.W65
  Korean
    Collections: PL973.2.L33
Lacandon dialect: PM3916
Lacheyel language: PM6333
Ladakhī language: PL3651.L3+
Lagoon languages: PL8430.L33
Laguna dialect: PM1645
Laha language (Vietnam): PL4251.L27
Lahcotah language: PM1021+
Lahu language (Asia): PL4001.L18+
Lahuli language: PL3651.L43+
Lai language (Chin): PL4001.L2
Lakes in literature
  Japanese
    Literary history: PL721.L34
Lakher language: PL4001.L28
Lala language: PL8430.L35+
Lālung language: PL4001.L3
Lamandau language: PL5340+
Lamano dialect: PM6336
Lamba language (Zambia and Congo):
  PL8431+
Lāmbichhōng language: PL3801.L2+
Lamé language (Cameroon): PL8433+
Lamisso dialect: PM6336
Lamista language: PM6341
Lampung language: PL5341+
Lanao-Moro dialect: PL5884
Lango language (Uganda): PL8437+
Language
  Esperanto texts: PM8284
Language acquisition
  Chinese: PL1074.85
  Korean: PL908.8, PL908.86

Language data processing
  Chinese: PL1074.5
  Korean: PL908.5
Language standardization and variation
  Chinese: PL1074.7
  Korean: PL908.8
Langue blue (Artificial language):
  PM8101+
Langue internationale naturelle (Artificial
  language): PM8128
Langue internationale néo-latine
  (Artificial language): PM8457
Lao language: PL4236+
Lao literature: PL4236.9.A+
Laqua language: PL4454.5
Larike-Wakasihu language: PL5342
Lashi language: PL4001.L4+
Latuka language: PL8441+
Lau language: PL6253.L38+
Laughter in literature
  Japanese
    Literary history: PL721.L39
Laven language: PL4454.7
Lavongai language: PL6253.L42+
Lavukaleve language: PL6621.L38
Law
  Chinese readers: PL1117.5.L38
  Esperanto texts: PM8280
Law in literature
  Chinese
    Literary history: PL2275.L38
  Japanese
    Literary history: PL721.L42
Lawa language (Thailand): PL4455
Lawangan language: PL5342.9
Lecan language: PM6348
Lefana language: PL8447+
Lega language: PL8380.K5+
Legal novels
  Chinese
    Literary history: PL2275.L38
Lele language (Chad): PL8453.15+
Lematang language: PL5342.93
Lembak Bilide dialects: PL5128.L4
Lenape language: PM1031+
Lenca language: PM3921
Lendu language: PL8453.18+

Lengua catolica (Artificial language): PM8501

Lengua dialect: PM6351

Lengua-Mascoi dialect: PM6351

Lengua universal (L. Selbor) (Artificial language): PM8504

Lenje language: PL8453.2+

Leno gi-nasu (Artificial language): PM8507

Lepcha language: PL3801.L4+

Lepers as authors
  Japanese literature
    Collections: PL756.L46

Lepers in literature
  Japanese
    Literary history: PL722.L46

Lesbians in literature
  Japanese
    Literary history: PL722.L47

Letter writing
  Chinese: PL1275

Letters
  Chinese
    Collections: PL2610
    Literary history: PL2400
    Chinese readers: PL1117.5.L48
  Japanese
    Collections: PL773+
    Literary history: PL743+
  Korean
    Collections: PL980.4
    Literary history: PL966.4

Leuangiua language: PL6459

Lexicography
  Chinese: PL1401+
  Korean: PL934+

Lexicology
  Chinese: PL1280

Lhasa dialect (Tibetan): PL3651.L45+

Lhomi language: PL3801.L54+

Lhōtā language: PL4001.L5

Li language (Tai): PL4251.L5

Liangmai Naga language: PL4001.L73+

Libertines in literature
  Japanese
    Literary history: PL722.L52

Life in literature
  Japanese
    Literary history: PL721.L52

Ligbi language: PL8453.8+

Lilima dialect: PL8348.595.L55

Lillovet language: PM1646.L7+

Lilowat language: PM1646.L7+

Limba language: PL8455

Limbu language: PL3801.L57+

Limbum language: PL8455.7+

Limilngan language: PL7101.L54

Lincos (Artificial language): PM8508

Ling (Artificial language): PM8509

Lingala language: PL8456+

Lingu franca nuova (Artificial language): PM8521

Lingu nov (Artificial language): PM8511

Lingua geral (Indian language): PM7171+

Lingua internazional (Artificial language): PM8531

Lingua italiana infinitiva (Artificial language): PM8535

Lingua lumina (Artificial language): PM8541

Lingua moderna (Artificial language): PM8551

Lingua philosophica (Artificial language): PM8563

Lingua universal (of Sotos Ochando) (Artificial language): PM8572

Lingvo internacia of Zamenhof (Artificial language): PM8201+

Lingvo internationa (Artificial language): PM8576+

Lintang dialect: PL5128.L54

Lipan language: PM1647

Lisu language: PL4001.L6+

Literary criticism, History of
  Japanese literature: PL712
  Korean literature: PL952.6

Literary landmarks
  Japanese literature: PL724+
  Korean literature: PL957.8

Literary relations of women
  Japanese literature: PL725
  Korean literature: PL957.9

Literary research
  Japanese literature: PL711.5
Literature
  Esperanto texts: PM8284.5+
Liyang language: PL4001.L73+
Llamaholot language: PL5339.98+
Lluru language: PM6356
Lo-yang shih (China) in literature
  Chinese
    Literary history: PL2275.L63
Logbara language: PL8458+
Loglan (Artificial language): PM8590
Logo language: PL8459.L26+
Logooli language: PL8459.L3+
Lōhorōng language: PL3801.L7+
Lolak language: PL5342.98
Loloish languages: PL3916+
Loma language: PL8459.L52+
Lomwe language (Malawi):
  PL8459.L534+
Loneliness in literature
  Chinese
    Literary history: PL2275.L65
  Japanese
    Literary history: PL721.L57
Longmen Caves in literature
  Chinese
    Literary history: PL2275.L85
Longuda language: PL8459.L55+
Loniu language: PL6253.L65+
Lonkengo language: PL8459.L63+
Lopa language (Nepal): PL3651.L65
Losengo language: PL8459.L66+
Love in literature
  Chinese
    Literary history: PL2275.L68
  Japanese
    Literary history: PL721.L6
  Korean
    Literary history: PL957.5.L68
Love poetry
  Chinese
    Collections: PL2519.L6
    Literary history: PL2309.L68
Lower Umpqua language: PM1598
Lozi language: PL8460+
Lu-ganda language: PL8201+

Lü language: PL4251.L8
Lu Mountains (China) in literature
  Chinese
    Literary history: PL2275.L83
Lü shi
  Chinese poetry
    Collections: PL2519.L83
    Literary history: PL2309.L83
Luba language: PL8461+
Lucazi language: PL8462+
Lucumbia language: PM6361
Luiseño language: PM1651
Lulé language: PM6366
Lule-Tonocoté language: PM6366
Lummi language: PM1656
Lunda language: PL8465+
Lundayeh language: PL5345+
Lung-men Caves in literature
  Chinese
    Literary history: PL2275.L85
Lungming language: PL4251.L85
Luo language (Kenya and Tanzania):
  PL8375+
Luoyang Shi (China) in literature
  Chinese
    Literary history: PL2275.L63
Lupaca dialect: PM6371
Luragoli language: PL8459.L3+
Lushai language: PL4001.L8+
Lusi language: PL6253.L85+
Lutau language: PL5895
Lutuamian languages: PM1661
Luvale language: PL8473+
Luyana language: PL8474.L78+
Luyia language: PL8474.L8+
Lyele language: PL8474.L92+
Lyric poetry
  Chinese
    Collections: PL2519.L93

M

Ma language (Africa): PL8474.M3+
Maanyan language: PL5347+
Maba language: PL8475+
Maban language: PL8477+
Maca language: PM6373

Masbateno language: PL5958+
Masenrempulu language: PL5408+
Mashco language: PM6464.M3+
Mashona language: PL8681+
Massachuset language: PM1736+
Master language (Artificial language):
  PM8612
Mataco languages: PM6466
Matagalpa language: PM3948
Mataguaya language: PM6471
Mathematics
  Esperanto texts: PM8286
Matlaltzinca language: PM4193
Matlame language: PM3951
Matlazahua language: PM3981
Matsukawa Railroad Accident, 1949, in
  literature
  Japanese
    Literary history: PL721.M38
Mattole language: PM1745.M3+
Matumbi language: PL8502.M38+
Maue language: PM6473
Maung language: PL7101.M3
Maxi dialect: PL8164.Z9M38
Ma'ya language (Indonesia): PL5410
Mayan languages: PM3961+
Mayapic languages: PL7101.M37
Mayna language: PM6476
Mayo dialect (Piman): PM3972
Mayogo language: PL8502.M42+
Mayoruna language: PM6479
Mazahua language: PM3981
Mazahui language: PM3981
Mazapili dialect: PM3986
Mazateco language: PM3991
Mbai language: PL8648+
Mbala language (Bandundu, Congo):
  PL8503.3+
Mbaya language: PM6485
Mbili language: PL8503.7+
Mbinsa language: PL8504+
Mbo language (Cameroon):
  PL8506.M36+
Mbuko language: PL8506.M38+
Mbukushu language: PL8507+
Mbum language: PL8508+

Mbunda language (Angola and Zambia):
  PL8509.M28+
Mbundu language (Luanda Provice,
  Angola): PL8381+
Mbya-Guarani language: PM6487
Mbya language: PM6487
Mdewakanton language: PM1751
Mech language: PL4001.B3+
Meco language (Mexico): PM3993
Medicine
  Chinese readers: PL1117.5.M43
  Esperanto texts: PM8288
Medicine in literature
  Japanese
    Literary history: PL721.M42
Mediotaguel language: PM3996
Medumba language: PL8510.M42+
Meepure dialect: PM6491
Megi language: PL8625+
Meithei language: PL4001.M31+
Mekongga language: PL5410.5
Melancholy in literature
  Japanese
    Literary history: PL721.M45
Melanesian languages: PL6191+
Mele-Fila language: PL6475
Melodrama in literature
  Japanese
    Literary history: PL721.M46
Memba language: PL4001.M37+
Memory in literature
  Korean
    Literary history: PL957.5.M46
Men authors
  Japanese literature
    Literary history: PL725.2.M45
Mende language (Africa): PL8511+
Mende language (Papua New Guinea):
  PL6621.M4
Menhari language: PM6496
Menominee language: PM1761
Mentawai language: PL5411+
Meque dialect: PM6501
Meratus dialect: PL5128.M47
Merchants in literature
  Chinese
    Literary history: PL2275.M49

Musical instruments in literature
  Chinese
    Literary history: PL2275.M87
Musicians in literature
  Chinese
    Literary history: PL2275.M87
Musima language: PM6631
Muskhogean languages: PM1971+
Muskogee language: PM991
Muslim authors
  Chinese
    Literary history: PL2278.5.M68
Muslim Kalagan language: PL5831+
Mutsun dialect: PM1976+
Muyska language: PM5811
Muyuw language: PL6258
Mwaghavul language: PL8536+
Mwamba language: PL8538+
Mwenyi language: PL8538.97+
Mwera language: PL8539+
Myrana (Artificial language): PM8643
Mystery stories
  Chinese
    Literary history: PL2275.D48
  Japanese
    Literary history: PL721.D45
  Korean
    Literary history: PL957.5.D48
Mysticism in literature
  Korean
    Literary history: PL957.5.M95
Mythology in literature
  Chinese
    Literary history: PL2275.M94
  Japanese
    Literary history: PL721.M85
  Korean
    Literary history: PL957.5.M98

N

Na-Dene languages: PM1980
Nāchherēng language: PL3801.N3+
Nachitoches language: PM1981
Nafaanra language: PL8540.4+
Naga Chothe language: PL4001.N24+
Nāgā languages: PL3881+

Naga Pidgin (Mixed language): PM7895.N3
Nagano-ken (Japan) in literature
  Japanese
    Literary history: PL721.N24
Nagasaki Bombardment, 1945, in literature
  Japanese
    Literary history: PL721.N248
Nagasaki-ken (Japan) in literature
  Japanese
    Literary history: PL721.N25
Nagauta (Texts)
  Japanese poetry
    Collections: PL762.N34
Nagrandan dialect: PM4051
Nahali language: PL4585+
Nahaunies language: PM1991
Nahuapo dialect: PM6641
Nahuatl language: PM4061+
Nahuatl literature: PM4068.9.A+
Nahuatl-Spanish dialect: PM4070
Nahuatlan languages: PM4060+
Nakanai language: PL6262
Nakara language: PL7101.N25
Nal bino (Artificial language): PM8651
Nalik language: PL6264
Nam language: PL3801.N4+
Nama language (Africa): PL8541+
Naman language (Vanuatu): PL6265
Nambicuara language: PM6643
Namia language: PL6621.N34
Nanai language: PL481.N34+
Nancowry language: PL4471.5
Nande language: PL8544+
Nandi language: PL8545+
Nandi languages: PL8545.97
Nanerua dialect: PM6646
Naniwabushi
  Japanese drama
    Literary history: PL738.N35
Nanjing (Jiansu Sheng, China) in literature
  Chinese
    Literary history: PL2275.N27
Nankina language: PL6621.N345
Nanticoke language: PM2001

Napeano dialect: PM6651
Napo language: PM6656
Napotoa language: PM6656
Napu language: PL5429+
Nara-ken (Japan) in literature
  Japanese
    Literary history: PL721.N27
Nara-shi (Japan) in literature
  Japanese
    Literary history: PL721.N27
Narak language: PL6621.N35
Narangga language: PL7101.N27
Narraganset language: PM2003
Narrative poetry
  Chinese
    Collections: PL2519.N47
    Literary history: PL2309.N47
  Korean
    Collections: PL975.46
    Literary history: PL960.46
Narrinyeri language: PL7101.N3
Naruto Strait (Japan) in literature
  Japanese
    Literary history: PL721.N28
Nascape language: PM2004.N3+
Nasgá language: PM2026.N3+
Nasioi language: PL6621.N36
Natchez language: PM2004.N4+
Nateni language: PL8547.N21+
Natick language: PM1736+
National characteristics in literature
  Japanese
    Literary history: PL721.N287
Nationalism in literature
  Korean
    Literary history: PL957.5.N38
Natural history
  Esperanto texts: PM8287
Naturalism in literature
  Japanese
    Literary history: PL721.N29
  Korean
    Literary history: PL957.5.N39
Nature in literature
  Chinese
    Literary history: PL2275.N3

Nature in literature
  Japanese
    Literary history: PL721.N3
  Korean
    Literary history: PL957.5.N4
Nauon dialect: PM6661
Navaho language: PM2006+
Naval science
  Esperanto texts: PM8296
Nawdm language: PL8547.N22+
Naxi language: PL4001.N35+
Nayarita language: PM3711+
Nchumburu language: PL8547.N25+
Ndali language: PL8547.N26+
Ndebele language (South Africa):
  PL8547.N27+
Ndebele language (Zimbabwe):
  PL8547.N28+
Ndogo-Sere languages: PL8547.N3
Ndonga language: PL8547.N4+
Ndu languages (Papuan): PL6621.N4
Ndumu language: PL8547.N5+
Negatives
  Korean: PL921.56
Negidal language: PL481.N45+
Nehaumis language: PM1991
Nek language: PL6621.N45
Neklakapamuk language: PM2045
Nembe language: PL8548
Nemi language: PL6267
Nenema language: PL6252.K78+
Nengone language: PL6268
Nenusa-Miangas dialect: PL5431
Neo (Artificial language): PM8670
Neo-Confucianism in literature
  Korean
    Literary history: PL957.5.N46
Neocoyo dialect: PM6666
Neoispano (Artificial language):
  PM8673
Neolatinus (Artificial language):
  PM8675
Nesahuaco language: PM6671
Nese language: PL6269
Netele language: PM2015
Netizcho language: PM4081

Northern Min dialects: PL1681+
Northern Paiute language: PM2094
Northern Pomo language: PM2043
Northern Sotho language: PL8690+
Northern Thai language: PL4251.N63+
Northwestern Turkic languages: PL61+
Nostalgia in literature
  Chinese
    Literary history: PL2275.N67
  Korean
    Literary history: PL957.5.N67
Noun
  Chinese: PL1232
  Korean: PL921.4
Nov Latin (Artificial language): PM8682
Novial (Artificial language): PM8685
Novolingua (Artificial language):
  PM8688
Nozi language: PM2641
Nsenga language: PL8656+
Ntlakyapamuk language: PM2045
Ntomba language: PL8568+
Nubi language: PM7895.N83
Nubian languages: PL8571+
Nuchistlan language: PM4101
Nuclear weapons in literature
  Japanese
    Literary history: PL721.A75
Nuer language: PL8576.N4+
Nufor language: PL6279
Nukahiva language: PL6471
Nukunu language: PL7101.N75
Nukuoro language: PL6485
Nula (Artificial language): PM8693
Numee language: PL6252.K35+
Numerals
  Chinese grammar: PL1238
Numipu language: PM2019
Nung language: PL4001.N8
Nunggubuyu language: PL7101.N8
Nunuma dialect: PL8576.N57+
Nupe language: PL8577+
Nutka language: PM2031
Nyabwa language: PL8579+
Nyah Kur language: PL4460
Nyai language: PL8727+
Nyalayu language: PL6280.N93+

Nyam-Nyam language: PL8828+
Nyambo language: PL8587+
Nyamkat dialect: PL3651.N8
Nyamwezi language: PL8591+
Nyandja language: PL8593+
Nyaneka language: PL8592.N3+
Nyanga language (Africa):
  PL8592.N43+
Nyangumata language: PL7101.N9
Nyanja language: PL8593+
Nyankole language: PL8594.N3+
Nyankore-Kiga language: PL8594.N45+
Nyoro language: PL8595+
Nyoro-Tooro language: PL8596.N9+
Nyunga dialects: PL7101.N97
Nyungwe language: PL8727+
Nzebi language: PL8596.N996+
Nzima language: PL8597+

O

O-mei Mountain (China) in literature
  Chinese
    Literary history: PL2275.O43
Oa language: PM6681
Obolo language: PL8598.O27+
Ocaina language: PM6682
Occidental (Artificial language):
  PM8702
Occupations in literature
  Japanese
    Literary history: PL721.O35
Oceania, Languages of: PL5001+
Oceanic languages: PL6171+
Ochwe'snicki jargon: PM7895.O3
Ocorona language: PM6683
Ocoroni language: PM4106
Ocotlan language: PM4111
Ocuiltec language: PM4116
Odors in literature
  Japanese
    Literary history: PL721.O37
Odual language (Nigeria):
  PL8598.O29+
Oedipus complex in literature
  Korean
    Literary history: PL957.5.O43

P

Paama language: PL6280.P32+
Pabo dialect: PM6721
Pacaguara language: PM7073
Pacao language (Texas): PM2097
Pacasa dialect: PM6726
Pacayu language: PM6731
Pachalaque language: PM2091.P3+
Pachera language: PM4151
Pacific Gulf Yupik language: PM92
Pacoh language: PL4462
Padam language: PL4001.P23
Paduba language: PM2091.P5+
Paduko language: PL8599.P28+
Paektu Mountain (Korea) in literature
  Korean
    Literary history: PL957.5.P33
Paes language: PM6736
Páez language: PM6736
Pahri dialect: PL3801.P34+
Pai language (China): PL4001.B16
Pai-shan shui tien chan (Hua-tien hsien,
  China) in literature
  Chinese
    Literary history: PL2275.P34
Paici language: PL6280.P35+
Paicone language: PM6741
Paipai language: PM4157
Paite language: PL4001.P28+
Paiute language: PM2094
Paiwan language: PL6157+
Pakaasnovos language: PM6743
Pakawa language (Texas): PM2097
Pakawan languages: PM4158
Paku language: PL5128.P35
Pala language: PL6281
Palaihnihan languages: PM2101
Palauan language: PL5434
Palaung language: PL4463
Palawanic languages: PL5985
Palawano language: PL5987+
Palenke language: PM6746
Paleosiberian languages: PM10+
Pame language: PM4161
Pamona language: PL5434.3+

Pampa del Sacramento language
  (Peru): PM5716
Pampa language: PM6751
Pampanga language: PL5991+
Pampanga literature: PL5994.A3+
Pamptikokes language: PM2111
Panajori dialect: PM6761
Panamane (Artificial language):
  PM8709
Panamint language: PM2115
Panare language: PM6763
Panayan language: PL5711+
Pandatoco dialect: PM6766
Pandaveque language: PM6771
Pangasinan language: PL6015
Pangwa language: PL8599.P33+
Paniquita language: PM6772.P3+
Panistock language: PM2121
Pānkhū language: PL4001.P3
Panoan languages: PM6773
Panteca language: PM4166
Pao-an language: PL431.B64+
Papabicotam dialect: PM2123
Papabuco language: PM4171
Papago dialect: PM2123
Papagol dialect: PM2123
Papaya language: PM6776
Paper in literature
  Japanese
    Literary history: PL721.P36
Papiamento (Mixed language):
  PM7895.P3+
Papinacho language: PM2125.P3+
Papuan languages: PL6601+
Parabá language: PM6781
Paracati language: PM6786
Paragoto dialect: PM6791
Paranapuro dialect: PM6796
Paratoa language: PM6801
Paraviane language: PM6806
Pareko dialect: PM6811
Parene dialect: PM6816
Parengi language: PL4586
Parentintim language: PM6818
Paresi language: PM6831
Päri language (Sudan): PL8599.P35+
Paria dialect: PM6821

Pariacota dialect: PM6826
Parisi language: PM6831
Parji language: PL4741+
Parodies
  Japanese poetry
    Collections: PL762.P3
Paronyms
  Chinese: PL1303
  Korean: PL933
Parra dialect: PM4181
Particle
  Korean: PL921.8
Particles
  Chinese grammar: PL1237
Parts of speech
  Chinese: PL1231.5+
  Korean: PL921+
Pascagoulas language: PM2125.P5+
Pasilingua (Artificial language):
  PM8712
Pasilogia (Artificial language): PM8732
Pasir dialect (Malay): PL5128.P368
Passa language: PM6836
Passamaquoddy language: PM2135
Pasto language: PM6838
Pastoral literature
  Chinese
    Literary history: PL2275.P36
Pastorals
  Chinese poetry
    Collections: PL2519.P37
    Literary history: PL2309.P37
Patacha language: PM6841
Patagonian language: PM7183
Patep language: PL6285
Pativa language: PM6851
Patnī language: PL3801.M2+
Patriotic poetry
  Chinese
    Collections: PL2519.P39
    Literary history: PL2309.P39
Patriotism in literature
  Chinese
    Literary history: PL2275.P37
  Japanese
    Literary history: PL721.P37

Patriotism in literature
  Korean
    Literary history: PL957.5.P37
Patronage and patrons in literature
  Japanese
    Literary history: PL721.P38
Pattani dialect (Malay): PL5128.P39
Pauná language: PM6856
Pauserna language: PM6859
Pawnee language: PM2137
Paya language: PM4183
Payagua language: PM6861
Payayace language: PM6866
Payure dialect: PM6871
Pazeh language: PL6158.5+
Peace in literature
  Japanese
    Literary history: PL721.P4
Pear language: PL4464
Peasantry in literature
  Japanese
    Literary history: PL722.P4
Peasants in literature
  Chinese
    Literary history: PL2275.P39
  Japanese
    Literary history: PL722.P4
  Korean
    Literary history: PL957.5.P42
Peaux-de-Lièvre dialect:
  PM2365.Z9K39
Peban language: PM6873
Pecuri language: PM2141
Peguan language: PL4331+
Pehuenche dialect: PM6876
Peking (China) in literature
  Chinese
    Literary history: PL2275.P42
Pelado language: PM6881
Pemón dialects: PM6885
Pencils in literature
  Japanese
    Literary history: PL721.P47
Pendau language: PL5434.34+
Penglai ge (China) in literature
  Chinese
    Literary history: PL2275.P43

Plants in literature
  Japanese
    Literary history: PL721.P5
Plateau languages (Benue-Congo): PL8600.P55
Plums in literature
  Chinese
    Literary history: PL2275.P55
Pochury language: PL4001.P63+
Pocoman language: PM4201
Poetry
  African
    Literary history: PL8010.4
  Chinese
    Collections: PL2517+
    Literary history: PL2306+
  Japanese
    Collections: PL757+
    Literary history: PL727+
  Korean
    Collections: PL974+
    Literary history: PL959+
Pogoro language: PL8601+
Pohnpeian language: PL6295
Pokomo language: PL8603+
Pokonchi language: PM4201
Police in literature
  Chinese
    Literary history: PL2275.P64
Police Motu language: PM7895.H5
Polindara language: PM6926
Political science
  Esperanto texts: PM8279
Politics in literature
  Korean
    Literary history: PL957.5.P64
Polygraphy
  Esperanto texts: PM8251
Polynesian languages: PL6401+
Pomo language, Northern: PM2043
Pomo languages: PM1601
Ponape language: PL6295
Ponca language: PM2181
Pōnnā language: PL4001.M31+
Ponosakan language: PL5434.45+
Popolaca language: PM4206
Popoloca language: PM4206

Popoluca language (Vera Cruz): PM4207
Popul vuh: PM4231.Z6
Port Sandwich language: PL6296.P66+
Portuguese-Tupi language: PM7171+
Postcolonialism in literature
  Korean
    Literary history: PL957.5.P65
Potawatomi language: PM2191
Potentu language: PM6931
Potiguare language: PM7170
Powhatan language: PM2194
Poya language (South America): PM6936
Prisoners as authors
  Chinese
    Collections: PL2515.5.P65
  Japanese literature
    Collections: PL756.P7
      Poetry: PL757.4.P74
Prizes
  Japanese literature: PL722.5+
  Korean literature: PL957.64+
Proletariat in literature
  Korean
    Literary history: PL957.5.P76
Pronoun
  Chinese: PL1234
  Korean: PL921.6
Pronunciation
  Chinese: PL1209
  Korean: PL915.4
Prophecies in literature
  Japanese
    Literary history: PL721.P72
Prose
  African
    Literary history: PL8010.6
  Japanese
    Collections: PL770+
    Literary history: PL740+
  Korean
    Collections: PL980+
    Literary history: PL965+
Prose poetry
  Chinese
    Collections: PL2519.P76

Reportage literature
  Korean
    Collections: PL980.45
Research, Literary
  Japanese literature: PL711.5
Resigero language: PM7003
Revenge in literature
  Chinese
    Literary history: PL2275.R48
  Japanese
    Literary history: PL721.R48
Revolutionary poetry
  Chinese
    Collections: PL2519.R48
    Literary history: PL2309.R48
Rhetoric
  Chinese: PL1271+
  Korean: PL927+
Rhythmics
  Chinese language: PL1279
  Korean language: PL929
Riang language (Mon-Khmer): PL4466
Rice wines in literature
  Japanese
    Literary history: PL721.R53
Rikbaktsa language: PM7004
Ritharrngu language: PL7101.R58
Ritual in literature
  Japanese
    Literary history: PL721.R56
Rivers in literature
  Chinese
    Literary history: PL2275.R58
  Japanese
    Literary history: PL721.R57
Ro (Artificial language): PM8751
Roads in literature
  Japanese
    Literary history: PL721.R62
Roamaino dialect: PM7006
Roanoak language: PM2227
Robbers in literature
  Korean
    Literary history: PL957.5.B74
Rocotona language: PM7009
Rōdōng language: PL3801.R6+
Roglai language: PL4498.R63+

Roh, Moo Hyun, 1946-2009, in literature
  Korean
    Literary history: PL957.5.R64
Roma language: PL5434.7+
Romanal (Artificial language): PM8753
Romance
  Japanese
    Collections
      Prose: PL774
    Literary history
      Prose: PL744
  Korean
    Collections
      Prose: PL980.5
    Literary history
      Prose: PL966.5
Románica (Artificial language):
  PM8753.5
Romanid (Artificial language): PM8754
Romanticism in literature
  Japanese
    Literary history: PL721.R64
Ron language: PL8607.R6+
Rong language: PL3801.L4+
Ronga language: PL8607.R73+
Rosaecrucian (Artificial language):
  PM8755
Rottinese language: PL5435
Rotuman language: PL6297
Roviana language: PL6298
Ruanababo dialect: PM7016
Ruanda language: PL8608+
Ruc language: PL4466.5
Rucouyenne language: PM6714
Rukai languages: PL6159+
Rundi language: PL8611+
Runga language: PL8613+
Rūngchhēnbūng dialect: PL3801.R8+
Rungus language: PL5435.36+
Ruri language: PL8615+
Russo-Japanese War, 1904-1905, in
  literature
  Japanese
    Literary history: PL721.R87
Ruund language: PL8618+

S

Saa language: PL6301
Saanich dialect: PM2235
Sabaibo language: PM4241
Sabanero language: PM4246
Sabaot language: PL8621+
Sabela language: PM7141
Saberi language: PL6621.S22
Sabuja language: PM7021
Sacacá language: PM7026
Sacapulteco language: PM4248
Saddharmapuṇḍarīka in literature
  Japanese
    Literary history: PL721.S23
Sado Island (Japan) in literature
  Japanese
    Literary history: PL721.S25
Saek language: PL4251.S23
Safaliba language: PL8624+
Sagara language: PL8625+
Sahaptin language: PM2243
Sahu language: PL6621.S24
Sailors as authors
  Japanese literature
    Collections
      Poetry: PL757.4.S24
Saiō in literature
  Japanese
    Literary history: PL721.S26
Sairang language: PL4001.S3
Sakalava dialect: PL5379.5.S25
Sakata language: PL8627+
Sakau language: PL6303
Saki language (America): PM2245
Salar language: PL54.4+
Salinan language: PM2251
Salish language: PM2261+
Salishan languages: PM2261+
Saliva language: PM7031
Salmano dialect: PM7036
Saluan language: PL5435.5+
Salvador (Artificial language): PM8777
Sama languages: PL6018
Sama Sibutu language: PL6019+
Samagota dialect: PM7038
Sambal language: PL6024.5+

Samburu language: PL8629+
Samo language (Western Province,
  Papua New Guinea): PL6621.S25
Samoan language: PL6501+
San qu
  Chinese literature
    Collections: PL2564.4
    Literary history: PL2354.4
Sanavironan language: PM7043
Sandawe language: PL8631+
Sangen language: PL5436+
Sangil language: PL5437+
Sangir language: PL5438+
Sango language (Ubangi Creole):
  PL8641+
Sāngpāng language: PL3801.S3+
Sangtam language: PL4001.S34+
Sangu language (Gabon): PL8642+
Santali language: PL4563+
Santee dialect: PM1021+
San'yō Region (Japan) in literature
  Japanese
    Literary history: PL721.S27
Sapibocono language: PM7046
Sapuan language: PL4466.7
Sara language: PL8644+
Sara languages: PL8645
Sara mbai language: PL8648+
Saramaccan language: PM7875.S27
Sarangani Manobo language: PL6029
Sarcee language: PM2275
Sarsi language: PM2275
Sarura language: PM7296
Sasak language: PL5439.13+
Sasŏl sijo
  Korean poetry
    Collections: PL975.5
    Literary history: PL960.5
Satawalese language: PL6303.5
Satire
  Chinese
    Collections: PL2613
  Japanese
    Collections
      Prose: PL776+
    Literary history
      Prose: PL746+

Satire
  Korean
    Collections
      Prose: PL980.7
    Literary history: PL957.5.W5
      Prose: PL966.7
Saukiyā Khun language: PL3801.R3+
Savaneric language: PM4246
Savara language: PL4587+
Savo language (Solomon Islands):
  PL6621.S3
Science
  Esperanto texts: PM8286
Science fiction
  Chinese
    Literary history: PL2275.S34
  Japanese
    Literary history: PL721.S3
  Korean
    Literary history: PL957.5.S35
Science in literature
  Japanese
    Literary history: PL721.S3
  Korean
    Literary history: PL957.5.S35
Script
  Chinese grammar: PL1171+
  Korean: PL910.5
Sea in literature
  Japanese
    Literary history: PL721.S38
  Korean
    Literary history: PL957.5.S42
Sea Islands Creole dialect: PM7875.G8
Seasons in literature
  Chinese
    Literary history: PL2275.S39
  Japanese
    Literary history: PL721.S4
Sechelt language: PM2280
Sechuana language: PL8747+
Secoffee language: PM2004.N3+
Secoya language: PM7049
Secret languages: PM9001+
Sedang language: PL4467
Sedik language: PL6161+
Seimat language: PL6304

Sekani language: PM2285
Sekkyōbushi
  Japanese drama
    Collections: PL768.J6
    Literary history: PL738.J6
Selepet language: PL6621.S4
Self in literature
  Chinese
    Literary history: PL2275.S44
  Japanese
    Literary history: PL721.S45
Self-instructors
  Korean language: PL913.4
Self-knowledge in literature
  Chinese
    Literary history: PL2275.S44
  Japanese
    Literary history: PL721.S45
Self-perception in literature
  Chinese
    Literary history: PL2275.S44
  Japanese
    Literary history: PL721.S45
Semā language: PL4001.S52+
Semai language: PL4467.5
Semantics
  Chinese: PL1291
  Korean: PL932
Sembla language: PL8653+
Semelai language: PL4467.6
Semendo dialect: PL5128.S46
Semigae dialect: PM7051
Semimaru, 10th cent.? in literature
  Japanese
    Literary history: PL721.S46
Seminole language: PM2291
Sena language: PL8655+
Seneca language: PM2296
Senga language: PL8656+
Senoic languages: PL4310.S45
Senryū
  Japanese poetry
    Collections: PL760
    Literary history: PL730
Sentani language: PL6621.S44
Senufo language: PL8658+

INDEX

Siamese literature: PL4200+
Siane language: PL6621.S5
Siar-Lak language: PL6304.5
Siberian Turkic languages: PL41+
Siberian Yupik language: PM94
Sibo language: PL481.S3+
Sibondoy language: PM5718.C3+
Sicaunies language: PM2285
Sichuan Sheng (China) in literature
  Chinese
    Literary history: PL2275.S95
Sick in literature
  Japanese
    Literary history: PL721.S542
Sicuane dialect: PM7063
Sijo
  Korean poetry
    Collections: PL975.6
    Literary history: PL960.6
Sikka language: PL5439.19+
Siksika language: PM2341+
Siladang dialect: PL5128.S55
Simelungun dialect: PL5439.2+
Simeulue language: PL5439.3+
Simigaecurari language: PM7066
Similatón dialect: PM4261
Simirenchi language: PM5818
Simte language: PL4001.S56+
Sin in literature
  Japanese
    Literary history: PL721.S547
Sinagoro language: PL6305,
  PL6621.S53
Sinaloense dialect: PM4266
Sindarin (Artificial language): PM8780
Singacuchuska language: PM7071
Singapore literature: PL3515+
Sino-Japanese War, 1937-1945, in
  literature
  Japanese
    Literary history: PL721.S55
Sino-Tibetan languages: PL3521+
Siona language: PM7072
Siouan languages: PM2351
Sipacapense language: PM4267
Sipibo language: PM7073
Sira language: PL8675+

Siriaño language: PM7074
Sirinek language: PM96
Siroi language: PL6621.S55
Sissala language: PL8682.S55+
Sissano language: PL6308
Situga dialect: PM7076
Situsa dialect: PM7076
Siuslaw language: PM2357
Siwai language: PL6621.S59
Siyin language: PL4001.S6
Skidegate language: PM1271+
Skittagetan language: PM1271+
Skwamish language (British Columbia):
  PM2381.S6+
Slang
  Chinese: PL1952+
  Korean: PL946+
Slave language (Indian): PM2365
Slavery in literature
  Korean
    Literary history: PL957.5.S55
Slavi language: PM2365
Snails in literature
  Japanese
    Literary history: PL721.S57
Snohomish language: PM2371
Snow in literature
  Japanese
    Literary history: PL721.S58
So language (Uganda): PL8682.S58+
Sobaihipure language: PM4271
Sobaipure language: PM4271
Sobojo language: PL5439.5
Social realism in literature
  Korean
    Literary history: PL957.5.S65
Social sciences
  Esperanto texts: PM8276+
Socialism in literature
  Japanese
    Literary history: PL721.S6
Socialist realism in literature
  Korean
    Literary history: PL957.5.S66
Society and literature
  Japanese
    Literary history: PL721.S62

Sociology
Esperanto texts: PM8278
Soembawa language: PL5445+
Soga language: PL8682.S62+
Soira dialect: PM6991
Sōka-shi (Japan) in literature
Japanese
Literary history: PL721.S63
Sokop language: PL5439.8+
Soldiers as authors
Chinese
Collections: PL2515.5.S6
Literary history: PL2278.5.S65
Japanese literature
Collections: PL756.S65
Korean
Collections: PL973.2.S65
Poetry: PL975.8.S62
Soldiers in literature
Japanese
Literary history: PL722.S64
Solresol (Artificial language): PM8790
Solteco language: PM4281
Somba language: PL8682.S64+
Sona (Artificial language): PM8795
Songe language: PL8683+
Songhai language: PL8685+
Songye language: PL8683+
Soninke language: PL8686+
Sonora language: PM4136
Sonsorol-Tobi language: PL6313
Sora language: PL4587+
Sōshi
Japanese
Collections
Prose: PL775
Literary history
Prose: PL745
Sotho language, Northern: PL8690+
Sotho language, Southern: PL8689+
Sotho-Tswana languages: PL8691
Sound in literature
Japanese
Literary history: PL721.S64
Korean
Literary history: PL957.5.S68

Sounds in literature
Korean
Literary history: PL957.5.S68
Southeastern Turkic languages: PL51+
Southern Arapesh language:
PL6621.S68
Southern Bullom language: PL8668+
Southern Epera language: PM7079
Southern Mande languages:
PL8490.M3595S68
Southern Min dialects: PL1701+
Southern Mofu language: PL8517
Southern Paiute language: PM2094
Southern Sotho language: PL8689+
Southern Tutchone language: PM2506
Southwestern Turkic languages: PL91+
Space and time in literature
Chinese
Literary history: PL2275.S6
Korean
Literary history: PL957.5.S69
Spelin (Artificial language): PM8802
Spies in literature
Korean
Literary history: PL957.5.S694
Spiti dialect (Tibetan): PL3651.S7
SPL (Artificial language): PM8815
Spokane language: PM2376
Spoken language
Chinese: PL1074.8
Korean: PL908.8, PL908.85
Spokil (Artificial language): PM8822
Sports and games
Esperanto texts: PM8275
Sports in literature
Chinese
Literary history: PL2275.S65
Japanese
Literary history: PL721.S66
Korean
Literary history: PL957.5.S696
Squawmish language (British
Columbia): PM2381.S6+
Sranan language: PM7875.S67+
Srê dialect: PL4453
Ssindang Kelingi language: PL5439.4+
Stalo language: PM2381.S8+

449

INDEX

Stars in literature
  Japanese
    Literary history: PL721.S72
State, The, in literature
  Japanese
    Literary history: PL721.S73
Stepmothers in literature
  Korean
    Literary history: PL957.5.S74
Stieng language: PL4341+
Student authors
  Japanese literature
    Collections: PL756.S85
  Korean
    Collections
      Poetry: PL975.8.S75
Style
  Chinese langauge: PL1271+
  Korean langauge: PL927+
Style in literature
  Japanese
    Literary history: PL721.S75
Subanun language: PL6035+
Subinha language: PM4285
Subiya language: PL8692.S86+
Subtiaban language: PM4286.S5+
Suchichi language: PM7081
Sudanian languages: PL8027
Suena language: PL6621.S92
Suerre language: PM4286.S7+
Sui language: PL4251.S95+
Suicide in literature
  Japanese
    Literary history: PL721.S76
Suk language (Africa): PL8692.S9+
Suku language (Congo): PL8693+
Sukuma language: PL8694.S94+
Sulka language: PL6621.S94
Sulu language: PL6041+
Sulung language: PL3801.S77+
Suma (Artificial language): PM8840
Sumba language: PL5443+
Sumbawa language: PL5445+
Sumbwa language: PL8694.S95+
Sumida River (Japan) in literature
  Japanese
    Literary history: PL721.S78

Sumo language: PM4286.S8+
Sundanese language: PL5451+
Sundanese literature: PL5454.A3+
Sunwār language: PL3801.S8+
Supernatural in literature
  Japanese
    Literary history: PL721.S8
  Korean
    Literary history: PL957.5.S96
Suppire language: PL8694.S96+
Surmic languages: PL8694.S97
Susu language: PL8695+
Suwawa language: PL5455+
Suzhou (Jiangsu Sheng, China) in
    literature
  Chinese
    Literary history: PL2275.S93
Swahili language: PL8701+
Swahili literature: PL8703.5+
Swazi language: PL8705+
Swordsmen in literature
  Japanese
    Literary history: PL721.S86
Syllabication
  Korean: PL918.8
Symbolism in literature
  Japanese
    Literary history: PL721.S94
  Korean
    Literary history: PL957.5.S97
Sympathy in literature
  Korean
    Literary history: PL957.5.S98
Synonyms
  Chinese: PL1301
  Korean: PL933
Szechwan Province (China) in literature
  Chinese
    Literary history: PL2275.S95
Szi Lepai dialect: PL4001.S8

T

Ta-li (China) in literature
  Chinese
    Literary history: PL2275.T27
Tabalosa language: PM7086

450

Tapuri language: PM7106
Tapuyan languages: PM7108
Tarahumare language: PM4291
Tarangan language: PL5456.86+
Taraon language: PL4001.D53
Tarascan language: PM4296+
Tariana language: PM7110
Tarok language: PL8711+
Tasio dialect: PM7111
Tatana language: PL5456.88+
Tatar language: PL73+
Tatche language: PM2381.T3+
Tatimolo dialect: PM4301
Tatiquilhati dialect: PM4306
Taurepan dialect: PM7113
Tausug language: PL6075+
Tauya language: PL6621.T35
Taverns in literature
  Japanese
    Literary history: PL721.H6
Taveta language: PL8715+
Tawakoni language: PM2421
Tawoyan language: PL5456.92+
Tay-Nung language: PL4251.T38+
Taying language: PL4001.D53
Tboli language: PL6078+
Tea ceremony, Japanese, in literature
  Japanese
    Literary history: PL721.J34
Tea in literature
  Chinese
    Literary history: PL2275.T42
  Japanese
    Literary history: PL721.T345
  Korean
    Literary history: PL957.5.T4
Teachers as authors
  Japanese literature
    Collections
      Prose: PL770.55.T4
  Korean
    Collections: PL973.2.T43
Teachers in literature
  Japanese
    Literary history: PL722.T4

Tears in literature
  Japanese
    Literary history: PL721.T348
Tebaca language: PM4316
Tebele language: PL8547.N28+
Technology
  Chinese readers: PL1117.5.T42
  Esperanto texts: PM8290
Technology in literature
  Japanese
    Literary history: PL721.T35
Teco language (Cuitlateco): PM3738
Tectiteco language: PM4319
Tecuexe language: PM4321
Tedaga language: PL8724+
Teenage authors
  Korean
    Collections: PL973.2.T45
Teguima language: PM4136
Tehua language: PM2431
Tehuantepecano language: PM4326
Tehueco language: PM4331
Teke language: PL8725
Telame language: PM2381.T3+
Telefol language: PL6621.T38
Telei language: PL6621.T4
Television
  Chinese readers: PL1117.5.T44
Television plays
  Chinese
    Collections: PL2579.T44
    Literary history: PL2368.T44
  Japanese
    Literary history: PL737.8
  Korean
    Collections: PL978.5.T44
    Literary history: PL963.5.T44
Telugu language: PL4771+
Telugu literature: PL4780+
Tem language: PL8725.15
Tembo language (Kivu, Zaire):
  PL8725.2
Temiar language: PL4468
Temne language: PL8735+
Temori language: PM4336

Utamakura in literature
Japanese
Literary history: PL721.U73
Ute language: PM2515
Utlateca language: PM4231
Uto-Aztecan languages: PM4479
Utopias in literature
Korean
Literary history: PL957.5.U85
Uvea language (Wallis Islands):
PL6551
Uwana language: PL8758+
Uzbek language: PL56+

V

Vacoregue language: PM3816
Vagala language: PL8759+
Vai language: PL8761+
Vaiphei language: PL4001.V34+
Valman language: PL6621.V3
Vaniva language: PM7236
Varogio language: PM4481
Varohio language: PM4481
Vayema language: PM4486
Vazevaco dialect: PM7238
Vegetables in literature
Japanese
Literary history: PL721.V39
Vejoso language: PM7241
Vejoz language: PM7241
Vela (Artificial language): PM8930
Velt-Deutsch (Artificial language):
PM8933
Veltlang (Artificial language): PM8937
Venda language: PL8771+
Verb
Chinese: PL1235
Korean: PL921.7
Versification in literature
Japanese
Literary history: PL721.V42
Veterans as authors
Japanese literature
Collections
Poetry: PL757.4.V48
Vicol language: PL5581+

Vietnam in literature
Chinese
Literary history: PL2275.V52
Vietnam War in literature
Chinese
Literary history: PL2275.V53
Vietnamese in literature
Chinese
Literary history: PL2275.V52
Vietnamese language: PL4371+
Vietnamese literature: PL4378.9.A+
Vige language: PL8773.V43+
Vilela language: PM7246
Vili language: PL8774+
Villmoluche dialect: PM7251
Violence in literature
Japanese
Literary history: PL721.V5
Violent deaths in literature
Japanese
Literary history: PL721.V5
Visaya language: PL5621+
Visona (Artificial language): PM8942
Vocabularies
African languages: PL8009
Volapük (Artificial language): PM8951+
Voldu (Artificial language): PM8961
Voto language: PM4487.V6+
Vowels
Chinese: PL1215
Korean: PL918.6
Voyages and travels
Chinese readers: PL1117.5.V68
Voyages to the otherworld in literature
Japanese
Literary history: PL721.V69
Vulum dialect: PL8535.95.V8
Vunjo language: PL8775.7+
Vute language: PL8775.9+

W

Wa language: PL4470
Waama language: PL8776+
Wabi language: PM3836
Wabnaki language: PM551
Wagap language: PL6227

Winds in literature
Japanese
Literary history: PL721.W55
Wine in literature
Chinese
Literary history: PL2275.W55
Wines, Rice, in literature
Japanese
Literary history: PL721.R53
Winnebago language: PM2591
Wintun languages: PM2595
Wirangu language: PL7101.W55
Wiru language: PL6621.W55
Wit and humor
Chinese
Collections: PL2613
Literary history: PL2403
Japanese
Collections
Prose: PL776+
Literary history
Prose: PL746+
Korean
Collections
Prose: PL980.7
Literary history: PL957.5.W5
Prose: PL966.7
Witoto language: PM7254
Witotoan languages: PM7254
Wives in literature
Japanese
Literary history: PL722.W58
Wiyot language: PM2605
Wobe language: PL8783+
Woccon language: PM2608
Wogeo language: PL6337.5
Woisika language: PL6621.W65
Woleai language: PL6338
Wolio language: PL5490+
Wolof language: PL8785+
Women authors
Chinese
Collections: PL2515
Literary history: PL2278
Japanese literature
Collections: PL756.W6
Prose: PL770.55.W64

Women authors
Japanese literature
Literary history: PL725
Korean
Collections: PL973
Poetry: PL975.8.W6
Prose: PL980.13.W65
Korean literature: PL957.9
Women in literature
Chinese
Literary history: PL2275.W65
Japanese
Literary history: PL722.W64
Korean
Literary history: PL957.5.W65
Wongaibon language: PL7101.W64
Word formation
Chinese: PL1231
Korean: PL919.4
Working class authors
Japanese literature
Collections: PL756.L33
Poetry: PL757.4.W67
Literary history: PL725.2.W65
Korean
Collections: PL973.2.L33
Poetry: PL975.8.W67
Korean literature
Literary history: PL957.95.W67
Working class in literature
Japanese
Literary history: PL722.L32
Korean
Literary history: PL957.5.W68
World English (Artificial language):
PM8981
World War II in literature
Japanese
Literary history: PL721.W65
Wororan languages: PL7101.W67
Wu-chih Mountains (China) in literature
Chinese
Literary history: PL2275.W82
Wu dialects: PL1931+
Wu-hsi shih (China) in literature
Chinese
Literary history: PL2275.W83

459

INDEX

Wu-i Mountains (China) in literature
  Chinese
    Literary history: PL2275.W84
Wu-t'ai Mountains in literature
  Chinese
    Literary history: PL2275.W85
Wu-tang Mountains in literature
  Chinese
    Literary history: PL2275.W87
Wudang Mountains (China) in literature
  Chinese
    Literary history: PL2275.W87
Wulguru language: PL7101.W85
Wutai Mountains (China) in literature
  Chinese
    Literary history: PL2275.W85
Wutun language: PL1900.W98
Wuvulu language: PL6339
Wuxi Shi (China) in literature
  Chinese
    Literary history: PL2275.W83
Wuyi Mountains (China) in literature
  Chinese
    Literary history: PL2275.W84
Wuzhi Mountains (China) in literature
  Chinese
    Literary history: PL2275.W82

X

Xaltepec language: PM4506
Xaquete dialect: PM7256
Xaracuu language: PL6218
Xaragure language: PL6340
Xebero language: PM6261
Xhosa language: PL8795+
Xiandao language: PL4001.X53+
Xiang dialects: PL1861+
Xiang sheng: PL2579.H8
  Chinese
    Literary history: PL2368.H75
Xicarolles language: PM1389
Xin (The Chinese word): PL1315.X56
Xinca language: PL4498.X3,
  PM4498.X3+

Xinjiang Uygur Zizhiqu in literature
  Chinese
    Literary history: PL2275.X56
Xixime language: PM4501
Xoquinoe dialect: PM3916
!Xu language: PL8796.6+
Xultepec language: PM4506
Xuzhou Shi (China) in literature
  Chinese
    Literary history: PL2275.H78

Y

Ya language: PL4251.Y32
Yacururé language: PM7261
Yagaria language: PL6621.Y27
Yagua language: PM7263
Yahgan language: PM7266
Yaka language (Congo and Angola):
  PL8796.8+
Yakan language (Philippines): PL6115
Yakanaku language: PM6896
Yākhā language: PL3801.Y3+
Yakima language: PM2611
Yakö language: PL8797+
Yakoma language: PL8799+
Yakonan languages: PM2621
Yakut language: PL361+
Yala language: PL8800.Y25+
Yalunka language: PL8800.Y29+
Yamanashi-ken (Japan) in literature
  Japanese
    Literary history: PL721.Y3
Yamassee language: PM2631
Yamba language (Cameroon and
  Nigeria): PL8800.Y33+
Yambeta language: PL8800.Y35+
Yamdena language: PL5495+
Yamea language: PM7269
Yami language: PL6120
Yamphu language: PL3801.Y43+
Yana language: PM2641
Yandruwandha language: PL7101.Y34
Yang-chou shih (China) in literature
  Chinese
    Literary history: PL2275.Y35

Yang, gui-fei, 719-756, in literature
  Japanese
    Literary history: PL721.Y35
Yangtze River Gorges in literature
  Chinese
    Literary history: PL2275.Y358
Yangtze River in literature
  Chinese
    Literary history: PL2275.Y358
Yangzhou Shi (China) in literature
  Chinese
    Literary history: PL2275.Y35
Yanhuitlan language: PM4521
Yankton dialect: PM1021+
Yanomamo language: PM7270
Yanzi language: PL8800.Y4+
Yao language (Africa): PL8801+
Yao language (Asia): PL4074+
Yao-Min language: PL4074+
Yaoi dialect: PM7271
Yaouré language: PL8805+
Yap language: PL6341
Yapua language: PM7286
Yaqay language: PL6621.Y29
Yaqui language: PM4526
Yareba language: PL6621.Y3
Yaro language: PM6126
Yarura language: PM7296
Yatasse language: PM2661
Yativera language: PM7301
Yaunde-Fang languages: PL8807
Yavapai language: PM2671
Yavipai language: PM2671
Yawa language: PL5497+
Yawelmani dialect: PM2681.Z9A+
Yawuru language: PL7101.Y39
Yebu dialect: PL8811+
Yekinahuer language: PM7306
Yele language: PL6621.Y35
Yellow River in literature
  Chinese
    Literary history: PL2275.Y45
Yellow Uigur language: PL45.Y44+
Yemba language: PL8813+
Yenesei inscriptions: PL31
Yenisei-Ostyak language: PM17
Yerava dialect: PL4719.5.Y47

Yerukala dialect: PL4797+
Yessan-Mayo language: PL6621.Y4
Yete dialect: PM7311
Yeyi language: PL8814.4+
Yi language: PL3311.Y5
Yidiny language: PL7101.Y53
Yimas language: PL6621.Y55
Yimchungru language: PL4001.Y38+
Yindjibarndi language: PL7101.Y54
Yindu dialect: PL4001.Y4
Yinggarda language: PL7101.Y55
Yir-Yoront language: PL7101.Y57
Yogad language: PL6135
Yogli dialect: PL4001.Y63+
Yokohama-shi (Japan) in literature
  Japanese
    Literary history: PL721.Y56
Yokuts language: PM2681
Yōkyoku
  Japanese drama
    Collections: PL765
    Literary history: PL735
Yom language: PL8814.8+
Yombe language (Congo and Angola):
  PL8815+
Yongkom language: PL6621.Y65
Yope language: PM3906
Yorta Yorta language: PL7101.Y65
Yoruba language: PL8821+
Yoshino Mountain (Japan) in literature
  Japanese
    Literary history: PL721.Y58
Youth as authors
  Chinese
    Collections: PL2515.5.Y68
    Literary history: PL2278.5.Y68
Youth in literature
  Japanese
    Literary history: PL722.Y67
Yova language: PM6556
Ypurinan languages: PM7314
Yualyai language: PL7101.Y83
Yuan Ming Yuan (Beijing, China) in
  literature
  Chinese
    Literary history: PL2275.Y83
Yucarari language: PM7321

Yucateco language: PM3961+
Yuchi language: PM2511
Yucuna language: PM7314.5
Yue dialects: PL1731+
Yue fu
  Chinese poetry
    Collections: PL2519.Y8
    Literary history: PL2309.Y8
Yugh language: PM19.5
Yuguguarana language: PM5983
Yui language: PL6621.Y8
Yuit language: PM94
Yukagir language: PM20+
Yuki language (California): PM2691
Yukian languages: PM2691
Yulu language: PL8826+
Yuman languages: PM2701
Yunca language: PM7316
Yunga language: PM7316
Yunnan Sheng (China) in literature
  Chinese
    Literary history: PL2275.Y85
Yupa language: PM7318
Yupik languages: PM80+
Yuracare language: PM7321
Yurimagua dialect: PM7326
Yurok language: PM2703

Z

Zaachilla dialect: PM4536
Zacapule language: PM4471
Zacateca language: PM4541
Zahao dialect: PL4001.Z3
Zakhring language: PL4001.Z33
Zaklohpakap language: PM3936
Zamucoan languages: PM7329
Zamucu language: PM7329
Zande language: PL8828+
Zantum (Artificial language): PM8995
Zapa language: PM7336
Zaparo language: PM7341
Zapotec language: PM4546+
Zarma dialect: PL8685.95.Z35
Zeguha language: PL8831+
Zeliang language: PL4001.Z44+
Zeona language: PM7346

Zepo dialect: PM7351
Zhangzhung language: PL3801.Z3+
Zhengzhou Shi (China) in literature
  Chinese
    Literary history: PL2275.Z75
Zhuang language: PL4251.C4+
Ziba language: PL8241+
Ziecoya dialect: PM7356
Zigula language: PL8831+
Zinantecan languages: PM3630
Zinza language: PL8835+
Zoe language: PM4551
Zoology
  Esperanto texts: PM8287
Zoque language: PM4556
Zotzil language: PM4466
Zotzlen language: PM4561
Zou dialect: PL4001.Z68+
Zuaque language: PM4331
Zuihitsu
  Japanese
    Collections
      Prose: PL772+
    Literary history
      Prose: PL742+
Zulgo language: PL8839+
Zulu language: PL8841+
Zuñi language: PM2711
Zutugil language: PM4471

GPO U.S. GOVERNMENT PRINTING OFFICE: 2010–350–024/60041